PERSONNEL and INDUSTRIAL RELATIONS
A MANAGERIAL APPROACH

PERSONNEL and INDUSTRIAL RELATIONS

A MANAGERIAL APPROACH
Third Edition

JOHN B. MINER
Research Professor of Management
Georgia State University

MARY GREEN MINER
Consulting Editor and Director, BNA Surveys
The Bureau of National Affairs, Inc.

Macmillan Publishing Co., Inc.
NEW YORK

Collier Macmillan Publishers
LONDON

Macmillan Publishing Co., Inc.
866 Third Avenue, New York, New York 10022

Collier Macmillan Canada, Ltd.

Library of Congress Cataloging in Publication Data

Miner, John B
  Personnel and industrial relations.

  Includes bibliographies and index.
  1. Personnel management. I. Miner, Mary Green, joint author. II. Title.
HF5549.M522   1977   658.3   76–10839
ISBN 0–02–381660–0

Printing: 3 4 5 6 7 8   Year: 8 9 0 1 2 3

Preface

In view of the variety of books written to provide an introduction to personnel management, it is important to indicate where within this dissimilar array the present volume falls. Our assumption is that personnel management represents a relatively circumscribed field within the broader organizational framework and that a student will take other courses dealing with the more general managerial functions and organizational processes. Thus subject matter that is commonly identified with such fields as organization theory, management, administrative science, organizational behavior, and human relations is given scant attention here.

Consistent with this approach, we have made a deliberate effort to distinguish this volume from the first author's *The Management Process*. The degree of overlap is minimal. In those few instances where particular subjects require treatment in both books, the approach and emphasis differ. In most cases those topics that are considered in both places are given major treatment in one and more circumscribed treatment in the other. Thus the objective has been to create two complementary but wholly independent volumes dealing with human resources utilization, rather than to present similar material in differing packages.

Organization theory has had an impact on this book almost entirely as it provides a framework for analysis and a method of defining the limits of the personnel management field. Used in this way, organization theory could perform the same function for books on other aspects of organizational operation—marketing, manufacturing, and accounting, for instance.

This emphasis on the organization as the unit of analysis yields some rather distinctive advantages. Among these the most significant appears to be the provision of a value system in terms of which the techniques and procedures of personnel management may be appraised. Throughout this book, reference to the fact that a personnel manager *should* do this or that means that doing so will in all probability contribute most effectively to the goals of the organization and thus to the fulfillment of managerial responsibilities. The frame of reference is the organization, the company, and not the individual employee or the total society. The values of the social system as a whole are reflected in what is described as the constraint and facilitator structure, but they do not provide a primary focus. It is this stress on the organization as the unit of analysis that leads to the subtitle "A Managerial Approach." The *manager's* job is to make his *organization* as effective as he possibly can.

An additional feature is a major concern with managerial problem solving, rather than descriptions of existing practice. The goal is to provide the reader with sufficient knowledge of approaches and relevant considerations so that he or she may develop appropriate strategies for solving a company's personnel problems.

Because much of our current knowledge in the personnel area derives from behavioral science research, this research has been incorporated extensively in many parts of the book. Yet the intent is to deal with problems of human resources utilization in all their manifestations. The behavioral sciences of psychology, sociology, political science, and cultural anthropology have contributed solutions to these problems in an extremely uneven manner. In some areas, behavioral science research provides practically all that is known; in other areas, behavioral scientists have conducted almost no research at all. Knowledge in the field of personnel and industrial relations derives from a host of disciplines. In what follows, every effort has been made to present the best information available, irrespective of its disciplinary origin.

The preparation of a new edition provides an opportunity to incorporate legislative changes and advances in research. Furthermore, as fields of study evolve, there are inevitably new topics that emerge on the horizon and increases in the salience of certain already existing concerns. The topic areas that have seen major new developments, which are therefore given increased or perhaps initial attention in this edition, are the following:

Careers in personnel and industrial relations
Individual differences
Group differences made important by legislation
Fair employment legislation (EEO)
Legal influences on benefits (ERISA)
National labor force trends
The Position Analysis Questionnaire
Job enlargement and enrichment
The four-day work week
Flexible working time
Human resource accounting
Error and bias in ratings

Scaled expectation method
Content and construct validity
Self-selection
Differential validity
Recruiting sources and strategy
Job search behavior
Affirmative action recruiting
The sentence completion technique
Job sampling procedures
Achievement motivation training
Behavior modification
Computer-assisted instruction
Personalized system of instruction
Career planning
Merit pay systems
Pay secrecy
Effects of safety legislation (OSHA)
Alcohol and drug problems
Public sector labor relations
Long-term disability insurance
Upward communications
Evaluation of personnel activities
Personnel management in small business

In addition, of course, new developments and information have resulted in numerous changes in what is said about many other topics already treated at length in the second edition.

A further point involves the order of presentation. The various topics are grouped in accordance with the dictates of the systems-oriented organizational model that provides the framework for the book and which is explicated in Chapter 3. The result is a sequence of chapters that departs in certain respects from traditional ordering. Some readers may desire to combine parts of Chapter 5, dealing with labor relations law, with Chapter 19 which covers other aspects of labor relations. Other aspects of Chapter 5 might be read in conjunction with Chapters 10 through 13, 16, and 17, again to combine legislation with certain relevant subject matter. For some purposes Chapter 4, on individual differences, might well be taken up along with Chapter 13, on psychological testing. Some would argue for a sequence running from jobs (Chapters 6 and 7), through filling jobs (Chapters 10, 11, 12, and 13), to training (Chapters 14 and 15), then to evaluation (Chapters 8 and 9), and finally to compensation (Chapter 16). There is nothing to prevent using the material in these varied ways. Yet, to the authors, the existing chapter sequence appears to be the most meaningful.

In revising the book, we have made extensive use of comments provided by Edwin Locke of the University of Maryland, Kenneth Van Voorhis of the University of South Florida, and James Wallace of Loyola College. We are most appreciative of their help. Barbara Williams of Georgia State University has contributed as a researcher and indexer and has also typed the complete manuscript. Also, the second author would like to thank her associates at the Bureau of National Affairs for providing her the opportunity to pursue her study of the personnel field.

J. B. M.
M. G. M.

Contents

THE NATURE AND EMERGENCE OF PERSONNEL MANAGEMENT

1 The Goals of Personnel and the Jobs of Personnel Managers

On what basis should one candidate for a job be hired and another rejected? What factors should be used in determining the pay rate for a particular position? What is the best way of training employees so they can achieve high levels of performance? How can understanding and acceptance of organizational goals be increased? These questions are heard every day in all types of organizations. They have stimulated, concerned, and at times plagued managers from time immemorial; they persist because the success of any enterprise depends in large part on the way in which they are answered.

People are the essential ingredient in all organizations, be the organizations business, educational, governmental, or religious, and the way in which people are recruited and utilized by the leadership largely determines whether the organization will achieve its objectives. It is not too surprising, therefore, that management is constantly concerned with the company's human resources—with the way in which these resources are developed and utilized, with the assumptions made about them, with the formulation of personnel policy, with the methods and procedures used in dealing with the work force.

A company should find and utilize the best available manpower in as effective a manner as possible, and it must do so within the constraints of ever-increasing governmental regulation affecting employee relations policies. By providing future managers a solid background in human resources management, it is hoped that this book will assist in the achievement of this objective.

THE GOALS OF PERSONNEL MANAGEMENT

Personnel management may be defined as the process of developing, applying, and evaluating policies, procedures, methods, and programs relating to the individual in the organization. This definition applies whether the specific employee is a maintenance mechanic, a file clerk, a research chemist, or a financial vice-president. Essentially, the personnel function is concerned with the management of the *human* resources of an organization, in contrast to the material or financial resources.

Another way to define personnel management is in terms of its goals, and in this sense the goals that personnel management seeks to achieve within the organization are the same as the goals of management in general. Although personnel managers carry out a unique set of activities having to do with the utilization of human resources, this work is done with a view to accomplishing exactly the same objective as is the work of other managers.

Task Goals

Two interrelated but distinct categories or types of organizational goals are involved here. The first of these is to maximize the productivity of the organization. This is not a new concept, of course; it has been generally recognized as a major goal of business and most other organizations for a long time. In the early years of industrialization, the maximization of productivity—and profit—often was the only goal worth mentioning.

In its most general sense, the productivity objective refers to the whole gamut of procedures and activities that management carries out to maximize the attainment of the stated purpose of the organization. This purpose may be to manufacture and sell automobiles, to provide a stock market investment counseling service, to administer a health care center, or to collect federal income taxes. Some of the larger corporations have become so complex and their product lines or services so diversified that a full statement of the productivity objective can become quite lengthy. Yet, in all instances, the organization is devoted to producing or providing something that presumably is necessary or has value for other people. In this sense, there always is a task objective.

In the business world, productivity is considered in relation to earnings, and what is produced or provided must have some prospect of yielding a long-term net profit. In the nonprofit sector of the economy, too, in such areas as government, health care, and education, management is concerned with achieving task goals, and productivity may be measured in terms of output per man-hour worked, as it often is in business firms. But the final balance sheet is not as crucial a factor. A city police department may end the fiscal year with a big budget surplus, but if the crime rate and number of unsolved murders have gone up 20 per cent during that year, the productivity objective is not being realized. Political and social pressures, rather than financial pressures, ultimately are likely to result in a change in leadership to bring about the achievement of the department's task goals.

Since the goals of personnel management are identical with those of the rest of the management team, the matter of productivity is a major concern of those engaged in carrying out the personnel function; it is their responsibility to develop and recommend policies and procedures that will contribute to this goal. For example, selection techniques can be devised that will result in the placement of people in jobs they can perform most effectively. Personnel managers also are frequently called upon to develop methods for measuring individual job performance, making it possible to obtain indexes of the contributions made by specific members to the productivity of the total organization. In situations where it is clear that performance needs improvement, the personnel department may design special training programs aimed at providing employees the skills they need to do a better job. Many of the personnel programs that will be discussed in later chapters obviously are tied to the achievement of the productivity goal.

Maintenance Goals

The second major type of organizational goal is one that is related to the first but can be distinguished from it quite clearly. It is of more recent origin and probably is still not nearly as likely to be given explicit statement as the productivity goal. Nevertheless, it is of equal, and in some situations even greater, importance. Stated most simply, this objective is to maintain the organization as an ongoing unit in the face of internal and external pressures and stress. The term *organizational maintenance* often is used to refer to this particular type of goal.

The importance of maintenance goals began to be appreciated in the late 1930s with the rise of a strong and militant labor movement and in the period following World War II, when shortages of talent developed and there was strong competition for the talent that was available. During this latter period, management began to realize that in order to maintain a loyal work force, an active effort would have to be made to establish working conditions that would contribute to job satisfaction and thus facilitate talent retention. As a result, management became much more aware that increased effort must be devoted to problems of organizational maintenance if the organization were to remain intact under the impact of a changing labor force and sweeping technological change.

In more recent years, beginning in the mid-1960s, changing values among younger workers and demands for social responsibility have added to the stresses on organizations. While social responsibility sometimes is described as a goal in and of itself, it appears more and more to be related to organizational survival. Areas of social responsibility that formerly were optional, such as equal employment opportunity and safety, now are part of the legal framework within which organizations must operate. Whether or not social pressures have been formalized into law, if they are strong enough an organization will have to be responsive to them in order to survive.

These changes have resulted in new organizational structures, and new employee groups have formed to demand positions within the existing hierarchy. At the same time, other groups, many with a declining role to play insofar as the company is concerned, have been striving to maintain their traditional status. As might be anticipated, personnel management has an extremely important role to play in creating conditions that will contribute to the stability of the organization. It is the responsibility of personnel managers more than any other group to recommend policies, procedures, and programs that will make the company an attractive place to work, will create an environment conducive to assimilating new types of employees, and at the same time will serve to minimize the internal conflict that could threaten the firm's very existence. When these efforts are successful, and internal stability has been achieved, the organization will be in a better position to maintain itself against external stress also.

As noted in the beginning of the discussion of the two types of goals, they are interrelated. If the maintenance goal is not achieved, the organization will cease to exist, and there will be no achievement of productivity goals. It is possible for an organization to continue to survive for a period of time without achieving its productivity or task goals; during a recession, production may be halted for weeks or even months while the organization structure remains intact. Over a long period, however, an organization that produces or provides nothing will have no reason to exist.

Just as the goals are interrelated, many of the programs carried out by the personnel department contribute to the achievement of both types of goals. Procedures aimed at reducing accident rates, for example, result in a safer, and thus more attractive, work environment and at the same time should improve the work group's productivity. The relationship between various personnel programs and goal achievement is discussed more fully in Chapter 3 and is a major emphasis throughout this book.

THE WORK OF PERSONNEL MANAGEMENT

The ultimate goals that personnel managers attempt to achieve are basically the same across organizations, but the specific activities carried out to achieve the goals may be quite different. The actual content of the work performed by the personnel staff may involve as many as 50 separate activities in large organizations, whereas in very small firms, personnel activities may be limited to a handful. Because the major part of this book is devoted to a detailed description of the activities that make up the practice of personnel management, only a brief list is presented here to indicate the activities that traditionally are the responsibility of the personnel department. These activities can be categorized as follows:

Planning—organization planning, manpower planning, employee information systems, job analysis.

Performance Appraisal—measuring productivity and other aspects of performance, management appraisal, and employee merit-rating.

Selection—recruiting, interviewing, testing, hiring, and placement of new employees.

Training and Development—orientation, on-the-job training, supervisory training, management development, organization development, and educational and scholarship programs.

Wage and Salary Administration—wage surveys, job evaluation, merit pay systems, incentive and bonus plans, and executive compensation.

Work Environment—safety programs, health and medical services, physical working conditions, and plant security.

Performance Control—counseling and discipline procedures, promotion, transfer, and separation.

Labor Relations—dealing with union organizing efforts, collective bargaining, grievances, and arbitration.

Benefits and Services—time off for vacation, holidays, or leaves, insurance, retirement plans, recreation and social activities, legal and financial aid, assistance with housing, moving, and transportation, and parking and feeding facilities.

Communications—employee publications, attitude surveys, suggestion systems, and community relations.

Research and Evaluation—reports, recordkeeping, and compiling facts and figures both for internal use and for compliance with government regulations.

Whether a particular activity will be performed by the personnel department in a specific organization depends on a number of variables. All employers need to have some procedures for hiring employees, for explaining what work is to be done, and for paying wages. But how much is done in areas such as planning, appraisal, benefits and services, and communications will depend on the size of the organization, whether it is located in an urban or rural setting, the type of industry, whether it is unionized, and the characteristics of the employee group with respect to age, sex, education, and skill levels.

The state of the economy is another factor influencing the activities of the personnel department. Within any organization, personnel activities may shift drastically from one year to another because of economic pressures. In times of full employment, training programs may be emphasized to make sure the company has an adequate supply of employees with the necessary skills. When there is a recession, however, training frequently all but disappears as a personnel activity. Thus, even in the largest organizations, the personnel function cannot remain static; it must be able to adjust to internal changes as well as to outside economic and social forces if it is indeed to contribute to the attainment of organizational goals.

PERSONNEL MANAGEMENT IN THE ORGANIZATIONAL CONTEXT

In view of the facts that personnel encompasses such a variety of activities, and that these activities differ from one organization to another, it is not surprising that there also are major differences in the size, structure, authority, and level of the personnel department from one organization to another. From one to another, even the name of the unit that is responsible for the management of human resources and the title of its head vary considerably. In a survey of 279 employers in the state of Indiana, 47 titles were used to identify the top personnel officer. The titles most frequently used were Personnel Manager, Personnel Director, Manager of Industrial Relations, Director of Industrial Relations, and Vice-President-Personnel. Some of the other titles noted included Supervisor of Personnel, Manager of Employee and Community Relations, and Administration Manager (15).

Effects of Company Size and Growth

The nature of the organizational unit responsible for personnel management depends in large measure on how long the company has existed and its size. In smaller firms, there frequently is no fully differentiated personnel function at all. Initially, personnel functions are performed by one or more managers whose primary duties are in other areas. As a firm grows, it typically reaches a point where a full-time personnel position is created, with the individual working in an "assistant to" capacity. He or she may be a staff assistant to the president or to some other officer of the company. Later still, a personnel department emerges as a separate entity.

There appears to be no clear pattern as to when the personnel function first becomes formalized. In one study, this happened in companies ranging from two to forty-three years of age and having from 70 to 520 employees (33). An analysis of the automotive parts industry indicated that the initial full-time personnel position appears on the average when the firm has just over 100 employees, and a personnel supervisory position when it has approximately 500 employees (10). In other industries, growth may progress somewhat further before there is a full-time personnel position, but in the majority of companies, such a job is now created at around the 200-employee level (29).

One might anticipate that the personnel job in such small firms would be very diverse and general with respect to activities. This is not actually the case. The initial "assistant to" position usually is created to maintain personal contact with employees, especially those with long service, because the firm has become so large that the president can no longer do this himself (33). Thus considerations related to organizational maintenance, welfare, and help with personal problems are primary. Such functions as labor relations, selection, compensation, and training remain in the hands of others and thus outside the personnel jurisdiction. As growth continues, these functions gravitate into personnel, and the work does become increasingly generalized, although what activities will be included is difficult to predict. In different companies, the president, other officers, and the line organization generally hold onto different functions. In the final stage of growth, there is a considerable differentiation of functions, and a multiplicity of specialist positions appears.

In large organizations, there may be separate personnel staffs at several organizational levels—the plant or departmental level, divisional level, and corporate level. One study of the personnel structure of 249 companies with 1,000 or more employees found that 80 per cent of them have multilevel personnel structures, most of them with different responsibilities at each level. The corporate level units, with between 15 and 40 people, have as their primary function the provision of advice on personnel policies to top management and of various services to other groups in the company (16).

In some companies, the employee relations function is split into two separate departments, one for handling relations with the union and the other with responsibility for nonunionized employee groups. Although a few large corporations like General Motors have divided their personnel function this way, relatively few organizations overall have done so; in one study of the personnel department, only 5 of 100 responding firms did not have a single top administrator in charge of all personnel and industrial relations activities (9).

Organizational Level and Size of Staff

As the titles of the top personnel officer indicate, the personnel function may vary in status from the supervisory level all the way to the vice-presidential level. In the years since World War II, it appears that personnel has experienced an upgrading in organizational status, and personnel executives at the vice-presidential level now are found in many companies (18). One study (2) reported that between 1959 and 1969, the number of vice-president positions in the personnel area in 100 major corporations increased from 28 to 43.

The figures in Table 1–1 suggest that the personnel executive's title is not necessarily an accurate reflection of his organizational level and influence. A comparison of the data for large versus small companies, for example, shows that while the personnel executive is a vice-president in 44 per cent of the large companies and only 17 per cent of the small ones, he or she reports directly to the top executive in 64 per cent of the small firms and 46 per cent of the large ones. No matter what the size or type of industry,

Table 1-1. *Organizational Level of Personnel Executives*

	Per Cent of Companies				
	All Companies (N = 107)	Large (N = 61) (1,000 employees or more)	Small (N = 46)	Manufacturing (N = 50)	Nonmanufacturing (N = 57)
Top personnel executive— Is a vice president	32	44	17	22	41
Reports directly to organization's highest official	54	46	64	58	50
Participates in overall company planning and policy determination	90	90	89	88	91

Source: Adapted from Bureau of National Affairs, Inc., "ASPA-BNA Survey No. 23: Planning and Budgeting the Personnel Program," *Bulletin to Management,* June 6, 1974, Part 2, p. 8.

however, about 9 out of 10 of the personnel officers participate in overall company planning and policy determination (8).

Compared to other functional units within organizations, personnel generally is one of the smallest. This is particularly true in manufacturing companies where the operating units—engineering, production—and marketing groups tend to have the largest divisions or departments. In one survey of more than 100 companies ranging in size from 100 to 15,000 employees, the size of the personnel department varied from one person to 150 (8).

A measure of the importance of the personnel department that has been used over the years is the "personnel staff ratio," which is the number of personnel staff people per hundred employees served. Usually, two ratios are determined—one for the total personnel staff and one for the professional and technical staff. In the survey cited above, for example, the median total personnel staff ratio for 101 companies is .89, while the professional/technical staff ratio is .46.

Studies of personnel staff ratios have been conducted periodically since 1948 by the University of Minnesota's Industrial Relations Center. These studies have shown that some of the factors influencing the size of the personnel department relative to the total number of employees are company size (the larger the operation, the fewer personnel staff per 100 employees), type of industry (utilities, banks, other financial institutions, and insurance have the highest ratios), and location (northwest states are highest; southwest and south central are lowest) (36).

Shared Decision-making Authority

A final aspect of the role of personnel management in the organization concerns the nature of its influence on the attainment of company goals. Personnel management has generally been considered, in traditional terms, a *staff* function within the organization. In the newer systems terminology, it is said to have a support role. This means that the job of personnel management is not to produce the goods and/or services that are the company's products. Activities of this kind are reserved to the *line* or primarily *operational* components. Rather, the aim of personnel management is to develop conditions within the firm that will facilitate the production of the goods and services in a manner that will be of optimal benefit to the organization. Thus, in an automobile manufacturing company, the personnel component might well recommend policies and procedures related to the training of production employees; it might even conduct such training, but it would not become directly involved in the actual process of manufacturing the automobiles.

Because personnel is essentially a staff function, decision-making authority typically must be shared with other managers outside the personnel department. This sharing occurs both on a vertical basis, with those at organizational levels above the top personnel executive, and horizontally, with

Table 1–2. Decision-making Authority of Personnel Executive

Responsibility Shared with	In Administration of These Activities
Top management	Planning general personnel policies Manpower planning Organization planning Vacations and holidays Military and other leaves
Salary committee	Nonmanagement pay policies Executive compensation
Company insurance department	Group insurance [a] Pensions [a] Health and medical services
Public relations department	Community relations
Employee organization	Recreation and social activities
Line supervisors	Recruiting and selection Performance appraisal Promotion, transfer, and separation Induction, orientation, and on-the-job training Supervisory training and management development Educational and scholarship programs Job evaluation Employee counseling Discipline and grievance handling Safety and working conditions Housing and moving services Union relations

Source: M. G. Miner and J. B. Miner, *A Guide to Personnel Management* (Washington, D.C.: BNA Books, 1973), p. 14. Reprinted with permission of Bureau of National Affairs, Inc.
[a] These functions are shared also with the Corporate Secretary and top management.

managers in other functions, particularly line functions. Table 1–2 shows the number of different people one personnel executive reports as sharing his decision-making authority and the activities for which responsibility is shared with others (22).

The need to share decision making obviously provides much potential for conflict, and this conflict has been a major source of concern among those studying the personnel field (28). One study indicates that the personnel job is viewed as heavily concerned with gathering and providing information (3), and a comparison of the authority of personnel managers and controllers shows clearly that the controllers are perceived to have considerably greater authority over a much wider range of matters (13). On the other hand, another study indicates that personnel managers perceive themselves as having somewhat more authority than others perceive them to have (11). Adding to the conflict potential is the finding of a survey among managers at different levels concerning which activities they want the personnel department to perform. There appeared to be considerable disagreement between executives at the top levels and the lower level line managers as to the desire for personnel involvement in various activities, with the line managers desiring more involvement than the executives viewed as appropriate (35). In such a situation, the personnel staff might find it difficult to know exactly what role it is expected to perform.

In actual practice, however, the limitations on the authority of the personnel function and real conflicts often are not nearly as pronounced as the staff designation would seem to imply. Although personnel managers may not have formal authority to enforce their recommendations, they frequently have an equally important type of authority. This derives from their specialized knowledge in the field of personnel management. Managerial jobs have become increasingly complex over the years, with the advent of both more advanced technology and increased government controls, and many managers have been only too happy to delegate certain aspects of their work to qualified specialists. There is evidence that both automation (27) and government regulation (7) have in fact contributed to greater responsibility and authority for the personnel function.

To the extent a personnel manager actually possesses superior competence in his field of specialization and can convince others of the value of his contribution, his "advice" may well acquire the ring of authority. As indicated by the results of the survey cited above (36), line managers often, although perhaps not universally, are glad to defer to the judgment of a person with expert knowledge when decisions with regard to human resources must be made.

Research data also indicate that when a personnel manager is working in certain areas, he can be expected to have more authority in decision making than in other areas. Another condition under which authority seems to be maximized is that of role conflict (28). When a personnel manager is faced with antithetical pressures from two directions, he is particularly likely to make an independent decision. This resort to independent action is most frequent when both pressures come from somewhat less powerful individuals, but it is clearly in evidence generally whenever role conflict exists. Apparently, the fact that others cannot agree leaves the personnel manager free to rely heavily on his own knowledge and judgment. When such disagreements regarding human resources problems exist, the personnel job can achieve considerable decision-making authority.

CAREERS IN PERSONNEL AND INDUSTRIAL RELATIONS

As an introduction to the field of personnel management, the discussion to this point has provided a view of the goals of personnel, a brief look at the work of personnel that will be expounded more fully throughout this volume, and an exploration of how the personnel function relates to the organization as a whole. For the student who may be studying the field of personnel management with the possibility in mind of making this field his or her career objective, the final section of this introductory chapter presents what is often termed vocational guidance information. Data on such matters as job opportunities, career patterns, salary levels, and educational and other qualifications for success in personnel and industrial relations are provided. This information is presented not so much for the purpose of influencing the reader to pursue a career in the personnel field as to provide objective data as a basis for realistic occupational choice—for making decisions that are likely to produce both satisfaction and accomplishments.

Occupational Outlook

In considering career choices, a basic question is what the outlook is for opportunity within a field. Are jobs readily available for persons interested in the personnel area? And what are the prospects for opportunities in the foreseeable future? According to U.S. government statistics, the personnel occupation was one of the major growth occupations during the 1960s, and continued growth and expansion is expected throughout the 1970s and at least to the mid-1980s.

The census figures reported in Table 1–3 show that during the 1960–1970 decade the number of personnel and labor relations workers nearly tripled, while the increase in the total labor force was about 20 per cent. Overall, the personnel occupation as a per cent of the total labor force doubled over the 10-year period. More recent figures from the U.S. Department of Labor's Bureau of Labor Statistics (BLS) provide forecasts of job openings in the field to the year 1985 (31). The BLS figures indicate that over the next 10 years, there will be an average of 20,800 job openings per year for personnel workers. Among the administrative and managerial positions covered in the report, only accountants are projected to have more job openings during the period of the forecast.

Additional information on the expected growth and expansion in personnel jobs is provided in the *Occupational Outlook Handbook* (30), which is published and periodically updated by the Labor Department. According to the *Handbook*, job prospects are particularly good for people trained in psychological testing and in handling work-related problems. At the present time, the majority of personnel jobs are in private industry, and within the private sector, the major projected growth in the personnel field is in service industries. Major growth also is expected in government personnel positions, particularly at the state government level (5).

This optimistic view of the future in personnel provided by government data is consistent with previous estimates from private sources (17, 18). Perhaps of equal importance with the question of *total* employment opportunity is the question of how far can an individual go in a personnel career. As noted in the discussion on the organizational level of the personnel

Table 1–3. Growth in Personnel and Labor Relations
Occupation, 1960–1970

	Employed Persons, 14 Years Old and Over (thousands)		
	1960 Census Figures	1970 Census Figures	Per Cent Change 1960–1970
Total labor force			
Male	43,467	48,139	10.7
Female	21,173	29,170	37.8
All	64,640	77,309	19.6
Personnel and labor relations workers			
Male	68	202	197.0
Female	34	89	161.8
All	102	291	185.3
PLR workers as per cent of total labor force			
Male	0.15	0.40	166.7
Female	0.16	0.30	87.5
All	0.15	0.30	100.0

Source: U.S. Department of Commerce, Bureau of the Census: 1970 Census of Population.

function, over the past 20 or 30 years there has been a decided upgrading of the field. It is clear that a person starting out in a personnel job today can attain a much higher-level position while remaining within the field than has been true in the past. Personnel executives in vice-presidential positions now are common, particularly in the larger companies, and there are recent reports of company presidents and other top corporate executives being appointed from the personnel component of the organization (25).

Career Patterns

While the ultimate career goal may be that of personnel vice-president in a large organization, or perhaps owner-director of a personnel consulting firm, the beginning personnel job is most likely to be in a specialized area within the broader field. Common entry positions include those of job analyst, employment interviewer, training specialist, wage and salary technician, labor relations assistant, communications assistant, and personnel trainee. From there, movement upward may occur within the various specialized areas of personnel, such as training and development or wage and salary administration. Another route involves more generalized positions in which the individual heads up personnel and industrial relations activities for various segments of an organization, such as a plant or product-line division. In some instances, people may shift back and forth from specialized personnel components to generalist positions. The career progression pattern used by one large chemical company is depicted in Figure 1–1 (23).

Those who enter personnel employment with a specialized background of training and experience are particularly likely to work at least initially in those areas related most closely to that background. They may subsequently

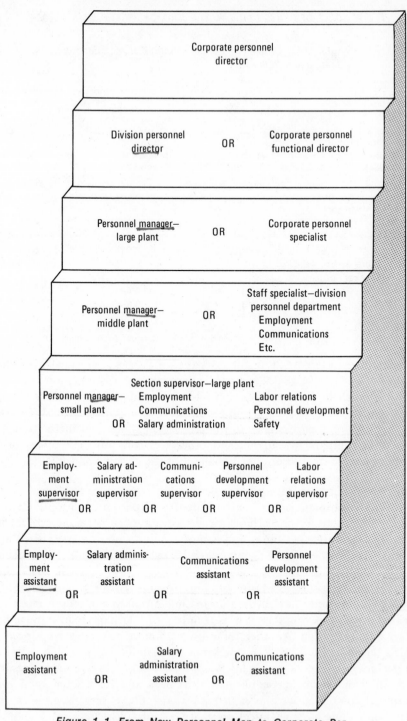

Figure 1–1. From New Personnel Man to Corporate Personnel Director.
Source: H. M. Mitchell, "Selecting and Developing Personnel Professionals," Personnel Journal, 49 : 587 (1970).

move to other specialized areas or to more general personnel positions, but many remain within their initial specialization, making a professional career for themselves within the organization. Thus, industrial psychologists are particularly identified with personnel research, lawyers with labor relations, accountants with employee benefit and retirement programs, those with a background in education with training and management development, labor economists with labor relations or wage and salary administration, physicians with industrial medicine, engineers with safety management, journalists with communications and publications, and clinical psychologists with counseling and appraisal. This plethora of professional specialists in the field represents both a boon and a problem. It brings a great deal of highly specialized knowledge to personnel decision making in many companies. At the same time, the presence of so many specialists, each with knowledge of a limited range of techniques as against the whole range of possible alternatives, tends to create a strong emphasis on techniques at the expense of broad problem solving (19). Often a technique is installed before the problem which it is intended to solve is even clearly identified.

One approach to this situation is to utilize consultants in the specialized areas, and thus to stress the actual employment within the company of more generalized human resources problem solvers, who do not have a primary commitment to some profession other than personnel and industrial relations. This trend is growing (6). As a result, an increasing number of personnel jobs are developing in professional and consulting organizations—law firms, accounting firms, benefits consultants, actuarial firms, psychological consulting firms, labor relations consultants, and the like. Many of the general management consulting firms do considerable work in the personnel area, especially in organization planning and executive compensation. There are also a number of personnel and industrial relations consulting organizations that offer services in a broad range of specialties.

Another source of such specialized assistance, and of employment in the personnel field as well, is the ranks of college and university faculties. Faculty members in such subject areas as labor economics, personnel management, industrial psychology, industrial relations, public personnel administration, industrial sociology, industrial engineering, organization theory, labor law, industrial education, and industrial medicine often are engaged either fully or in part in work within the personnel and industrial relations field.

Salary Levels

Salaries for college graduates in beginning personnel positions generally are comparable with those for graduates with other business administration majors. A survey of selected white-collar occupations conducted by the Bureau of Labor Statistics (BLS) in March 1975 provides average salaries for several categories and levels of professional groups in private industry. One of the beginning personnel positions, that of Job Analyst II, paid an average annual salary of $12,543; comparable figures for Accountants II and Auditors II were $12,758 and $12,587, respectively (32).

At the top levels of most organizations, however, personnel executives traditionally have not been the highest paid, although there is evidence that in recent years the compensation of top personnel officers has been moving up at a more rapid rate than that for executives in other areas of management (24). The most comprehensive data on salaries of personnel executives are provided in surveys conducted every two years by the American Society for Personnel Administration (ASPA) among its membership. Data from the 1974–1975 survey (1) are shown in Table 1–4.

The ASPA survey is based on figures provided by more than 5,000 members who are in the position of Personnel Director, Personnel Manager, Director of Industrial Relations, Manager of Employee Relations, or Manager of Industrial Relations. All are generalists rather than specialists in particular aspects of personnel, and the levels of their positions range from the single plant unit to corporate headquarters. Salary data shown in Table 1–4 include base salary plus bonuses or other cash payments paid in 1974.

Table 1–4. Cash Compensation—Personnel Managers, 1974

Group	Lowest	First Quartile	Median	Third Quartile	Highest
Total (N = 5005)	$5,700	$16,151	$20,157	$25,783	$170,000
By Length of Experience in Personnel Administration					
Less than 2 years (N = 342)	$5,700	$10,623	$13,647	$17,136	$ 39,500
2–5 years (N = 947)	7,000	13,542	16,057	19,234	86,000
6–10 years (N = 1374)	9,000	16,310	19,180	22,754	102,000
11–15 years (N = 885)	9,420	18,354	22,235	27,798	170,000
Over 15 (N = 1457)	6,500	20,451	25,213	31,228	107,000
By Level of Education					
High School (N = 1221)	$6,760	$12,276	$16,146	$20,146	$ 52,500
College—no degree (N = 816)	5,700	13,548	17,077	21,525	70,000
Bachelor's degree (N = 1726)	6,500	16,130	19,650	24,859	99,000
Graduate training—no degree (N = 1131)	7,560	17,188	20,947	26,385	64,500
Graduate degree (N = 1111)	8,400	18,855	23,750	29,569	170,000

Source: American Society for Personnel Administration, 1974–1975 Salary Survey (Berea, Ohio, 1975), pp. 17–18.

The data shown indicate clearly that experience in the field and educational level make a difference. Other data from the survey show that age, length of service, level of position, and size of company also are reflected in salary levels. For example, the median income for personnel managers responsible for one unit of a company with less than 1,000 employees at that location was $17,163 in 1974 compared to a median income of $37,500 for personnel managers with responsibility for servicing an entire company with more than 15,000 employees.

Requirements for Success

As is true for most occupations, there is no definitive formula for assuring success as a personnel professional. Over the years, however, a number of surveys have been conducted to determine certain characteristics of people working in personnel jobs. Because these surveys have used different samples, they have not always produced identical results. Yet there is enough consistency so that a reasonably stable picture of people in personnel and industrial relations positions can be constructed.

EDUCATION

The great majority of personnel managers have college degrees; many have graduate degrees. As indicated by the salary data of Table 1–4, the more successful personnel executives are the ones with the highest level of education. The major field in college varies considerably, although in recent years a degree in business administration has been increasing in popularity and now appears to be the most common undergraduate degree for people in personnel (15, 26). Other majors frequently mentioned include psychology, economics, and engineering (12, 15). Graduate degrees of personnel executives most often are in business administration, with some in law, psychology, economics, and education (15).

Personnel managers tend to have taken certain courses in college with considerable frequency, no matter what their major field of study. Data on this point are shown in Table 1–5. The core subjects appear to be industrial psychology, an introductory course in personnel management, an introduction to labor relations, and human relations or organizational behavior (12). Results of other surveys (15, 34) support the view that personnel managers most often have a background of knowledge in industrial psychology, personnel, labor relations, and organizational behavior.

Because of the projected growth of the personnel occupation mentioned previously, there has been some concern about the lack of college-level courses in personnel management in many parts of the country. One study of 242 major colleges and universities indicated that they offer an average of fewer than three courses pertaining directly to personnel management, and there are 44 schools that had no personnel courses at all (4). As an aid to students interested in pursuing a personnel or industrial relations major at

Table 1–5. College Courses Related to Personnel Taken by Personnel Managers

Course	Number of Managers by Organization Level			
	Plant (N = 21)	Division (N = 20)	Corporate (N = 53)	All (N = 94)
Industrial psychology	9	16	36	61
Personnel administration	12	12	30	54
Labor problems	11	11	27	49
Human relations	8	13	23	44
Job evaluation	4	6	20	30
Problems in personnel administration	5	9	16	30
Wage and salary administration	5	8	17	30
Collective bargaining	5	5	19	29
Time and motion study	7	8	10	25
Industrial sociology	2	5	9	16
Psychological testing	3	0	4	7
Counseling and interviewing	2	0	3	5

Source: O. J. Harris, "Personnel Administrators—The Truth About Their Backgrounds," *MSU Business Topics*, 17, Summer 1969, p. 28. Reprinted by permission of the publisher, The Division of Research, Graduate School of Business Administration, Michigan State University, East Lansing.

the undergraduate or graduate level, the American Society for Personnel Administration has prepared a directory of nearly 200 colleges and universities in the United States and Canada offering such programs and listing the programs, faculties, and courses available (14).

WORK EXPERIENCE

One of the most frequent criticisms voiced by top executives in other areas regarding personnel managers is that they lack line or general management experience and thus do not understand many problems outside their own area of specialization (18). Among one group of top personnel executives, slightly less than half had had line experience at some point in their careers. On the average, for those who had worked in line positions, the duration of such employment was approximately five years; very few had over 10 years' experience. Thus, the top personnel executive is rarely a line manager who has been rotated into personnel for a limited period of time. Typically, he is a staff specialist who has spent considerable time in the personnel area.

Surveys including personnel managers at lower levels generally indicate that about two thirds have had experience outside personnel, although not always in a line management capacity (12, 28). There is no one area that is particularly frequent—accounting, production, sales, engineering, and many other jobs are noted (15). Often these are first jobs, in some cases rotating trainee assignments, from which the individual moves into personnel rather quickly. A career pattern entirely within the field of personnel and industrial relations is more prevalent among the younger people in the field (26).

OTHER REQUIREMENTS FOR SUCCESS

Most of what is known about the requirements for success in the personnel field other than education and experience is judgmental in nature. There is one study of a group of 101 personnel executives that does indicate that the more successful ones are similar to other successful high-level managers in such attributes as motivation to manage, supervisory ability, intelligence, and initiative (21). Compared to managers overall, however, personnel managers generally are somewhat lower in motivation to manage, particularly with respect to assertiveness (20).

Because relatively little of a scientific nature is known about what kind of person is most likely to succeed and what kind will fail, advisers tend to rely on rather general statements. An example of such statements concerning personal attributes desirable for personnel work is found in the *Occupational Outlook Handbook:*

Personnel workers should speak and write effectively and be able to work with people of all levels of intelligence and experience. They also must be able to see both the employee's and the employer's points of view. In addition, personnel workers should be able to work as part of a team. They need supervisory abilities and must be able to accept responsibility. A personnel worker should like detail, be persuasive, and have a congenial personality. (30, p. 147)

Support for some of the characteristics noted in the *Handbook* is found in a study of personnel executives who were asked to list the five personal characteristics they considered most essential for success in the field. The characteristics mentioned most frequently were integrity and effective communications, intelligence, and genuine interest in people (15). Since people—the organization's human resources—are what personnel management is all about, it does seem reasonable that a "genuine interest in people" may be crucial to success in personnel. It seems clear that a certain level of intelligence, an appropriate educational background, and motivation to manage also are necessary ingredients for making it to the top.

With this brief look at the opportunities for careers in personnel, we turn now to the historical development of the field. An appreciation of the traditions of and precedents from the various disciplines influencing present personnel practice will provide a background for viewing the various aspects of the work of personnel.

QUESTIONS

1. What are the most important productivity goals of a large city bank? What types of measures might be used to determine whether the human resources of the bank are contributing effectively to the achievement of these goals? What personnel programs would you suggest to improve the contribution of the human resources to the achievement of productivity goals?
2. Consider some of the changes in attitudes toward work that appear to have occurred in the past 10 to 20 years. What effect might these changes have on the types of personnel programs a company undertakes? Describe specific programs that could result from these changes.
3. What activities performed by the personnel department are likely to be found in all organizations regardless of type or size? What are some of the factors that determine whether certain personnel activities will be performed in a particular organization?
4. How does the fact that personnel is primarily a staff function affect the authority of the personnel manager?
5. Imagine that you are the president of a small manufacturing company that has grown to the point where you feel the need to hire a personnel manager. What qualifications—specific skills, education, experience, aspects of personality—would you look for? Where would you go to recruit such a person?

REFERENCES

1. American Society for Personnel Administration. *1974–1975 Salary Survey.* Berea, Ohio: the Society, 1975.
2. Battalia, Lotz, and Associates. *A Decade of Change in Top Management Organization and Executive Job Titles.* New York: Battalia, Lotz, and Associates, 1969.
3. Belasco, J. A., and J. A. Alutto. "Line Staff Conflicts: Some Empirical Insights." *Academy of Management Journal,* 12 (1969), 469–477.
4. Belt, J. A., and J. A. Richardson. "Academic Preparation for Personnel Management." *Personnel Journal,* 52 (1973), 373–380.
5. Boynton, R. E. "Where Can We Find a Good Personnel Man?" *Personnel Administrator,* 15 (1970), No. 5, 34–36.
6. Bureau of National Affairs, Inc. "ASPA-BNA Survey: Use of Consultants." *Bulletin to Management,* March 4, 1971, Part 2.
7. Bureau of National Affairs, Inc. "ASPA-BNA Survey: Trends in Personnel Management." *Bulletin to Management,* June 7, 1973, Part 2.
8. Bureau of National Affairs, Inc. "ASPA-BNA Survey No. 23: Planning and Budgeting the Personnel Program." *Bulletin to Management,* June 6, 1974, Part 2.
9. Bureau of National Affairs, Inc. *The Personnel Department,* Personnel Policies Forum Survey No. 92. Washington, D.C.: BNA, Inc., 1970.

10. DeSpelder, B. E. *Ratios of Staff to Line Personnel.* Columbus, Ohio: Bureau of Business Research, Ohio State University, 1962.
11. French, W., and D. A. Henning. "The Authority-influence Role of the Functional Specialist in Management." *Academy of Management Journal,* 9 (1966), 187–203.
12. Harris, O. J. "Personnel Administrators—The Truth About Their Backgrounds." *MSU Business Topics,* 17 (1969), No. 3, 22–29.
13. Henning, D. A., and R. L. Moseley. "Authority Role of a Functional Manager: The Controller." *Administrative Science Quarterly,* 15 (1970), 482–489.
14. Herman, Georgianna, Ed. *Personnel and Industrial Relations Colleges: An ASPA Directory.* Berea, Ohio: American Society for Personnel Administration, 1974.
15. Indiana State Chamber of Commerce. "Personnel Administration in Indiana." Indianapolis: the Chamber of Commerce, 1973.
16. Janger, A. R. *Personnel Administration: Changing Scope and Organization,* Studies in Personnel Policy No. 203. New York: National Industrial Conference Board, 1966.
17. Lecht, L. A. *Manpower Needs for National Goals in the 1970s.* New York: Praeger Publishers, Inc., 1969.
18. McFarland, D. E. *Company Officers Assess the Personnel Function,* AMA Research Study 79. New York: American Management Association, Inc., 1967.
19. Miner, J. B. "An Input-Output Model for Personnel Strategies." *Business Horizons,* 12 (1969), No. 3, 71–78.
20. Miner, J. B. "Levels of Motivation to Manage Among Personnel and Industrial Relations Managers." *Journal of Applied Psychology,* 61 (1976), 419–427.
21. Miner, J. B., and M. G. Miner. "Motivational Characteristics of Personnel Managers." *Industrial Relations,* 15 (1976), 225–234.
22. Miner, M. G., and J. B. Miner. *A Guide to Personnel Management.* Washington, D.C.: BNA Books, 1973.
23. Mitchell, H. M. "Selecting and Developing Personnel Professionals." *Personnel Journal,* 49 (1970), 583–589.
24. Patton, A. "Executive Compensation Inequities." *Business Horizons,* 13 (1970), No. 2, 73–84.
25. "Personnel—Fast Track to the Top." *Dun's Review,* 105 (April 1975), No. 4, 74–77.
26. Ramser, C. "The Personnel Executive: A Pilot Study." *North Texas State University Business Studies,* Fall (1968), 59–62.
27. Rezler, J. "Automation: Its Impact on the Organization and Functions of Personnel Management," in J. J. Famularo (ed.), *Handbook of Modern Personnel Administration.* New York: McGraw-Hill Book Company, 1972, Chapter 63.

28. Ritzer, G., and H. M. Trice. *An Occupation in Conflict: A Study of the Personnel Manager.* Ithaca, N.Y.: New York State School of Industrial and Labor Relations, Cornell University, 1969.

29. Simonds, R. H. "Human Resources Administration: In the Small Manufacturing Concern," in W. J. Wasmuth, R. H. Simonds, R. L. Hilgert, and H. C. Lee, *Human Resources Administration: Problems of Growth and Change.* Boston: Houghton Mifflin Company, 1970, pp. 105–184.

30. U.S. Department of Labor. *Occupational Outlook Handbook, 1974–1975 ed.*, Bureau of Labor Statistics Bulletin 1785. Washington, D.C.: Government Printing Office, 1974, pp. 146–147.

31. U.S. Department of Labor, Bureau of Labor Statistics. *Occupational Manpower and Training Needs,* Bulletin 1824. Washington, D.C.: Government Printing Office, 1974.

32. U.S. Department of Labor, Bureau of Labor Statistics. *National Survey of Professional, Administrative, Technical, and Clerical Pay, March 1975.* Washington, D.C.: Government Printing Office, 1975.

33. Wasmuth, W. J. "Human Resources Administration: Dilemmas of Growth," in W. J. Wasmuth, R. H. Simonds, R. L. Hilgert, and H. C. Lee, *Human Resources Administration: Problems of Growth and Change.* Boston: Houghton Mifflin Company, 1970, pp. 1–103.

34. Wheelen, T. L. "Graduate Business Education for Personnel Management Executives." *Personnel Journal,* 49 (1970), 932–934.

35. White, H. C., and R. E. Boynton. "Role of Personnel: A Management View." *Arizona Business,* 21 (1974), No. 8, pp. 17–21.

36. Yoder, D. "Personnel Ratios 1970." *Personnel Administrator,* 15 (1970), No. 6, 36–37.

2 The Historical Development of Personnel Management

There are probably few fields of organized human endeavor that have developed in a really pure state, uninfluenced by other areas of knowledge. Sociology was affected by history and social work, psychology developed from a merging of philosophy and physiology, and engineering is primarily an amalgam formed out of the traditional physical sciences, such as physics and chemistry, combined with the demands of the business enterprise. Many other examples could be cited.

Personnel management is no exception. The field as it currently exists represents a crystallization of a variety of historical and contemporary influences, among them economics, psychology, social work, engineering, and accounting. Together these influences have combined in a complex fashion to bring the profession to its current position in the management framework. The purpose of this chapter is to trace these historical roots and show how they have contributed to the growth and current status of personnel management.

In general, it appears that there have been two major traditions or trends within personnel management over the years. One of these, stemming largely from economics and accounting, has emphasized a hardheaded, profit-minded approach to the utilization of human resources; the other, with its origins in social work and certain subfields within psychology, has taken more of a social welfare viewpoint. This duality of approach appears to have hampered the development of the profession within certain segments of American industry, and the signs of the split have still not entirely disappeared (15). The social welfare tradition has been viewed as antithetical to the "real" organizational goal of productivity by many managers both within and outside the personnel field. On the other hand, the feeling among those with a social welfare orientation has been that management generally emphasized productivity and profit at the expense of employee satisfaction.

THE BEGINNINGS

Interest in, and concern with, the utilization and organization of human resources have been in evidence since antiquity (8). The topic appears in the philosophic, religious, and military writings of both ancient and medieval times, and certain aspects of current practice can be traced directly to origins in Europe during the 1400s (13). Yet the history of personnel management as a distinct managerial specialty does not extend back nearly that far. In fact, the field as a separate entity is actually of relatively recent origin. Its development had to await the growth of the business unit and the consequent emergence of at least some degree of managerial specialization. This type of growth did not begin to occur until the years between the close of the Civil War and the early part of the 20th century (6).

It was during this period that a significant increase in the size of the organizational unit began to take place, and it was then that departments devoted to such specialties as finance and accounting, production, and marketing came on the scene. These three were the most common subdivisions at that time. There is no evidence that separate departments devoted to the personnel function were in existence during this post–Civil War period (6).

Scientific Management

A small group of managers who were very much concerned with developing techniques for the maximization of the productivity goal through the effective utilization of human resources did begin to emerge, however. These were the industrial engineers, among whom Frederick W. Taylor (19) is perhaps best known. According to these people, the contribution of the human factor to the attainment of high productivity levels could be increased sizably through the appropriate use of selection, training, and monetary incentives.

Although Taylor and the other industrial engineers of the time, such as Frank and Lillian Gilbreth and Henry Gantt, had little interest in the formation of personnel departments as such, they did make a major contribution to that end through their insistence that management must pay attention to such matters as the selection of employees, proper training methods, and the development of appropriate compensation programs. This was in relation to a predominant concern with how machinery might be used most effectively.

The key components of this early industrial engineering approach were the emphasis on identifying the ideal physical conditions and methods of work and the concern with developing monetary incentives for the worker that would be both satisfying and effective. In this way, it was felt that there would be benefits to both the company and the individual. This movement, which was named "scientific management" by Taylor, became an extremely important force in American industry during the latter part of the 19th century and the early 20th century. By the time of World War I, scientific management had spread abroad and was applied to problems of improving productivity in France and England (23).

Scientific management constituted the first real attempt, originating from within management itself, to achieve a means of utilizing human resources that would be optimal from both the company and individual viewpoints. Nevertheless, scientific management was a continuing object of attack by workers and unions for many years, in spite of the fact that it gave important consideration to the welfare of the individual employee (10). Among management scholars, in fact, the motives behind Taylor's approach still are the subject of debate (7).

The Labor Movement

A second major influence during this period was the growth of the organized labor movement in the United States. Because the new unions were continually making demands for economic concessions from management, the history of the labor movement becomes almost inevitably intertwined with the history of personnel management. To understand the nature of these employee demands, why they became largely economic rather than social in nature, it is necessary to review, at least briefly, the background of unionism in the United States.

A trade-union movement can be found in this country as far back as the late 18th century, when organizations were formed in a number of cities to represent the printers, carpenters, and shoemakers. These unions were local in nature, with few financial resources to call on, although they did resort to strikes on a number of occasions even in those early years (1786, 1799, and 1809). They operated under one major handicap, however, during this period. All unions were considered under the English common law to be conspiracies against the public, because it was presumed that their purpose was to benefit the membership at the expense of society. Not until 1842, in the famous case of *Commonwealth* v. *Hunt,* did this interpretation of the legal status of trade unionism begin to change. At this time, a precedent was established that a union was no longer illegal in and of itself, but the means that it used to gain its ends (strikes, boycotts, and so on) might well provide a basis for legal action.

As a result of this decision and the rapid industrial expansion of the mid-19th century, the number of trade unions increased significantly, both along the eastern seaboard and in the developing areas around the Great Lakes. By the end of the Civil War, there were approximately 300 local unions, and national organizations had been formed by such groups as the printers, stonecutters, hat finishers, machinists, locomotive engineers, plasterers, cigar makers, and bricklayers.

The next step was the development of some type of national labor federation, and in 1886 a number of unions formed the American Federation of Labor (AFL). In contrast to some earlier, unsuccessful efforts to unify various union groups, undertaken primarily for political purposes of a socialist nature, the AFL was devoted to the purely economic objectives of increased wages and better working conditions and composed largely of unions organized along craft lines (cigar makers, printers, carpenters, and so on). The spokesman for the organization was Samuel Gompers, and under his presidency it grew rapidly in size and solidified its position despite considerable employer opposition. By 1917, total union membership in the United States, most of it within the AFL, was over 3 million. The growth of the union movement during this period produced an increasing concern throughout American industry with questions relating to manpower utilization and with what we would now call personnel policy.

The Welfare Secretaries

One response to this growth of trade unionism was the emergence of the so-called social, or welfare, secretaries, starting just prior to 1900. Although the major stimulus for the creation of these positions was without doubt management's need to find some means of stemming the union tide, it is also true that employers were increasingly concerned over the growing size of their organizations and the fact that it was becoming more and more difficult to maintain close personal contact with employees.

The welfare secretaries were expected to assist the workers by suggesting improvements in working conditions and in any other way that they could. It is largely from these individuals that the social welfare tradition in personnel management first developed. The welfare secretaries concerned themselves with helping workers with such matters as housing, medical care, educational facilities, and recreational activities, and in the various other areas that have become the province of the social workers of today (20). They were, in actual fact, engaged almost entirely in promoting the organizational maintenance objective, although this was not widely recognized.

The Early Personnel Departments

It was from a merging of these various developments that the first recognizable personnel departments began to appear in the period between the turn of the century and World War I. In 1902, the National Cash Register Company established a Labor Department that was responsible for such matters as wage administration, grievances, employment, sanitary and working conditions, record keeping, and worker improvement (6). Other companies gradually followed suit, and by 1912 the first employment managers association was founded (3). By 1917, this increased to 10 associations, with over 1,000 member companies (21).

Although the work performed in these early departments varied somewhat from company to company, there was a common core of activities that were almost invariably present. These were selection, recruiting, record keeping, training, time and motion studies, welfare, and, generally, union relations. The primary stated goal of the personnel function in this pre–World War I period, as with most other aspects of the business enterprise, appears to have been productivity, or profit. Welfare activities as well as methods improvements were evaluated either explicitly or implicitly in terms of their contribution to this objective. The organizational maintenance goal as such was not widely recognized or accepted, except among a rather limited group of individuals within the personnel area itself.

EARLY INDUSTRIAL PSYCHOLOGY

During this same period, some developments were occurring within certain American universities that were to have a profound impact on the future course of personnel management. The science of psychology had had its beginning on the European continent as a combination of physiology and philosophy. By 1900, it had penetrated the United States and had become well established in a number of major universities. Although originally defined as the study of consciousness, or conscious experience, this emphasis soon began to fade in the utility-minded American environment (4). Men like James Angell and John Dewey at the University of Chicago started to talk about the *uses* of consciousness and its functions. And psychology began to move to a much greater concern with practical problems.

Cattell and Muensterberg

This utilitarian approach was taken up shortly on the East Coast, particularly by James McKeen Cattell at Columbia University and by Hugo Muensterberg at Harvard. Both of these men made significant contributions to early industrial psychology in the period when the possibility of applying the still adolescent science to industrial problems was just beginning to be recognized. Subsequently, their ideas became part of the developing body of knowledge in the field of personnel management as well.

Although Cattell was a psychologist whose early training was in the German laboratories, where a purely descriptive, nonutilitarian approach to the study of conscious experience prevailed, he soon directed his attention almost entirely to ways in which psychology could be of use to society. By 1890, he had coined the term *mental test* and had assumed the chairmanship of the psychology department at Columbia University. During the ensuing years at Columbia, Cattell continued to actively encourage research and interest in the applications of psychology to practical problems. In his later years, he founded the Psychological Corporation, one of the first consulting firms providing psychological services to the business world and a major publisher of psychological tests for industrial use.

In an even more direct line with the development of personnel management are the activities of Hugo Muensterberg at Harvard University. During the first 15 years of the 20th century, Muensterberg developed an extremely active interest in seeking out ways in which psychology could be applied to the problems of business and industry and wrote extensively, expounding his views (16). He was also able to put a number of his ideas to good use within several firms in the Boston area. Perhaps his most famous study involved the development of a selection test for electric-streetcar operators. Throughout Muensterberg's research and writings, a strong emphasis on empirical analysis and statistical validation inheres. This emphasis has now rather thoroughly permeated the methodology of personnel research.

Psychology in World War I

The most historically significant contributions that psychology made to the origins of the personnel field occurred during World War I. Cattell and Muensterberg were important, but it was not until the war period that objective psychological tests were used on a major scale to facilitate the effective utilization of human resources within a large organization.

The U.S. Army was faced with the problem of deciding what to do with the millions of men being drafted into service. Which ones should go to Officer Candidate School, and which ones should get technical training? A special committee of psychologists constructed a short intelligence test known as the Army Alpha. Based on an experimental instrument being developed by Arthur Otis, a Cleveland psychologist, the Alpha was the first group intelligence test and a milestone in the methodology of psychological test construction.

During the course of administering the Army Alpha, it became apparent that a surprisingly large number of recruits were scoring at the zero point or very close to it. Investigation revealed that many of these individuals were illiterate, and that Army Alpha presumed a certain amount of literacy. This led to the construction of a second test, Army Beta, designed specifically to provide information regarding the intelligence of those who were not able to read and write well enough to complete Army Alpha. The new instrument proved invaluable as an aid in the placement of less-well-educated recruits. It subsequently found wide usage in the postwar years in the testing of immigrants who came to the United States with little knowledge of the English language.

THE INTERVAL BETWEEN THE WARS
The 1920s

As a result of steadily increasing growth prior to the war, the success of the Army personnel program, and the general business boom, personnel management grew rapidly during the 1920s. Many companies added personnel departments for the first time, and a number of colleges and universities began to offer training in the area. Personnel consulting firms began to appear, one of the first being the Scott Company, which was formed by a group of people who had worked on the Army Alpha and Beta during the war years. Personnel research studies were initiated in a variety of settings.

The personnel departments of this period looked much like many that exist today. The major areas of specialization were selection, recruiting, training, methods improvement, and employee welfare. The last activity was strongly supported during the 1920s, which often is referred to as the "age of paternalism" in personnel management. One aspect of employee welfare that received special emphasis in this period concerned employee safety and health, which resulted from the recent enactment of state workers' compensation laws (9).

Probably the most important factor contributing to the welfare emphasis was the very intensive campaign that management mounted to discourage the growth of the labor unions. This became possible after the government-sponsored and government-enforced agreements that had been in effect during the war period were permitted to expire. Many companies used both positive incentives, such as benefit and recreation programs, and negative sanctions in their efforts to keep the unions out. This was the period of the so-called yellow-dog contracts, under which the worker agreed, as a condition of employment, not to join a union. At this time also *company unionism* reached its peak. Management-sponsored employee groups of this kind were particularly prevalent in the petroleum industry.

Thus, the welfare programs of the 1920s represented in large part an attempt to eliminate employee dissatisfaction, thereby minimizing the conflict-producing impact of the union movement. But this conflict-reduction objective was not the only one involved here. There was a general feeling, which is still popular in some quarters today, that "a happy employee is a productive employee." Thus, the welfare programs were considered to be good for productivity and were justified as such by the personnel departments of the period.

Toward the end of the 1920s, a series of experiments began at the Hawthorne plant of the Western Electric Company, near Chicago, that was to extend over several years and to have a substantial impact on the field of personnel management. Briefly, these experiments, which have been described and discussed at length in other publications (12, 18, 23), were initiated in order to study the effects of physical factors such as lighting and ventilation on worker productivity. As time went on, it became increasingly apparent that productivity was primarily affected by the emotional state of the employee; by his relationship with other people, particularly those with whom he worked; and by the amount and kind of attention he received from his superiors.

These findings served as the basis for what has since come to be called the *human relations* movement in American industry. For our purposes, however, it is most important that they provided personnel managers with a major justification for their welfare programs. Here was some real evidence that factors in the realm of employee attitudes and motivation did make a difference insofar as performance and productivity and profits were concerned.

The Depression Years

Whereas the 1920s was a time of growth, the 1930s was just the reverse. With the great reduction in business activity throughout the world came a sharp emphasis on cutbacks and savings (17). Managements were almost universally interested in doing all they could to reduce costs and to eliminate activities that were not absolutely necessary. The welfare programs of personnel management had had some difficulty justifying their existence in times of prosperity; in a time of depression, they were clearly in serious trouble. In many companies, it soon became apparent that they were definitely expendable.

Gradually, therefore, the welfare tradition began to lose out within personnel management, and in many cases whole personnel departments went with it. Those that remained were in most instances rather drastically reoriented and reorganized. The stimulus for this change came in part from government, both federal and state, and in part from the labor unions.

Under the pressures of the depression, a number of laws were passed that placed the unions in a much more advantageous position than that which they had held previously. Among the most important of these were the Norris-La Guardia Act of 1932 and the Wagner Act of 1935. The former drastically limited the use of court injunctions as a method of preventing work stoppages. The Wagner Act went much further and guaranteed the right of workers to organize into labor unions and to bargain collectively with their employers. (These laws will be discussed further in Chapter 5.)

The stimulus provided by this new legal environment produced mass unionization drives in a number of industries that had never previously been organized—the automotive, aluminum, and rubber industries, among others. These new unions were in many instances of a very different nature than those that had existed since the 19th century. Increasingly, management found itself faced with demands from *industrial unions* that included all types of workers from a given industry, regardless of specific occupation. Almost all unions, previously, had been of the *craft* variety, containing workers in a single occupation irrespective of the industry in which they worked.

By 1941, the total number of union members had increased from the 1933 low of 2,973,000 to a very respectable 8,614,000 (2), and there were now two major national labor federations, the American Federation of Labor and the Congress of Industrial Organizations (CIO). The former still stressed the old concept of craft unionism, whereas the CIO was made up in large part of a group of industrial unions that had seceded from the AFL in 1935.

As a consequence of this tremendous growth in the size and power of the union movement, major changes had to be made in whatever remnants of the earlier personnel departments remained by the mid-1930s. Increasingly, personnel managers found that they had to concern themselves with developing recommendations and evaluating policies designed to deal with the resurgent labor unions. Individuals with legal training began to find positions in personnel departments, and the attention of the personnel field as a whole became riveted on the labor relations problem.

WORLD WAR II

Although World War I had a sizable impact on the development of personnel management, the significance of World War II was infinitely greater. One reason was that World War II was conducted on a considerably larger scale and, as a result, the need for effective manpower utilization was much more pronounced. Second, the demand was not only greater in a quantitative sense, but more complex in a qualitative sense. Weapons and machinery were of a much more advanced design, and the airplane in particular had introduced a new set of manpower problems.

As in World War I, personnel researchers were called on to help solve the problems of the armed forces in the placement of the vast numbers of draftees and volunteers; the task had become much more complex because of the tremendous increase in the number of technical specialties. The result was a great variety of psychological tests developed to aid in the process of allocating individuals to training programs and to specific duty assignments; many of these tests later were adapted for industry use (1). Military researchers also did considerable work in the applied science of learning and in human engineering as they sought better ways of designing military equipment and more effective ways of teaching people how to use it. Many of the techniques introduced by the armed services subsequently found their way into the business world and had a profound influence on industrial training and management development (13).

For the personnel function, however, the effect of World War II was not limited to developments in the military sector; there was a much more direct impact as the federal government asserted control over various programs relating to personnel management throughout the economy. The activities affected most directly were training and development, which was influenced primarily by the administration of the War Manpower Commission, and compensation and labor relations, which were under the control of the War Labor Board.

Developments in the Training Field

To meet the need for effective utilization of manpower in the United States, the War Manpower Commission was established to find ways of locating, training, and assigning people with appropriate skills not only for the military, but also for civilian government agencies, business, and agriculture. A major problem was how to train the large numbers of individuals who flocked into the defense plants, many of them women and older people with no factory experience, so they would become satisfactory workers within a relatively short period of time. The problem was complicated by the fact that there was a shortage of experienced instructors to provide the training. The solution was the development of a program of Job Instruction Training (JIT) sessions, conducted by the Commission's Training Within Industry Division, which were highly successful in training inexperienced trainers. The JIT guidelines, using some of the same principles of applied learning theory as those used by the military psychologists, were developed in considerable detail and became the basis of many industrial on-the-job training programs still in use.

A second type of training program that was stimulated by the War was the development program for managers and executives. Under government sponsorship, more than 200 colleges and universities began to offer courses for businessmen on such topics as office management and personnel administration, and in 1943 the Advanced Management Program was established at Harvard. Prior to World War II, the training effort in most companies was limited to manual skills, and many training programs that had existed earlier were abandoned during the depression; by the end of the War, training had become a well-established part of the personnel function (9).

The War Labor Board

At the time of the United States involvement in World War II, the unions were continuing their organizing efforts on a large scale, often with rival unions trying to organize workers at the same plant. Because these jurisdictional disputes were a potential threat to achieving production goals, the mission of the National War Labor Board was to prevent these and other types of labor disputes, a mission in which the Board was highly successful.

It was in the effort to prevent inflation and disputes over wages that the War Labor Board had the most direct impact on personnel management.

In the administration of wage and salary controls, the Board exerted authority over all employers with nine or more employees regardless of whether they were represented by a union. Regulations issued by the Board limited the amounts of wage increases employers could grant and also specified what other types of compensation were permissible. One effect of limiting pay increases was that employers increasingly offered extra payments in the form of paid holidays and vacations; it was during this period that these so-called fringe benefits became a major payroll cost for most employers.

For the typical personnel department, the major effect of the War Labor Board's existence was the setting up of a formal wage and salary administration program. Because the Board permitted adjustments without prior approval if they were made under an established plan for wage progression, many companies established such plans for the first time. Just as most companies had no formal training programs before World War II, wage and salary administration programs also were rare but became well established during the wartime period. Two lasting effects of the War Labor Board's regulations are the concepts of adjusting wages to changes in the cost of living and using wage surveys to determine whether the wages paid by one company are fair compared to those paid by other companies (13).

1945–1970: A QUARTER-CENTURY OF GROWTH

The overall impact of World War II on personnel management was that the scope of activities handled by the personnel department increased substantially, and the personnel manager became a much more visible part of the organization. To make sure the company was in compliance with government regulations, and also because of pressures from the unions, personnel administrators increasingly found themselves taking over many responsibilities that traditionally had belonged to the line supervisors. By the end of the war, personnel was recognized and established as a specialized function of management, and the major activities comprising the personnel function as we know it today had been introduced.

The Postwar Decade

In the postwar period, personnel management had reached what one writer called its "adolescence," with the role of personnel differing widely from one organization to another and no general agreement on what its role should be "when it grows up" (22). However, the decade following the war was a period of almost constant expansion in nearly every segment of the economy, and the field of personnel administration shared in this growth. One result of the continued economic growth in the 1950s was that serious shortages of technical and engineering manpower developed, and personnel people were called upon for solutions to the problem. A solution for many of the nation's large corporations involved extensive college recruiting programs of the kind still found at most large universities.

Labor unrest in the period following World War II was another factor affecting personnel administration. From 1941 to 1945, union membership had increased by 5 million to nearly 13 million; with the end of the war and the end of wage controls, the unions became particularly militant and made increasing demands on industry for health and welfare programs, pensions, and other fringe benefits that were extremely costly to management. Many of these demands were finally granted, but only after extended negotiations and some long and bitter strikes. Public alarm at the obvious power of the unions during this period finally resulted in the enactment of the Taft-Hartley Act to curb the abuses of union power (14). Even with the Taft-Hartley law in effect, unions continued to grow and had more than 17 million members by 1954. In 1955, the 20-year split in the labor movement came to an end when the two major groups of unions united to form the AFL-CIO; despite the merger, however, jurisdictional disputes between unions continued to create problems for management.

Government regulation also continued to have an impact on personnel. Companies were required by law to provide reemployment rights to veterans of both World War II and the Korean conflict, and wage and salary controls were reinstituted in the early 1950s, when inflational pressures mounted as a result of the Korean involvement. The combination of manpower shortages, labor relations, and government relations contributed to the increasing influence and expansion of personnel management and also to increasing awareness of organizational maintenance as an important management goal. At the same time, it became apparent that many of the traditional approaches of personnel administrators to the problems of selection and training were no longer viable because of changes in the composition of the work force and in the nature of the work to be done. Compared to earlier generations of workers, the postwar labor force was much better educated and had a much broader spectrum of experiences; increasing numbers of women also were seeking employment in the business world. Technological changes and automated production processes called for quite different skills; extensive retraining often was required, and in many instances companies were completely restructured as a result of technological innovations.

By the mid-1950s, it became clear that the solutions to problems of human resources management could not easily be found in the personnel policies and techniques existing in most companies. Fortunately for management, the academic world had begun to take an interest in questions relating to the management of human resources, and it was from the universities, and particularly from behavioral scientists, that the solutions began to emerge.

The Role of the Universities

Courses in personnel management at the college level date back to the 1920s in a number of universities, but it was not until the post–World War II period that they became widespread. During this period, there was a sharp increase in the number of courses dealing with manpower utilization and with other aspects of the personnel function, and a major in personnel management was being offered in most schools of business administration. Graduate programs, in particular, were attracting sizable numbers of students.

In conjunction with the increase in course offerings in the personnel area, a second major development was the establishment at a number of universities of various research centers and institutes devoted specifically to the study of manpower problems (13). A few industrial relations centers that were supported primarily by sources outside the universities themselves had been established in the 1930s, but during the 1940s and 1950s nearly 50 research centers were founded, and many of them were financed by university or public funds. Among the first of these were the School of Industrial and Labor Relations at Cornell University (1944), the Institute of Labor and Industrial Relations at the University of Illinois (1946), and the Industrial Relations Center at the University of Minnesota (1945).

Although these centers have been most important in their role as agents in the search for basic knowledge, they have also made a significant contribution in attracting a number of capable individuals to the personnel field. Scholars from a variety of disciplines have been brought together in the industrial relations centers, with the result that a multidimensional approach to the problems of the field has been encouraged. Most prominent among the participants have been economists, psychologists, sociologists, industrial engineers, political scientists, and lawyers. The research emerging from this amalgamation of basic disciplines has proved to be of inestimable value to the practitioners of personnel management.

The Impact of Behavioral Science Research

Applications of the results of behavioral science research to the solution of personnel problems began with the work of the psychologists in World War I. During the 1920s many large corporations established personnel research units that set up selection testing and performance appraisal programs similar to the ones that had been so effective in the military. However, the research conducted by these in-house groups was not generally publicized outside the company, so the results did not contribute to the advancement of knowledge in the area.

The Hawthorne studies of the late 1920s, noted earlier, were the first behavioral science studies of industrial workers to receive widespread dissemination, but it was not until the 1940s that they had any real impact on industry. The findings of the Hawthorne researchers, which suggested that a permissive, or democratic, style of leadership was more effective than the traditional authoritarian leadership, received support from another series of studies on leadership techniques conducted by researchers at the University of Iowa under the direction of Kurt Lewin. These and other studies led to a new emphasis in human relations training for supervisors and higher-level managers in programs that were adopted on a large scale in industry during the 1950s.

While the human relations movement obviously was tied to organizational maintenance goals and fostered by the welfare tradition in personnel, it was also argued that productivity goals would be affected positively. According to proponents of the human relations approach, democratic leadership would result in employees who were more satisfied with their jobs and thus would perform more effectively and contribute more to the achievement of the organization's productivity goals. The relationship between employee job satisfaction and productivity became the focus for a vast amount of scientific research in the 1950s and 1960s as it became increasingly clear that the human relations approach does not necessarily result in greater productivity. This relationship still is being investigated, but the consensus at present seems to be that it is possible to improve either productivity or job satisfaction, but not both at the same time (11).

While it is true the behavioral scientists have not solved the productivity-satisfaction dilemma, their efforts have resulted in the development of better techniques and innovative approaches in many areas of personnel practice. In addition to the contributions of those in the academic world, researchers in the employ of major companies have begun to publish much of their research so that others can benefit from their results. Increasingly, however, the researchers are finding that what works in one organization may not be the most effective approach in another; more and more research is being directed to determining what policies and practices will contribute to the most effective utilization of human resources in a specific company.

Professional Activities

While developments within the universities and among the behavioral scientists were contributing to the academic respectability of personnel management, significant changes also were taking place for those involved in personnel practice. As more people moved into personnel administration, they began to have an increasing sense of identity and increasing concern over matters of ethical personnel practice. For those in personnel practice, there have been two major areas of expansion in professional activities over the past 20 to 30 years—professional associations and publications.

Among the professional groups in personnel, the largest is the American Society for Personnel Administration, which has grown from fewer than 100 members at its founding in 1948 to nearly 15,000 in 1975. Another group, made up primarily of personnel administrators in the public sector, is the International Personnel Management Association (IPMA), formed in 1973 through a merger of two existing personnel groups oriented toward government and other public institutions. There are also many associations made up of people interested in special areas of personnel, such as the

American Society of Training Directors and the American Compensation Association, that have expanded their activities over the years. Two groups that include large numbers of university professors and that have contributed to the advancement of knowledge in the field are the Industrial Relations Research Association, which includes mostly economists and labor relations experts, and the Division of Industrial and Organizational Psychology (Division 14) of the American Psychological Association, which includes personnel researchers from private industry and the government as well as most academics in personnel psychology. All these associations have had a significant impact on personnel management through their meetings, their sponsorship of research projects, and their publications.

Among the most widely read publications in the field, two began in the early 1920s—*Personnel,* which is published bimonthly by the American Management Association, and *Personnel Journal,* a monthly published privately. In the period following World War II, several new publications appeared. Some of these were sponsored by the newly established university centers, such as the quarterly *Industrial and Labor Relations Review,* begun in 1947 by the Cornell School of Industrial and Labor Relations, and *Industrial Relations,* published by the University of California's Institute of Industrial Relations since 1961. In the behavioral sciences, reports of results of personnel research appear in *Personnel Psychology,* published quarterly since 1948; research relevant to personnel also frequently is found in the *Journal of Applied Psychology,* which has been published for more than 50 years by the American Psychological Association. The major personnel associations also have their own periodicals—*The Personnel Administrator,* published by ASPA, and *Public Personnel Management,* published by IPMA. In addition, there are many periodicals for management in general that publish articles relevant for personnel people; the number and scope of these publications also have expanded greatly in the period since World War II.

THE RECENT PAST

In recent years, the growth in personnel management has continued in spite of, or in some cases because of, outside social and economic forces that have created a multitude of problems for management in general. As noted in Chapter 1, the 1960s witnessed a growth both in numbers of people working in personnel administration and in the level and importance of personnel as an organizational function, and the forecast is that this growth will continue well into the 1980s. One aspect of this growth has been the extension of personnel administration from the large corporations and the federal government to smaller business organizations and to state and local government agencies.

A major factor contributing to the need for even small employers to have a personnel officer is the tremendous increase in laws and government regulations affecting one personnel activity or another that have gone into effect in the last 5 to 10 years. A detailed discussion of the legal influences on personnel management is presented in Chapter 5; it is important to note, however, that the overall impact of the legislation of recent years has been to bring matters relating to human resources utilization to the attention of the highest levels of management. Achievement of organizational goals, in both productivity and maintenance areas, is directly at stake when a company faces a possible million-dollar lawsuit because of failure to comply with the requirements of legislation, such as that relating to equal employment opportunity.

The expansion in governmental influence on personnel management has resulted in large measure from changing values of society. Increasingly, in recent years, the view has been expressed that management, particularly business management, should concern itself with such matters as social responsibility and service to society (15). Legislation concerning fair employment practices, occupational safety and health, and pollution control represents the government's expanding role in exerting pressure on business and other institutions to act in accordance with society's changing values.

Major changes in personnel practice in areas such as selection and training have resulted from these changes in values and from the efforts of employers to achieve organizational maintenance goals by adapting to society's pressures. Just as results were beginning to be realized in the realm of social responsibility, however, economic difficulties—inflation and recession—beset American industry. By the mid-1970s, productivity and survival once again became the paramount concerns of management, and social goals became a source of conflict; in many companies, programs in the area of social responsibility came to a standstill, at least temporarily (5).

While it is not yet clear what the long-range impact of the current social and economic forces will be as far as personnel management is concerned, the indications are that personnel is more than ever in the forefront of management. People with expertise in solving people problems are being asked to participate in the top-level decision making of today's organizations to a greater extent than ever before.

QUESTIONS

1. Listed below are a number of activities that come under the responsibility of the personnel department in most organizations. For each activity listed, (a) indicate the decade of this century in which it became widespread as a personnel function, and (b) discuss the social, economic, or political pressures that led to its introduction as a major component of personnel programs.
   a. Wage and salary administration.
   b. Safety and health programs.
   c. Selection testing.
   d. Management development programs.

e. Labor relations.

f. College recruiting.

g. Human relations training.

2. What are the major factors contributing to the increased responsibility and visibility of personnel as a management function over the past 10 to 20 years?

3. List four professional associations that have been influential in the development of personnel management, and indicate the type of person who would be likely to be a member of each association.

4. If you were asked to write a paper tracing the development of one aspect of personnel administration over the past 50 years, what two periodicals would most likely be the best sources of information?

5. What is the significance of each of the following in the development of personnel management:

a. Welfare secretaries.

b. Western Electric Company-Hawthorne Plant.

c. The War Labor Board.

d. Job Instruction Training (JIT).

e. Industrial unions.

REFERENCES

1. Bellows, R. *Psychology of Personnel in Business and Industry.* Englewood Cliffs, N.J.: Prentice-Hall, Inc., 1961.

2. Bernstein, I. "The Growth of American Unions." *American Economic Review,* 44 (1954), 303–304.

3. Bloomfield, M. "The Aim and Work of the Employment Managers' Associations." *Annals, American Academy of Political and Social Science,* 65 (1916), 77.

4. Boring, E. J. *A History of Experimental Psychology.* New York: Appleton-Century-Crofts, 1950.

5. Bureau of National Affairs, Inc. "ASPA-BNA Survey No. 29: Economic Pressures and Employee Relations Programs." *Bulletin to Management,* August 14, 1975, Part 2.

6. Eilbert, H. "The Development of Personnel Management in the United States." *Business History Review,* 33 (1959), 345–364.

7. Fry, L. W. "Frederick W. Taylor—Organizational Behaviorist?," in A. G. Bedeian, A. A. Armenakis, W. H. Holley, Jr., and H. S. Feild, Jr., Eds. *Proceedings, Thirty-fifth Annual Meeting of the Academy of Management,* 1975, pp. 1–3.

8. George, C. S. *The History of Management Thought.* Englewood Cliffs, N.J.: Prentice-Hall, Inc., 1972.

9. Kahler, G. E., and A. C. Johnson. *The Development of Personnel Administration, 1923–1945.* Madison, Wis.: Bureau of Business Research and Services, Graduate School of Business (Monograph No. 3), 1971.

10. Kakar, S. *Frederick Taylor: A Study in Personality and Innovation.* Cambridge, Mass.: The MIT Press, 1970.
11. Katzell, R. A., and D. Yankelovich. *Work, Productivity, and Job Satisfaction.* New York: Psychological Corporation, 1975.
12. Landsberger, H. *Hawthorne Revisited.* Ithaca, N.Y.: Cornell University Press, 1958.
13. Ling, C. C. *The Management of Personnel Relations—History and Origins.* Homewood, Ill.: Richard D. Irwin, Inc., 1965.
14. Macdonald, Robert M. "Collective Bargaining in the Postwar Period." *Industrial and Labor Relations Review,* 20 (1967), 553–577. Reprinted in A. N. Nash and J. B. Miner, *Personnel and Labor Relations: An Evolutionary Approach.* New York: Macmillan Publishing Co., Inc., 1973, 414–438.
15. Milton, C. R. *Ethics and Expediency in Personnel Management: A Critical History of Personnel Philosophy.* Columbia, S.C.: University of South Carolina Press, 1970.
16. Muensterberg, H. *Psychology and Industrial Efficiency.* Boston: Houghton Mifflin Company, 1913.
17. Nash, A. N., and J. B. Miner. *Personnel and Labor Relations: An Evolutionary Approach.* New York: Macmillan Publishing Co., Inc., 1973.
18. Roethlisberger, F. J., and W. J. Dickson. *Management and the Worker.* Cambridge, Mass.: Harvard University Press, 1939.
19. Taylor, F. W. *The Principles of Scientific Management.* New York: W. W. Norton & Company, Inc., 1967.
20. "Welfare Work in Company Towns." *Monthly Labor Review,* 25 (1927), 314–321. Reprinted in A. N. Nash and J. B. Miner, *Personnel and Labor Relations: An Evolutionary Approach.* New York: Macmillan Publishing Co., Inc., 1973, pp. 19–25.
21. Willits, J. H. "Development of Employment Managers' Associations." *Monthly Labor Review,* 5 (1917), 497–499.
22. Worthy, James C. "Changing Concepts of the Personnel Function." *Personnel,* 25 (November 1948), 166–175. Reprinted in A. N. Nash and J. B. Miner, *Personnel and Labor Relations: An Evolutionary Approach.* New York: Macmillan Publishing Co., Inc., 1973, pp. 153–163.
23. Wren, D. A. *The Evolution of Management Thought.* New York: The Ronald Press Company, 1972.

3 — *A Model of the Personnel Management Function*

One major criticism leveled at personnel management as it is actually practiced in organizations, especially those of a business nature, is that it is technique bound (3, 6). The field has attracted many individuals who are strongly committed to particular techniques rather than to broad managerial problem solving. Characteristically, because of the nature of their training and experience, these individuals are truly conversant with only a limited range of personnel techniques. Thus, they are in a poor position to make meaningful choices among multiple alternatives. They tend to take the techniques and approaches they know as givens and then apply them to as many problem situations as they possibly can, rather than start with the problem and then select the particular technique that will yield the best solution.

There is no question that personnel management has long suffered from a continuing succession of fads and cure-alls—its own particular collection of patent medicines. This emphasis on techniques rather than problems tends to produce a situation in which the techniques are applied indiscriminately, whether or not they are appropriate to a company's particular human resource problems. Approaches may be continued long after they have outlived any possible usefulness. There is little incentive to develop personnel strategies specifically tailored to changing demands from the outside world, or to internal problems, when the techniques themselves assume greater importance than the problems to be solved.

This is not to say that personnel management does not need the techniques; in fact it needs them badly, and it needs as many useful ones as it can get. But it is important that these techniques become the servants of comprehensive decision making and wide-ranging strategy formulation, rather than ends in themselves. Toward this objective the model of the personnel function contained in this chapter has been developed. The intent in presenting it here, at this early point in the book, is to direct attention away from the specific techniques per se and toward broad problem solving and the making of choices from among multiple alternatives. Similar models designed to foster strategy formulation are appearing with increasing frequency in the personnel literature (1, 2).

GOALS, CONSTRAINTS, AND FACILITATORS

The basic assumption underlying the model is that organizations have certain goals that provide a degree of focus for their activities, and that to the extent a company achieves an integration of effort behind meaningful goals, it is likely to be effective and successful. Discussions in Chapters 1 and 2 have already considered these goals in some detail and some of the historical problems of personnel management associated with them, so only a brief review is required here. At least in an official sense, goals are established by the next larger social unit, the society, rather than from within the organization itself. However, the actual, operative goals which apply within the organization may deviate in varying degrees from these official expectations. In one sense, the goals of a company are the role prescriptions established for organizations of its particular type within the framework of the total social structure. They provide a definition of what the organization is expected to contribute (7, 8).

At the same time that society specifies goals for its constituent organizations, indicating how necessary functions are to be allocated among the various societal sectors, it also establishes control over many of the means used to reach these objectives. In effect, certain activities are constrained and restricted, while others are facilitated and fostered. Thus, society operates both to set the goals of business firms and to introduce forces that establish, or at least make particularly attractive, certain paths to goal attainment.

Company Goals

Business organizations, comprising the economic sector, as previously noted, operate with two primary types of goals under a capitalistic system. To the extent a firm is attaining both of these, it may be presumed to justify its creation and existence within society. These goals serve to guide all facets of organizational activity. That being so, they are relevant for personnel management, just as they are for marketing, manufacturing, accounting, and other functions.

THE PRODUCTIVITY GOAL

All organizations have one or more task objectives. In the United States, the economic sector of society is expected to operate in accordance with the capitalistic system. Thus, the task objective of business organizations is closely allied not only to the production of goods and services, but to the maximization of long-term net profit as well. Society expects business firms to produce as much as possible and make as much profit as possible within the limitations imposed by existing constraints and the organizational maintenance goal.

THE ORGANIZATIONAL MAINTENANCE GOAL

At the same time that companies are productive, they must also take steps to ensure survival on other grounds. The organization must be maintained as an ongoing social unit in the face of both internal and external pressures and stresses. Internal stress derives from intergroup conflict, low morale, and widespread dissatisfaction. It may under extreme circumstances result in a total disintegration of the organization, as members leave and subunits split off. Such matters have been the special concern of psychologists and sociologists. External stress, on the other hand, derives from the pressures imposed by governments, public opinion, and other economic organizations. Here economists and political scientists have been particularly concerned.

Constraints and Facilitators for Personnel Decisions

Decisions made to implement the attainment of company goals are influenced by a host of constraints and facilitators. There are a number of things that, at a given point in space and time, a personnel manager can and cannot do in carrying out his function. Certain actions may be physically impossible, or the consequences may be such as to make them distinctly unattractive; others may be very attractive. These forces, which impinge upon decision making in the personnel area, are of two kinds.

INTERNAL FACTORS

The major internal factors that serve to influence personnel decisions are the characteristics of the company's labor force, the existing structure of role prescriptions, and the union contract currently in effect. Individual differences, as they are reflected in a particular work force, in all probability have the most pronounced impact.

At a particular point in time, a company's employees are characterized by specific distributions of abilities and personalities. These distributions may act to facilitate particular kinds of personnel actions; they may provide the basis for the success of certain current operations. At the same time, other alternative decisions may be limited, although later the internal constraints thus imposed can be overcome through the hiring of new employees, training, and other procedures. Many companies have experienced serious difficulties because the constraints introduced by the nature of an existing work force have not been fully recognized. The very internal factors that facilitate present approaches may restrict change. Thus, rapid shifts to new products, automated procedures, or a strong research orientation may fail because current employees do not have the required capabilities and cannot adapt fast enough.

Restrictions are also imposed by the existing procedures for segmenting the total work effort, as a result of organization planning, manpower planning, and job analysis. These procedures may make it very easy to get the things done that they were set up to facilitate. But when a particular structure has been developed, with certain prescribed lines of authority, status, and communications, it may be difficult to get other types of things done. The limitations can be overcome through a restructuring of the organization or through job redesign, but at any one time they represent a clearcut constraint system. Similarly, the union contract specifies what can and cannot be done in certain areas, with regard to the utilization of human resources. It, too, can be changed, but rarely with ease, and then only when the next occasion for collective bargaining presents itself.

EXTERNAL FACTORS

Forces from outside the organization are even more resistant to change than those of an internal nature. This is particularly true of external forces introduced by the culture. In Japan, discharging a man for incompetence has long been considered reprehensible, and the particular equalitarian value system of the communist countries has served effectively to bar almost all psychological testing. Similarly, the high incidence of illiteracy in many underdeveloped countries tends to restrict company training efforts severely.

Within a country, geographical differences may also introduce significant constraints. Existing attitudes may place major barriers in the way of hiring particular groups of individuals for certain types of jobs. Differences in the educational, intellectual, and other characteristics of regional populations may force much more intensive recruiting efforts, expanded training, or even a curtailment of expansion plans.

Similar constraint systems may characterize entire industries. Differences in the propensity to strike impose limitations on the extent to which organizational maintenance considerations can be ignored. In years past, in industries such as mining and lumber, it was essential to devote considerable effort to such matters; in agriculture and the utilities, it was much less so. Again, in fields such as petroleum refining, where advancing technology has markedly reduced manpower needs, selection is not available in most cases as a means of upgrading a labor force; new refinery workers are only rarely hired. Industry constraints of much the same kind operate in other sectors of the economy.

Finally, there is the great variety of legal constraints that serve to restrict personnel actions. Perhaps most widely known are the federal labor laws, the Wagner Act and the Taft-Hartley Act. But there are also numerous state laws in the labor relations area, as well as laws that limit employment decisions, at all levels of government. The Fair Labor Standards Act, fair employment practices legislation, the Social Security Act, Workmen's Compensation, and so on, in addition to various court and commission rulings, can be cited as examples. These laws and rulings impose constraints on the payment of wages, working hours, selection procedures, separations, safety procedures, the utilization of older workers, and employment in a research capacity.

Yet it is no more appropriate to view external forces as introducing constraints only than it is to so view internal forces. Many external forces serve to facilitate particular kinds of decisions. Thus, the passage and subsequent enforcement of civil rights legislation has in fact made it much easier to hire minority group members. The laws have served to mitigate the influence of previously dominant attitudes in many communities, thus facilitating decisions to hire highly qualified women, blacks, and others for positions that were previously not available to them. Even the existence of very low educational levels in a particular area or country may have positive consequences in certain types of situations. Thus, a company needing large numbers of minimally skilled workers may find hiring easier under these circumstances.

INPUTS AND OUTPUTS

Internal and external factors operate on an organization, which may be most appropriately viewed as a behavioral system, performing in accordance with the input-output model (4, 5). Insofar as the personnel function is concerned, the input side deals primarily with people, although for other purposes financial resources, materials, facilities, and technology may also be treated as inputs. People become available to the organization as a result of the employment process. They enter the firm with abilities, skills, personality characteristics, and cultural values that, as previously noted, operate to impose certain constraints on personnel decisions. But individual differences are also the raw materials, in a human resources sense, through which productivity and maintenance goals are achieved.

On the output side, the major consideration insofar as personnel management is concerned is the behavior of employed individuals as organization members. This behavior involves three aspects: (a) the things that people who work for the company say and do, (b) the things that people who work for the company are expected to say and do, and (c) the relationships between expectations and what members of the organization actually say and do.

Role Prescriptions

The things that people who work for a company are expected to do may be labeled as role prescriptions. These role prescriptions are developed to contribute most effectively to goal attainment. At least this is the intent. Unhappily, exact methods of determining whether a given structure of organizational roles is maximally supportive of productivity and maintenance goals are not generally available. Thus, there is usually considerable guesswork involved, even though experience can be a useful guide.

Nevertheless, after such role prescriptions are established, they become at a given point in space and time a set of internal constraints on related decisions. They impose limitations on personnel actions, just as individual differences do. At the managerial level, a major contributor in introducing role expectations is the process of organization planning. At lower levels in the company, some form of job analysis is used to perform this function, although on occasion aspects of a formal job analysis program are extended upward into the ranks of management. Manpower planning also establishes role prescriptions.

At all levels, it is important that the role prescriptions established be clear and that they be accepted within the organization as legitimate. In part, this is necessary as a means to gaining the full advantages of division of labor in the pursuit of maximal productivity. But clear-cut jurisdictions, with little overlap and widespread acceptance, are also an important means to internal conflict reduction. Thus, the process of setting role prescriptions can make a sizable contribution to both major types of organizational goals.

Role Behavior

The things people are expected to do on the job are known as role prescriptions; the things they actually do are known as role behaviors. To the extent these role behaviors approximate a perfect match with the appropriate role prescriptions, an individual is said to be effective or successful. It is assumed that he is in fact contributing to company goal achievement.

Performance evaluation is essentially a matter of determining the degree of this matching. It is an attempt to take organizational goal attainment down to the level of the individual contribution. Or, put somewhat differently, it represents an evaluation of the behavioral output in terms of its contribution to the total firm. What is really important, insofar as an organization is concerned, is not how much an individual does, but how much of what he does is organizationally relevant as determined by his role.

As with the establishing of role expectations, the evaluation of role behaviors tends to be differentiated on a vertical scale. Management-appraisal techniques are utilized at the upper levels, as is employee evaluation at the submanagerial levels. In the former instance, considerable emphasis is usually placed on the performance of the group managed as well as on the performance of the manager himself; below the ranks of management, only the performance, or role behavior, of the individual himself is of concern.

The Input Side

In the presentation of this theoretical model, the output side is discussed first, because the selection of individual inputs must be carried out with a view to maximizing future role prescription–role behavior matching. An organization should pick those individuals for membership who subsequently will be most effective on the job. To fully understand personnel selection, then, one must be aware of what the concept of effective performance implies.

This means that studies should be conducted to establish procedures that will in fact identify those individuals within an applicant group who are most likely to succeed. Unfortunately, some firms use a cumbersome and often very expensive selection apparatus that falls far short of accomplishing this objective. In such cases, the selection process may contribute only very minimally to goal attainment. Certainly, there is little point in extensive recruiting if a company does not select from among those recruited the specific individuals who will contribute most on an organizationally relevant basis.

This requirement that selection techniques be evaluated in terms of their contribution to the company holds for all approaches. Such techniques for the evaluation of individual inputs to an organization are of two types. First, there are those that utilize information on past behavior to predict future behavior. Among these are most selection interviews, application blanks, biographical inventories, and reference checks and the more comprehensive background investigations. Second, there are the techniques that utilize information on current behavior and functioning to predict future behavior. Among these are physical examinations, ability testing, personality testing, and skill or achievement testing.

THE INPUT-OUTPUT MEDIATORS

A final aspect of the model, perhaps the most important in that it covers more different types of personnel activities, is that of the input-output mediator. Such techniques are used to sustain or improve upon the original input so that the output comes as close to being maximized as possible. These mediators may be grouped in several ways.

Structural and Functional Mediators

One basis for grouping is in terms of structural and functional characteristics. The structural mediators are the previously discussed techniques for establishing role requirements. These techniques provide a basis for evaluating role behaviors, but only the role behaviors themselves represent actual organizational outputs. The structural mediators are procedures for grouping organizational tasks and establishing role requirements so as to channel the behaviors of organization members in the direction of goal attainment. This is accomplished through manpower and organization planning, and job analysis. After these role prescriptions are set, they represent internal constraints.

The functional mediators influence organization members through procedures that impinge on the individual directly, rather than through role prescriptions. Included in this category are management development, training, wage and salary administration, safety management, counseling, discipline, medical treatment, labor relations activities, fringe benefits, and employee communications. All the techniques used to influence organizational input discussed in this book, with the exception of human resources and organization planning, and job analysis, are functional in character. Yet the current listing is not meant to be definitive. Fifty years from now, approaches that at present are not even under consideration may well have achieved widespread acceptance.

Productivity-oriented and Maintenance-oriented Mediators

As previously indicated, the structural mediators normally serve both types of organization goals. They segment work, permitting specialization and thus more efficient productivity, while establishing jurisdictions that serve to limit internal conflict. Although in any given firm the major emphasis in developing role prescriptions may be on productivity or on maintenance considerations, both factors are likely to receive some recognition.

The functional mediators, on the other hand, appear to be much more susceptible to differentiation in terms of the type of organizational goal fostered. Yet even here there may be some overlap. Thus, although management development techniques generally appear to be strongly oriented toward productivity, certain human relations programs as well as sensitivity training are clearly directed toward organizational maintenance. This suggests that, at least potentially, many of the functional mediators could be focused on either type of goal or on both. In actual practice, however, there has been a tendency to use a particular type of mediator primarily for one purpose or the other.

Thus, management development, training, wage and salary administration, safety management, medical procedures, counseling, discipline, and the like tend to be applied most frequently toward the end of increasing productivity. The various approaches in the labor relations area, employee benefits and services, and communications procedures are characteristically maintenance-oriented.

Input-improving, -sustaining, and -controlling Mediators

In many of its applications, the input-output model has included a feedback, or control, procedure. Thus, when the operation of part or all of the system drops below a certain level, or deviates too much from certain predetermined standards, corrective forces are activated, much as a thermostat serves to activate a heating system when the temperature falls below a preset level.

Although this feedback, or control, concept is useful in understanding the functioning of some input-output mediators, it is not adequate to the task of explaining the whole gamut of techniques. At least two other types of mediators must be considered. These two categories, along with the control concept, provide a way of viewing mediators as they relate to the input side of the system.

One group of mediators is oriented toward the improvement of inputs so that role behavior eventually exceeds the level that could have been anticipated merely from a knowledge of the original input. Thus, the objective is to improve performance above and beyond what was manifest at the time of hiring. The structural mediators certainly contribute to this process, because in channeling effort and motivating individuals, they attempt to maximize output in the form of role behavior. The most obvious examples of input-improving mediators, however, are management development and training. Here, an effort is made to change the individual in some way, so that he now either is more capable of performing effectively or has a greater desire to do so. Various payment plans are also initiated with a view to mobilizing individual motivation behind organizational goal attainment. In all these instances, the primary stress is not so much on correcting deviations from a preestablished standard, as on actually making the individual more effective than he was when he entered the organization.

Second, there is a group of mediators that serve primarily to sustain the behavior potential existing in the input. Such approaches are essentially preventive. They attempt to keep the situation from getting worse, rather than to make it much better. Most of what is done in the organizational maintenance area is basically of this kind. Approaches in labor relations, employee benefit programs, and communications efforts tend to focus on protecting the organization against stresses that might threaten its survival. Few firms are concerned with totally eradicating internal conflict or maximizing employee satisfaction. It is sufficient to establish conditions and utilize procedures that prevent internal stresses from becoming disruptive and that keep people at least as satisfied as they were when they joined the company. Similarly, activities in the areas of safety management and preventive medicine are of an input-sustaining nature. The objective is to maintain the individual in the same state, insofar as his performance potential is concerned, as existed at the time of hiring.

Finally, there are mediators that operate selectively to control negatively deviant cases. In these instances, the feedback concept is adequate to explain what occurs. Individuals whose behavior departs from role requirements so markedly as to fall below a preestablished standard are identified, the sources of the failure are determined, and an appropriate corrective process is set in motion. Medical treatment, discipline, much reassignment,

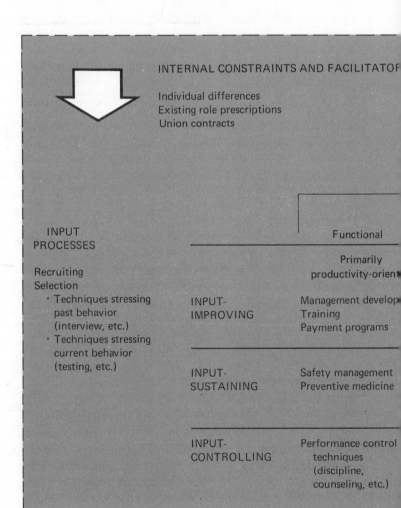

EXTERNAL CONSTRAINTS AND FACILITATO

. Cultural, geographical,
    and industry characteristics
Labor relations laws
Employment laws

INTERNAL CONSTRAINTS AND FACILITATOF

Individual differences
Existing role prescriptions
Union contracts

INPUT
PROCESSES

Recruiting
Selection
· Techniques stressing
  past behavior
  (interview, etc.)
· Techniques stressing
  current behavior
  (testing, etc.)

Functional

Primarily
productivity-orien

INPUT-
IMPROVING

Management develop
Training
Payment programs

INPUT-
SUSTAINING

Safety management
Preventive medicine

INPUT-
CONTROLLING

Performance control
   techniques
   (discipline,
   counseling, etc.)

*Figure 3–1.
The Model
of the Per-
sonnel Man-
agement
Function.*

and employee counseling operate in this manner. On occasion, mediators that are more commonly applied in an input-improving or input-sustaining context may also be utilized in a corrective sense and thus fulfill a control function. Thus, job redesign, training, payment procedures, and the like may be used at times for purposes of performance control.

The various elements of the total model are presented in Figure 3–1.

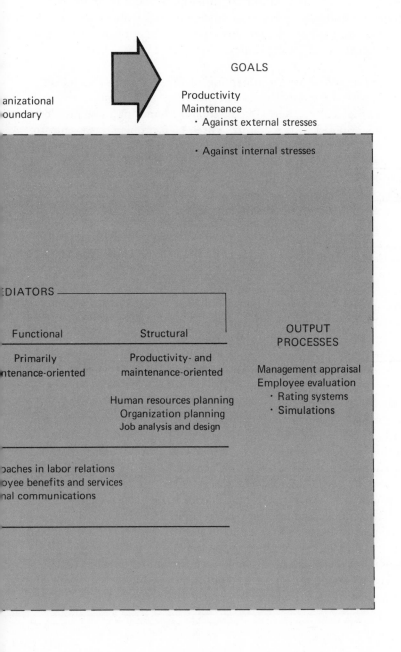

THE PROBLEM-SOLVING APPROACH TO
PERSONNEL MANAGEMENT

The model that has been developed implies a problem-solving approach to the personnel field. Specific strategies must be designed, depending upon the particular task objectives and constraint structure of a given organization. The input processes, mediators, and output processes that will maximize goal attainment in one situation are unlikely to do so in another. It is in the development and implementation of such overall strategies for corporate human resource utilization that the managerial approach to the personnel field achieves its fullest expression.

Implications for Organization of the Personnel Function

The model serves to emphasize broad problem areas and views techniques as interdependent or alternative methods of handling these problems · within the limits imposed by constraints. Three such problem areas emerge:

1. The input problem—How can recruiting and selection procedures be used to maximize goal attainment most effectively?
2. The mediator problem—What techniques can be used to improve, sustain, and control a firm's human resources so as to maximize goal attainment?
3. The output problem—How can role prescriptions be established and role behaviors evaluated so as to maximize goal attainment?

If these problem areas are to remain superordinate to the techniques for solving them, responsibility for problem solution should be assigned at a high level in the personnel organization. Thus, there would be three managers, one each responsible for employment (input processes), personnel services (mediators), and performance evaluation (output processes), reporting to the vice-president-personnel. Each would have various unit heads under him in charge of groups segmented on either a geographical or technique basis, or both.

With such an arrangement, a particular technique can be phased in or out, given a large budget or a small one, depending on its current adequacy for the solution of one of the three basic personnel problems, and on the overall human resources strategies of the firm. The choice of a technique would depend also on the state of knowledge regarding it and on existing constraint structures. Changes in technique can be made without affecting the top-level personnel organization. At the same time, the way is opened for truly creative thinking about basic personnel problems and for the development of original approaches to their solution. An approach that shows promise can be encouraged by budgeting more money for it, by allotting it greater manpower, and by establishing a higher salary for the manager in charge of it. Unfortunately, such organizational forms, which clearly subordinate techniques to problems, are rarely found in today's personnel departments.

Implications for Personnel Strategies

The implications of the input-output model for strategy are even more significant than they are for organization. Assuming that the objective is to utilize human resources most effectively, with the least cost in time, money, and effort, the model provides a basis for developing specific strategies tailored to the needs of various-sized organizations, occupational groups, and organizational units.

For example, in the case of professionals, scientists, or other highly trained employees, a major emphasis on input processes is most appropriate. To emphasize mediators at the same time usually is wasteful; only relatively small increments in performance can be expected. What is important is to hire people who are the best obtainable products of universities and other training institutions. If this is done effectively, there is little to be gained by investing heavily in further training, by capping high starting salaries (necessary for recruiting) with generous salary increments, and so on. In most cases where an input-maximizing strategy is employed, input-improving mediators should be deemphasized. Those of the sustaining and control type should be entirely adequate.

The problem of effectively utilizing employees at a low-skill level, on the other hand, normally calls for a different approach. Assuming conditions of minimal constraints on firing, a strong output emphasis usually offers the best solution. It is most important to retain those individuals who perform well. Here, the major investment should be in establishing clear role prescriptions against which role behavior may be evaluated frequently and reliably. A performance evaluation system that yields a continuing posthiring screen should be developed, instituted, and maintained. With such emphasis on output processes, there is little need to invest heavily in input processes or in control mediators as long as there is the possibility of discharging those who do not perform effectively.

Increasingly, however, legal constraints, labor union contracts, and cultural values have made discharge more difficult. As a consequence, an output process emphasis may not be the appropriate strategy for dealing with low-skill manpower. There is now a need to make the most of existing human resources. Performance control as a means of restoring effective performance in those who drop below acceptable levels becomes important. So, too, do input-improving mediators relating to work motivation—the structural mediators and payment processes.

Developing strategies to deal with specific constraints is one of the most pressing problems in the personnel area at the present time. In particular, the constraints imposed by advancing technology and fair employment practices legislation have demanded attention. In many industries, automation has resulted in a sizable decrease in manufacturing work forces. Hiring has been reduced so drastically that strategies emphasizing input processes become meaningless. At the same time, layoffs based on seniority have produced a work group considerably older than in the past. Under such circumstances, strategies that stress input-sustaining and input-improving mediators take on a new importance. In the case of the input-improving techniques, however, it is important to invest most heavily in those individuals who will remain employed longest. With an older work force, this requires an additional continuing concern with output processes, especially as they relate to physical functioning and capabilities.

Fair employment practices legislation coupled with other factors that foster the employment of minority group members also may call for strategies emphasizing input-improving mediators. In the initial stages, the tendency has been to rely mostly on recruiting and selection to obtain the better-educated individuals. However, limits on the number of such individuals inevitably will drive up the cost of this approach to the point where those who employ large numbers of minority group members must seek alternatives. At that point, the emphasis in relation to input processes should shift from productivity to organizational maintenance, and input-improving mediators such as training should be used to provide the major contributions in the productivity area.

Thus, the formulation of strategies to deal with human resources problems should not be limited to productivity considerations. Just as major emphasis may be given to input processes, various kinds of mediators, and/or output processes in developing strategies to achieve the productivity goal, a similar choice among alternatives may be made in the case of organizational maintenance. Traditionally, the most difficult problem has been union-management conflict. Various types of input-sustaining mediators have been used to deal with it. Long-standing legal constraints have made it almost impossible to use strategies that are primarily either input- or output-oriented in the labor relations area. The days of yellow-dog contracts and large-scale dismissal for union activity are long past.

Outside the area of union involvement, however, legal constraints are not yet as extensive. Within management ranks, for instance, dissension may be held in check by emphasizing selection of less contentious people, by evaluating performance against very explicit role prescriptions in this area, or by introducing human relations or sensitivity training. Which strategy might prove most fruitful will depend on the constraints imposed by the characteristics of the present management group, the number of new openings occurring in management, the value structure of the company, and so on.

It is important that strategies be developed to deal with various known sources of conflict and dissatisfaction and that these strategies be appropriate to the specific group of employees concerned. A strategy that works for unionized production workers is unlikely to be appropriate for research scientists or top-level management.

These examples of how the input-output model of the personnel process may be used are not in any sense all-inclusive. Strategies should be formulated in terms of specific existing constraint structures. Each group within a company, which is affected by constraints differing significantly from those affecting any other group, should have its own strategy. Thus the number of approaches, even within a single company, may be quite large. In the chapters that follow, this model will be used to point up the interrelationships among techniques and the diverse strategies that may be used. It provides a framework for discussing the personnel and industrial relations function and is particularly useful in delineating the differences in strategies appropriate to the small business enterprise and the large corporation (9).

QUESTIONS

1. In what sense do constraints operate as facilitators also? Discuss with reference to specific internal and external constraints on the personnel function.
2. Differentiate between role prescriptions and role behavior, and give examples of each.
3. Describe each of the following personnel activities in terms of the components of the model of the personnel management function, indicating in each instance what it is about the activity that causes it to be classified as it is within the model:
   a. Disciplinary actions.
   b. Management appraisal.
   c. Job analysis.
   d. Preventive medicine.
   e. Recruiting.
4. How might the model of the personnel management function be used to organize a personnel department? What are the advantages of doing this?
5. What is meant by personnel strategy? Give examples of strategies with an input emphasis; a mediator emphasis; an output emphasis.

REFERENCES

1. Beatty, R. W. "Personnel Systems and Human Performance." *Personnel Journal,* 52 (1973), 307–312.
2. Blakeney, R. N., M. T. Matteson, and J. Huff. "The Personnel Function: A Systemic View." *Public Personnel Management,* 3 (1974), No. 1, 83–86.
3. Dunnette, M. D., and B. M. Bass. "Behavioral Scientists and Personnel Management." *Industrial Relations,* 2 (1963), 115–130.

4. Kast, F. E., and J. E. Rosenzweig. *Contingency Views of Organization and Management*. Chicago: Science Research Associates, Inc., 1973.
5. Katz, D., and R. L. Kahn. *The Social Psychology of Organizations*. New York: John Wiley & Sons, Inc., 1966.
6. Miner, J. B. "An Input-Output Model for Personnel Strategies." *Business Horizons*, 12 (1969), No. 3, 71–78.
7. Miner, J. B. *Management Theory*. New York: Macmillan Publishing Co., Inc., 1971.
8. Miner, J. B. *The Management Process: Theory, Research, and Practice*. New York: Macmillan Publishing Co., Inc., 1973.
9. Miner, J. B. "Personnel Strategies in the Small Business Organization." *Journal of Small Business Management*, 11 (1973), No. 3, 13–16.

CONSTRAINTS AND FACILITATORS FOR PERSONNEL DECISIONS

4   *Individual Differences and Cultural Contexts*

The model of the personnel function presented in Chapter 3 indicates several different types of constraints and facilitators that may influence personnel decisions. A number of these factors are given more extended consideration in this and the following chapters of Part II; others are discussed in later chapters, since they serve in a dual role—both as mediators and as determinants of decisions related to human resources.

In Figure 3–1 (see Chapter 3), the external constraints and facilitators listed are cultural, geographical, and industry characteristics as well as various laws enacted by governmental bodies, in particular the laws relating to labor relations and employment practices. Of these influences, those emanating from cultures and societies, including the laws established by societies, require the most discussion. The present chapter deals at some length with the ways in which varying cultural contexts can condition personnel decisions. Chapter 5 delineates the laws currently operating in the United States as external influences on such decisions.

Figure 3–1 also notes three types of constraints and facilitators that are internal to the organization; these are individual differences, existing role prescriptions, and union contracts. The latter two also may be viewed as mediators and accordingly are considered in appropriate chapters later in the book. Existing role prescriptions are the topics of Chapters 6 and 7, dealing with organization and manpower planning, and job analysis and structuring. Union contracts are dealt with in Chapter 19, on labor relations. Individual differences are a major concern in the present chapter.

INDIVIDUAL DIFFERENCES

People differ from one another. They differ in an almost infinite number of respects, including aspects of their intelligence, personality, and physical makeup. This fact of difference is something of which we are all so aware that we generally tend to take it for granted, yet the practice of personnel management is influenced as much by this diversity of human characteristics as by any other factor.

At a given point in space and time, the decision alternatives realistically available to a personnel manager are strongly influenced by the specific nature of the human resources available within the organization. The people employed provide a particular set of abilities, specialized knowledges, motives, and physical skills. These serve to facilitate certain kinds of decisions, if the employees have the characteristics needed to carry out particular kinds of tasks quickly and efficiently. But the personnel manager's freedom to implement other kinds of decisions may be severely restricted. A major scientific research effort, for instance, cannot be undertaken immediately by a firm devoid of individuals with advanced training in the sciences.

At a given point in time, with one's perspective limited to a specific organization and the individuals constituting it, these constraints may appear to be insurmountable. But given a longer time span and the possibility of utilizing human resources outside the existing firm, many constraints can be made to disappear. Thus, it is important to know not only how people differ in those characteristics that are related to the attainment of organizational goals, but also how various types of individuals may be changed—at what cost, under what circumstances, and in how short a period of time.

Relative Importance of Individual and Group Differences

The best way to understand the nature and extent of individual differences is to consider a distribution showing where people fall on some measure of a human characteristic. Table 4–1 shows such a distribution for performance on a rather difficult test of vocabulary knowledge that was administered to a representative sample of people throughout the United States by Gallup Poll interviewers (28). This particular test turns out to be closely related to some of the more comprehensive and widely used indexes of general intelligence (26). Thus, the scores reflect an aspect of people that

Table 4-1. Distribution of Verbal-ability Scores for Individuals Other Than Students with Low and High Levels of Education

Test Score	Total Nonstudent Sample	Six Years or Less of Schooling	College Graduates
0			
1			
2	4	3	
3	10	8	
4	20	15	
5	36	23	
6	58	23	
7	85	21	1
8	105	33 ← Median	
9	126	29	3
10	125	25	5
11	139 ← Median	18	3
12	128	12	4
13	114	10	7
14	98	4	13
15	65	3	12 ← Median
16	60	3	13
17	35	1	10
18	27		9
19	8		1
20	6		3
Mean	10.95	8.23	14.73

Source: Adapted from J. B. Miner, *Intelligence in the United States* (Westport, Conn.: Greenwood Press, Inc., 1973), pp. 148–149.

is important in our society and often does make a difference in the kind of work people do and how well they do it (24).

Yet the distribution of results for individuals no longer in school spreads over almost the whole range of possible scores. There are people who get only 2 of the items right, and there are other people who get all 20 right, although there are not very many in either category. A comparison of individuals at the extremes, those with scores of 2, 3, or 4 with those scoring 18, 19, or 20, would reveal very different kinds of people with sharply differing work capabilities. This is what is meant by individual differences.

On the other hand, it should be noted that a large proportion of the people do not differ very much at all. If one focuses on the middle range in Table 4-1, it becomes apparent that over 50 per cent of the population scores in the 5-point range from 9 through 13. Clearly, individual differences on a characteristic are of importance only to the extent that there are significant numbers of people out at the extremes. It turns out, however, that this is in fact the case with regard to a great many aspects of human beings. The so-called *normal distribution,* with its typical, bell-shaped form, has been found with very high frequency (1, 44).

GROUP DIFFERENCES

Table 4–1 contains not only the distribution of test scores for the total sample, but within this the distributions for individuals with the lowest and the highest levels of education. On the average, these two groups differ considerably, by six or seven points. This is because people with limited verbal ability tend not to go very far in school, while those with greater verbal ability are selected for advanced education; it is also because the mere fact of educational exposure tends to produce an increase in verbal ability (28).

But what is true on the average is not true of every individual. Some relatively high-intelligence people leave school early for a variety of reasons, and some who are overachievers relative to their basic abilities make it through college on pure hard work. Thus, the range of scores within both the very-low-education and the college-graduate groups is roughly twice as large as the difference between the average scores of the two groups. Generalizing from knowledge about a group to specific individuals within the group can become a rather hazardous affair (20).

For example, in the case of the data presented in Table 4–1, where the differences in the means for the groups are unusually large, 45 per cent of those with very little education appear to be capable intellectually of making it through college (assuming a score of 9 as the bare minimum requirement). Furthermore, if one were a personnel manager in search of raw intellectual talent, and not necessarily the knowledge a particular college degree could provide, the place to look would not necessarily be among college graduates. There are 105 people who have the very lowest level of schooling noted in Table 4–1 who score 9 or above; there are only 83 college graduates. One would have to search more widely among those at lower educational levels, while practically all college graduates would prove acceptable, but the actual pool of intellectual talent is larger among those with little education, and the competition for this talent from other employers can be assumed to be much less intense.

This does not say that college graduates are not required for many purposes. But if what is desired is bright people, who are trainable, in large numbers, the college graduate population may not be the best place to look, this in spite of the fact that exclusive reliance on known differences in group means might lead to opposite conclusions.

A similar point may be made with reference to the data of Table 4–2, where the group differences are of the magnitude more commonly found. Motivation to manage is an important ingredient in managerial success in medium- and large-sized organizations (27, 32). The average manager, irrespective of level or functional area, has a test score of 0, which is roughly

Table 4–2. Distributions of Motivation-to-manage Scores for Middle- and Top-level Personnel and Industrial Relations Managers

Test Score	Middle-level Managers	Top-level Managers
−8		
−7	2	
−6	1	
−5	3	1
−4	4	1
−3	7	5
−2	6	8
−1	6 ← Median	7
0	10	7 ← Median
+1	6	4
+2	3	7
+3	1	4
+4		2
+5		
+6		1
+7		
+8		
Mean	−1.55	−.04

the same as the average for top-level personnel managers in Table 4–2. Thus, the data, which are taken from a study of personnel managers nationwide, indicate somewhat higher levels of motivation to manage outside the personnel field (31). However, within the samples considered in Table 4–2, 53 per cent of the top-level group have the average amount of managerial motivation or more than 41 per cent of the middle-level group have that amount.

The two managerial groups do differ in mean motivation levels (with a high degree of statistical significance), but there is still so much overlap that it would be very misleading to substitute a knowledge of a person's position level for an actual measurement of motivation to manage. This point can be illustrated over and over again; <u>individual differences tend to be consistently greater than group differences</u>. Only a relatively small part of the individual differences on any human characteristic can be expected to be accounted for by a particular group membership.

BASES FOR FORMING GROUPS

What has been said about the relationship between group and individual differences does not imply that some kind of grouping may not be useful for certain purposes, but it does indicate that a knowledge of group membership cannot be substituted, without considerable probability of error, for actual knowledge regarding a specific performance-related characteristic. It cannot be assumed that a person with only four years of schooling will necessarily have below-average intelligence, for example.

Furthermore, serious questions may be raised regarding the usefulness of many of the traditional bases for grouping people that have been used in the personnel field and in psychology (12). These include such factors as sex, race, age, and geographical area of origin. These turn out to be very broad categories, and the range of human variability on important work-related characteristics within such groups is often almost as large as in the population as a whole. Increasingly, it is becoming clear that these kinds of groupings are so far removed from the characteristics of people that matter, such as intelligence and motivation, that they are very nearly worthless to a personnel manager insofar as his or her direct contribution to organizational goal attainment is concerned. On the other hand, legal enactments over the past 15 years have made such groupings considerably important for other reasons.

The relative usefulness of different ways of grouping people may be illustrated from the research on the relationship between satisfaction with one's job and the degree to which that job provides variety and freedom (job enlargement). Variety and freedom appear to be a source of considerable satisfaction to some people, but not others. If one tries to pin down exactly which people, it turns out that the best way to describe them is in terms of the possession of strong motives involving self-expression and autonomy in the use of skills. People with these motives are very likely to enjoy enlarged jobs; others are not particularly likely to enjoy them (45). In contrast, an earlier attempt, on the basis of rural-urban origins, to identify people who experience satisfaction with job enlargement proved much less useful. A rural background provided only a very rough designation of the people who might be expected to respond to enlarged jobs.

Groupings based on factors that are close to on-the-job attitudes and behaviors, factors that are internal to the individual in a psychological sense, appear to be much more useful to personnel managers than groupings in terms of more remote characteristics, such as rural-urban origins, sex, or race. This is another way of saying it is the individual differences directly underlying job attitudes and behavior that really matter.

Important Types of Individual Differences

What are the crucial kinds of individual differences to which personnel managers should direct their attention? The discussion to this point has noted verbal ability and several kinds of motivation. What else is involved?

CLASSIFICATIONS OF INDIVIDUAL DIFFERENCES

One system of classifying the individual differences that relate to work uses the three major categories of mental capabilities, manual and physical response capabilities, and interpersonal skills and personality (34). Within mental capabilities, numerical ability and verbal ability are differentiated. Manual and physical response capabilities are specified as the capabilities of this type needed to perform a given job successfully. However, it is further noted that no truly adequate classification system for human physical abilities exists at present. Interpersonal skills and personality also suffer from the lack of a widely accepted classification system. The major differentiation made is between response capabilities, such as a learned skill in handling interpersonal situations, and behavioral predispositions, such as the various motives already considered. These reflect the "can do" and "want to" aspects of personality.

Another, slightly different, approach was developed originally to provide insight into the various factors that contribute to unsatisfactory job performance and failure (30). This approach is discussed in some detail in Chapter 18, on performance control. At this point, it is necessary only to specify the kinds of individual differences that are considered:

Intelligence and job knowledge
    Verbal ability
    Special abilities—numerical, spatial, mechanical
    Organizational and specific job knowledge
    Capabilities for judgment and memory
Emotional characteristics
    Emotionality with regard to anger, anxiety, excitement, and other emotions
    Emotional health as distinct from—
        Neurosis
        Psychosis
        Alcohol and drug problems
Motivational characteristics
    Motive strength with regard to success and failure, dominance, conformity, social interaction, and other motives
    Methods used to satisfy motives as related to job requirements
    Level of personal work standards
    Generalized work motivation
Physical characteristics
    Physical health and illness or disability
    Physical health as distinct from physical disorders of emotional origin
    Physical characteristics such as height and weight
    Muscular and sensory abilities and skills

Although this classification scheme is more differentiated than the preceding one, it covers essentially the same ground—intellectual factors, personality (emotions and motives), and physical factors. Other classification systems have been proposed, but almost without exception they utilize these three broad categories of individual differences, while differing in their more detailed breakdowns. The specific factors that are important will differ, of course, from job to job, depending upon the particular requirements of the position.

INDIVIDUAL DIFFERENCES INFLUENCING COMPETENCE IN MANAGERIAL DECISION MAKING

An idea of how certain individual differences may constrain company actions can be obtained by considering what is known about the factors that influence individual managerial decision-making skills. Assume that a company is in a phase of rapid expansion involving both new products and new markets. In order to maintain this growth effectively, it is necessary to have a large number of managers who can make decisions and establish policies on matters that have not previously been of concern to the company. Such managers might be found and/or developed internally, or they might be hired from the outside, but either way if people with the characteristics needed to make effective decisions in this kind of situation cannot be located, projected growth rates are unlikely to be realized. In fact, in view of the known riskiness of the new products/new markets strategy, the company may well face financial disaster.

A recent review of research dealing directly with individual factors in decision making, strategy development, and policy formation provides an idea of the kinds of individual differences a personnel manager might want to emphasize in staffing under growth conditions of this kind (43). Because we are dealing with decision making, the main emphasis is on intellectual and cognitive factors. Job knowledge is an important factor, and in the case under consideration, this knowledge should relate directly to the new products and markets. General intelligence is another important intellectual variable. Studies also indicate that differences in what has been called cognitive style are significant in this kind of decison making. The more cognitively complex person is better at searching out and using a great deal of information, thus exploring a large number of alternatives. Many aspects of a problem are differentiated and then integrated in a solution. The result appears to be a potential for much greater effectiveness in policy formulation than the less cognitively complex person possesses (21).

In addition to these intellectual considerations, there are others that fall in the personality domain. Decisions are influenced by values. In the business world, pragmatic, achievement-related, and action-oriented values have been found to be particularly important (8). Also, risk-taking propensities are related to decision success, although not always in a positive direction; it all depends on the situation. In the case of the new products/new markets growth company, however, a willingness to take some risks appears essential. Finally, a capacity for original, creative thinking, a characteristic that has both intellectual and personality ingredients, is important (43). When a company is thrusting itself into a whole new environment, it badly needs new types of problem solutions.

These are some of the types of factors that influence managerial decision making and on which individuals differ significantly. In the situation under consideration, if these factors are not taken into account either explicitly or implicitly, the risks of company failure are high; certainly many individual managers will fail. Yet, in other circumstances, with other jobs and different work requirements, a completely new set of individual factors can become important for decisions regarding human resources.

Group Differences Made Important by Legislation

The thrust of the discussion to this point is that major emphasis should be placed on individual differences and on differences between groups formed on the basis of psychological variables that are very close to the individual level. Everything that is currently known suggests that such an approach represents the best personnel practice. However, it is also true that legislative enactments over the past 15 years have served to emphasize certain group differences. In view of these laws, and the court decisions related to them, it has become increasingly important for the personnel manager to understand how certain groups differ. The laws involved are considered in the following chapter; the group differences are considered here. In particular, the legal concern is with groupings based on race, color, religion, national origin, sex, and age. Since most decisions that personnel managers are currently facing involve the male-female, black-white, and younger (under 40)-older (40–65) distinctions, these are given primary consideration here.

DIFFERENCES BETWEEN THE SEXES

Recently, an extremely comprehensive review of the research on male-female differences has been completed by Eleanor Maccoby and Carol Jacklin (22), and this review provides the primary basis for what follows. These authors note a number of "unfounded beliefs" about sex differences that turn out not to be supported by the data. Thus, there appear to be no consistent mean differences between the sexes with regard to such factors as sociability, suggestibility, self-esteem, rote-learning ability, analytic skills, achievement motivation, and auditory orientation. There are, however, well-established differences of the following types:

1. Girls have greater verbal ability than boys.
2. Boys excel in visual-spatial ability.
3. Boys excel in mathematical ability.
4. Males are more aggressive (22, pp. 351–352).

Maccoby and Jacklin do not reach a definite conclusion as to whether the greater aggressiveness of males results in stronger tendencies toward dominance, competitiveness, assertiveness, and motivation to manage. However, there are other, more recent, findings that provide some answers in this regard. When actual practicing male and female managers are compared, there appear to be few differences (3, 32). Furthermore, these characteristics appear to be associated with successful leadership among females just as they are with males (2, 32). On the other hand, there is evidence that on the average these "managerial" characteristics are less prevalent among females than males when the research focus is on nonmanagerial groups (32). Presumably, this finding is an indirect reflection of the difference in aggressiveness. Nevertheless, the data on practicing managers indicate that there are many women with high levels of managerial motivation.

BLACK-WHITE DIFFERENCES

There has been a great deal of controversy surrounding the whole issue of black-white differences in the intellectual sphere. This controversy has centered around the issue of environmental versus hereditary causation and the appropriateness of standardized general intelligence tests for black people, in particular. Neither of these matters can be said to have been settled by the currently available data. However, it can be said that measures now in use, whether they do or do not tap hereditary factors and whether they are or are not appropriate for use with blacks, do tend to yield higher scores for whites on the average. A very comprehensive review of the research in this area by Joseph Matarazzo (24) leads him to the following conclusions:

The results are almost identical across all age samples: blacks, *on the average,* earned a mean IQ about 11 points *lower* than whites. Wide individual differences around this mean were found in all samples, however (pp. 340–341).

Thus, in spite of recent advances, it remains true that in most areas of the country, general-ability tests will yield lower average scores for black job applicants than for whites (33, 37). Data on this point are given in Table 4–3. On the test of learning ability, when blacks and whites of the same educational level and age are compared, there is only one instance where the blacks have higher scores, and this is at the advanced college level where whites with high scores are not likely to seek refinery work. Black-white differences are particularly marked at the refinery location in the Southwest. Although not always as pronounced, much the same pattern emerges on the mechanical comprehension and nonverbal reasoning measures, as well. It seems clear that if only applicants with test scores above certain specified levels are hired, a white person will have a much better chance for employment than a black.

In contrast, studies among managers indicate that the blacks tend to have more of the positive kinds of motivation that make for success as managers.

Table 4–3. Mean Test Scores for Black and White Job
Applicants at Two Geographically Dispersed Refineries

Test Measure	Educational Level	Location			
		Southwest		Northeast	
		Black	White	Black	White
Learning ability	High school graduate	23.2	35.3	32.7	37.1
	Less than 2 years college	28.6	36.6	32.2	38.8
	More than 2 years college	28.2	37.9	39.7	34.5
Mechanical comprehension	High school graduate	14.3	26.5	14.6	19.4
	Less than 2 years college	18.6	27.5	16.8	25.1
	More than 2 years college	17.1	27.2	15.2	21.2
Nonverbal reasoning	High school graduate	5.8	12.2	10.3	12.6
	Less than 2 years college	7.9	10.7	11.2	14.8
	More than 2 years college	8.1	9.9	12.0	14.3

Source: C. L. Moore, J. F. MacNaughton, and H. G. Osburn, "Ethnic Differences Within an Industrial Selection Battery," Personnel Psychology, 22 : 478 (1969).

They have been found to be more ambitious and upwardly mobile than their white counterparts (5, 10); they also have been found to possess a greater motivation to manage (32). Although data on black-white differences in general, not just among managers, are less conclusive, they do point in the same direction. Responses to national surveys indicate that blacks want high incomes from their jobs more and work that is important and gives a feeling of accomplishment less than whites (46). This finding is not just a function of financial deprivation; it is just as true of blacks who are financially well-off as of those who are not. Thus, blacks as a group appear to be more motivated by a desire for pragmatic rewards, while whites seem to be more willing to settle for rewards of a psychic nature.

AGE DIFFERENCES

For many years, the belief among psychologists and educators in this country was that general intelligence shows a steady rise until the late teens and then begins a decline that extends throughout the rest of life. Advances in research methodology and a greater sophistication in the use of research tools, however, have led to a drastic revision of this belief. It is now recognized that those studies which seemed to demonstrate a decrease in intelligence with increasing age may have turned out as they did largely because older people in our society usually have less education. When the older and younger groups are equated in terms of education, no evidence of decline can be found. (28). In fact, it appears that, at least among those with high school or college training, there is actually a slight tendency for intelligence to rise throughout adult life. Many such people apparently have greater ability toward the end of their occupational careers than at the beginning. These findings have received support from other studies, in which the same individuals were tested at various times over the life span (24).

Thus, at present, there seems little reason to expect any decline in general intelligence or verbal ability with age, and in fact at the higher occupational, educational, and intellectual levels, there should be an increase. On the other hand, it is true that, because of somewhat lower average educational levels, older people generally do score below the peak age group (individuals in their late thirties and early forties).

Other abilities do not follow quite the same pattern; there does seem to be a decline in many cases (11). In most areas other than verbal, people tend to become somewhat less competent after their mid-twenties, although in individual cases where the skills are continually practiced, this drop-off may well not occur. A rather pronounced decrement with age is particularly likely to appear on tasks that emphasize speed (19, 30). Here, there seems little doubt that significant decreases do occur—partly as a consequence of reduced efficiency in visual perception and of visual falloff, partly as a result of a falloff in the rapidity with which muscular responses can be carried out.

None of this should be taken to imply that older workers cannot be taught new skills. Such problems as do arise in this regard appear to be primarily attributable to inappropriate motivation rather than to lack of the ability required for learning. Older people have had an opportunity to develop rather definite attitudes as a result of their extensive work experience. Over the years, beliefs regarding the correct way to do things have been reinforced again and again, to the point where they become firmly entrenched in the personality. For this reason, individuals who have been in the labor force for a considerable period may fail to appreciate the value of new techniques and procedures. They fail to learn new skills largely because they do not believe such learning is desirable, rather than because of a lack of ability.

Insofar as work performance is concerned, it seems clear that problems are most likely to arise when an older worker is employed in a factory job or similar work that requires extensive physical activity. After the age of about forty-five, it becomes very difficult to carry out repetitive physical activities at a rapid pace (30). Thus, the quality of work done may be maintained at a high level, but the quantity of output is likely to fall off. In office jobs, however, and in managerial or professional positions, where intellectual and, particularly, verbal abilities take on more significance, performance should not decline with age. In fact, in many managerial positions, there may be a steady improvement as a result of increased verbal competence and experience.

The view that older workers are characteristically more satisfied with their job in its various aspects is generally confirmed by the research that deals with measures of job satisfaction obtained from employees themselves (13). However, there is one major proviso. When *skill obsolescence* is in the picture, so that an individual feels that the pace of advancing knowledge in his field is more rapid than his capacity or opportunity to absorb it, he is likely to experience considerable strain and much less satisfaction. Thus, for instance, engineers may become *less* satisfied as they become older, if they remain in a rapidly changing engineering occupation. The result can be a return to school at a relatively advanced age with a view to starting a new career (16). The degree to which obsolescence of this kind occurs is closely tied to a variety of positive motives (39). Obsolescence is less frequent when ambition and achievement motivation are high.

WHY THESE GROUP DIFFERENCES ARE IMPORTANT

The reason personnel managers need to know about the group differences noted is that the existence of these differences may serve to hamper the hiring and upgrading of women, blacks, and older workers. At the same time, many companies are under strong governmental pressure, including in certain cases court orders, to hire and promote these same people in disproportionate numbers to compensate for any past failures in this regard.

The details of the legal aspects of this problem will be considered in Chapter 5, and applications in the area of psychological testing in Chapter 13. Insofar as individual and group differences are concerned, however, the important point is that when a constant hiring standard is maintained, and no special recruiting efforts are mounted, groups that are significantly lacking in a given characteristic are not likely to show up in large numbers in the company work force. At least they will not show up in the same numbers as groups in which the characteristic is more predominant.

Thus, if measures of visual-spatial ability, numerical ability, and aggressiveness are used in the selection process, proportionately fewer female applicants and more male applicants will be hired. Similarly, the use of general intelligence and other intellectual measures tends to yield disproportionately fewer black hires and the use of highly speeded perceptual and muscular measures will yield fewer people over age forty. In all of these cases, the lower average scores in a group mean that there are likely to be fewer members who will exceed any minimum acceptable level applied in selecting among applicants. To eliminate this effect and hire more females, blacks, or older workers, one either would have to recruit a disproportionately large number of applicants from these population groups or use different minimum acceptable levels for the different groups. Thus, if there were a need to hire more females, one might use the male average on an aggressiveness measure as a minimum level for male hires, but the lower female average for females, thus bringing in 50 per cent of both groups rather than, say, a 70 to 30 ratio of males to females.

In any event, in order to adopt either of these strategies, it is essential to know about any group differences in the characteristics used as a basis for selection. This is why a knowledge of black-white, male-female, and age differences is important in the practice of personnel management.

Removing Individual-difference Constraints

If a firm appears to need more people with a particular type of ability, motivation, or other characteristic, there are three possible approaches to removing the constraint imposed by the apparent lack:

1. Go outside the company and find people with the needed characteristic.
2. Change existing employees, so that they will have the characteristic.
3. Change existing job requirements, so that the characteristic that appeared to be in short supply is no longer as crucial.

Succeeding chapters consider in detail the feasibility of various recruiting and selection, training and development, and job design and structuring approaches. The need here is to obtain a general understanding of the degree to which these approaches are applicable to various types of individual difference constraints.

What are the chances that constraints can be removed by changing people? In general, the prospects, insofar as various intellectual abilities are concerned, do not appear to be very good. Although learning is clearly involved here, this learning tends to occur at the most rapid rate during the formative years, while the individual is devoting his energies almost entirely to his education. Probably if a smaller amount of time were allocated to the learning process in adult life, changes could be produced then, and many people could develop their abilities to a much higher level. This assumes, however, that they would also *want* to learn this much. In actual fact, the time involved and the problem of motivation present almost insurmountable barriers in adult life as our society is now structured.

The usual practice now when intellectual abilities are needed is to go outside the company to find them, although historically many companies have also simplified their jobs through increased specialization to reduce the intellectual demand. The reason for using this job-simplification strategy was that the same individual difference constraints that existed within the firm characterized the immediate outside labor force also. Thus, the constraints were both internal and external in nature. Currently, however, companies tend to recruit in broader labor markets and to recruit more intensively. Advances in transportation and communication have made this possible. Thus, it is possible to locate and hire the kinds of people needed by drawing on a larger human resource pool and combing it more thoroughly.

Similarly, motivational and other personality characteristics are typically built up in an organization through selective hiring and retention. On the other hand, there is considerable evidence that training and development procedures that focus on attitude and motivational change can produce substantial results (27). The level of motivation to manage can be raised in many people, for instance, and this is just as true of females as of males. Also, companies are using the job-redesign strategy, and job enlargement in particular, to make work requirements more compatible with motivational patterns (45). Thus, both individual change and job change are feasible approaches in dealing with constraints imposed by personality-based individual differences.

In the physical area, the constraints often are associated with handicaps or advancing age and are not reversible within the individual even with the most expert medical treatment. Thus, alternative strategies are called for.

Declines in visual perception of the kind that usually come with age need not result in a major decrement in performance on the part of the worker. To a considerable extent, job restructuring and design can mitigate the effects of these losses in perceptual abilities. Such restructuring now appears to be possible in many cases where it was not considered feasible previously. To take an example, an individual may be required to react to various dials on a dashboard and have difficulty doing so accurately and quickly. A simple repainting of the dashboard may serve to make the dials stand out more vividly and thus reduce the effects of poor visual perception.

Similarly, reduced muscular speed may be compensated for by emphasizing the penchant for accuracy that often appears to develop at the same time. In many instances, a lower quantity of output per individual becomes acceptable if waste and breakage are almost completely avoided and errors are rare. Often, a separate inspection job can be eliminated when older or handicapped workers are engaged in the production process; the duties of the inspector are taken over by the production workers themselves, thus reducing the need for extremely high output rates.

In addition to such job redesign, employees can be effectively retrained for new jobs more suited to their capabilities, although resistance at the outset may serve to discourage attempts along these lines. Actually, once they start a program of retraining, older workers are more likely to complete it than are those of a younger age (20). The greatest problem is to bring about a change in attitudes such that the retraining will be undertaken in the first place. This attitude change may be required not only in the employee himself, but also on the part of a management that believes that age precludes new learning.

VARYING CULTURAL CONTEXTS

Knowledge regarding the influence that differences in national culture may have upon personnel management is of considerable importance to American companies today. International trade has reached a record peak with the countries of Europe, Latin America, and the Far East and promises to attain even higher levels as the developing nations move toward economic self-sufficiency and higher standards of living. Thus, large numbers of American firms are faced with the problem of staffing overseas offices and in many cases manning major production and distribution facilities in foreign countries (35). If these international operations are to be managed in a way that will maximize organizational productivity and maintenance, a very high priority must be given to the development and utilization of knowledge that might indicate how the management process should be varied in the light of cultural considerations.

That cultural variations do exist, even at the managerial level, can no longer be doubted. In one study of managerial attitudes, sharp differences were found between Nordic-European countries (Norway, Denmark, Germany, and Sweden), Latin-European countries (France, Spain, Italy, and Belgium), the United States and Great Britain, a group of developing countries (Argentina, Chile, and India), and Japan, which stood alone. Managers in these countries did hold many attitudes in common, but there were also a number of specific findings characteristic within each cultural grouping (14). Subsequent research has extended these analyses to Australia (4) and Greece (6). The former matches the Anglo-American grouping most closely, and the latter the Latin-European, but both countries show unique patterns associated with their own cultures and their stages of industrialization.

The direct relevance of such consideration for the personnel field is demonstrated in a study of collective bargaining behavior (38). Sizable differences in basic strategies and approaches to dealing with a union were found between American managers on the one hand and Danes, Dutchmen, Germans, and Britons on the other. In general, the Americans were likely to settle more rapidly and thus avoid deadlocks, to give up more in cash settlements, and to resort to trade-offs among items more frequently. Such differences suggest that the injection of an American bargaining team into German negotiations, for example, might at the very least produce some unexpected results.

In actual fact, almost any aspect of personnel management may be influenced by cultural and national differences of this kind. Thus, there are major culture-based variations in personnel practice, even in two countries as generally similar as Canada and the United States (17). People in various parts of the world may view things very differently, and in particular they may have widely varying value-based conceptions of what is right and what is wrong. The following examples provide a sampling of these differences.

The patterns noted operate as *external* constraints and facilitators as they pressure companies toward certain types of policies and decisions. But they are also *internal* in nature to the extent that they characterize the company workforce.

Japanese Culture

A good example of the way in which cultural considerations may serve to condition personnel decisions comes from Japan. In connection with a research study, some two thousand production workers, divided equally between the United States and Japan, were surveyed (47). The firms studied in the two countries were essentially comparable. Some of the questions dealing with personnel practices and policies that were asked of the workers in both countries are noted in Table 4–4.

Table 4–4. Differences Between Japanese and American Employees' Cultural Values

Questionnaire Items	United States (per cent)	Japan (per cent)
I believe workers are willing to work hard on their job because		
they want to live up to the expectation of their family, friends, and society.	10	41
they feel it is their responsibility to the company and to co-workers to do whatever work is assigned to them.	61	37
the harder they work, the more likely they are to be promoted over others to positions of greater responsibility.	9	11
the harder they work, the more money they expect to earn.	20	11
I think of my company as		
the central concern in my life and of greater importance than my personal life.	1	9
a part of my life at least equal in importance to my personal life.	22	57
a place for me to work with management, during work hours, to accomplish mutual goals.	54	26
strictly a place to work and entirely separate from my personal life.	23	8
If a worker, although willing, proves to be unqualified on his job, management should feel a responsibility		
to continue his employment until he retires or dies.	23	55
to continue his employment for as long as one year so that he may look for another job.	19	23
to continue his employment for three months so that he may look for another job.	38	18
to terminate the employment of unqualified workers after giving about two weeks' notice.	20	4

Table 4–4. (Continued)

Questionnaire Items	United States (per cent)	Japan (per cent)
When a worker wishes to marry, I think his (her) superior should		
help select a possible mate and serve as a go-between.	2	6
offer personal advice to the worker if requested.	29	70
merely present a small gift from the company.	9	19
not be involved in such a personal matter.	60	5
If my immediate supervisor enters a crowded bus on which I am riding, I should		
always offer him my seat, since he is my superior.	2	10
offer him my seat unless I am not feeling well.	2	44
remain seated and offer to hold any packages he may have.	33	41
remain seated, since a fair rule is "first come, first served."	63	5
Decisions on problems concerning promotion, transfer, wage increases, and hours of work should be made on the basis of		
judgment of the supervisor in charge of the workers involved at the time each such problem arises.	15	5
discussions among supervisors and managers concerning each such problem at the time it arises.	21	49
a general policy which is interpreted in each case by the supervisor in charge of the workers involved.	4	11
a clearly stated written policy which provides a guide for settling such problems according to predetermined criteria.	60	35
Regarding the practice of comparing workers through merit rating, I am		
unwilling to be compared through merit rating.	9	33
willing to be compared, provided the procedure is set with participation of the union.	41	51
willing to be compared, provided it is on the basis of procedures long established and widely recognized in other companies.	33	10
willing to be compared according to a procedure set at management's discretion.	17	6
In deciding upon promotion to various supervisory levels, higher management should		
secure agreement from subordinates who will be affected.	6	38
secure agreement from the labor union on all such decisions.	6	14
consult the labor union before making such decisions.	20	10
make such decisions carefully on its own judgment.	68	37

Source: A. M. Whitehill and S. Takezawa, *The Other Worker* (Honolulu: East-West Center Press, 1968), pp. 106, 111, 139, 171, 176, 297, 302, and 308.

An examination of the responses to the first five questions indicates that a Japanese worker has a very different relationship to his job and his superiors than has a worker in the United States. Expectations in the larger society are a major source of work effort, and work assumes a more central role in Japan. There is more of a melding of life off the job with the world of work; respect for authority is high, but in return the Japanese worker appears to expect considerable job security.

There is no reason why such a culture pattern should not produce as great a contribution to productivity as does the United States culture pattern, although the bases of work motivation appear to be somewhat different. Organizational maintenance should come particularly easily, and turnover would be expected to be low. Studies indicate that in fact Japanese workers are somewhat more stable than United States workers. Moving from one firm to another is most infrequent among the older, better-educated, higher-status, and better-paid males in larger firms (23). Thus, it seems that commitment to the employing organization is not entirely a moral obligation. It is also a reciprocation for status and other rewards received. A personnel manager in Japan can expect a highly motivated and loyal work force, but he must give considerable attention to meeting culture-based expectations.

The last three questions in Table 4–4 bring out a somewhat different aspect of Japanese culture—the value placed on shared decision making. Managers should include subordinates, the union, and other managers in their decision-making processes. The result of this view is that many decisions in Japanese industry are in fact long-drawn-out. Once a decision does emerge, however, acceptance has already been obtained, and implementation presents few problems. The fact that more successful managers in Japan value loyalty highly and place a low value on self-interest appears to facilitate this shared decision-making process (9).

Indian Culture

Data on what Indian workers want from their jobs, derived from 11 separate surveys as given in Table 4–5, provide some interesting comparisons with results obtained in the United States (7). Clearly, in India, job security and opportunity for advancement are relatively more important, while sympathetic supervision and adequate benefits are much less so. In part, these differentials can be accounted for in terms of the very high unemployment rates that have plagued India. It is not surprising that job security is so important, and advancement may well represent protection against dismissal in this context. But a very different attitude toward authority in the two cultures also is reflected. Thus, increased consideration and kindness from supervisors, and benevolence on the part of management in general, would seem to be much less effective as a way of building commitment to the company in India than in the United States.

Table 4–5. Comparison of Rankings of Job Factors by
Indian and American Workers

Job Factor	Ranking Among Indian Workers	Ranking Among American Workers
Adequate earning	1	1
Job security	2	4
Opportunity for advancement	3	6
Suitable type of work	4	5
Sympathetic supervision	5	3
Adequate personal benefits	6	2
Comfortable working conditions	7	7

Source: Adapted from A. M. Dolke, "Factors in Job Satisfaction of Indian Workers," in S. K. Roy and A. S. Menon (eds.), *Motivation and Organizational Effectiveness* (New Delhi, India: Shri Ram Centre for Industrial Relations and Human Resources, 1974), pp. 87–88.

A tendency toward a punitive-paternalistic, rather authoritarian ap-proach on the part of Indian executives has been noted (36). There is, in fact, extensive evidence that a kind of dependence-proneness coupled with authoritarianism permeates the Indian culture (41). What those in authority wish to do is very likely to be accepted. This may facilitate policy imple-mentation, but it also places tremendous responsibility in the hands of top-level executives. What they choose to do is unlikely to be counteracted.

Mexican Culture

Studies comparing the United States and Mexico indicate sizable cultural differences. One such study utilized operative employees of the same glass company in both countries (42). The Mexican workers emerged as having consistently greater motive satisfaction. This was particularly true in such areas as self-realization, security, and esteem. In addition, all motives were considered more important in Mexico. The Mexicans appear to have stronger motives in general, but in large part these motives are satisfied—they get what they want.

A second study comparing Mexican, Mexican-American, and American bank employees suggests a reason for this finding (48). There was evidence of a greater emphasis on interpersonal experience and friendships with others for the group studied, the more involved it was in the Mexican cul-ture. This is consistent with the finding of a strong emphasis on social motivation and a lower interest in achievement in Mexico than in the United States (25). Apparently, Mexican culture serves to stress social relationships, friendships, and a concern for people as individuals rather than for the position held. This motive is not only important, but also highly satisfied—thus, the high satisfaction of Mexican workers. This stress on social interaction as an end rather than a means appears to serve as a limitation on productivity. In Mexico, decisions to implement organizational maintenance may be easily achieved, but those related to productivity and profits may be quite another matter.

The Developing Countries

Many other examples could be given to indicate how cultural factors can act to limit certain courses of action and foster others. However, it is probably more appropriate at this point to turn to the difficulties that may be encountered in the underdeveloped countries of the world. These appear to be of two general types—ideological and educational.

In one comparative study of 34 nations, an attempt was made to relate the level of economic development to the values and motivational patterns of the people (25). A major portion of these findings is of direct relevance here, because they indicate that there are certain countries where, because of the value systems, organizational productivity may be relatively easy to achieve and organizational maintenance difficult; there are others where the reverse is true. In those countries that had maintained high levels of economic growth, the people were marked by a strong emphasis on hard work and achievement and, perhaps even more important, by the view that social relationships should occur with some specific purpose in mind, such as a business deal, rather than for purely social reasons. Such a culture pattern should facilitate the productivity goal, but it would appear that special measures would have to be taken so that individuals of this kind could work together in a cooperative manner. It seems less likely that they would spontaneously create the feelings of camaraderie and friendship that are necessary to a stable organization, one that will continually resist both internal and external stresses.

On the other hand, in those countries where economic growth was slow, social relationships tended to be valued for their own sake, as in Mexico, and people did not need particular purposes or goals to engage in them. Here, organizational maintenance might be expected to come more easily, but the lower level of achievement motivation would suggest that commitment to a company's productivity and profit objectives might be much more difficult to obtain. Countries where the desire to achieve was low and where economic growth was minimal were by no means all in the category that would be called underdeveloped, however. Many had experienced considerable growth in the past, but not in the last few decades. This low group included such diverse nations as Belgium, Algeria, Denmark, Chile, and Switzerland. In these and other countries, the values necessary to productivity and continued economic growth are lacking.

A deficiency in the required values is not the only factor that may serve to limit goal achievement in the underdeveloped areas. An equally important factor is education, at least insofar as productivity is concerned (15). In many countries of the world, certain types of personnel programs are out of the question, merely because the labor market does not contain individuals with the necessary basic education, skills, or professional training. Countries such as Afghanistan, Ethiopia, and Haiti not only have a very limited economic capacity, but they lack the educated personnel needed for advancement.

Dealing with Constraints

In general, the approach here has been one of pointing out some of the constraints within which personnel decisions must be made in foreign countries. Little has been said about the possibility of circumventing these restrictions, largely because this is not easily done. An obvious procedure is to move the business operation to a cultural context where the limitations no longer exist. This may or may not be feasible on other grounds. Personnel considerations are not always paramount. Or it may be possible to staff the organization in large part from outside the culture that imposes the restrictions, perhaps with United States citizens. This may or may not solve the problem.

Another alternative involves inducing change in the culture itself (29). Because of the widespread support for cultural values within a society, this is not easily done. But it is possible, and societies and cultures do change. Managers can play a role in this process and have in fact often done so. A personnel manager may do much to foster change through the development of appropriate training and communications programs within the company. Similarly, he may serve as a public relations agent within the external community by discussing the virtues of the desired change. Although these attempts to modify attitudes may meet with only limited success in and of themselves, they can contribute a great deal to an ongoing change process. Combined with other socioeconomic and political forces in the culture, they can make a very real difference.

GEOGRAPHICAL AND INDUSTRY CHARACTERISTICS

As indicated early in this chapter, cultural factors require the most explanation among the various constraints and facilitators that are primarily external. The effects of geographical and industry characteristics tend to be more obvious; in addition, some attention is given to such considerations in Chapter 18, on performance control.

One type of geographical constraint is the availability of public transportation. Continuous shift operation is very difficult, for instance, in the New York City area, where many people do not have automobiles and rely heavily on public transportation, because schedules are extremely light in the late-night and early-morning hours.

Many companies have found that to attract qualified technical and professional employees to research and development installations and to other facilities requiring high-talent personnel, it is often necessary to offer an opportunity for continuing education at the undergraduate level and particularly at the graduate level. When university facilities are not available in the area, recruiting can become extremely difficult. It may in fact be impossible to operate certain kinds of installations efficiently in locations where appropriate business, scientific, and technical courses are not available.

There are certain restrictions on personnel decisions that result directly from the fact that a firm has chosen a suburban, rather than a downtown, location for its facilities. One major constraint arises because placing a facility in a suburb of a major city can be looked on as situating it on the edge, or perimeter, of a circle. Thus, the distance between the facility and the diametrically opposite side of the circle is twice as great as would be the distance between that side and a facility located in the center, or in the downtown area. Even more important, from a practical viewpoint, is the fact that crossing a city in this manner normally takes much longer than traveling the same distance in open country. As a result, the labor market available in a suburban area tends to be restricted considerably compared to that which could be tapped from a downtown location. A further restraint is imposed as a result of the normal urban direction of transportation flow. Most public transport routes go inward, like the spokes of a wheel. As a result, getting from one suburban point to another, even on the same side of the city, can be difficult if one does not have an automobile. This may prove to be a problem in recruiting young workers.

In addition to these various geographical considerations, there are others associated with particular industries. Industries differ in the geographical locations from which their new materials derive, in their technologies, in their traditions, in the types of human resources available to them, and in many other respects. All these factors can have considerable significance for practice in the personnel area.

One example of such industry differences is provided by the propensity to strike, which historically has varied considerably from one industry to another (18). Data in this regard are provided in Table 4–6. It is apparent that industrial relations policies and practices may be affected drastically by such differences in union behavior.

The various technologies and the types of materials utilized in different industries have a marked influence on the way jobs are structured and organizations designed. Thus, a personnel manager in one industry may well find himself limited to markedly different alternatives, insofar as dividing up the work, job analysis, and organization planning are concerned, from those realistically available to a personnel manager in another industry.

Additional examples could be cited, but what has been said should be sufficient to demonstrate the role industry differences can play. Overcoming industry-related constraints, as with those of a geographical nature, can be difficult, but is by no means impossible. Various possibilities will become apparent as we move on to a discussion of various personnel techniques and

Table 4–6. General Pattern of Strike Propensities

Propensity to Strike	Industry
High	Mining, maritime, and longshore
Medium high	Lumber, textile
Medium	Chemical, printing, leather, manufacturing (general), construction, food, and kindred products
Medium low	Clothing, gas, water, electricity, services (hotels, restaurants, etc.)
Low	Railroad, agriculture, trade

Source: C. Kerr and A. Siegel, "The Inter-industry Propensity to Strike—An International Comparison," in A. Kornhauser, R. Dubin, and A. M. Ross, eds., *Industrial Conflict*, p. 190. Copyright 1954 by McGraw-Hill Book Company, Inc. Used by permission of McGraw-Hill Book Company.

procedures in later chapters. Again, it is important to emphasize that a good personnel manager cannot afford to be lacking in ingenuity. Perhaps, on occasion, he may need to be really creative, in the same sense that outstanding research scientists are.

QUESTIONS

1. Under what circumstances might individual differences that are operating as internal constraints prove to be external constraints also?
2. What are some of the ways in which individual differences have been classified? Which types do you think are most important to personnel managers? Why?
3. In what sense are group differences relatively unimportant to personnel management, and in what sense are they, or at least some of them, very important? Support your answer with examples.
4. In what ways do workers in the United States appear to differ from workers in various other parts of the world?
5. Describe several geographical or industry characteristics, other than those considered in the text, that might operate as constraints and facilitators. Show how each may influence personnel decisions.

REFERENCES

1. Anastasi, A. *Individual Differences.* New York: John Wiley & Sons, Inc., 1965.
2. Bartol, K. M. "Male Versus Female Leaders: The Effect of Leader Need for Dominance on Follower Satisfaction." *Academy of Management Journal,* 17 (1974), 225–233.
3. Chapman, J. B. "Comparison of Male and Female Leadership Styles." *Academy of Management Journal,* 18 (1975), 645–650.
4. Clark, A. W., and S. McCabe. "The Motivation and Satisfaction of Australian Managers." *Personnel Psychology,* 25 (1972), 625–638.

5. Crane, Donald P. "How Blacks Become Managers in Atlanta, Georgia, Companies." *Training in Business and Industry,* 8 (1971), No. 6, 21–26.

6. Cummings, L. L., and S. M. Schmidt. "Managerial Attitudes of Greeks: The Roles of Culture and Industrialization." *Administrative Science Quarterly,* 17 (1972), 265–272.

7. Dolke, A. M. "Factors in Job Satisfaction of Indian Workers," in S. K. Roy and A. S. Menon (eds.), *Motivation and Organizational Effectiveness.* New Delhi, India: Shri Ram Centre for Industrial Relations and Human Resources, 1974, pp. 75–103.

8. England, G. W. "Personal Value Systems of Managers and Administrators." *Academy of Management Proceedings* (1973), 81–88.

9. England, G. W., and R. Lee. "The Relationship Between Managerial Values and Managerial Success in the United States, Japan, India, and Australia." *Journal of Applied Psychology,* 59 (1974), 411–419.

10. Fernandez, J. P. *Black Managers in White Corporations.* New York: John Wiley & Sons, Inc., 1975.

11. Fozard, J. L., and R. L. Nuttall. "General Aptitude Test Battery Scores for Men Differing in Age and Socioeconomic Status." *Journal of Applied Psychology,* 55 (1971), 372–379.

12. Ghiselli, E. E. "Some Perspectives for Industrial Psychology." *American Psychologist,* 29 (1974), 80–87.

13. Gibson, J. L., and S. M. Klein. "Employee Attitudes as a Function of Age and Length of Service: A Reconceptualization." *Academy of Management Journal,* 13 (1970), 411–425.

14. Haire, M., E. E. Ghiselli, and L. W. Porter. *Managerial Thinking: An International Study.* New York: John Wiley & Sons, Inc., 1966.

15. Harbison, F. H. "Human Resources and the Development of Modernizing Nations," in G. G. Somers (ed.), *The Next Twenty-five Years of Industrial Relations.* Madison, Wis.: Industrial Relations Research Association, 1973, pp. 177–186.

16. Hiestand, D. L. *Changing Careers After Thirty-five.* New York: Columbia University Press, 1971.

17. Jain, H. C. *Contemporary Issues in Canadian Personnel Administration.* Scarborough, Ontario: Prentice-Hall of Canada Ltd., 1974.

18. Kerr, C., and A. Siegel. "The Inter-industry Propensity to Strike—An International Comparison," in A. Kornhauser, R. Dubin, and A. M. Ross, (eds.), *Industrial Conflict.* New York: McGraw-Hill Book Company, 1954, pp. 189–212.

19. Laufer, A. C., and W. M. Fowler. "Work Potential of the Aging." *Personnel Administration,* 34 (1971), No. 2, 20–25.

20. Lofquist, L. H., and R. V. Dawis. *Adjustment to Work.* New York: Appleton-Century-Crofts, 1969.

21. Lundberg, O., and M. D. Richards. "A Relationship Between Cognitive

Style and Complex Decision Making: Implications for Business Policy." *Academy of Management Proceedings* (1972), 95–98.

22. Maccoby, E. E., and C. N. Jacklin. *The Psychology of Sex Differences.* Stanford, Calif.: Stanford University Press, 1974.

23. Marsh, R. M., and H. Mannari. "Lifetime Commitment in Japan: Roles, Norms, and Values." *American Journal of Sociology,* 76 (1971), 795–812.

24. Matarazzo, J. D. *Wechsler's Measurement and Appraisal of Adult Intelligence.* Baltimore: The Williams & Wilkins Company, 1972.

25. McClelland, D. C. *The Achieving Society.* New York: Van Nostrand Reinhold Company, 1961.

26. Miner, J. B. "On the Use of a Short Vocabulary Test to Measure General Intelligence." *Journal of Educational Psychology,* 52 (1961), 157–160.

27. Miner, J. B. *Studies in Management Education.* New York: Springer Publishing Company, 1965.

28. Miner, J. B. *Intelligence in the United States.* Westport, Conn.: Greenwood Press, Inc., 1973.

29. Miner, J. B. "The Cross-cultural Perspective to Work Motivation," in S. K. Roy and A. S. Menon (eds.), *Motivation and Organizational Effectiveness.* New Delhi, India: Shri Ram Centre for Industrial Relations and Human Resources, 1974, pp. 29–42.

30. Miner, J. B. *The Challenge of Managing.* Philadelphia: W. B. Saunders Company, 1975.

31. Miner, J. B. "Levels of Motivation to Manage Among Personnel and Industrial Relations Managers." *Journal of Applied Psychology,* 61 (1976), 419–427.

32. Miner, J. B. *Motivation to Manage.* Atlanta, Ga.: Organizational Measurement Systems Press, 1977.

33. Moore, C. L., J. F. MacNaughton, and H. G. Osburn. "Ethnic Differences Within an Industrial Selection Battery." *Personnel Psychology,* 22 (1969), 473–482.

34. Porter, L. W., E. E. Lawler, and J. R. Hackman. *Behavior in Organizations.* New York: McGraw-Hill Book Company, 1975.

35. Root, F. R., and D. A. Heenan. "Staffing the Overseas Unit," in Joseph J. Famularo (ed.), *Handbook of Modern Personnel Administration,* New York: McGraw-Hill Book Company, 1972, pp. 56:3–16.

36. Roy, S. K. "Personnel Management in Indian Business and Industry." *Personnel Administration,* 34 (1971), No. 2, 14–19.

37. Ruda, E., and L. E. Albright. "Racial Differences on Selection Instruments Related to Subsequent Job Performance." *Personnel Psychology,* 21 (1968), 31–41.

38. Shapira, Z., and B. M. Bass. "Settling Strikes in Real Life and Simula-

tions in North America and Different Regions of Europe." *Journal of Applied Psychology,* 60 (1975), 466–471.

39. Shearer, R. L., and J. A. Steger. "Manpower Obsolescence: A New Definition and Empirical Investigation of Personal Variables." *Academy of Management Journal,* 18 (1975), 263–275.

40. Sheppard, H. L. *New Perspectives on Older Workers.* Kalamazoo, Mich.: W. E. Upjohn Institute for Employment Research, 1971.

41. Sinha, J. B. "The Psycho-social Background and Work Motivation," in S. K. Roy and A. S. Menon (eds.), *Motivation and Organizational Effectiveness.* New Delhi, India: Shri Ram Centre for Industrial Relations and Human Resources, 1974, pp. 1–28.

42. Slocum, J. W. "A Comparative Study of the Satisfaction of American and Mexican Operatives." *Academy of Management Journal,* 14 (1971), 89–97.

43. Steiner, G. A., and J. B. Miner. *Management Policy and Strategy.* New York: Macmillan Publishing Co., Inc., 1977.

44. Tyler, L. E. *Individual Differences: Abilities and Motivational Directions.* New York: Appleton-Century-Crofts, 1974.

45. Wanous, J. P. "Individual Differences and Reactions to Job Characteristics." *Journal of Applied Psychology,* 59 (1974), 616–622.

46. Weaver, C. N. "Black-White Differences in Attitudes Toward Job Characteristics." *Journal of Applied Psychology,* 60 (1975), 438–441.

47. Whitehill, A. M., and S. Takezawa. *The Other Worker.* Honolulu: East-West Center Press, 1968.

48. Zurcher, L. A. "Particularism and Organizational Position: A Cross-cultural Analysis." *Journal of Applied Psychology,* 52 (1968), 139–144.

5   *Legal Influences*

The value system of the United States is such that it is a constant source of pride to us that we have been able to build a very prosperous society while still keeping relatively free of governmental constraints. There can be no doubt, however, that over the past half-century, management's freedom has been eroded substantially by a continued growth in the amount of legislation bearing on the employment relationship. Selection procedures, strikes, collective bargaining, firings, wages, hours of work, working conditions—these and many other aspects of personnel management have been increasingly influenced by various types of governmental action. Whatever one's own feelings about the need for such legislation, there can be no doubt that from the viewpoint of the business organization, there has been a marked increase in the number of legal influences that both constrain and facilitate personnel decision making.

The purpose of this chapter is to trace the development of these influences as they operate in different areas of the total personnel function. Because this topic is extensive, it is not possible to treat in a comprehensive manner all the legal statutes that are relevant. The discussion is intended to provide a general coverage only, and even then it will be limited to those legal requirements that specifically affect managerial decisions. Laws that bear on the activities of union officers, union members, and the general public may have indirect implications for the practice of personnel management, but they are not of central concern and thus are more appropriately left to an intensive course in the field of labor law.

THE EXTENT OF LEGAL INFLUENCE ON PERSONNEL DECISIONS

An indication of the extent of influence of federal laws on personnel management appears in Table 5–1, which outlines the coverage and basic requirements of and the record-keeping obligations imposed by several federal statutes. Regulations under most of these laws also include a require-ment that the employer post an official notice informing employees of their coverage and rights under the particular law (15). A further requirement of some legislation involves reports that must be filed with various government agencies. One example is that employers of one hundred or more employees covered by the Civil Rights Act must file annual information reports on the sex and racial characteristics of their work force.

The impact of regulation by the federal government on areas of personnel management has grown tremendously over the past decade. Perhaps a peak was reached with the wage-price freeze of 1971, when employers were prohibited from granting wage increases for a period of three months. The result was that a very large and important aspect of personnel activity in most firms was at a virtual standstill due to federal regulation.

In addition to federal legislation affecting personnel matters, there are a large number of state laws that must be taken into account. A number of the state laws impose additional record-keeping and reporting requirements, as well as the payment of certain payroll taxes. In some instances, employers find that they are covered by conflicting provisions at the state and federal levels; it may take several years of litigation in the courts before such issues are resolved (24). This type of situation is most likely to occur shortly after

Table 5–1. Coverage and Requirements of Selected Federal Laws

Statute	Coverage	Basic Requirements	Records to Be Retained
1. Fair Labor Standards Act (1938)	Employers engaged in interstate commerce	Pay minimum hourly rate and 1½ for hours after 40 per week; also covers equal pay, child labor, and homework	Employee's name, address, birth date (if under age 19), sex, and occupation. Hour and day when employee's work week begins, hours worked each day and each work week. Basis on which wages are paid (e.g., $3 per hour), regular hourly rate for any overtime work, amount and nature of payment excluded from the regular rate, total daily or weekly straight-time earnings, total overtime earnings for work week, all wage additions or deductions and total wages paid each pay period, dates of payment and of pay period.
2. Civil Rights Act of 1964 (Title VII) (1964, as amended 1972)	Employers of 15 or more employees and engaged in interstate commerce	No job discrimination based on race, color, religion, sex, or national origin	(a) Any personnel or employment record kept by employer, including application forms and records having to do with hiring, promotion, demotion, transfer, layoff or termination, rates of pay, or other terms of compensation, and selection for training or apprenticeship. (b) Personnel records relevant to charge of discrimination or action brought against employer, including, for example, records relating to charging party and to all other employees holding similar positions, application forms or test papers completed by unsuccessful applicant and by all other candidates for same position. (c) Those required to file apprenticeship reports shall maintain (1) chronological list of names and addresses of all applicants, dates of application, sex, and minority group identification or (2) file of written applications containing same information.

3. Age Discrimination Act (1967)	Employers of 25 or more employees and engaged in interstate commerce	No job discrimination based on age 40 to 65 years	(a) Payroll records containing each employee's name, address, date of birth, occupation, rate of pay, and compensation earned per week. (b) Personnel records relating to (1) job applications, resumés, or other replies to job advertisements, including records pertaining to failure to hire; (2) promotion, demotion, transfer, selection for training, layoff, recall, or discharge; (3) job orders submitted to employment agency or union; (4) test papers in connection with employer-administered aptitude or other employment tests; (5) physical examination results; (6) job advertisements or notices to employees regarding openings, promotions, training programs, or opportunities for overtime work. (c) Employee benefit plans, written seniority or merit rating systems.
4. Occupational Safety and Health Act (1970)	Employers engaged in interstate commerce	Employers must furnish employees a place of employment free from recognized hazards that might cause serious injury or death. Employers must comply with the specific safety and health standards issued by the Department of Labor. Employees must comply with safety and health standards, rules, regulations, and orders issued under the Act.	(a) Occupational Injury and Illness Log, briefly describing injury or illness and its extent or outcome. (b) Supplementary Record, containing more detailed information on the injury or illness. (c) Annual Summary.

Table 5-1. (Continued)

Statute	Coverage	Basic Requirements	Records to Be Retained
5. Pension Reform Law (1974)	All employee benefit plans of employers engaged in interstate commerce	Benefit plans must meet certain minimum standards for employee participation, vesting rights, funding, reporting, and disclosure	As necessary to make required reports: (a) To employees—a summary description of the pension plan, a copy of the statements and schedules from the annual report, a statement of accrued and vested benefits, information on their vested benefits. (b) To the Secretary of Labor—a financial statement, an actuarial report, and an insured plan report.

Source: Compiled from Bureau of National Affairs, Inc., *Personnel Management* (Washington, D.C., 1976), 251: 751–756.

the enactment of a federal law covering aspects of employment already subject to state regulation.

Not only has there been a marked increase in the different types of personnel decisions subject to federal regulation, but the types of organizations covered under federal law also have increased. Before 1966, for example, personnel policies and practices in institutions of higher learning were not subject to any federal standards. Since then, changes in the laws and regulations as well as court actions have resulted in large colleges and universities being governed by the same rules as any other employer (29).

It is interesting to note that the history of state and federal legislation in areas affecting personnel management has followed a similar pattern over the years. What usually has happened is that a number of states—generally those that are the most heavily industrialized or considered the most progressive—have statutes on the books for many years before Congress passes a law setting standards for employers throughout the country. Congressional enactment follows a buildup of political pressure because of the states that do not set standards, or do not enforce them, in certain areas.

In many instances, the passage of a federal law facilitates personnel decision making. Before the federal law on occupational health and safety went into effect in 1971, for example, companies in some states did not provide certain safety equipment because the cost of doing so would put them at a competitive disadvantage, even though they wanted to do so from an employee relations and organizational maintenance point of view. Once all employers involved in the same type of work are subject to the same safety requirements, the competitive disadvantage disappears.

For companies with manufacturing plants or other facilities in several states, the advantages of federal standards in personnel matters are obvious. Nevertheless, there still are certain aspects of employment in which the state laws have a large influence. In this chapter, some of these state laws will be discussed along with the federal laws with reference to the types of personnel decisions they affect.

LEGAL ASPECTS OF SELECTION DECISIONS

The area of personnel activity that has seen the greatest impact from a legal point of view since the mid-1960s is that of hiring. Prior to the enactment and enforcement of fair employment legislation, employers were largely free to select anyone they wanted as employees. Most legal influences in the personnel area involved the employment relationship with those already on the payroll. Now the selection process itself is subject to legal scrutiny from several angles. The major influences stem from laws prohibiting discrimination in employment because of race, sex, or age, at the local, state, and federal levels. Other legal influences on hiring discussed in this section include those resulting from employment contracts and trade secrets, and privacy rights as protected under consumer credit law.

Fair Employment Legislation

The first fair employment practice statute was enacted by New York State in 1945, and over the next 20 years, half the states followed suit. The biggest impetus to equal opportunity in employment, however, came with passage of the Civil Rights Act of 1964, Title VII of which prohibits discrimination in employment based on race, color, religion, national origin, or sex, and which applies to employers, labor unions, and employment agencies. In the years that the Civil Rights Law has been in operation, the number of complaints of job discrimination has grown steadily, from 8,800 in fiscal year 1966 to 55,900 in fiscal year 1974 (21).

Title VII is enforced by the Equal Employment Opportunity Commission (EEOC). Under the original law, the EEOC tried to effect compliance by conferences with the parties involved, conciliation, and persuasion. If these efforts failed, the EEOC could ask the Attorney General to bring a civil suit against the employer. These enforcement procedures proved to be slow and cumbersome and resulted in the passage of amendments to the Act, in 1972, giving EEOC the power to bring enforcement actions directly through the federal courts (18). The Commission continues to attempt to push enforcement of equal opportunity through the use of conciliation agreements and consent decrees; the fact that EEOC now can go directly to court and has had settlements involving large amounts of back pay upheld by the courts is a major factor influencing managerial decisions in the human resources area (17).

Another program the federal government has available for policing employment discrimination is provided for under executive orders that apply to government contractors. Such orders date back to World War II, but the one that has had the most significant impact is Order No. 11246, issued in 1965. The order not only prohibits government contractors from discrimination in employment, but also requires that they take "affirmative action" to make sure such discrimination does not exist (31). The order is implemented by the Office of Federal Contract Compliance Programs (OFCCP) in the U.S. Department of Labor, which has authority to terminate contracts and to debar companies from bidding on government contracts in the future.

In view of the sanctions available to OFCCP and the fact that the executive order applies to some ninety thousand establishments, employing about one-third of the American labor force, the potential impact would appear to be greater than that of the EEOC. Over the years, however, the program has suffered from lack of personnel, inefficiency, and administrative conflicts between OFCCP and EEOC (26).

Racial Discrimination

The areas of personnel decision making that may be affected by FEP regulation are not limited to the hiring process. Complaints to the EEOC have involved promotion opportunities and seniority systems, and there is increasing concern with the lack of minorities and women in the higher-paying occupations or managerial positions. Initially, however, the major thrust was against *hiring* practices that result in discrimination, whether deliberate or inadvertent. Rulings by the EEOC that have been upheld in the federal courts, for example, include one that prohibits an employer from using arrest records as a basis for hiring decisions, even though the policy is applied objectively and fairly as between applicants of various races (15). Such a policy results in discrimination against black candidates, because blacks are arrested substantially more frequently than whites.[1]

Although the total selection process, including recruiting and interviewing, is subject to scrutiny under FEP regulations, the employment practice that has come in for the greatest criticism is that of psychological testing (4). Of the early complaints filed with the EEOC, which numbered some forty thousand from 1967 through 1970, about 20 per cent concerned the use of tests, and both EEOC and OFCCP issued detailed guidelines related to the use of tests and testing procedures (16). This concern with the use of tests was anticipated by various members of Congress when the Civil Rights Act was passed, and Title VII includes a provision indicating that testing for selection purposes is legal as long as the test is not specifically designed, intended, or used to discriminate. The provision was added as an outgrowth of a case in the early 1960s in which the Illinois Fair Employment Practices Commission questioned the use of a standard verbal-ability test by the Motorola Company (6).

Despite this provision in the law, the crucial issue in the use of tests and other hiring practices, according to the U.S. Supreme Court, is not the employer's intent but the result. If the practice results in discrimination against a minority group and cannot be shown to be related to job performance, then the practice is prohibited. The significance of this ruling for employers is that they must be able to show that tests and other hiring procedures are proved measures of job performance. In the Court's words, "What Congress has commanded is that any tests used must measure the person for the job and not the person in the abstract." [2]

Another area in which the EEOC and other government agencies began to take action involved the operation of seniority systems, many of them long-established in unionized industries, that had the effect of denying promotion opportunities to minorities and, in some cases, women (46). One large-scale effort by the government resulted in an agreement involving the nation's major steel producers and the Steelworkers union; it not only called for a complete revamping of the seniority system in nearly 250 plants, but also set up a back-pay fund of more than $30 million for the victims of past discrimination. The steel industry consent decrees were attacked by both civil rights and women's rights groups but were upheld in the federal

---

[1] *Gregory v. Litton Systems, Inc.,* USDC CenCalif 1970, 2 FEP Cases 821.
[2] *Griggs v. Duke Power Co.,* U.S. SupCt 1971, 3 FEP Cases 175.

courts.[3] The whole matter of the effect of seniority systems became even more crucial during the recession of the mid-1970s, when many recently hired minority group members became the first to be laid off; employers often found themselves caught between the requirements of a union contract and the provisions of affirmative action programs agreed to with government agencies (49).

Sex Discrimination

During the early 1970s, problems relating to sex discrimination emerged as another major concern for personnel management. The inclusion of sex as a basis of discrimination to be prohibited by Title VII of the Civil Rights Act was an apparent effort to defeat the bill at the time it was passed, and its inclusion was even opposed by the Women's Bureau of the U.S. Department of Labor (10). The interpretation of this provision has proved to be one of the most difficult problems for the EEOC, as it has faced an increasing number of sex discrimination complaints over the years (48).

One basis for the difficulties in enforcing the ban on sex discrimination in employment is that such discrimination may be permissible where sex is a "bona fide occupational qualification" (BFOQ), necessary to the employer's normal operation. The BFOQ exception also applies to discrimination based on religion or nationality, but not to racial discrimination. What constitutes a BFOQ has been subject to different interpretations in various courts, although the EEOC itself maintains that this exception should be interpreted narrowly (45). Jobs may be restricted to one sex for reasons of authenticity, as, for example, actresses or models portraying women, or on the basis of community standards of morality or propriety, as in the case of rest room attendants, but not on the basis of general assumptions of characteristics or stereotypes of men or women in general. Thus, the EEOC has said a refusal to hire women as salespeople because they are considered less aggressive than men is not based on a bona fide occupational qualification (15).

An issue that arose very early under the sex discrimination ban was that of jobs traditionally denied women because of certain physical aspects of the work, such as strenuous lifting. In general, the courts upheld the EEOC position that such weight-lifting requirements do not constitute bona fide occupational qualifications.[4] This problem was confounded by the presence in many states of so-called protective laws, many dating back to the early 1900s, limiting the number of hours women can work or the weights they can be required to lift. At first EEOC evaluated such laws on a case-by-case basis on the assumption that the ban on sex discrimination was not intended to disturb the state laws that have the effect of protecting women. Finally,

---

[3] *U.S. v. Allegheny-Ludlum Industries, Inc.*, CA 5 (1975), 11 FEP Cases 167.
[4] *Weeks v. Southern Bell Telephone Co.*, CA 5 (1969), 1 FEP Cases 656; *Bowe v. Colgate-Palmolive Co.*, CA 7 (1969), 2 FEP Cases 121.

the EEOC decided that because these laws treat all women as a group and do not take individual differences into account, they cannot be used as a basis for denying jobs to women. As a result, many of the protective laws have been ruled by the courts as in conflict with the federal law and thus invalid, and by 1975 only 6 states had retained maximum hours laws unchanged, out of the 40 that had such laws before the Civil Rights Act went into effect (15).

Age Discrimination

Public policy with respect to the employment of older workers changed considerably between the depression period of the 1930s and the civil rights era of the 1960s and 1970s. Legislation enacted during the early period, as illustrated by the Social Security Act of 1935, was designed to encourage older people to retire from the labor market by the age of sixty-five at the very latest by providing at least a minimum retirement income. In the years since, more and more workers have become covered by Social Security, and most employers have augmented these federal benefits with private pension payments. The overall effect of the combined public and private programs has been to achieve the goal of reducing the proportion of older workers in the work force (33). As indicated in Table 5–2, while the proportion of men working or available for work decreased by about seven percentage points from 1947 to 1975, the drop in the proportion of men sixty-five and over was more than three times as great. Similarly, although female participation in the labor force has been increasing steadily since World War II, the net change among women sixty-five and over has been minimal, with some decline over the past decade.

By the mid-1960s, there were signs that the public policy of encouraging older workers to leave the labor force was having some negative effects. The percentage of older people in the population was increasing steadily, yet the job opportunities for men and women diminished markedly when they reached age forty-five, one reason being the high cost of funding adequate retirement benefits for the older worker. As a result of the diminishing job opportunities, by 1964 there were approximately 750,000 unemployed workers aged forty-five or older, and half the nation's poverty-stricken families were headed by persons over forty-five years old (50).

There were some proposals to provide relief for the older worker under the Civil Rights Act of 1964, but in the end, age was not included as one of the bases of job discrimination prohibited by Title VII. Three years later, however, Congress did enact the Age Discrimination Act of 1967, providing many of the same provisions against discrimination in employment for persons aged forty to sixty-five that Title VII provided with respect to race, sex, religion, and national origin (25). There are certain exceptions for bona fide occupational qualifications based on age, such as the federal regulations that impose age limits for jobs as airline pilots. The Age Discrimination

Table 5–2. Labor Force Participation Rates for Persons
Sixteen Years and Over

Year	All Males	Males 65 and Over	All Females	Females 65 and Over
1947	86.8	47.8	31.8	8.1
1948	87.0	46.8	32.7	9.1
1949	86.9	46.9	33.2	9.6
1950	86.8	45.8	33.9	9.7
1951	87.3	44.9	34.7	8.9
1952	87.2	42.6	34.8	9.1
1953	86.9	41.6	34.5	10.0
1954	86.4	40.5	34.6	9.3
1955	86.2	39.6	35.7	10.6
1956	86.3	40.0	36.9	10.9
1957	85.5	37.5	36.9	10.5
1958	85.0	35.6	37.1	10.3
1959	84.5	34.2	37.2	10.2
1960	84.0	33.1	37.8	10.8
1961	83.6	31.7	38.1	10.7
1962	82.8	30.3	39.0	9.9
1963	82.2	28.4	38.3	9.6
1964	81.9	28.0	38.7	10.1
1965	81.5	27.9	39.3	10.0
1966	81.4	27.0	40.3	9.6
1967	81.5	27.1	41.1	9.6
1968	81.2	27.3	41.6	9.6
1969	80.9	27.2	42.7	9.9
1970	80.6	26.8	43.4	9.7
1971	80.0	25.5	43.4	9.5
1972	79.7	24.4	43.9	9.3
1973	79.5	22.8	44.7	8.9
1974	79.4	22.4	45.7	8.2

Source: Manpower Report of the President (Washington, D.C.: Government Printing Office, 1975), p. 205.

Act is not enforced by the EEOC but is administered by the U.S. Department of Labor.

The initial enforcement of the Act was aimed at reducing the number of newspaper advertisements for job vacancies that list a maximum age or use terms such as "young person" or "recent college graduate" (34). More recently, the Labor Department, going to court on behalf of older workers who were forced into early retirement, has succeeded in getting some of these workers reinstated in their jobs and obtaining substantial amounts of back pay for them (11).

Other Antidiscrimination Legislation

Many employers are subject to federal antidiscrimination laws in addition to the Civil Rights and Age Discrimination acts; often these laws apply specifically to government contractors or any employers receiving any kind of federal assistance. Examples of this type of legislation include the Rehabilitation Act of 1973, barring discrimination against the handicapped, and the Vietnam Era Veterans Readjustment Act of 1974 (18).

As indicated in the preceding discussion, a number of states (and some cities) also have passed FEP laws outlawing discrimination on the basis of race, color, religion, or national origin. These laws vary considerably in enforcement provisions and applicable penalties and have been subject to considerable change over the years. In addition, a number of states have passed legislation barring discrimination on the basis of age or sex, when the job requirements do not appear to have an age- or sex-related basis. States having statutes constraining employment decisions in these various ways are noted in Table 5–3. This table is complete through 1976.

In many instances state FEP legislation has more impact on employers than the federal law because the state agencies usually are empowered to take direct action against violators. One provision of the federal law is that in states having fair employment practice laws with such enforcement powers, complaints of discrimination must be brought first to the state agency, with a wait of 60 days before taking the complaint to the federal EEOC. While there is considerable potential for confusion between state and federal authorities in FEP matters, federal requirements take precedence if there are inconsistencies (24). A crucial matter for the personnel manager, for example, is the question of identifying an applicant's or employee's race in personnel records. Under a number of state laws, this practice is illegal, but even in these states the federal government requires employers of one hundred or more people to obtain this information and report it. Such information is useful to the EEOC and other government agencies in determining where discrimination does in fact exist (16).

The effect of FEP legislation, both national and local, on the personnel practices of individual employers has varied considerably, but it is clear that there have been changes in recruiting patterns, selection standards, use of psychological tests, and the like as a result. The overall effect in terms of the long-term goals of such legislation is more difficult to determine. Although change has been extremely slow, there was some measurable gain in the achievement of greater racial integration by the end of the 1960s (8). Reports from the EEOC in the mid-1970s, as indicated in Table 5–4, did show both minorities and women with higher percentages of jobs both overall and in the upper-level professional and managerial positions. The figures in Table 5–4 are based on the annual reports required to be filed with EEOC by all organizations employing 100 persons or more.

Other Legal Aspects of Selection Decisions

Besides the laws and regulations concerned with fair employment practices, there are a number of other legal considerations that may affect the selection process. Two of these involve trade secrets and privacy rights.

Table 5–3. State Fair Employment Practice Laws

State	Type of Illegal Discrimination			
	Racial, Religious	Sex	Age	Handicapped
Alabama	—	—	—	—
Alaska	X	X	X	X
Arizona	X	X	—	—
Arkansas	—	—	—	—
California	X	X	X	X
Colorado	X	X	X	—
Connecticut	X	X	X	—
Delaware	X	X	X	—
District of Columbia	X	X	—	—
Florida	X	X	—	—
Georgia	X	—	X	—
Hawaii	X	X	X	X
Idaho	X	X	X	—
Illinois	X	X	X	X
Indiana	X	X	X	X
Iowa	X	X	X	X
Kansas	X	X	—	X
Kentucky	X	X	X	—
Louisiana	X	—	X	—
Maine	X	X	X	X
Maryland	X	X	X	—
Massachusetts	X	X	X	X
Michigan	X	X	X	—
Minnesota	X	X	—	X
Mississippi	—	—	—	—
Missouri	X	X	—	—
Montana	X	X	X	X
Nebraska	X	X	X	X
Nevada	X	X	—	X
New Hampshire	X	X	X	X
New Jersey	X	X	X	X
New Mexico	X	X	X	X
New York	X	X	X	X
North Carolina	X	X	—	X
North Dakota	X	—	X	—
Ohio	X	X	X	X
Oklahoma	X	X	X	—
Oregon	X	X	X	X
Pennsylvania	X	X	X	X
Puerto Rico	X	X	X	—
Rhode Island	X	X	X	X
South Carolina	—	—	—	—
South Dakota	X	X	—	—
Tennessee	—	—	—	—
Texas	—	X	—	—
Utah	X	X	X	—
Vermont	X	X	—	—
Virginia	—	—	—	X
Washington	X	X	X	X
West Virginia	X	X	X	X
Wisconsin	X	X	X	X
Wyoming	X	X	—	—

Source: Compiled from Bureau of National Affairs, Inc., *Fair Employment Practices* (Washington, D.C., 1976), 451: 25–28.

Table 5–4. Changes in the Job Picture by Race and by
Sex, 1966 and 1974

Occupation	White	All Minority	Men	Women
Total				
1966—Number	22,652,796	2,917,809	17,514,626	8,055,979
Per cent	88.6	11.4	68.5	31.5
1974—Number	26,403,667	5,199,124	20,011,129	11,591,662
Per cent	83.5	16.5	63.3	36.7
Officials and managers				
1966	98.1	1.9	90.4	9.4
1974	95.0	5.0	87.0	13.0
Professionals				
1966	96.5	3.5	86.0	14.0
1974	92.8	7.2	71.2	28.8
Technicians				
1966	93.5	6.5	68.9	31.1
1974	88.4	11.6	68.8	31.2
Sales workers				
1966	95.6	4.4	61.2	38.8
1974	90.9	9.1	53.4	46.6
Office and clerical workers				
1966	94.1	5.9	27.6	72.4
1974	86.3	13.7	20.7	79.3
Craft workers				
1966	93.8	6.2	93.6	6.4
1974	88.6	11.4	92.3	7.7
Operatives				
1966	85.6	14.4	72.3	27.7
1974	77.9	22.1	68.6	31.4
Laborers				
1966	71.8	28.2	76.1	23.9
1974	69.0	31.0	68.7	31.3
Service workers				
1966	71.9	28.1	56.7	43.3
1974	68.5	31.5	47.8	52.2

Source: EEO-1 Reports, 1966 and 1974.

TRADE SECRETS AND EMPLOYMENT CONTRACTS

The employment of an individual currently working for a competing company in a job involving access to trade secrets has posed legal problems for many years (42). These problems became pronounced in the 1950s, when most large companies were investing heavily in research and development activities. At issue is the question of whether employees can be prohibited from moving to another company and bettering their position simply because they have access to knowledge that might be used to competitive advantage by the new employer. In most controversies related to this issue, there is no state or federal legislation that is applicable, although a few states do have laws that prohibit such restraints on future employment (36).

Even in the absence of legislation, a number of cases involving trade secrets have reached the courts. One of the most famous of these was *Goodrich Company v. Wohlgemuth.*[5] Wohlgemuth, a chemical engineer, was manager of Goodrich's space suit division at the time he left to work for International Latex Corporation, on *its* space suit program, at a higher salary. Goodrich sued to prevent him from taking the new job, on the grounds that this would result in the transfer of Goodrich trade secrets to Latex. After a bitter and extended court battle, Wohlgemuth was allowed to take the job at International Latex but was prohibited from passing on any trade secrets (41).

In general, courts have been increasingly loath to keep employees from moving to better jobs merely to preserve trade secrets, even in situations where an employee has signed a preemployment contract stipulating that trade secrets will remain the property of the company. However, such contracts may still prove useful in preventing the disclosure of trade secrets or in collecting damages if disclosure does occur when an employee goes to work for a competitor (35).

PRIVACY RIGHTS

Various practices that may be involved in the hiring process have come under legal regulation in efforts to protect the privacy rights of employees and job applicants (23). In roughly a dozen states, for example, it is against the law to require preemployment polygraph (lie detector) tests. Another hiring practice, which is more common than the use of lie detectors, is to obtain information on job applicants through a consumer credit reporting service. As a result of widespread concern over the prospect of damaging but incorrect information being used as the basis for employment decisions, Congress passed the Fair Credit Reporting Act, which took effect in 1971. One aspect of the law covers the use of consumer credit reports in checking on job applicants or candidates for promotion and requires employers to notify individuals if their applications are denied on the basis of information from such a report. If the reporting service conducts a large-scale investigation, involving interviews with friends, neighbors, and associates of the applicant, he must be notified in advance. In neither case does the employer have to disclose the contents of the report he receives, but he does have to tell the applicant the name of the company providing the report. The law gives individuals the right to obtain information on the report from the credit agency (15).

---

[5] *Goodrich Co. v. Donald W. Wohlgemuth*, Ct of Appeals of Ohio, Summit City (1963).

LEGAL ASPECTS OF COMPENSATION

In contrast to the legal influences on hiring, which are mostly of relatively recent origin, wage and salary payments have been subject to legal regulation under laws setting a minimum wage since the 1910s in some states and since the 1930s on the federal level. A more recent type of legislation, both federal and state, affecting wage payments is that of equal pay laws.

Another type of government regulation that has even more direct consequences for personnel management is the imposition of controls on the payment of wages, salaries, and employee benefits. Over the years, this has occurred as a result of the inflationary pressures of wartime economies and during the "economic emergency" of the early 1970s.

Other aspects of employee compensation are subject to a variety of legal influences. Plans providing certain pension and welfare benefits are subject to standards legislated by the federal government, and both the federal and state governments have programs providing payments such as social security, unemployment compensation, and temporary disability benefits. Overall, the personnel administrator needs to weigh a number of kinds of legal considerations in formulating and implementing policies relating to compensation.

Minimum Wage Laws

Governmental interest in and control of wage rates date back to a law passed in Massachusetts in 1912. The most important of the minimum wage laws is the Fair Labor Standards Act, which was passed by Congress in 1938 and amended in 1949, 1955, 1961, 1966 and 1974. At the time of the original enactment, the law (which also has an hours-of-work provision, to be discussed later) set as its goal a national minimum wage of 40 cents per hour by 1945. However, this target was reached considerably before the date specified, as a result of increases during World War II. As indicated in Table 5–5, over the years the specified minimum wage has gone up progressively to the present level of $2.30 per hour.

With the 1966 amendments, employees of nearly all businesses in interstate commerce, except those with a very small dollar volume, were made subject to the federal minimum wage; the 1974 amendments extended coverage to large groups of government employees and domestic workers (20). The largest groups still exempt from the law's coverage are executive, administrative, and professional employees, outside salespeople, and self-employed workers. Presumably, most individuals in these categories are currently at rates above the minimum, and for this reason the exemptions are most meaningful as they relate to the hours and overtime provisions of the Act, to be discussed later in this chapter.

Two other federal laws that establish minimum wage rates are the Davis-Bacon Act of 1931, known as the Prevailing Wage Law and applying

Table 5–5. Federal Minimum Wage Legislation—Fair
Labor Standards Act

Legislation	Minimum Hourly Wage ($)	Minimum Hourly Wage for Employees Not Previously Covered ($)	Minimum Hourly Wage for New Farm Coverage ($)
Original enactment—1938			
Effective 1938	.25		
Effective 1940	.30		
Effective 1945	.40		
1949 Amendments	.75		
1955 Amendments	1.00		
1961 Amendments			
Effective September 1961	1.15	1.00	
Effective September 1963	1.25	—	
Effective September 1964	—	1.15	
Effective September 1965	—	1.25	
1966 Amendments			
Effective February 1967	1.40	1.00	1.00
Effective February 1968	1.60	1.15	1.15
Effective February 1969	—	1.30	1.30
Effective February 1970	—	1.45	—
Effective February 1971	—	1.60	—
1974 Amendments			
Effective May 1974	2.00	1.90	1.60
Effective January 1975	2.10	2.00	1.80
Effective January 1976	2.30	2.20	2.00
Effective January 1977	—	2.30	2.20
Effective January 1978	—	—	2.30

to federal construction project contractors, and the Walsh-Healey Public Contracts Act of 1936, which applies to other government contractors. Minimum wage legislation at the state level, as indicated, has a considerably longer history than at the federal level. At the present time, all but seven states, mostly in the Southeast, have minimum wage laws; in a few states, these laws apply only to females and minors (15). The state laws do cover a number of workers who fall outside the jurisdiction of the federal legislation, in particular those employed by companies not in interstate commerce.

Equal Pay Laws

Proposals for equal pay laws were considered by Congress in every session from 1945 until 1963, when the Equal Pay Act was passed, in the form of an amendment to the Fair Labor Standards Act (50). At that time, several states had such laws in effect, and since then many more have adopted them; by the end of 1975, nine-tenths of the states had such laws (15). In general, the effect is to outlaw any pay differentials based on sex.

In implementing the federal law, the government has taken the position that the jobs in question do not have to be identical but only "substantially equal" to require the same rate of pay. In several instances, groups of women employees have been awarded large sums of back pay when it was found that they were performing essentially the same jobs as men with different job titles.

One reason women were paid lower wages than men for the same type of work was that employers viewed their long-term potential as less, because the probability of turnover was considered to be higher for women than for men (32). This view often was used as a basis for excluding females from trainee positions. Banks, for example, frequently paid women tellers less than male tellers because the males were being groomed for promotion to officer positions. This practice is now illegal under the Equal Pay Act, and a federal court upheld the position that women cannot be paid less than men for such jobs in the absence of any visible training program open to both sexes (38).[6]

In its enforcement efforts, the Labor Department often has joined forces with the EEOC to reach agreements with employers designed to remedy the effects of past discrimination related to pay and promotion policies (28). One of the most publicized and far-reaching of these agreements involved AT&T and called for payments of $15 million to 13,000 women and 2,000 minority men at nonmanagement levels who had been denied pay and promotion opportunities. A second agreement with AT&T extended the provisions to cover several thousand management employees and specified that salary increases for these employees were not to be made on the basis of their former pay, because this practice had the effect of perpetuating past discrimination in pay (19).

Wage and Salary Controls

Direct controls on wage and salary payments were in effect during the World War II period from 1942 to 1945 and again during the Korean War

---

[6] *Shultz v. First Victoria National Bank,* CA 5 (1969), 19 WH Cases 275.

from 1951 to 1953. In both these instances, the controls were aimed at stabilizing the potential inflationary pressures of a wartime economy by establishing limits on increases permitted in wage and salary rates. The World War II limit on general wage increases was 15 per cent, and during the Korean period it was 10 per cent. During both periods, a long series of regulations outlined the permissibility of other types of wage increases, such as cost-of-living increases, bonus payments, and adjustments in fringe benefits.

The United States's most recent experience with economic controls lasted from 1971 through mid-1974 and began with a three-month wage-price freeze during which no general wage or salary adjustments were permitted, and only a few individual raises were authorized. The controls were relaxed gradually over the next two years and during the last year of the program applied only to certain industries and to top executive pay. In 1974, the controls program ended, and a Council on Wage and Price Stability was given the function of monitoring the nation's economy (15).

The 1970s controls program followed a decade of widespread concern over the inflationary effects of wage and price increases and was instituted in an effort to combat what was called an "inflationary psychology." Wage earners, particularly those represented by large unions, had come to expect increasingly generous wage raises each year, in part, at least, to offset continuing escalation of the cost of living. Experience under the controls program indicated, however, the relationships were more complex, and as the program ended, the nation was faced with continuing inflation as well as an increasing unemployment problem (37).

Legal Influences on Benefits

An important part of the total compensation paid employees consists of benefits in the form of time off with pay or outside payments such as insurance premiums. These payments often are affected in one way or another by federal or state legislation. One example involves the size of monthly payments under the federal Social Security program, which may well be taken into account in establishing the level of benefits employers pay under their own pension plans. An example at the state level might be the laws providing for temporary disability payments, found in a few jurisdictions. The existence of these laws has considerable impact on the type of sick leave program a company establishes for its employees.

A recent addition to the myriad of federal laws affecting employee benefits is the Employee Retirement Income Security Act of 1974, commonly referred to as ERISA or the Pension Reform Law. The law's basic purpose is to provide a number of protections and guarantees for the payment of benefits under private industry plans and to set standards in the areas of participation, vesting of benefits, and funding (12). While the legislation is designed to afford protection to employees covered by pension plans, at the time of its enactment there was concern that the costs to employers of meeting the new standards might result in smaller companies' deciding to abandon their benefit programs, with the result that fewer workers would be eligible for private pension benefits (27). Whatever the long-term results in terms of overall pension coverage, the reporting and other requirements of ERISA impose an additional legal burden related to the management of an organization's human resources.

WORKING HOUR CONSTRAINTS

Closely tied to the growth of legislation dealing with the regulation of wages has been the spread of legal constraints on hours of work. To a large extent, legislation that has specified allowable wage structures has also contained certain restrictions on the amount of time certain people can spend at work. As with the wage limitations, working hour laws passed at the federal level apply to firms engaged in interstate commerce, and those at the state level to companies operating on an intrastate basis.

Among the federal laws discussed in the previous section, both the Fair Labor Standards Act, as amended, and the Walsh-Healey Public Contracts Act have provisions governing the working hours of employees. A major intent of these laws is to limit the length of the work week indirectly, by requiring premium pay for time worked in excess of a specific standard.

Most important for our purposes is the Fair Labor Standards Act, which requires the payment of time and one half for all work in excess of 40 hours per week in most covered industries. A work week is defined as a recurring period of 168 hours (7 consecutive 24-hour periods). It need not be the same as the calendar week, and it may begin at any hour of the day.

As noted earlier, several categories of employees are exempt from both the minimum wage and overtime provisions of the Fair Labor Standards Act, notably executive, administrative, and professional employees paid on a salaried rather than an hourly wage basis. In addition, employees in certain specified businesses are exempt only from the overtime provisions. The number of these exemptions has been narrowed considerably since the initial law was enacted in 1938.

At the state level, legal constraints on working hours have a much longer history, dating back to the early 1800s, and they are much more direct. While the federal government restricts hours of work primarily through overtime payment provisions, the states specifically limit the amount of time that can be worked. The reason for this is that the state laws controlling hours of work have been based more on humane considerations and were passed originally for the specific purpose of preventing the exploitation of child and female employees.

At the present time, all the states have laws regulating the employment of minors (defined as persons under twenty-one years of age in some states, under eighteen in some, and under sixteen years in others), with provisions limiting the number of hours that can be worked within a given time period and sometimes restricting or prohibiting night work (15). Most states also have laws regulating working hours for both men and women in certain types of employment where public safety is a major consideration or where there are extremely hazardous working conditions. State laws controlling hours of work for female employees only, which once were found in nearly all the states, generally have been repealed or ruled unenforceable since the passage of the Civil Rights Act.

LEGISLATION AFFECTING THE WORK ENVIRONMENT

While some of the earliest legislation related to hours of work was based on considerations of employee safety and health, other types of legislation have a much more direct effect on the work environment and employee health and safety. These are the state workers' compensation laws and federal and state occupational safety and health laws.

Workers' Compensation

The development of state statutes providing compensation for employees injured on the job or to families of employees who are killed in industrial accidents occurred many years after the advent of industrialization. In the early years, an employer was protected from costs associated with accidents by employer liability laws stemming from three major aspects of common law:

1. The doctrine of contributory negligence: Employers were not liable if an accident resulted from an employee's negligence.
2. The doctrine of the assumption of risk: An employee who accepted a job also accepted the risks involved.
3. The doctrine of the fellow-servant rule: If an employee was injured by a fellow employee, the employer was not responsible.

This legal structure proved increasingly unsatisfactory on a number of counts. The employer was constantly harassed with suits to determine liability, and the employee was faced with a major loss of income unless he could win a legal battle that inevitably involved considerable expense. These earlier laws also proved inadequate from the point of view of society as a whole, in that they forced many accident victims onto the public relief rolls (30).

For these reasons, a somewhat different way of looking at accidents, and the manner in which their costs should be borne, began to achieve acceptance. Instead of attempting to determine causation and liability, the new idea was that accidents were a cost of production and therefore should be passed on to the consumer. The result was the development of a variety of *workers' compensation* plans, which are essentially insurance systems with the benefits payable to employees who are accident victims. Every state in the union, as well as the District of Columbia and Puerto Rico, now has such a plan. In addition, the federal government has a workers' compensation arrangement for its employees and for longshore and harbor workers.

Because each state has its own plan, details vary greatly and are constantly changing. However, nearly all have as a common feature the provision of benefits as a percentage of wages up to a maximum amount and for a specified period. Allowances are usually provided for hospital expenses and for benefits to survivors in case of death. In the typical plan, also, the employee does not have to initiate a claim; this is done by a state commission at little or no cost to the injured person.

Most significant for our purposes is the fact that nearly all the laws adjust the rates to be paid by the company in terms of the firm's safety record. Thus, strong pressures are put on management to develop policies and procedures that will foster employee safety. It is in this sense that workers' compensation legislation has served most markedly to influence personnel decisions. This adjusting of the payment rate in terms of the number and costliness of accidents tends to be the usual practice whether the system used is a state-operated insurance plan or one that utilizes a private insurer.

In addition, most states have encouraged the employment of handicapped workers by passing legislation that specifies that the employer is to have charged against him only those injuries that actually occur within his firm. The reason for this is that if an already handicapped worker were to be injured, the result might well be a total disability. Should such a situation result in a total disability accident's being charged against the firm, the impact on the workers' compensation rate might be sizable, and management would be under some pressure to avoid hiring the handicapped. The laws, as now written, however, indicate that only the specific injury is to be charged. The disabled worker is paid out of a special state fund that is not dependent on employer contributions.

All but three of the state workers' compensation laws were enacted before 1920, and there has been some concern that many of them are out of date. Certain types of injuries and occupational diseases that did not exist in earlier years often are not covered at all; in nearly all states, the level of benefits payable has lagged considerably behind actual wage levels. In 1970, Congress authorized a national commission to study these problems, with a view to taking action to remedy them (13); to date, however, there have been no major changes in the state systems.

Occupational Health and Safety Laws

In most states, the implementation of the workers' compensation law involves requirements, such as factory inspections, that have a direct impact on a company's safety programs. Some states have additional regulations establishing health and safety standards and procedures; these date back as far as 1852, when Massachusetts passed the nation's first safety law, setting standards relating to the operation of steam engines (30). Even in states where such laws do exist, their administration and enforcement have been variable, and during the 1960s, the nation's record in industrial safety began to decline significantly after several decades of improvement.

Besides the increase in accidents, industry was faced with another problem during this period—the problem of how to handle the dangers of new chemicals and other agents whose potentially harmful effects were largely unknown. For many years, the federal government's authority to deal with safety and health problems was limited to jurisdiction in coal-mining operations and regulations covering companies working on government contracts. The first comprehensive occupational health and safety bill was proposed to Congress in 1968, but only after two years of testimony and heated debate was the Occupational Safety and Health Act (of 1970) actually passed (24).

The Act gives the federal government authority to set and enforce rigorous nationwide safety and health standards for employees of all business enterprises in interstate commerce. Government agents may conduct inspections and investigations of work facilities, and the courts may condemn conditions or practices that constitute an imminent danger to employees' health or safety. The federal law also includes provisions for permitting the states to take over enforcement of safety and health standards where the state standards appear to be as effective in protecting the health and safety of employees as the federal standards (13).

The first few years of federal enforcement of OSHA have been viewed as "developmental" and marked by controversy over such issues as what standards should be adopted, legal procedures for making inspections and issuing fines, and record-keeping requirements (1); it is too soon to see the long-term effects of the law. One indication that it is achieving its purpose is found in the statistics relating to the five industries the Labor Department chose for its initial major enforcement efforts. These target industries—longshoring, roofing and sheet metal, meat and meat products, miscellaneous transportation equipment, and lumber and wood products—are those with the worst safety records at the time OSHA was enacted. As indicated by the figures in Table 5–6, all five of these industries experienced a decline in accident rates from 1972 to 1973 (47).

LEGAL INFLUENCES ON SEPARATIONS— UNEMPLOYMENT COMPENSATION

Just as employers do not always have complete freedom to hire anyone they please, there also are instances when they may not be able to fire anyone they please. The most restrictive legal considerations relating to discharge are those involving union members and union activity, which will be discussed in the next section. Other restrictions stem from humanitarian reasons, as in cases where courts have ruled that employees cannot be forced

Table 5–6. Recordable Occupational Injury and Illness Incidence Rates for Target Industries, United States, 1973 and 1972

| Industry | Incidence Rates per 100 Full-time Workers | | Per Cent of Change |
| | Total Recordable Cases | | |
	1973	1972	
Roofing and sheet-metal work	27.7	28.9	−4.2
Metal products	27.2	28.2	−3.5
Lumber and wood products	24.1	25.4	−5.1
Miscellaneous transportation equipment	35.5	36.5	−2.7
Water transportation services	26.2	26.9	−2.6

Source: U.S. Department of Labor, Occupational Injuries and Illnesses in the United States, by Industry, 1973 (Washington, D.C., 1975), p. 3.

to retire early when there are no pension benefits available to them and they are not old enough to qualify for Social Security payments. A further legal influence on separation policies is provided under the unemployment compensation system.

To encourage employers to stabilize their employment policies and keep individual workers on the job, every state has an unemployment compensation program that is financed by taxing employers according to the extent to which their companies have contributed to the unemployment rolls. These programs have other objectives as well—to keep purchasing power at a high level and thus assist the economy, and to minimize the impact of unemployment as it may affect the individual and his family. However, it is because unemployment compensation laws influence personnel policy by encouraging employment stabilization and a minimal number of separations that they are included in this chapter.

Although the first law in the United States was on the state level, in Wisconsin in 1932, the real impetus to the growth of unemployment insurance came in 1935, in the midst of the depression, when the Social Security Act was passed. An important provision of this act was a federal tax on payrolls, of which 90 per cent was to be refunded to the states if they passed acceptable unemployment compensation programs. By July 1937, all of the states and the District of Columbia had enacted laws of this kind.

The common characteristics of the various systems are that:

1. There must usually be a waiting period (generally one week) before unemployment benefits are paid to the worker who has just lost his job, although in recent years a few states have abolished the waiting period.
2. The person who receives benefits must establish his eligibility for unemployment payments by virtue of previous employment and earnings;

these then determine the amount of the subsequent weekly benefit payments and the number of weeks the payments will continue.

3. The person who receives benefits must be ready, willing, and able to work in his "usual line of work" should a suitable position be located for him.

4. Individuals may be disqualified from benefits for quitting without cause or for being fired with cause (for justified disciplinary reasons).

5. Strikers are usually disqualified from benefits entirely, although in some states unemployment benefits can be paid after a limited period on strike.

Under the experience-rating provisions of state laws, employers who minimize their layoffs and firings benefit in terms of a lower tax rate; unemployment compensation payroll taxes can be reduced considerably by companies that can schedule the work evenly. Employers also are encouraged to contest any unemployment insurance claim that might be without merit. On the other hand, there are times when individual employers have little control over business conditions.

One problem with the present system is that the payroll taxes go up and workers run out of benefit coverage during the periods of greatest unemployment. Federal amendments passed in the high unemployment year of 1970 created a means for states to extend benefit durations for persons who exhaust regular benefits during periods of acute unemployment. In most states, the maximum number of weeks benefits are payable is 26; the new provisions permit up to 39 weeks of benefits, financed partly by the federal government.

Another issue over the years has involved the level of UC benefits, which vary considerably from state to state, and the increases in benefits, which generally have lagged behind increases in the cost of living. These considerations have resulted in numerous proposals for the federal government to step in and enforce standards for benefit levels, but these proposals have not been adopted (43).

Although the result of governmental intervention in this area might seem to be a contribution to organizational maintenance, this need not invariably be the case. The employees retained may represent a source of considerable dissension within the firm. Also, the maintenance goal may be achieved at great cost, in terms of profits, if there is not sufficient work to keep employees busy or if the retained employees are ineffective performers whose deficiencies are beyond the power of management to correct.

LEGAL INFLUENCES ON LABOR RELATIONS

Among the areas of activity with which the personnel manager is typically concerned in his everyday work, there is probably none in which the government takes a greater interest or attempts to exert more control than the labor-management relationship. A company's efforts to achieve the goal of organizational maintenance are circumscribed by a considerably more extensive barrier of legal restraints than are its efforts relative to the productivity objective. In many respects, the current legal framework in the labor relations area operates to sustain labor-management conflict through its concern with maintaining a balance of power; thus, it inevitably serves to frustrate, at least partially, efforts to promote organizational maintenance.

Federal Legislation

As indicated during the discussion of the development of personnel management in Chapter 2, the United States has some very strong traditions relating to the importance of private property rights and freedom of the individual. These values and beliefs are deeply embedded in the fabric of our society; they are supported throughout the socioeconomic hierarchy. Thus, it is not surprising that our common law (which is based on the accumulated decisions of the judiciary over a very long period of time) was directly opposed to the idea of imposing constraints on management's freedom to operate a business as it saw fit throughout the early part of the country's history.

This basic philosophy of noninterference with the rights of the employer remained strong through the first third of the 20th century. The philosophy manifested itself increasingly through the use of the injunction, a legal procedure under which employers could obtain a court order prohibiting certain actions by unions, such as strikes. Along with the use of the injunction, there also was judicial support for yellow-dog contracts, in which workers agreed at the time of their employment that they would not join a labor union or engage in any union activity.

This philosophy achieved what would appear to be a high point in 1917, when the Supreme Court ruled that an injunction could be issued forbidding all attempts to organize workers who had signed contracts agreeing not to join unions.[7] In this case, the principle of governmental support for the doctrine of minimal constraint on the managerial process is clearly evident.

RAILWAY LABOR ACT OF 1926

One exception to the prevailing attitude in the pre-1932 era involved the railroad industry. Several years of labor strife that followed government operation of the railroads during World War I led to the passage of the National Railway Labor Act in 1926. This law resulted from a joint effort by representatives of railroad management and the unions, and established procedures for collective bargaining and disputes settlement. Since 1936, the air transport industry also has been covered by the Act. In recent years, the effectiveness of the Act has been seriously questioned because of the need of

---

[7] *Hitchman Coal and Coke Company v. Mitchell*, 245 U.S. 229, 38 SupCt 65 (1917).

the federal government to intervene before any settlements are reached, and a number of proposals have been made for its amendment or outright repeal (40).

1932—NORRIS-LA GUARDIA ACT

The first step away from the no-constraint philosophy relating to industry in general came in 1932, when the depression was at its peak. The disillusionment of the depression years served to stimulate a widespread tendency to question existing values and assumptions. This questioning eventually produced some marked changes in the country's legal position regarding labor unions and union activity. Thus it was that in 1932 Congress passed the Norris-La Guardia Anti-injunction Act, the first of a number of laws effectively restricting management's freedom in dealing with labor unions.

The logic of the Norris-La Guardia Act, which is still operative today, is very simple, yet the import of the Act has been tremendous. It essentially affirms a laissez-faire philosophy in that it specifies that government should not impose constraints upon the conduct of the union-management relationship or interfere with it *in any way*, unless there has been actual violence or damage to tangible property. It thus expressly forbids the enforcement of yellow-dog contracts by the courts and the use of the injunction in cases where damage *might* ensue. Instead, the injunction can be granted only in cases where there is actual damage or violence, and even then its use is severely limited.

1935—NATIONAL LABOR RELATIONS ACT (WAGNER ACT)

The passing of the Wagner Act in 1935 marks the beginning of active *federal* intervention in labor-management disputes with the express purpose of constraining the activities of one of the participants—in this case, management. The stated purpose of the act was to (a) encourage trade union growth and (b) restrain management from interfering in any way with this growth. Although the Norris-La Guardia Act was prolabor in spirit, it was essentially laissez-faire in its basic nature. Its intent was to *stop* certain types of governmental intervention.

The Wagner Act went much further. It stated that the government could not remain neutral and that it must take an active role in union-management relationships by constraining the activities of one group (management) in order to advance the fortunes of the other (the unions). The spirit of the act can best be seen by reading the concluding paragraph of its introduction:

It is hereby declared to be the policy of the United States to eliminate the causes of certain substantial obstructions to the free flow of commerce and to mitigate and eliminate these obstructions when they have occurred, by encouraging the practice and procedure of collective bargaining and by protecting the exercise by workers of full freedom of association, self-organization, and designation of representatives of their own choosing, for the purpose of negotiating the terms and conditions of their employment or other mutual aid or protection.

To fulfill this stated purpose, the Wagner Act did two things. It set up machinery to facilitate the choice of a labor union by a group of workers. More important for our purposes, however, it enunciated a list of activities that were forbidden to management. These activities, which in the act are defined as unfair labor practices, were considered to be inimical to the purpose of the act, the encouragement of labor union growth, and hence were specifically proscribed. They comprise the first major set of direct, governmentally imposed constraints on management in the area of union-management relations.

The administrative power inherent in the act was vested in a three-man National Labor Relations Board and a staff of lawyers, investigators, and other personnel, who were responsible to the Board. It was the function of this governmental unit to set up election machinery, upon request, to determine if the majority of a given group of workers wished to have a particular union as a bargaining representative and to investigate complaints regarding unfair labor practices.

The provisions of the Wagner Act that were devoted to imposing specific constraints on the practices of management in order to stimulate union growth were important, wide-ranging, and outstandingly successful. During the twelve years when the Wagner Act was the basic law of the land (1935–1947), union membership increased from 3 million to over 15 million, and the trade unions assumed a position among the largest and strongest social institutions in the country (9). In fact, the growth was so phenomenal, and the power of the labor movement became so great, that strong sentiment began to develop in favor of correcting the inherently one-sided viewpoint of the Wagner Act. Many came to feel that a legal situation in which all constraint was placed on one side and the government took its place with the other was intolerable. By 1947, public opinion in support of change had become so strong that Congress responded with the Taft-Hartley Act.

1947—TAFT-HARTLEY ACT

On June 23, 1947, the Congress of the United States passed an amendment to the Wagner Act known as the Labor-Management Relations Act, or, as it is popularly known, the Taft-Hartley Act. With this piece of legislation, a new philosophy regarding the proper role of government in the conduct of union-management affairs achieved formal acceptance. This was the concept of the impartial umpire. The explicit prounion bias of the Wagner Act was repudiated, and the basic position, at least in theory, now was that government should not take sides, but rather should stand aside like an umpire, taking care to observe that the collective bargaining process took place fairly and according to the rules, and that the interests of the general public were preserved. The essential neutrality of spirit that characterized this law is exemplified by the following wording:

> Employees shall have the right to self-organization . . . for the purpose of collective bargaining or other mutual aid or protection, and shall also have the right to refrain from any or all of such activities.

For 30 years, the Taft-Hartley Act has been the most important labor law in this country (2). As a result of it, the government was officially placed in the middle, neither encouraging nor discouraging union organization. The employee could either seek union representation or reject it, and the government backed this right of free choice.

Administration of the law was left in the hands of the National Labor Relations Board, but the Board was enlarged from three to five members. A General Counsel was added to aid the Board, and an explicit policy of decentralized decision making was stated. At the present time, this means that all representation elections are conducted and all representation decisions rendered by the regional directors. The Board in Washington will consider appeals only under a limited set of specified conditions. Unfair labor practices cases have not been decentralized, and all are decided in Washington.

NLRB INTERPRETATION OF THE LABOR RELATIONS ACTS

From the point of view of influence on managerial actions, the limitations set forth in the labor relations statutes have been subject to various interpretations at various points in time. It has been noted frequently over the years that the NLRB, whose members are appointed by the President for a five-year term of office, tends to change character with changes in the political party in power in Washington. This sometimes has resulted in reversals by the NLRB itself of long-standing precedents used as the basis for its decision making (3).

Another uncertainty in the implementation of the labor laws is that many NLRB decisions have been reversed in the federal courts, and the process of judicial review usually takes many years. In a number of instances, employers have been successful in getting the courts to agree that the NLRB has gone too far, especially in interfering with the day-to-day bargaining relationship of the company and union involved (22). By the time the court decision is handed down, however, the parties will have had to come to some resolution on their own, or the relationship is likely to have disintegrated and organizational maintenance suffered severely.

Over the years, NLRB has built up sets of precedent that indicate the direction its decisions will take and the degree of influence the federal labor laws may have on managerial decisions (5, 14). Some of these precedents will be discussed in Chapter 19, on labor relations; many of them involve legal technicalities more properly covered in courses on labor law.

One area of concern has involved NLRB's jurisdictional standards. The limitedness of the funds with which the Board has always had to operate has made it impossible to regulate all the cases involving interstate commerce, which both the Wagner and Taft-Hartley acts specifically delegated to it. To cope with this problem, the Board has established certain standards, based on a firm's volume of business, to determine whether it will accept jurisdiction. These standards are set forth in Table 5–7 (39).

Table 5–7. NLRB Standards for Asserting Jurisdiction

1. Nonretail business: Direct sales of goods to customers in other States, or indirect sales through others (called outflow), of at least $50,000 a year; or direct purchases of goods from suppliers in other States, or indirect purchases through others (called inflow), of at least $50,000 a year.
2. Office buildings: Total annual revenue of $100,000, of which $25,000 or more is derived from organizations which meet any of the standards except the indirect outflow and indirect inflow standards established for nonretail enterprises.
3. Retail enterprises: At least $500,000 total annual volume of business.
4. Public utilities: At least $250,000 total annual volume of business, or $50,000 direct or indirect outflow or inflow.
5. Newspapers: At least $200,000 total annual volume of business.
6. Radio, telegraph, television, and telephone enterprises: At least $100,000 total annual volume of business.
7. Hotels, motels, and residential apartment houses: At least $500,000 total annual volume of business.
8. Privately owned hospitals and nursing homes operated for profit: At least $250,000 total annual volume of business for hospitals; at least $100,000 for nursing homes.
9. Transportation enterprises, links and channels of interstate commerce: At least $50,000 total annual income from furnishing interstate passenger and freight transportation services; also performing services valued at $50,000 or more for businesses which meet any of the jurisdictional standards except the indirect outflow and indirect inflow standards established for nonretail enterprises.
10. Transit systems: At least $250,000 total annual volume of business.
11. Taxicab companies: At least $500,000 total annual volume of business.
12. Associations: These are regarded as a single employer in that the annual business of all association members is totaled to determine whether any of the standards apply.
13. Enterprises in the Territories and the District of Columbia: The jurisdictional standards apply in the Territories; all businesses in the District of Columbia come under NLRB jurisdiction.
14. National defense: Jurisdiction is asserted over all enterprises affecting commerce when their operations have a substantial impact on national defense, whether or not their enterprises satisfy any other standard.
15. Private nonprofit universities and colleges: At least $1,000.000 gross annual revenue from all sources (excluding contributions not available for operating expenses because of limitations imposed by the grantor).

Through enactment of the Postal Reorganization Act in 1970, jurisdiction of the NLRB was extended to the United States Postal Service, effective July 1, 1971.

Source: National Labor Relations Board, Summary of the National Labor Relations Act (Washington, D.C.: Government Printing Office, 1971).

For a number of years, employers in interstate commerce too small to meet the NLRB standards were not covered by the federal law. Nor, as a result of a series of Supreme Court decisions, were they covered by the various state labor relations acts (in those states having them). This situation was remedied by the Landrum-Griffin Act of 1959, which is discussed in the next section. This act gives the states jurisdiction over those cases that might fall under federal law but that the NLRB has chosen not to accept primarily because the firm involved does not have the necessary volume of business.

1959—LANDRUM-GRIFFIN ACT

During the late 1950s, a series of Congressional investigations resulted in some rather sweeping disclosures indicating that union members were being victimized both physically and financially by their elected union officials. There were also some instances in which employers appeared to be guilty of racketeering practices (44). The result was the passage of the Labor-Management Reporting and Disclosure Act of 1959, known as the Landrum-Griffin Act.

This act had as its major purpose the regulation of the internal affairs of unions and the relationships between union leaders and members. However, since the investigations had also indicated that employers were in some cases engaging in undesirable practices, the act did contain a number of clauses aimed at regulating managerial activity.

These constraints were of two major types (1). For one thing, the law required employers to report to the Secretary of Labor any payments or loans made to unions, their officials, or members. Excluded from this requirement were payments made for some valid reason such as (a) payments to a union officer because of his services as an employee, (b) payments resulting from some legal action, (c) payments into valid benefit funds, and (d) payments as a result of the purchase of an article at the prevailing market value. The purpose of this provision was to eliminate what have been called *sweetheart contracts,* under which the employer and union agree to terms that maintain substandard working conditions to their mutual advantage.

Another group of limitations imposed under the law required a variety of other reports from employers as to any payments made to employees, if these payments were for reasons that fall generally under the heading of influencing employees concerning their right to organize and bargain collectively. There was also a provision calling for reports on payments made to labor consultants, if the payments were made in order to purchase influence over the behavior of employees.

State Legislation

In addition to the federal laws, there also has been a considerable amount of legislation at the state level, beginning in 1937. Relatively few states—

Table 5–8. Checklist of State Labor Laws

State	State Labor Relations Acts	Public Employees: Collective Bargaining	Right-to-work Laws	Strikes	Picketing, Boycotts
Alabama	—	X	X	X	X
Alaska	—	X	—	X	—
Arizona	—	X	X	X	X
Arkansas	—	—	X	X	X
California	—	X	—	X	X
Colorado	X	X	—	X	X
Connecticut	X	X	—	X	X
Delaware	—	X	—	X	X
District of Columbia	—	—	—	X	X
Florida	—	X	X	X	X
Georgia	—	—	X	X	X
Hawaii	X	X	—	X	X
Idaho	—	X	—	X	X
Illinois	—	—	—	X	X
Indiana	—	X	—	X	X
Iowa	—	—	X	X	—
Kansas	X	X	X	X	X
Kentucky	—	—	—	X	X
Louisiana	—	X	X	—	X
Maine	—	X	—	X	X
Maryland	—	X	—	X	X
Massachusetts	X	X	—	X	X
Michigan	X	X	—	X	X
Minnesota	X	X	—	X	X
Mississippi	—	—	X	—	X
Missouri	—	X	—	X	X
Montana	—	X	—	X	X
Nebraska	—	X	X	X	X
Nevada	—	X	X	X	—
New Hampshire	—	X	—	X	X
New Jersey	—	X	—	X	X
New Mexico	—	—	—	X	X
New York	X	X	—	X	X
North Carolina	—	—	X	—	X
North Dakota	X	X	X	X	X
Ohio	—	—	—	X	X
Oklahoma	—	X	—	X	X
Oregon	X	X	—	X	X
Pennsylvania	X	X	—	X	X
Puerto Rico	X	—	—	X	X
Rhode Island	X	X	—	X	X
South Carolina	—	—	X	X	X
South Dakota	X	X	X	X	X
Tennessee	—	—	X	X	X
Texas	—	—	X	X	X
Utah	X	—	X	X	X
Vermont	X	X	—	X	X
Virginia	—	—	X	X	X
Washington	—	X	—	X	X
West Virginia	X	—	—	X	X
Wisconsin	X	X	—	X	X
Wyoming	—	X	X	X	X

Source: Bureau of National Affairs, Inc. Labor Relations (Washington, D.C., 1976), pp. 87: 19–20.

about one-third—have enacted labor legislation designed to accomplish on the state level what the Wagner and Taft-Hartley acts had done on the federal level. These acts usually cover interstate cases for which the NLRB has refused to accept jurisdiction and also intrastate commerce.

Even in states that do not have comprehensive labor relations laws, however, many aspects of labor relations activities are covered under more limited laws and regulations (15). Several of these aspects, as well as the state labor relations acts, are listed in Table 5–8.

These state laws differ from one another considerably in both coverage and provisions, and include constraints on unions as well as on management. Of particular interest are the growing number of state laws regulating labor relations for public employees. In light of recent increases in union activities among such groups as teachers and other employees of state and local governments, these laws have taken on considerable significance.

QUESTIONS

1. What are the various groups of people covered by federal fair employment legislation? Can you think of any other groups that might be covered by future legislation? Why?
2. Which of the federal laws related to personnel matters have been passed since 1965? What do these laws have in common?
3. What federal laws deal with each of the following?
   a. Overtime pay.
   b. EEOC.
   c. Yellow-dog contract.
   d. Firing.
   e. Payments to labor union officials.
4. How does the developing pattern of legislation relate to organizational maintenance considerations? Discuss with reference to laws dealing with fair employment practices, unemployment, and labor relations.
5. What appears to be the historical relationship between state and federal legislation in the personnel area? Can you identify any geographical areas of the country where certain kinds of laws tend to be absent? If so, what factors might account for this situation?

REFERENCES

1. Aaron, B. J. "The Labor Management Reporting and Disclosure Act of 1959." *Harvard Business Review,* 73 (1960), Nos. 5 and 6.
2. Aaron, B. "Legal Framework of Industrial Relations," in *The Next Twenty-five Years of Industrial Relations.* Madison, Wis.: Industrial Relations Research Association, 1973.
3. Aaron, B. J., and P. S. Meyer. "Public Policy and Labor-Management Relations," in B. J. Aaron, P. S. Meyer, J. Crispo, G. L. Mangum, and

J. S. Stern, *A Review of Industrial Research,* Vol. 2. Madison, Wis.: Industrial Relations Research Association, 1971, pp. 1–60.

4. Ace, M. E. "Psychological Testing: Unfair Discrimination?" *Industrial Relations,* 10 (1971), 301–315.

5. Anderson, H. J. *Primer of Labor Relations,* 20th ed. Washington, D.C.: Bureau of National Affairs, Inc., 1975.

6. Ash, P. "The Implications of the Civil Rights Act of 1964 for Psychological Assessment in Industry." *American Psychologist,* 21 (1966), 797–803.

7. Barnako, F. R., A. J. Reis, and M. Wood. "An Assessment of Three Years of OSHA," in J. L. Stern and B. D. Dennis (eds.), *Proceedings of the Twenty-seventh Annual Winter Meeting.* Madison, Wis.: Industrial Relations Research Association, 1975.

8. Bergmann, B. R., and W. R. Krause. "Evaluating and Forecasting Progress in Racial Integration of Employment." *Industrial and Labor Relations Review,* 25 (1972), 399–409.

9. Bernstein, I. "The Growth of American Unions." *American Economic Review,* 44 (1954), 308–317.

10. Bureau of National Affairs, Inc. *Civil Rights Act of 1964.* Washington, D.C.: BNA, Inc., 1964.

11. Bureau of National Affairs, Inc. *Daily Labor Report,* No. 42 (1975), pp. D-1, D-2.

12. Bureau of National Affairs, Inc. *Highlights of the New Pension Reform Law.* Washington, D.C.: BNA, Inc., 1974.

13. Bureau of National Affairs, Inc. *Job Safety and Health Act of 1973.* Washington, D.C.: BNA, Inc., 1971.

14. Bureau of National Affairs, Inc. *Major Labor-law Principles Established by the NLRB and the Courts.* Washington, D.C.: BNA, Inc., 1974.

15. Bureau of National Affairs, Inc. *Policy and Practice Series* (Labor Relations, Personnel Management, Fair Employment Practices, Compensation). Washington, D.C.: BNA, Inc., 1976.

16. Byham, W. C., and M. E. Spitzer. *The Law and Personnel Testing.* New York: American Management Association, 1971.

17. Chayes, A. H. "Make Your Equal Opportunity Program Court-proof." *Harvard Business Review,* Vol. 32, No. 5 (1974), 81–89.

18. Commerce Clearing House. *1975 Guidebook to Fair Employment Practices.* Chicago: CCH, Inc., 1975.

19. Cook, A. H. "Equal Pay: Where Is It?" *Industrial Relations,* 14 (1975), 158–177.

20. Elder, P. "The 1974 Amendments to the Federal Minimum Wage Law." *Monthly Labor Review,* 97 (1974), No. 7, 33–37.

21. Equal Employment Opportunity Commission. *Ninth Annual Report.* Washington, D.C.: The Commission, 1975.

22. Fanning, J. H. "Remedies for Unfair Labor Practices," in G. G. Somers (ed.), *Proceedings of the Twenty-third Annual Meeting.* Madison, Wis.: Industrial Relations Research Association, 1971, pp. 244–253.
23. Goldstein, R. C., and R. L. Nolan. "Personal Privacy vs. the Corporate Computer." *Harvard Business Review,* 53 (1975), No. 2, 62–70.
24. Greenman, R. L., and E. J. Schmertz. *Personnel Administration and the Law.* Washington, D.C.: Bureau of National Affairs, Inc., 1972.
25. Grunewald, R. J. "The Age Discrimination in Employment Act of 1967." *Industrial Gerontology,* No. 15 (1972), 1–11.
26. *Harvard Law Review.* "Developments in the Law—Employment Discrimination and Title VII of the Civil Rights Act of 1964." *Harvard Law Review,* 84 (1971), 1109–1316.
27. Henle, P., and R. Schmitt. "Pension Reform: The Long, Hard Road to Enactment." *Monthly Labor Review,* 97 (1974), No. 11, 3–12.
28. Kilberg, W. J. "Progress and Problems in Equal Employment Opportunity." *Labor Law Journal,* 24 (1973), 651–661.
29. Knodle, L. L. "Federal Involvement in College and University Personnel Administration." *Journal of College and University Personnel Administration,* 22 (1971), No. 3, 92–98.
30. Ling, C. C. *The Management of Personnel Relations.* Homewood, Ill.: Richard D. Irwin, Inc., 1965.
31. Lockwood, H. C. "Equal Employment Opportunities," in D. Yoder and H. G. Heneman (eds.), *Staffing Policies and Strategies.* Washington, D.C.: Bureau of National Affairs, Inc., 1974.
32. Mancke, R. B. "Lower Pay for Women: A Case of Economic Discrimination?" *Industrial Relations,* 10 (1971), 316–326.
33. *Manpower Report of the President.* Washington, D.C.: Government Printing Office, 1975.
34. Marcus, S., and J. Christoffersen. "Discrimination and the Older Worker." *Business Horizons,* 12 (1969), No. 5, 83–89.
35. Meyer, P. "When to Use Employment Contracts." *Harvard Business Review,* 49 (1971), No. 6, 70–72.
36. Milgrim, R. M. "Getting the Most Out of Your Trade Secrets." *Harvard Business Review,* 52 (1974), No. 6, 105–112.
37. Mills, D. Q. *Government, Labor, and Inflation: Wage Stabilization in the United States.* Chicago: University of Chicago Press, 1975.
38. Moran, R. D. "Reducing Discrimination: Role of the Equal Pay Act." *Monthly Labor Review,* 93 (1970), No. 6, 30–34.
39. National Labor Relations Board. *Summary of the National Labor Relations Act.* Washington, D.C.: Government Printing Office, 1971.
40. Northrup, H. R. "The Railway Labor Act: A Critical Reappraisal." *Industrial and Labor Relations Review,* 25 (1971), 3–31.
41. O'Meara, J. R. *Employee Patent and Secrecy Agreements.* New York: National Industrial Conference Board, 1965.

42. O'Meara, J. R. *How Smaller Companies Protect Their Trade Secrets.* New York: Conference Board, 1971.

43. Papier, W. "Standards for Improving Maximum Unemployment Insurance Benefits." *Industrial and Labor Relations Review,* 27 (1974), 376–390.

44. Saposs, D. J. "Labor Racketeering—Evolution and Solutions." *Social Research,* 25 (1958), 253–370.

45. Shaeffer, R. G. *Nondiscrimination in Employment: Changing Perspectives, 1963–1972.* New York: Conference Board, 1973.

46. Smith, A. B., Jr. "The Impact on Collective Bargaining of Equal Employment Opportunity Remedies." *Industrial and Labor Relations Review,* 28 (1975), 376–394.

47. U.S. Department of Labor. *Occupational Injuries and Illnesses in the United States by Industry, 1973.* Washington, D.C.: Government Printing Office, 1975.

48. Walsh, E. B. "Sex Discrimination and the Impact of Title VII." *Labor Law Journal,* 25 (1974), 150–154.

49. Wood, Norman J. "Equal Employment Opportunity and Seniority: Rights in Conflict." *Labor Law Journal,* 26 (1975), 345–349.

50. Wortman, M. S. *Critical Issues in Labor.* New York: Macmillan Publishing Co., Inc., 1969.

ROLE PRESCRIPTIONS AND ROLE BEHAVIOR: THE EVALUATION OF INDIVIDUAL OUTPUTS

6   *Organization and Human Resource Planning*

In this chapter and the next, attention will be given to the matter of establishing expected patterns of behavior-role prescriptions. Organization planning does this for managers; it indicates what managerial positions are to exist and what types of role behavior are to be expected of each manager. Human resource planning establishes role prescriptions within the personnel component; it states what kind of people, and how many, must be recruited, selected, trained, and perhaps laid off at various points in the future. Job analysis, which is the concern of the following chapter, typically focuses on positions below the managerial level, although it may be carried some distance up the managerial hierarchy on occasion.

In the remaining two chapters of this section, the focus will be on techniques that may be used to determine whether individuals actually do approximate the established role prescriptions for their positions. When a person acts in a way that is highly congruent with the expected pattern, he is normally defined as successful or effective. When he deviates too far from existing role prescriptions, he is likely to be considered unsuccessful or ineffective. The process of establishing role requirements and determining the degree of deviation from them in actual behavior is what is meant when we speak of *the evaluation of individual outputs*.

It may seem strange that a discussion of the output side has been placed ahead of any description of input processes, such as recruitment, selection, and placement. There is, in fact, some logical inconsistency in this approach. Yet to do otherwise would be even more confusing. The individuals selected for employment must be those who will most closely approximate in their work behavior the role prescriptions for the positions they will fill. Hiring should be oriented toward obtaining successful people who will contribute the most to the company's goals. But this cannot be done without a full understanding of what kinds of behavioral outputs are desired, of how success is defined in a given job and in a given company. Thus, the discussion of what we select *for* must precede any detailed treatment of *how* we select.

ORGANIZATION PLANNING AS ESTABLISHING MANAGERIAL ROLE PRESCRIPTIONS

Psychological research provides considerable evidence that there are certain role prescriptions that operate with a rather high degree of consistency across a great variety of managerial positions in the business world (22, 25). Because of their prevalence and their nature, these requirements are not likely to be specifically designated when organization plans are drawn up and managerial job descriptions devised. Yet when people are selected for managerial work, there is a high probability that an individual's ability and desire to behave in accord with these prescriptions will be an important consideration, irrespective of the specific position to be filled.

The evidence indicates that managers, as managers, are expected to have a relatively favorable attitude to their superiors (those in positions of authority over them). In their relationships with other managers at comparable levels, the role prescriptions call for a generally competitive attitude and thus a desire to do better than the others. Finally, managers are expected to impose their own wishes on subordinates and to exercise power over them. The nature of the managerial role is such that incumbents are supposed to get those who work for them to do what they want.

These are general prescriptions that are likely to appear no matter what the particular position, as long as it is essentially managerial, and that we shall return to again in connection with the discussion of management appraisal. But there are also specific role requirements that are unique to a given job or a group of jobs. They are the major concern of those involved in the process of structuring and restructuring organizations.

The Organization Planning Group

The actual work of organization planning units can vary considerably depending on the degree to which top management has relinquished its control over decisions in this area. In some instances, the planning is carried out by the chief executive himself, perhaps with the help of other corporate officers or an outside consultant. Here, the organization planning group, if it exists at all, prepares position guides, policy manuals, organization charts, and the like, that have as their essential purpose the implementation of decisions made at higher levels.

Other companies use their organization units more directly for the specific purpose of restructuring the company. In such cases, the units have much greater authority to actually establish role prescriptions for managerial personnel and to decide who is supposed to do what.

Under the latter set of circumstances, the organization planning process becomes extremely complex if the company is large and the types of work performed are varied. There is, first, the necessity of spelling out the task or productivity objective of the company in detail—products, services, markets, and so on. Then, a clear picture of existing managerial role prescriptions must be obtained and maintained. This requires extensive interviewing of managers throughout the company, often coupled with the use of written questionnaires. Special attention is given to identifying necessary functions that have not been provided for and to investigating what might be unnecessary duplication of activities. Organization and policy manuals are prepared as a result. These represent a complex amalgam of what is and what should be (2).

Many firms also develop an ideal plan as a goal for the future (2). For a variety of reasons, this specific organizational structure may not be feasible at present. Yet it is considered that it would be the most suitable for attaining productivity objectives if organizational maintenance considerations and the limitations of currently available manpower could be ignored. Often the ideal plan includes human resource planning data, such as inventories of existing managerial talent, future skill requirements, and anticipated rates of development for current managers. Phase plans are developed that spell out in detail how and when the ideal structure might be achieved. Theoretically, all that is needed is for the organization planning group to implement changes and issue new organization charts in accord with the phase plans. In actual fact, however, organizational change is a much more complex process than this, a process that is heavily invested with "the art of the possible." In many instances, the ideal structure is changed long before it is attained.

Organization Development

In contradistinction to the type of organization planning group just described is another type that characteristically uses the title organization development. Organization development is an amalgam of certain approaches in management development and organization planning. Groups of this kind place much greater emphasis on training for better group or team development and for better interpersonal relations. They are concerned initially with changing the attitudes, values, and opinions of managers; the new organization structure emerges as an outgrowth of these shifts on the part of the managers themselves (10, 20).

Typically, the organization structures that emerge from this approach tend to foster decision making at lower levels in the hierarchy, thus encouraging what has come to be called participative management. Project or matrix structures designed to facilitate communication and interaction between groups and departments on a horizontal basis are another common outcome. In general, the organization development approach is more concerned with the process of obtaining acceptance of change by dealing with resistances initially than more traditional organization planning, which often merely assumes that what top management supports will in fact be implemented. Relatively few companies currently resort to organization development in its pure form with the objective of organizational restructuring. However, a number of other personnel activities, particularly in the areas of job analysis, training, and development, are often carried out in the name of organization development (15).

Considerations in Organization Planning

The primary consideration in developing a company structure is that the organization pattern selected be one that will contribute to the attainment of the firm's goals—that will facilitate coping with the uncertainties of the environment, within existing constraints. Ideally, the structure in effect at any given time will be the one that can make a maximal contribution. The difficulty is that no one knows exactly what this ideal is. The great diversity of organizational patterns to be found in American industry today reflects in part the diversity of the problems faced by different companies. But even more it reflects the diversity of opinion among those responsible for organization planning. It would appear to be primarily because of these opinion differences that many firms undergo major reorganizations quite frequently.

There are several considerations that can provide some guidance and thus permit an organizational design at least approximating the ideal. One of these is the role that organization structures and the resulting managerial prescriptions play in reducing conflict and thus fostering the maintenance objective. When role prescriptions are unclear and ambiguous, considerable stress inevitably will be generated within an organization as managers fight to gain control over new activities and thus build their empires (21). This kind of conflict can be minimized if it is possible to establish clear role prescriptions that are accepted as legitimate throughout the firm.

The important thing is to gain acceptance for areas of jurisdiction or realms of authority before a power conflict has developed and thus before intense emotions are aroused. If this is done, then certain activities will be viewed as within the legitimate domain of certain managers, and controversy will be held to a minimum. The existing role prescriptions will have the support of managers throughout the company, and personal power plays aimed at extending the authority of a given manager will be discouraged.

This means that an organization planning group has to give particular attention to areas of overlapping jurisdiction. Every effort should be made to have as clear a statement as possible regarding which manager has which set of responsibilities. Without this, the organizational maintenance objective will almost certainly suffer as a consequence of internal disputes. It is also important that the role prescriptions established by the organization planning group be accepted and viewed as legitimate throughout the firm. Far too many companies have moved from a centralized to a decentralized structure only to face chaos rather than increased effectiveness as a result. Old role prescriptions and patterns of authority may not be relinquished, and the new structure may not achieve widespread acceptance. Thus, those responsible for organization planning must take steps to gain support for the new designs they introduce. Organization development can be one approach to dealing with this problem.

Another major consideration in organization planning involves the constraints imposed by individual differences. There has in the past been some tendency to conceptualize the "good" organizational structure quite apart from any thought about the people who might be available to fill the positions created. As a result, the disparity between role prescription and role behavior has on occasion been rather large, and ineffective performance has been the result.

Increasingly, the need to design organizational structures and establish role prescriptions that are in accord with existing abilities, skills, and personality characteristics has become apparent. For example, two vice-presidents might be equally competent in most spheres, but whereas one is a very sociable individual who functions most effectively when he is surrounded by people, the other is somewhat withdrawn and is really comfortable only with a few individuals whom he has known for many years. In the former instance, a relatively wide span of control with a number of people reporting directly to the vice-president would seem to be appropriate. But this type of organizational structure would almost guarantee trouble in the second case. In the latter instance, an additional level could be introduced so that perhaps two individuals report *directly* to the vice-president; the remainder would report only through these two.

This means that organization planning must be done with considerable knowledge of the people who will be filling the various positions and with a full understanding of the various organizational arrangements that are possible. To put these two together in an effective manner requires a high level of ingenuity.

In this connection, particular attention must be given to the trained combinations of knowledge that are developed by educational institutions. As the structure of knowledge becomes increasingly complex with each new scientific advance, the universities are forced more and more into making certain rather basic decisions for society. When a specific curriculum is decided upon for a given professional training program or for any other type of occupational preparation, this curriculum serves to predetermine the combinations of knowledge that a company can acquire. Certain fields of specialization will be found regularly in conjunction with one another, but other patterns are very unlikely to emerge at all.

These trained combinations of knowledge, which result from curriculum planning at the university level, have major implications for organization structure. It is pointless to establish role prescriptions for a position that are at variance with the patterns of specialization the universities have created. Certain types of groupings are almost forced on companies as a result of the constraints imposed by the educational process. As a result, it is common practice to have physical science research units, accounting units, legal units, and so on, in a manner that parallels the various university curriculums and to have these units headed by persons who are trained specialists in these areas. To introduce role prescriptions that require combinations of knowledge that people do not possess will almost inevitably produce a less effective organization.

A final consideration in organization planning relates to the nature of the work to be done. To achieve their goals, various companies must carry out certain tasks in certain ways; the structure of external constraints and pressures is such as to almost demand particular activities and approaches. When this is the case, particular organization structures may be especially appropriate. Thus, the development of complex computers that are extremely expensive and that must be fully utilized to be economically feasible has militated in favor of considerable centralization of accounting functions.

On the other hand, intense price competition at the local level often can be most effectively handled through a decentralized marketing organization with decision making moved down to relatively low levels. When much of the work is of a project nature, a systems type of structure is particularly appropriate. The evidence suggests that where the production process is on a single-unit basis, the ideal is a rather flat organizational structure. As the technology shifts to batch production, assembly-line mass production, and finally continuous-process production of the kind utilized in much of the chemical industry, the number of hierarchic levels required tends to increase, at least in smaller firms (37). Clearly, as the nature of an industry's technology changes, comparable changes in organization structure may well become necessary.

This discussion of organization planning has been concerned with the process of adopting a structure that, it is hoped, will maximize goal attainment. But it is also apparent that company structures and the role prescriptions that are indigenous to them can operate as internal constraints on decision making after they have been introduced and have won widespread acceptance (18). Thus, individual differences are not the only source of restriction within the firm itself. The way in which an organization has been designed will impose certain patterns of communication and characteristically indicates which managers must be contacted to make and implement particular types of decisions. The constraints imposed by organizational structure can of course be overcome through a change in the existing pattern of managerial role prescriptions, but that takes time and may or may not be feasible.

VARIABLES IN ORGANIZATION PLANNING

The topic of organization planning is as much, if not more, an aspect of general management as of personnel management. Among the various management functions, *organizing* is often mentioned as a major feature of the work of managers in general, and not just those in the personnel area. Furthermore, as Table 6–1 indicates, those who head up organization planning groups, many of whom are vice-presidents themselves, most frequently report directly to the top—to the chairman of the board or president—rather than to someone at the second or third level. Since the individual in charge of personnel would be either a vice-president or director, it is apparent that in a great many firms, and in particular in those of small or medium size, organization planning typically occurs outside the personnel jurisdiction (12). In view of this, the discussion here will merely highlight some of the major variables that may be incorporated in different organization plans and structures. Detailed consideration will be left to a more comprehensive treatment of the management process (23).

A feeling for the diversity that may characterize structures may be gained from the schematic representations of Figure 6–1. Here the authors have placed seven different, but frequently overlapping, forms on a continuum

Table 6–1. Reporting Relationships of Organization Planning Department Heads in 117 Companies

Levels Reported to	Industrial Companies			Nonindustrial Companies	All Companies
	Large Firms	Medium-sized Firms	Smaller Firms		
First (chairman of board or president)	21	18	23	24	86
Second (vice-president)	10	3	4	8	25
Third (director)	5	1	0	0	6

Source: Reprinted by permission of the publisher from AMA Research Study No. 106, *Organization Planning and Development*, by W. F. Glueck, © 1971 by the American Management Association, Inc.

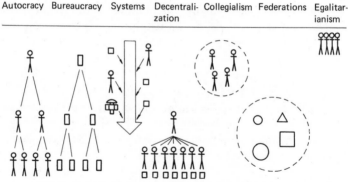

Autocracy Bureaucracy Systems Decentrali- Collegialism Federations Egalitar-
                                  zation   ianism

Figure 6–1. Distribution of Organization Forms.
Source: G. H. Rice and D. W. Bishoprick, *Conceptual Models
of Organization* (New York: Appleton-Century-Crofts, 1971),
p. 208.

from the most autocratic and coercive on the left to the most democratic
and egalitarian on the right (29). It is clear from this analysis that the distribution of power and authority is one of the major factors that differentiate one organization structure from another.

Vertical Aspects

Organization structures may be viewed in terms of both their vertical and
horizontal dimensions. Variations on the vertical dimension often have to
do with the level at which decisions are made and role behaviors occur;
thus, the variations relate to such matters as autonomy of decision making,
delegation, centralization, and decentralization. Another type of vertical
variation has to do with the length of the *chain of command,* the number of
levels in the hierarchy stretching from the lowest production worker to the
chief executive. This matter of how tall or flat the organization structure is,
is directly related to the number of individuals reporting to a manager, the
span of control. A structure with many individuals under each manager,
and thus wide spans of control, will yield a flatter hierarchy than would exist
if the same firm were organized with narrow spans.

In addition, there are a number of different types of vertical relationships
that may exist at the very top of an organization. The board of directors
may exercise considerable authority over company officers or very little. The
chairman of the board may be the chief executive officer, or the president
may hold this role, or authority may be shared among several members of a
chief executive office. This latter form of group control at the top appears to
be growing in popularity (1).

Horizontal Aspects

In addition to choosing among these various aspects of vertical structure,
those concerned with planning organization forms must also consider a

number of different horizontal alternatives. Although differences in power and authority relationships are a consideration here, there is a somewhat greater concern with who does what, and thus with how the work is divided. Jobs may be structured very narrowly (simplification), or they may cover quite a range of activities (enlargement). This concept of division of labor also applies to departments. How many departments should there be? Of what size? On what basis should departments occur?

Horizontal differentials may also be introduced with regard to line and staff status. Some groups, among them those in the personnel and industrial relations area, are characteristically labeled as staff in contrast to line units, such as those in manufacturing. Generally, the staff units exercise less authority over decisions. Some companies have moved away from line-staff to project structures, or superimposed product or project management on the existing structure to form a matrix. These relatively newer forms permit considerable flexibility, since project teams can be phased in and out as needed. Another horizontal variation has to do with the use of committees constituted of individuals selected from various groups across the organization. Some firms utilize such committees extensively; others, rarely or not at all.

It is clear that the variables and the variations to be considered in organization planning are numerous. We are only beginning to fully comprehend that the form, or combination of managerial role prescriptions, that is most effective under one set of circumstances may very well be much less effective in a different market environment or with a different technological base (27). However, a foundation of research that will permit a more scientific choice of structural aspects appropriate to a particular organizational context is beginning to emerge.

HUMAN RESOURCE PLANNING AS ESTABLISHING PERSONNEL ROLE PRESCRIPTIONS

Human resource planning may be described as a process which seeks to ensure that the right number and kinds of people will be at the right places at the right time in the future, capable of doing those things which are needed so that the organization can continue to achieve its goals.

Essential to the overall process are four component processes (36), although on occasion a company may fail to develop procedures in all four areas and still consider itself to be engaged in human resource planning (35). The four processes are as follows:

1. Forecasting future needs for different kinds of skills and different types of human resources.
2. Inventorying existing human resources.
3. Projecting present resources into the future and comparing the anticipated future position against the needs that have been forecast.

4. Planning the necessary activities, such as recruiting, selection, training, compensation, and placement, required to meet future human resource requirements.

It is in the fourth area that human resource planning clearly becomes a matter of developing role prescriptions for personnel managers. The first three activities may require considerable involvement from outside the personnel function, but the end result is a set of specifications indicating what personnel activities must be carried out if future human resource needs are to be met. Without clear and precise role prescriptions of this kind, human resource planning can become a futile intellectual exercise.

Human Resource Forecasting

Practically all firms engage in at least *short-term* human resource forecasting. Here, the exigencies of the present situation exert a controlling influence. Inventories of available talent and counts of vacant positions, sometimes supplemented by estimates of losses through turnover, retirement, and so forth, are the usual approaches (34). Although it is not possible to specify an exact time span for such short-range forecasts in all companies, there is a point at which somewhat different and more complex procedures are required. Such *midrange* forecasting is distinguished from longer-range efforts by the fact that human resource demands can be determined from actions the company has already taken. Thus, a decision to build a new plant in a given location will mean that at some point, perhaps a year or so in the future, the personnel needed to operate such a plant must be available. Forecasts based on known manufacturing technology and previous staffing experiences can be developed with considerable precision in such cases.

Long-range forecasting, extending five or ten years into the future, is a much more difficult and hazardous affair. Here, no definite decisions have yet been made as to whether a new plant will be built or whether the firm will expand into a new product area. It is long-range forecasting that will be our major concern here, although a number of the approaches considered can be and are applied in midrange forecasting as well.

THE FUTURE DEMAND

The first, and in many ways the most difficult, step in human resource planning is to forecast needs for various types of resources at various points in the future. Such human resource needs, or demands, are closely tied to the company's general business plan; as a result, this aspect of human resource planning is highly dependent on the total business planning effort (31). In addition, it typically is carried out using historical data on relationships known to have existed in the past.

The usual approach is to select a business factor with the dual characteristics that (a) it is closely related to the basic nature of the business, and thus utilized in general business planning, and (b) it is highly correlated with human resource requirements. Sales or production forecasts are commonly used (16), and some very detailed procedures for estimating future labor productivity have been developed for this purpose (35). In some firms, it has proved necessary to select somewhat different business factors for different segments of the work force. One reason for this is the basic requirement that historical data be available so that relationships between the business factor and manpower levels in the past can be established. Developing such a data base often is a costly and time-consuming process.

Once the basic data are obtained, the usual practice is to adjust historical relationships between the business factor and utilization of different types of human resources for any special circumstances that existed in the past, and then to project the relationship into the future, again adjusting for anticipated events that are a part of the firm's overall long-range plan (36). There is in all this a good deal of subjective modification of existing statistical relationships, based on the judgments not only of personnel people but of managers in other functional areas as well. A major factor serving to modify statistical relationships, especially at the managerial level, may be the organizational structures planned for the future. Subjective modifications of this kind have been found to contribute substantially to the accuracy of projections from historical data (8). What finally emerges is a statement of the number of people needed at various future times in certain specified categories of employment.

INTERNAL SUPPLY

To determine what special personnel efforts may be needed in the future, the forecast of demand must be compared with a forecast of labor supply, assuming existing policies and procedures remain in effect. The essence of what is involved is given in Figure 6–2, using one segment of a company as the planning unit (11).

The starting point is an inventory of existing personnel in whatever categories are required to make direct comparisons with the demand data. With the existing organization structure assumed as a constant, the next step is to obtain estimates of outmovements over the planning period, using information provided by unit managers, statistics on past movements, and in some cases actuarial data. Included are the estimated number of:

1. Voluntary quits.
2. Retirements (both early and regular).
3. Dismissals.
4. Promotions, demotions, and transfers out.
5. Layoffs.
6. Deaths.

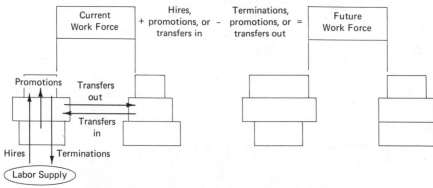

Figure 6–2. Overview of a Human Resource Planning
System.
Source: R. H. Fulton, "A Company Technique for Estimating
Future Manpower Requirements," in R. A. Beaumont, ed.,
Manpower and Planning (New York: Industrial Relations
Counselors, 1970), p. 42.

The estimated outmovements are set against estimates of inmovement
from hiring and from personnel actions such as promotion, demotion, and
transfer in from other company components. The result is a statement of
what the employment situation will be at a point in the future if things
continue in the present pattern. The supply-and-demand comparison may
then indicate that (a) the two will be largely in balance, or (b) supply will
exceed demand, in which case some type of force reductions will be required, or (c) the need will outdistance the supply. This latter instance is
the "reason to be" for human resource planning. Given this situation, projected outmovement and inmovement data must be combined to determine
how many and what types of new people must be obtained over the planning
period to achieve the future work force that has been forecast. In this area
of forecasting internal human resource supplies, a good deal of work has
been done to develop mathematical modeling procedures that take into
account the transitional probabilities for various kinds of inmovements and
outmovements. In fact, the whole area of human resource planning and
projection has proved to be a particularly attractive one for those concerned
with developing quantitative models (3).

Developing Personnel Role Prescriptions

Where the forecast indicates that a certain number of people will be required in various skill categories at some specified time in the future, and
these people may not be readily available, the major planning question
becomes one of determining how to achieve the desired position. Put somewhat differently, what personnel strategies should be used to reach the
desired situation? How should the gap between anticipated demand and

anticipated supply be filled? What role prescriptions for personnel should be developed?

The most obvious source of needed people is direct recruiting from the outside labor force into positions where vacancies are anticipated. Whether or not this strategy will succeed depends on whether the external supply of qualified people is adequate and whether this supply meets the demand of industry as a whole. It is entirely possible that a large number of individuals may be preparing to enter a particular field, but shortages will still emerge if too many companies want this particular set of skills (36). Many of the data needed to make this kind of determination derive from governmental forecasts of the kind discussed later in this chapter.

In view of certain expected states of future human resource availability, a decision may be reached to start recruiting immediately at compensation levels somewhat above the existing market. This strategy is most appropriate for high-talent personnel, such as research scientists, who cannot be acquired through internal efforts (35). An alternative strategy, when shortages of certain needed skills in the labor force are anticipated, is to break down a given job into somewhat simpler component tasks and recruit from less-well-trained sources than previously.

In addition to job redesign, companies may resort to training and development efforts, given the extensive lead time that effective human resource planning permits. This becomes particularly important where major technological changes are anticipated (4). For some jobs, such as those of research scientists, most companies cannot do the necessary training themselves. However, even in these cases, they can stimulate an increased external human resource supply through the funding of university fellowships and through other procedures calculated to expand the number of students in particular programs of study. In many instances, a demand-supply gap may exist in occupations that do permit internal development. Thus, with the foreknowledge permitted by human resources planning, college graduates may be recruited and developed to fill future managerial vacancies, and the less skilled may be hired with the expectation that following training they can move up to fill gaps in more highly skilled occupations.

When tightness in the existing labor market is anticipated, companies may expand into new markets. One approach, common during wartime, is to attempt to attract housewives. Another is to move into the ranks of the culturally disadvantaged and the hard-core unemployed. Particularly in the last instance, special training may be required.

Just what strategies will be developed and what personnel role prescriptions established depend on the type of employees involved and the labor market conditions projected. It is apparent, however, that human resource planning does not stop once forecasting has been completed. In fact, it is only then that personnel management takes over fully. What is done on the basis of the forecasts, in terms of alternative investments in input processes, mediating processes, and output processes, is primarily a concern of the personnel function.

The Costs Versus Return on Investment

The literature on human resource planning almost without exception extols its virtues and advocates universal application. Yet a great many companies do not engage in long-term forecasting of the kind just discussed and in fact do little that could be considered as human resource planning by any definition. A survey of 84 companies revealed that only 24 engaged in human resource planning (36). Another study indicated that of 69 firms in Minnesota, 72 per cent forecast demand, but only 36 per cent forecast internal supplies (16).

Studies of this kind consistently indicate that human resource planning is much less prevalent in small companies. Given the fact that effective human resource planning with a sufficiently comprehensive data base is very costly in terms of both time and money, the failure of many small firms to engage in formal planning makes considerable sense. Even if a sizable demand-supply gap in percentage terms is identified in some occupational grouping, the actual number of individuals needed will be small simply because the company as a whole does not have a large number of employees. Finding a few new salesmen in the existing labor market, for instance, when the need first becomes apparent should not represent a major recruiting problem.

On the other hand, the same percentage gap in the sales force of a large corporation might mean finding thousands of people—an impossible task to achieve without the lead time provided by planning. Yet the total costs to do an effective job of human resource planning can be expected to be very nearly as great in the small firm as in the large one. The small firm should be just as well off using the strategy of a rapid recruiting response at the point when a need becomes apparent. Such a strategy would leave the large firm seriously understaffed. Clearly, the investment in human resource planning makes sense for the large company; for the small one, the alternative strategy seems more appropriate. Only when massive growth is anticipated does human resource planning seem likely to offer an adequate return for the small organization.

There are additional instances in which investment in formal human resource planning must be questioned. If, in advance, there are good reasons for expecting that demand-supply gaps will be minimal, and no major redistribution of skills within the company can be anticipated, the planning may not be worth the cost. It is the anticipation of shortages, the exact nature and extent of which are as yet unknown, that should and usually does provide the impetus for human resource planning (16).

Second, adequate human resource planning requires adequate forecasting. There are clearly major differences between industries in terms of their stability and predictability (36). Thus, some companies have been unable to keep their margins of error within the 10 percent or so generally considered acceptable, irrespective of what they have tried. In part this may be due to the wrong choice of a business factor, in part it may be attributable to the lack of an adequate historical base of data relating changes in the business factor to employment levels, but there are other instances when the problems extend beyond these causes. In any event, when the forecasting error can be expected to be large, or the lead time must be reduced to a period so short as to be meaningless to obtain an adequate forecast, the cost of human resource planning is unlikely to be returned, and some other strategy seems preferable. Among the other alternatives are crash recruiting programs and deliberate stockpiling of personnel.

THE NATIONAL LABOR FORCE

As previously noted, decisions as to exactly how anticipated future human resource shortages are to be eliminated are conditioned by expectations regarding future resource availability in the external labor force. In part, this is a matter of the distribution of individual differences in abilities and personality characteristics in the labor markets on which a company can draw. But it is also a function of the trained capacities, the occupational qualification, of the people in these labor markets. Thus, some knowledge of occupational trends in the labor force is essential to effective human resource planning. If the country as well as the company is likely to suffer shortages in a given occupation, direct recruiting is unlikely to be the answer to the company's problem. Similarly, organization planning must also take labor force trends into account. It is pointless to design the structure of managerial positions in such a way as to make staffing practically impossible.

General Trends

During the 1960s, the national labor force increased at an average rate of 1.6 per cent a year. A growth rate of 1.7 per cent is projected to 1980 and then some leveling off is expected, with a 1.1 per cent average growth rate for the 1980–1985 period (17). Expansion of this kind in the number of people available for work does not guarantee against shortages in specific occupations in the future, but from an employer viewpoint it represents a positive development.

The specific nature of anticipated changes within this labor force also has positive implications. Throughout the 1970s, the teenage labor force will expand somewhat less rapidly than in the past, while the twenty to thirty-four age group will grow rapidly. Thus, a greater number of people in the prime working years will be available. The proportion of women in the labor force increased from 32.3 per cent in 1960 to 37.4 per cent in 1972. That proportion is expected to reach 38.5 percent by 1980 and then level

Education Level

off. The overall educational level of the labor force should continue to increase.

These projections, and those of an occupational nature to be presented in the next section, are based on data from the U.S. Department of Labor. Analyses of projections made in the past indicate considerable precision. Total labor force growth has been predicted with very little error, although recently women have contributed more to the increase than had been anticipated (30). Projections for individual industries and occupations have also been surprisingly close to the mark.

Occupational Projections

Data on the demand for workers in different industries and occupational groupings are provided in Tables 6-2 and 6-3. The greatest projected growth in demand is in the service and government categories in which growth was also greatest in the past (19). The demand for professional and technical workers and for clerical workers will increase the most among the various major occupational groups. Table 6-4 contains a listing of certain specific high-growth occupations as determined from analyses of census data (7).

From a human resource planning viewpoint, these demand projections become fully useful only as they relate to anticipated supply. Will there be enough people ready to meet the demand? Will shortages hit a number of firms? In the lower-level occupations, this may not be a major problem, at least to the extent that training periods are relatively short, but at higher levels the consequences can be drastic.

While demand figures are calculated by breaking down gross national product projections, supply is determined from educational enrollments and anticipated losses due to deaths, retirements, and transfers (23). The age distribution in an occupation is an important consideration. An occupation such as carpentry, which has had little recent growth, has many older workers and thus a high rate of loss by death and retirement. Among electricians, who are generally younger, this source of loss is minimal.

For some time, the greatest supply shortages have been anticipated in professions such as architecture, dentistry, engineering, law, medicine, optometry, pharmacy, and veterinary medicine. However, a number of factors now make this prospect less imminent. Growth in demand has not been as great in these professions as in some others (see Table 6-4), in part because of the increasing availability of paraprofessionals and technicians. Furthermore, the expansion in education generally has been reflected at the professional level as well, and women are now entering professional training in much greater numbers than they have in the past (28). Perhaps even more important, however, is the fact that increasing numbers of young people are being attracted to the professions. This shift is occurring at the expense of managerial occupations in large organizations and presages a

Table 6–2. Employment (Jobs) by Major Industry Sector for 1960 and 1972, and Projected Demand for 1980 and 1985 (numbers in thousands)

Industry Sector	1960		1972		1980		1985	
	Number	Per Cent	Number	Per Cent	Number	Per Cent	Number	Per Cent
Government	8,353	12.1	13,290	15.5	16,610	16.4	18,800	17.5
Agriculture	5,389	7.8	3,450	4.0	2,300	2.3	1,900	1.8
Mining	748	1.1	645	.8	655	.6	632	.6
Contract construction	3,654	5.3	4,352	5.1	4,908	4.8	5,184	4.8
Manufacturing	17,197	25.0	19,281	22.5	22,923	22.6	23,499	21.8
Transportation and public utilities	4,214	6.1	4,726	5.5	5,321	5.2	5,368	5.0
Wholesale and retail trade	14,177	20.6	18,432	21.5	21,695	21.4	22,381	20.8
Finance, insurance and real estate	2,985	4.3	4,303	5.0	5,349	5.3	5,932	5.5
Other services	12,152	17.6	17,118	20.0	21,815	21.5	23,913	22.2

Source: Manpower Report of the President (Washington, D.C.: Government Printing Office, 1975), p. 314.

Table 6–3. Employment by Occupational Group for 1960 and 1972, and Projected for 1980 and 1985 (numbers in thousands)

Occupational Group	1960		1972		1980		1985	
	Number	Per Cent	Number	Per Cent	Number	Per Cent	Number	Per Cent
Professional and technical	7,469	11.4	11,459	14.0	15,000	15.7	17,000	16.8
Managers and administrators	7,067	10.7	8,032	9.8	10,100	10.5	10,500	10.3
Sales workers	4,224	6.4	5,354	6.6	6,300	6.6	6,500	6.4
Clerical workers	9,762	14.8	14,247	17.4	17,900	18.7	19,700	19.4
Craft and kindred workers	8,554	13.0	10,810	13.2	12,300	12.8	13,000	12.8
Operatives	11,950	18.2	13,549	16.6	15,000	15.6	15,300	15.1
Nonfarm laborers	3,553	5.4	4,217	5.2	4,500	4.7	4,500	4.4
Service workers	8,023	12.2	10,966	13.4	12,700	13.3	13,400	13.2
Farmers and farm laborers	5,176	7.9	3,069	3.8	2,000	2.1	1,600	1.6

Source: Manpower Report of the President (Washington, D.C.: Government Printing Office, 1975), p. 314.

Table 6–4. Major Occupations Experiencing Rapid
Growth in Employment

Occupation	Per Cent Increase, 1960–1970
Professional and technical	
Computer specialists	1997
Operations and systems researchers and analysts	246
Personnel and labor relations workers	185
Health technologists and technicians	106
Social scientists	162
Social and recreation workers	121
Teachers, college and university	152
Technicians, except health, and engineering and science	118
Vocational and educational counselors	236
Managers and administrators	
Bank officers and financial managers	1196
Health administrators	1089
Sales managers, except retail trade	275
Sales workers	
Stock and bond sales agents	185
Clerical workers	
Billing clerks	146
Clerical supervisors	108
File clerks	148
Library attendants and assistants	246
Office machine operators, computer and peripheral equipment	5985
Teachers aides	675
Service workers	
Child care workers, except private household	278

Source: C. B. DiCesare, "Changes in the Occupational Structure of U.S. Jobs," Monthly Labor Review, 98 (1975), No. 3, pp. 26–30.

developing shortage in this area (24). Changes in attitudes and values among college students extending back into the early 1960s can be expected to have a direct impact on the availability of managerial talent; as a result, the manager and administrator category should reflect the greatest supply shortages over the next decade.

EMPLOYEE INFORMATION SYSTEMS AND SKILLS INVENTORIES

As previously indicated, comprehensive forecasting, as well as effective utilization of internal resources to meet forecast needs, requires a tremendous amount of information regarding the numbers, characteristics, skills, effectiveness, and promotion potential of existing employees. Extensive information is also needed as a basis for developing strategies to tap external markets to fill projected manpower needs—data on preferable recruiting sources, types of individuals with good retention potential, and the like. Increasingly, these information requirements are being met through the use of computerized systems that permit the storage of extensive data, as well as rapid search and analysis.

Personnel Computer Systems

One conception of a computerized system for human resources utilization is given in Figure 6–3. Such a system is in certain respects much more comprehensive than those generally in use today (14). Most systems have not been established to provide this much information, primarily because of the costs involved.

Many of the early applications of computers in the personnel field were related to compensation, payrolls, and fringe benefits, as well as employee records (26). More recent surveys indicate that these areas still predominate (5, 33, 34). Applications in such areas as determining training needs, human resource planning, and collective bargaining, although increasing, are still relatively uncommon, even though the potential value of employee information systems in these areas is considerable. For a number of reasons, computer applications in the personnel area have tended to lag behind those in other parts of the company. The most sophisticated and compre-

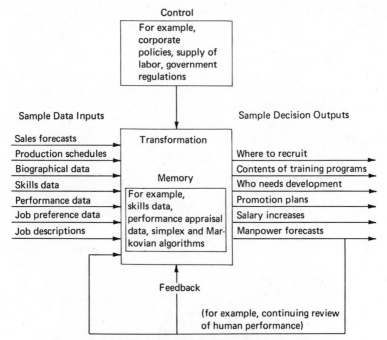

Figure 6–3. A Personnel Information Decision System.
Source: P. S. Greenlaw and R. D. Smith, *Personnel Management: A Management Science Approach* (New York: Thomas Y. Crowell Company, 1970), p. 2.

hensive systems are to be found in various federal government departments, with state governments and private business slightly behind; the least effective systems are to be found in county and city government (33). At the present time, in the personnel and industrial relations area, there appears to be very little use of computerized personnel data in conjunction with operations research techniques employed as an aid to top-level decision making.

Skills Inventories

One major potential computer application in personnel management for purposes of both organization and human resource planning is the skills inventory. Usually the initial data are derived from forms completed by employees and checked by their superiors and/or the personnel department. Data on education, training, prior employment, language capabilities, and specialized skills are fed into the computer. The result is a comprehensive statement of the jobs present employees are capable of performing.

Searches to fill vacancies may be conducted rapidly and with ease. All that is needed is that the requirements for the position be put into the computer. The outcome will be a list of all individuals in the company who meet these requirements. As a result, companies can quickly determine their own internal capacity for correcting occupational shortages and thus the extent to which outside recruiting efforts or internal training is necessary.

Return on the Investment

As with human resource planning as a whole, it is appropriate to ask to what extent employee information systems in general and computerized skills inventories in particular are worth the time, money, and effort involved. The answer once again is that it depends on the circumstances.

Although a great majority of the largest companies either have personnel computer systems in operation or "in process," there are a number that have discontinued them or given up on the updating of their skills inventories (6). Often the skills inventories simply are not used. In many instances, the computers are programmed to hold masses of data that no one wants. The problem of a lack of mesh between what is put into the computer and what is needed for personnel decision making is a common one. The result is that costly systems are established with little return insofar as actual use is concerned (9, 26).

Experience indicates that skills inventories are of less value when the organization is structured almost entirely on a functional basis so that people with the same skills are very likely to be in the same units. Under these circumstances, there is little need to go to a computer to locate certain skills; one can go to the appropriate unit. Furthermore, a certain amount of resistance often develops to skills inventories and to other computerized employee information systems as well, especially in decentralized companies in which the units guard their autonomy jealously. The computer systems permit a great deal of centralized decision making, if they are well constructed to include appropriate information. Outlying units may resent this intrusion on their prerogatives and take steps to undermine the system (33).

It seems apparent that employee information systems are most likely to pay their way in large companies that are labor-, rather than capital-, intensive (6). Banks, life insurance companies, financial service organizations, and retail chains seem particularly well suited. Within manufacturing, the larger firms certainly can benefit from such systems, but there is a point in terms of size where the more conventional personnel file coupled with the knowledge managers have of their subordinates becomes entirely adequate, and the expense of an employee information system is not warranted.

Experience indicates that the most immediate benefit from the installation of a computerized system is the greater accuracy of the data available. Savings over prior methods tend to be sizable in many instances. These savings occur more in the form of increased capability and cost avoidance than in personnel staff reduction. The truly significant value appears to be quick access to information, which frees the time of personnel managers and staff for activities other than routine information search (32).

QUESTIONS

1. What aspects of organization structure may be characterized as vertical in nature and what aspects horizontal?
2. In what ways does role theory contribute to an understanding of organization planning and its effective implementation?
3. What are the key components of human resource planning and what problems may arise with regard to each?
4. What appear to be the major changes in the characteristics of the national labor force that can be expected in the next 10 years? What staffing problems will these changes create for companies?
5. What is the current status of computer applications in the personnel area? What applications do you envisage for the future that are currently rare?

REFERENCES

1. Bagley, E. R. *Beyond the Conglomerates.* New York: Amacom, 1975.
2. Brockhaus, W. L. "Planning for Change with Organization Charts." *Business Horizons,* 17 (1974), No. 2, 47–51.
3. Bryant, D. R., M. J. Maggard, and R. P. Taylor. "Manpower Planning Models and Techniques." *Business Horizons,* 16 (1973), No. 2, 69–78.
4. Burack, E. H., and T. J. McNichols. *Human Resource Planning: Technology, Policy, Change.* Kent, Ohio: Comparative Administration Research Institute, Kent State University, 1973.
5. Bureau of National Affairs, Inc. "ASPA-BNA Survey: Manpower Programs." *Bulletin to Management,* December 14, 1972.

6. Cheek, L. M. "Personnel Computer Systems." *Business Horizons,* 14 (1971), No. 4, 69–76.
7. DiCesare, C. B. "Changes in the Occupational Structure of U.S. Jobs." *Monthly Labor Review,* 98 (1975), No. 3, 24–33.
8. Drandell, M. "A Composite Forecasting Methodology for Manpower Planning Utilizing Objective and Subjective Criteria." *Academy of Management Journal,* 18 (1975), 510–519.
9. Foltman, F. F. *Manpower Information for Effective Management.* Ithaca, N.Y.: New York State School of Industrial and Labor Relations, Cornell University, 1973.
10. Friedlander, F., and L. D. Brown. "Organization Development." *Annual Review of Psychology,* 25 (1974), 313–341.
11. Fulton, R. H. "A Company Technique for Estimating Future Manpower Requirements," in R. A. Beaumont (ed.), *Manpower and Planning.* New York: Industrial Relations Counselors, 1970, pp. 39–64.
12. Glueck, W. F. *Organization Planning and Development.* New York: American Management Association, Inc., 1971.
13. Goldstein, H. "Government Techniques for Projecting Occupational Manpower Needs," in R. A. Beaumont (ed.), *Manpower and Planning.* New York: Industrial Relations Counselors, 1970, pp. 23–25.
14. Greenlaw, P. S., and R. D. Smith. *Personnel Management: A Management Science Approach.* New York: Thomas Y. Crowell Company, 1970.
15. Heisler, W. J. "Patterns of OD in Practice." *Business Horizons,* 18 (1975), No. 1, 77–84.
16. Heneman, H. G., and G. Seltzer. *Employer Manpower Planning and Forecasting.* U.S. Department of Labor Manpower Research Monograph No. 19. Washington, D.C.: Government Printing Office, 1970.
17. Johnston, D. F. "The United States Economy in 1985: Population and Labor Force Projections." *Monthly Labor Review,* 96 (1973), No. 12, 8–17.
18. Labovitz, G. H. "Organizing for Adaptation." *Business Horizons,* 14 (1971), No. 3, 19–26.
19. *Manpower Report of the President.* Washington, D.C.: Government Printing Office, 1975.
20. Miles, R. E. "Organization Development," in G. Strauss et al. (eds.), *Organizational Behavior: Research and Issues.* Madison, Wis.: Industrial Relations Research Association, 1974, pp. 165–191.
21. Miles, R. H., and M. M. Petty. "Relationships Between Role Clarity, Need for Clarity, and Job Tension and Satisfaction for Supervisory and Nonsupervisory Roles." *Academy of Management Journal,* 18 (1975), 877–883.
22. Miner, J. B. *Studies in Management Education.* New York: Springer Publishing Co., Inc., 1965.

23. Miner, J. B. *The Management Process: Theory, Research, and Practice.* New York: Macmillan Publishing Co., Inc., 1973.
24. Miner, J. B. *The Human Constraint: The Coming Shortage of Managerial Talent.* Washington, D.C.: BNA Books, 1974.
25. Miner, J. B. *Motivation to Manage.* Atlanta, Ga.: Organizational Measurement Systems Press, 1977.
26. Morrison, E. J. *Developing Computer-based Employee Information Systems.* New York: American Management Association, Inc., 1969.
27. Ouchi, W. G., and R. T. Harris. "Structure, Technology, and Environment," in G. Strauss et al. (eds.), *Organizational Behavior: Research and Issues.* Madison, Wis.: Industrial Relations Research Association, 1974, pp. 107–140.
28. Parrish, J. B. "Women in Professional Training." *Monthly Labor Review,* 97 (1974), No. 5, 41–43.
29. Rice, G. H., and D. W. Bishoprick. *Conceptual Models of Organizations.* New York: Appleton-Century-Crofts, 1971.
30. Rosenblum, M. "On the Accuracy of Labor Force Projections." *Monthly Labor Review,* 95 (1972), No. 10, 22–29.
31. Steiner, G. A., and J. B. Miner. *Management Policy and Strategy.* New York: Macmillan Publishing Co., Inc., 1977.
32. Tetz, F. F. "Evaluating Computer-based Human Resource Information Systems: Cost vs. Benefits." *Personnel Journal,* 52 (1973), 451–455.
33. Tomeski, E. A., and H. Lazarus. *People-oriented Computer Systems: The Computer in Crisis.* New York: Van Nostrand Reinhold Company, 1975.
34. Towers, Perrin, Forster, and Crosby. *Corporate Manpower Planning.* Philadelphia: TPF/C, 1971.
35. Vetter, E. W. *Manpower Planning for High Talent Personnel.* Ann Arbor, Mich.: Bureau of Industrial Relations, University of Michigan, 1967.
36. Wikstrom, W. S. *Manpower Planning: Evolving Systems.* New York: Conference Board, 1971.
37. Woodward, J. *Industrial Organization: Theory and Practice.* New York: Oxford University Press, Inc., 1965.

Organization planning } *knowledge of job structure*
job analysis

7   *Job Analysis and Design* *(Lower level)*

DEFINITIONS AND USES

A personnel manager must rely heavily on a knowledge of the existing job structure in developing and administering programs designed to provide effective utilization of human resources within a company. In part, as indicated in the preceding chapter, this knowledge is developed through the process of organization planning; in part, it is a product of job analysis.

Organization planning is concerned basically with role prescriptions at the upper levels and with defining expected behavior within the managerial hierarchy. Job analysis carries this process down through the rest of the organization, usually with a much greater degree of specificity and detail than is provided by organization planning. Because this type of detail often is helpful in the case of managerial jobs as well, a number of companies utilize job analysis techniques to establish role prescriptions for many positions at the managerial level also. Thus, some degree of overlap between the two techniques can develop. When this happens, it is important that the managerial role prescriptions derived from the two sources be closely coordinated, so that disparities do not emerge.

In any event, job analysis, like organization planning, is a method of establishing a base against which the actual behavior of a firm's employees may be evaluated. It helps to provide a picture of each job and of the interrelationships between jobs. The results of organization planning and job analysis taken together yield a comprehensive and detailed view of how a company has structured itself to achieve its objectives.

The Terminology of Occupational Study

Before turning to a discussion of the methods and procedures employed in performing a job analysis, it is essential that we establish an understanding of some of the terms that will be used. This will help to prevent considerable confusion later on. The definitions that follow constitute what has come to be the generally accepted terminology in the personnel literature (25).

A *task* is a distinct work activity carried out for a specific purpose. An example is that of a retail clerk in a department store dusting merchandise. Another example would be the same clerk setting up the same merchandise in an attractive display. When there are enough such related activities, a position is created.

A *position* is a specific set of tasks and duties performed by a given individual in a given firm at a given time. The number of positions in a company at one time is equal to the number of employees at the same time.

A *job* is normally made up of a number of similar positions in a given company. However, a job may involve only one such position at a given time. For example, a store may have one retail hardware clerk or many, depending on the size of the store and the scope of its business.

An *occupation* is a number of similar jobs existing in different companies and at different times. Examples of occupations are carpenters and civil engineers.

A *job description* is a written statement of the tasks, duties, and behaviors required in a given job, plus the personal qualifications that all candidates for the job must possess. (The latter aspect often is referred to separately as the *job specification*.)

A *job family* is a collection of two or more jobs that either require similar worker characteristics or contain parallel tasks, as determined by the job analysis.

When a study is made of the tasks performed by a single person, the term *position analysis* is usually employed. When the scope is broadened to include two or more positions that are similar enough to be considered one job, it is more characteristic to speak of *job analysis*. Because in the business world, at least at lower levels, there are usually two or more similar positions within a firm, the designation job analysis typically is used. This analysis provides information about the job, the necessary activities and personal requirements involved, and its relationship to other jobs. It results in the job description and job specification.

It is important to understand that although the job analysis frequently utilizes the actual behavior of incumbents, the job description, nevertheless, provides a statement of what *should* be; it is a set of role prescriptions or requirements. Job analysts develop their descriptions from information that is derived from people actually doing the work, just as organization analysts do, but this does not mean that the final result is necessarily a specific statement of what any individual actually is doing. It is instead an idealized statement of what that person and others holding the position are expected to do.

On occasion job descriptions are written well before the company actually has employed anyone in positions of a particular type. In such instances the role prescriptions cannot be based in any way on the actual behavior of incumbents. Perhaps the most striking example of this derives from the field of space travel. Before each astronaut started out on his flight, a detailed job description was developed specifying exactly what he was expected to do and when. Because of the physical and psychological stresses involved, a great variety of factors had to be considered in constructing such role prescriptions. In many instances simulated conditions were devised to determine which behaviors would contribute most effectively to goal attainment. Here, there can be no question but that an *ideal* behavior pattern was developed (16).

The Uses of Job Analysis

As noted previously, the data derived from job analyses aid considerably in evaluating the behavior of individual organization members as this behavior contributes to the attainment of company goals. Jobs are structured in a way that is intended to contribute maximally to productivity and maintenance goals; then individual behaviors are compared against these expected patterns. In this way, an evaluation of the individual outputs of the organization is obtained (6). This contribution to the appraisal and evaluation process is an important function of job analysis, but it is by no means the only use to which this information may be put.

Job evaluation is perhaps the most widespread application of the data of job analysis. Job descriptions are used to evaluate jobs in terms of their worth to the company. Wage and salary differentials are then established to reflect the existing differences in job requirements. In this connection, it is important to make a clear distinction between job analysis, job evaluation, and individual evaluation. The first refers to the establishment of role prescriptions, the second to the rating of *jobs* for payment purposes, and the third to the rating of *people* in relation to role prescriptions.

Job descriptions are of considerable value as guides to hiring and placement practices. People who will be most successful, who will most closely approximate role requirements, should be selected for employment and assigned to appropriate kinds of work. Therefore, selection procedures must be developed on the basis of a detailed knowledge of position requirements. This is the consideration that led us to take up the evaluation of individual outputs prior to discussing the evaluation of inputs into the organization. The use of job analysis in this manner is not only good personnel practice; it is also a necessary step in establishing the job relatedness of selection procedures under equal opportunity laws and executive orders (32).

Job analysis provides an indication of the needs that training and management development must fulfill. Training programs should be devised to provide skills, knowledge, and motives that are lacking but that are required for effective or outstanding performance and adequate morale. Training should be along the lines required to generate a close match between actual and expected behavior.

The safety director can utilize the data of job analysis to identify job hazards and dangerous working conditions. In fact, many job descriptions include this information as an integral aspect. With this information, steps can be taken to minimize the possibility that an accident will occur.

By providing a means to common understanding between management and the labor unions with regard to the duties of each position, job analysis eliminates, or at least reduces, one type of employee grievance. Suspicion of favoritism is considerably reduced to the extent pay differentials are based on clear differences in job duties. Thus, job analysis contributes to reduced internal conflict once the program is well established and widely accepted; the organizational maintenance goal is thereby fostered.

The data of job analysis provide an index of what are presumed to be the most appropriate work procedures, given the existing equipment. But after a job has been studied in this amount of detail, it may become apparent that certain changes in the person-machine balance are economically feasible and desirable. Automatic equipment may be introduced, or on occasion human actions may be substituted for machinery. Thus, job analysis can provide a basis for reengineering the positions involved.

Job descriptions from different companies provide a method of comparing rates of pay within occupations. With such information, it is possible to be reasonably certain that the jobs compared are in fact similar. A company may determine how its pay scales jibe with those of others in the community, for comparable work, and adjust its rates to a desired level.

Counseling, of course, is largely an application outside the company itself. Yet job descriptions, such as those developed by the U.S. Employment Service, and occupational information based on extensive job analyses can have considerable value in areas such as vocational guidance and rehabilitation counseling. With this type of data, it is possible to guide the inexperienced and the disabled into occupations where they are most likely to succeed.

THE SCOPE OF THE JOB ANALYSIS

What are the kinds of information that must be obtained in connection with a job analysis? There is no simple answer to this question, because the specific job under consideration, the company, and the purpose to which the data are to be put all exert an influence. Different jobs have quite different salient aspects, and companies develop varying procedures for a number of reasons. If the primary purpose is to prepare a set of training guidelines, the information sought may well differ considerably from that desired should the objective be to construct a wage system. Yet there are certain types of data that are included in most analyses, although in by no means all, and it is these that have been singled out for discussion here. Exactly where a particular type of information may appear within a given job description is subject to considerable variation: A specific item may well initiate one job description and come at the end of another. There are almost as many variants as there are companies with job analysis programs.

Elements of the Job Description

JOB TITLE

All job descriptions contain a specific job title or name, because this is needed for bookkeeping purposes within the firm and to facilitate reporting of the firm's activities to the government and to other data-collection agencies. In many cases, alternative or slang titles also are noted.

WORK ACTIVITIES AND PROCEDURES

The segment of the job description covering work activities and procedures is devoted to describing, in whatever detail is necessary, the tasks and duties to be performed on the job, the materials used in carrying them out, the machinery operated, if any, the kinds of formal interactions with other workers required, and the nature and extent of the supervision given or received.

PHYSICAL ENVIRONMENT

The section on physical environment contains a complete description of the physical working conditions where the work is to be performed. Among the factors that should be noted are the normal heat, lighting, noise levels, and ventilation in the work situation. In addition, it is sometimes desirable to indicate the location of the work in terms of a rural-urban or some other geographical designation, because this may be of relevance in recruiting and for other purposes. Any particular accident hazards also are described.

SOCIAL ENVIRONMENT

An increasingly common part of the job description is a section devoted to specifying the social conditions under which the work will be carried out. The types of information included tend to vary considerably from company to company. Often there is a statement regarding the number of individuals in the working environment of the particular job, and information on certain characteristics of these work associates. Thus, some idea may be gained regarding the homogeneity or heterogeneity of the individuals who will be employed together.

Physical aspects of the job that have a bearing on the social aspects may also be noted—time of work hours (night or day), work location (city, suburban, or rural), availability of noncompany facilities (stores, restaurants, and so on), and availability of recreation (company-sponsored or not). These and other features of the social environment are significant in relation to the organizational maintenance goal. Role prescriptions in the areas of conflict minimization, cooperation with superiors, maintaining continued employment uninterrupted by excessive absenteeism, and the like always exist, even though these requirements may not be explicitly stated in the job description. Knowledge of the social environment can be extremely helpful in minimizing disparities between prescriptions of this kind and actual behavior.

CONDITIONS OF EMPLOYMENT

The aspect of the job description dealing with conditions of employment is concerned with the place of the job in the formal organization, in such terms as the wage structure, working hours, method of payment, permanency of the positions, seasonal or part-time nature of the work, allowable fringe benefits, relation to other jobs, and opportunities for promotion or transfer. Although efforts should always be made to write statements in a job description clearly and precisely, this is particularly important when the conditions of employment are being described, because of the possible legal implications of many of the items.

In Tables 7–1 and 7–2 two somewhat different types of job descriptions are presented. The first utilized the form that has been developed by the U.S. Manpower Administration of the Department of Labor, an organization that has had more experience in job analysis activities than any other, public or private. The job analyses are used in the various service activities of the Manpower Administration, including placement, training, and job

Table 7–1. A Typical Completed Job-analysis Schedule Using the United States Manpower Administration Form

OMB 44–R0722

U.S. Department of Labor
Manpower Administration

Estab. & Sched. No. 071–3120–423

JOB ANALYSIS SCHEDULE

1. Estab. Job Title INFORMATION DESK CLERK, receptionist-clerk

2. Ind. Assign. ret. tr.

3. SIC Code(s) and Title(s) 5311 Department Stores

DOT Title Code 237.568

Ind. Desig. WTA Group Information Gathering, Dispensing, Verifying, and Related Work p. 258

4. JOB SUMMARY:

Answers inquiries and gives directions to customers, authorizes cashing of customers' checks, records and returns lost charge cards, sorts and reviews new credit applications, and requisitions supplies, working at Information Desk in department store Credit Office.

5. WORK PERFORMED RATINGS:

	(D)	(P)	T
Worker Functions	Data	People	Things
	5	6	7

Work Field 282-Information Giving 231-Recording

M.P.S.M.S. 890-Business Service

6. WORKER TRAITS RATINGS:

GED 1 2 (3) 4 5 6

SVP 1 2 (3) 4 5 6 7 8 9

Aptitudes G 3 V 3 N 3 S 4 P 4 Q 3 K 4 F 3 M 4 E 5 C 5

Temperaments D F I J (M) (P) R S T (V)

Interests 1a (1b) (2a) 2b 3a 3b 4a 4b 5a 5b

Phys. Demands (S) L M H V 2 3 (4) (5) 6

Environ. Cond. (I) O B 2 3 4 5 6 7

Table 7–1. (Continued)

---

7. General Education
    a. Elementary 6 High School none Courses _____
    b. College none Courses _____

8. Vocational Preparation
    a. College none Courses _____
    _____
    b. Vocational Education none Courses _____
    c. Apprenticeship none _____
    _____
    d. Inplant Training none _____
    e. On-the-Job Training 3 to 5 weeks by Credit Interviewer _____
    f. Performance on Other Jobs none _____

9. Experience none _____

10. Orientation 1 week _____

11. Licenses, etc. none _____

12. Relation to Other Jobs and Workers
    Promotion: From this is an entry job To CREDIT INTERVIEWER _____
    Transfers: From none To none _____
    Supervision Received CREDIT MANAGER _____
    Supervision Given none _____
    _____

13. Machines, Tools, Equipment, and Work Aids
    Impressing Device—Small Hand-operated device, of similar construction to stapler with a nonmoving base and a moveable upper arm containing inked rollers which Impressing Device are moved by a lever in the upper arm. Charge card is placed in a groove in the base, stand-up print facing up, and paper or bill positioned over card, then the upper arm is brought down and lever depressed to bring inked rollers over paper to make impress of card's print.

14. Materials and Products
    none

15. Description of Tasks:
    1. Answers inquiries and gives direction to customers: Greets customers at Information Desk and ascertains reason for visit to Credit Office. Sends customer to Credit Interviewer to open credit account, to Cashier to pay bills, to Adjustment Department to obtain correction of error in billing. Directs customer to other store departments on request, referring to store directory. (50%)
    2. Authorizes cashing of checks: Authorizes cashing of personal or payroll checks

Table 7–1. (Continued)

(up to a specified amount) by customers desiring to make payment on credit account. Requests identification, such as driver's license or charge card, from customers, and examines check to verify date, amount, signature, and endorsement. Initials check, and sends customer to Cashier. Refers customer presenting Stale Date Check to bank. (5%)

3. Performs routine clerical tasks in the processing of mailed change of address requests: Fills out Change of Address form, based on customer's letter, and submits to Head Authorizer for processing. Files customer's letter. Contacts customer to obtain delivery address if omitted from letter. (10%)

4. Answers telephone calls from customers reporting lost or stolen charge cards and arranges details of cancellation of former card and replacement: Obtains all possible details from customer regarding lost or stolen card, and requests letter of confirmation. Notifies Authorizer immediately to prevent fraudulent use of missing card. Orders replacement card for customer when confirming letter is received. (10%)

5. Records charge cards which have inadvertently been left in sales departments and returns them to customer: Stamps imprint of card on sheet of paper, using Imprinting Device. Dates sheet and retains for own records. Fills out form, posting data such as customer's name and address and date card was returned, and submits to Authorizer. Makes impression of card on face of envelope, inserts card in envelope, and mails to customer. (5%)

6. Sorts and records new credit applications daily: Separates regular Charge Account applications from Budget Accounts. Breaks down Charge Account applications into local and out-of-town applications and arranges applications alphabetically within groups. Counts number of applications in each group and records in Daily Record Book. Binds each group of applications with rubber band, and transmits to Tabulating Room (10%)

7. Prepares requisitions and stores supplies: Copies amounts of supplies requested by Credit Department personnel onto requisition forms. Submits forms to Purchasing Officer or Supply Room. Receives supplies and places them on shelves in department store storeroom. (10%)

16. Definition of Terms
    Stale Date Checks—More than 30 days old

17. General Comments
    none

18. Analyst   A. Yessarian   Date   7/25/70   Editor   M. Major   Date 7/26/70

Reviewed By   John Milton   Title, Org.   Credit Manager

National Office Reviewer   W. Irving

Source: U.S. Department of Labor. *Handbook for Analyzing Jobs.* (Washington, D.C. Government Printing Office, 1972), pp. 37–41.

Table 7–2. A Typical Job Description for a Specific
Position in a Specific Firm: Dealer Sales Supervisor for
a Petroleum Company

Title: Dealer Sales Supervisor

Salary grade: 12

Department: Domestic Marketing

Title of immediate supervisor: District Manager

Duties: Under direction, supervises 6–15 salesmen engaged in selling and stimulating resale of company products to and/or by assigned accounts, acquiring new business, and in developing stations. Plans and supervises direct marketing activities within district or assigned territory in order to acquire and maintain maximum amount of profitable business by securing and retaining superior operation of service stations, developing dealers, acquisition of new direct marketing accounts, etc.

1. Performs supervisory duties; assigns work, answers questions, etc.; follows current activities by review of reports, discussions with subordinates, etc. Interviews job applicants, and makes selection subject to District Manager's approval. Handles minor disciplinary matters. Is consulted relative to promotions, transfers, salary treatment, etc. Endorses expense and mileage accounts.

2. Plans and supervises direct marketing activities within the district or territory in order to acquire and maintain maximum amount of profitable business by securing and retaining superior operation of service stations, developing dealers, acquisition of new direct marketing accounts, etc. Receives occasional special assignments from District Manager, consults him as necessary on policy problems, and keeps him advised as to direct marketing activities; otherwise works independently in accordance with established policies. Keeps informed of current activities by field observations, advice of subordinates, etc.

   a. Recruits new dealers through personal contacts, newspaper ads, etc.; interviews candidates in conjunction with salesmen and recommends selection to District Manager. Gathers necessary credit information and personal references. Schedules trainees in training school and reviews periodic progress reports. Attempts to place graduate trainees awaiting station with established dealer for further training. Indoctrinates and motivates new dealers; makes in-station inspections to check on training, answer questions, etc. Upon request, arranges for dealer employee clinics to be held within the district and assigns service salesmen as instructors; acts as faculty member of Dealer Training Schools.

   b. Reviews monthly profit-and-loss statement and housekeeping reports prepared by salesmen on each financed dealer; looks for possible trouble spots, such as excessive personal accounts receivable expenses, personal loans, unbalanced sales, etc.; discusses weak points with salesmen, recommends remedial measures, and follows for correction. Participates in annual district reviews of dealers for purpose of discussing past performance, planning future programs and goals, pointing out weak spots in operation, and offering advice relative to elimination. Prepares dealer lease analysis forms recommending future rental treatment, and discusses with District Manager.

   c. Trains, coaches, and assists salesmen in selling and acquiring accounts, training their dealers, investigating and settling complaints, overcoming problems, negotiating contracts, planning and executing sales promotions, etc., by double teaming with them in the field. Requests assistance from regional staff personnel and supplier's representatives, and handles necessary liaison duties.

d. Inspects stations in conjunction with District Manager; checks on appearance, service rendered, personnel's working knowledge, customer contacts, etc.; prepares written report, and follows for correction of noted deficiencies. In daily travels around territory, makes casual inspections of stations, and advises others of items needing correction. Follows closely and handles nonroutine matters in connection with dealer changeovers.

e. Performs sundry related duties; plans and may conduct periodic sales meetings. Attends district's staff meetings. Handles correspondence with regional and home office personnel, dealers, etc., relative to matters supervised. Contributes to district's monthly marketing letter. Assists District Manager in preparation of service station site justifications, budgets, quotas, performance reports, etc. Speaks at local service organizations and may serve as member of various industry and trade associations and committees.

3. As individually assigned, substitutes partially for District Manager during vacations and other absences to the extent of signing forms, reports, etc., normally signed by District Manager, and handling familiar matters according to District Manager's known views or his handling of similar problems in past; refers questionable matters to Regional Office for advice or decisions; advises District Manager of matters handled.

Educational requirements: High school graduate.

Speciflc knowledge to start: General knowledge of dealer marketing; company products; district organization and facilities; company marketing policies and procedures; service station operation. Supervisory experience.

Where experience required: 4–5 years' experience in dealer marketing with at least 1–2 years as Dealer Salesman.

Knowledge acquired on job: Experience in motivating, training, and supervising salesmen: learn to develop and apply effective selling programs; familiarity with company and competitive marketing activities in district; learn responsibility limits of positions. (6–9 months to acquire.)

Physical effort: Semiactive; drives car approximately 1,100 to 2,000 miles/month.

Responsibility:
Men—Supervision of 6–15 salesmen.
Materials—Economical use of office supplies.
Equipment—Care and use of office machines; inspection of service stations.
Markets—Acquiring and efficient servicing of accounts; occasional public relations contacts.
Money—Economical use of company expense funds by self and subordinates.
Methods—Execution, selection, and control of methods used in direct marketing.
Records—Preparation, analysis, and endorsement of records, reports, and forms relative to direct marketing activities.

Working conditions:
Regular working hours 8:30 to 5:00 five days a week.
Surroundings and hazards:
10–60 per cent normal office conditions.
40–90 per cent field and travel conditions, with related hazards.

counseling. However, this format may be adapted to the needs of employing organizations and in fact has been found useful as a basis for developing affirmative action plans in compliance with governmental directives (4). The Work Performed Ratings and Worker Traits Ratings are based upon detailed procedures set forth in the *Handbook for Analyzing Jobs* (37).

The job description for a dealer sales supervisor given in Table 7–2 is tailored to the needs of a particular company, which utilizes this information in staffing and as a basis for developing compensation rates. Considerable attention is given to differentiating between what the sales supervisor is expected to do and what is expected of his superior, the district manager. In this instance, the job description has been coordinated with the organization planning function.

The Job Specification

The job specification part of the job description may not be labeled separately or, if it is, it may well appear under the heading of qualifications. It contains information on the personal characteristics that are believed necessary for the performance of the job. Included are such factors as educational background, experience, and personal qualifications.

Although the job specification is not universally treated as a separate entity within the job description, there are strong arguments for so treating it. The reason is that it performs an entirely different function from the other components. The job specification neither states role prescriptions nor describes the conditions of work. Instead, it attempts to indicate what kind of people can be expected to most closely approximate the role requirements. Thus, it is basically concerned with matters of selection, screening, and placement.

A detailed discussion of problems in the selection area is presented in Part IV. Nevertheless, it is important to note here that job specifications are often written with little real knowledge as to their actual relationship to work performance. Thus, it has become common practice to require high school graduation for a great variety of positions. Yet this is often done without trying out individuals who have not graduated from high school in the particular type of work to determine if they are capable of effective performance. In most jobs, it seems likely that a person of reasonable intelligence and emotional maturity who has not finished high school will do as well as the graduate who lacks one or both of these characteristics.

Numerous other examples could be given. The point is that job specifications often serve to artificially restrict the labor market, so that it is very difficult to find anyone who meets all the requirements. This sort of thing is fine—if the specifications must in fact be met to assume satisfactory performance. But frequently the information that would indicate whether this is true or not has not been obtained. Specifications often are written without the intensive study that should precede the introduction of any selection

procedure. If under these conditions they operate to exclude disproportionate numbers of minority group members, they may very well be declared
illegal.

THE METHODS OF JOB ANALYSIS

The methods used to gather information about a job vary greatly in
comprehensiveness and systematic rigor. In the discussions that follow, an
effort will be made to explain some of the more commonly used techniques.
Emphasis will be placed on the advantages and disadvantages of each approach, and an attempt will be made to cite typical occupations for which
the particular procedure is most useful.

Observation of the Job Occupant

Observation of the job occupant is a frequently used method of identifying the tasks and duties actually involved in fulfilling the demands of a
particular job. It requires merely that the job analyst observe a number of
job occupants, as they perform the job in a normal, workaday manner, and
that these observations be recorded in some systematic manner. This may be
done either by writing down what was done in narrative form or by selecting what is relevant from among alternatives on some sort of checklist. The
checklist approach, of course, requires some prior knowledge of the particular job and jobs closely related to it. The job description is then written to
include any new role prescriptions that may be desired. It is important that
more than one job occupant be watched at work, because to do otherwise
might result in the highly idiosyncratic and unique behaviors of a specific
individual being written into the description.

Unfortunately, the simplicity of this approach is somewhat misleading.
There are certain related problems that can be very significant in the business situation. First, the use of this method requires the assumption that the
act of observing an individual at work does not have an impact on the work
behavior itself. For the method to be of value, the worker must do the
same things in the same way when he is being watched as when he is not. In
many instances, this requirement is clearly not fulfilled.

Many people have a tendency to show off under circumstances such as
this; others become anxious. Activities that are expected to yield approval
often are exaggerated. If the worker feels he is being observed in order to
set his wage rate (as may well be the case), it is very likely that he will pattern his activities so as to obtain as favorable a rate as possible. These difficulties can, of course, be avoided by setting up a procedure whereby the
worker may be observed without his knowledge. This is not easily accomplished, however. If the subterfuge is found out, labor relations problems
can be anticipated, and considerable damage to morale is almost inevitable.
All in all, it would seem that some distortion of normal behavior as a function of observation is very likely in most instances.

A second difficulty with the direct observation method of job analysis is that it becomes almost meaningless in the case of work that is primarily mental in nature. Thus, there are many positions ranging from private secretary to chairman of the board that are not really subject to this type of study. Observation alone will not yield a clear and meaningful picture of what the individual is doing. It should be noted, also, that the general trend with the introduction of technology is for the amount of physical behavior to decrease, whereas mental activities increase as a factor in job performance.

A final problem with observation is that it is not very practical when the job cycle is rather long, that is, when the time from the beginning to the end of a specific task extends over a considerable period of time. For example, the individual who has only to punch holes in some material with the aid of a machine may have a cycle of 10 or 20 seconds. But the skilled machinist who is making up an extremely complex and sensitive die may have a cycle of three to six months. In any instance where a specific action occurs only infrequently, it is very uneconomical to attempt a complete job description based on observation alone.

For the reasons stated, it appears that the observation technique should be employed only when the work is largely automatically controlled (as with a conveyor belt system), when it is primarily physical, and when the job cycle is rather short (as with certain lower-level clerical jobs and many unskilled and semiskilled factory jobs).

Interview of the Job Occupant

Many of the objections to observation as a method of establishing the tasks, duties, and responsibilities of a job can be overcome by utilizing the interview as a source of information. The job cycle problem is largely eliminated, because the worker can observe himself and briefly summarize, in words, behaviors that were spread over a long time span. Similarly, an individual can monitor his own mental processes even though an observer cannot. As a result, the difficulty with nonphysical tasks is minimized; mental and behavioral activities both can be described. Furthermore, the employee is made an active participant in the information-gathering process, with the result that negative attitudes and resistances are much less likely to develop. Finally, this procedure utilizes the often considerable information the worker has about his job, information that may not be available to the job analyst from any other source.

It is desirable that this procedure be utilized only after considerable preplanning and forethought. The individual doing the interviewing, the job analyst, must be thoroughly trained in the techniques of interviewing. Questions should be worked out in advance, and there should be a clear concept of exactly what information is desired.

The job analyst needs to be able to gain *rapport* with the worker whose job is being studied. Confidence must be elicited, and the worker must be induced to accept the usefulness of the job analysis procedure. This is not easily done. Sometimes, it is impossible. But the difficulties are compounded when, for instance, a college-trained job analyst goes into a plant to interview a blue-collar worker with only a minimum of formal schooling and uses a vocabulary that is well above the level that the worker can adequately comprehend. In such cases misunderstanding is inevitable, and resentment very likely. The information-gathering function will probably not be adequately served.

A second possible source of difficulty is the distorted picture of his position that the person being interviewed may present, consciously or unconsciously. He may, for example, attempt to portray his work as more difficult and important than it really is, in the hope that his pay and status will be increased accordingly. Interview data derived from a number of individuals performing the same or very similar tasks can be used to correct this tendency in part, but it is sometimes difficult to fit several disparate interviews together to form a comprehensive picture. The important thing is that the job analyst retain a clear conception of his own role—that he keep constantly in mind the fact that he is supposed to establish a set of role prescriptions. These will only rarely be identical with any one incumbent's statements regarding his work behavior. Thus, job descriptions must go beyond mere interview data to effectively structure the whole pattern of work within the organization.

It is important to note that observation and interview procedures do not consistently yield the same results. In one comparison study conducted over a wide range of jobs in three organizations, the median correlation between structured observation and interview measures was only .33 (23). Agreement was best on such matters as the variety inherent in the work and the level of skills required; it was least good on the extent to which the work was perceived as uncertain in nature and on the extent to which cooperation with others was required.

Since individual interview, and individual observation, procedures tend to be expensive, some companies have employed group interviews with job incumbents (32). Usually, four to six people are included. The job analyst may interview a cross-section of incumbents, or a technical conference approach may be utilized, with the job analyst coordinating a discussion among highly experienced personnel. Undoubtedly, these approaches lose something as against a composite derived from individual interviews, but they do conserve the time of job analysts.

Job Occupant Description

Job occupant description is similar in intent and procedure to the interview, except that the occupant either writes a narrative description or fills out a questionnaire, rather than giving the information orally. Usually, he is expected to go into considerable detail regarding the tasks performed, the conditions of work, and the materials and equipment employed. Examples of items that can be used in a checklist to be filled out by job occupants are given in Table 7–3 (38).

As might be expected, this technique has many of the advantages and disadvantages of the interview. It is, however, somewhat more economical of time and effort, because the services of an interviewer are not required. On the other hand, there is a loss in flexibility, which means that mistaken impressions can go uncorrected or require considerable time to correct. Also, the benefits of a face-to-face discussion, as they may contribute to rapport and consequently to the correctness of the information obtained, are lost.

Both the interview and the written description suffer from the fact that job occupants may report incorrectly regarding their work. Probably the most effective way to compensate for any such bias is to have the data obtained from the incumbent reviewed by his immediate superior. If the superior has actually performed the work in the past, he is likely to be particularly helpful. Even without such personal experience, however, he can be presumed to possess considerable knowledge, merely because of the nature of his relationship to the incumbent and to the job. Because the objectives of the worker himself and those of his superior are likely to be somewhat different, this review may well provide a valuable antidote to the worker's statements in certain areas. Although research in which the various methods of job analysis are compared have produced mixed results, the studies have indicated that several different job occupants can be quite consistent in their description of the same job. On the other hand, investigations aimed at determining the degree of agreement between job incumbents and their superiors have not always produced evidence of a high relationship (29). It is apparent that the worker and the manager may see and stress somewhat different aspects of the job.

In general, the methods involving the securing of information directly from the job occupant have a considerable advantage when the job analyses cover positions at middle or relatively high levels, where the work is not very repetitive. Individuals in these types of jobs are also those with whom the typical job analyst is likely to be most capable of gaining rapport.

Examination of Previous Job Descriptions

Another way of gathering information about a job is to determine what is already known about it. This cuts down on duplication of effort and can provide a substantial base for subsequent study. Thus, for those companies that have them, previous job descriptions can be of real benefit. Before utilizing such information, however, or any job descriptions that may be available from other firms, it is important to look into the analysis procedures employed. A poorly prepared job description may well do more harm than good. Also, the possibility that technological and other changes may

Table 7–3. Selected Examples of Items from a Job Description Checklist for Mechanical Repairing and Related Work

---

What the Worker Does

Listed below are activities that might be involved in a job-worker situation. Record
an "x" after each activity relating to the job being analyzed.

Estimates cost of mechanical maintenance and repair.   ☐
Examines parts for defects.   ☐
Fabricates replacement parts.   ☐
Requisitions parts and materials.   ☐

(58 items)

Communication Responsibilities

Record an "x" to indicate communication responsibilities.

Management   ☐
Customers   ☐

(5 items)

Education and Training

Record an "x" to indicate education or training required.

High school   ☐
Junior college   ☐
On-the-job training   ☐

(9 items)

Mechanical Repair Apprenticeships

Record an "x" to indicate type of apprenticeship training.

Automotive mechanic
    Diesel mechanic   ☐
Textile machine mechanic
    Weaving room mechanic   ☐
Millwright   ☐

(39 items)

Subjects and Courses

Record an "x" to indicate subjects or courses that develop skills for occupation:

Trade-related subjects
    Blueprint reading   ☐
    Hydraulics   ☐
Trade theory
    Aircraft mechanics
        Ignition systems   ☐
    Power house mechanic
        Boiler testing   ☐

(184 items)

Licensure, Certificates, etc.

Record an "x" to indicate license or certification required.

FAA license   ☐
Stationary engineer   ☐

(7 items)

Table 7–3. (Continued)

Union Affiliation

Record an "x" to indicate union affiliation.

Aluminum Workers International Union ☐
United Rubber Workers Union ☐
Company union ☐

(19 items)

Machines and Equipment

Record an "x" to indicate type of machines or equipment repaired.

Oil field machinery and equipment ☐
Film laboratory equipment ☐
Auxiliary systems
   Pneumatic systems ☐

(132 items)

Tools and Work Aids

Record an "x" to indicate tools and work aids used.

Handtools
   Blow torches ☐
   Box wrenches ☐
Measuring devices
   Depth micrometer ☐
Technical manuals ☐

(74 items)

Environmental Setting

Record an "x" after each item to indicate where the work is performed.

Agriculture ☐
Commercial
   Business service ☐
   Printing and publishing ☐
Military ☐
Other (specify) ☐

(32 items)

Source: U.S. Department of Labor. Task Analysis Inventories. (Washington, D.C.: Government Printing Office, 1973), pp. 77–85.

have altered the job considerably should be considered. Many job descriptions prepared in the past are in fact obsolete, insofar as present day activities are concerned, even though the job titles may have remained the same.

There are several other sources of occupational information that can be of help. Perhaps most important among these is the Dictionary of Occupational Titles, published by the U.S. Department of Labor (36). This contains very brief job descriptions of over twenty thousand jobs. Almost any job title in normal usage can be found there. The job descriptions, however, are quite short and are based on multicompany studies. Thus, they may well not be appropriate for establishing role prescriptions in connection with a specific job in a specific company.

Two other sources are the Alphabetical Index of Industries and Occupa-

tions, put out by the Bureau of the Census (35), and the *International Standard Classification of Occupations* (20). Both are intended primarily for use in connection with a census of population and thus provide only minimal information about each job in the job description sense. However, by providing classification information, they do indicate the general type of work to which each job title refers.

Examination of Work Materials

In some cases, it is possible to gain important information concerning the tasks and duties of a particular job by examining the materials typically used during work performance. A good example would be the tools of a carpenter, or perhaps the typewriter used by a secretary. The usefulness of this method is, of course, quite limited, but it can be of considerable supplementary value in certain instances.

Performance of Work Activities

It has long been said that the best way to learn about something is to do it. More recently, this assumption has received considerable support from laboratory research in the field of psychology. Thus, it seems apparent that one of the best ways for a job analyst to obtain information about a job is to take on its duties himself.

In many cases, this is entirely feasible. Such jobs as retail clerk and truck-driver can be learned rather rapidly, as can many others requiring relatively limited skills. However, it is obvious that this is a technique of rather restricted usefulness and generality, because many jobs take years of training. For positions of the latter type, the procedure is obviously of little value. Probably, as the complexity of our knowledge increases, there will be fewer and fewer jobs that can be studied by actually performing them, but the advantages of the approach where it can be used are considerable.

DEVELOPING JOB FAMILIES

One of the primary goals of a job analysis program is to develop systematic knowledge of how the jobs in a given company are related to one another in terms of either the required tasks, the necessary personal characteristics, or both. Such information can be of considerable value in planning training programs, selection, transfer, promotion, and other personnel activities. If certain jobs can be shown to group together, the occupants of these similar positions can be treated as a unit for a number of purposes. Groupings of this kind are particularly valuable as a guide in the placement of employees and in developing compensation schedules.

The Position Analysis Questionnaire

One of the more promising approaches to developing job groupings is the Position Analysis Questionnaire (25, 26). This questionnaire contains 194 job elements presented in checklist form that incumbents evaluate relative to their work. The elements are of six types—information input (e.g., use of written materials), mental processes (e.g., coding/decoding), work output (e.g., use of keyboard devices), relationships with other persons (e.g., interviewing), job context (e.g., working in high temperature), and other job characteristics (e.g., irregular hours). The approach has the advantage that a large range of jobs may be studied and described in terms of the extent to which the various elements are or are not present.

Through the use of the statistical technique known as factor analysis, 32 basic dimensions have been identified on which jobs vary. Scores on each of these dimensions may be computed for any job using the responses of incumbents to the 194 job element items. The result is a profile that describes the job on each of the 32 dimensions, which range from Watching Devices/Materials for Information to Dealing with the Public to Working on a Variable vs. Regular Schedule. Jobs may then be grouped on the basis of the degree of similarity of their profiles.

The extent to which this technique can be applied effectively to all types of jobs, at all levels, remains something of a question. The developers of the questionnaire indicate that it can be completed by individuals with as little as 10 to 12 years of formal education. However, analyses of its reading level indicate that the words used are sufficiently difficult so that full understanding could not be anticipated below the college-graduate level (2). It therefore appears that the instrument should be used only for jobs requiring higher education or should be completed by a job analyst on the basis of interview/observation data.

Career Ladders

Approaches such as the Position Analysis Questionnaire tend to emphasize job families constituted on a horizontal basis. An alternative procedure, illustrated in Figure 7–1, establishes grouping on a vertical basis to constitute career ladders (11, 12). Jobs are viewed as varying in the extent to which they require dealing with data, people, and things. Within each of these areas, levels of activities exist. Higher-level activities are presumed to incorporate all those within the area that are placed at a lower level, but lower-level activities preclude those above them.

Thus, career programming is viewed as movement upward in one or more of the three areas to the performance of higher-level activities and thus to a higher-level position. Education and training are a means to movement to higher-level activities. This approach is of particular value in eliminating dead-end jobs at lower levels from which movement upward is virtually impossible. Grouping jobs on a vertical basis into those requiring skills related to data, people, or things primarily permits the specification of a career ladder extending upward from all entry-level positions. Of course,

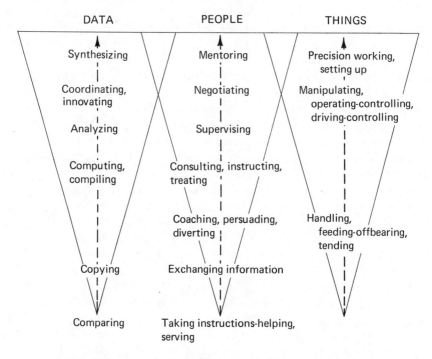

Note: Each successive function reading down usually or typically involves all those that follow it. The functions separated by a comma are separate functions on the same level, separately defined. They are on the same level because empirical evidence does not make a hierarchical distinction clear. The hyphenated functions: taking instructions-helping operating-controlling, driving-controlling, and feeding-offbearing are single functions. Setting up, operating-controlling, driving-controlling, feeding-offbearing and tending are special cases involving machines and equipment of precision working, manipulating, and handling, respectively, and hence are indented under them.

Figure 7–1. Scales Indicating Levels of Job Activities for Purposes of Establishing Career Ladders.
Source: S. A. Fine and W. W. Wiley, An Introduction to Functional Job Analysis: A Scaling of Selected Tasks from the Social Welfare Field (Kalamazoo, Mich.: W. E. Upjohn Institute for Employment Research, 1971), p. 31.

opportunities to engage in higher-level activities may be quite limited within any one organization.

Recent concern for the upgrading of minorities and others with limited occupational skills has sparked a sizable body of research on job families, and on career ladders in particular (39). In certain industries, such as health care, these studies have raised serious questions regarding the essential nature of license, certification, and degree requirements that effectively block upward movement on the job and that may necessitate a greater investment in education than performance of particular tasks requires. These research findings have been embraced by a number of pressure groups, with the result that a major attack on "credentialism" now appears to be under way. It is too early, however, to determine what the results will be.

MODIFICATIONS DERIVED FROM JOB REDESIGN
AND MANAGEMENT BY OBJECTIVES

Although job analysis as described here is widely used in business organizations, it has been the subject of continuing criticism almost from its inception. There are those who believe that such analyses are far too restrictive in nature—that they are not desirable because the job is largely what an individual makes of it. According to this viewpoint, job descriptions and the role prescriptions they contain impose undue limitations on the development or growth of the individual in his or her job. *Job redesign* and *management by objectives* are two approaches that have introduced major modifications into job descriptions and job analysis procedures along the lines advocated by the critics of traditional practices.

Job Enlargement and Enrichment

One major emphasis has been on the expansion of jobs to make them include more tasks and thus, in most instances, a greater degree of discretion for the worker. This expansion may be horizontal; for example, the worker becomes responsible for a larger segment of a product and thus takes on additional role prescriptions previously assigned to others at essentially the same level. It may also be vertical, in that duties of a superior now accrue to the worker. Almost invariably, horizontal enlargement involves some changes of a vertical nature, as well, simply because incorporating more sequential tasks of the kind involved in an assembly line also requires more coordination of efforts by the individual. The term job enlargement is usually used with reference to predominantly horizontal redesign. Job enrichment is usually applied to vertical expansion.

In spite of considerable positive evidence from research studies, of which the AT&T investigations are probably the best known (13, 14), not all research indicates that job expansion will contribute to greater goal attainment. In some instances, merely changing the job description and thus the role prescriptions has been found to be a source of positive results; the change need not be in the direction of enlargement (5).

A number of reports of research in this area have been seriously questioned both as to the analytic approaches used and the interpretations of results (10). A major problem is that there is a tendency to introduce a variety of other changes at the same time as the job redesign, with the result that it is not possible to say with certainty what the real cause of any improvements might be. In particular, it appears that concomitant pay increases may be a factor in the attractiveness of redesigned jobs, rather than the revised nature of the work itself (33).

In any event, what does seem to be clear is that not all people respond the same way to expanded jobs. Such positive effects as do occur appear to be restricted to people with strong motives involving self-expression and autonomy in the use of skills and primarily intrinsic work values (17, 31, 42).

This means that measures of employee readiness for enriched or enlarged jobs should be obtained prior to undertaking a major redesign project. An instrument has been developed for assessing such readiness in an employee group as well as for diagnosing existing jobs to determine where redesign might be feasible and evaluating the effects of job changes on employees (18).

Actually, there is nothing inherent in the job redesign concept that is antithetical to job analysis as such. Job descriptions can be written to include many tasks and considerable personal discretion, or- they may be established on a much narrower basis. The attack of the job expansion advocates appears to be more on the way job analysis has often been used in the past than on the process itself. Research to date merely indicates that job analysts should give considerable attention to horizontal and vertical divisions of labor. There appears to be an optimum on both dimensions that is in part at least a function of emotional, motivational, and mental ability differences among individuals. Thus, it would appear that job analysis, like organization planning, should take into account the nature of the job incumbent.

Management by Objectives

In contrast to job enlargement, management by objectives (MBO), in some of its applications, can turn out to be the antithesis of job analysis as it has typically been performed. Even when considerable information is obtained directly from the job incumbent, the role prescriptions of job analysis are ultimately set by someone else. It is the essence of the job analysis procedure that jobs can be coordinated with each other so that the duties of each can be clearly differentiated. This planning of what *should* be in each job is a personnel function. In contrast, MBO may involve the use of self-established prescriptions, wherein the individual largely establishes for himself what he is to do. Under such conditions, the official job description, if it exists at all, may be totally ignored.

In essence, management by objectives requires that an individual and his superior work out a precise statement of performance objectives in a variety of areas, each with a clearly stated accomplishment date. Subsequently, when this date arrives, performance is compared against objectives, and accomplishments as well as variances are discussed. Superior and subordinate then establish a new set of objectives for a new time span, and the cycle is repeated. Such a procedure may be used for a variety of purposes (8, 30). By comparing role prescriptions, stated as objectives, with performance, an appraisal, or evaluation, of the individual's work may be obtained. Compensation may be tied to the extent to which objectives are attained. The goal-setting process provides an opportunity for considerable coaching and training by the superior. Basically, however, MBO is a procedure for planning. As a planning process, it yields role prescriptions. That is the aspect which is of primary significance for job analysis.

At least in its early applications, MBO was essentially a method of self-evaluation, in contrast to evaluation by superiors, calculated to maximize individual motivation. Goal setting was a highly participative process with self-established role prescriptions the usual result. The research evidence clearly indicates that the fact of establishing definite goals is, in fact, a positive motivational force (24). However, it is not always true that this goal setting must be done entirely by the individual to obtain the full motivational impact (8). The motivational potential of MBO appears to be more in the goal-setting aspect than in the resort to self-established role prescriptions.

In its current applications, some companies continue to stress the self-establishment of role prescriptions; some do not. It appears that certain kinds of individuals are much more responsive to this aspect than others, just as some people respond favorably to job expansion, and others do not. The major problem arising out of incorporating self-established role prescriptions into MBO as a central feature below the very top managerial levels is that of coordination and integration of efforts. Often self-established role prescriptions turn out to be overlapping, or basic tasks are left unperformed. The objectives established may have little relationship to overall organizational goals.

The evidence to date with regard to the effectiveness of MBO programs as actually used by companies is mixed. Sometimes, positive results are obtained (21), and sometimes they are not (28). It appears that in many cases managers merely go through the motions and little real goal setting and planning occurs (34). In any event, incorporating self-establishment of role prescriptions to the point where job analysis in its usual form is either eliminated or ignored does not seem necessary or even desirable. It would seem preferable to stress interview and job occupant description methods of job analysis, and thus to obtain considerable input from the individual as a basis for establishing role prescriptions for his job. There is, in fact, no reason why much greater use cannot be made of position analysis, so that the work is adjusted to the individual. However, the need for some overall coordination of the job structure, presumably as a function of personnel management, remains apparent. It does not seem desirable to extend MBO in such a way as to substitute it for job analysis.

VARIATIONS IN HOURS OF WORK

Most job descriptions specify the hours during which the work is to be performed or the method by which decisions in this regard are to be made. As noted in Chapter 5, legislation has introduced some pressures and constraints in this area, but it is apparent that a great deal of managerial discretion still exists. It is also apparent that the normal, expected hours to be worked each week have been declining for a number of years throughout the world, although sizable differences still exist from country to country (9).

Historically, two of the major variations in hours of work have been part-time as opposed to full-time jobs and varying shift schedules. More recently, the four- and even three-day week has come to the scene, as have flexible and variable scheduling of hours. Because these newer approaches are being advocated widely and are not well understood, they are given particular attention here.

Staffing jobs with part-time workers has the advantage of flexibility and access to a labor force, consisting of housewives and retired people, that would not otherwise be available (43). Certain types of jobs are ideally suited to the part-time approach. This is particularly true where the nature of the work causes it to be concentrated in a limited period of the day, as with certain mail room and janitorial tasks.

Variations in hours of work associated with multiple shift schedules take a variety of forms. Originally, shift work was used primarily to meet technological requirements in industries where the production process required continuous operation. In such cases, a three-shift schedule is now characteristic. Increasingly, however, shift work is being introduced for economic reasons—to obtain a greater return on capital investments, such as large computer installations, where two or three shifts may be employed.

Although rotating shift assignments are widely used for a number of jobs, usually with weekly rotation, there is an increasing body of evidence that this procedure may have detrimental consequences for certain employees (27). Clearly, physiological and psychological problems may result. Normal biological rhythms are disrupted, and there may not be adequate time between rotations for readjustment. In addition, sleep disturbances and gastric disorders, often of a psychosomatic nature, may develop. Because of this, relatively permanent shift assignments may represent a more desirable alternative. However, night shift jobs should be staffed with individuals who do not mind such an assignment, and reviews of physiological and psychological adjustment should be conducted at regular intervals.

The Four-day Work Week

As weekly hours of work have declined to 40 and below, it has become increasingly feasible to reduce the work week to less than five days. The most frequently used approach of this kind, and the only one that has been studied with any degree of adequacy, is the four-day week with work days of 10 or perhaps slightly less hours. A schedule of this kind permits a three-day weekend.

Several well-controlled studies have been conducted comparing this approach with the more conventional five-day week (7, 22). In general, it appears that job satisfaction is increased, at least in some respects, and job-related tension reduced. Performance may be unaffected, or it may increase. Probably the major source of any increased output is the elimination of start-up and shut-down periods in the fifth day, for jobs where these times are of sufficient duration to cut into production significantly. Absenteeism

Table 7–4. Per Cent of Nonfarm Workers Who Usually
Work Full Time Related to Usual Number of Days
Worked per Week

Days Worked	Per Cent
3	0.3
4	1.1
4½	0.4
5	82.2
5½	4.3
6	9.7
7	1.9

Source: J. N. Hedges, "How Many Days Make a Work
Week?" Monthly Labor Review, 98 (1975), No. 4, p. 31.

seems to be totally unaffected by the shift to a four-day week; however, the
proportion of workers holding a second job tends to be substantially greater
among those on a four-day schedule (19).

As indicated in Table 7–4, the four-day week has not as yet achieved
widespread adoption in the United States, in spite of its apparent advantages for many types of work. There is evidence that the number of workers
on three- and four-day weeks is increasing, but so is the number on a five-day
week. The most pronounced trends are the shifts away from work weeks
extending beyond five days. These long work weeks are most characteristic
of managerial and sales jobs (19).

Flexible Working Time

In contrast to the four-day work week, the approaches to flexible and
variable working time currently being advocated involve a resort to self-
defined role prescriptions insofar as hours of work are concerned. The extent of this employee discretion varies considerably under the different
plans. The term *flexible* is normally applied to cases where employee discretion is only partial, in that attendance during certain core hours is required. The term *variable* is used where the employee has complete freedom to choose the specific hours to be worked, although not the number.

Flexible working hour systems characteristically provide discretion as to
starting time, lunch hour scheduling, and leaving time, but establish set
role prescriptions regarding the late morning and early afternoon core
hours (1). The discretionary hours may be scheduled in advance by the
employee, or they may be established from day to day. Some systems require
that a given number of hours be worked each day, while others permit the
accumulation of credits and debits over a period of time, such as a month.
A number of methods have been developed for recording actual hours
worked, handling overtime, and dealing with absenteeism.

The flexible working time concept appears to have achieved much greater acceptance in Europe, where it was initiated, than in the United States (3, 40). It was originally introduced to deal with transportation difficulties but is now viewed as offering a number of other advantages. Although the approach seems most applicable to R&D operations, professionals, and clerical work, it has been applied to a variety of production operations also. Under such circumstances, it may be necessary to accumulate rather sizable in-process inventories.

The descriptions of European systems offer convincing testimonials to the effectiveness of the flexible, and to a lesser degree the variable, approaches. Certainly, a great deal of ingenuity has been shown by personnel managers in overcoming possible obstacles. Yet well-controlled research is not widely available, although such work as has been done is encouraging (15, 41). Tentatively, it can be concluded that where the work is suitable, these approaches do not have major negative effects and may have a number of positive ones. It may very well be that individual workers choose to work when they can work best. They tend to carry forward credits in hours worked rather than debits, and necessary activities do appear to be covered (41).

All in all, the recent approaches to varying hours of work would seem to offer a prime example of creative personnel management. They are entirely consistent with the concept of job analysis set forth in this chapter and can easily be incorporated within such a framework. In addition, certain of the variants, like job redesign, mesh well with variations with regard to individual differences.

QUESTIONS

1. How does job analysis contribute to the following areas?
   a. Labor relations.
   b. Job evaluation.
   c. Training need analysis.
   d. Employee evaluation.
   e. Selection.
2. What is a job specification? What special problems are involved? Can you think of any laws a job specification might violate?
3. What is the relationship between management by objectives and job analysis? Can MBO provide an adequate substitute for job analysis? Explain.
4. Compare the four-day work week and such approaches as flexible and variable working time. What are the advantages and disadvantages of each? Give examples of situations where these approaches might not be feasible.
5. What special problems is the Positive Analysis Questionnaire designed to solve? What method of obtaining job analysis information does it

employ? How might this approach be used as an aid in job enlargement? In job evaluation?

REFERENCES

1. Allenspach, H. *Flexible Working Hours.* Geneva, Switzerland: International Labour Office, 1975.
2. Ash, R. A., and S. L. Edgell. "A Note on the Readability of the Position Analysis Questionnaire." *Journal of Applied Psychology,* 60 (1975), 765–766.
3. Baum, S. J., and W. M. Young. *A Practical Guide to Flexible Working Hours.* Park Ridge, N.J.: Noyes Data Corporation, 1974.
4. Berwitz, C. J. *The Job Analysis Approach to Affirmative Action.* New York: John Wiley & Sons, Inc., 1975.
5. Bishop, R. C., and J. W. Hill. "Effects of Job Enlargement and Job Changes on Contiguous but Nonmanipulated Jobs as a Function of Workers' Status." *Journal of Applied Psychology,* 55 (1971), 175–181.
6. Brumback, G. B. "Consolidating Job Descriptions, Performance Appraisals, and Manpower Reports." *Personnel Journal,* 50 (1971), 604–610.
7. Calvasina, E. J., and W. R. Boxx. "Efficiency of Workers on the Four-day Work Week." *Academy of Management Journal,* 18 (1975), 604–610.
8. Carroll, S. J., and H. L. Tosi. *Management by Objectives: Applications and Research.* New York: Macmillan Publishing Co., Inc., 1973.
9. Evans, A. A. *Hours of Work in Industrialized Countries.* Geneva, Switzerland: International Labour Office, 1975.
10. Fein, M., "Job Enrichment Does Not Work." *Atlanta Economic Review,* 25 (1975), No. 6, 50–54.
11. Fine, S. A. "Functional Job Analysis: An Approach to a Technology for Manpower Planning." *Personnel Journal,* 53 (1974), 813–818.
12. Fine, S. A., and W. W. Wiley. *An Introduction to Functional Job Analysis: A Scaling of Selected Tasks from the Social Welfare Field.* Kalamazoo, Mich.: W. E. Upjohn Institute for Employment Research, 1971.
13. Ford, R. N. *Motivation Through the Work Itself.* New York: American Management Association, Inc., 1969.
14. Ford, R. N. "Job Enrichment Lessons from AT&T." *Harvard Business Review,* 51 (1973), No. 1, 96–106.
15. Golembiewski, R. T., S. Yeager, and R. Hilles. "Factor Analysis of Some Flexitime Effects: Attitudinal and Behavioral Consequences of a Structural Intervention." *Academy of Management Journal,* 18 (1975), 500–509.
16. Grether, W. F. "Psychology and the Space Frontier." *American Psychologist,* 17 (1962), 92–101.
17. Hackman, J. R., and E. E. Lawler. "Employee Reactions to Job Char-

acteristics." *Journal of Applied Psychology Monographs,* 55 (1971), No. 3, 259–286.

18. Hackman, J. R., and G. R. Oldham. "Development of the Job Diagnostic Survey." *Journal of Applied Psychology,* 60 (1975), 159–170.

19. Hedges, J. N. "How Many Days Make a Work Week?" *Monthly Labor Review,* 98 (1975), No. 4, 29–36.

20. International Labour Office. *International Standard Classification of Occupations.* Geneva, Switzerland: International Labour Office, 1969.

21. Ivancevich, J. M. "Changes in Performance in a Management by Objectives Program." *Administrative Science Quarterly,* 19 (1974), 563–574.

22. Ivancevich, J. M. "Effects of the Shorter Work Week on Selected Satisfaction and Performance Measures." *Journal of Applied Psychology,* 59 (1974), 717–721.

23. Jenkins, G. D., D. A. Nadler, E. E. Lawler, and C. Cammann. "Standardized Observations: An Approach to Measuring the Nature of Jobs." *Journal of Applied Psychology,* 60 (1975), 171–181.

24. Locke, E. A. "Personnel Attitudes and Motivation." *Annual Review of Psychology,* 26 (1975), 457–480.

25. McCormick, E. J. "Job Information: Its Development and Applications," in D. Yoder and H. G. Heneman (eds.), *Staffing Policies and Strategies.* Washington, D.C.: Bureau of National Affairs, Inc., 1974, pp. 35–83.

26. McCormick, E. J., P. R. Jeanneret, and R. C. Mecham. "A Study of Job Characteristics and Job Dimensions as Based on the Position Analysis Questionnaire (PAQ)." *Journal of Applied Psychology Monograph,* 56 (1972), 347–368.

27. Maurice, M. *Shift Work.* Geneva, Switzerland: International Labour Office, 1975.

28. Muczyk, J. P. "A Controlled Field Experiment Measuring the Impact of MBO on Performance Data." *Academy of Management Proceedings,* 1975, 363–365.

29. Prien, E. P., and W. W. Ronan. "Job Analysis: A Review of Research Findings." *Personnel Psychology,* 24 (1971), 371–396.

30. Raia, A. P. *Managing by Objectives.* Glenview, Ill.: Scott, Foresman and Company, 1974.

31. Robey, D. "Task Design, Work Values, and Worker Responses: An Experimental Test." *Organizational Behavior and Human Performance,* 12 (1974), 264–273.

32. Rouleau, E. J., and B. F. Krain. "Using Job Analysis to Design Selection Procedures." *Public Personnel Management,* 4 (1975), 300–304.

33. Simonds, R. H., and J. N. Orife. "Worker Behavior Versus Enrichment Theory." *Administrative Science Quarterly,* 20 (1975), 606–612.

34. Singular, S. "Has MBO Failed?" *MBA,* 9 (1975), No. 9, 47–50.

35. U.S. Department of Commerce, Bureau of the Census. *Alphabetical In-*

dex of Industries and Occupations. Washington, D.C.: Government Printing Office, 1971.

36. U.S. Department of Labor. *Dictionary of Occupational Titles,* 3rd ed. Washington, D.C.: Government Printing Office, 1965.
37. U.S. Department of Labor. *Handbook for Analyzing Jobs.* Washington, D.C.: Government Printing Office, 1972.
38. U.S. Department of Labor. *Task Analysis Inventories.* Washington, D.C.: Government Printing Office, 1973.
39. U.S. Department of Labor. *Job Analysis for Human Resource Management: A Review of Selected Research and Development.* Manpower Research Monograph No. 36. Washington, D.C.: Government Printing Office, 1974.
40. Wade, M. *Flexible Working Hours in Practice.* New York: John Wiley & Sons, Inc., 1973.
41. Walker, J., C. Fletcher, and D. McLeod. "Flexible Working Hours in Two British Government Offices." *Public Personnel Management,* 4 (1975), 216–222.
42. Wanous, J. P. "Individual Differences and Reactions to Job Characteristics." *Journal of Applied Psychology,* 59 (1974), 616–622.
43. Werther, W. B. "Part-timers: Overlooked and Undervalued." *Business Horizons,* 18 (1975), No. 1, 13–20.

8 *Management Appraisal*

In the two preceding chapters, some of the methods used to establish and formalize role prescriptions have been discussed at length. Let us now turn to the various methods that have been developed to evaluate individuals relative to these role prescriptions—more especially, in this chapter, to the evaluation of managerial personnel.

It should be understood at the outset that the fact of evaluation in some form is inevitable. All organizations make some effort to determine whether individual members are contributing to the attainment of objectives. This may be done in an offhand way by the top person or through the use of a complex, formal appraisal and evaluation system. The evaluations may be precise and accurate or vague and almost entirely in error. But whether we like it or not, we can almost certainly expect to be judged in some way when we join an organization, especially if it is an employing organization that rewards its members with money for their efforts in its behalf.

There are a great variety of techniques and procedures that have been devised to aid in this process of evaluation and appraisal. All have in common the fact that they attempt to provide some indication of the extent to which an individual's behavior matches a conception of what he is expected to do. The basic consideration in appraisal is whether the behavior of a person is so integrated with established role requirements that he is considered a success or so much at variance with them that he is considered a failure. Ideally, this means an evaluation in terms of contribution to organizational goals (11).

Because any given position is likely to have a number of different role prescriptions, we can expect that job-related behavior will be evaluated in a number of different aspects. Particularly in the case of managers, it is not a matter of doing one or even a few things correctly, but of doing a great variety of different things, all designed to meet one role prescription or another. Accordingly, an individual may be considered a great success in one regard only to fall down badly in some other area, relative to some other requirement (28).

It is characteristic to evaluate people in terms of various aspects of their behavior, or dimensions of performance. Generally, the major concern is with actual behavior, with the things a person does or says. But on occasion, evaluation systems move one step back into the individual and attempt to deal with the abilities, motives, and emotional patterns that cause or determine the behavior. The most general approach is to establish the extent of the match to a role prescription, or the degree of success. But often *standards* are introduced, so that behavioral output is considered only as it relates to some minimal acceptable level. Either the person is above standard in a particular regard or below it.

Individual appraisal is carried out to determine what actions should be taken with regard to a person—in the present instance, a manager. The result may be a decision to increase his pay, or decrease it, or leave it the same. Or the evaluation may be used as a basis for a placement decision: promotion, demotion, transfer, retention in the same job, or even separation. Management-appraisal data are also used to guide management-development activities, either directly, through a feedback of the conclusions to the person evaluated, or indirectly, as an indicator of future educational needs. Finally, the evaluations may be used to provide *criterion* data when selection procedures are being developed. This topic will be a primary concern in Part IV. It is sufficient to note here that a company normally tries to select from among job applicants those who have characteristics similar to the characteristics of its more successful employees and to screen out applicants who appear to be like unsuccessful workers of the past.

JUDGMENTAL APPRAISAL

Probably the most widespread method of evaluating managers is to obtain some type of judgment regarding their effectiveness. This may be done as required whenever a manager is being considered in connection with some personnel action, such as promotion or a proposed development activity. Or the appraisals may be conducted at regular intervals, so that all managers are considered within a specified time span. Ideally, this would be done at least once a year. Anything longer than that is likely to produce considerable error, because managers do change, and consequently evaluations that are badly outdated may be employed to guide personnel actions. A recent survey indicates that over 90 per cent of companies have some kind of management appraisal program. In almost all cases, judgmental aspects are involved, and evaluations are obtained from the immediate superior, although other sources may be used as well (5).

In this chapter, little attention will be given to the specific rating procedures and the types of judgmental errors that may occur. It is sufficient here to cover the different sources of appraisal data and the relative merits of each. The details of rating scale construction and use will be taken up in Chapter 9. It is important to recognize, however, that what is said there regarding the techniques used with lower-level employees is equally applicable to judgments regarding managers. Many management-appraisal systems utilize rating systems that are identical in format to those discussed in the next chapter, although the variables, or dimensions measured, may be different (because managerial work is different).

Appraisal by Superiors

One of the first questions that arise in constructing any management appraisal system is whether to use the judgments of a single superior or of several. On this point, the evidence is clear (21). The average of several evaluations made by equally competent raters is far superior to a single rating. This means that, if at all possible, several levels of supervision should be tapped, provided of course that all the individuals involved are in a good position to observe the work behavior of the person being appraised. Sometimes it is possible to utilize managers at higher levels who are not in the direct chain of command—an individual who works in close spatial proximity, a staff manager with whom he often deals, or similar people. Multiple ratings appear to be preferable, even if the immediate superior is the only person who is really knowledgeable regarding the individual. Thus, the average of several successive evaluations made by the same superior over a period of perhaps six months is generally superior to a single report.

The difficulty with using managers at various higher levels to obtain multiple ratings is that the condition of equal competence is frequently not met. A manager several levels above the individual being appraised may well lack a really adequate opportunity to observe. Thus, his conclusions may be based on a limited number of isolated incidents, plus hearsay. Often immediate superiors, because of a greater amount of acquaintance, are in a better position to make evaluations of their people than those above them. In any averaging of ratings, one would want to give their opinion much greater weight.

This raises an additional problem with regard to multiple ratings by superiors. Many companies conduct what they call appraisal sessions, where several of the manager's superiors meet and discuss his work in detail. They then make what amounts to a group rating, which is the particular composite of their individual opinions that they can agree on or that the majority favors. This composite is likely to be heavily weighted with the views of the highest-level individual present, or the highest-level person who clearly states his opinions. Yet, as we have seen, this person may not be in the best position to appraise the manager. As a result, the degree of error can be considerable.

To overcome this difficulty, it is generally considered desirable to have the evaluations made separately and to record all of them in the personnel office before any group appraisal session is conducted. If a composite rating is then made by the group, it can be checked against the average of the independent ratings to see if it represents a shift in the direction of the highest-level person, who unfortunately may not be in a position to keep himself as well informed as he believes. Since people at different levels typically are in a position to observe different aspects of an individual's performance, it may also be desirable to determine what these aspects are in advance and then to obtain evaluations only on dimensions appropriate to the level of the manager doing the rating (3).

THE APPRAISAL SUMMARY

In companies that maintain an ongoing appraisal system with periodic evaluations, the typical procedure is for a member of the personnel department to write up the findings in an appraisal summary. This summary may be merely a brief synopsis, but in some firms it takes the form of an extensive and detailed description of the individual. An outline for an appraisal summary of this latter type is presented in Table 8–1.

The data used to write the appraisal summary on a specific individual are derived in large part from the individual's superiors. But, in addition, the typical program utilizes psychological tests, a personal history form to be filled out by the manager himself, and in many cases a personal interview with the manager conducted by a personnel representative. The summary itself is characteristically considered confidential and is made available only to the manager's direct-line superiors and to appropriate personnel managers.

THE MANAGEMENT INVENTORY

As indicated in Chapter 6, effective manpower planning requires that projections be made of internal supplies of various types of talents. At the management level, these projections are usually based on a composite analysis

Table 8–1. Outline Covering Items Included in a Typical
Appraisal Summary

1. Personal Background:
   Age
   Family background
     Marital status
     Children
   Education
     Types of specialization and degrees
     Extracurricular activities and offices
   Military experience
     Period of service
     Rank at start and end
     Nature of chief assignments
     Campaigns and decorations
   Work history
     Employers
     Position titles and duties
   Special accomplishments
     Honors and awards
     Professional or trade organization memberships and offices
     Community and church activities and offices
     Publications
   Special limitations
     Health
     Family problems
   Hobbies and recreational activities
2. Nature of Work:
   Generalized statement based on organization planning and job analysis data
   Committee assignments
   Number and titles of people supervised
3. Job Performance and Personal Qualifications:
   General statement of value to company and probable future contribution
   Technical performance
     Evaluation against expectations in each of the key areas noted in job description
     Specific achievements in each of key duties
   Motivation in current position
     Attitude toward superiors, company, and job
     Acceptance of and desire for responsibility
     Personal desire for accomplishment and drive
     Self-reliance in making decisions
     Degree and fairness of competition
     Loyalty to company and general managerial orientation
   Intelligence as manifested on the job
     Selection of realistic goals and methods of goal attainment
     Ability to learn new techniques
     Resourcefulness in new and trying situations
     Quality and speed of thinking
     Organizational and planning ability
     Judgment
     Thoroughness and accuracy
     Ability to sell ideas

Table 8–1. (Continued)

Flexibility in dealing with ideas of others
Creativity
Emotional stability
    Adjustment to frustrations and constraints
    Capacity to take calculated risks
    Ability to get along with others
    Reaction to criticism and pressure
    Objectivity and freedom from prejudice
    Excessive emotionality
    Impairments caused by off-the-job problems
Leadership skills
    Ability to elicit cooperation from subordinates
    Ability to criticize and give orders if necessary
    Skill as a team worker with other organizational units
    Development of subordinates
    Delegation and use of controls
    Capacity to establish and publicize performance standards
    Type of subordinates sought and ability to appraise
Three accomplishments in present job that indicate what he or she is capable of
Summarizing snapshot covering major strengths and weaknesses
4. Overall Performance Rating:
Individual rating relative to what is expected
Ranking among others at same level doing similar work
5. Potentiality:
Promotability and expected rate (or timetable) of progress
Actual job or job types (job families) qualified for
Long-range potential
6. Recommended Actions:
Changes in placement
Ideal duration of current placement
Development needs and plans based on comparison against following list of
management knowledges and skills
    Knowledge of: Technical information bearing on job
                   Related specialties and jobs
                   Labor relations and labor law
                   Business economics
                   Company and departmental objectives
                   Job evaluation and payment policies
                   Safety
                   Employee benefits and privileges
                   Company organizational structure
                   Legal constraints
                   Industry practices and competitive picture
    Skill in: Delegation to subordinates
                   Coaching subordinates
                   Setting performance standards
                   Establishing controls and follow-up
                   Long-range planning
                   Decision making
                   Selling ideas
                   Negotiation

Table 8–1. (Continued)

Evaluation of individuals and groups
Taking disciplinary action
Maintaining morale
Communications
Analyzing accounting reports and other data
Cost control
Discussion leadership
Report and letter writing
Public speaking
Interviewing and meeting people
Developing budgets
Reading (speed and comprehension)

of data derived from the management appraisal process. When all the appraisal summaries are completed in a given company unit, it is common practice to prepare a management personnel inventory indicating future replacement needs and listing the candidates who may qualify for anticipated vacancies, immediately or after further development. Anticipated needs for at least five years are usually considered, based on performance, expected promotions, retirement schedules, health, and projected organizational changes.

Replacement candidates are obtained not only from the specific unit but from other segments of the company as well. It is entirely possible that an individual may appear as a candidate on inventory lists for several units, depending on the breadth of his training and experience. The lists are maintained on a continuing basis and are reviewed and updated frequently. On occasion, the management inventory is developed in chart form along the lines of Figure 8–1.

Appraisal by Peers or Subordinates

During World War II a technique known as *buddy rating* was developed by Navy psychologists. This procedure requires that each member of a group rate all other members on certain aspects of their work performance. The ratings on each individual are then averaged to provide an index of the person's competence.

In the years since these initial applications, much has been written about the advantages of this technique, especially as an aid in the evaluation of managers. Either all managers at a comparable level in a given unit, perhaps all first-line foremen in a small manufacturing plant, rate each other, or as a variant each manager is rated by his subordinates. In this way, it is possible to obtain evaluations from those who are likely to be well acquainted with the person being appraised, to have observed his or her work closely over a long period, and thus to be capable of making extremely accurate ratings.

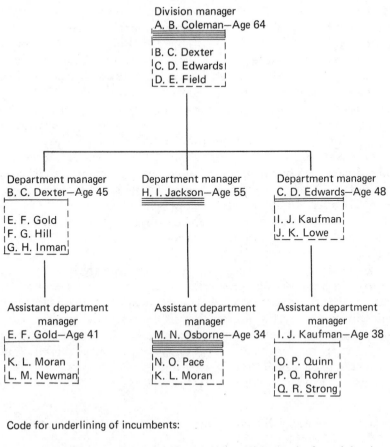

Division manager
A. B. Coleman—Age 64

B. C. Dexter
C. D. Edwards
D. E. Field

Department manager
B. C. Dexter—Age 45

E. F. Gold
F. G. Hill
G. H. Inman

Department manager
H. I. Jackson—Age 55

Department manager
C. D. Edwards—Age 48

I. J. Kaufman
J. K. Lowe

Assistant department
manager
E. F. Gold—Age 41

K. L. Moran
L. M. Newman

Assistant department
manager
M. N. Osborne—Age 34

N. O. Pace
K. L. Moran

Assistant department
manager
I. J. Kaufman—Age 38

O. P. Quinn
P. Q. Rohrer
Q. R. Strong

Code for underlining of incumbents:

——— Outstanding potential. Ready for job above. High promise for unit head.
═══ Good potential. Fair promise for unit head.
▤▤▤ Potential for some growth. Not likely to make unit head.
▦▦▦ Not likely to advance beyond present position.
▩▩▩ Age or health make replacement necessary within five years.
▤▤▤ Unsatisfactory performance. Replacement needed.

Figure 8–1. Management Inventory Chart.

Despite these apparent advantages, however, buddy-rating procedures have not achieved widespread acceptance in the business world. There are a number of reasons for this. For one thing, people at the same level in the managerial hierarchy are apt to be either friends or rivals. In the former instance, the ratings may be elevated inappropriately; in the latter, they may be depressed. Also, where there is mutual rating, there is always the possibility of a deal, such that both parties agree to do well by each other.

Other problems arise where subordinates are asked to evaluate their superiors. There is, for one thing, the anticipation of reprisal, whether justified or not. As a result, only the reckless or those who are on the verge of quitting may be willing to express a negative opinion. Furthermore, sub-ordinates are likely to have personal objectives that differ from corporate objectives and that may exert an undue influence on the ratings. This is a problem in any rating system, but its impact tends to be increased when evaluations are made by people far removed from the policy-making level in the organization. Subordinates may well view a superior in terms of the degree to which he has served to satisfy or frustrate their own personal motives, rather than in terms of his contribution to company goals (8).

Of the two approaches, peer ratings appear to be more useful than rating by subordinates. On occasion, peer ratings have been found to yield results quite similar to those obtained with superiors doing the rating; in other cases, the two have differed considerably (15). There appear to be major variations among situations and companies that may serve to reduce or to increase the differences between perceptions of role behavior by peers and superiors.

It is apparent that peer ratings can also be used effectively to predict sub-sequent job performance and promotion. This is true even when those doing the rating are fully aware that what they say about the individual may have considerable impact on his future career (16). These data, taken as a whole, indicate that many of the potential sources of bias inherent in the peer rating procedure may not actually operate as frequently as has been assumed. The evidence to date indicates that peer ratings can very well serve as a use-ful adjunct to the more traditional evaluations by superiors.

Appraisal Systems Involving Personnel Managers and Psychologists

FIELD REVIEW

One variant on the standard methods of appraisal, to which the name *field review* is often applied, involves much more active participation on the part of the personnel department. In this approach, the appraisal data are collected orally rather than through the use of written forms. Normally, a personnel representative will go to the office of the manager's superior with a specific list of questions. Answers to these questions are obtained in con-versation and recorded in note form. The notes are then converted to a written description after the personnel representative returns to his own office. A draft of this written description is reviewed by the superior, and then it is put in final form. All this can, of course, be a time-consuming and costly process.

The advantages of this approach are inherent in the fact that an oral procedure is more likely to elicit specific information regarding the person being appraised. Superiors will say things about a person in a free discussion of this kind that they will not put in writing. In addition, the fact that a personnel representative will actually spend an hour or more conducting the interview conveys the impression that the appraisal process is considered quite important. Thus, the kind of superficial, hurried response that written rating forms sometimes produce is much less common. The manager being interviewed tends to feel that if the personnel people are willing to go to this much trouble to obtain his opinions, he should at least try to provide as considered a judgment as possible.

Finally, this technique has the advantage that the personnel representative can maintain similar standards of evaluation across a large number of interviews. He can establish what amounts to a set of ground rules, which are held constant for all managers appraised. He can introduce the conditions necessary for true comparability among ratings. This control over the general level of ratings and of the factors to be considered is much more difficult to exercise when written forms are used or when appraisal sessions are conducted by differing groups of managers, each constituted to judge a particular individual.

In the latter instance, it has become common practice to have a management-appraisal specialist from the personnel department sit in on the group meetings for just this reason. Usually, this person writes the appraisal summary also. Such an individual can establish common standards for the ratings within a department or division or across the company as a whole. If he feels a particular group of superiors is being excessively lenient, or harsh, as compared with other such groups, he can take steps to correct this variation in standards, either by inducing the group to change its views or by introducing compensating statements into the final appraisal summary.

PSYCHOLOGICAL APPRAISAL

A markedly different type of appraisal is typically carried out by industrial psychologists who have had some training in the techniques of personality assessment. These appraisals usually involve extensive interviewing coupled with individual psychological testing. They are often employed in conjunction with other evaluation procedures. But even if this is not the case, efforts are made to integrate the test and interview data with information available from personnel files and other sources. The psychologist attempts to get as clear an understanding as he can of the underlying intellectual, emotional, and motivational characteristics of the individual and then converts this into a picture of how such a person might be expected to behave. The resulting psychological description, as the example of Table 8-2 indicates, is not so much a summary of actual behavior as a prediction of anticipated behavior under certain specified circumstances.

Evaluations of this kind are particularly helpful when decisions must be made regarding promotion or transfer, because they provide information regarding how the individual might be expected to act in the new position relative to revised role prescriptions. However, psychological procedures are

Table 8–2. Example of a Psychological Description on a Candidate for Promotion

---

Albert W. Woodworth, sales training representative

Mr. Woodworth appears to be the outstanding individual among the four candidates for District Marketing Manager evaluated. The evidence suggests that Mr. Woodworth would not only make a major contribution in the position for which he is currently being considered, but that he also has the potential to perform very effectively at higher levels in the company. The following strengths are apparent:

1. Mr. Woodworth's general verbal intelligence level is very high. He has a Wechsler Verbal IQ of 136. This is the top score obtained among the 31 members of marketing management who have been evaluated to date. This showing is particularly surprising in view of the fact that Mr. Woodworth has no formal college education. Reasoning and problem-solving ability are also at a high level, as indicated by the results of the Terman Concept Mastery Test. Apparently, Mr. Woodworth has not only accumulated a great deal of knowledge—he is capable of bringing his intellectual abilities to bear in the solution of complex problems.
2. Mr. Woodworth is very strong on problem solving in the numerical area, being particularly adept in quickly grasping a problem and coming up with a solution. He should be outstanding in drawing inferences from an analysis of sales figures and in the accounting aspects of his work.
3. Mr. Woodworth's mechanical ability is at a very high level. In fact, his ability in this area is actually quite outstanding.
4. Mr. Woodworth has very wide interests and keeps himself informed in a great variety of fields. This breadth of interest plus his capacity for very rapid learning should permit Mr. Woodworth to adapt readily to new situations. It is unlikely that he will require a very long training period if promoted.
5. From the Picture Arrangement Test, it is apparent that Mr. Woodworth has very strong work motivation. He can be counted on to push himself hard. He has the capacity to get things done and will keep at a problem until he has it licked. He appears to be happiest when he is working hard and effectively.
6. Mr. Woodworth is a rather independent person. He is unlikely to lean on others and is quite capable of reaching his own decisions. He would much prefer to figure out problems himself and do things his own way. Although he will on occasion follow the advice of others, he tends to distrust it. However, he can be counted on to follow directions and company policy meticulously when this is necessary. There is little question that Mr. Woodworth will do his best work when given a free hand.
7. It is evident from the Thematic Apperception Test stories that Mr. Woodworth is an extremely competent planner and organizer. He will take risks but prefers to do so only after he has made a careful analysis of the alternatives. He has his own ideas about how things should be done, and these ideas are likely to be both original and practical.

Although these strengths taken as a whole seem to argue very strongly for Mr. Woodworth's selection as District Marketing Manager, there are two problems which should be mentioned:

1. At the present time, Mr. Woodworth is somewhat uncertain about his own ability. Although he seems to enjoy management responsibilities and likes to participate in the solution of complex marketing problems, he has no clear conception of his own capacities and tends to underestimate them. He realizes that he has never held a job that has really challenged him, but, on the other hand, perhaps because of this

Table 8–2. (Continued)

lack of challenge, he has no idea of the level at which he might be able to function. It seems probable that Mr. Woodworth is the type of person who will perform more effectively the higher he rises in the organization. He needs to find out how good he really is, and only by facing greater challenges is he likely to gain confidence in his own ability. He needs to prove himself to himself, and only after he has done this is he likely to realize his full potential. This entire problem came out quite clearly during the course of the interview.

2. Mr. Woodworth tends to be rather impatient with mediocrity. He holds himself to very high standards and expects others to perform at the same high level. He may find it hard to delegate to people whom he feels are not as competent as he would wish. As a result, he may try to do too much himself and thereby fail to develop his subordinates to the full. He is also unlikely to establish warm relationships with his subordinates, tending to remain somewhat at a distance from people. Mr. Woodworth is well aware of these problems but appears to be incapable of solving them at the present time. As Mr. Woodworth becomes more confident of his own abilities, he may well feel freer to let subordinates learn through an occasional failure and become capable of greater freedom in his own emotional relationships. This problem, like the other, should largely solve itself if Mr. Woodworth rises to higher levels of management responsibility. Nevertheless, it should be recognized that Mr. Woodworth will probably never be as effective in his handling of people as he is in problem-solving and organizing efforts.

---

also used by many companies in connection with a regular, periodic appraisal program. Although some companies do maintain an internal staff of industrial psychologists to conduct assessments of this type, a large proportion of the work is done by outside consultants.

Research on the success with which subsequent performance has been predicted from such evaluations has yielded varied results. A number of studies have produced findings that indicate that the psychological descriptions are highly accurate and that they can be used to identify those who will succeed or fail in a given company (21). However, it appears that whether these performance predictions will prove correct depends in large part on the psychologist's knowledge of the organization, its role prescriptions, and its value structure. When this knowledge is lacking, the psychologist may have to rely on misconceptions about what makes for success in the firm, or he may make judgments based on his own view of the individual's emotional health alone. In either case, he is unlikely to predict very well (22). In such circumstances, there may be large differences among psychologists in the extent to which their recommendations are favorable, irrespective of any actual differences between individuals.

The data of Table 8–3 are derived from a study of six psychologists' evaluations of candidates for consulting positions. Psychologist 3 tends to make a disproportionately large number of favorable recommendations, while Psychologists 2 and 6 tend to be unfavorable. These differences are statistically significant and suggest a generalized tendency for certain psy-

Table 8–3. Mean Psychological Evaluation Scores and
Recommendation Percentages for Six Psychologists

Psychologist	Individuals Evaluated	Mean Evaluation Score (range 1–4)	Per Cent Favorable Recommendations (scores of 3 and 4)
Firm A			
Psychologist 1	38	2.26	53
Psychologist 2	25	1.76	32
Firm B			
Psychologist 3	32	2.88	69
Psychologist 4	29	2.28	55
Psychologist 5	20	2.40	55
Psychologist 6	12	2.08	25

Source: J. B. Miner, "Psychological Evaluations as Predictors of Consulting Success," *Personnel Psychology*, 23 : 401 (1970).

chologists to respond positively or negatively independent of the qualifications of the person evaluated.

Self-appraisal

Self-appraisal appears to be a useful method of stimulating managers to change and improve their performance; when they are dealing with their own expressed opinions, they are less likely to be defensive than when a superior tells them what he thinks (1). Accordingly, they are more likely to do something about the situation, at least in those areas where they recognize deficiencies. However, it seems clear that self-appraisal cannot be substituted for other approaches when the evaluation is desired for purposes other than development. The evidence on this is quite strong.

For one thing, self-appraisals tend to be considerably more favorable than ratings by superiors under the usual conditions of personnel practice, although when the ratings are obtained under research conditions, this need not be true (12). Studies in which self-ratings and supervisory ratings were correlated indicate that the two measure quite different things. In one instance, ratings by superiors and self-ratings (12) yielded correlations ranging from .02 to .39 on different scales, with a median of .26. Another study (15) yielded a median correlation of .05. Clearly, the individuals were not evaluating themselves in terms of the same type of standards their superiors employed.

Appraisal Applications of Management by Objectives

As noted in Chapter 7, MBO has been viewed, at least in part, as a method of management appraisal since its inception. This tie between appraisal and MBO arose out of certain dissatisfactions with conventional procedures of evaluation by superiors, and in particular out of dissatisfaction with the consequences when managers were required to feed back appraisal data to their subordinates with a view to encouraging more effective performance.

Intensive studies of appraisal interviews conducted at General Electric indicate that any criticism by a superior is usually rejected as incorrect (20). Defensiveness was the characteristic attitude among the subordinates, and indications of a desire to actually improve performance occurred less than once per interview. Yet without the development of carefully stated goals for improvement, criticism was unlikely to produce an increase in effectiveness. Clearly, feedback procedures may well yield a considerable loss insofar as the organizational maintenance goal is concerned and very little, if any, improvement in productivity.

In addition, the experience of many companies has been that it is very difficult to get managers to conduct appraisal interviews with their subordinates. Because the situation is perceived as an unpleasant one, managers avoid it, and the interviews are held only after considerable pressure and dissension. Many are never held in any real sense at all.

Another response to the anticipated unpleasantness of feeding back negative evaluations is a distortion of the ratings. In one study, the average rating on 485 supervisors moved from a score of 60, under normal nonfeedback conditions, to 84 when a rerating to be combined with appraisal interviews was obtained two weeks later (31). One way of making the ratings easier to report to others is to make them more favorable. Obviously, evaluations that are to be used for development purposes in an appraisal interview should not be used for other purposes, such as pay or promotion.

Because of these deficiencies in the feedback approach, it has been suggested that the development goal can be better served if managers appraise themselves (17). Although the various advocates differ somewhat on the specifics, the usual approach is for the individual to sit down with his immediate superior and establish a series of targets or objectives for the next six months or for some other appropriate time period. Then, at the end of the specified interval, the two have a second discussion during which the person evaluates his performance relative to his objectives, attempts to solve any problems that he now recognizes, and sets new objectives for the next period. Throughout this process, the superior assumes the role of a listener, and on occasion a guide, but never that of a critic. Because there is no external criticism, there is no defensiveness. To the extent the individual criticizes himself, the basis for a change in his behavior has presumably been established.

With this type of emphasis, management appraisal and MBO became primarily procedures for developing the individual. However, self-established role prescriptions and self-appraisal are not essential to the use of an MBO approach to evaluation; accordingly, MBO-based appraisals can be conducted in such a way as to serve other goals than those of management development. A number of companies utilize procedures under which higher levels of management above the individual exercise considerable control over the role prescriptions that are established. The evaluation of performance against objectives subsequently is done by the superior, not the individual. Thus, the MBO approach to performance appraisal should not be identified entirely with self-appraisal; it may involve appraisal by superiors as well.

Even so, there appears to be a widespread consensus among managers that MBO appraisals should not replace the more traditional approaches. There is considerable feeling that the fact that MBO is tailored to the individual makes it unsatisfactory as a method for making comparisons across managers (26). According to this view, MBO's greatest strengths are in the goal setting, and thus in motivation and development, and in the emphasis on planning for the future. The most frequently mentioned problem with MBO among those using it is that the measurement process tends to partially distort the realities of the job (30). Thus, there is a tendency to establish objectives in areas where measurement of accomplishments is relatively easy, especially quantitative measurement. These may not be the most important areas. Such problems can become crucial in professional, service, and staff activities where the measurement of key functions in quantitative terms is often difficult. Consistent with these interpretations is the finding that achievement of objectively defined MBO goals is relatively unrelated to overall assessments of managerial effectiveness (2). In short, as practiced, MBO assessment does not cover all that should be expected from a management appraisal system.

Assessment Centers

A second type of appraisal that involves judgments derived from multiple sources is the *assessment center* approach. Although assessment centers have a relatively long history in the field of psychology, the impetus for their current popularity in the appraisal of managers derives from applications initiated at AT&T in the mid-1950s (4). An idea of the nature of this approach may be gained from the schedule for a three-day assessment given in Figure 8–2. This is followed by two days in which the management representatives and the psychologists, who also participate in the assessments, rate the managers who have undergone evaluation on a variety of dimensions (9).

In this particular program at the Standard Oil Company of Ohio, 12 managers were evaluated each week by 3 managers several levels above them and by 2 psychologists. The evaluations are not made on the job, but rather are based on observations of behavior and on test results obtained in a special setting designed specifically for purposes of appraisal. The ratings are made from personal history forms completed by the assessees, the results of interviews conducted by one of the management representatives, observed and recorded performance on the situational exercises, analyses of projective

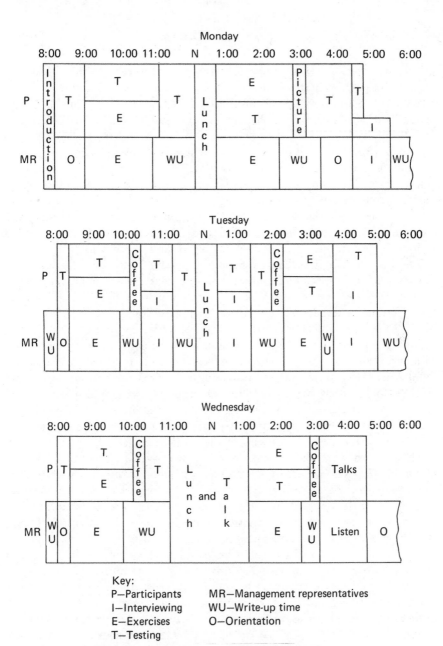

Figure 8–2. Schedule for an Assessment Center.
Source: R. B. Finkle and W. S. Jones, *Assessing Corporate Talent: A Key to Managerial Manpower Planning* (New York: John Wiley & Sons, Inc., 1970), p. 51.

personality tests made by clinical psychologists, other psychological test results, the peer evaluations of other assessees, and personal impressions derived from both formal and informal contacts during assessment. Thus, elements of superior appraisal, peer ratings, and psychological evaluation are all involved.

The end result is a set of composite ratings made by the superior managers and psychologists on various job-related factors bearing on placement considerations, the appropriate supervisory climate for the person, developmental needs, and potential for advancement. For each individual assessed, there is a written report for managers throughout the company, a quantitative output adapted for computer storage for manpower planning, and a technical file for use by personnel managers and psychologists.

The unique aspect of these assessment centers is the use of situational exercises such as special interviews, management games, in-basket performance, leaderless group discussions, case analyses, individual fact-finding and decision-making exercises, and oral presentations as a basis for assessment. These are typically tailored to the particular corporate environment. Many have proved to be highly predictive of subsequent managerial performance. For example, a special exercise which required managers to handle materials in a simulated in-basket on their desks was developed specifically for Unit Managers of Shop Operations at General Electric (19). Ratings, derived from this exercise, of ability to prepare adequately for decision making and of capacity to organize systematically were significantly associated with subsequent success in the Unit Manager job.

Although such special exercises have often proved to be good indicators of on-the-job effectiveness in later years, so have the other aspects of the total assessment center process. Reviews of the extensive research that has been done in the area consistently conclude that the procedure appears to be very effective in the early identification of managerial potential (13, 14, 18). On the other hand, the process is extremely costly, both in terms of the time of the raters and of the lost work of managers who are assessed. It is probably most beneficial for large firms, where communication regarding sources of managerial talent across units is difficult. In smaller firms, other appraisal methods and more informal communication procedures may be quite adequate. There seems to be little difference whether the ratings are made by professional psychologists or experienced manager observers. Also, the assessment center approach appears to be just as valuable when applied in identifying managerial talent among females as with males (25).

OBJECTIVE MEASURES OF PRODUCTIVITY AND PROFIT

Although subjective rating procedures are probably the most widely used in evaluating managers, at least in connection with formal appraisal programs, a variety of hard or objective indexes may also be employed.

These characteristically are based on the behavior of the unit under the manager being appraised. If productivity and contribution to profit of a unit are high, then the manager is considered effective. If the average level of stress originating within a unit is low, and the capacity to reduce external stresses high, the manager is also evaluated favorably.

At the present time, various productivity and profit indexes are more frequently obtained than are measures of organizational maintenance. This is particularly true at the higher levels of management. There seems to be a tendency to assume that maintenance considerations are primarily a matter of concern for lower-level supervisors, and that profitability should weigh more heavily in the role prescriptions of managers toward the top of the hierarchy. This situation may well change in the future, but currently it does appear to be a fact of business life. A recent survey of chief executive officers indicated that profit performance was by far the most important criterion used in evaluating their immediate subordinates at the vice-presidential level (27).

Nonfinancial Measures

Largely because of the central interests of the industrial engineers who have made major contributions in this area, objective indexes related to manufacturing output are available in the greatest number. Some of these measures of group performance that can be used to evaluate the effectiveness of a manager are the following:

1. Units produced.
2. Number of rejects.
3. Training time to reach standard production.
4. Meeting of production schedules.
5. Machine down time.
6. Scrappage.

Many of these indexes, when on an individual basis and attributed to a single worker, are more relevant to the considerations of the next chapter than to management appraisal. Only when such individual measures are combined to provide a group statistic can they be used to evaluate the competence of supervision.

The same holds for the evaluation of managers in areas of work other than the direct production of a product. Thus, the total sales figures, or gains and losses over a prior period, for a group of salesmen can be used to evaluate sales managers and so, too, can the number of customer complaints. Research and development managers may be appraised using variables such as the number of patents resulting from the efforts of their subordinates or the number of assigned projects that move to actual completion. Office managers may be considered in terms of subordinate activities, such as words typed, filing errors, and IBM cards punched.

The important thing is that these indexes must be relevant to the role prescriptions for the specific position, and that measures of some kind must be developed for all important role prescriptions. It is unfortunately easier to establish objective, numerical measures in some areas than others. The result is that these areas may receive undue emphasis, purely because of their measurability, whereas other factors included in the job description are entirely neglected in the appraisal. If this happens, as it apparently often does in MBO applications, a manager can easily learn to direct his efforts toward those requirements of his job that can form a basis for evaluation. The consequence may be a major imbalance in the distribution of work, especially if a number of managerial jobs have similar role prescriptions and are evaluated in the same manner. This is why it is crucial that appraisal systems be developed by working back from a knowledge of the total job and its requirements, rather than by utilizing a few easily obtained measures that appear to have some relevance. It is also absolutely essential that the factors selected be subject to the influence and control of the manager.

Some companies have gone to considerable lengths to establish comprehensive evaluation systems of this kind for managerial jobs, introducing very specific criteria to indicate what are to be considered acceptable levels of performance. Thus, one may find such standards as the following:

1. Warehouse turnover is greater than 200 per cent per year.
2. Frequency of vehicle accidents is less than .35 per hundred thousand miles.
3. Operating overtime hours are less than 2.5 per cent of scheduled hours worked.
4. Training sessions are held once each month.

Accounting Measures

In recent years, some major developments in the field of accounting, especially cost accounting, have made it increasingly feasible to evaluate managers in terms of their contributions to profits. It has long been common practice to establish budgets for various groups and to consider managers who unnecessarily exceed these budgetary allocations as unsatisfactory in this particular regard. Similarly, many companies have evaluated wastage, equipment maintenance, and labor in terms of the costs involved.

Much more sophisticated procedures are being introduced now in an effort to deal with the entire gamut of factors influencing profitability in a single comprehensive analysis. Thus, cost centers may be established to coincide with the divisional boundaries of a company that has decentralized along product lines. The division is then treated as a separate firm, and the manager is evaluated in terms of share of the market, net sales, profit as per cent of sales or invested capital, and the like. If, in such cases, the divisional unit utilizes services, materials, or components from other segments of the company outside the manager's jurisdiction, transfer prices are negotiated in terms of market values (6).

Increasingly, these procedures are being moved down through the managerial hierarchy, so that the contributions to profit achieved by lower-level managers, especially those within the line organization, can be determined. Standard costs are established for labor, materials, and overhead on the basis of prior experience and judgment. Cost variances are then computed by comparing actual figures with these standards, and managers are evaluated in accordance with the direction and amount of these variances. The technique requires a detailed organization plan with clear-cut designation of areas of responsibility. Also, there is a very considerable element of subjectivity inherent in setting the standard costs. Yet variance analysis of this kind does appear to provide an extremely valuable tool in appraising managers.

An extension of this approach involves the use of data derived from *human resource accounting* in the evaluation of managers. Such a procedure serves to give a manager credit for increasing his investment in human resources and charges him for using up that investment (7, 23). Thus, the manager who recruits and develops outstanding people whose current performance and performance potential have considerable value to the company is in fact credited with these contributions in the calculation of the profitability of his operation. At the same time, managers who squander human resources either by failing to utilize personnel effectively, or by provoking high turnover rates among their more talented subordinates, or by failing to train and develop people to their full potential, are penalized in the calculation of profit performance. This procedure has the advantage that it tends to forestall, or at least devalue, managerial approaches that achieve high short-term profitability at the cost of using up the organization's human capital, and thus at the expense of the long-term profit potential of a unit. Although human resource accounting in general, and in particular its applications in management appraisal, are still in a developmental stage, a considerable amount of progress has been made (10).

OBJECTIVE INDEXES IN THE MAINTENANCE AREA

As with productivity, organizational maintenance measures taken within the group or unit that is a particular manager's responsibility may also be used for purposes of appraisal. This assumes that a major factor contributing to any lack of job satisfaction, or sense of attachment to the work organization, can be the behavior of the manager in charge. If the various indexes suggest that a certain manager has a highly dissatisfied group, the undesirable situation can be attributed to him and an unfavorable evaluation result.

Unfortunately, the use of this type of information in evaluating individual managers has not been developed to the level of sophistication achieved in the productivity and profit areas. Immediate supervision is not the only factor that must be considered in identifying sources of variation in maintenance indexes.

Clearly, policies and decisions made at a variety of managerial levels can have an impact. Yet very few companies have worked out their role prescriptions and allocations of responsibility among the various levels of management with the same precision in the organizational maintenance area that they have achieved when dealing with productivity and profits. There appears to be a tendency at the present time to exaggerate the role of immediate supervision, when higher-level management may actually be exerting greater influence. Therefore, the various maintenance indexes should be used with caution when appraising individual managers. It is important to know who or what actually is responsible for the existing state of affairs. Yet some measures of this kind are essential because of their relationship to an important company goal.

Measures of Withdrawal from the Job

There are a number of indexes that seem to reflect the tendency of people to avoid or escape from that which they experience as unpleasant. In units where dissatisfaction is marked and there is little sense of belongingness or cohesion pulling them to the group, employees may be expected to seek out various ways of leaving the specific work situation, either temporarily or permanently.

SEPARATIONS AND TURNOVER

Research indicates that employees who experience a sense of deprivation on the job insofar as important motives are concerned are particularly likely to leave the firm (23). Turnover has been demonstrated to bear a close relationship to the level of satisfaction at work and to the degree to which work interferes with other satisfactions. Whether or not, however, the sources of frustration involved are under the control of any particular manager must be ascertained separately in each individual case.

A variety of different procedures are used to compute turnover. For purposes of evaluating managers, it is generally desirable to eliminate involuntary separations, such as those caused by death, illness, and mandatory retirement, from the statistics, because these causes are not normally subject to managerial influence. Often a ratio such as the following is computed for each unit:

$$\text{turnover} = \frac{\text{number of separations}}{\text{midmonth employment}} \times 100$$

It is important in evaluating statistics of this kind to utilize data collected over a period of time to eliminate the effects of seasonal and other temporary fluctuations. Only when a manager has consistently high turnover figures month after month should the possibility that he is ineffective be actively considered. Also, it is important to hold the general type of occupation and certain employee characteristics relatively constant in evaluating these figures. Turnover among young female clerical employees, for instance, is almost invariably high because of marriage, family moves, returning to school, pregnancy, and other factors that are less likely to operate in other groups.

ABSENTEEISM

Although it is by no means universal practice to keep absence statistics for the various individual work units, these data can be of considerable value in appraising managers. One way of avoiding an unpleasant work environment is to stay away from the job as much as possible. There are a variety of types of excused absences—sick leaves, military leaves, and the like—that normally do not reflect a desire to withdraw from a disturbing situation. Nevertheless, much that passes for sickness is probably not, and many illnesses are emotionally caused. It does seem appropriate to consider a manager unsatisfactory in the maintenance area if his group has a continuing, disproportionately high, absenteeism rate.

As with turnover, a variety of formulas are used to indicate absence rates. A common approach is the following:

$$\text{absenteeism} = \frac{\begin{array}{c}\text{number of man-days lost through} \\ \text{job absence during period}\end{array}}{\begin{array}{c}\text{average number of employees} \times \\ \text{number of work days}\end{array}} \times 100$$

Some firms keep records covering not only the number of days lost, but the number of times, also. Usually, older work groups will have a higher number of days lost from work than those containing largely younger employees, but the actual frequency of separate incidents of absenteeism may not be as great.

Closely related is the use of tardiness statistics, which may well reflect a similar withdrawal tendency and which are easily obtained for any group that punches time cards. However, measures of lateness are probably much less frequently maintained on a regular basis than absenteeism data. Certainly, they are less commonly used to evaluate managers.

INJURIES AND DISPENSARY VISITS

Although the use of accident statistics as indexes of managerial competence is probably more appropriately explained in terms of the direct relationship to profits and out of humane considerations, it is nevertheless true that people who are more upset and disturbed at work are particularly susceptible to injury. Thus, maintenance considerations can be involved.

In the case of dispensary visits, the relationship is still clearer. A common method of escaping an unpleasant work environment is to seek medical attention. At the most, one might be sent home; at the least, one will be away from the work place for a period.

In many cases, injuries that involve lost time are recorded separately from those that do not require that the individual be sent home. Both lost time and minor injuries are expressed as a frequency per man-hours worked in the unit. Although statistics on dispensary visits are only rarely maintained as a basis for evaluating managers, a count of the number of initial visits for a new complaint within some specified time span can be an effective method of identifying a widespread desire to avoid a particular work situation.

Measures of Resistance Against Management

Another way in which internal stress may manifest itself within a work unit is through direct resistance and conflict. Group members who are dissatisfied may not avoid the situation that disturbs them; rather, they may attack the management that they see as causing their difficulties. Such resistance may be covert or overt. In any event, the manager who heads up a unit where signs of resistance are numerous can find himself judged less competent; whether this is justified or not must depend on the degree of influence he has over the situation.

DISCIPLINARY ACTIONS

One way in which dissatisfaction may appear is through overt flouting of work rules and intentional deviation from role prescriptions. Such behavior characteristically results in a warning, suspension, or discharge, after a formal disciplinary hearing. When such formal disciplinary actions occur frequently within a given unit, it may well be that the manager has provoked considerable resentment by his actions. Among the behaviors that may elicit formal action of this kind by the company are the following:

1. Unauthorized absence.
2. Insubordination or impertinence.
3. Loafing or sleeping.
4. Misrepresentation, such as tampering with time cards or records.
5. Smoking when forbidden.
6. Drinking or carrying liquor.
7. Dishonesty or stealing.
8. Fighting on the job.
9. Gambling.
10. Willful breach of safety rules.
11. Repeated lateness.
12. Leaving the job without permission.
13. Immoral conduct.
14. Drug abuse.

GRIEVANCES

Another commonly used index is the number of grievances filed by employees within a given time period. Although complaints of any kind can theoretically be used, the usual procedure is to count the number of separate, formal grievances filed in writing under the terms of the union contract.

By filing a grievance, an employee is taking an action that he is well aware management does not wish him to take. Furthermore, in most cases, the grievance statement is directly critical of some managerial behavior. The union may make this particular outlet for dissatisfaction readily available and may even ask the employee to take the action. Yet it is doubtful that many grievances occur in the complete absence of some measure of discontent. Thus, a manager with a high grievance rate can be presumed to have a group that represents some threat to the integrity of the firm.

OTHER INDICATIONS OF RESISTANCE

There are several other possible measures that may or may not be appropriate, depending on the company and situation. Among these are the number of man-hours lost from work due to work stoppages, strikes, slowdowns, and the like—or the total number of separate incidents of this kind. The manager who experiences a high incidence of such occurrences is not likely to be fulfilling the requirements of his job, whether or not the resistance behavior is union-inspired—provided that he is in a position to exert some influence over such events.

Actually, any failure to behave in ways that management is widely known to desire, if it is prevalent enough in a group, may yield evidence regarding the extent of dissatisfaction. Thus, a consistent refusal to join the company retirement system or to participate in group insurance plans might be used as an index in evaluating managers. So, too, may the extent of participation in suggestion systems and in company-sponsored recreational programs. Obviously, the more relatively independent indexes that are developed, the more certain one can be in describing a particular manager as successful or unsuccessful in his efforts to foster organizational maintenance.

APPRAISAL BY ATTITUDE SURVEY

A final procedure for evaluating managers is the attitude survey. In general, the results of these surveys tend to be closely related to other maintenance-related measures, such as turnover and absenteeism, although they do not necessarily yield a high correlation with measures of productivity and profits.

When used to evaluate managers or to predict labor relations problems, attitude surveys are normally handled on a group basis. That is, it is not so much the feelings of a particular individual that are of concern, but the overall level of morale in a given unit. For this reason, the surveys are usually conducted on an anonymous basis, and on occasion only a sample of the employees in a group is measured. In the latter instance, it is important that the sample be truly representative. The usual procedure is to select the sample at random, so that each individual in the unit has an equal chance of showing up in the survey group.

Although a detailed discussion of attitude measurement techniques must await later chapters, several points should be made here. For one thing, surveys of this kind normally contain questions dealing with working conditions, supervisory behavior, attitude toward the job itself, loyalty to the company as a whole, company policies, and other considerations. If the questionnaire is this broad in scope, it is inappropriate to use the total result to evaluate immediate supervision. The various sections of the survey form must be sorted out in terms of the particular level of management with the appropriate responsibility. One cannot expect a manager whose role prescriptions do not call for action in a given area to exert influence over attitudes in that area.

Second, a decision as to whether a particular unit is satisfied or dissatisfied should be based on information that can be presumed to be valid and that is characteristic of the group as a whole. To do otherwise can only produce a biased evaluation of the unit's management. Thus, there must be reason to believe that the people surveyed have in fact given evidence of their true feelings, a topic that we shall cover in greater detail later. And the survey should include all, or nearly all, members of the unit. If a sample is used, the respondents should not be permitted to select themselves. Replies obtained from the 30 or 40 per cent who may take the trouble to return a mailed questionnaire can well reflect only the attitudes of those who are relatively satisfied. It is essential to obtain evidence regarding the attitudes of those who did not reply originally, in such instances, and correct the results accordingly. This is a difficult and time-consuming process, but only after it has been done can a manager be appraised correctly through the use of attitude survey findings.

CAREER APPRAISAL

Although management appraisal is normally concerned with determining how well a person is doing on his present job relative to a given set of role prescriptions, there are instances where a measure of overall career success to date is desired. This is a particularly important consideration when evaluation data are being used to provide a criterion for use in developing selection procedures. Usually, it is more desirable to select management trainees who will achieve continuing success in a variety of positions, rather than those who will do an outstanding job as trainees or in their first subsequent assignment.

Perhaps the most frequently used career index is the managerial level attained. Most firms maintain a system of salary grades, with each job from assistant foreman to president assigned to some point on the scale. The particular grade for the position held by an individual then becomes a measure of his success.

Because these grade levels may be closely related to age or seniority, and because they are strongly influenced by the level at which a person started with the company, it is more desirable to employ some index of grade progression than the absolute level. Thus, one can use a promotion rate measure such as the following:

$$\text{success} = \frac{\text{present grade} - \text{starting grade}}{\text{total years of employment}}$$

There has also been considerable interest in the use of salary data as a basis for evaluation (24, 29). Certainly such a measure is consistent with popular sentiment. It appears to offer a number of advantages when employed within a single company that awards salary increases on grounds of merit and that maintains a stable salary scale utilizing comparable standards for all managers. Usually, when salary is employed as a success index, some correction for age or tenure is introduced to produce a change rate rather than an absolute amount. On occasion, more complex statistical procedures are developed to provide data on the degree to which each person's salary deviates from the figure to be expected for people of his age and experience.

Rating procedures may also be used to evaluate career success as well as success on the current job. The most commonly used technique is some kind of promotability index of the type noted in Figure 8–1. When a person is said to have outstanding potential for advancement, a major determinant of this evaluation is likely to be a pattern of consistent accomplishment in prior positions. Thus, predictions of future progress are in large part predicated on past success. Of course, potential ratings are conditioned to some degree by age, and thus should not be used to evaluate career success among individuals over fifty. An individual of fifty-five may have little prospect of progressing further in the remaining ten years with the company and yet have had a very outstanding career.

QUESTIONS

1. What special problems are associated with ratings by the following groups?
   a. Superiors several levels up.
   b. Peers.
   c. Subordinates.
   d. Immediate superiors who feed the ratings back to the employees.
   e. The employees themselves.
2. How do psychological appraisal and assessment centers differ from other approaches to appraisal?
3. Evaluate management by objectives as an appraisal procedure. How might objective measures be utilized with this approach?

4. What special advantages does human resource accounting appear to offer in connection with management appraisal? Would you expect this approach to be used widely? Explain.
5. Distinguish between the following:
   a. Measures of withdrawal and measures of resistance.
   b. Field review and the appraisal by superiors.
   c. Career appraisal and the management inventory.

REFERENCES

1. Bassett, G. A., and H. H. Meyer. "Performance Appraisal Based on Self-review." *Personnel Psychology*, 21 (1968), 421–430.
2. Bishop, R. C. "The Relationship Between Objective Criteria and Subjective Judgments in Performance Appraisal." *Academy of Management Journal*, 17 (1974), 558–563.
3. Borman, W. C. "The Rating of Individuals in Organizations: An Alternative Approach." *Organizational Behavior and Human Performance*, 12 (1974), 105–124.
4. Bray, D. W., R. J. Campbell, and D. L. Grant. *Formative Years in Business: A Long-term AT&T Study of Managerial Lives.* New York: John Wiley & Sons, Inc., 1974.
5. Bureau of National Affairs, Inc. *Management Performance Appraisal Programs.* Personnel Policies Forum Survey No. 104, January 1974.
6. Burns, T. J. *The Behavioral Aspects of Accounting Data for Performance Evaluation.* Columbus, Ohio: College of Administrative Science, The Ohio State University, 1970.
7. Caplan, E. H. *Management Accounting and Behavioral Science.* Reading, Mass.: Addison-Wesley Publishing Co., Inc., 1971.
8. Cummings, L. L., and D. P. Schwab. *Performance in Organizations: Determinants and Appraisal.* Glenview, Ill.: Scott, Foresman and Company, 1973.
9. Finkle, R. B., and W. S. Jones. *Assessing Corporate Talent.* New York: John Wiley & Sons, Inc., 1970.
10. Flamholtz, E. *Human Resource Accounting.* Encino, Calif.: Dickenson Pub. Co., Inc., 1974.
11. Ghorpade, J. *Assessment of Organizational Effectiveness.* Pacific Palisades, Calif.: Goodyear Publishing Co., Inc., 1971.
12. Heneman, H. G., III. "Comparisons of Self- and Superior Ratings of Managerial Performance." *Journal of Applied Psychology*, 59 (1974), 638–642.
13. Howard, A. "An Assessment of Assessment Centers." *Academy of Management Journal*, 17 (1974), 115–134.
14. Huck, J. R. "Assessment Centers: A Review of the External and Internal Validities." *Personnel Psychology*, 26 (1973), 191–212.
15. Klimoski, R. J., and M. London. "Role of the Rater in Performance Appraisal." *Journal of Applied Psychology*, 59 (1974), 445–451.

16. Kraut, A. I. "Prediction of Managerial Success by Peer and Training-staff Ratings." *Journal of Applied Psychology,* 60 (1975), 14–19.
17. McGregor, D. "An Uneasy Look at Performance Appraisal." *Harvard Business Review,* 35 (1957), No. 3, 89–94.
18. MacKinnon, D. W. *An Overview of Assessment Centers.* Greensboro, N.C.: Center for Creative Leadership, 1975.
19. Meyer, H. H. "The Validity of the In-basket Test as a Measure of Managerial Performance." *Personnel Psychology,* 23 (1970), 297–307.
20. Meyer, H. H., E. Kay, and J. R. P. French. "Split Roles in Performance Appraisal." *Harvard Business Review,* 43 (1965), No. 1, 123–129.
21. Miner, J. B. "Management Appraisal: A Capsule Review and Current References." *Business Horizons,* 11 (1968), No. 5, 83–96.
22. Miner, J. B. "Psychological Evaluations as Predictors of Consulting Success." *Personnel Psychology,* 23 (1970), 393–405.
23. Miner, J. B. *The Management Process: Theory, Research, and Practice.* New York: Macmillan Publishing Co., Inc., 1973.
24. Mitchel, J. O. "Assessment Center Validity: A Longitudinal Study." *Journal of Applied Psychology,* 60 (1975), 573–579.
25. Moses, J. L., and V. R. Boehm. "Relationship of Assessment-center Performance to Management Progress of Women." *Journal of Applied Psychology,* 60 (1975), 527–529.
26. Patz, A. L. "Performance Appraisal: Useful but Still Resisted." *Harvard Business Review,* 53 (1975), No. 3, 74–80.
27. Reeser, C. "Executive Performance Appraisal—The View from the Top." *Personnel Journal,* 54 (1975), 42–46, 66–68.
28. Schmidt, F. L., and L. B. Kaplan. "Composite vs. Multiple Criteria: A Review and Resolution of the Controversy." *Personnel Psychology,* 24 (1971), 419–434.
29. Srinivason, V., A. D. Shocker, and A. G. Weinstein. "Measurement of a Composite Criterion of Managerial Success." *Organizational Behavior and Human Performance,* 9 (1973), 147–167.
30. Stein, C. I. "Objective Management Systems: Two to Five Years After Implementation." *Personnel Journal,* 54 (1975), 525–528, 548.
31. Stockford, L., and H. W. Bissell. "Factors Involved in Establishing a Merit-rating Scale." *Personnel,* 26 (1949), 94–116.

9

Employee Evaluation Systems

BEHAVIORAL SPECIFICITY OF RATING SYSTEMS
    Evaluation Against Formal Role Prescriptions
    Evaluation Against Informal Role Prescriptions
ERROR AND BIAS IN RATINGS
    Halo
    Constant Error
    Recency Error
    Error of Central Tendency
    Personal Bias
    Bias and Equal Employment Opportunity
    Reducing Error Through Training
TYPES OF RATING METHODS
    Rating Scales
    Employee Comparison Systems
        RANKING
        PAIRED COMPARISONS
        FORCED DISTRIBUTION
        COMBINING EMPLOYEE COMPARISON DATA
    Behavior Checklists
        FORCED-CHOICE PROCEDURES
        CRITICAL INCIDENT RATING
        METHODS OF SCALED EXPECTATION
    Essay Evaluations
THE USE OF SIMULATIONS IN EVALUATION
RESISTANCE TO EVALUATION
    Seniority and Union Resistance
    Overcoming Resistance
PERSONNEL STRATEGY AND THE EVALUATION OF
INDIVIDUAL OUTPUTS

Because the preceding chapter devoted considerable space to the so-called hard, or objective, measures of productivity and maintenance, there is little need to recapitulate here what has been said already. It is important to remember, however, that in evaluating managers, at least insofar as their supervisory skills are concerned, we were interested primarily in average or total measures for the subordinate group as a whole. Now, as we move to nonmanagerial employees, we are concerned with the number of units produced or the number of absences or the number of disciplinary actions for each individual.

Although the preceding discussion covered the hard measures in some detail, it did not deal with the specifics of rating-scale construction and the techniques of judgmental evaluation. These will be of primary concern in this chapter. One of the tasks that nearly every personnel manager must perform at one time or another is to construct a new rating form, or to revise an old one that is not working properly. At first glance, this may seem to be a relatively simple task, but there are a number of pitfalls. It is extremely helpful to have some familiarity with the relevant research and with the experience of others.

In addition, we will be concerned with the various obstacles and resistances that may obstruct the effective utilization of these techniques. For various reasons, the systematic evaluation of employee behavior relative to role prescriptions may face a number of difficulties and become a source of considerable internal conflict itself. It is important that a personnel manager be sensitive to these problems, especially as they relate to seniority provisions in union contracts.

BEHAVIORAL SPECIFICITY OF RATING SYSTEMS

An important dimension on which rating systems vary is the degree of specificity with which actual behavior on the job is described. The rating measure itself may incorporate detailed descriptions of behavior derived from job analysis. In this situation, all important formal role prescriptions are spelled out, and evaluation becomes a matter of merely indicating the extent to which these desired role behaviors are exhibited. At the other extreme is the rating measure that simply asks whether an individual is a good or bad performer, with little or no reference to the specific role prescriptions for the job.

Generally, rating systems that are highly behaviorally specific have been viewed as preferable. It has been assumed that different raters will be more likely to agree when more specific measures are used, and that the various errors to which rating systems are prone will be less likely to occur. However, a review of the research on this issue brings out strong evidence that less behaviorally specific measures may prove just as effective as those that are closely tied to formal role prescriptions (14). It appears that scales with varying degrees of behavioral specificity can be used with profit, although the different types of scales may in fact turn out to be measuring quite different things.

Evaluation Against Formal Role Prescriptions

The behaviorally specific measures that incorporate formal role prescriptions invariably are based on some kind of job analysis. Frequently, the role prescriptions are grouped into rating dimensions by the statistical technique of factor analysis, which identifies those behavior descriptions that are most closely associated with each other (7).

Examples of some behavior descriptions associated with the role prescriptions for grocery clerks are (11)

1. By knowing the price of items, the checker can be expected to look for mismarked and unmarked items.
2. The checker organizes the order when checking it out by placing all soft goods like bread, cake, and so on, to one side of the counter, all meats, produce, frozen foods, to the other side, thereby leaving the center of the counter for canned foods, boxed goods, and so on.

Examples for department managers in a department store are (10)

1. Could be expected to smooth things over beautifully with an irate customer who returned a sweater with a hole in it and turn her into a satisfied customer.
2. Could be expected always to maintain complete and accurate merchandising records in his area, thereby ensuring profitable cleanups and reducing the proportion of markdowns.

One requirement for rating systems of this kind is that the evaluations be made by a person who has had ample opportunity to observe job behavior closely over a considerable period. Furthermore, separate rating forms must be constructed for each job, because each job has different role prescriptions. Where there are some overlapping role prescriptions across jobs, the magnitude of this task may be reduced, but it is nevertheless true that to develop behaviorally specific measures for all jobs in a company is a time-consuming and costly process. It may well be worth all the time and money involved, however, if an output process emphasis is an important factor in the company's personnel strategy.

Evaluation Against Informal Role Prescriptions

At the other extreme is the global rating system, which asks only whether an individual is outstanding, average, or unsatisfactory, whether performance is above standard or below, and/or whether potential is high or low. There may be many gradations or few in the scale used, but there is nothing to indicate exactly which role behaviors are associated with a high rating and which with a low one. This is entirely up to the rater. While he may utilize formal role prescriptions based on an extensive job analysis in making his judgments, these are likely to be tempered to a marked degree by any generalized concepts of good and bad performance or good and bad people existing in the organization. If aggressive selling, for instance, is valued generally in a company, such behavior will contribute to a high rating, but so too might such factors as nationality, church membership, educational background, race, or sex. Obviously, there is a potential for illegal discrimination in the use of such procedures, which will be considered shortly. On the other hand, discrimination is not an inevitable concomitant: It depends on the value system of the organization and of the individual rater.

Measures of this global type can be used effectively for a great variety of jobs with little or no modification. This is partly because the rater is being asked to take into account his perception of the role requirements for each job as he makes his evaluations; thus, the rating scale does not change from job to job, but the rater's reference points do. Perhaps even more important, however, is the fact that informal role prescriptions do not vary much across jobs. If high intelligence, or a tendency to work hard, is valued, this will be true irrespective of the particular job held; thus, no revision of the rating measure used is needed in shifting from evaluations of sales personnel, for example, to those of clerical workers.

Although some companies use only a single rating of overall performance, perhaps supplemented by a rating of potential for promotion, others move slightly farther in the direction of behavioral specificity by utilizing several measures dealing with various aspects of performance, such as quality of work produced, quantity, cooperativeness in dealing with others, and the like. Many of these are aspects of all jobs; some, such as effectiveness in dealing with customers, important for all sales personnel, are associated with job families. On occasion, certain personal traits assumed to be of importance in the work are included as well. Generally, ratings of an individual on the separate dimensions are highly correlated with each other. It is as if the employee were really being rated on the same dimension each time. He probably is—the dimension being his degree of fit with the organization's value structure. The labels, such as quantity of work, quality, or even creativity or competitiveness, attached to measures that have little behavioral specificity, do not seem to be very meaningful in and of themselves (21).

ERROR AND BIAS IN RATINGS

A number of different types of rating methods have been developed. Some tend to be quite behaviorally specific, others are not, and a few can be one or the other depending on how they are used. Since most of the newer methods in the field have been introduced in an effort to reduce or eliminate various presumed sources of error or bias in the rating process, the discussion will turn to these types of error first.

Halo

Halo is the tendency to evaluate a person in a similar manner, favorably or unfavorably, on all or most of the dimensions of a rating form because a general overall impression colors the ratings. There is thus a bias that causes the independent dimensions to be less measures of what their labels state than of a single all-pervasive view of the individual. When correlations between the various component measures of a rating form are consistently high, there is reason to suspect halo error.

Whether a halo effect should really be considered error, however, depends on several considerations. If the rating scale does in fact measure characteristics that are important to job success, the selection and retention process can be expected to produce in its own right rather sizable correlations that are not due to bias. Also, error is involved only to the extent a true measure relative to a specific role prescription is desired. Thus, for behaviorally specific measurement, halo is a problem; for more general ratings which attempt to evaluate congruence with organizational value systems of an informal nature, the high intercorrelations are no problem at all. In fact, they may be one indication of a desirable degree of integration within the firm (21).

Constant Error

There is a tendency for superiors to use somewhat different sets of standards in judging subordinates. The situation is essentially the same as that existing in colleges and universities, where every student is familiar with the existence of difficult and easy graders. When evaluations made by different managers are compared, as they must be, this tendency can introduce considerable error. All those rated by one manager may score below those rated by another, even though the two groups are in actual fact very similar. The differences obtained are due to differences in managerial standards, not in performance. Although the literature tends to devote more attention to leniency errors, it should be recognized that severity errors can occur as well.

The tendency to be consistently lenient is characteristic of those managers who utilize a supervisory style manifesting considerable kindness, helpfulness, and consideration toward subordinates generally (16). It appears that in giving a high rating to those who work for them, they are merely providing another indication of their usual kindness. This tendency to be lenient is most pronounced when the ratings are to be used for administrative purposes, rather than for research, and thus might actually affect the person's future. It is also more pronounced when the ratings must be reported to and justified to the subordinate (27).

Recency Error

Most ratings are intended to cover a preceding period of time, perhaps six months or a year. Ideally, they should represent the average or typical behavior for this period. There is a tendency, however, to base ratings on what is most easily remembered, that is, the most recent behavior. This may well not be characteristic of the total period, especially if the employee is aware of the approximate date when he will be evaluated.

Error of Central Tendency

Whatever the level of the standards employed by a given superior, there is a possibility that he will rate all subordinates within a narrow range. For one reason or another, the difference between the best and the worst employee on a particular scale often turns out to be minimal, even though much larger differences do in fact exist. In small units, it is not unheard of to find the whole group clustered at one point on the scale. Errors of this kind tend in large part to obviate the value of the evaluations. This clustering is commonly toward the middle of a scale, and it is this particular tendency that is implied by the error of central tendency. The rater does not place anyone very far from the midpoint, in either a positive or a negative direction.

Personal Bias

Perhaps the most important error of all arises from the fact that few people are capable of carrying out objective judgments entirely independent of their values, prejudices, and stereotypes. All kinds of inappropriate criteria and standards may be introduced into the evaluation process with the result that, on occasion, ratings relate not so much to company goals as to the personal goals of a particular manager. Thus, evaluations can be influenced by factors such as an employee's racial or ethnic background, physical attractiveness, religion, manner of dress, alcoholic consumption, social standing, treatment of wife and children, and ancestry, which are normally of little significance for the achievement of organizational goals.

Bias and Equal Employment Opportunity

To the extent race, sex, national origin, or religion enters into ratings, so that certain kinds of people are consistently rated lower than their true performance would warrant, with the result that promotions are denied and pay raises are not forthcoming, bias is transformed into illegal discrimination. Court-ordered back-pay awards can result, and in the case of class action judgments, these may be very large indeed. Bias of this kind in performance evaluations may also be transformed into discrimination in hiring if the performance measure is used as a criterion in a validity study to identify measures for use as selection instruments.

Research indicates that attitudes toward blacks can influence performance evaluations. These effects, with blacks rated lower by the more prejudiced individuals, are most pronounced with regard to ratings of human relations skills; they are less in evidence with regard to administrative and technical skills (24). It can be assumed that similarly biased attitudes with regard to sex, or religion, or nationality can have comparable effects. On the other hand, it is also clear that biasing effects of this kind cannot always be assumed. White supervisors in a bank have been found to rate black subordinates just as high as whites (2), and a study of peer ratings among foremen trainees also failed to reveal black-white differences (25). In these particular cases, it may be that discriminatory attitudes were minimal or that the raters were able to consciously counteract any manifestation of their attitudes in the ratings.

Reducing Error Through Training

One procedure that has been found quite effective in reducing many of these types of errors is training the raters to recognize and counteract the biasing tendencies. Such training may take a variety of forms. Both group discussions among managers and workshops incorporating videotape feedback have been found useful (17). Even a very short presentation aimed at sensitizing managers to the nature of halo error and to its consequences for performance evaluation has been found to enhance the accuracy of ratings (5).

The key requirements in any such training appear to be that the raters are provided an opportunity to identify and learn about sources of error and bias, and that they become motivated to do something about these problems in carrying out their own evaluations. Far too frequently, performance evaluation programs are introduced without any attempt to achieve either of these objectives; forms are merely sent out. The available evidence makes it apparent that even when scales are designed with considerable effort to reduce errors in rating, additional increments of effectiveness can be anticipated from training (5).

TYPES OF RATING METHODS

Although a variety of classifications of judgmental procedures exist (1, 3), the one used here employs rating scales, employee comparison systems, checklists, and free-written essays as the primary categories. This approach covers all of the techniques in widespread use. Written essays are most common, and rating scales are not far behind, followed by the checklist. The other techniques are relatively much less frequent (9).

Rating Scales

Rating scales may take various forms, but the primary characteristic is the requirement that a check be placed at some point along a scale of value. There may be a line along which a manager is to place a mark (the graphic scale), or numbers may be used, one of which is to be circled, or the approach may be that of Figure 9-1. The high and low ends are identified as such, and intermediate points may be defined through the use of appropriate adjectives. Research indicates that however identified, the distinct scale points should number at least five (18).

Scales of this kind are widely used, primarily because they are so simple to construct. Yet in most cases no provision is made for reducing halo, constant error, and errors of central tendency, all of which can have a consider-

Name: Date:
Department: Seniority Date:
Job Title:

Quantity	Quality	Cooperation
Output of satisfactory work	Accuracy, thoroughness, and effectiveness of work	Ability to get along with supervisors and other employees
Quantity far below typical; requires improvement ☐	Quality far below typical; requires improvement ☐	Cooperation far below typical; requires improvement ☐
Quantity below typical performance ☐	Quality below typical performance ☐	Cooperation below typical performance ☐
Quantity within typical performance ☐	Quality within typical performance ☐	Cooperation within typical performance ☐
Quantity above typical performance ☐	Quality above typical performance ☐	Cooperation above typical performance ☐
Quantity outstanding, far above typical performance ☐	Quality outstanding, far above typical performance ☐	Cooperation outstanding, far above typical performance ☐

Comments:

Figure 9–1. A Typical Rating Scale.

able impact. To the extent that they become behaviorally specific, error may be reduced, but simplicity of construction is lost as well.

Given an adequate awareness of the factors that introduce bias and a desire to overcome them, rating scales apparently can be employed effectively by managers in evaluating their subordinates. In actual practice, this degree of freedom from error may not be too common. This is particularly true if the rater is asked to mark a great variety of scales, which appear frequently to be overlapping, on each individual. When the number of dimensions is over ten, at most, the prospect of appropriate motivation in the rater becomes rather low.

Figure 9–2 presents a rating scale that has been constructed for a slightly different purpose than the scale of Figure 9–1. This particular measure is designed to obtain information regarding whether or not an employee

---

Name: Current Date:

Department: Date Probationary Period Ends:

Job Title:

Please check the appropriate statement or statements in each area to indicate extent of employee's progress.

Quantity of Work:

  Slow to learn _____

  Has to be pushed on occasion _____

  Consistently meets requirements _____

  Does more than required _____

Quality of Work:

  Not really very good _____

  Sometimes drops below acceptable level _____

  Acceptable _____

  An accurate worker _____

Personal Characteristics:

  Does not cooperate with other workers _____   Cooperates _____

  Is absent frequently _____   Is rarely absent _____

  Wastes time _____   Does not waste time _____

  Is not a safe worker _____   Is a safe worker _____

  Demands frequent supervision _____   Can work alone _____

  A troublemaker _____   Does not stir up trouble _____

Are you satisfied to have the employee remain working for you? _____

If not suitable for retention in present job, would you recommend another

  job? _____

Comments:

Figure 9–2. Typical Probationary Employee Evaluation.

should be retained at the end of the initial probationary period, usually from two to six months. It has a strong negative orientation, because the major concern is to identify those who will not be capable of effective performance. Perhaps the greatest value of scales of this kind is that they help to remind a manager of the great variety of behaviors that must be compared against role requirements in reaching a decision on retention. Notice that this decision is not actually requested until the end of the scale, after all the various aspects of the employee's behavior have been considered.

Employee Comparison Systems

Employee comparison systems do not require the use of an absolute standard, as do the rating scales. Instead of comparing each worker against some generalized concept of acceptable behavior, the rater makes comparisons among the various individuals being evaluated. Thus, other workers provide reference points for the ratings, and the result is a relative evaluation.

RANKING

With ranking, the manager merely orders his subordinates on as many dimensions, or characteristics, as are required. Each dimension is treated separately. Various aids have been developed for this purpose, because ranking may not be an easy task when a relatively large number of employees is involved.

One of these, called the alternation-ranking method, represents an attempt to get the easier discriminations, those involving the poorer and better individuals, out of the way first, so that the rater can concentrate on the middle range, where decisions are more difficult. Thus, the best person is selected first, then the worst, then the next best, the next worst, and so on, working inward, until the last person noted is the one in the median position.

An alternative approach involves having the manager assume a hypothetical role as the head of a newly formed firm. He is then asked to select the one individual from among his present subordinates whom, on the basis of performance and potential, he would like to have as his vice-president. This name is recorded. Next, the manager is asked to assume this particular individual has refused the appointment, and to select a second person from among his current group. This procedure is repeated until all members have been ranked. The problem with this and similar nomination techniques is that they provide only a single measure on an overall effectiveness scale.

The major advantage of any type of ranking is that it spreads individuals out over the whole range of performance. The error of central tendency is eliminated, and constant errors cannot occur as such. In addition, halo appears to be minimized when the dimensions are ranked separately, and person-to-person comparisons made on each. The biggest problems arise when there is a need to combine ratings made by different supervisors on different groups. It is always possible, although not probable, that the best person in one group is actually below the poorest in another. This difficulty will be discussed in more detail shortly.

PAIRED COMPARISONS

A second method of employee comparison produces a ranking as a final result but requires only that the superiority of one individual over another be established by judgment. From a series of such comparisons of pairs, a

Table 9–1. Instructions to Raters Used in the Tabulating Machine Operator Study

---

The purpose of these rating forms is to see how the various members of the group you supervise compare with each other in important aspects of tabulating machine operation.

In making the ratings, compare the employees under you on the following aspects of tabulating machine operation:

1. *Application.* Which employee is stronger in his application to the job? Which shows more interest in the work and strives to do well in it?
2. *Accuracy.* Which employee produces more consistently accurate work? Which do you feel you do not have to check on as much?
3. *Speed.* Which employee gets his assigned jobs done faster? Which one can produce more in a given time?
4. *Cooperation.* Which employee demonstrates a greater spirit of cooperation with his fellow workers and his supervisor? Which gets along better with people on the job?
5. *Overall effectiveness.* Considering the four factors above, and others not mentioned, that are important in tabulating work, which employee would you say is a more effective tabulating machine operator?

A separate form for each of these aspects on which you will rate your employees is attached. In completing these forms, you are to compare each employee with every other employee once on each of the five aspects.

1. In the column running down the left side of each form are the names of employees in your group who do the tabulating work. The same names in the same order appear in the row running across the top of the form.
2. No ratings are required in the blanks below the diagonal line running from the top left to the bottom right corner of the sheet, because you cannot compare any individual with himself.
3. Beginning with the name of the first employee in the left column, you are to compare him with each of the other employees whose names appear in the upper row. If, in your opinion, the employee whose name is to the left is better in the aspect of the job that is being judged, place a "1" in the square made by the intersection of the column and the row. If you feel the employee whose name is in the upper row is better, place a "0" in the square.
4. Repeat the process for the succeeding names in the left column until the form is finished.
5. Even though two employees may be nearly equal on any characteristic, you must decide who is better and assign a "1" or "0."
6. Leave no blank spaces and use only "1's" or "0's."

Aspect: *Overall effectiveness.* If you consider application, accuracy, speed, cooperation, and any other aspects that are important in tabulating work, which employee would you say is a more effective tabulating machine operator?

Figure 9–3. A Typical Completed Paired Comparison Rating Form from the Tabulating Machine Operator Study.

rank ordering may be constructed. The nature of the technique is illustrated in Table 9–1 and Figure 9–3, which are derived from a study in which ratings of office tabulating machine operators were employed to establish criteria for use in setting up a selection testing program (19, 20).

In Figure 9–3, a group of five operators are rated on one dimension by their superior. If the number of "better" evaluations is totaled for each person, the results are as follows:

Cooper	4
Adams	3
Dalton	2
Baker	1
Emory	0

These data provide a ranking within this particular group, with Cooper the most effective worker and Emory the least. The actual study involved the combining of similar information on four different tabulating units, most of them considerably larger than this one.

Table 9–2 provides information on the similarity between the paired comparison ranking of the same individuals by pairs of superiors and on the similarity between ratings made by the same superior at an interval of one year. The results suggest that the procedure is generally effective, but that the cooperation ratings, at least relatively, are defective. This may well be due to certain inadequacies of the instructions to raters (Table 9–1) in this particular area. Placing cooperation with fellow workers and with superiors together in one dimension may produce some ambiguity, with the raters

Table 9–2. Correlations Between Paired Comparison Ratings Made by Two Superiors and Between Ratings of Tabulating Machine Operators Made at a One-year Interval

Aspects Rated	Average Correlations Between Ratings of Two Superiors (average $N = 16$)	Correlations Between Ratings Separated by One-year Interval ($N = 35$)
Application	.85	.75
Accuracy	.79	.72
Speed	.81	.78
Cooperation	.67	.64
Overall effectiveness	.79	.75

emphasizing one aspect at one time, another aspect at another. If fellow workers and superiors had been separated by setting up two different dimensions, this would probably have produced more satisfactory results.

FORCED DISTRIBUTION

One of the difficulties with ranking, and particularly paired comparisons, is that when the unit to be evaluated is large, for example over 25, it is often necessary to break down the total group into subgroups for purposes of rating. An alternative to this is a forced distribution.

In a sense, this is a variant of the rating scale procedure, with a provision eliminating constant errors and errors of central tendency. Managers are instructed to place their subordinates in categories on each dimension according to certain predesignated proportions. The common distribution is

low 10%   next 20%   middle 40%   next 20%   high 10%

Thus, for a unit of 46 people, the foreman would be asked to sort them as follows:

low 5   next 9   middle 18   next 9   high 5

Notice that no assumption is made regarding the absolute level of performance. The lowest five are not necessarily unsatisfactory, only relatively less effective.

COMBINING EMPLOYEE COMPARISON DATA

The major difficulty with all the techniques discussed in this section is that although the relative position of each *person* within a group is established, there is no provision for determining the relative status of various groups. Two rankings on separate work units by their separate supervisors do not reflect any existing differences between the groups. One unit may have many more outstanding performers than the other, yet the ranking data will not indicate this fact.

The most common approach has been to assume that the groups to be compared or combined do not differ appreciably. If the groups are of different size, the ranks obtained from ranking or paired comparisons are translated into *standard scores* through the use of conversion tables and then combined into a single list. Sometimes rating-scale data are obtained along with the employee comparisons as a check on the assumption of equality of groups. If an average on a rating scale for one group should closely approximate that for another group, it is considered appropriate to combine the two.

Where there is good reason to believe real group differences exist, the employee comparison approaches have only limited application. The major exception is where a few individuals can be included in the evaluations of more than one rater. These key individuals serve to provide reference points around which the data for the various groups in which they have been included may be combined. It is important, however, that all who rate these key individuals be well acquainted with their work.

Behavior Checklists

The essential characteristic of the checklist procedures is that they deal with on-the-job behaviors; they are by definition quite behaviorally specific. The manager actually reports on or describes the behavior of his subordinates rather than evaluating it. This means that separate checklists must be developed for each position that differs to any sizable degree in role prescriptions from other positions.

Because the manager provides only a number of checked behaviors that serve to describe a particular person, the actual evaluation process must be carried out elsewhere. The behavior descriptions included in the checklist must be categorized in terms of the degree to which they match role prescriptions. This is normally done by people who are familiar with the specific type of work—various levels of supervision, job analysts, personnel specialists, and perhaps industrial engineers or others who serve in a staff capacity relative to the positions under consideration.

These evaluations of checklist items may be carried out in a rough manner or by using more precise scaling techniques. In any event, the result is a designation of certain behaviors as good or desirable and others as less so. If the good behaviors are consistently checked by the superior of a particular employee, and the less desirable behaviors are not, then the employee is considered to have been given an outstanding rating. The weights or evaluations attached to items are not normally known to the supervisors doing the rating.

FORCED-CHOICE PROCEDURES

A variant of the checklist technique has been developed that almost eliminates the personal bias problem and most other sources of error as well. Unfortunately, it accomplishes this result while introducing a situation in which those doing the rating have no idea whether they are evaluating a person favorably or not. The consequence has been that many managers have developed considerable resistance to this approach—called the forced-choice procedure—so much so that very few firms are now using it. Yet it is desirable to have some familiarity with the forced-choice procedure, if only because of the extensive discussions it has provoked within personnel management.

The basic elements of the measure are a series of blocks of two or more behavior descriptions. The descriptions within each block are selected so as to be approximately equal in their degree of favorableness, but markedly different in the degree to which they have been found in prior studies to be associated with effective or ineffective performance, as defined by some other, external criterion. Thus, a block of items used in one of the early developmental studies for rating training skills and containing favorable descriptions is

1. Patient with slow learners.
2. Lectures with confidence.
3. Keeps interest and attention of class.
4. Acquaints classes with objective for each lesson in advance.

A block of unfavorable items is

1. Does not answer all questions to the satisfaction of students.
2. Does not use proper voice volume.
3. Supporting details are not relevant.

Within each of these blocks, certain items have been found to discriminate between poor and good teachers, whereas others have little relation to success (4).

CRITICAL INCIDENT RATING

The Critical Incident Rating is best described by reference to a system developed some years ago for evaluating salesmen at the Minnesota Mining and Manufacturing Company (15). Initially, sales managers in the various divisions were asked to submit short stories or anecdotes, called critical incidents, that illustrated what they considered particularly effective or ineffective salesman behavior. The result was 61 instances of effective performance and 35 instances of ineffective performance. Analysis of these data revealed that 15 basic types of behavior were involved, such as following up, carrying out promises, and communicating all necessary information to sales managers.

A rating sheet was then constructed covering these 15 areas, based on items as closely allied to the original critical incidents as possible. The rater was asked to indicate the extent of his agreement or disagreement should he hear a particular statement used to describe the salesman being evaluated. Examples of these statements based on critical selling incidents are

1. Follows up quickly on requests from customers.
2. Promises too much to customers.
3. Writes poor sales reports.

The major advantages of this technique are in establishing comprehensive definitions of role requirements, if these are not available from other sources, and in providing items that, because they are close to on-the-job behavior, can serve to reduce personal bias.

METHODS OF SCALED EXPECTATION

An approach that has achieved considerable popularity in the research literature, although not yet in personnel practice, is the scaled expectation, or behaviorally anchored, procedure. There are several variants of this method, but all have much in common with the critical incident and other checklist rating systems, while retaining certain common elements with the rating scales as well. Overall, the method of scaled expectation must be viewed as the behaviorally specific rating system *par excellence*.

Although the order in which they are carried out may vary, the following steps are characteristic in the scaled expectation method:

1. Managers with knowledge of the work to be rated identify and define a number of dimensions or aspects of the job, such as communicating relevant information, diagnosing problems, and meeting day-to-day deadlines. In essence this is a type of job analysis.

2. These same managers develop a number of statements illustrating effective and ineffective job behaviors along each of these dimensions. This step is analogous to the critical incident rating procedure.

3. Another group of managers, equally knowledgeable regarding the work, is given the definitions of dimensions from step 1 and the critical incidents from step 2 separately and asked to assign each incident to the most appropriate dimension. This is a matter of retranslation to see if the original incident-dimension fit will hold up. If it does not, the incident is discarded.

4. The second group of managers scales each remaining incident as to the degree of effectiveness-ineffectiveness of the behavior, usually on either a seven- or nine-point scale. Where disagreement regarding scale values is pronounced, the incident is discarded.

5. The final rating form contains a series of scales, perhaps ten, anchored by behaviorally specific incidents at points along each scale, obtained by averaging the values obtained in step 4. Figure 9–4 presents one such scale for the communication effectiveness of workers in a production unit (29). The anchoring incidents are recast in an expectation format, and the rater is to check the scale value that best describes the worker.

Communications—the ability to present information clearly to co-workers

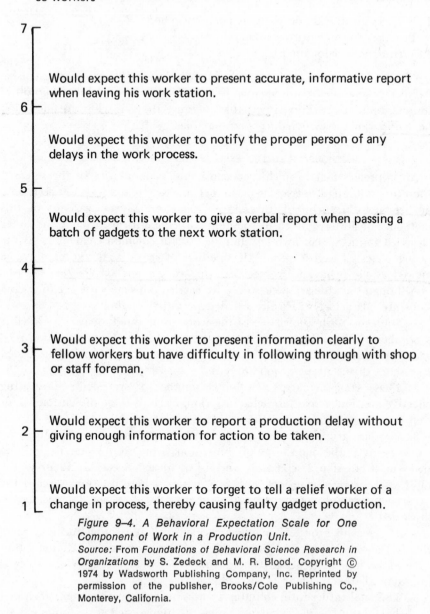

Figure 9–4. A Behavioral Expectation Scale for One Component of Work in a Production Unit.
Source: From *Foundations of Behavioral Science Research in Organizations* by S. Zedeck and M. R. Blood. Copyright © 1974 by Wadsworth Publishing Company, Inc. Reprinted by permission of the publisher, Brooks/Cole Publishing Co., Monterey, California.

This is a time-consuming and costly process. Theoretically, at least, it should serve to drastically reduce errors such as halo, leniency, and central tendency. Yet the accumulated research evidence does not support such a conclusion (6, 26). Improvements over the simpler rating scales can be expected, but the amount of error reduction is not as great as had been anticipated, and it may not be sufficient to justify the time, effort, and cost involved. This is particularly true if adequate job-analysis data are already available, and the use of the scaled expectation method accordingly contributes little to an understanding of job requirements and performance.

Essay Evaluations

In another method, the essay evaluation, the superior merely writes out what he thinks of the subordinate, usually with very little by way of guidelines as to what points should be covered. An example is presented in Figure 9-5.

This approach does little to reduce the various types of error that may influence the evaluation process. Personal bias, in particular, may be marked, because the manager selects his own grounds for judging his subordinate. Comparisons between individuals become difficult, because one person may be evaluated in one regard, and another person on a completely different basis.

Specific role prescriptions may be introduced, and free-written statements requested, in each area. If this is done, however, a rating scale is normally much easier to employ.

THE USE OF SIMULATIONS IN EVALUATION

Because of the many possible sources of bias and error that may serve to distort evaluations based on performance in the actual workplace, there has been an increasing tendency to utilize various kinds of work simulations as a source of evaluation. These often are similar to the situational exercises employed in the assessment centers; in fact, ratings derived from the in-basket exercise, which is widely used in assessment centers, have been used as independent performance measures.

Advocates of the simulation approach to evaluation argue that day-to-day performance is not usually a good measure of what a person can do, because it is influenced by such factors as the nature of supervision, peer pressures to control output, individual motivation, and the like (13). Factors of this kind can be held at approximately the same level for all who participate in the simulation, and thus valid comparisons can be made between one person's proficiency and that of another.

Although some simulations are little more than knowledge tests indicating how much the individual knows about the job, others go far beyond this, providing an opportunity to perform most of the tasks that would be performed in the actual work setting. The difference is that performance occurs in a highly controlled, or "purified," environment, established so as to facilitate accurate measurement. Thus, an exercise used by the American Telephone and Telegraph Company requires an operator to handle a standardized set of calls using actual equipment over an hour-long period

Name: Date:

Department: Seniority Date:

Job Title:

                    Type of Review

New employee _____   Annual _____

Special _____   Separation _____

Transfer _____   Promotion _____

Employee's strong points:

Employee's weak points—areas where improvement is needed:

Comments with regard to any contemplated separation, transfer,
    or promotion:

Figure 9–5. A Typical Essay Evaluation.

(12). A supervisor observes performance. Evaluations are made in terms of (a) a productivity measure that accounts for the number of activities and the complexity of each call handled and (b) the number of mistakes or deviations from accepted practice.

The problem with this type of purification of the evaluation situation is that it may emphasize the effectiveness of measurement at the expense of what needs to be measured. The simulation may in fact be unreal and artificial. It may have little to do with the actual job, and, even if it is highly job-related, the employee is most likely to exhibit his maximum performance capability, rather than what might be expected to be typical on a day-to-day basis. These considerations suggest that simulation evaluations should not be considered as identical to error-free on-the-job evaluations, unless some evidence of this effect is available. In many instances, the two will be measuring somewhat different things. Nevertheless, indexes derived from simulations can prove useful for certain purposes, such as determining the extent to which learning has occurred in a training program.

RESISTANCE TO EVALUATION

In spite of the obvious significance of employee evaluation for the attainment of company goals, there are a number of sources of resistance that may make it difficult to install and maintain systems of this kind. This problem appears to be particularly acute among production employees. While the great majority of other employee groups are covered by some kind of performance evaluation system, this is true for only about half of all production workers (9).

One major difficulty is that employees who do not anticipate a favorable rating are likely to be opposed to the whole evaluation process, which is perceived as a personal threat. Managers and supervisors may experience considerable group pressure in this regard, with the result that many of them, especially those who are particularly sensitive about such matters, may find it very difficult to actually do the ratings. Thus, there may be delays and other difficulties that, although probably not intentional, do reflect the conflicting pressures to which lower-level managers are exposed. It should be emphasized, however, that the problems for raters and ratees alike revolve around negative evaluations. Both parties appear to enjoy the process when the outcome is positive (28).

Seniority and Union Resistance

Perhaps the greatest present source of difficulty in the area of employee evaluation stems from the unions. Rating procedures are almost universally condemned as being inconsistent with a long-standing labor union commitment to the seniority principle.

When seniority holds for purposes of layoff, promotion, shift selection, eligibility for overtime, work assignments, and the like, it is the senior employee in terms of service with the company, or in the seniority unit, who gets the preferred treatment. This tends to eliminate most, if not all, need for a merit rating system.

Union contracts contain a variety of provisions insofar as seniority is concerned. In the most extreme case, seniority only is mentioned. Other contracts say that seniority governs, provided the senior employee is minimally capable of doing the work. Still others indicate that seniority shall be the deciding factor where ability is equal. This, of course, places the burden of proof on management. Evidence must be presented that a person with less seniority is the more capable, if, for instance, he is to be promoted. Even in the latter case, close inspection of actual practices often reveals that merit characteristically takes a position secondary to seniority.

A recent survey indicated that seniority was mentioned in 92 per cent of the union contracts. As regards layoffs, it was the sole or determining factor in 72 per cent of the contracts. For promotion, it was equally influential in 38 per cent (8).

Union contracts contain widely varying provisions regarding the date that seniority starts to accumulate, loss of seniority, individuals who are exempt from the standard seniority provisions, and so on. It is almost impossible to generalize on these matters. There are also wide differences in the way the seniority unit is defined. Seniority may be company-wide or plant-wide. It may hold only within certain occupational groups or departments or even pay ranges.

In general, management prefers to keep the seniority unit as small as possible. The reason for this is that when layoffs must occur and higher-level positions are eliminated, it is common practice to permit *bumping* within the unit; that is, an employee with seniority may demand the job of another employee with less seniority. This can extend down through the unit until the person with the least seniority, in the lowest-level job, is the one laid off. Where seniority is company-wide and a highly skilled position is eliminated, the amount of dislocation occasioned by successive bumping can be considerable. Where the seniority unit is small, changes in the job structure are much more easily accomplished. Nevertheless, many companies have been forced to move to plant-wide seniority in recent years because of court actions and government pressure related to equal employment opportunity considerations.

One final point should be made regarding the union and rating procedures. Even where seniority provisions have not obviated the need for employee evaluation, the union may exercise a certain degree of control over an existing rating system. Thus, some contracts call for a review procedure under which a combined union-management committee reconsiders certain supervisory evaluations and may in fact change them. Among office employees, roughly half have access to some kind of appeal procedure; among production workers, when an evaluation system does exist, appeal or protest safeguards are even more prevalent (9). In a number of cases, the regular grievance machinery is used for this purpose.

It is apparent, therefore, that when employee evaluation systems are installed, the personnel manager will have to be sensitive not only to possible sources of individual resistance, but to union attitudes as well.

Overcoming Resistance

Resistance may serve to block the initiation of an evaluation system, but it is also likely to emerge after the system has been established and there are specific details to attack. The result may well be a gradual erosion of the program and in some cases eventual abandonment.

The greater the resistance exhibited, the more those who are administering the program need to move toward those who do the rating, if the program is to survive. One method of moving toward the raters involves having personnel representatives actually go out and collect the data in a face-to-face situation, as in the field review method, rather than merely sending out forms and waiting for them to come back. Such an approach demonstrates the willingness of personnel management to do a sizable share of the work in order to ensure a successful program.

Another approach is to involve those who will do the rating in the construction of the evaluation system. In this way it becomes *their* system, and they have an investment in its success. Such an approach is directly built into the scaled expectation method, but it can become a part of the development of other types of performance evaluation systems as well. Resistance can also be avoided by deliberately designing the evaluation system with a view to minimizing it, as indicated by the following examples.

1. Managers strongly oppose peer and subordinate ratings, but will accept superior ratings.
2. Whereas a procedure requiring the feedback of results to subordinates may elicit major resistance, one without the feedback requirement is much less likely to be opposed.
3. Forced-choice and forced-distribution methods are often a source of resistance because the manager feels manipulated and *forced* into something he may not want to do. Where resistance is anticipated, the system can be tailored to gain maximum acceptance.

Finally, there is evidence that where a performance evaluation program is initially acceptable, it can be maintained over a number of years as a viable, functioning entity by training managers in its use and by constant monitoring for evidence of erosion (23). This latter process involves a higher-level review of all ratings made by a given manager with a view to early identification of any shift toward errors of central tendency, leniency, severity, and the like. Summary data for all ratings made in a given period are fed back to each manager and discussed with him. Given continuing attention of this kind, the various sources of resistance need not be insurmountable.

PERSONNEL STRATEGY AND THE EVALUATION OF INDIVIDUAL OUTPUTS

The choice of an appraisal, or evaluation, approach may be conditioned by the resistances anticipated, but it is also important to use whatever approach is most appropriate to the use to be made of the data obtained. The technique selected should be the one that will serve a particular purpose best (22). This may well mean having several different evaluation sys-

Table 9–3. Recommended Evaluation Procedures for
Various Purposes

Purpose	Recommended Approaches
1. Help or prod supervisors to observe their subordinates more closely and to do a better coaching job.	Critical incident technique Appraisal applications of management by objectives
2. Motivate employees by providing feedback on how they are doing.	Appraisal applications of management by objectives Objective measures and indexes Critical incident technique
3. Provide backup data for management decisions concerning merit increases, promotions, transfers, dismissals, and so on.	Forced-choice procedures Assessment center Rating scales Field review Ranking Paired comparisons
4. Improve organization development by identifying people with promotion potential and pinpointing development needs.	Forced-choice procedures Assessment center Rating scales
5. Establish a reference and research base for personnel decisions.	Rating scales Ranking

Source: Adapted from W. Oberg, "Making Performance Appraisal Relevant," *Harvard Business Review*, 50, No. 1 : 61–67 (1972).

tems. It is not uncommon that a single approach simply will not serve all desired objectives.

One view of the most appropriate approaches for various purposes is given in Table 9–3. To this should be added the fact that rating systems with little behavioral specificity are most appropriate for identifying informal role prescriptions and organizational value structures. If the major objective is to carry out an organizational analysis to find out what characteristics and behaviors are valued in an organization, then measures of individual qualities and job behaviors should be correlated with these global ratings across many different types of jobs. On the other hand, if the objective is to evaluate performance against formal role prescriptions of the type job analysis yields, much more behaviorally specific procedures of the kind produced by critical incident techniques or the scaled expectation procedure should be used.

Finally, there is the question of how much emphasis should be placed on the evaluation of individual outputs—how much time, money, and effort should be invested in this type of activity. One reason for investing in output processes is that this investment is a means to implementing some other strategy. Thus, if it seems appropriate to stress input processes, one has to obtain reasonably good measures of current performance in order to find out what types of people can be expected to succeed later on. Similarly, if such input-improving mediators as management development, training, and payment programs are to be emphasized, performance evaluation becomes important as a means of stimulating maximum motivation. Results of the evaluations are fed back either through developmental and coaching interviews or through variations in the amount of individual wage and salary increases. In either event, it is important that a degree of accuracy be present; without it, acceptance and motivation are not likely to be maximized.

Input-sustaining mediators require an evaluation process that focuses on the lower part of the range. It is important, for instance, to determine whether accident and injury rates are getting too high or employee dissatisfaction is so marked that labor difficulties can be anticipated. For an input-controlling emphasis, the concern is entirely with the cutting point where performance falls above or below some minimum acceptable standard. Thus, strategies emphasizing the different types of mediators call for special emphases on different segments of a performance scale. To be useful with regard to the mediating processes, it is necessary to have a scale that will be sensitive throughout its range, at and below the average, or around the minimum standard, depending on the type of mediator to be emphasized in connection with a particular personnel strategy.

However, output process feedback is not the only reason for investing in the evaluation of individual outputs. There is a personnel strategy that involves delayed selection. In this instance, investment in input processes is minimal, and as a result, almost anyone who is recruited or applies for a job is hired, assuming certain very basic qualifications are met. At some later point, a comprehensive output evaluation is introduced. This may be in connection with an "up-or-out" policy, whereby the individual is either promoted or dismissed. The evaluation may also be used only for purposes of deciding upon promotion, as against retention at the present level. Or it may be introduced to discriminate between those who will be retained and those to be separated at the end of a probationary period. Whatever the objective of delayed selection, it is a substitute for an input-process emphasis and requires a heavy investment in output processes to be successful.

Similarly, an output emphasis is called for when there is a policy of separating anyone who falls below a certain minimum performance level irrespective of the point in the person's career when this happens. It is important to be right about these evaluations, so that acceptable performers are not dismissed and poor ones retained.

QUESTIONS

1. How may discrimination against minorities or women become manifest in performance ratings? What are the consequences when this occurs?
2. Distinguish between constant errors and errors of central tendency. Would you expect one to yield more halo error? Explain.

3. It has been claimed that the best rating methods are the least widely used, and the worst methods are the most popular. Why might this be?
4. Distinguish between the following rating methods:
   a. Paired comparison and forced choice.
   b. Scaled expectation and forced distribution.
   c. Rating scales and employee comparison systems.
5. If you were faced with the problem of introducing a performance evaluation system into a unionized production unit where high levels of resistance were to be anticipated from first-line supervision and the union, what approach would you take?

REFERENCES

1. Baggaley, A. R. "A Scheme for Classifying Rating Methods." *Personnel Psychology*, 27 (1974), 139–144.
2. Bass, A. R., and J. N. Turner. "Ethnic Group Differences in Relationships Among Criteria of Job Performance." *Journal of Applied Psychology*, 57 (1973), 101–109.
3. Baylie, T. N., C. J. Kujawski, and D. M. Young. "Appraisals of People Resources," in D. Yoder and H. G. Heneman (eds.), *Staffing Policies and Strategies*. Washington, D.C.: Bureau of National Affairs, Inc., 1974, pp. 4-159 to 4-201.
4. Berkshire, J. R., and R. W. Highland. "Forced-choice Performance Rating: A Methodological Study." *Personnel Psychology*, 6 (1953), 355–378.
5. Borman, W. C. "Effects of Instructions to Avoid Halo Error on Reliability and Validity of Performance Evaluation Ratings." *Journal of Applied Psychology*, 60 (1975), 556–560.
6. Borman, W. C., and M. D. Dunnette. "Behavior-based Versus Trait-oriented Performance Ratings: An Empirical Study." *Journal of Applied Psychology*, 60 (1975), 561–565.
7. Brumback, G. B., and J. W. Vincent. "Jobs and Appraisal of Performance." *Personnel Administration*, 33 (1970), No. 4, 26–30.
8. Bureau of National Affairs, Inc. *Basic Patterns in Union Contracts*. Washington, D.C.: BNA, Inc., 1975.
9. Bureau of National Affairs, Inc. *Employee Performance: Evaluation and Control*. Personnel Policies Forum Survey No. 108, February 1975.
10. Dunnette, M. D. "Managerial Effectiveness: Its Definition and Measurement." *Studies in Personnel Psychology*, 2 (1970), No. 2, 6–20.
11. Fogli, L., C. L. Hulin, and M. R. Blood. "Development of First-level Behavioral Job Criteria." *Journal of Applied Psychology*, 55 (1971), 3–8.
12. Gael, S., and D. L. Grant. "Validation of a General Learning Ability Test for Selecting Telephone Operators." *American Psychological Association Experimental Publication System*, Issue 10 (1971), February, MS. No. 351-2.
13. Grant, D. L., and D. W. Bray. "Validation of Employment Tests for

Telephone Company Installation and Repair Occupations." *Journal of Applied Psychology,* 54 (1970), 7–14.

14. Kavanagh, M. J. "Rejoinder to Brumback—The Content Issue in Performance Appraisal: A Review." *Personnel Psychology,* 26 (1973), 163–166.

15. Kirchner, W. K., and M. D. Dunnette. "Identifying the Critical Factors in Successful Salesmanship." *Personnel,* 34 (1957), No. 2, 54–59.

16. Klores, M. S. "Rater Bias in Forced-distribution Performance Ratings." *Personnel Psychology,* 19 (1966), 411–421.

17. Latham, G. P., K. N. Wexley, and E. D. Pursell. "Training Managers to Minimize Rating Errors in the Observation of Behavior." *Journal of Applied Psychology,* 60 (1975), 550–555.

18. Lissitz, R. W., and S. B. Green. "Effect of the Number of Scale Points on Reliability: A Monte Carlo Approach." *Journal of Applied Psychology,* 60 (1975), 10–13.

19. Miner, J. B. "The Concurrent Validity of the Picture Arrangement Test in the Selection of Tabulating Machine Operators." *Journal of Projective Techniques,* 24 (1960), 409–418.

20. Miner, J. B. "The Validity of the Picture Arrangement Test in the Selection of Tabulating Machine Operators: An Analysis of Predictive Power." *Journal of Projective Techniques,* 25 (1961), 330–333.

21. Miner, J. B. "Bridging the Gulf in Organizational Performance." *Harvard Business Review,* 46 (1968), No. 4, 102–110.

22. Oberg, W. "Making Performance Appraisal Relevant." *Harvard Business Review,* 50 (1972), No. 1, 61–67.

23. Prather, R. L. "Extending the Life of Performance Appraisal Programs." *Personnel Journal,* 53 (1974), 739–743.

24. Richards, S. A., and C. L. Jaffee. "Blacks Supervising Whites: A Study of Interracial Difficulties in Working Together in a Simulated Organization." *Journal of Applied Psychology,* 56 (1972), 234–240.

25. Schmidt, F. L., and R. H. Johnson. "Effect of Race on Peer Ratings in an Industrial Situation." *Journal of Applied Psychology,* 57 (1973), 237–241.

26. Schwab, D. P., H. Heneman, III, and T. A. DeCotiis. "Behaviorally Anchored Rating Scales: A Review of the Literature." *Academy of Management Proceedings,* 1975, pp. 222–224.

27. Sharon, A. T., and C. J. Bartlett. "Effect of Instructional Conditions in Producing Leniency on Two Types of Rating Scales." *Personnel Psychology,* 22 (1969), 251–263.

28. Stone, T. H. "An Examination of Six Prevalent Assumptions Concerning Performance Appraisal." *Public Personnel Management,* 2 (1973), 408–414.

29. Zedeck, S., and M. R. Blood. *Foundations of Behavioral Science Research in Organizations.* Monterey, Calif.: Brooks/Cole Publishing Co., 1974.

IV SCREENING AND SELECTION: THE EVALUATION OF INDIVIDUAL INPUTS

The Logic of Selection

The matter of dealing with the individual human inputs to a company is basically a personnel function. First, a pool of applicants or potential employees (perhaps candidates is the best word) must be recruited. Information must then be collected on these individuals, in terms of which some will be selected for employment, and others screened out. The primary consideration in reaching such a decision on employment is whether or not the individual is likely to achieve success in the organization, that is, whether he can be expected to make a sizable contribution to the attainment of organizational objectives.

Part III discussed at some length the various ways in which the behavioral outputs of managers and other employees can be measured and evaluated. Thus, a person could be rated high or low on the quality of his work, he could have a good absenteeism record or a poor one, and so on. Part IV will take up the techniques—interviews, psychological tests, reference checks, physical examinations, application blanks—that are used to select people who are most likely to obtain favorable evaluations on these various indexes of success.

This chapter will be devoted to a general treatment of the logic of selection. Much of our knowledge in this area was originally developed with reference to psychological testing. However, these approaches have much wider applicability, and the considerations involved are just as relevant for interviews, application blanks, and the other selection procedures as they are for psychological tests. Basically, we shall be concerned with the various methods used to relate the preemployment, or preplacement, data on an individual to indexes of the degree of matching between role behaviors and role prescriptions. The latter measures usually are referred to as *criteria* in the selection context.

THE LONGITUDINAL PREDICTION MODEL

The logic of the selection process has been most completely developed in what is called the longitudinal prediction model (16). When a selection measure meets the requirements of this model, it is said to possess *predictive validity*. There are two major variants, or cases, involved.

Case 1—Single Predictor

Step 1. Study the job or group of related jobs for which selection is to occur in order to identify characteristics that might be related to success. These may be intellectual abilities, personality factors, types of prior experience, physical attributes, or anything else that can be measured prior to actual job placement.

Step 2. Decide on the specific measures of these characteristics to be used. If verbal ability is a potential predictor, is it to be estimated from an interview or measured by a test? If a test, which particular one?

Step 3. Obtain these predictor measures on a relatively large group of job applicants or candidates. Then hire from this group without reference to the predictor data. That is, select the individuals to be employed without looking at the measures obtained and without taking this information into account in any way. This normally means that employment decisions should be made by a person other than the one conducting the study. If, on the other hand, the measures are used to select those who will be hired at this initial stage, and these predictors do have some validity, only relatively good performers will be found on the job, and the possibility of identifying predictors that differentiate between good and poor performers will be to that degree lost. The sample may be accumulated over time as hirings occur, but there should be a bare minimum of 30 individuals in the hired group and preferably many more.

Step 4. Gather criterion data on the individuals hired, after such information becomes available. The measure used may be any of those discussed in Chapters 8 and 9. Usually these data are not suitable for use as criteria until after the individual has been on the job long enough for his performance level to stabilize.

Step 5. Determine the degree of relationship between the predictor values and the criterion values. Usually, a correlation coefficient is used to indicate the degree of this relationship. The specific statistical index of correlation may vary depending on the distribution of predictor and criterion values in the group, but in any event, the result will be a coefficient ranging from −1.00 through 0 to +1.00, with the larger values, both negative and positive, indicating a closer relationship between predictor and criterion. The larger the coefficient, the greater the predictive validity of the measure taken before hiring.

A simple chart of the relationship may be established if a summary statement of the kind a correlation coefficient provides is not needed. Thus, at each level on the predictor index, the number of people falling at each point on the criterion would be indicated as follows, assuming a sample of 50:

Predictor Values	Criterion Values				
	1	2	3	4	5
5			1	2	2
4		2	1	4	3
3	2	2	12	4	
2	1	5	4		
1	2	1	2		

It is not necessary to compute a correlation coefficient from this chart to ascertain that a predictor is rather closely and positively related to a criterion.

Step 6. If the results of step 5 indicate a relatively good predictive validity, then under most circumstances a second study should be carried out on the same job using the same predictor and criterion measures. This is called the *cross-validation* and is undertaken because any relationship established in the first group might have been due to a mere chance fluctuation. A second study is done to be more confident that the relationship is there, and that it can be relied on subsequently when people who obtain high values on the predictor are actually selected for employment.

Obtaining a cross-validation sample is not always easy, especially if there is some urgency about getting the selection procedure into use as soon as possible. Under these circumstances, it is relatively common practice to collect data on both groups at once. Thus, if 100 persons are hired for a job, the total group may be split in half, with the initial validation done on one subsample and the cross-validation on the other. In any event, step 6 should be carried out. It is particularly crucial when a number of different predictor measures have been tested for a relation to a criterion, and only one or two have produced significant results. Under these circumstances, chance may well be operative, and the one or two predictors that seemed to work in the first group may not work in the second (33).

Case 2—Multiple Predictors

Most jobs are not so simple that a single measure of a single predictor is sufficient to yield maximum results. Normally, the best predictions are obtained when a number of predictors measuring a variety of characteristics are combined in some manner.

Steps 1 through 4 are essentially the same under multiple prediction as they are when predictors are validated separately. The major difference emerges in step 5. Some solution must be developed to the problem of combining the various factors in such a way as to maximally predict job success. There are a number of approaches to this problem.

MULTIPLE CORRELATION

In multiple correlation, the correlations between the predictors are computed, as well as the correlations between various predictors and the criterion. A multiple correlation coefficient is then derived that represents a maximal index of the relationship, one that automatically weights the separate predictors so as to yield the best prediction of the criterion. So-called *regression weights* may then be developed. The values obtained by an individual on the various measures may be multiplied by these weights and then combined to produce a maximum estimate of the chances for job success. Because this procedure is particularly sensitive to chance fluctuations, it is essential that step 6, cross-validation, be carried out.

ADDITIVE CORRELATION

Additive correlation is essentially an approximation procedure for the multiple correlation coefficient. It involves adding the values obtained by an individual on all the predictors together and then computing the correlation between this composite index and the criterion. Rather surprisingly, this technique does yield a close approximation to the results obtained from the multiple correlation approach.

MULTIPLE CUTOFF PREDICTION

In multiple cutoff prediction, the predictors are utilized one at a time rather than in combination. Thus, correlations are computed as in case 1 for each of the predictors with the cross-validation step included. Then the predictor that consistently produced the highest relationship with the criterion is identified, and some value is established as minimally satisfactory for employment. All candidates who fall below this value are screened out; all others continue as candidates. These remaining individuals must then meet a similar test based on the predictor having the second highest correlation with the criterion. This process of successive screening out is continued until all predictors exhibiting a consistent relationship to the criterion are exhausted. Those who at least equal the minimum satisfactory value on all predictors are hired. Normally, three or four such hurdles are all that are required. Beyond that, very little predictive power is added.

PROFILE MATCHING SYSTEM

In profile matching, the scores on all valid predictors for those particular employees who prove to be successful are averaged (5). These average scores then serve to describe what a successful employee would look like; they may be used to constitute an ideal profile for comparison purposes, as in Figure 10–1. Candidates are matched against this profile, and those whose scores most nearly approximate the ideal on the predictors included in the profile are selected for employment. The degree of match may be calculated by simply adding the absolute values of all deviations from the ideal values.

CLINICAL PREDICTION

With clinical prediction, the combining of predictors is accomplished by the personnel manager or psychologist on the basis of personal experience and without resort to statistical aids. The result is a decision that takes into account all the information available but weights the different measures and factors on a largely intuitive basis. Selection decisions of this kind have been successfully simulated on a computer (29) and at least under certain circumstances have proved as valid as those of a more statistical nature (15).

A study of decision processes used by experienced managers in selecting individuals for international assignments provides an example of clinical

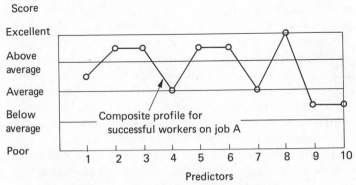

Figure 10–1. Example of a Hypothetical Profile Composed of the Average Scores for All Workers Considered Successful on Job A for Each of 10 Predictors.
Source: M. L. Blum and J. C. Naylor, Industrial Psychology: Its Theoretical and Social Foundations (New York: Harper & Row, Publishers, 1968), p. 72.

prediction (18). Such considerations as proved performance in a similar job, leadership skills and the ability to command respect, general perceptiveness and grasp of problems, and administrative skills were consistently weighted heavily in reaching the selection decision. In contrast, spouses' attitudes toward overseas assignment, past performance overseas, ability to work with foreign employees, and potential for advancement to a more responsible position were viewed as much less important and had relatively little influence on the assignment decision. Whether or not these are the most appropriate priorities, it is clear that the *process* involved here operates in a manner not unlike the use of statistical regression weights.

THE CONCURRENT MODEL

The concurrent approach is identical to that of longitudinal prediction, with one very important exception: The predictor and criterion measures are obtained at roughly the same point in time, usually on individuals who have been employed for a considerable period in the job to be studied. Thus, there is no long wait after the predictor data have been obtained to collect the criterion information. Either case 1 or case 2 may be applied, and the cross-validation is done on a second sample of employees selected from the current group.

This procedure is admittedly a shortcut and as such has certain rather marked deficiencies. For one thing, the motivation of present employees in taking a test or filling out a questionnaire or even in an interview situation may be quite different from that of job applicants: They may not try as hard. Yet the results are to be applied to an applicant group. This can introduce considerable error into the selection process, especially when measures of interests and certain kinds of personality tests are used. With physical examinations, intelligence tests, application blank data, and the like, it probably matters very little.

Second, the results obtained from certain measures may be largely a function of job tenure. Thus, indexes of job knowledge may yield higher scores the longer the person has been on the job. This can produce rather misleading results when the job knowledge measure is used as a predictor in an applicant group, none of whom have had prior experience in that particular type of work. If, however, one is aware of this problem, appropriate statistical procedures can be used to take the effects of job tenure out of the results. Thus, this potential source of error can be eliminated.

Finally, it is possible with some predictors that success or failure on the job may serve to determine the values obtained, rather than the reverse. For instance, in one study, decreases in personal satisfaction were found over eight years of employment among less successful managers, but there were increases among the more successful (7). Clearly, any predictor-criterion relationship involving personal satisfaction established from a concurrent study would not necessarily appear under the more exacting conditions of a longitudinal prediction study. This problem of "what causes what" is particularly common when measures of certain attitudes, interests, and personality characteristics are used as predictors. Often, a review of the relevant research literature will reveal whether or not a particular predictor should be trusted, based on evidence of concurrent validity.

Example of the Concurrent Model with Multiple Predictors

As good an example of the concurrent method as exists in the literature is provided by a study carried out at IBM (30). The first task of personnel researchers was to study thoroughly the role requirements of the lower-level factory manager jobs through interviews with a number of incumbents. These interviews suggested that knowledge of the work done was not as important as such factors as supervisory interest, decision-making skill, and employee orientation. Accordingly, a number of predictors in these areas were selected for trial and administered to the managers.

The predictors that gave any hint of possessing value are described in generalized terms in Table 10–1. Several other measures were used but have not been noted because of the consistently negative results. The criteria were, first, the average of the performance ratings made by a number of fellow managers. This index proved to be of only limited value because the peer ratings on the same manager were not generally in very close agreement. Second was a corrected salary figure that was constructed to eliminate the influence of seniority with the company and as a manager. Finally, there were ratings by superiors, which, like the peer ratings, suffered from considerable unreliability.

In the first sample of 42 managers, as Table 10–1 indicates, a number of predictors yielded some evidence of concurrent validity. Six measures pro-

Table 10–1. Correlation Coefficients Showing Relationships Between Predictors and Criteria. First Sample
$(N = 42)$

Predictors	Criteria		
	Peer Rating	Corrected Salary	Superior Rating
Intelligence test	.26	.40	.13
Personality test			
Ascendancy	.29	.28	.22
Responsibility	.02	.25	.09
Emotional stability	−.03	.08	−.07
Sociability	.08	.07	.07
Total score	.19	.39	.22
Supervisory test	.11	.04	.12
Biographical questionnaire	.03	.23	.19
Age	−.16	−.47	−.16

Source: Adapted from M. E. Spitzer and W. J. McNamara, "A Managerial Selection Study," *Personnel Psychology,* 17 : 32 (1964).

Table 10–2. Correlation Coefficients Showing Relationships Between Predictors and Criteria. Cross-validation
Sample (N = 42)

Predictors	Criteria		
	Peer Rating	Corrected Salary	Superior Rating
Intelligence test	.14	.36	.11
Personality test			
Ascendancy	−.02	.16	.11
Responsibility	−.17	.09	.07
Emotional stability	−.06	.23	.17
Sociability	−.06	−.14	−.12
Total score	−.09	.12	.04
Supervisory test	.13	.17	.33
Biographical questionnaire	.34	.35	.24
Age	.13	−.03	.25

Source: Adapted from M. E. Spitzer and W. J. McNamara, "A Managerial Selection Study,"
Personnel Psychology, 17 : 32 (1964).

duced coefficients above .20. The corrected salary criterion proved the most
predictable, as might be expected in view of the deficiencies in the other
indexes.

As so often happens, however, cross-validation washed out a number of
these initial findings—the relationships were not consistently present in
these managerial positions, and thus the predictors could not be relied upon
in a selection system. (See Table 10–2.) As a consequence, the measures of
ascendancy, responsibility, personality test total score, and age had to be
abandoned. Emotional stability and the supervisory test showed some new
strength as predictors, but because both were totally ineffective in the first
sample, these later findings had to be discounted. Only the intelligence
measure and the biographical questionnaire, which resembled an application blank and contained questions dealing with personal experiences and
interests, held up in cross-validation, primarily in relation to the salary
criterion.

When these two predictors were combined to yield a multiple-correlation
coefficient, the value obtained in the first managerial sample was .43. In the
cross-validation group, it was .41. If the top 25 per cent of the managers,
based on the weighted combination of intelligence and biographical measures, had been selected for these positions, 68 per cent of them would have
proved to be above-average performers. Thus, the new selection system
yields an improvement of 36 per cent over existing procedures. In view of
the nature of the predictors identified, there is little reason to believe a
longitudinal study would have produced differing results.

An idea of what such a longitudinal study can produce may be derived
from the data of Table 10–3. In this instance, biographical data obtained
prior to hiring were analyzed, related to subsequent success criteria, cross-

Table 10–3. Probability of Success and Failure for Management Consultants According to Initial Score on a Biographical Questionnaire

Biographical Questionnaire Score	Number of Consultants in Score Range	Per Cent Unsuccessful— Separated Without Election to Partnership	Per Cent Successful— Elected to Partnership
22–26	13	38	62
17–21	55	53	47
12–16	73	77	23
7–11	32	94	6
2–6	7	100	0
Total Ns	180	127	53

validated, and finally combined into a predictive score (19). The criterion is whether or not the consultant achieved the goal of election to partnership in the firm. Most of those who were separated either were asked to leave or had good reason to believe they would not be elected. Although high scores on the biographical questionnaire do not guarantee success, low scores carry a very high probability of failure. A cutting score between 11 and 12 would assure that practically no potentially successful candidate would be lost. On the other hand, if fewer partners were needed, a higher cutting score could be employed.

OTHER APPROACHES IN VALIDATION

Although the methods described above are the most widely used in personnel selection, certain other approaches to validation require discussion. Several of these approaches have taken on particular significance because they have been mentioned in the various guidelines for compliance with equal employment opportunity legislation issued by federal enforcement agencies. Others represent extensions or variants of the basic criterion-related approaches that have particular value in special circumstances or for solving certain kinds of problems.

Content and Construct Validity

There are two types of rational validation for selection procedures that are recognized in compliance guidelines (3, 31). The first of these, _content validity_, involves a systematic study of a job to establish the knowledge, skills, and behaviors that are required; an appropriate selection procedure is then developed on a judgmental basis. Most of the tests of job knowledge utilized by the government in connection with meeting civil service requirements rely on such content validity. Another example might be a typing test used to select people for jobs in a typing pool.

It is important to distinguish this approach from _face validity_. Content validity involves a judgment by an expert that the selection procedure is in fact job-related. Face validity, on the other hand, involves merely an impression of appropriateness on the part of the person completing a measure. Thus, numerical items may be written with reference to actual store products and prices to make them look appropriate to applicants for positions as retail sales clerks. This is face validity. But the computations involved could be so much more complex than those actually required on the job that the test items are totally irrelevant. Under such circumstances, one would have face validity without content validity. Normally, content-valid procedures do appear face valid, but the reverse need not be true.

Construct validity refers not so much to job behaviors and skills as to underlying characteristics of the job performer, such as verbal ability or achievement motivation. For construct validity to apply, the theoretical construct must be well defined, the selection procedure must be known to be a measure of the construct, and an important aspect of job behavior must involve the construct. Establishing such validity involves rational inference from a body of research. Thus, a measure of achievement motivation must be shown to relate to other measures of the same construct while having less relationship to other motivational constructs—social motivation, conformity motivation, and the like. At the same time, there must be good reason to believe the construct is important in a certain kind of work, as achievement motivation is in entrepreneurial activities, for instance. In many cases, this may in fact require the conduct of criterion-related studies, either predictive or concurrent (3).

Synthetic Validity

One of the major disadvantages of the longitudinal and concurrent models is that both require a relatively large number of employees doing similar work. They are thus of limited value in small companies and in larger firms wherever the number of people employed in a given type of activity is small. The synthetic validity model was developed for application in such situations (9, 33). The approach is analogous to that of the methods engineer who, when developing a standard time for a specific job, combines the various estimated times for separate elements of the operation.

First, various work elements, or job requirements, must be identified, using job analysis procedures. Then, the predictor measures must be validated on a number of jobs having a particular work element or job requirement in common. If a sizable relationship between the values on a given predictor and those on some criterion index can be established for these jobs having a common characteristic, then the predictor can be used in selecting individuals for all jobs with the same work elements or requirements. The essence of the approach is that a high level of accomplishment on a predictor is almost invariably associated with a high level on a certain type of job behavior. If this can be established, the predictor can be used for any job where the behavior is required and important. Essentially, what is involved is the combining of a number of different jobs with something in common to obtain a large enough group for study so that criterion-related validation is possible.

The Decision Model in Selection

A second approach that has fostered considerable discussion, even though because of its complexity it has not been widely applied, derives from mathematical decision theory (10, 11). According to this view, the ultimate purpose of any predictor is to assist in making a *decision* as to what should be done with a given applicant or candidate, and therefore the soundest approach to evaluating a measure is through determining the benefits that accrue to the total organization as a result of a particular decision. The utility concept is used to provide an index of value. Utility is defined in terms of the benefits that accrue from a given set of decisions, less the total costs incurred in the decision-making process.

Although a detailed mathematical treatment is not contemplated here, it is possible to describe the basic elements of this approach. There is, first, certain information regarding the individual—interview data, a completed application blank, test scores, and the like. Second, there are various treatments that may be utilized depending on the decision made—hire the applicant; reject the applicant; collect further information. Third, the outcomes of decisions are expressed in terms of various criterion values, which may be based on ratings and objective indexes. Finally, there are the utilities attached to the various outcomes; the benefits, less the costs, derived from having an individual perform effectively in a given type of work or the net benefit derived from rejecting an individual with somewhat different characteristics.

Probabilities are attached to these factors and a matrix constructed, so that it is possible to evaluate each applicant in terms of his expected value to the firm should he be hired for a particular position. One difficulty with this approach is that good measures of the utilities associated with various decision outcomes may not be available. Solutions to this problem have been developed, however, and it may well be that the future will see a much wider application of the decision model in personnel selection.

Moderator Variables

Moderator variables are characteristics used to divide a sample of employees into two or more groups, so that predictor-criterion correlations may be calculated in each group separately. The reason for doing this is that a predictor may be very effective in one group, but when this group is combined with another in which the predictor is not effective, the overall result can be useless for selection purposes. Thus, for a group as a whole, the predictor-criterion correlation might be .19. When this group is divided into two subgroups, however, on the basis of some moderator variable, the results might be as follows:

subgroup 1 $r = .48$
subgroup 2 $r = .04$

In this instance, the initial correlation of .19 would appear to be of little practical significance; the correlation of .04 for subgroup 2 is even worse. But for subgroup 1, a truly effective predictor has been identified (provided cross-validation yields a similar result). Thus, one would use this predictor for selecting among job applicants of the type represented by subgroup 1 and then would attempt to identify some other predictor that could be used with applicants of the subgroup 2 type.

A number of different types of moderator variables have been used. Under the impact of equal employment opportunity legislation, race has been used often, with separate validities calculated for blacks and whites. Job satisfaction has been utilized to separate out subgroups that are more and less satisfied. Various measures of motivation have also been used so as to permit validation of predictors separately for highly motivated workers and for those with less motivation.

Perhaps the greatest problem with this approach is that it may identify a number of good predictors for one subgroup yet leave another subgroup practically devoid of useful measures for selection purposes. It may prove impossible to find procedures that can be shown to be valid for a sizable subset within the normal applicant population. In addition, the use of moderator variables requires a large number of individuals to start with. By the time two or three subgroups have been formed for both first and cross-validation samples, each group may be so small that the results have little meaning. Where sufficient individuals are available for study, however, the use of moderator variables can be a very valuable adjunct to the longitudinal and concurrent models (1).

THE LIMITATIONS OF SELECTION

It should be apparent from the correlations between predictors and criteria noted previously, such as those in Tables 10–1 and 10–2, that available selection techniques are not a panacea. Effectively utilized, they can increase the level of goal attainment in a company, but instances of performance failure and individual discontent will inevitably remain. There are certain inherent limitations in selection models and technology that may never be completely overcome.

The Use of Selection Procedures

One major problem, and this will become increasingly apparent after the discussions in Chapters 12 and 13, is that the available predictors are far from perfect. They do not always reveal a characteristic that is important in determining job behavior, nor do they consistently specify correctly the degree to which it may be present. Interviews, psychological tests, physical examinations, and all the other techniques may not yield the information they should, and on occasion they may produce erroneous information.

Another difficulty is associated not so much with the techniques themselves as with the people who use them. Human error is almost inevitable, even though it can be reduced through effective selection and training of personnel managers and workers. In one instance, the author had a sample of several hundred answer sheets for the psychological tests used in a company's selection battery rescored at a later date. Although in most cases the divergence was not large, there were tests that had clearly been scored with considerable error—sufficiently so to produce an inappropriate selection decision. Similar errors, because of the misunderstanding of an interview statement or the misreading of some physical measure, occur more often than is generally recognized.

Considerations of economy are also relevant. The physical exam is a good example. Increasingly, medical science is developing complex procedures for the detection of various diseases. Many of these diagnostic aids are extremely costly and require highly trained personnel to use them; some necessitate hospitalization during the period that tests are carried out. There can be no question that these techniques have considerable value in predicting subsequent events. Yet companies rarely use them in connection with the preemployment physical examination. They are too costly in time and money, and the disorders they identify are frequently rather rare. As a result, a decision has been made in many instances to risk future absenteeism and perhaps ineffective job behavior rather than invest in the available selection techniques.

The investment decision here is analogous to that involved in a deferred maintenance policy as applied to equipment and machinery. Instead of attempting to spot potential breakdowns and correcting the situation, one allows the breakdown to develop, on the assumption that the resulting costs will be less than those that preventive maintenance would necessitate. Many companies have not adopted psychological testing programs and other selection procedures for much the same type of reason. They assume that a sizable investment in selection procedures is not warranted, because any difficulties that develop can be handled later. Thus, emphasis is concentrated on the output processes rather than on organizational inputs.

In addition to these limitations associated with the selection procedures themselves, there are other problems. One of the major reasons for the failure of selection predictions is that people change in unexpected ways. A physical disorder may develop, personality changes may occur, and so on. Marital difficulties may produce discontent that is subsequently transferred to the job. Or financial problems may arise that could not have been anticipated but that leave the employee preoccupied and upset. The list of possibilities is endless. The point is that things happen to people over the years of employment that leave them changed individuals. When these are added to the normal alterations associated with aging, it is obvious that selection procedures have a potential that realistically must be considered somewhat limited. Certainly, prediction in the short run is much better than it is over a long period.

This problem of change is not restricted to the individual himself, however. Jobs change, too. A person who was quite effective on an assembly line may not do so well when his job is automated more fully. A salesman who can sell one type of product in one market may run into difficulty when competitive pressures force the company to shift to a somewhat different consumer market or product. It is difficult if not impossible to select for the jobs of the future, especially when at the same time one must select for the still existing jobs of the present.

Change may also occur across jobs rather than within them. That is, a person may shift from job to job within the company rather than be faced with a change in the role prescriptions of a given position. Some amount of career change is the general rule rather than the exception. Certainly, this is the case among college-educated employees and within the ranks of management. This matter of career prediction is one of the most difficult in the entire field of personnel selection. It requires that predictors be validated against career criteria and that longitudinal studies extend over long time periods. It is not too difficult to successfully predict whether a person will do well during his training period or in his initial placement with the company. It is quite another matter to predict that he will perform effectively 20 years hence in a position whose level and nature are something of a mystery. Yet there is no question that career selection of this kind is what most companies need, at least for a sizable proportion of the people they hire.

A final source of error has already been mentioned in a different context. Two managers may not evaluate their subordinates in exactly the same way, using the same criteria and standards. This is particularly true when organization planning and job analysis have had only minimal application, with the result that role prescriptions are ambiguous and uncertain. A worker who is considered satisfactory by one superior may be rated considerably lower by another, even though his behavior has not changed. Two workers whose role behaviors are almost identical can be evaluated quite differently. Obviously, when criteria are unstable and unreliable in this manner, selection techniques will not come out looking very effective.

All these limitations are superimposed on the constraints imposed by the available manpower pool and the restrictions created by the nature and extent of the recruiting process. No selection procedure can yield an effective work force if the recruitment procedures cannot, or do not, provide an adequate group of candidates from which selection can occur. Recruitment, then, becomes the sine qua non for selection. If the number of possible hires equals the number of jobs to be filled, there is no selection. Therefore, it is crucial to develop recruiting procedures that will provide a sufficiently large and varied candidate manpower pool so that the selection techniques can at least achieve their maximum potential. Actually, any valid selection technique will perform quite effectively if it can be used to skim the cream off a very large candidate group. As the number of candidates available begins to approach the number to be hired, however, a personnel strategy emphasizing input processes becomes less and less appropriate.

Self-selection

The procedures considered to this point assume that the decision to hire is made by a manager who possesses information regarding the candidate, the job, and the relationship between the two. But what if the candidate makes the decision? What if the candidate is provided with detailed information regarding the job, and perhaps even regarding validity relationships? How is this kind of self-selection likely to work out? Here we are in a kind of no-man's-land between recruiting and selection, where the candidate supply could be severely restricted simply because those who might otherwise be candidates are not any longer, since they possess information that causes them to select themselves out. Clearly, selection on the part of the company can be limited under such circumstances, if it occurs at all, as a result of the reduced number of people who really want the job.

One method of providing candidates with the requisite information for self-selection is through a computerized information system (28). Another approach that has been used is a detailed and highly realistic film (32). Whether such procedures actually serve to reduce the candidate pool appears to depend on the unemployment rate. If there are few jobs available, the provision of detailed job information makes little difference; candidates will accept the job if it is offered, even if they know enough about it to have serious doubts regarding their interest. On the other hand, even under conditions of limited employment opportunities, providing information to permit valid self-selection can relate to job survival. Those who make realistic self-selection decisions based on comprehensive knowledge of the job are more likely to want to stay.

The answer to our question appears to be that self-selection is no more valid than any other approach. People take jobs they do not want because of pressures in the labor market, and they may miscalculate their own interests and capabilities. Ultimately, those who make employment decisions based on realistic information are more likely to stay on (32), but there is no certainty that they will make valid self-selection decisions. In spite of some strong advocacy of the self-selection approach (12), the limitations of selection are no less in evidence when that approach is used.

SELECTION AND FAIR EMPLOYMENT

In Chapter 5, the various laws, court decisions, executive orders, and governmental guidelines that affect input processes were discussed. The overall impact of the law in this area on personnel practice has been sizable; in particular, actions taken to reduce racial and sex discrimination have had an impact on practices with regard to psychological testing. In actuality, the legal enactments relate equally to all types of selection procedures, but the focus of enforcement to date has been primarily on testing and on various application blank items.

Because judgments made by courts and federal regulatory agencies with regard to discrimination in employment can result in very large payments in the form of damages to the parties discriminated against, and since the cost of a legal defense can be considerable, the net effect of FEP legislation has been to raise decision making with regard to selection procedures to the highest corporate levels. Here is an area where personnel management can have a clear and highly visible impact on corporate profits. Fair employment legislation has greatly enhanced the importance of personnel expertise.

Validation Requirements

The consideration that has contributed most to the implication of psychological testing in FEP matters is the finding that black applicants on the average usually score well below whites on various ability tests (8). Research on this point was discussed in Chapter 4. As a consequence of this situation, an employer who wished to minimize the number of blacks on his payroll could do so merely by requiring that all people hired score above a given level on a test of intellectual ability, without regard to whether the test was job related (had predictive or concurrent validity) or not. By setting the cutting score quite high, one can ensure in most labor markets that a much greater proportion of white than black applicants will "pass." In some instances, it might even be possible to hire no blacks at all, because none apply who score at the required level in the period during which sufficient whites are being screened to fill the available openings.

It should be emphasized that a low proportion of minority group members is not in and of itself evidence of discrimination. Only if the existing labor market for a given occupational group, when defined in a reasonable manner, proves to contain a considerably higher proportion of minority group members than a company's labor force is there a basis for a charge of unfair hiring practices. If under such circumstances the company is using selection procedures that contribute to this situation, it must show that they are in fact job related—that is, that any tendency to screen out minority group members that the use of the selection procedure introduces is justified, because these individuals could not be expected to perform the work effectively. In practice, this often means that the company must demonstrate validity among both whites and minority group members (2, 3).

Differential Validity

One response to governmental pressures has been to cease using techniques such as psychological tests or to suspend their use temporarily. Some companies have chosen this route on the grounds that they are not sure what will satisfy legal requirements and that complex validation studies of the type required are too expensive to justify the costs (23). On the other hand, if validity for blacks and whites can be demonstrated, a company is then in a good position to protect itself against any charge of discrimination that a government examiner may bring. Thus, an input strategy that emphasizes validation can well be a much more effective approach than merely abandoning tests or application blanks. In view of the sizable increases in validation research over the last 10 years, it appears to be a strategy that has achieved widespread acceptance (22).

In essence, validating separately for blacks and whites or males and females involves the use of the moderator variable design where race or sex is the moderator. One might ask why this is necessary. Would not a measure that proves valid for one group be expected to be valid for the other? The answer is that over a wide range of circumstances this does turn out to be the case (6, 20, 21). However, there are exceptions.

Table 10–4 provides an example of such differential validity. In this instance, the test is highly predictive of turnover for whites $(r = .34)$; the high scorers leave. For blacks, the direction of the correlation changes completely, although the coefficient is low $(r = -.10)$; the high scorers tend to stay (25). Findings of this kind are not common, but they do tend to support the requirement that measures be validated separately for any groups that

Table 10–4. Number and Percentages of Employees Remaining After 10 Weeks or More by Wonderlic Test Score

Group	Test-score Range	Number Hired	Number Remaining	Per Cent Remaining
Whites	32 and above	40	16	40.6
	27–31	41	19	46.3
	24–26	32	19	59.4
	12–23	36	30	83.3
Blacks	27 and above	15	11	73.3
	23–26	12	9	75.0
	20–22	11	9	81.8
	12–19	13	9	69.2

Source: E. Ruda and L. E. Albright, "Racial Differences on Selection Instruments Related to Subsequent Job Performance," Personnel Psychology, 21 : 38 (1968).

may be discriminated against, at least until we have a clearer picture of when such differences in validity coefficients can be expected.

FACTORS INFLUENCING THE USE OF AN INPUT-ORIENTED STRATEGY

One factor that may influence decisions with regard to emphasizing recruiting and selection as major components of a company's overall personnel strategy is the pressure exerted as a result of FEP legislation. If the cost of doing validation studies appears excessive, or if after extensive study valid, nondiscriminatory predictors cannot be identified, then a firm may want to resort to a strategy of hiring practically anyone who applies. Investments in mediator and/or output processes would then be used to upgrade the company labor force.

Legal considerations are not the only factors that may influence decisions regarding the degree of input-process emphasis, however. A number of other factors must be taken into account. Among these, the invasion of privacy issue, union positions, and the matter of return on investment require particular attention.

The Invasion of Privacy Question

Industry generally has been under considerable ethical pressure in the area of selection. Several congressional investigations have been conducted with a view to imposing constraints on the use of psychological tests, although no legislation has been passed. Also, a number of books and articles have been written that attack the use of tests, as well as of computerized personnel data banks (13).

A major concern in all these instances is that personality testing and related techniques represent an invasion of privacy: that individuals are called upon to reveal things that they might not wish to reveal; that they often do not even know what they are revealing about themselves; that information obtained is not held to a confidential psychologist-applicant relationship, but imparted to a third party, the company's management. These actions are felt to be unethical. Those who attack such procedures and who feel that perhaps legal constraints should be imposed in this area believe that individual freedoms are being violated.

What seems to be not clearly understood in all this is that the selection situation is not synonymous with the physician-patient relationship or that of lawyer to client. Except with self-selection, it is not the applicant who wants information or assistance, but the company. Furthermore, the applicant is aware of the purpose of the various selection procedures. If he takes a test, he recognizes that this experience is germane to his being considered for employment. The applicant presumably wants something from the potential employer and understands quite clearly that he must provide certain information to have a chance of obtaining what he wants. Thus, he trades information about himself for the opportunity of being hired. This is a long way from coercion, and it is coerced invasion of privacy, where the individual has no choice, that is normally considered unethical.

This is not to say that information obtained from psychological tests, physical examinations, or other selection tools, whether stored in a computer data bank or not, cannot be misused by unscrupulous individuals. There are important security problems here, and there can be a major ethical problem as well if information is used for some purpose other than that anticipated by the applicant, that is, the evaluation of his qualifications for employment. To protect the public against such misuse of employment data, psychologists and others have devoted considerable time and energy to the formulation and the enforcement of appropriate ethical controls. Nevertheless, the pressures in this area are a reality, and should they derive from sources, such as consumers, lending institutions, and the like, that are of central significance to a company, they can be sufficiently strong to prevail. There is evidence to indicate that those who are by nature shy and retiring, critical of others, and relatively unassertive are particularly likely to be concerned regarding invasion of their privacy in the employment situation (24).

Union Pressures

Another source of pressure to limit or eliminate the use of tests, and on occasion other selection techniques as well, can be a union (14). This may be because the union wishes to establish seniority as the only basis for promotion, assignment, and layoff. The existence of test data would provide objective support for ability or merit claims and thus might be used to override seniority considerations (4). In addition, some unions have been able to exert considerable influence, if not outright control, over the hiring process, in spite of the outlawing of the closed shop. To the extent selection techniques might threaten this influence, they have been opposed.

Some firms have agreed to contract terms that effectively proscribe testing and other selection techniques as well. In general, such agreement appears to occur in a context of minimal input emphasis, and thus the company is giving away something it cares little about, probably to gain some concession viewed as more significant. On the other hand, agreeing to severe constraints on selection procedures can prove to be self-defeating, if at some later point an input-oriented strategy appears to be called for. Certainly, if a company desires to utilize an input strategy for unionized jobs, every effort should be made to retain as much freedom in the use of selection techniques as possible. Where this freedom is severely constrained by union agreements, some alternative strategy should be emphasized.

Return on the Investment

Throughout this chapter, a considerable amount of evidence regarding the validity of various measurement procedures has been presented. There can be little doubt that selection tools offer an opportunity to regulate the human input to an organization in such a way as to make a very sizable contribution to goal attainment. Given adequate research, it is possible for management to contribute a great deal toward both productivity and organizational maintenance through the use of appropriate selection techniques. These procedures do work; not perfectly, but they work.

Further evidence on this point, in dollars and cents terms, comes from an early study carried out on the selection of telephone operators in the San Francisco area (26). A test battery containing numerical and clerical ability measures was used as a predictor. The savings attributable to the fact that many operators who would have failed if hired did not have to be trained were calculated. The following figures correct these training savings for the additional recruiting costs the tests introduce. Scores on the test battery may range from 0 to 80, and the minimum score for hiring could, of course, be set at any point between, depending on the availability of applicants in the labor market and the degree of selectivity desired. This study was published in 1956; the savings would be much greater today. Two studies involving the use of weighted application blanks indicate savings of $234,000 (27) and $250,000 (17) in the 1973–1974 period.

Minimum Score for Hiring	Net Saving ($)
30	8,000
40	35,000
50	47,000
60	50,000

It is apparent from these data that good selection procedures developed with reference to organizationally meaningful criteria can yield very sizable savings. The real strength of human measurement techniques in selection is that when correctly validated they place primary emphasis on merit rather than on the biases and moods of the person doing the selection.

Given this potential for both validity and savings, when should a major investment in input strategies be attempted? At least one such condition occurs when people are prepared for their work primarily outside the organization. This would normally be true of professionals, secretaries, and many other occupational groups who learn most of what they will do on the job in some segment of the educational system. Here stress should be placed on attracting the best possible people and selecting from among them those most likely to succeed, thus investing disproportionately more in input processes. On the other hand, when jobs requiring considerable knowledge and skill that are practically unique to the particular company or industry are involved, the input emphasis can be decreased considerably. What is most needed in this situation is the best possible internal training effort.

Another consideration is whether an input emphasis can really be made to work. Is it possible for the company to recruit top talent? Can really effective selection devices be developed and applied? In many instances, accomplishing these goals at reasonable cost is much easier for larger firms than small ones. The larger companies are more likely to be widely known and thus have a recruiting edge based on goodwill. They are also more likely to be able to justify the personnel research staff needed to conduct fruitful validation studies. In small companies, such research is more difficult because of small numbers of employees in the various occupations and limited numbers of new hires. Also, the total number of employees and hires may not be sufficient to warrant the investment in personnel research. Given these considerations, many small companies would do well to emphasize strategies other than those of an input-oriented nature, unless their employees are primarily professionals.

QUESTIONS

1. What are the major differences between concurrent and predictive validity? What possible sources of error in interpreting the results does the predictive approach avoid?
2. Differentiate among construct, content, and face validity. Which is more likely to elicit employee acceptance of a testing program? Which is more likely to elicit acceptance by an industrial psychologist?
3. What are the major limitations of selection? Self-selection has been proposed as a panacea for these limitations of selection. Compare it against each of the limitations and indicate your conclusions.
4. Why do you suppose the matter of differential validity has become such a source of controversy? Why should EEOC favor it, and many employers oppose it?
5. If you were faced with the problem of convincing the management of a company that has heretofore hired almost entirely on a first-come-first-served basis to invest in an extensive selection program, what arguments would you present? What counterarguments would you anticipate from the company's management?

REFERENCES

1. Ash, P., and L. P. Kroeker. "Personnel Selection, Classification, and Placement." *Annual Review of Psychology,* 26 (1975), 481–507.
2. Bassford, G. L. "Job Testing—Alternative to Employment Quotas." *Business Horizons,* 17 (1974), No. 1, 37–47.
3. Baxter, B. "Review of Selected Federal and Professional Positions on the Use of Tests in Employment." *American Psychological Association Journal Supplement Abstract Service Document,* Ms. No. 802, 1974.
4. Biddle, R. E., and L. M. Jacobs. "Under What Circumstances Can a Unionized Company Use Testing for Promotion?" *Personnel Psychology,* 21 (1968), 149–177.

5. Blum, M. L., and J. C. Naylor. *Industrial Psychology: Its Theoretical and Social Foundations.* New York: Harper & Row, Publishers, 1968.

6. Boehm, V. R. "Negro-White Differences in Validity of Employment and Training Selection Procedures: Summary of Research Evidence." *Journal of Applied Psychology,* 56 (1972), 33–39.

7. Bray, D. W., R. J. Campbell, and D. L. Grant. *Formative Years in Business: A Long-term AT&T Study of Managerial Lives.* New York: John Wiley & Sons, Inc., 1974.

8. Bray, D. W., and J. L. Moses. "Personnel Selection." *Annual Review of Psychology,* 23 (1972), 545–576.

9. Campbell, J. P., M. D. Dunnette, E. E. Lawler, and K. E. Weick. *Managerial Behavior, Performance, and Effectiveness.* New York: McGraw-Hill Book Company, 1970.

10. Cronbach, L. J., and G. C. Gleser. *Psychological Tests and Personnel Decisions.* Urbana, Ill.: University of Illinois Press, 1965.

11. Cronbach, L. J., G. C. Gleser, H. Nanda, and N. Rajarantam. *The Dependability of Behavioral Measurements.* New York: John Wiley & Sons, Inc., 1972.

12. Fine, S. A. "What's Wrong with the Hiring System?" *Organizational Dynamics,* 4 (1975), No. 2, 55–67.

13. Goldstein, R. C., and R. L. Nolan. "Personal Privacy Versus the Corporate Computer." *Harvard Business Review,* 53 (1975), No. 2, 62–70.

14. Hagglund, G., and D. Thompson. *Psychological Testing and Industrial Relations.* Iowa City: University of Iowa, 1969.

15. Holt, R. R. "Yet Another Look at Clinical and Statistical Prediction: Or, Is Clinical Psychology Worthwhile?" *American Psychologist,* 25 (1970), 337–349.

16. Korman, A. K. *Industrial and Organizational Psychology.* Englewood Cliffs, N.J.: Prentice-Hall, Inc., 1971.

17. Lee, R., and J. M. Booth. "A Utility Analysis of a Weighted Application Blank Designed to Predict Turnover for Clerical Employees." *Journal of Applied Psychology,* 59 (1974), 516–518.

18. Miller, E. L. "The International Selection Decision: A Study of Some Dimensions of Managerial Behavior in the Selection Decision Process." *Academy of Management Journal,* 16 (1973), 239–252.

19. Miner, J. B. "Success in Management Consulting and the Concept of Eliteness Motivation." *Academy of Management Journal,* 14 (1971), 367–378.

20. Miner, J. B. "Psychological Testing and Fair Employment Practices: A Testing Program That Does Not Discriminate." *Personnel Psychology,* 27 (1974), 49–62.

21. O'Connor, E. J., K. N. Wexley, and R. A. Alexander. "Single-group Validity: Fact or Fallacy?" *Journal of Applied Psychology,* 60 (1975), 352–355.

22. Peterson, D. J. "The Impact of Duke Power on Testing." *Personnel,* 51 (1974), No. 2, 30–37.
23. Prentice-Hall, Inc. "P-H/ASPA Survey: Employee Testing and Selection Procedures—Where Are They Headed?" *Personnel Management: Policies and Practices.* Englewood Cliffs, N.J.: Prentice-Hall, Inc., 1975, 649–680.
24. Rosenbaum, B. L. "Attitude Toward Invasion of Privacy in the Personnel Selection Process and Job Applicant Demographic and Personality Correlates." *Journal of Applied Psychology,* 58 (1973), 333–338.
25. Ruda, E., and L. E. Albright. "Racial Differences on Selection Instruments Related to Subsequent Job Performance." *Personnel Psychology,* 21 (1968), 31–41.
26. Rusmore, J. T., and G. J. Toorenaar. "Reducing Training Costs by Employment Testing." *Personnel Psychology,* 9 (1956), 39–44.
27. Schmidt, F. L., and B. Hoffman. "An Empirical Comparison of Three Methods of Assessing the Utility of a Selection Device." *Journal of Industrial and Organizational Psychology,* 1 (1973), 1–11.
28. Smith, R. D. "Models for Personnel Selection Decisions." *Personnel Journal,* 52 (1973), 688–695.
29. Smith, R. D., and P. S. Greenlaw. "Simulation of a Psychological Decision Process in Personnel Selection." *Management Science,* 13 (1967), 409–419.
30. Spitzer, M. E., and W. J. McNamara. "A Managerial Selection Study." *Personnel Psychology,* 17 (1964), 19–40.
31. Stone, C. H., and F. L. Ruch. "Selection, Interviewing, and Testing," in D. Yoder and H. G. Heneman (eds.), *Staffing Policies and Strategies.* Washington, D.C.: Bureau of National Affairs, Inc., 1974.
32. Wanous, J. P. "Effects of a Realistic Job Preview on Job Acceptance, Job Attitudes, and Job Survival." *Journal of Applied Psychology,* 58 (1973), 327–332.
33. Zedeck, S., and M. R. Blood. *Foundations of Behavioral Science Research in Organizations.* Monterey, Calif.: Brooks/Cole Publishing Co., 1974.

11 The Recruitment Process

The first step of the input procedure involves the process of recruitment. As noted in Chapter 10, unless an organization has more qualified candidates for jobs than there are positions to fill, there is no selection; any person who can do the work, at any level of performance, will be hired. For the personnel function to maximize its contribution to organizational effectiveness, it must undertake programs that will ensure there will be a pool of potential employees with the education, skills, or other requirements of the available jobs. Without some kind of recruiting efforts—internal, external, or both—there is no way a company can continue to achieve its goals.

The nature and extent of the recruiting program depends on a multitude of factors, including the skill levels required, the state of the labor market and general economic conditions, and the image of the employer in the outside world. A company that has a general reputation of paying fair wages, providing good employee benefits, and taking an interest in employee welfare may attract all the job applicants it needs without going to any extra recruiting effort at all. Furthermore, small companies that hire only a few people a year may not need to do more than spread the word around the plant or office that there is a job vacancy.

In recent years, however, societal pressures and governmental regulations have added a new dimension to the recruitment process. This is the concept of *affirmative action*; as this concept has been applied to recruiting, it has resulted in programs requiring employers to go out and actively seek job applicants from groups of people who might not otherwise apply for employment, because they have been denied such employment in the past. Companies that in the past did not have to engage in extensive recruiting efforts are now frequently required to do so; these affirmative action recruiting programs are discussed in the last section of this chapter.

RECRUITING STRATEGY

The appropriate strategy for a company to follow in its recruiting activities is dictated by the results of its activities in the areas of organization and human resource planning as discussed in Chapter 6. If the plans indicate no anticipated growth and little attrition in the near future as a result of retirements or other known factors, recruiting can be kept at a minimal level. Where the opposite is true—if a major expansion is under way and/or large numbers of employees are approaching retirement age, for example —then major recruiting programs are called for.

For the nation's largest employers—including the federal and state governments and utilities and transportation companies, as well as the biggest manufacturing companies—recruiting is a continuous large-scale enterprise. These employers know from experience, and from their human resource planning data, that they are likely to have hundreds or even thousands of openings for certain job categories every year. It is only the medium-sized or small company that can afford to turn its recruiting efforts off and on; whether active recruiting programs will be required or not frequently depends on the nature of the labor market.

The results of a classic study of the effect of labor market conditions on employers' recruiting practices are shown in Table 11-1. As the results indicate, the tighter the labor market, the wider the area from which companies look for new employees (28). A more recent study of labor market conditions and employer hiring standards also emphasizes the effect of outside economic conditions on recruiting needs. This study indicates that in an area with relatively high unemployment, employees hired had higher levels of schooling and higher performance on preemployment tests than did a similar group of employees in the same jobs for the same company at a location in an area of relatively low unemployment (17). The implications for the company recruiter are that the standards specified as a requirement for filling a particular job may have to be modified, and the recruiting source changed accordingly. If it is no longer feasible to require a high-

Table 11–1. Recruiting Practices and the Firm's Position in the Labor Market

Degree of Tightness in the Labor Market	Sources Used in Recruiting	Area Covered in Recruiting
Most loose	Direct hiring	Immediate vicinity
Intermediate	Unions Friends and relatives Private and public agencies	Part of the metropolitan industrial area
Tight	Advertising Nearby special sources (business colleges, private agencies with employer paying fee)	All of the metropolitan area
Most tight	Labor scouting	Regional and national

Source: F. T. Malm, "Recruiting Patterns and the Functioning of Labor Markets," *Industrial and Labor Relations Review*, 7 : 518 (1954).

school diploma or a college degree for certain jobs, then the recruiter will need to go to sources other than high schools and colleges.

Use of the Job Specification

Information derived from human resource planning indicates the *extent* to which recruiting programs should be undertaken; the *nature* of the programs, or what recruiting should be emphasized, are dictated by the results of job analysis. In particular, the job specification, as described in Chapter 7, for positions in which vacancies are anticipated provides the clues to where recruiting efforts are most likely to be successful.

In the previous chapter, it was noted that the more information candidates are given about the realities of the job they apply for, the lower the turnover rate among those who accept employment. It has been suggested that part of the recruiter's job is to give prospective employees as clear a picture as possible of what they can look forward to if they are hired (39). One way to do this is to include more details in the job specification to help job seekers make intelligent choices. A "multiperspective" job specification, which has been advocated by one writer, would emphasize the tasks of the job, the personal content of the job, and the extent and types of relationships necessary to perform the job effectively (36). This type of job specification would provide a clearer definition of the role of the position as well as the tasks of the position.

At the point at which an opening occurs for a specific position, most employers use a special job-requisition form filled out by the supervisor of the unit that has the vacancy; the form usually requires the approval of a higher-level manager (42). In addition to information from the job specification for the position, particularly educational qualifications or skills required, the job requisition indicates the starting date and pay rate, whether it is a permanent or temporary, full-time or part-time job, and whether it can be filled by an internal transfer. The receipt of the job requisition in the company employment office is the recruiter's signal for action.

Recruitment from Within

When a vacancy occurs, the normal practice in many firms is to carry out a search within the company to identify possible candidates before turning to the various outside sources. Individuals may be considered for *promotion* into the position or for *lateral transfer* or in some cases for *demotion,* although the latter is relatively rare.

Recruitment from within of this kind appears to be the primary method of obtaining candidates at the management level (28). There are some firms, however, that place considerable reliance on outside sources in filling managerial vacancies. Management inventory charts of the kind discussed in Chapter 8 are particularly helpful when an effort is being made to recruit within the company. If an up-to-date employee information system is maintained, it can be of considerable assistance in rapidly identifying those with the necessary qualifications.

At the lower levels, however, seniority lists may well exercise considerable control over the internal recruiting process. As indicated in Chapter 9, many companies are required by the terms of their contract with the union to obtain candidates from among the longest-service employees within the particular seniority unit where the vacancy exists.

It is also common practice below the management level to post vacancies by advertising them widely throughout the firm. A candidate pool is then constructed out of those who bid on the advertised position. This procedure has the disadvantage that many well-qualified individuals may fail to volunteer for consideration because they fear reprisal on the part of their superiors. This is a particular problem where the change in position would represent a lateral transfer. Many supervisors do, in fact, consider such an attempt to leave their unit as a slap in the face on the part of the subordinate.

A closely related procedure is the talent search. Usually, this is used when a company anticipates a number of future vacancies at the highly skilled and lower management levels and wishes to recruit candidates for promotion from within the firm. The search is widely advertised, and employees are asked to notify the personnel office if they wish to be considered for various training programs that will qualify them for promotion. Those who indicate interest are administered an extensive battery of psychological tests and evaluated in various other ways. The people finally selected are given appropriate training and then placed in a reserve talent pool while continuing on in their regular jobs until selected for promotion. A variant of this procedure involves the use of a short battery of psychological tests, emphasizing verbal ability, that is given to all lower-level employees. Candidates for the more refined screening are then identified on the basis of test scores rather than through a bidding process.

Recruitment-from-within policies, involving job posting, talent searches, and special training programs, have received increasing attention under the pressures for equal employment opportunity (25). Government agencies reviewing employment policies frequently require companies that previously did not post job vacancies and solicit inside candidates to do so. The ultimate goal of such procedures is to keep minorities and women from being "locked in" the lower-paying, often dead-end, entry-level jobs.

Use of Temporary and Part-time Employees

In some situations, the appropriate strategy is other than one of embarking on a large-scale recruiting program, even though there may be many jobs to be filled. This is the case where the vacancies will not be permanent, because the regular employees are on vacation or on leave and plan to return, or where additional personnel are needed to assist with a special short-term project or to handle the work load in peak seasons. For these purposes, many employers call on temporary help, often provided through an outside agency that already has done the recruiting. Occasionally, temporary employees are used to fill vacancies for jobs particularly difficult to fill until a permanent employee can be found (2).

There are both positive and negative aspects to the use of temporary employees in terms of costs and of contributions to achievement of productivity goals (16); from an organizational maintenance viewpoint, however, one could anticipate some negative consequences from frequent resort to temporary help for the same types of jobs or the use of temporaries for extended periods of time. Permanent employees generally are viewed as having a much greater degree of identification with the organization and its goals.

As noted in Chapter 7, hiring employees on a part-time basis can achieve greater flexibility in work scheduling. The use of part-timers is a popular method of coping with peak work loads on certain days of the week or at certain hours of the day in many nonmanufacturing industries, such as restaurants and retail trade. Although temporary help often is recruited by outside agencies, many companies recruit part-timers just as full-time employees are recruited, using many of the same sources.

RECRUITING SOURCES

A large range of recruiting sources, some practically free of expense to the employer and others very costly, are available to employers seeking job applicants. All companies make use of internal sources to some extent; whether or not outside sources also are used depends on the variables discussed previously—the number of recruits needed, the type of jobs to be filled, and the condition of the labor market.

Internal Sources

Internal sources for recruiting job applicants can be relied on to fill many jobs that do not require special skills or educational backgrounds. One internal source is the file of *walk-in candidates* maintained by the employment office in most companies of any size. Particularly when jobs are scarce, persons looking for work will check the employment office of as many firms as possible. No matter what the condition of the labor market, there will be some walk-in applicants—people entering the labor force for the first time or exploring the chances of improving their job situation.

Whether or not a firm can rely heavily on individuals who come in seeking work or who call in depends in large part on the extent to which the company is widely known in an area and on its reputation as an employer. Normally, the smaller company will not be in as good a position to utilize this source as the larger one, although in some instances the effects of size on visibility can be overcome through product advertising and the introduction of unusually attractive employment practices.

Employee referrals—friends or relatives of present employees—often are a good source of applicants, although small companies that might be able to rely on this source exclusively have had to guard against conflict-of-interest problems. When the labor market is very tight, large employers frequently offer their employees bonuses or prizes for any referrals who are hired and stay with the company for a specified length of time. Some companies also maintain a file of *former employees* whose work records were good to contact when there are job openings for which they qualify.

The Union

Another source of applicants that may be tapped before advertising or going to employment agencies is the union, if employees are organized. The use of labor unions in recruiting usually is limited to manual jobs and varies considerably from one industry to another. Although the Taft-Hartley Act specifically forbids the *closed shop*, which requires that employers hire only union members, there are numerous cases where in fact recruiting is restricted almost entirely to the unions. In the maritime industry, union hiring halls represent practically the only labor source. Similarly, union control of the labor pool is characteristic in construction, printing, and the operating aspects of wholesale trade. In other industries, the union is contacted only rarely for recruiting purposes.

Advertising

There are two common forms of recruitment advertising. The first is the "help wanted" ad that appears in the classified advertising pages in local newspapers throughout the country; such ads are used by large and small employers to fill specific job openings. In addition, some employers run classified recruiting ads on a continuous basis for job categories with high turnover and frequent vacancies.

The second type of recruitment advertising is the large display notice, prepared by professional company advertising personnel or agencies, that frequently appear in the financial or sports sections of large metropolitan newspapers (7). These ads are used by large employers recruiting on a nationwide basis, particularly for people with skills that are in short supply. They may appear in journals of trade and professional associations as well as in newspapers.

While newspaper advertising is widely used, there are certain drawbacks that should be recognized. After the ad appears, there is no way of controlling the number of applicants. As a result, firms have been flooded with people seeking advertised positions, to the point where personnel resources were not adequate to cope with the influx. Yet it is very poor public relations policy to turn people away at such times without at least a brief interview. For this reason, many of the larger companies place primary emphasis on techniques other than advertising in recruiting clerical and manual workers, especially when a labor surplus is known to exist in the employment area. On the other hand, the number of applicants responding to a recruitment advertisement will be limited to those qualified and genuinely interested if the ad is worded effectively (5).

Private Employment Agencies

Private employment agencies—both local and those that operate on a nationwide basis—are used for obtaining job applicants for many types of positions; they are used most frequently for clerical workers and professional and managerial personnel. An employment agency can be particularly helpful in situations where an employer requires only one or two people a year in certain job classifications, but people who have specific skills. In effect, the agency does the recruiting, usually through advertising, and the initial screening of candidates, including testing for skills, such as typing. By using an agency to perform these functions, the company employment staff can be kept to a minimum.

For an employment agency to be effective for the employer, the agency must have accurate information about the jobs to be filled and about the company as a place to work. The agency needs to be provided definitions, job specifications, and honest salary data for vacant positions. Some companies invite agency personnel to tour their facilities and include agencies on their mailing lists for company publications, such as annual reports, so they can provide a better picture for prospective candidates (28).

The United States Employment Service

A major recruiting source is the network of public employment agencies that operate in the various states under the general guidance of the U.S. Employment Service (USES). There are more than 2,400 such offices that are staffed with state employees, although funds are provided by the federal government. Because the USES offices have the responsibility for administering state unemployment benefit systems, there have been charges that they sometimes refer workers who are not qualified for the jobs to be filled in an attempt to get them off the state unemployment rolls. One survey of nearly 200 employers indicates, however, that three-fourths of the companies use USES regularly, and 5 per cent occasionally, as a recruiting source (4). As indicated by the figures in Table 11–2, lower-level jobs are listed with USES by employers more frequently than higher-skilled positions.

The USES offices make a variety of services available to employers in addition to the referral of job applicants. These include psychological testing, the furnishing of occupational information, and advice on turnover and absenteeism problems. During the 1960s, the public employment offices became particularly active in making referrals to federally sponsored human resource training programs for the disadvantaged, of the kind discussed in Chapter 14. This emphasis on the placement of the human resource program trainees and on dealing with other "social" problems has been pointed out as one cause of the decline in job placements by the government employment service during the 1960s (32).

Another activity undertaken by the USES in recent years is the development of computerized job market information systems, or *job banks.* Job orders are listed in a computer; the bank includes brief descriptions of all job openings known to the USES in a specified area. Each morning, the computer prints out a book of current orders for distribution to all offices in the area; referrals to employers are controlled by telephone from a central office to avoid referring too many applicants for a particular job. Each evening, filled jobs are deleted, and new openings received are added.

The first job bank went into operation in 1968 in Baltimore, Maryland; within three years, the number of local job banks had reached more than 100 and included nearly all cities with a population of 250,000 or more. Statewide job banks also have been developed with the goal of eventually forming an integrated national computer job bank that would provide

Table 11–2. Job Categories Listed with USES

Job Category	Per Cent of Companies Listing with USES
Office employees	70
Unskilled laborers	63
Production workers	67
Trained technicians	46
Professionals	36
Supervisors	26
Managers	17

Source: Compiled from Bureau of National Affairs, Inc., "Special Report: Use of USES," *Bulletin to Management,* March 23, 1972, Part 2, p. 1.

more extensive job information and speed up the placement process. An assessment of progress with the job bank program indicates that while some individual local systems have been successful, there is little evidence so far that the computerized systems have improved or speeded up the placement process to any meaningful degree (37).

Schools

Many employers recruit candidates directly from high schools or vocational schools in the local area for jobs that do not require higher levels of education. Companies that need large numbers of such employees frequently maintain continuous contact with guidance counselors and teachers of business and vocational subjects. Work-study programs provide an opportunity for local students to work part-time while they finish their schooling; these students may well become full-time employees upon graduation.

There are a number of other public relations or community relations programs employers may undertake to enhance their image with the local schools. Sometimes they donate used equipment for training classes or provide speakers for school programs. One widely known nationwide program for business-education cooperation is Junior Achievement, under which local businessmen act as sponsors for student organizations formed to undertake the running of a small business enterprise. A major goal of all these programs is to make recruiting easier.

RECRUITING FOR MANAGERIAL AND PROFESSIONAL TALENT
College Recruiting

For most of the nation's medium and large corporations, as well as the major nonbusiness employers, college graduates are the prime source of their managerial, professional, and sales personnel, and campus recruiting is an extensive operation. As Table 11–3 indicates, graduates at both the bachelor's and master's level in a variety of disciplines are sought by the company recruiters (9). Almost all colleges have at least one placement office to coordinate the visits of company representatives and arrange interviews with students. Some have created specialized facilities within various professional schools as well.

Although few studies have been conducted that would indicate the specific techniques most likely to yield a sizable return on an investment in this area, certain guidelines have achieved widespread acceptance. Most firms prepare brochures describing the organization and its jobs and distribute them to college placement offices before the interviewer arrives. In general, companies attempt to maintain continuing contact with college placement officials and to recruit regularly each year. When a company is a steady recruiter on a particular campus, it is more likely to be offered

Table 11–3. Employment of Inexperienced College Men During 1974 and Estimated for 1975 by 140 Companies

Degree/Major	1974		1975	
	Number of Companies	Number of Men	Number of Companies	Number of Men
Bachelor's level				
Engineering	83	3658	84	3777
Accounting	80	2582	83	2843
Sales—marketing	55	1391	59	1483
Business administration	69	1644	72	1454
Liberal arts	47	726	39	654
Production management	20	88	24	100
Chemistry	24	87	22	111
Mathematics—statistics	48	372	43	300
Economics—finance	36	209	35	165
Other fields	36	343	33	299
Master's level				
Engineering	32	475	28	423
Other technical fields	22	145	19	114
MBA with technical BS	22	144	23	155
MBA with nontechnical BA	50	437	45	400
Accounting	14	773	15	817
Other nontechnical fields	18	143	12	131

Source: F. S. Endicott, 1975 Trends in Employment of College and University Graduates in Business and Industry (Berea, Ohio: American Society for Personnel Administration, 1974), p. 3.

desirable interview dates by the placement office and to obtain assistance in other forms.

Most campus interviews are conducted only for the purpose of initial screening and to provide the candidate with information regarding the job and/or training program for which he is being considered. The list in Table 11–4 provides an idea of the types of questions college students are asked most frequently by company recruiters during the initial campus interview (9). Normally, a visit to some company facility follows, and it is there that the selection decision is actually made. In some instances, job offers are made on the basis of the campus contact alone, although rarely at the actual time of the interview.

Companies sometimes go beyond the placement office contact in their search for candidates. Many utilize summer or part-time employment opportunities to attract college students who might later be considered for permanent positions (22). There is a widespread effort to get through to the professors directly to solicit information on students with outstanding potential. On occasion, professors are retained as consultants, with this as the primary objective.

Table 11–4. Questions Asked by Employers During the
Interview with College Seniors

General Classification of Questions	Number of Companies Asking Questions in This Classification
Goals and purposes—Life purposes—Career objectives	36
Type of work desired—Kind of job—Job expectations	33
Reasons for selection of company—Knowledge of company	29
Personal qualifications—Strengths and weaknesses	27
Career choice—Reasons for decisions	23
Qualifications for the job—How college education has prepared the candidate	22
Educational choices and plans—Choice of college—Choice of major	21
Geographical preferences—Willingness to relocate	21
Major achievement and accomplishments	20
Extracurricular activities—Extent of participation	6
Academic strengths and weaknesses—Grades	5
College subjects—Those liked most and least	5
Summer and part-time employment—What interested candidate most	5
Willingness to travel	3
Others	2

Source: F. S. Endicott, 1975 Trends in Employment of College and University Graduates in Business and Industry (Berea, Ohio: American Society for Personnel Administration, 1974), p. 8.

Most firms maintain detailed statistics with regard to the campus recruiting process. Comparisons are usually made from year to year and, where possible, with other companies. Some of the more common ratios are

$$\frac{\text{number of invitations to visit company}}{\text{number of campus interviews}}$$

$$\frac{\text{number of invitation acceptances}}{\text{number of invitations to visit company}}$$

$$\frac{\text{number of job offers}}{\text{number of company visits}}$$

$$\frac{\text{number of job acceptances}}{\text{number of decisions to hire}}$$

Probably the major factor contributing to an unsatisfactory result when statistics of this kind are computed is some type of deficiency in the campus contact process itself. College recruiting is often a grueling and, for some people, a boring process. The result is that a person who is potentially a very effective interviewer may not actually live up to this potential out in the campus placement office. What is needed is an individual who is interested in working with college students and who is enthusiastic about the company. Given these requirements, it probably matters very little whether he is a representative of a line unit, temporarily detached to recruit in his area of expertise, or a personnel man assigned regularly to this type of work. Most large companies appear to utilize individuals of both types.

Special Problems in College Recruiting

Several additional problems associated with the recruiting of college graduates have been more clearly identified as a result of research. On-campus recruiting is conducted almost exclusively by the larger companies; small companies fill their more limited needs in other ways. The result is that many individuals who might otherwise prefer a smaller firm are attracted to the larger ones simply because they have practically no opportunity for exposure to small firms in the college placement office. With more experience in the business world, they tend to gravitate to the smaller companies. Thus, organizations that do extensive college recruiting often experience very high turnover rates in that sector of their work force that has been perhaps the most expensive to recruit. Many of those hired become very disillusioned with their initial employer (38).

A second problem is that even those who accept job offers often back out before arriving to start work. In one company, this rate was running at over 16 per cent of all acceptances (21). Although there is evidence that such rates can be reduced through the use of a systematic schedule of telephone contacts during the intervening period, this places an additional burden on the total recruiting process.

The limited and often superficial nature of contacts in the college placement office appears to introduce further difficulties. One study found that among a group of interviewers on a college campus, scholastic standing of applicants was the most important of three variables, but where scholastic standing of applicants was the same, the interviewers clearly preferred the more physically attractive applicants and male rather than female applicants for a managerial position (8). The results of another study of the factors considered most important in the evaluation of college graduate job applicants also indicate that "general appearance" is the criterion with the highest ranking (23).

Student Attitudes

An important factor in the success of any college recruiting effort is the sum of the attitudes, values, and expectations that students have as regards business in general and the specific organization in particular. On this score, too, companies have encountered added difficulties since the middle 1960s. Over the past decade, the attitudes and values of college students appear to have changed in several dimensions; in particular, the students seem to have developed increasingly negative attitudes toward pursuing managerial careers in business. One suggestion for overcoming these attitudes is that business take steps to influence college students in their early student years through the sponsorship of seminars and work-study programs; often, the only information college students get about business careers comes from professors or peers with no real industry experience (31).

While negative attitudes toward business may result in some difficulty in companies' hiring their quota of college graduates, this problem will be crucial only when jobs are plentiful and applicants scarce. At the present time and for the foreseeable future, most companies should have little difficulty in filling lower-level managerial and professional positions. Evidence of other changes in the attitudes of college students indicates a problem that may become more acute as the current generation of college recruits move up the managerial hierarchy (30).

The data in Table 11-5 show the decline in overall motivation to manage and various attitudes related to such activities among MBA students between 1964 and 1973 (29). In large corporations and other bureaucratic organizations, it has been found that motivation to manage is related to

Table 11-5. Decline in Motivation to Manage Among Graduate Business Administration (MBA) Students: 1964-1973

	Years	
	1964	1972-1973
Motivation to manage		
High motivation	29 (58%)	4 (15%)
Low motivation	21 (42%)	22 (85%)
Favorable attitude toward authority		
High motivation	28 (56%)	5 (19%)
Low motivation	22 (44%)	21 (81%)
Desire to compete		
High motivation	25 (50%)	9 (35%)
Low motivation	25 (50%)	17 (65%)
Assertive motivation		
High motivation	38 (76%)	11 (42%)
Low motivation	12 (24%)	15 (58%)
Desire to exercise power		
High motivation	30 (60%)	15 (58%)
Low motivation	20 (40%)	11 (42%)
Desire for a distinctive position		
High motivation	32 (64%)	10 (38%)
Low motivation	18 (36%)	16 (62%)
Sense of responsibility		
High motivation	23 (46%)	6 (23%)
Low motivation	27 (54%)	20 (77%)

Source: J. B. Miner, The Human Constraint: The Coming Shortage of Managerial Talent (Washington, D.C.: Bureau of National Affairs, Inc., 1974), p. 60.

success in the managerial role. With the overall decline in such motivation indicated among college students, including those in business schools, serious shortages of managerial talent can be anticipated. A comprehensive study of recent graduates of the Harvard Business School reinforces this forecast (40).

Other Sources of Professional and Managerial Talent

Although many companies secure their professional and managerial people through campus recruiting, there are times when limited supplies of talent and rapid growth have forced a number of firms into the open market. In contrast to the college placement office, recruiting in the open market can be turned on and off as needed.

During the 1960s, when shortages of engineers became acute, a number of approaches became common. Company representatives attended meetings of professional societies for recruiting purposes as well as for updating their knowledge. Advertisements appeared in the newspapers of cities where large numbers of the desired type of professionals were known to work, indicating that a personnel representative would be in a given hotel for a specified period. Some firms paid particular attention to canceled government contracts or other indications of declining business and would send recruiters to interview displaced employees on the premises of the company reducing its professional force.

With the cutbacks in the space program and other government contracts in the early 1970s, these types of recruiting activities became less prevalent. Most companies have been able to fill their recruiting needs for higher-level personnel through campus recruiting.

Computerized Job Market Information Systems

In instances where professional people with experience are desired, there are a number of computer storage and retrieval systems that can be used. Although the specific items stored vary considerably from one job market information system to another, the basic approach is the same as that used in internal employee information systems. The difference is that the resumés that provide the input come from individuals who are seeking work rather than from the employees of a single company. When a company desires a particular type of employee, job specifications and requirements are fed into the computer, where they are matched against the resumé data stored there. The output is a set of resumés for individuals who meet the requirements.

These systems operate on a national basis and are limited to professional and managerial positions in contrast to the local and state job banks of the USES. One of the most successful national computer job-applicant matching systems is one developed by the College Placement Council; called GRAD, it has been in operation since 1966. Some of the others that have been tried over the years have suffered from a variety of problems similar to these mentioned with reference to employee skills inventories and information systems (14). With further development, however, this approach offers the prospect of providing a useful adjunct to the recruiting process. Costs to the employer are not large and, as job banks are built up to an adequate size, this method may prove to be an extremely valuable one for identifying candidates for hard-to-fill positions requiring unusual combinations of skills.

Executive Search Firms

In the years since World War II, there has been what appears to be an increasing tendency to hire managers, especially manager-specialists, away from other firms—a practice referred to as pirating. In some instances, these candidates come to a company's attention as a result of contacts initiated by the candidates themselves, either in response to advertising or unsolicited. More commonly, they are sought out directly by the firm or by its representatives.

There are a number of companies that fill the majority of their managerial positions through pirating. The more common practice is to rely primarily on promotion from within and to resort to recruiting from other firms only in unusual instances. In the latter cases, companies may carry out the recruiting largely on their own. But where hiring on the outside is frequent, the usual practice is to utilize employment agencies, consulting organizations, and search firms to keep the company name out of the picture until the individual is clearly a strong candidate.

In recent years, the prime source of outside hiring has been the search organization, which devotes all its energies to management recruiting. The largest of these firms are based in New York City, but there are others throughout the country. These organizations guarantee to produce at least three qualified candidates in return for a fee consisting of 15 to 30 per cent of the first year's salary, which must be paid, in many instances, whether a person is actually hired or not (26). Often these firms make their initial contact with a prospective candidate through a letter that describes the job in some detail and asks for recommended candidates. If the individual recommends himself, then he places himself in a position to be seriously considered for the job.

RECRUITING EFFECTIVENESS

To date there has been little in the published literature reporting research on why employers choose one recruiting method over another for finding applicants for certain types of jobs (10). While many large employers undoubtedly conduct research on questions such as which college campuses tend to produce the best recruits or which employment agencies send the most qualified applicants, the results of this research rarely find their way into the published sources.

One of the few studies reported shows the relationships between recruiting source and subsequent turnover of clerical employees of a New York City bank and provides evidence that employees from certain sources are more likely to continue on the job. Those more likely to stay were re-employed former workers, those referred by their high school, those referred by their present employer, or walk-ins. Rapid turnover characterized those obtained through employment agencies and newspaper advertisements (15).

Job Search Behavior

Some recent studies of job search methods used by individuals seeking employment do provide some information that may be useful to employers trying to decide the best recruiting source for certain types of employees (33, 35). Data from one of these studies, presented in Table 11–6, show that direct application is the most frequent method for obtaining jobs in all job categories. The second most frequent method differs considerably among occupations, however, with those in managerial occupations more likely to answer ads, clerical workers more likely to use a private employment agency, and craft workers more likely to ask their friends about jobs where they work.

Another study of the labor market experience of college graduates indicates the search methods considered most useful and points up some differences between male and female graduates in this regard (43). As in the previous study, direct application to the employer was the method most frequently used by both sexes; it was considered the *most useful* method by 50 per cent of the female graduates, compared to only 37 per cent of the males. According to 20 per cent of the women and 17 per cent of the men, the most useful method was application to the college placement office or professors; friends or relatives were rated most useful as a source of jobs by 26 per cent of the men and 15 per cent of the women. Information on job search behavior of persons in the labor market is particularly useful when it is analyzed in this way; the results can indicate where employers' recruiting efforts as related to affirmative action programs should be most successful.

AFFIRMATIVE ACTION RECRUITING

Some of the most widespread changes in company recruiting practices have occurred over the past decade as a result of pressures for equal employment opportunity. As discussed in Chapter 5, the enactment of the Civil Rights Act of 1964 and its subsequent enforcement have affected personnel practice drastically; recruiting is an area that has been affected most directly.

The impetus for changes in recruiting has occurred primarily through requirements for company *affirmative action* programs under agreements with EEOC or OFCCP. The philosophy behind these programs is that it is not sufficient that there is no *intent* to discriminate in hiring and promo-

Table 11–6. *Method by Which Current Job Was Obtained by Occupation, January 1973*

Method by Which Job Was Obtained (percentage distribution for each occupation)

Occupation	Applied Directly to Employer	Asked Friends About Jobs		Asked Relatives About Jobs		Answered Ads in Local Paper	Private Employment Agency	State Employment Service	School Placement Office	Civil Service Test	All Other Methods
		Where They Worked	Elsewhere	Where They Worked	Elsewhere						
Total, all persons	34.9	12.4	5.5	6.1	2.2	12.2	5.6	5.1	3.0	2.1	10.9
Professional and managerial	29.0	8.3	8.7	2.9	1.8	11.0	7.0	1.8	8.0	3.7	17.8
Professional	30.7	8.6	7.8	2.5	1.4	9.0	5.6	1.6	10.2	4.0	18.5
Managerial	24.3	7.6	11.1	3.9	2.7	16.5	10.9	2.5	1.9	3.1	15.5
Clerical and sales	29.7	11.9	4.3	4.8	2.1	15.1	12.4	5.6	2.5	3.3	8.4
Sales	42.8	12.3	5.8	3.8	1.9	16.8	4.3	2.2	1.9	—	8.4
Clerical	25.4	11.8	3.9	5.1	2.1	14.5	15.1	6.7	2.7	4.3	8.4
Craft workers, total	41.1	14.4	4.8	7.1	1.9	9.5	1.5	4.2	.6	.4	14.6
Union members	30.9	10.3	5.6	5.3	2.3	7.6	.7	3.3	.7	—	33.2
Nonunion members	45.4	16.1	4.5	7.8	1.7	10.3	1.8	4.6	.6	.6	6.7
Operatives, total	41.5	13.6	4.6	8.8	2.2	10.8	1.2	7.0	1.1	.4	8.6
Union members	41.0	11.4	5.4	5.2	1.4	11.1	1.4	8.2	—	.5	14.4
Nonunion members	41.6	14.1	4.4	9.7	2.4	10.7	1.2	6.7	1.4	.4	7.3
Nonfarm laborers	40.1	15.1	4.3	9.6	7.1	6.4	.5	5.9	1.1	.7	9.4
Service workers, except private household	38.7	15.4	5.6	6.9	1.2	14.8	1.3	5.7	2.2	2.0	6.2

Source: C. Rosenfeld, "Job-seeking Methods Used by American Workers," *Monthly Labor Review,* 98 (1975), No. 8, p. 41.

Table 11–7. Most Effective Recruiting Sources for Minority and Female Applicants (N = 160 companies)

Recruiting Source	Per Cent of Companies Noting Source as Effective for	
	Minority Applicants	Female Applicants
Community action agencies	44	19
Referrals from present employees	32	29
Colleges with large enrollments of minorities or females	28	30
Advertisements in media with minority or female appeal	26	34
Employment agencies— U.S. Employment Service	24	12
Agencies specializing in minority or female applicants	19	11
Regular private agencies	13	19

Source: Bureau of National Affairs, Inc., *Equal Employment Opportunity: Programs & Results,* Personnel Policies Forum Survey No. 112, March 1976, p. 3.

tion; if a company's personnel practices result in an adverse effect on a protected group, such as blacks or women, then affirmative action must be taken to eliminate the adverse effect (25). For many companies with superior records in employment matters, this has meant engaging in outside recruiting efforts for the first time; in particular, firms that in the past were able to fill all their recruiting needs through walk-in candidates or word-of-mouth referrals by friends or relatives on the payroll found themselves in trouble, because all-white or all-male work groups tended to perpetuate themselves.

Table 11–7 indicates the sources a number of employers have found most effective in their affirmative action efforts to recruit minority workers and women, particularly for professional or managerial positions (3). In addition to the traditional sources, minority or women's colleges, employment agencies specializing in certain groups, community action groups, and advertisements in minority or women's publications are being solicited or used for recruiting applicants. A number of other sources for managerial talent have been suggested, including ministers, government officials who have been involved with human resource programs, and teachers and educational administrators (20).

Implementing Affirmative Action

For the personnel executive, the implementation of an affirmative action program presents a number of difficulties even with the use of broader recruiting sources. One basic problem involves the process of establishing goals for the employment of minorities and women. As required by the government, this process becomes extremely complicated, because the goals are determined by comparing present employment by department and job level with data on the availability of talent in the relevant labor market. For lower-level jobs, the relevant labor market would be the local area; for certain professional or managerial positions, the data would be drawn from the entire nation, and recruiting would be called for on a nationwide basis (19).

For affirmative action recruiting at the lower levels, particularly with regard to minorities, there are differences in attitudes toward work and in work search behavior that might affect the relative success of certain types of recruiting efforts. Results of the research on job search methods noted above indicate that blacks are less likely than whites to apply directly to employers or to answer local newspaper advertisements but are more likely to ask friends or relatives about jobs, take Civil Service tests, use the USES, and work through community action organizations (35). Another study of race and economic class and the intention to work found that blacks are more likely to seek employment through enrollment in human resource training programs (12).

Research on differences in attitudes toward characteristics of the job and the work environment indicates that blacks attach more importance to salary level and job security and are less likely than whites to prefer work that is important or provides a feeling of accomplishment (41). These differences appear to hold for newly hired college graduates as well as for employees at lower levels. One study found that while both black and white groups of college graduates view opportunity for future development as the most important aspect of their jobs, blacks were more concerned than whites with such factors as security and salary (1).

Even if a company is successful in recruiting large numbers of qualified minority and/or female candidates for positions where they are needed to fulfill affirmative action goals, another problem frequently emerges. This is the problem of long-standing attitudes concerning traditional roles and the influence of stereotypes in making selection decisions (6). One area where this type of problem has made change difficult is that of hiring women for what are viewed as traditionally male jobs at lower levels, particularly jobs that are hazardous or require physical strength (11). Particularly noteworthy is the small percentage of women in the skilled trades; in 1970, only 5 per cent of the jobs in these trades were held by women, even though there had been an 80 per cent increase since 1960 (18).

The matter of sex-role stereotyping with regard to managerial positions appears to be even more pronounced. Studies have been conducted involving hiring or promotion decisions for management jobs in which two identical applications or work histories have been used except that one would carry a male name and the other a female name. The results typically indicate the existence of antifemale biases with regard to the ability to handle higher-level responsibilities (34).

Equally demanding is the problem of getting support for affirmative action efforts throughout the organization. It frequently is argued that lower-level supervision is where the most resistance is likely to be encountered, because it is there that the problems of integrating new types of workers into the group are most acute. There is evidence, however, that this resistance is greatest at the top levels of management (13).

To deal with these problems of attitudes and resistance to equal opportunity efforts, the personnel executive faced with governmental, and perhaps, societal, pressures may need more than just extensive recruiting programs. Special training for supervisors and managers and company-wide communications programs often are considered essential aspects of affirmative action endeavors. Despite the apprehension commonly expressed by both managers and lower-level employees when change is in the offing, there is evidence that it may be unwarranted when the change involves providing equal job opportunity. One report concerns the experience of IBM in hiring blacks for jobs as salesmen and repairmen that involved customer contact and previously had been held only by whites. It was found that once the program was under way, black employees were accepted by fellow employees and by the public and required no more training or other help than whites (24).

QUESTIONS

1. What recruiting strategies and approaches tend to be used when qualified employees are readily available? What changes can be expected when scarcities develop?
2. What problems are companies likely to face in campus recruiting? Can you think of any alternative approaches that companies might better use to achieve the same objectives?
3. What changes have affirmative action plans introduced into company recruiting procedures? What difficulties would you expect companies to face in this area?
4. One way a company can improve its recruiting effectiveness is to identify its best sources and concentrate its efforts there. How might a study to identify these "best sources" be designed and carried out?
5. Why might a company make extensive use of temporary employees? In what kinds of jobs and for what purposes would their use appear to be a sound strategy?

REFERENCES

1. Alper, S. W. "Racial Differences in Job and Work Environment Priorities Among Newly Hired College Graduates." *Journal of Applied Psychology*, 60 (1975), 132–134.
2. Bureau of National Affairs, Inc. "ASPA-BNA Survey No. 25—Part-time and Temporary Employees." *Bulletin to Management*, December 5, 1974, Part 2, 1–8.

3. Bureau of National Affairs, Inc. *Equal Employment Opportunity: Programs & Results.* Personnel Policies Forum Survey No. 112, March 1976.
4. Bureau of National Affairs, Inc. "Special Report: Use of USES." *Bulletin to Management,* March 23, 1972, No. 1154—Part 2, 1–6.
5. Burrow, E. E., and E. J. Leslie. "Adding the Professional Touch to Classified Advertising." *Personnel Journal,* 52 (1973), 705–709, 734.
6. Cohen, S. L., and K. A. Bunker. "Subtle Effects of Sex Role Stereotypes on Recruiters' Hiring Decisions." *Journal of Applied Psychology,* 60 (1975), 566–572.
7. Coss, F. *Recruitment Advertising.* New York: American Management Association, Inc., 1968.
8. Dipboye, R. L., H. L. Fromkin and K. Wiback. "Relative Importance of Applicant Sex, Attractiveness, and Scholastic Standing in Evaluation of Job Applicant Résumés." *Journal of Applied Psychology,* 60 (1975), 39–43.
9. Endicott, F. S. *1975 Trends in Employment of College and University Graduates in Business and Industry.* Berea, Ohio: American Society for Personnel Administration, 1974.
10. Ericson, R. W. "Recruitment: Some Unanswered Questions." *Personnel Journal,* 53 (1974), 136–140, 147.
11. Evans, V. M. "Unisex Jobs and Nontraditional Employment." *Personnel,* 52 (1975), No. 6, 31–37.
12. Feldman, J. "Race, Economic Class, and the Intention to Work: Some Normative and Attitudinal Correlates." *Journal of Applied Psychology,* 59 (1974), 179–186.
13. Fernandez, J. P. *Black Managers in White Corporations.* New York: John Wiley & Sons, Inc., 1975.
14. Foltman, F. F. *Manpower Information for Effective Management, Part 2: Skills Inventories and Manpower Planning.* Ithaca, N.Y.: New York State School of Industrial and Labor Relations, 1973.
15. Gannon, M. J. "Sources of Referral and Employee Turnover." *Journal of Applied Psychology,* 55 (1971), 226–228.
16. Gannon, M. J. "A Profile of the Temporary Help Industry and Its Workers." *Monthly Labor Review,* 97 (1974), 44–49.
17. Gaston, R. J. "Labor Market Conditions and Employer Hiring Standards." *Industrial Relations,* 11 (1972), 272–278.
18. Hedges, J. N., and S. E. Bemis. "Sex Stereotyping: Its Decline in Skilled Trades." *Monthly Labor Review,* Vol. 97 (1974), No. 5, 14–22.
19. Higgins, J. M. "The Complicated Process of Establishing Goals for Equal Employment." *Personnel Journal,* 54 (1975), 631–637.
20. Iacobelli, J. L., and J. P. Muczyk. "Overlooked Talent Sources and Corporate Strategies for Affirmative Action." *Personnel Journal,* 54 (1975), 532–535, 549, 575–577, 587.

21. Ivancevich, J. M., and J. H. Donnelly. "Job Offer Acceptance Behavior and Reinforcement." *Journal of Applied Psychology,* 55 (1971), 119–122.
22. Kane, S. E. "Summer Employment Can Pay Off as a Recruiting Tool." *Journal of College Placement,* 33 (1973), No. 4, 69–73.
23. Kohn, M. "Hiring College Graduates Through Off-campus Selection Interviewing." *Public Personnel Management,* 4 (1975), No. 1, 23–31.
24. Kraut, A. I. "The Entrance of Black Employees into Traditionally White Jobs." *Academy of Management Journal,* 18 (1975), 610–615.
25. Lockwood, H. C. "Equal Employment Opportunities," in D. Yoder and H. G. Heneman (eds.), *Staffing Policies and Strategies.* Washington, D.C.: Bureau of National Affairs, Inc., 1974.
26. Lopez, F. M. *The Making of a Manager.* New York: American Management Association, Inc., 1970.
27. McBrearty, J. J. "Myths About Employment Agencies." *Personnel Administrator,* 19 (1974), No. 6, 51–54.
28. Malm, F. T. "Recruiting Patterns and the Functioning of Labor Markets." *Industrial and Labor Relations Review,* 7 (1954), 507–525.
29. Miner, J. B. *The Human Constraint: The Coming Shortage of Managerial Talent.* Washington, D.C.: Bureau of National Affairs, Inc., 1974.
30. Miner, J. B. "Student Attitudes Toward Bureaucratic Role Prescriptions and Prospects for Managerial Talent Shortages." *Personnel Psychology,* 27 (1974), 605–613.
31. Mitchell, T. R., and B. W. Knudsen. "Instrumentality Theory Predictions of Students' Attitudes Towards Business and Their Choice of Business as an Occupation." *Academy of Management Journal,* 16 (1973), 41–52.
32. Nordlund, W. J. "Employment Service Placement in the Sixties." *Industrial Relations,* 13 (1974), 213–217.
33. Reid, G. L. "Job Search and the Effectiveness of Job-finding Methods." *Industrial and Labor Relations Review,* 25 (1972), 479–495.
34. Rosen, B., and T. H. Jerdee. "Sex Stereotyping in the Executive Suite." *Harvard Business Review,* 52 (1974), No. 2, 45–58.
35. Rosenfeld, C. "Jobseeking Methods Used by American Workers." *Monthly Labor Review,* 98 (1975), No. 8, 39–42.
36. Spencer, H. "Task Definition: The Catalyst in the Matching Process." *Personnel Journal,* 53 (1974), 428–434.
37. Ullman, J. C., and G. P. Huber. "Are Job Banks Improving the Labor Market Information System?" *Industrial and Labor Relations Review,* 27 (1974), 171–185.
38. Vroom, V. H., and E. L. Deci. "The Stability of Post-decision Dissonance: A Follow-up Study of the Job Attitudes of Business School Graduates." *Organizational Behavior and Human Performance,* 6 (1971), 36–49.

39. Wanous, J. P. "A Job Preview Makes Recruiting More Effective." *Harvard Business Review*, 53 (1975), No. 5, 16, 166, 168.
40. Ward, L. B., and A. G. Athos. *Student Expectations of Corporate Life*. Boston: Harvard Business School, Division of Research, 1972.
41. Weaver, C. N. "Black-White Differences in Attitudes Toward Job Characteristics." *Journal of Applied Psychology*, 60 (1975), 438–441.
42. Wernimont, P. F. "Recruitment Policies and Practices," in D. Yoder and H. G. Heneman (eds.), *Staffing Policies and Strategies*. Washington, D.C.: Bureau of National Affairs, Inc., 1974.
43. Young, A. M. "Labor Market Experience of Recent College Graduates." *Monthly Labor Review*, 97 (1974), No. 10, 33–40.

12   *The Employment Interview and Related Techniques*

There are two approaches that characteristically provide a basis for selection decisions. One relies heavily on the assumption that a candidate's past behavior can serve as a guide for predicting his future. Accordingly, extensive information is collected regarding the person's previous behavior in various educational, occupational, and perhaps other situations. Then, this information is evaluated relative to the role requirements of the position to be filled—or of several positions, if career considerations are involved. The expectation is that the individual will remain much the same person in the future that he was in the past; that he will retain the same or similar characteristics and will behave in accordance with the previous pattern.

This rationale underlies many of the procedures regularly employed in the selection interview. It also underlies most biographical inventories, application blanks, medical history forms, and reference-checking techniques. In all these instances, the primary, although not exclusive, emphasis is on accumulating valid information about the past to provide a basis for selecting the particular human inputs to the organization that will maximize future effectiveness.

A very different rationale underlies most psychological testing, the physical examination, and certain adaptations of the interview and the application blank. As we shall see, these adaptations make the particular interviews and application blanks very similar to psychological tests. This second approach relies heavily on the sampling of present behavior as a basis for prediction. Relatively standardized situations that presumably have some relation to the job or jobs are established, and candidates are asked to behave within these contexts. It is assumed that their behavior in these limited situations is typical of their total present behavior, and that they will remain sufficiently unchanged in the future to permit effective prediction.

The present chapter will take up the selection procedures that have their primary roots in an evaluation of the candidate's past: the interview, the various adaptations of the application blank procedure, and reference checks. In the next chapter, attention will be focused on techniques of sampling current behavior to obtain information on intellectual and physical functioning and on personality characteristics.

THE INTERVIEW

Although it should be evident that interview procedures are widely used for a variety of purposes, the primary concern here is with specific applications in the evaluation of human inputs to a business organization. Therefore, applications in such areas as marketing research, employee counseling, management appraisal, and attitude surveys will receive very little attention.

Even within the input context, the interview serves a number of purposes: it is much more than a selection device. This is probably why it has survived and even thrived in the face of extended attacks by industrial psychologists and others and in the face of considerable evidence that, as commonly used, it is often not a very effective selection technique.

There are, in fact, a number of requirements connected with the input process that at present cannot be accomplished in any other way, although telephone and written communication might be substituted in certain instances. One of these roles has already been noted in the preceding chapter. Interviews are used as often to sell the company and thus recruit candidates for employment as to select. A single interview frequently involves both selection and recruiting aspects. Furthermore, terms of employment are characteristically negotiated in the interview situation, and an important public relations function is performed. Applicants who must be rejected are particularly likely to leave with very negative attitudes toward the company if they have not had an opportunity to talk with a responsible representative.

Even when the focus is directly on the selection process, the interview appears to possess certain unique values, which may account for its continued widespread use. For one thing, the great flexibility of the technique, which can contribute to limited validity in some selection situations, may represent a major asset in other situations. The interview is the method *par excellence* for filling in the gaps between other selection techniques— gaps that could not have been foreseen until the other techniques were actually applied. Responses on the application blank may make clear the need for further information regarding the circumstances surrounding certain previous employment and separation decisions. An interview can be of considerable help in providing such information.

It is also clear that the interview is widely used to determine whether an applicant is the type of person who can be expected to fit in and get along in the particular firm. Its use with reference to such organizational maintenance considerations is probably much more widespread than in predicting productivity. This is not to imply that other selection techniques cannot be used to predict maintenance criteria, but for various reasons they often are not given the same emphasis as the interview. There is something about the process of personal judgment that produces a strong feeling of validity, even when validity is not present (6). It is not surprising, therefore, that many companies place heavy emphasis on interviewing when attempting to predict whether a person will be a source of conflict, will have a negative impact on others, or will be an extremely unhappy employee.

Finally, there are situations, especially when managerial and professional positions are involved, where the interview is the only major selection technique that realistically *can* be used. When a person who already has a good job, who gives every evidence of being a good prospect, and who does not have a strong initial incentive to make a move is faced with extensive psychological testing, a physical exam, and an application blank (above and beyond the résumé he has already submitted), he may shy away. If this seems likely, it is often wiser to rely on the interview, reference checks, and the like in spite of their shortcomings, rather than face the prospect of losing the individual.

What Is Known About the Selection Interview

A great deal has been written regarding the techniques of interviewing for various purposes (8, 16). Much of this, however, derives from the expertise and opinion of specific individuals. What is really known, in the sense that it is based on studies using selection models of the kind discussed in Chapter 10 and on other scientific research procedures, is considerably less.

The discussion here will be restricted to what is known in this scientific sense. Unfortunately, when this is done, a great deal is left to the discretion of the individual interviewer. Yet there is little point in continuing to perpetuate much of the existing lore, which in many instances has been developed out of situations far removed from the company employment office and which may therefore be quite erroneous when applied to a selection interview in the business world.

CONSISTENCY OF INTERVIEWER JUDGMENTS

There is considerable evidence to indicate that, although an interviewer will himself exhibit consistency in successive evaluations of the same individual, different interviewers are likely to come to quite disparate conclusions. Thus, when two employment interviewers utilize their own idiosyncratic interview procedures on the same applicant, the probability is that they will come to differing decisions. They will normally elicit information on different matters, and even when the topics covered do overlap, one individual will weight the applicant's responses in a way that varies considerably from that employed by another (30).

These problems can be overcome. Interviewers can be trained to follow similar patterns in their questioning and to evaluate responses using the same standards. When more structured interview techniques are used, when the questions asked are standardized and responses are recorded in some systematic manner, the consistency of the judgmental process increases markedly (4, 27). Within limits, it does not matter which interviewer is used; the results tend to be similar. Also, this kind of reliability of decision is sharply increased by providing the interviewer with detailed information regarding the nature of the jobs to be filled (14). Unfortunately, however, structuring of a kind that will increase the consistency of judgments appears to be the exception rather than the rule in most personnel offices. Thus, where strong reliance is placed on the interview, the final selection decision often depends as much on which interviewer is used as on the characteristics of the applicant. On the other hand, agreement does not guarantee accuracy of prediction; there can be great consistency in picking the wrong people.

ACCURACY OF INTERVIEW INFORMATION

Studies to determine the accuracy of work-history statements made in the interview indicate that reporting errors may occur. Thus, in one instance, when a check was made with employers, information given by the interviewees regarding job titles was found to be invalid in 24 per cent of the cases. Job duties were incorrectly reported by 10 per cent, and pay was incorrectly reported by 22 per cent (33). In general, the tendency was to upgrade rather than downgrade prior work experience.

In many employment situations, interview distortion may not be as prevalent as the preceding figures suggest. Yet in any given instance, an interviewer may be faced with an applicant who deliberately, or perhaps unconsciously, falsifies his report. In such cases, the usual tendency is for the person to make his record look better than it is. It can be assumed, also, that many applicants will attempt to avoid discussing previous instances of ineffective work performance. Where valid data are essential, it is usually desirable to check interview statements against outside sources.

ACCURACY OF INTERVIEWER JUDGMENTS

The inevitable conclusion derived from a number of investigations is that interview judgments, as they are usually made in the employment situation, are not closely related to independent measures of the characteristics judged.

Nor are they closely related to measures of success on the job. In an overall sense, the evidence regarding the validity of the selection interview yields a distinctly disappointing picture (34).

Yet there are conditions under which the interview exhibits considerable strength as a selection device, and there are some characteristics that are capable of being judged more effectively than others. Evidence on this point is contained in Table 12–1, based on selection interviews conducted by a management consulting firm (18). The data are for interviews carried out by personnel managers and by partners in the firm; more junior consultants turned out to be poor interviewers. The firm had an "up-or-out" policy, and thus subsequent promotion indicated a very favorable performance evaluation and a desire to retain the individual in the organization. The most valuable predictor proved to be the tone (whether positive or negative) of any overall comments the interviewer wrote in at the end of the report form—in other words, a "gut" reaction to the fit between individual and organization. Ratings of practical judgment, self-confidence, and promotion potential also correlated well with subsequent promotion: there was some validity for problem-solving ability, imagination, and the recommendation whether to hire or not. Yet other items on the interview report form were totally unrelated to subsequent success.

In another series of studies, rather sizable predictive validities were reported for overall interviewer estimates of suitability for employment when a highly structured, patterned interview approach was followed (17). When validated against duration of employment for the 587 people who left the company within an 18-month period, the interviews yielded a correlation

Table 12–1. Correlations Between Interview Rating Form Items and Subsequent Promotion

Interview Item	r
Personal impression	.13
Effectiveness with people	.04
Firm acceptance	−.03
Mental ability for problem solving	.23
Imagination	.27
Initiative and sustained drive	.14
Practical judgment	.37
Technical competence	−.10
Character and habits	−.12
Self-confidence, maturity, and emotional stability	.40
Potential as a clientele builder	.05
Promotion potential	.36
Employment recommendation	.28
Special comments	.54

Source: J. B. Miner, "Executive and Personnel Interviews as Predictors of Consulting Success," *Personnel Psychology*, 23 : 534 (1970).

of .43. The employees rated higher initially in the employment interview stayed longer. The 407 employees who were still on the job 18 months after hiring were rated for performance effectiveness by their superiors and the results compared with the earlier interview judgments. A predictive validity coefficient of .68 was obtained. Subsequent studies using the same patterned interview format produced correlations with success criteria that were consistently in the range of the .60s.

It is evident that the interview can be quite effective when used in a relatively standardized manner and when individualized interviewer approaches and biases are controlled. Under such standardized conditions, the interview takes on certain characteristics of the application blank or a psychological test. It becomes in many respects an oral version of the common written selection procedures, although still with greater flexibility. There is nothing in what has been said to imply that less structured (and less directive) interviews may not yield equally good validities under certain circumstances and with certain interviewers, but without further research, it is not possible to specify exactly what these requisite conditions are.

STUDIES OF DECISION MAKING IN THE INTERVIEW

Certain other conclusions regarding the decision-making process in the interview have been developed as a result of a series of studies initiated at McGill University (32). The early research found that in the actual employment situation, most interviewers tend to make an accept-reject decision early in the interview. They do not wait until all the information is in. Rather, a bias is developed and stabilized shortly after the discussion starts. This bias serves to color the remainder of the interview and is not usually reversed. However, more recent research indicates that this temporal bias can be overcome when interviewers have detailed information regarding the job and what makes for success in it (24).

Interviewers also are much more influenced by unfavorable than by favorable data. If any shift in viewpoint occurs during the interview, it is much more likely to be in the direction of rejection. Apparently, selection interviewers tend to maintain rather clear-cut conceptions regarding the role requirements of the jobs for which they are interviewing. They compare candidates against these stereotypes in the sense of looking for deviant characteristics and thus for negative evidence with regard to hiring. Positive evidence is given much less weight (15).

These findings suggest certain guidelines for maximizing the effectiveness of employment interviewing. For one thing, the data repeatedly indicate that if an interviewer knows a lot about the *job* he is interviewing for and what kind of people tend to succeed in it, he or she will be more objective and the result will be better. If it is intended that the interview should make a *unique* contribution to the selection process, however, the interviewing ought to be done with relatively little foreknowledge of the *candidate*. Thus, contrary to common practice, application blanks, test scores, and the like should be withheld until after the initial selection interview. Personal history data should be obtained directly from the candidate in oral form, even if written versions are available. This approach will serve to delay decision making in the interview, with the result that information obtained during the latter part of the discussion can be effectively utilized in reaching a judgment. If data are needed to fill in the gaps between the various selection techniques, these can be obtained from a second interview. Thus, the interview as an independent selection tool should be clearly differentiated from the interview as a means of following up on leads provided by other devices. The interviewer should be clear in his own mind as to which objective he is seeking.

When the interview is used as an independent procedure, information obtained from the various sources should be combined and evaluated subsequently to reach a final selection decision, rather than during the interview proper. When the interview is used to supplement application blank, medical history, and psychological test data, it should be considered as an information-gathering device only, not as an ideally constituted selection procedure. In neither case should it assume the proportions of a final arbiter, superseding all other techniques and sources of information.

Types of Employment Interviews

It is evident that the content of the selection interview may be varied. Different interviewers may ask different questions, concentrate on different parts of the person's prior experience, and attempt to develop estimates of different characteristics. It is also true that the basic technique or procedure may be varied.

PATTERNED, OR STRUCTURED, INTERVIEWS

This approach has already been noted in connection with the discussions of the consistency and accuracy of interviewer judgments. Often a detailed form is used, with the specific questions to be asked noted and space provided for the answers. The form is completed either during the interview or from memory immediately afterward. In other cases, only the areas to be covered are established in advance, the order of coverage and actual question wording being left to the interviewer. Either way, the more structured approach offers distinct advantages over the usual procedure, in which different interviewers may go off in completely different directions, depending on their own and the candidate's predilections. On the other hand, it should be recognized that information loss may occur because of a lack of flexibility.

NONDIRECTIVE PROCEDURES

The nondirective approach derives originally from psychotherapy and counseling. It permits the person being interviewed considerable leeway in determining the topics to be covered. The basic role of the interviewer is to reflect the feelings of the other person and to restate or repeat key words and phrases. This tends to elicit more detailed information from the interviewee, especially with reference to his emotional reactions, attitudes, and opinions. Because the candidate actually controls the content of the interview, this procedure may take the discussion far afield from what the interviewer might wish to treat. It frequently yields a great deal of information about the prior experiences, early family life, and interpersonal relationships of the individual, but much of this often has no clear relationship to the employment decision. For this reason, the nondirective technique is usually mixed with a more directive, questioning approach when it is used in the selection interview.

MULTIPLE AND GROUP INTERVIEWS

Another procedure, which has on occasion proved to yield very good validity, involves the use of more than one interviewer. Either the candidate spends time talking to several different people separately, or he meets with a panel, or board, whose members alternate in asking him questions (13). The latter approach can easily be integrated into a patterned or structured format, and when this is done, the resulting decisions and evaluations appear to maximize prediction of subsequent performance. Normally, the group evaluation is derived after discussion among the various interviewers, but independent estimates can be obtained from each person, and these then averaged to achieve a final decision. The major disadvantage of any multiple-interviewer procedure is that it can become very costly in terms of the total number of working hours required. For this reason, it is usually reserved for use in selecting people for the higher-level positions in a company.

STRESS INTERVIEWS

The stress approach achieved some acceptance in the business world after World War II as a result of its use during the war to select men for espionage work with the Office of Strategic Services. As used in industry, this procedure usually involves the induction of failure stress. The interviewer rather suddenly becomes quite aggressive, belittles the candidate, and throws him on the defensive. Reactions to this type of treatment are then observed.

Because it utilizes a sample of present behavior to formulate predictions, rather than focusing on past behavior, the stress interview is in many ways more like a situational test than a selection interview. It has the disadvantage that rejected candidates who are subjected to this process can leave with a very negative image of the company, and even those whom the company may wish to hire can become so embittered that they will not accept an offer. This does not happen often, and usually a subsequent explanation can serve to eradicate any bad feelings. Yet when the fact that there is little positive evidence on the predictive power of the stress interview is added to these considerations, it seems very difficult to justify its use under normal circumstances. The selection situation alone appears to be anxiety-provoking enough for most people.

The Interview and Selection Models

It seems absolutely essential that the interviewer receive some systematic feedback on the validity of his decisions if a company is to make effective use of the selection interview. To accomplish this, written evaluations of each candidate must be recorded. These interview ratings can be compared at a later date with criterion information provided by the employee's immediate superior or derived from some other source. In this way, the interviewer can modify his technique over time to maximize his predictive validity.

This approach suffers from the fact that no follow-up can be made on applicants who are not hired. Yet in most companies, personnel recommendations are not followed religiously. For various reasons, those recommended for rejection are hired on occasion. In addition, other selection procedures may outweigh a negative interview impression. Thus, there will be individuals in the follow-up group who have received rather low ratings, although the preponderant number will have had generally favorable evaluations in the interview.

One should not expect perfect success from these studies. Yet an interview should contribute something above what might be obtained by chance alone and from the use of other techniques. Also, if a standardized interview form is used, individual questions can be analyzed to see if they discriminate between effective and ineffective employees, as in Table 12–1. If certain questions appear not to be contributing to the predictive process, others can be substituted and evaluated in a similar manner.

APPLICATION BLANKS AND BIOGRAPHICAL INVENTORIES

Probably the most widely used selection device is some type of written statement regarding the applicant's prior experiences and behavior. This may take the form of the conventional application blank, or an extended biographical inventory utilizing a great variety of multiple-choice questions may be employed. On occasion the form and content of the statement are determined by the applicant rather than the company. Such resumés are particularly likely to be used when the applicant is at the professional or managerial level.

Application Blanks

The actual items included on the application blank vary considerably from company to company. Many firms maintain several different versions for various positions. It is particularly common to have a separate blank for professional and technical employees, but it may be expedient to develop special forms for any group of jobs that are similar in their requirements and for which applications are received frequently.

In addition to such routine matters as name, address, telephone number, date of birth, social security number, marital status, children, and citizenship, most forms request information on education and previous employment. Items dealing with education normally emphasize the extent of training rather than the quality of the work done. Information on grades, if it is desired, is better obtained from the educational institution itself.

Work history data may be requested in a variety of forms. Usually, it is desirable to determine not only job title, but duties and also the level of the position within the employing organization. Salary data can be helpful in negotiating a salary figure with those who will be entering positions that do not have a set starting rate. Questions regarding the reasons for leaving previous employers are often unrevealing, but on occasion they do yield valuable information.

It is important in constructing an application blank to obtain only data that will be used. There is a tendency for these forms to grow in length over the years, to the point where they can well serve to discourage applicants who, at least initially, are not strongly motivated for employment. It is also important to be sure that the information requested is not in violation of federal and state fair employment practices legislation. Items such as arrest history, educational level, and children born to unmarried mothers may be interpreted as discriminatory, unless clear evidence can be presented that they are job related. Data for minority group members are likely to be different, and an employer has to show that these matters are as important to job performance for one group as the other.

The important consideration insofar as legal restrictions are concerned is that data related to race, sex, national origin, religion, and age not be used to discriminate against certain groups (20). In order to clear themselves of any suspicion in this area, a number of employers have eliminated many application blank items that had previously been standard. Yet data in these sensitive areas can be collected for research purposes and are in fact essential to the conduct of differential validity studies (29). As noted in previous discussions of these matters, the crucial requirement is that the company be able to show in some manner that it is not discriminating.

Although the validity of information reported in application blanks has been studied less frequently than the accuracy of interview information, the findings are much the same (11). In some instances, previous employers listed by the applicant indicated that the individual never had worked for them. Reasons for leaving were at variance in 25 per cent of the cases. Time spent in previous employment often was overestimated, as was the rate of payment. At least among applicants for lower-level positions, some degree of distortion of application-blank statements can be anticipated.

Weighting Application-blank Items

The scoring of application blanks in accord with the demands of the selection model dates back to the early 1920s. The basic requirement is that responses to the various items on the blank be related to some criterion of job success. Studies have been done using job tenure, success ratings, salary increases, and a variety of other indexes. Application blank data are widely used in predicting turnover. One advantage of this approach is that, because application blanks are almost universally filled out by all applicants, it is possible to carry out weighting studies at any time. All that is required is a search of the files for the application blanks of people hired for a given type of work during a specified period. These blanks may then be related to available measures of success or turnover.

A variety of techniques for weighting application blank items have been developed, some of them quite statistically complex (7, 12). In general, however, the more involved procedures do not add a great deal as long as the number of cases used in the analysis is sufficiently large. The much simpler horizontal per cent method, as illustrated in Figure 12–1, appears to be perfectly adequate for most purposes. All that is needed is a sample of employees that may be divided, usually at the median, into a high and a low group on some criterion index. Application blanks filled out previously, at the time of employment, are then checked to determine how many in the low and high groups selected each alternative on a given item. The per cent of those responding in a particular way who also fall in the high group on the criterion is then computed. This percentage is converted to a weight by rounding to a single number. High values are associated with the desired performance, and low values with that which is not desired. A total score for the blank is obtained by adding up the weights on the individual items.

In the hypothetical example of Figure 12–1, it is clear that the married group tends to produce more than its share of effective employees. Accordingly, this response on the application blank receives a high score. The divorced and separated responses, being associated with less-effective performance, receive a low score, whereas those who report themselves as single or widowed receive only a slightly negative weight. Education does not serve to discriminate very well between the high and low groups, although there is some slight advantage associated with the very highest levels of educational accomplishment. A sales or managerial background, on the other hand, appears to be highly desirable, whereas a lack of previous work experience, or employment in areas other than those listed, perhaps farming, yields low weights. Military service does not matter one way or the other. Using these four questions only, a married person with college education, immediately preceding experience in sales, and military service would have a total score of 26. This is well above the 14 obtained by a divorced high school graduate with no previous work experience and no military service.

After weights have been developed in this manner, it is important that the

Response Categories	Low Group	High Group	Total Number	Per Cent High	Weight
Marital Status					
Single	35	19	54	35	4
Married	52	97	149	65	7
Divorced	25	8	33	24	2
Separated	15	6	21	29	3
Widowed	13	10	23	43	4
	140	140	280		
Education					
Grade school	13	14	27	52	5
High school incomplete	28	23	51	45	5
High school graduate	56	46	102	45	5
College incomplete	18	16	34	47	5
College graduate	16	25	41	61	6
Graduate work	9	16	25	64	6
	140	140	280		
Most Recent Work Experience					
None	18	5	23	22	2
Production	40	30	70	43	4
Clerical	38	28	66	42	4
Sales	8	35	43	81	8
Managerial	5	17	22	77	8
Professional	13	16	29	55	6
Other	18	9	27	33	3
	140	140	280		
Military Service					
Yes	77	86	163	53	5
No	63	54	117	46	5
	140	140	280		

Figure 12–1. Form for Weighting Application Blank Responses by the Horizontal Per Cent Method (Hypothetical Data).

scoring be cross-validated on another sample drawn from the same employee group. This is essential in constructing a weighted application blank, because many of the differences in weights may not reflect real differences but only chance fluctuations. When a large number of items are weighted in this manner, cross-validation may yield validity coefficients well below what the analysis of the original sample seemed to suggest: these coefficients may even shrink to zero (28).

Additional cross-validations should also be conducted at periodic intervals after the weighting procedure has actually been introduced into the selection process, especially if any major changes in the jobs involved, personnel policies, or labor market have occurred in the interim since the weights were originally established (26). Continuing studies of the relationship between weighted scores and job performance should also be made when the weights used are widely known in the company. An initially entirely satisfactory validity can shrink to zero if managers, anxious to find replacements and familiar with the weights, are tempted to guide applicants into the desired responses.

It should be emphasized that studies done to date do not yield support for the view that certain responses on an application blank are universally predictive of future success, irrespective of the job and the situation. In fact, the responses that contribute the most to the relationship with a criterion are often difficult to explain in any manner.

On the other hand, some studies have produced very significant patterns of predictive responses. An analysis of application-blank responses of boys doing direct door-to-door selling indicated that such items as owning a bicycle, family receives a newspaper, attending a show or circus with parents, having a telephone in the home, and saving money earned were highly predictive of success (1). The data consistently indicated that boys of higher socioeconomic status were more successful.

Similarly, a study of application-blank data in a consulting firm showed that the more successful consultants had held commissioned officer's rank in service, had previously been members of management in a business firm, were graduates of a private preparatory school, were graduates of a small private college, had obtained a graduate degree from the Harvard Business School or some other prestige school, and had served in the Navy or Air Force; yet their fathers were of relatively low educational and occupational level. The data taken as a whole suggest a strong desire to seek out elite associations and to move upward from lower socioeconomic backgrounds (19).

Biographical Inventories

The distinction between a weighted application blank and a biographical inventory is by no means clear-cut. However, the typical biographical inventory contains a somewhat larger number of items, utilizes a multiple-choice format exclusively, and deals with matters that would not normally be covered in an application form. Often, there are questions dealing with early life experiences, hobbies, health, social relations, and so on, that go well beyond the application blank in their detailed coverage of prior experiences (9). In some instances, questions on attitudes, interests, values, opinions, and self-impressions are included. When this occurs, the biographical inventory begins to approximate a test. Thus, selection instruments of this kind, although they tend to place primary emphasis on the

Classification Data
What is your present marital status?
    1. Single.
    2. Married, no children.
    3. Married, one or more children.
    4. Widowed.
    5. Separated or divorced.

Habits and Attitudes
How often do you tell jokes?
    1. Very frequently.
    2. Frequently.
    3. Occasionally.
    4. Seldom.
    5. Cannot remember jokes.

Health
Have you ever suffered from:
    1. Allergies?
    2. Asthma?
    3. High blood pressure?
    4. Ulcers?
    5. Headaches?
    6. None of these.

Human Relations
How do you regard your neighbors?
    1. Not interested in your neighbors.
    2. Like them but seldom see them.
    3. Visit in each others' homes occasionally.
    4. Spend a lot of time together.

Money
How much life insurance, other than company group insurance, do you carry on your own life?
    1. None.
    2. $1,000 to $7,500.
    3. $7,500 to $12,500.
    4. $12,500 to $25,000.
    5. Over $25,000.

Parental Home: Childhood, Teens
During most of the time before you were 18, with whom did you live?
    1. Both parents.
    2. One parent.
    3. A relative.
    4. Foster parents or nonrelatives.
    5. In a home or institution.

Personal Attributes
How creative do you feel you are?
    1. Highly creative.
    2. Somewhat more creative than most in your field.
    3. Moderately creative.
    4. Somewhat less creative than most in your field.

Figure 12–2. Typical Biographical Inventory Questions.
Source: J. R. Glennon, L. E. Albright, and W. A. Owens,
A Catalog of Life History Items (Washington, D.C.; Division
14, American Psychological Association).

Present Home, Spouse, and Children
Regarding moving from location to location, my wife:
1. Would go willingly wherever my job takes me.
2. Would not move under any circumstances.
3. Would move only if it were absolutely necessary.
4. Has not told me how she feels about moving.
5. Not married.

Recreation, Hobbies, and Interests
Have you ever belonged to:
1. A high school fraternity or its equivalent?
2. A college fraternity?
3. Both a high school and a college fraternity?
4. None of the above.

School and Education
How old were you when you graduated from high school?
1. Younger than 15.
2. 15 to 16.
3. 17 to 18.
4. 19 or older.
5. Did not graduate from high school.

Self-impressions
Do you generally do your best:
1. At whatever job you are doing?
2. Only in what you are interested?
3. Only when it is demanded of you?

Values, Opinions, and Preferences
Which one of the following seems most important to you?
1. Having a pleasant home and family life.
2. Obtaining a challenging and exciting job.
3. Getting ahead in the world.
4. Being active and accepted in community affairs.
5. Making the most of your particular ability.

Work
How do you feel about traveling in your work?
1. Would enjoy it tremendously.
2. Would like to do some traveling.
3. Would travel if it were necessary.
4. Definitely dislike traveling.

Figure 12–2. (Continued.)

past as a predictor of the future, can also serve to sample present behavior and functioning to achieve their predictive purpose. Examples of the various kinds of items currently in use are presented in Figure 12–2.

Biographical inventories are usually constructed for the specific purpose of predicting success in a given type of work. The items included are those that the person conducting the analysis believes have some potential as predictors. The mechanics of weighting are essentially the same as those described for the weighted application blank. Usually, however, items that do not discriminate between high and low performers are dropped from the final measure. Thus, the validation and cross-validation process serves as a means of item selection.

When cross-validation is successfully carried out, a weighted score across a number of items is obtained, and the items deal with historical events that are potentially verifiable, the biographical inventory appears to be a highly effective selection procedure (2). When biographical inventories of this kind are compared with psychological tests, they tend to yield considerably higher validities in relation to job performance and tenure criteria. The crucial requirement for achieving such results, however, is the conduct of adequate research to identify the specific items that have predictive power.

REFERENCES AND BACKGROUND CHECKS

A final method of obtaining information on an applicant's prior behavior utilizes not the individual himself, but those who have associated with him and been in a position to observe him. Often, a written evaluation is obtained, but telephone interviews appear to be most frequent (25).

Although the use of references, usually individuals named by the applicant, is widespread in the business world, the available research does not provide much basis for optimism insofar as this approach to the selection problem is concerned. One study related scores obtained from a standardized recommendation questionnaire to subsequent supervisory ratings of performance (21). The questionnaire contained items on occupational ability, character and reputation, and employability. On the average, two completed questionnaires were returned on each individual included in the study, and the scores on these were averaged for the purpose of computing validity coefficients. The recommendations came from previous employers, supervisors, personnel managers, co-workers, and acquaintances. The men evaluated were all civil service employees working in various skilled trades. Results are presented in Table 12–2.

Only the correlations in the .20s have any predictive significance, and these are still low. Since only 5 of the 12 values reach even this level, the findings cannot be interpreted as providing much support for the use of recommendations. The major difficulty is that the responses were almost without exception very positive. Thus, the range of scores was narrow, and discrimination among applicants minimal. This appears to be a typical difficulty with recommendations. However, there is some evidence that when references are obtained in letter form, rather than by standardized questionnaire, different types of positive statements can have differential significance (23). When positive statements regarding only such characteristics as cooperation, consideration, and urbanity appear in the letter, there is a good chance the person writing the reference has some doubts regarding the applicant's qualifications. If, on the other hand, there are positive statements in the areas of mental agility, vigor, dependability, and reliability,

Table 12–2. Correlation of Employee Recommendation Scores with Supervisors' Ratings

Trade	N	r
Carpenter	51	.01
Equipment repairman	40	.23
Machinist	100	.24
Machine operator	108	−.10
Ordnanceman (torpedo)	125	−.01
Radio mechanic	107	.29
Aviation metalsmith	94	.24
Highlift-fork operator	108	.21
Auto mechanic	98	.09
Painter	70	.07
Ordnanceman	100	.10
Printer	116	.11

Source: J. N. Mosel and H. W. Goheen, "The Validity of the Employment Recommendation Questionnaire in Personnel Selection," *Personnel Psychology*, 11 : 484 (1958).

then it can be assumed that a favorable opinion regarding performance potential really exists.

A question may arise concerning the source of the recommendations. Is it possible that certain types of people, having had particular kinds of relationships with an applicant, will provide more valid information than other types? A study to check on this hypothesis has been conducted using public school teachers (3). Employment recommendation questionnaires were correlated with performance ratings given at the end of the first year of employment by each teacher's principal. The results, given in Table 12–3, are very similar to those of Table 12–2. Only correlations of about .20 and higher

Table 12–3. Correlation of Reference Ratings with Subsequent Performance Ratings by Source of Reference

Reference Source	N	r
Last superintendent	147	.08
Last principal	340	.19
Last supervisor	96	.23
Other superintendent	111	.22
Other principal	407	.07
Other supervisor	53	.06
Head of college education department	150	.21
Professor of practice teaching	68	−.03
Cooperating teacher of practice teaching	184	.09

Source: R. C. Browning, "Validity of Reference Ratings from Previous Employers," *Personnel Psychology*, 21 : 391 (1968).

have any predictive significance, and there are few of these. The data do not suggest that any particular sources are clearly preferable.

Somewhat more encouraging results have been obtained from a study that attempted to determine whether references might yield substantial validity under certain circumstances, but not others (5, 22). This proved to be the case. The references were most accurate when received from immediate supervisors who supervised the candidate for a considerable time period in a job much the same as that in which the later employment occurred. However, references from supervisors of the same sex, race, or country of origin as the individual evaluated often had an upward bias that made them less useful. Thus, if characteristics of the source and of the relationship between the applicant and the reference source can be taken into account, the reference check does appear to have considerable value. Unfortunately, as with many moderator variable studies of this kind, the findings of this investigation provide no guides with regard to the large group of candidates whose references have a very good chance of being inaccurate.

A final question involves the relationship between written recommendations and more intensive field investigations, which attempt to develop a picture of an individual's background from personal interviews with a variety of people who have known him or her. A study in this area dealt with government employees hired to fill positions as economists, budget examiners, and training officers (10). Field interviews were conducted with from three to six people who knew the applicant, and the results of these interviews were combined into an overall field evaluation. The latter investigation report ratings were then correlated with previously obtained ratings on a standardized recommendation questionnaire dealing with the applicants' personality, skill, knowledge, human relations competence, and occupational development.

As Table 12–4 indicates, there was a positive relationship between the written recommendations and the more intensive field investigations. What the table does not indicate is the amount of information that came out in the interviews but not in the letters. Such matters as gross incompetence, alcoholism, and homosexuality were practically never mentioned in writing. Yet the field interviews often led to the identification of such factors. It seems clear, therefore, that the more effort one puts into an investigation of

Table 12–4. Correlation of Employee Recommendation Scores and Investigation Report Ratings

Position	N	r
Economist	41	.22
Budget examiner	21	.54
Training officer	47	.45

Source: H. W. Goheen and J. N. Mosel, "Validity of Employment Recommendation Questionnaire: II. Comparison with Field Investigations," *Personnel Psychology*, 12 : 300 (1959).

an applicant's background, the greater the probability that meaningful results will be obtained. Letters to friends identified by the applicant are in all probability not even worth the cost of mailing. Intensive interviews with former superiors, and others who know the person well, may be worth the effort.

It should be emphasized that field investigations of the type described are not restricted to government employees. Bonding and security clearance investigations are frequently carried out on industrial employees. Many firms regularly obtain credit evaluations on applicants, and the credit agencies often provide detailed information on other matters as well. For a rather nominal price, checks are carried out on court records, educational credentials, prior work experiences, and places of residence. On occasion, detective agencies are used to investigate managerial candidates. It is common practice to speak either on the telephone or in person with mutual acquaintances, especially those with occupational skills similar to the applicant's. Although the evidence on the matter is sparse, it seems likely that all these techniques, if they are used in a systematic manner with cross-checks between sources, will be more valuable and valid than written references. Nevertheless, it is important to maintain an ongoing validation effort to determine whether all types of preemployment information are related to subsequent success.

As noted in Chapter 5, various laws and court decisions increasingly are constraining the use of references and background investigations in order to protect individual rights to privacy and to prevent blacklisting in employment. There are not only the federal limitations on the use of credit investigations without adequate reporting to job candidates, but also a number of state laws that make former employers liable for damages under certain circumstances. Such liability may occur when statements by a former employer can be shown to have wrongfully barred a candidate from a subsequent position with another employer as a result of blacklisting, false statement, or misrepresentation.

Thus, a personnel executive in California recommends, "if a company elects to answer an employment inquiry, the answer should be limited to a very concise and truthful statement of facts pertaining to the reasons for the particular termination in question. . . . Many businesses are verifying dates of employment and last position only. . . . It would probably be best not to respond to the rating part of the inquiry, since ratings are quite subjective. In addition, it would not be advisable to state whether the employee was eligible for rehire" (31, pp. 46–47). Obviously, if this advice is widely followed, reference checks of the kind that have been used so extensively in the past may well practically disappear.

QUESTIONS

1. What things can be done to increase the reliability and validity of decisions based on selection interviews?

2. In what ways are the construction and use of application blanks constrained by legal considerations? Explain.
3. Why is cross-validation so important with weighted application blanks? How would you go about constructing and cross-validating such a measure?
4. A number of considerations suggest that written reference checks may be becoming a thing of the past, and that this is not an entirely undesirable development. What are these considerations?
5. Define what is meant by each of the following and evaluate the effectiveness of each:
   a. Nondirective interview.
   b. Stress interview.
   c. Biographical inventory.
   d. Field investigation.

REFERENCES

1. Appel, V., and M. R. Feinberg. "Recruiting Door-to-door Salesmen by Mail." *Journal of Applied Psychology*, 53 (1969), 362–366.
2. Asher, J. J. "The Biographical Item: Can It Be Improved?" *Personnel Psychology*, 25 (1972), 251–269.
3. Browning, R. C. "Validity of Reference Ratings from Previous Employers." *Personnel Psychology*, 21 (1968), 389–393.
4. Carlson, R. E., P. W. Thayer, E. C. Mayfield, and D. A. Peterson. "Improvements in the Selection Interview." *Personnel Journal*, 50 (1971), 268–275, 317.
5. Carroll, S. J., and A. N. Nash. "Effectiveness of a Forced-choice Reference Check." *Personnel Administration*, 35 (1972), No. 2, 42–46.
6. Downs, C. W. "A Content Analysis of Twenty Selection Interviews." *Personnel Administration and Public Personnel Review*, 1 (1972), No. 2, 24–31.
7. England, G. W. *Development and Use of Weighted Application Blanks.* Minneapolis, Minn.: Industrial Relations Center, University of Minnesota, 1969.
8. Fear, R. A. *The Evaluation Interview.* New York: McGraw-Hill Book Company, 1973.
9. Glennon, J. R., L. E. Albright, and W. A. Owens. *A Catalog of Life History Items.* Washington, D.C.: Division 14, American Psychological Association (undated).
10. Goheen, H. W., and J. N. Mosel. "Validity of the Employment Recommendation Questionnaire: II. Comparison with Field Investigations." *Personnel Psychology*, 12 (1959), 297–301.
11. Goldstein, I. L. "The Application Blank: How Honest Are the Responses?" *Journal of Applied Psychology*, 55 (1971), 491–492.
12. Guion, R. M. *Personnel Testing.* New York: McGraw-Hill Book Company, 1965.

13. Karras, E. J., and J. H. Zimmerman. "Dimension Interviewing." *Personnel Journal,* 51 (1972), 733–736.
14. Langdale, J. A., and J. Weitz. "Estimating the Influence of Job Information on Interviewer Agreement." *Journal of Applied Psychology,* 57 (1973), 23–27.
15. London, M., and M. D. Hakel. "Effects of Applicant Stereotypes, Order, and Information on Interview Impressions." *Journal of Applied Psychology,* 59 (1974), 157–162.
16. Lopez, F. M. *Personnel Interviewing.* New York: McGraw-Hill Book Company, 1975.
17. McMurry, R. N. "Validating the Patterned Interview." *Personnel,* 23 (1947), 263–272.
18. Miner, J. B. "Executive and Personnel Interviews as Predictors of Consulting Success." *Personnel Psychology,* 23 (1970), 521–538.
19. Miner, J. B. "Success in Management Consulting and the Concept of Eliteness Motivation." *Academy of Management Journal,* 14 (1971), 367–378.
20. Minter, R. L. "Human Rights Laws and Pre-employment Inquiries." *Personnel Journal,* 51 (1972), 431–433.
21. Mosel, J. N., and H. W. Goheen. "The Validity of the Employment Recommendation Questionnaire in Personnel Selection." *Personnel Psychology,* 11 (1958), 481–490.
22. Nash, A. N., and S. J. Carroll. "A Hard Look at the Reference Check." *Business Horizons,* 13 (1970), No. 5, 43–49.
23. Peres, S. H., and J. R. Garcia. "Validity and Dimensions of Descriptive Adjectives Used in Reference Letters for Engineering Applicants." *Personnel Psychology,* 15 (1962), 279–286.
24. Peters, L. H., and J. R. Terborg. "The Effects of Temporal Placement of Unfavorable Information and of Attitude Similarity on Personnel Decisions." *Organizational Behavior and Human Performance,* 13 (1975), 279–293.
25. Pyron, H. C. "The Use and Misuse of Previous Employer References in Hiring." *Management of Personnel Quarterly,* 9 (1970), No. 2, 15–22.
26. Roach, D. E. "Double Cross-validation of a Weighted Application Blank over Time." *Journal of Applied Psychology,* 55 (1971), 157–160.
27. Schwab, D. P., and H. G. Heneman, III. "Relationship Between Interview Structure and Interinterviewer Reliability in an Employment Situation." *Journal of Applied Psychology,* 53 (1969), 214–217.
28. Schwab, D. P., and R. L. Oliver. "Predicting Tenure with Biographical Data: Exhuming Buried Evidence." *Personnel Psychology,* 27 (1974), 125–128.
29. Stone, C. H., and F. L. Ruch. "Selection, Interviewing, and Testing," in D. Yoder and H. G. Heneman (eds.), *Staffing Policies and Strategies.* Washington, D.C.: Bureau of National Affairs, Inc., 1974.
30. Valenzi, E., and I. R. Andrews. "Individual Differences in the Decision

Process of Employment Interviewers." *Journal of Applied Psychology,* 58 (1973), 49–53.

31. Wangler, L. A. "The Employee Reference Request: A Road to Misdemeanor?" *Personnel Administrator,* 18 (1973), No. 6, 45–47.
32. Webster, E. C. *Decision Making in the Employment Interview.* Montreal, Canada: Industrial Relations Centre, McGill University, 1964.
33. Weiss, D. J., and R. V. Dawis. "An Objective Validation of Factual Interview Data." *Journal of Applied Psychology,* 44 (1960), 381–385.
34. Wright, O. R. "Summary of Research on the Selection Interview Since 1964." *Personnel Psychology,* 22 (1969), 391–413.

13

The Physical Examination and Psychological Testing

In this final chapter on the selection process, the coverage will be restricted to the methods of regulating the human inputs to an organization that place primary stress on samples of current activity. Both the physical examination and psychological testing attempt to develop an estimate of future effectiveness from an analysis of present functioning in a particular sphere.

The parallel between the two does not end there, however. Both techniques normally require the services of a specialist, medical or psychological, although certain types of psychological testing can be carried out by individuals without the professional degree, as can certain aspects of the physical exam. Both have also become embroiled in a certain amount of controversy related to the invasion-of-privacy question, as discussed in Chapter 10.

THE PHYSICAL EXAMINATION AND RELATED MEASURES

As with a number of other selection tools, the preemployment physical examination is characteristically utilized with more than a single purpose in mind. True, these procedures are normally intended as a method of eliminating individuals who might not be physically capable of performing effectively. Thus, the selection goal is an important one. But there are a number of other objectives that no doubt would induce many firms to continue using physical examinations for job candidates, even if the examination procedures were known to have very limited predictive validity.

For one thing, information on physical functioning can be helpful in determining the specific type of position in which a person might perform most effectively and with the least likelihood of injury. Thus, a placement as well as a selection role may be involved. Some industrial physicians appear to believe that the physical examination should rarely be used for purposes of rejection, but primarily to establish a suitable placement. This, however, does not appear to be the dominant viewpoint (19).

On the other hand, rejections on medical grounds do not normally run as high as for other reasons. The data of Table 13–1 are probably typical. In this instance, the physical examination clearly served to guide a placement decision in 10 per cent of the cases and to bar employment in 12 per cent. The latter were largely applicants for work in oil fields and refineries who exhibited abnormalities in back X rays.

Another goal has to do entirely with safety. Data from the physical examination can be used to sensitize a person to his limitations. Thus, he may be in a better position to protect himself against accident and injury. Closely related is the fact that a physical examination given just prior to employment can provide a base against which to evaluate any subsequent workers' compensation claims. From a management viewpoint, it is important to know whether any injuries, defects, or diseases that may appear in an employee were present before the individual started working for the company, or whether they could be a direct result of the conditions of employ-

Table 13–1. Classification Based on 7,500 Preplacement Physical Examinations Conducted by Mobil Oil Company

Class		Per Cent
A	Physically fit for any work	20
B	Defect negligible or correctable: otherwise fit for any work	58
C	Defect limits fitness for certain work and/or requires medical control	10
D	Defect requires medical control or attention and disqualifies for employment	12

Source: E. P. Luongo, "The Preplacement Physical Examination in Industry—Its Values," *Archives of Environmental Health,* 5 : 359 (1962).

ment. The existence of accurate preemployment data can serve to limit the company's liability for a subsequent disability.

Finally, there are circumstances under which a physical examination *must* be given to applicants. For example, the Interstate Commerce Commission requires such an examination for truck drivers and states specific physical criteria for employment in this type of work. Visual defects in particular are likely to lead to rejection.

Reports of company practice with regard to the use of preemployment physical examinations indicate widespread usage, especially in manufacturing industries, where 90 per cent of the firms utilize the procedure. The percentage for all employers is approximately 80. As one personnel manager notes, "the cost of preemployment physicals is more than repaid through elimination of high-risk hires who have a high incidence of sick time and time off the job, and who increase the cost of the medical program" (10, p. 3). Presumably, it is attitudes such as this that account for the popularity of the physical examination in selection.

The physical examination does not take an identical form in all companies and for all jobs. Where the nature of the work is such that a specific type of disability will almost inevitably restrict effectiveness, this particular sphere tends to receive greater attention, and more detailed medical tests are normally carried out. Thus, the preemployment physical examination is in reality a battery of tests, which should be selected with a view to maximizing predictive effectiveness in the particular situation while at the same time keeping related costs to a minimum. Some of the measures that may be used are a serological test, blood counts, roentgenograms of the chest, electrocardiograms, a metabolism test, measures of sensory functioning, a urinalysis, the electroencephalogram, and tests of neuromuscular reactions. Such tests have been used quite widely to detect drug addiction (9).

Consistency and Validity of Physical Tests

Research carried out some years ago dealing with the consistency of preemployment physical examinations given applicants for positions as airline pilots was rather discouraging (22). Repeated examinations did not yield the same results. In one instance, even when comparisons were restricted to items on which the same tests were used, and items, such as weight, that might have changed between the two examinations were eliminated, only 16 per cent of the total number of defects noted were listed as similar by two different medical examiners. In another case, 43 per cent of a group of pilot applicants who had already passed a Civil Aeronautics Administration physical exam were subsequently found to have disqualifying defects. A major problem seems to be the tendency of physicians to be very strict with regard to their own specialties and considerably less so in other areas.

There have been a number of improvements in the objectivity and standardization of the various medical tests in recent years, and greater consistency than that found in the studies just described can now be expected. Yet it is still possible in some instances to memorize an eye chart with glasses on before being asked to read the chart without glasses. If the results of such a test are compared with those obtained when a person is required to remove his glasses before entering the test room, the conclusions derived from the two measurements are not likely to be similar. Clearly, the consistency of results obtained in actual practice from various medical tests is far from perfect.

In addition to consistency, it is also important to demonstrate validity—the actual contribution of the selection physical examination to lowered workers' compensation costs, improved performance, and reduced accident rates and absenteeism. A series of studies that permit a comparison of accident rates among airplane pilots who did and did not possess certain physical defects at the time of employment is relevant to this issue (22).

The first investigation was carried out on a group of Pan American World Airways ferry pilots during World War II. Because of shortages of available personnel, only 9 of 281 applicants were rejected. Of those accepted, 75 had one or more defects that would normally be disqualifying—poor visual acuity, defective color vision, overweight or underweight, high blood pressure or pulse rate, hay fever, hearing loss, and structural defect. In spite of these physical inadequacies, there were only five fatal accidents in the ensuing operations. Of the 10 pilots killed, only 5 had physical defects at the time of employment, and none of these defects appeared to be causally related to the accident.

In another case, a group of 114 Lockheed test pilots was studied. On the average, these men had 3 separate physical defects. Over a 5-year period, however, there were only 19 accidents causing destruction of aircraft. The physical condition of the pilot did not appear to be a causative factor in any of these instances.

Finally, the RAF conducted a comparison between a group of 106 pilot applicants with known physical defects and a matched group who met all screening standards. At the end of 10 years, almost exactly half of each group were still flying. There were no reliable differences in the number of accidents while flying.

It should be emphasized that in none of these cases were the "physically unfit" men totally unselected. Extreme disabilities were disqualifying in all instances. Yet it does appear that standards may often be set much higher than is necessary, and that many tests having no relation to job performance are used. Under such circumstances, the predictive validity of the physical examination does not appear to be very high.

This situation has led some to the conclusion that in many cases physical examinations should be abandoned and health questionnaires substituted. Under such circumstances, little effort would be made to improve the predictive power of physical tests, to establish validities and minimum standards on an empirical basis. Rather, physical examinations would be played down in the selection process and given only in certain special cases or when required by law.

HEALTH QUESTIONNAIRES

The available evidence on the use of health questionnaires in the selection situation is rather encouraging. Considerable research has been conducted with the Cornell Medical Index-Health Questionnaire, which contains 195 Yes-No items dealing with disorders of the eyes and ears, respiratory system, cardiovascular system, digestive tract, musculoskeletal system, skin, nervous system, and genitourinary system, as well as fatigability, frequency of illness, miscellaneous diseases, habits, and mood patterns. The questions cover both present physical functioning and the past medical history. They are very similar to those a physician would ask in an interview situation.

When this questionniare was used as a selection device in a factory of the Benson and Hedges Tobacco Company, it was found that the applicants indicated considerably fewer complaints than are normally noted on the measure (15). Presumably, many were attempting to hide disorders that they felt might be disqualifying. Yet, when physical examinations were given to the applicants and the rejected group was compared with those who surmounted this last hurdle and were hired, the ones who failed to pass the physical exam did indicate significantly more complaints on the health questionnaire. Furthermore, among those hired, correlations of .40 for men and .26 for women were found between the number of complaints and the frequency of absenteeism after employment. More recently, a similar level of validity has been reported for the questionnaire in the selection of Navy enlisted men for underwater demolition training (18).

It is apparent that medical questionnaires can provide a useful adjunct to the selection process. On the other hand, elimination of the physical examination does not seem wise. Perhaps appropriate research based on selection models will reveal that the examination can be shortened in many cases and testing restricted to the particular measures that are known to possess predictive validity for the particular job under consideration. This could mean putting together a markedly different set of medical tests to constitute the total examination in one situation as opposed to another. Such an approach is widely used in psychological testing.

The Polygraph and Lie Detection

Although not normally incorporated in the physical examination, the polygraph provides measures of physiological functioning of essentially the same kind as those often obtained in connection with the physical examination. The standard polygraph used in the United States records blood pressure and pulse, respiratory patterns, and sweat gland activity simultaneously (20). The lie-detection examination differs from the physical examination in that its objective is to identify dishonesty or criminal behavior, rather than disability or illness; the measurement processes involved are basically the same, however.

In lie detection, a series of questions are asked while at the same time the polygraph records physiological variations. Control questions are used to establish base-line patterns under conditions of no dissimulation. These patterns are compared to those for relevant questions from which particular reactions are expected if deception is attempted. Conducting a lie-detection examination requires considerable skill both in asking the questions and in interpreting the polygraph recordings. Most of the work is done by private firms specializing in this area. It is rare for a company to conduct its own examinations.

Lie-detection examinations are not widely used in the business world, and when they are used it is more likely to be in solving suspected employee thefts than in preemployment screening. Use is most extensive in wholesale and retail trade; it is also relatively common among financial, insurance, and real estate establishments. In the selection context, the major emphasis is on determining the extent of honesty in completing the application blank. The most common concern is to establish whether the individual might be expected to steal from his employer if hired. It is not at all uncommon for people to admit previous thefts to the examiner during the course of the lie-detection examination.

PROBLEMS OF VALIDITY

Many arguments have been advanced, both pro and con, regarding the use of lie detection. Ethical considerations have been explored at length, and many case examples have been presented to document particular positions. It is apparent that a number of inexperienced and untrained examiners have entered the field; in some cases, the examinations have been very poorly conducted (20). As a result, certain states have passed licensing laws to improve the quality of work in the field. About the same number have attempted to solve problems of validity by outlawing polygraph use by business firms.

Given this environment of controversy, how valid can lie detection be when carried out by a highly qualified examiner? Although the research evidence is limited, the available data indicate that very high levels of validity can be obtained. In one instance, polygraph examiner conclusions regarding the presence of deception were compared with the findings of a panel of judges who read entire trial transcriptions (with polygraph reports deleted) and made decisions as to whether they believed the individual to be guilty or not (7). In the instances where the four judges were in complete agreement, the lie-detection examination was in accord on over 90 per cent of the cases. Where only a majority of the judges concluded for or against guilt, the polygraph report agreed 75 per cent of the time.

Validity of this kind presupposes that experienced polygraph examiners will agree in their identification of diagnostic physiological responses. Separate studies of the reliability of identification support this conclusion, with the average agreement level being 95 per cent (13).

CRIMINAL BEHAVIOR QUESTIONNAIRES

Just as health questionnaires have been developed to supplement and in some cases replace preemployment physical examinations, questionnaires have also been developed to predict criminal behavior, particularly theft. The questionnaires are of special importance in the states that have passed laws barring the use of polygraph examinations.

One such instrument that has been studied quite extensively contains questions regarding attitudes toward punishment for crimes and attitudes toward one's own criminal behavior. Additional questions deal more specifically with any criminal activities in which the individual may have participated (3, 4). Surprisingly, job applicants in significant numbers actually do admit to a wide range of criminal behaviors. Furthermore, results obtained with the questionnaires have been compared with those from polygraph examinations. Agreement is quite close, sufficiently so to recommend the questionnaire as a device for screening out individuals who may subsequently steal from their employer.

PSYCHOLOGICAL TESTING: ABILITIES

In the following sections, a number of different types of psychological tests will be discussed. From among the measures that have had considerable business application, examples will be drawn in a manner intended to illustrate the diversity of approaches taken, rather than to indicate the most widespread usage. At the end of each section, a general review will be attempted of the validities obtained with each type of test in various business positions. More detailed information on the tests noted can be found in *The Seventh Mental Measurements Yearbook* (11).

Multiability Tests

One approach in psychological measurement has been to incorporate a number of quite varied subtests in a comprehensive test battery. The batteries typically yield an overall index of intelligence plus subscores for specific mental abilities.

WECHSLER ADULT INTELLIGENCE SCALE

The Wechsler Adult Intelligence Test is an individually administered test, with questions asked orally by a psychologist of the person tested and answers recorded on a special test form (23). Because it is time-consuming and costly to administer, the Wechsler is not widely used for personnel selection except at the higher levels. There are 11 subtests in all:

Verbal

1. Information. A series of open-ended questions dealing with the kinds of factual data people normally pick up in their ordinary contacts.
2. Comprehension. Another series of open-ended questions covering the individual's understanding of the need for social rules.
3. Arithmetic. All the questions are of the story, or problem, type. Scoring is for the correctness of solutions and the time to respond.
4. Digit span. Here a group of numbers is read off, and the subject repeats them from memory, sometimes backward.
5. Similarities. Pairs of terms are read off, and a common property, or characteristic, must be abstracted.
6. Vocabulary. A series of words that must be defined in the subject's own terms.

Performance

7. Picture completion. A number of pictures are presented in which the subject must identify the missing component.
8. Picture arrangement. Items require that a series of pictures be arranged as rapidly as possible in the order that makes the most sense.
9. Object assembly. Jigsaw puzzles that must be put together within a given time limit.
10. Block design. Working with a set of small blocks having red, white, or red and white faces, the subject attempts to duplicate various printed designs as quickly as possible.
11. Digit symbol. The subject is given a series of paired symbols and numbers as a code. He is then to write as many correct numbers as he can for each of a whole series of scrambled symbols within a set time period.

DIFFERENTIAL APTITUDE TESTS

One of the most carefully constructed sets of tests currently available is the Differential Aptitude Tests, which take about four hours to administer. Eight separate aptitude measures are included. With the exception of the clerical test, all have liberal time limits, with the result that older applicants are not unduly penalized. For most purposes, it would probably not be necessary to administer the entire battery, but rather only those tests that have proved to have relevance for the particular position under consideration. The aptitudes measured are

1. Verbal reasoning. These are a series of verbal analogies. A good background of general information is required.
2. Numerical ability. Arithmetic computations with a multiple-choice format. The choices are structured in such a way that the answers must actually be computed.
3. Abstract reasoning. The items are made up of sets of four "problem figures" that constitute a logical sequence of some kind. A fifth figure must

then be selected from among five "answer figures" to complete the sequence.

4. Space relations. A series of items requiring visualization of forms in space. A key pattern must be matched in some way with one or more of five multiple-choice forms.
5. Mechanical reasoning. Pictures are shown depicting various mechanical problems. A number of questions are then asked to determine if the subject understands the mechanical processes involved. This is the typical item type in mechanical ability measures.
6. Clerical speed and accuracy. Five pairs of numbers and/or letters are shown, one of which is underlined. On an answer sheet the same pairs are shown, but in a different order. The task is to pick out the underlined pair on the answer sheet. The test is timed, and the score is based on the number of items completed correctly.
7. Language usage, spelling. A series of words, some spelled correctly and some not. The subject must indicate which are right.
8. Language usage, sentences. A measure of the degree to which an individual understands the formal rules of grammar.

GENERAL APTITUDE TEST BATTERY

A battery of psychological tests constructed by the USES, the General Aptitude Test Battery, has had wide distribution because of its use in the state employment offices. It is aimed primarily at the lower job levels and contains 12 separately timed tests. Scores from these tests are combined to yield measures of various individual aptitudes, plus an index of general intelligence. The special aptitudes measured are verbal, numerical, spatial, form perception, clerical perception, coordination, finger dexterity, and manual dexterity.

The test has been used extensively in occupational research conducted by the USES and in these studies has typically yielded good validity. However, it is clear that the aptitudes that are related to success in one type of work are not always the same as those that are associated with success in another. Furthermore, the USES studies indicate that although success in training is best predicted with measures of general intelligence and of verbal and numerical ability, aptitudes such as coordination, finger dexterity, and manual dexterity are relatively more important in predicting job proficiency (6). The results reported in USES may of course overstate what can be expected in a single application at a particular location. Thus, a recent company study with coil winders failed to replicate the validation of .25 to .40 previously reported for that occupation (2).

Tests of Special Intellectual Abilities

A number of separately published tests measure one, or at most two, of the various mental abilities. In many respects, they are similar to specific

Table 13–2. Correlations Between General Intelligence
Tests in a Sample of 108 Sales Employees

Test	Mean Score	Vocabulary Test G-T		Concept Mastery	WAIS Score
		Form A	Form B		
Vocabulary Test G-T, Forms A and B (40 items)	27.64	.89	.89	.73	.56
Vocabulary Test G-T, Form A (20 items)	13.03		.59	.64	.47
Vocabulary Test G-T, Form B (20 items)	14.61			.67	.54
Concept Mastery Test	61.50				.54
WAIS Score	67.22				

Source: J. B. Miner, "On the Use of a Short Vocabulary Test to Measure General Intelligence," *Journal of Educational Psychology*, 52 : 158 (1961). Copyright 1961 by the American Psychological Association, and reproduced by permission.

subtests of the multiability batteries. There are independent measures of clerical ability, mechanical ability, creative ability, spatial ability, numerical ability, verbal ability, and others.

Certain of these tests are considered as measures of general intelligence. These usually are pure verbal ability tests, although in certain instances numerical items are included as well. Available evidence appears to support the general intelligence designation, even when the verbal ability measures are quite short (24). In Table 13–2, correlations among a short vocabulary test, the Concept Mastery Test, a much longer measure containing some numerical as well as verbal items, and the Wechsler Adult Intelligence Scale are reported. All the correlations are substantial. Thus, when a score is referred to as an index of *general intelligence,* either a verbal ability test score, a verbal and numerical score, or a comprehensive score derived from a multiability test may be indicated. The common bond appears to be a strong emphasis on material normally learned in school.

Psychomotor Tests

The coordination and dexterity tests of the General Aptitude Test Battery have already been mentioned. Other typical psychomotor measures are the MacQuarrie Test for Mechanical Ability and the O'Connor Finger and Tweezer Dexterity Tests. In addition, there are a number of special coordination measures and apparatus tests that tap muscular skills of a grosser nature.

Although most psychomotor tests require some kind of special equipment, the MacQuarrie utilizes only pencil and paper. There are seven subtests:

1. *Tracing.* The subject draws a continuous line from a start through gaps in a series of vertical lines to a finish point.
2. *Tapping.* The subject makes dots on a paper as quickly as possible.
3. *Dotting.* Dots are made within small irregularly placed circles.

4. *Copying.* Simple designs are copied by connecting the appropriate dots from among a much larger number.
5. *Location.* The subject is required to locate specific points in a smaller version of a large stimulus.
6. *Blocks.* Piled blocks are shown in two dimensions, and the total number in the pile must be determined.
7. *Pursuit.* The subject visually traces lines through a maze.

This type of test appears to measure something rather different than the psychomotor tests utilizing special equipment. There is also reason to believe that the latter are more likely to yield adequate predictions in the selection situation (17). Yet tests such as those in the MacQuarrie have proved valid for occupations such as aviation mechanic and stenographer.

The O'Connor tests require a board with 100 small holes in rows of 10 and a shallow tray in which a number of pins are placed. The subject's job is to fill the holes with pins using either his fingers or, in some instances, tweezers. The score is the amount of time required to complete the task. This is the traditional type of measure used to obtain an index of finger dexterity. Similar pegboards with screws, nuts and bolts, and so on, provide a measure of more comprehensive psychomotor skills of the kind subsumed under the title manual dexterity.

The O'Connor measures have been found valid as predictors of success among power sewing-machine operators and also for dental students, as well as for a variety of other manipulative tasks. The pegboard format is the most widely used among the psychomotor tests. It has in general proved to be a highly effective one in the selection situation.

In the coordination area, the most typical measure probably is the pursuit rotor, which establishes aiming skill, or, perhaps more appropriately, motor coordination. The task here is to follow a dot on a rotating disk, using a stylus. The test measures electronically record the number of seconds the stylus is actually on the moving point.

Much more complex apparatus tests requiring a subject to pull certain levers, push certain pedals, and so on, when a given pattern of lights appears, have also been developed. Such apparatus techniques, although they have not been widely used in industry, do appear to possess considerable potential. Unfortunately, separate procedures must be developed for each job, or perhaps on occasion for a job family. This is costly and requires considerable research. In fact, further research seems to be needed in the area of psychomotor abilities generally. The various tests are not closely related, and a measure that will predict for one job often does not do so for another that on the surface would seem to be very similar.

General Pattern of Validities: Abilities

The most comprehensive and up-to-date summary of previous research available at the present time breaks the ability measures into intelligence, spatial and mechanical, clerical, and psychomotor types (16). Under intelligence are placed not only studies involving the use of the multiability tests, but also those employing specific measures of numerical and verbal abilities.

In general, the various measures of intelligence and of spatial and mechanical abilities seem to achieve their greatest predictive effectiveness when used to select individuals for training programs. Used in this capacity, they far excel other types of ability measures. However, when prediction goes beyond the training period and moves to actual on-the-job performance, tests of intelligence and of spatial and mechanical abilities appear to do only as well as the clerical and psychomotor measures. This would suggest that generally, where there is particular concern about selecting people who will be able to get through a training period, emphasis can best be placed on intelligence, spatial, or mechanical measures, as appropriate to the particular jobs under consideration. Tests of this kind deal with the capacity to learn and thus are particularly suited to predicting success in training or educational programs. Job effectiveness, on the other hand, requires these "learning" abilities no more than abilities of other kinds.

When attention is focused on specific types of occupations and the tests that will predict success in training for these occupations, the differential significance of the various abilities begins to appear. Success in training for clerical positions is best predicted with the intelligence measures and with the job-specific clerical ability tests. In addition, the indexes of spatial and mechanical abilities also yield good validities.

In selecting people for training in service occupations, such as waiters and hospital attendants, it seems best, in view of the validities obtained, to concentrate on intelligence, spatial, and mechanical tests. These measures are also effective in predicting training success for the skilled industrial occupations, as are measures of clerical ability. At the semiskilled level, the highest validities against training criteria have been obtained with the psychomotor ability tests and the spatial and mechanical measures. Success in training for unskilled occupations is not as well predicted by any of the ability tests; no particular ability stands out.

When we shift from success in training to effectiveness on the job, a greater number of studies are available and more occupations have been investigated. At the managerial level, measures of intelligence and also those of a clerical nature appear to work best. Success in clerical work is predicted about equally well by intelligence and clerical indexes. In the sales occupations, abilities are not generally very important. An exception to this generalization can be made, however, in the case of the higher-level jobs, such as industrial and insurance sales, where intelligence, and to a lesser degree clerical ability, are important. In the lower-level positions, especially among salesclerks, ability tests do not seem to carry any validity at all. Effective performance in the protective service occupations, such as policeman and fireman, is about equally well predicted by all types of ability measures. Performance in the other service occupations, however, appears to be more closely related to intelligence. Success in the various industrial positions at the skilled, semiskilled, and unskilled levels can be predicted with all types of ability measures, although generally the validity coefficients tend to be lower than those obtained with managers, clerical workers, and higher-level sales personnel.

PSYCHOLOGICAL TESTING: PERSONALITY

The majority of the personality tests currently on the market ask the respondent to describe himself in some way, and these self-reports are either taken at face value or related to some group with known characteristics to obtain a score. A second approach utilizes the projective rationale. Tests of this kind obtain descriptions or reactions, not with reference to the self in the here and now, but to some far-removed situation or stimulus. Inferences are then made back to the individual's personality pattern.

The major problem in personality testing is the tendency to portray oneself in the most favorable light. This problem becomes acute in the selection situation. Although the desire to make a good impression may represent a positive contribution when abilities are measured, because it ensures that the applicant will do his best on the tests, such a desire may produce only a distorted and atypical picture in the personality area. Much of the work that has been done in the field of personality testing over the past 30 years has been concerned with the effort to find a solution to this problem (14).

Self-report Techniques

Perhaps the most widely used self-report measures are those that provide information on the degree of interest in various types of activities, primarily those of an occupational nature. The major titles are the Strong Vocational Interest Blank and the Kuder Preference Records. There are, in addition, a number of tests that yield scores on several personality characteristics, usually at least 4 and in some instances as many as 18. Among these self-report tests are the Edwards Personal Preference Schedule and the Minnesota Multiphasic Personality Inventory.

INTEREST MEASURES

In the interest measures, items typically deal with what the individual likes to do or with reports on his own behavior. The Strong Vocational Interest Blank is scored in terms of the similarity between an individual's responses and those of people actually in a given occupation. Thus, a high score on a particular scale means that the person has interests like those of people in that occupation. It does not necessarily mean that he has directly indicated a marked interest in performing in that occupation. This indirect measurement procedure is intended to at least reduce the amount of distortion. Studies indicate, however, that the Strong Vocational Interest Blank still *can* be distorted to produce a desired picture; on the other hand, in the actual selection situation, the amount of distortion occurring appears to be much less (1).

One of the Kuder Preference Records yields occupational scores in the same manner as the Strong Vocational Interest Blank. Another deals with interest areas, such as mechanical or artistic, rather than specific occupations. In both instances, the person must select from three listed activities the one he likes the most and the one he likes the least. Of the two Kuder measures described here, the latter appears most likely to be distorted.

PERSONALITY MEASURES

A different approach to the elimination of bias is reflected in the Edwards Personal Preference Schedule. This is a forced-choice procedure (see Chapter 9) requiring the subject to choose between paired alternatives, the majority of which have been selected so as to be matched in terms of their social desirability. Thus, on most items, the subject cannot respond so as to present a "good" image, because he must choose between two equally "good" alternatives. The test measures some 15 motives: the need or desire for achievement, deference, order, exhibition, autonomy, affiliation, intraception, succorance, dominance, abasement, nurturance, change, endurance, heterosexuality, and aggression. It takes approximately 40 minutes to administer.

The Edwards has rather consistently yielded reliable correlations when studied in relation to various indexes of occupational success (17). Yet, again, as with the Strong Vocational Interest Blank, the procedures introduced to handle distortion do not appear to have been entirely successful. The test can be answered in such a way as to present a good impression (8); in the real-life selection situation, however, only a fraction of this distortion potential appears to be realized (28).

The Minnesota Multiphasic Personality Inventory is a quite different type of self-report measure. Here, an attempt is made to handle distortion by including certain items intended to indicate whether the individual has understood what is to be done and cooperated in completing the test. When these items are answered in certain ways, the other scores obtained become suspect. These scores deal with various types of emotional pathology—depression, hysteria, and the like. The items are scored in terms of the tendency to respond in ways differing from the responses of the normally adjusted. Thus, the end result is a profile indicating similarity to the emotionally disturbed for different diagnosed disorders.

Projective Techniques

The projective procedures approach the problem of bias in a very different manner than the self-report techniques. A projective test is constructed so that the uninformed person cannot determine what is being measured.

The subject simply does not know what he is revealing about himself when he responds to a test item. As a consequence, he cannot bias his response so as to present a socially desirable picture or a picture that seems to be congruent with job expectations.

In theory, at least, this would appear to be the ideal solution to the bias problem. The subject does not describe himself; he reacts, and by reacting in a particular manner reveals what type of person he is. In practice, this approach has encountered sizable difficulties. The problem is that the very procedures that keep the subject from understanding his own responses also make it difficult for the test administrator to understand them. Thus, the projective approach in conquering the bias problem introduces the new problem of interpretation. Work with techniques such as the Rorschach Test, the Thematic Apperception Test, the Rosenzweig Picture-Frustration Study, the various sentence completion measures, the Tomkins-Horn Picture Arrangement Test, and the Worthington Personal History has resulted in some real progress in this area. Yet there can be no question that much more must be learned about the various ways in which people reveal themselves through their test responses before the projective tests can achieve their full potential as personnel selection techniques.

THE THEMATIC APPERCEPTION TECHNIQUE

The TAT, as originally developed, contained 20 pictures, many of them quite ambiguous. In many instances, however, fewer pictures are employed, especially in the industrial situation. Furthermore, a number of special versions of the TAT have been conceived, often using pictures of a much clearer and more structured nature than those originally utilized in the test. In all instances, the subject is asked to tell a story using the picture as a starting point. He is to describe the people, tell what is happening, and develop both the past and the future of the scene depicted. Because he must go beyond the picture itself, his own personal imaginative and fantasy processes are brought into play.

Very little evidence is available regarding the relationship between the TAT in its original form and job performance. Furthermore, although the test may be given in a group situation, with the subjects writing their stories, analysis remains a time-consuming process. For these reasons, the original TAT cannot be recommended as a selection technique under most circumstances.

On the other hand, research has been done with certain special versions of the technique, and relatively simple and objective scoring systems have been developed. Thus, a set of pictures selected to measure a desire for achievement has been found to produce responses that can be scored rapidly, with minimal error. This achievement motivation measure has been shown to yield consistent relationships with various indexes of entrepreneurial success in this country and abroad (21).

Another approach that is closely related to the TAT is the Tomkins-

Horn Picture Arrangement Test (PAT). In this instance, the subject is presented with three pictures at a time that he must arrange to produce a sequence that makes a logical story. Then the brief story describing this pattern of events is written below the pictures. There are 25 such items. Very impressive results have been obtained with this measure, especially in predicting success in sales and consulting occupations (30).

THE SENTENCE-COMPLETION TECHNIQUE

Sentence-completion tests, of which there are a number available, present a series of verbal stems, or beginnings of sentences, that the person is asked to complete. Usually, there is an additional request that in finishing the sentences he express his real feelings. Although some of the items may elicit completions of a self-report nature, the tests are usually constructed so that inferences regarding personality characteristics can be made in terms of the symbolic significance of the responses. Thus, the self-reports are not accepted at face value.

There is reason to believe this technique may prove valuable as a selection device. Unlike most other projectives discussed, it is easy both to administer and to score. Studies with the Miner Sentence Completion Scale, which has been devised specifically for use with management personnel, have consistently indicated that this instrument has both predictive and concurrent validity when used with managerial groups (25, 26). Table 13-3 provides a summary of these findings.

General Pattern of Validities: Personality

Studies relating personality measures, whether self-report or projective, to indexes of success during the training period have almost uniformly yielded disappointing results (16). In groups where any sizable amount of research has been done, which includes clerical, protective service, and skilled occupations, the reported validities have consistently been well below those obtained with certain types of ability measures.

Table 13–3. Validity Data for the Miner Sentence Completion Scale

Managerial Group Studied	N	Criterion Measure	Correlation
R&D managers	81	Potential rating	.43
Marketing managers	81	Promotion rate	.39
Varied managers	61	Rehire rating	.69
Department store managers	70	Managerial level	.42
School administrators	82	Composite rating	.42
R&D managers	117	Peer rating	.55
Personnel managers	101	Managerial level and pay	.28

Source: Adapted from John B. Miner, Studies in Management Education, New York: Springer, 1965; Motivation to Manage, Atlanta, Ga.: Organizational Measurement Systems Press, 1977.

When the focus shifts to on-the-job performance, this picture changes. Managerial success is best predicted by clerical and general intelligence tests, but personality measures are nearly as effective. Among clerical employees, the personality measures again come right behind the intelligence and clerical tests. It is in the sales area, however, that personality tests have proved most useful, primarily because here their contribution is almost unique. Ability measures appear to have little relationship to sales success, except for the intelligence measure among those in higher-level sales positions. Personality measures, on the other hand, have consistently turned out to be good predictors at all levels of sales employment. Among salesclerks, they are the only kind of test that yields positive relationships.

Within the various service occupations, personality tests, although not nearly as effective as in the sales area, achieve validities that are often superior to those reported for ability measures. Job performance in the industrial occupations generally is no better predicted by personality measures than ability measures, but comparable validities can be expected. In general, the evidence indicates that personality measures can make a valuable contribution to the selection process.

PSYCHOLOGICAL TESTING: SKILLS AND ACHIEVEMENTS

Measures of skills and achievements are derived directly from the job and thus tend to be specific to the occupation for which selection is to occur. Either a job sample is developed, as with the various typing and stenographic tests, or a series of questions are asked regarding the job. In some instances, tests of this type are available on a commercial basis, but it is also common practice to construct homegrown measures that are specifically suited to the needs of a particular company. Although criterion-related validity may be studied, the primary emphasis is on content validity.

Job-sampling Procedures

Job-sampling tests are feasible only where the role prescriptions for a job form a rather homogeneous unit. If the job is complex, requiring many different types of activities, all of which are equally important to success, any truly inclusive job-sample test would be so lengthy and cumbersome that its use in a selection battery would not normally be expedient. Even with the more homogeneous jobs, most such tests tend to be only similar to the actual work situation and not exact duplicates of it.

Traditionally, the use of job-sample testing has been restricted to positions that have been designed with rather simple role requirements or for which only previously trained or experienced applicants are hired. This is because testing a group of inexperienced individuals on a complex job sample is of little value, since all will obtain low scores. Under such circumstances, ability measures are much more likely to discriminate within the groups and predict which individuals will learn rapidly and achieve job success. More recently, approaches have been developed which include an opportunity to demonstrate one's ability to learn certain parts of the job; thus, evaluation follows a brief learning experience (29). As a result, inexperienced candidates can be tested, and meaningful differences among them established.

A number of firms have developed job-sample tests for skilled and semi-skilled positions. In some instances, special equipment simulating that used on the job has been constructed. In other cases, a standardized test situation utilizing actual equipment is employed. In any event, it is crucial that all people tested be required to perform the same tasks under the same conditions in the same period of time. Job samples of this kind have been developed for a variety of positions in such areas as punch-press operation, inspection, packaging, fork-lift operation, and truck driving and in certain kinds of special machine operation.

Job-sampling procedures have also had widespread use in the clerical field. Here, where jobs tend to be highly standardized across a great many firms, regular commercial tests are much more common than for blue-collar workers. Among those available are the Blackstone Stenographic Proficiency Tests, the Thurstone Examination in Typing, and the Seashore-Bennett Stenographic Proficiency Tests. These require that applicants take dictation and/or type, using materials that are the same for everybody. Scoring procedures have been worked out, and the scores obtained by a given applicant can be compared with those for a large number of clerical workers who have taken the test.

Although managerial work is generally less suitable for job sampling, certain aspects of the job have been simulated with some success, as with the In-basket Test, which was previously discussed as a simulation to be used for appraisal purposes.

Although the job-sampling approach is probably most widely used to screen initial applicants, especially those who have gone through apprenticeship, vocational, or secretarial training programs prior to applying for a job, it is also used in connection with promotions. Job-sample tests have proved particularly valuable in instances where the union contract placed limitations on the promotion process. If, for instance, the contract says seniority shall govern, provided the senior person is qualified to perform the higher-level job, it is important to determine whether he is qualified. Job samples can be very helpful in this regard. In other cases, management has more freedom of action and can promote the most qualified employee, provided that where capability is equal the senior person will be moved up. Here, also, the level of qualification can best be demonstrated with a job-sample test. The advantage of using job samples in these situations is that they do tend to be predictive of subsequent performance, *and* they are usually acceptable to the union. An equally valid projective personality measure would normally be of much less value for this purpose because of the *apparent* disparity between the test and the job.

The advent of the equal employment opportunity legislation and its enforcement has provided a spur to the development of job-sample procedures (27). The need for a preliminary job analysis, the content validity, and the fact that adverse impacts are less likely all make the approach particularly attractive from a fair employment viewpoint. Typically, a good job-sample measure will not yield the same disproportionately high ratio of white to minority hires that the conventional mental ability tests do. Furthermore, in many of the kinds of jobs for which job-sample measures are characteristically developed, the job samples prove to be better predictors of later success than ability and personality tests (5, 12). Tests that involve actual physical manipulation rather than verbal performance appear to be particularly effective.

Achievement Tests

Achievement tests differ from job samples in that they deal with the knowledge or information required to perform a job. Instead of demonstrating his skill, the applicant answers written or oral questions about the work. There is considerable overlap between the two procedures.

Measures of this kind have proved particularly useful in discriminating between those who are and those who are not qualified to perform a given type of work. Because they are relatively easy to construct and administer, they are usually more appropriate for this purpose than job samples. It is not at all uncommon for a job applicant to claim prior work experience, as a carpenter, machinist, engineer, or accountant, when he has actually performed in a less-skilled capacity. Either the person intends to bluff his way into a higher-level position, or there is some ambiguity in the true meaning of the occupational title. In any event, a test of job knowledge can be very helpful.

So-called trade tests have been developed along these lines by the U.S. Employment Service for a number of skilled occupations. These are oral tests, usually containing 15 questions. The questions are selected by administering a much larger number of questions to three groups of workers: journeymen, apprentices and helpers in the trade, and individuals employed outside the trade in positions that are part of the same job family. A good question, one that is retained in the final test, should yield consistently correct responses in the first group and practically no correct responses in the third group. When a number of questions of this kind are put together in a test, experienced journeymen can easily be identified, because they will obtain total scores at a level almost never obtained by those in the other two groups. Tests of this type have also demonstrated considerable validity as predictors of the degree to which an individual's behavior actually matches the role prescriptions for a job.

Achievement testing need not be restricted to short oral tests. Written tests have been developed by a number of firms for a whole range of positions. Tests of accounting knowledge, policies and procedures, human relations, business law, and economics, which cover segments of a job rather than the totality of information required, have also been constructed. Most civil service tests are of this kind.

Although, in general, achievement measures are constructed by the company to fit its own specific needs, some commercial tests are available. The Occupational Research Center at Purdue University has developed a number of these for the skilled trades. They are measures of information regarding such occupations as electrician, lathe operator, carpenter, sheet-metal worker, and welder. More specific tests also deal with industrial mathematics, blueprint reading, and scale reading.

QUESTIONS

1. Both the preemployment physical examination and the use of polygraphs have produced considerable criticism. Is there any basis for these negative reactions? What alternative procedures might be used? Explain.
2. What are the strengths and weaknesses, the advantages and disadvantages, of the following as selection tests?
   a. General Aptitude Test Battery.
   b. Complex apparatus tests.
   c. Edwards Personal Preference Schedule.
   d. Sentence-completion technique.
   e. Trade tests.
3. How do self-report and projective personality tests differ? Can you give any explanation for the fact that many industrial psychologists prefer the former, and many clinical psychologists the latter?
4. What types of tests are most valid for predicting success in training, and what types for predicting on-the-job success? Why do you suppose these differences exist?
5. Job-sampling procedures appear to be increasing considerably in popularity. What factors might account for this?

REFERENCES

1. Abrahams, N. M., I. Neumann, and W. H. Githens. "Faking Vocational Interests: Simulated Versus Real Life Motivation." *Personnel Psychology*, 24 (1971), 5–12.
2. Anderson, H. E., S. L. Roush, and J. E. McClary. "Relationships Among Ratings, Production, Efficiency, and the General Aptitude Test Battery Scales in an Industrial Setting." *Journal of Applied Psychology*, 58 (1973), 77–82.
3. Ash, P. "Validation of an Instrument to Predict the Likelihood of Em-

ployee Theft." *Proceedings, Seventy-eighth Annual Convention, American Psychological Association,* 1970, 579–580.

4. Ash, P. "Screening Employment Applicants for Attitudes Toward Theft." *Journal of Applied Psychology,* 55 (1971), 161–164.

5. Asher, J. J., and J. A. Sciarrino. "Realistic Work Sample Tests. A Review." *Personnel Psychology,* 27 (1974), 519–533.

6. Bemis, S. S. "Occupational Validity of the General Aptitude Test Battery." *Journal of Applied Psychology,* 52 (1968), 240–244.

7. Bersh, P. J. "A Validation Study of Polygraph Examiner Judgments." *Journal of Applied Psychology,* 53 (1969), 399–403.

8. Blumenfeld, W. S. "Effects of Various Instructions on Personality Inventory Scores." *Personnel Administration and Public Personnel Review,* 7 (1972), No. 2, 67–71.

9. Bureau of National Affairs, Inc. "ASPA-BNA Survey: The Employee with Problems." *Bulletin to Management,* December 10, 1970, 1–10.

10. Bureau of National Affairs, Inc. *Services for Employees.* Personnel Policies Forum Survey No. 105. Washington, D.C.: BNA, Inc., 1974.

11. Buros, O. K., ed. *The Seventh Mental Measurements Yearbook.* Highland Park, N.J.: Gryphon Press, 1972.

12. Campion, J. E. "Work Sampling for Personnel Selection." *Journal of Applied Psychology,* 56 (1972), 40–44.

13. Edel, E. C., and J. Jacoby. "Examiner Reliability in Polygraph Chart Analysis: Identification of Physiological Responses." *Journal of Applied Psychology,* 60 (1975), 632–634.

14. Edwards, A. L., and R. D. Abbott. "Measurement of Personality Traits: Theory and Technique." *Annual Review of Psychology,* 24 (1973), 241–278.

15. Erdmann, A. J., K. Brodman, J. Deutschberger, and H. G. Wolff. "Health Questionnaire Use in an Industrial Medical Department." *Industrial Medicine and Surgery,* 22 (1953), 355–357.

16. Ghiselli, E. E. "The Validity of Aptitude Tests in Personnel Selection." *Personnel Psychology,* 26 (1973), 461–477.

17. Guion, R. M. *Personnel Testing.* New York: McGraw-Hill Book Company, 1965.

18. Gunderson, E. K. E., R. H. Rahe, and R. J. Arthur. "Prediction of Performance in Stressful Underwater Demolition Training." *Journal of Applied Psychology,* 56 (1972), 430–432.

19. Luongo, E. P. "The Preplacement Physical Examination in Industry— Its Values." *Archives of Environmental Health,* 5 (1962), 358–364.

20. Lykken, D. T. "Psychology and the Lie Detector Industry." *American Psychologist,* 29 (1974), 725–739.

21. McClelland, D. C., and D. G. Winter. *Motivating Economic Achievement.* New York: The Free Press, 1969.

22. McFarland, R. A. *Human Factors in Air Transportation*. New York: McGraw-Hill Book Company, 1953.

23. Matarazzo, J. D. *Wechsler's Measurement and Appraisal of Adult Intelligence*. Baltimore, Md.: The Williams and Wilkins Co., 1972.

24. Miner, J. B. "On the Use of a Short Vocabulary Test to Measure General Intelligence." *Journal of Educational Psychology*, 52 (1961), 157–160.

25. Miner, J. B. *Studies in Management Education*. New York: Springer Publishing Company, 1965.

26. Miner, J. B. *Motivation to Manage*. Atlanta, Ga.: Organizational Measurement Systems Press, 1977.

27. Muchinsky, P. M. "Utility of Work Samples." *Personnel Journal*, 54 (1975), 218–220.

28. Orpen, C. "The Fakability of the Edwards Personal Preference Schedule in Personnel Selection." *Personnel Psychology*, 24 (1971), 1–4.

29. Siegel, A. I., and B. A. Bergman. "A Job Learning Approach to Performance Prediction." *Personnel Psychology*, 28 (1975), 325–339.

30. Wittreich, W. J., and J. B. Miner. "People: The Most Mismanaged Asset." *Business Horizons*, 14 (1971), No. 2, 69–77.

V INPUT-OUTPUT MEDIATORS: TECHNIQUES FOSTERING PRODUCTIVITY AND PROFIT

14 *Management Development*

In Parts V and VI, we shall take up the various personnel techniques that have been developed to mediate between the human inputs to a firm and the behavioral outputs that contribute to goal attainment. The primary intention in utilizing these techniques is to change and improve the input so as to maximize the amount of productivity and profit and at the same time ensure the continued stability of the organization itself. In some instances, however, mediators are used merely to sustain the effective functioning of the input against forces that might otherwise drastically reduce the level of output. Thus, the most efficient company is viewed as the one that selects the best applicants and then introduces mediating techniques that at least maintain, and ideally improve upon, the quality of this input, while also inducing members to devote their greatest efforts toward achieving the organization's goals. Mediators can be, along with selection procedures, a means of at least partially overcoming any constraints imposed by individual differences.

The five chapters of this part discuss the functional mediators that are oriented primarily toward the productivity goal. The following part will take up functional mediators oriented toward organizational maintenance. Although the classification in terms of the type of company goal served is generally appropriate, there are instances where the categorization must be considered somewhat arbitrary. Thus, although management-development activities are in most cases intended as methods of increasing the overall productivity of the organization, there are certain types of management-development procedures that appear to be directed primarily toward the reduction of conflict within managerial ranks, and that thus ameliorate internal stresses. Yet it seems undesirable to split the discussion of educational processes in the way that strict adherence to this goal dichotomy would require. Rather than do this, instances where particular procedures contribute to an alternative goal will be noted as they occur.

Chapters 14 and 15 are concerned with the various educational techniques used to raise the level of performance of organization members. This may be achieved either by providing new knowledge and information relevant to a job, by teaching new skills of a psychomotor nature, or by imbuing an individual with new attitudes, values, motives, and other personality characteristics. Often these techniques are utilized with segments of a work force irrespective of the existing performance level. Thus, a given work group or managerial component may be given a particular course with a view to improving the role behavior of all members, the outstanding as well as the less effective. On occasion, training is focused on those who, either because they are new to the type of work or for other reasons, are not immediately in a position to achieve a successful level of performance.

As has been the custom previously with discussions of procedures for developing role prescriptions and of methods used to evaluate organization members, a split will be made in terms of the company hierarchy. Thus, this chapter will deal with training techniques normally used with managerial and other employees in the upper segment of the organization. Chapter 15 directs itself to employees at lower levels.

EVALUATION OF CHANGE MODELS

Just as when a new selection procedure is introduced it should be validated against existing criteria of success in the organization, so when a new training program is introduced, it should be studied to determine whether it really is contributing to improved performance. There is a strong temptation on the part of many personnel managers to avoid this step, because the evaluation of a program always raises the possibility that it will turn out to have been worthless and thus a waste of a good deal of time and money. In fact, studies indicate that evaluations by training personnel of the relative effectiveness of various management development procedures are quite unrelated to the quality of the evidence available to them (5). Yet from an overall company viewpoint, evaluation through research is essential if there is any prospect that the same or a similar course might be repeated in the future. As with validity studies in selection, however, there are cost considerations. Validation makes sense only if enough people are to be hired for the particular type of work to justify the expense of the research. Similarly, training evaluation is warranted only when a sufficient number of people are to be trained in a particular way.

It is important that a personnel manager be capable of carrying out change evaluation studies on his own programs when appropriate and that he be familiar with the studies that have been done by others on the various types of courses that he may be considering. This necessitates a sufficient knowledge of the logic of evaluation to permit discrimination between a good study and a poor one. The discussion in this section should provide this knowledge. In addition, it will introduce a basis for determining the effectiveness of the various development techniques to be considered later in this chapter. In what follows, it is taken for granted that merely asking participants or their superiors for their reactions to training proves little about training effectiveness, even though this is by far the most frequently used approach to evaluation (40).

The Before-After Model

The basic question that may be asked with regard to any training effort is whether it does in fact yield a change in the people exposed to it. Normally, an experimental design for answering this question would involve a pretest, then exposure to training, and then a posttest. The pre- and postmeasurements are made using indexes that are closely related to what the course is expected to accomplish. Thus, an attempt to improve understanding of company policies would presumably be evaluated by using a test of knowledge regarding policy before the course started and the same or a very similar test afterward. Should there be a statistically reliable increase in score for the group as a whole from pretest to posttest, this would provide the type of evidence for change that might permit generalization to other applications of the same course.

It would still remain to be demonstrated, however, that such a change had been caused by the course itself, and not by some external factor. For instance, it might be that the change in knowledge of policy identified actually resulted not so much from the training as from the fact that a revised policy manual was issued to all management personnel shortly after the course

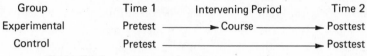

Figure 14–1

started. To check on this kind of possibility, one would have to carry out the same pretest-posttest procedure on a *control group* consisting of managers like those exposed to training but differing in that they did not take the course in company policy. Should this control group increase in knowledge of policy as much as the *experimental group*, who had had the course, this would support the view that some extratraining factor such as the new manual was the major cause of change. On the other hand, a statistically reliable increase in knowledge in the experimental group coupled with a complete lack of change in the control group would provide evidence that the training was in fact achieving its objective.

In selecting such a control group, it is important to use people as similar to those in the experimental group as possible and to make certain that the two groups have much the same types of experiences over the period of training. The only difference should be that one group is exposed to the course, and the other is not. To demonstrate that the training has been effective, one must show that the addition of this single factor to one of two otherwise similar groups is sufficient to create a real difference at some later point in time. This before-after model is outlined in Figure 14–1.

The After-Only Model

An alternative approach that offers certain advantages, as well as dis-advantages, is outlined in Figure 14–2. Here the experimental and control groups are selected in the same manner as in the before-after approach, but only posttests are administered. Change is presumed to have occurred if there is a statistically significant difference between the two groups at the time the measurement occurs. This assumes that the two groups were identical originally.

The problem is that in most ongoing business situations, it is extremely difficult to determine whether identical groups have been selected without employing a pretest to be sure. Thus, there is always the possibility, when the after-only model is used, that any differences between the two groups established after training might have been present before. What appears to be change might only be a long-standing group difference.

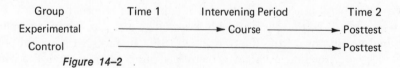

Figure 14–2

Yet the simplicity of the after-only design is appealing, and there are circumstances under which one can feel reasonably confident that relatively good initial matching has occurred. Thus, this approach is used on occasion, although probably not as frequently as the before-after model. It has the additional advantage that there is no possibility of a pretest's sensitizing those who take the course to certain specific aspects of the training. Managers may learn certain things only because they get the impression from a pretest that they should learn these particular things (23). The posttest then reveals a change. But in subsequent administrations of the course, without a pretest (or posttest either, for that matter), this learning does not occur, and the change can well be negligible. The after-only design avoids this source of error.

This pretest sensitizing effect can be a real problem, especially when the measures used contain items practically identical to material covered in training. In such cases, the ideal evaluation design is a combination of the before-after and after-only approaches, using at least three groups (3). This permits the identification of any pseudochanges resulting from the sensitizing effects of a pretest through a comparison of the two experimental groups taking the course. Unfortunately, studies of this kind that eliminate practically all sources of error are rarely conducted. They are too complex and require more subjects for inclusion in the various experimental and control conditions than are normally available.

The Retention and Organizational-relevance Factors

Although the demonstration of a change caused by the educational process is the first step in any evaluation study, this is not all that is required. To be of much value to a company, the change must be retained, and it must be clearly of a kind that contributes to goal attainment.

Retention is normally determined by taking a third measurement at some point in time well after training has been completed, perhaps as long as a year later. Or the posttest itself may be delayed so that retention and change are measured at one and the same time. In the latter instance, if a pretest-posttest change is not found, there is no way of knowing whether the course was totally ineffective or a real change was vitiated by events occurring subsequent to training.

It is clear that such vitiation of change does occur. The consequence is what is known as *encapsulated training*. Within the education situation itself, considerable change occurs, but none of this is actually carried back to the job. Because the training process is eventually terminated, all change will inevitably disappear also.

This type of encapsulation seems to be particularly frequent when there is a disparity between the actual role prescriptions for the job and those taught in the course. Management development may emphasize being kind and considerate toward subordinates, whereas the established role prescrip-

negatives of training

tions for a manager, which are enforced by his superiors, emphasize pressure for production and the frequent use of negative sanctions. One solution to the dilemma thus produced is to accept the training values, but only for purposes of training—not back on the job. Because the entire reward structure built around the job is calculated to obtain a close match between role behavior and the established role prescriptions, and because the training emphasis if incorporated in behavior would tend to widen this gap and thus reduce the chances of being considered a success, the manager is careful not to let any training effects manifest themselves in the actual work situation.

Another type of reaction may occur when the role requirements presented in the training situation are distinctly different from those characterizing the job situation. On occasion, the two sets of expectations are carried into the work environment together, with the result that the manager does not know what he is supposed to do and what kind of behavior will be considered as evidence of success. The result is what is known as *role conflict.* Under such circumstances, the changes produced by training are retained, but at considerable cost to the individual in terms of anxiety and confusion. The consequence for the organization is likely to be internal conflict and in many cases the eventual loss of a potentially valuable manager.

The solution to problems of encapsulated training and training-produced role conflict is to be sure that the role requirements taught in the course and those existing in the job situation are not divergent. This can be accomplished by synchronizing the course with existing role prescriptions. When this is done, it can be assumed that the training will be reinforced by subsequent work experiences, and changes will be retained. On the other hand, if the training is intended as a procedure for introducing alternative role prescriptions and thus moving managerial behavior toward a new pattern of expectations, the new role prescriptions should be made part of the job context as well. Thus, the changes should be organizational in nature and not restricted to a given management-development experience. It is for this reason that most training directors first attempt to expose the company's top management to any course emphasizing new role prescriptions. Then they work down through the successive levels of the hierarchy. In this way, a climate favorable to the new behaviors is created from the outset, and retention of change is fostered.

MEASURING ORGANIZATIONAL RELEVANCE

The final step in the evaluation model, and one that is far too often neglected, involves tying the change to organizational goals or to the role prescriptions that mediate goal attainment. Thus, if a knowledge change is produced, it must be demonstrated that the knowledge actually helps those who possess it to perform more effectively. If a change in attitudes occurs, there must be reason to believe these attitudes are associated with success on the job.

Methods of accomplishing this final step vary considerably. The ideal procedure is to use various judgmental or objective appraisal measures at pretest and posttest. Thus, the profit performance of cost centers or the turn-over rate in work groups pre- and posttraining might be compared, or ratings might be obtained from superiors at the two points in time. Unfortunately, obtaining comparable objective measures for all members of both experimental and control groups is often difficult. And when ratings are obtained from superiors who know the composition of experimental and control groups, the possibility of bias is pronounced. The wish, even though entirely unconscious, to justify the decision to invest in a training program may well distort the posttest evaluations in favor of the experimenal group.

For these reasons, it has become common practice to use various tests, attitude measures, and the like as pretest and posttest measures. However, these must be shown to have a positive relationship with success on the job. Thus, validity studies, in many cases predictive validity studies, must be carried out. The models discussed in Chapter 10 are the appropriate ones for this purpose. The point is that there must be good reason to believe that the development procedure has moved a number of individuals along some dimension that is known to yield *role behavior* that is positively valued within the organization (19).

CLASSROOM-TYPE DEVELOPMENT TECHNIQUES

A variety of training procedures require that the participants leave their jobs and engage in some kind of learning effort, usually of a group nature. These classroom-type development techniques should be contrasted with the more individualized approaches that involve building the developmental aspect directly into the job itself—job rotation, special committee assignments, and so on. The latter procedures will be taken up in the following section.

Among the various classroom procedures in common use are human relations training, lectures, group discussions, T-Group or laboratory techniques, conference leadership and coaching training, creativity and problem-solution training, motivation training, film and TV presentations, university management-development programs, case analysis, business games and other types of simulation techniques, role playing, and behavior modification. Obviously, many of these designations overlap.

Human Relations Training

Although the human relations programs had their origins in the Hawthorne studies of the post–World War I period, it was the advent of research in the area of democratic leadership during and immediately after World War II that actually sparked their widespread application. Since these beginnings, the programs have consistently operated within the welfare tradition of personnel management, emphasizing as they do the crucial significance of consideration and kindness as part of the supervisory process. The result can well be that power and influence are shifted downward, away from management to lower levels (2).

Originally, the view was that through human relations training, a more satisfied employee group could be achieved, with the result that productivity would increase. Thus, in basic conception, the programs were intended to foster productivity and profit. In all probability, they do contribute to this goal indirectly through a reduction in strikes, slowdowns, and the like. Yet it is also true that there is no necessary direct relationship between job satisfaction and productive output. The recognition of this fact has gradually led to a reconceptualization of the role of human relations training. Increasingly, such programs are viewed as valuable for the specific contribution they make to reduced conflict within the organization and thus to the maintenance objective alone. At the same time, however, other more productivity-oriented subject matter has been included with the specifically human relations content.

Thus, the "human relations package" now may include such topics as safety, production control, union contract administration, company policies, cost control, economics, company organization, job evaluation, methods improvement, and incentive payment, as well as the more typical material on employee motivation and attitudes, group dynamics, communications, counseling, and democratic leadership (40). In this comprehensive form, the human relations program is clearly directed toward both productivity and maintenance considerations.

THE RESULTS OF EVALUATION

Rather consistently, training of this kind has been found effective in producing change—in knowledge, in attitudes, and in leadership behaviors (32). Yet such research as has been done suggests that there is a very considerable risk involved. There is no question but that human relations training can become encapsulated, or that it can produce role conflict. The emphasis on consideration and democratic procedures may be inconsistent with existing role prescriptions and values (29).

Changes appear to occur irrespective of whether the training is conducted primarily by the lecture method or through group discussion, although training directors tend to believe that the lecture approach is inferior (10). The research evidence does not support this tendency to devalue the lecture. However, discussion techniques do appear to be more widely employed in industry. The method uses a small group who work with a leader to develop discussion about human relations problems. Usually, there are 10 to 20 people in each group. Members must have practical experience with the subject being considered to be able to participate actively.

Actual practice differs considerably insofar as the role of the discussion leader is concerned. In some instances, the leader has the conference content outlined in advance and the major conclusions to be reached already clearly established in his mind. He then guides the group by questions and comments, so that the preestablished points are covered. In other cases, the approach is much more nondirective, with the group developing its own framework for discussion. Here, the leader serves primarily to encourage members to participate and as a resource person. Which procedure is best depends on the goal of the training and on the skill of the leader. The effective guidance of a discussion to a predetermined conclusion is a difficult art.

Changes resulting from a week-long course in the human relations tradition are presented in Table 14–1. In this instance, the same trainer taught two different groups of managers using considerably different approaches and styles with each. With one group, the learning process was highly structured, lectures were used a great deal, discussion was limited to specific issues, and feedback on performance was given. In the other, much greater latitude was given to the participants, lectures were infrequent, discussions were freewheeling, and feedback was minimal. It would appear from Table 14–1 that both approaches were successful in producing changes of the kind human relations programs aspire to, although an untrained control group is needed to be absolutely certain of this. But what is more significant is that on all four measures, the change in the group exposed to structured lectures was distinctly greater than in the free-discussion group (17).

In the case of the data presented in Table 14–1, the posttest was taken at the end of the course. Other studies have focused more directly on the retention problem. In one instance, changes of the kind human relations training tends to foster were found to be still in evidence 18 months after the program ended; in fact, they were more distinct then than they had

Table 14–1. Comparison of Effects of Structured-lecture vs. Free-discussion Approach to Management Development

Factor Measured	Pretest Mean Score	Posttest Mean Score	Change
Group cohesiveness			
Lecture	20.3	45.2	24.9
Discussion	19.0	34.7	15.7
Openness of communication			
Lecture	25.5	46.1	20.6
Discussion	25.0	24.9	−.1
Productivity of groups			
Lecture	9.0	37.4	21.4
Discussion	10.3	26.3	16.0
Attitudes toward trainer			
Lecture	19.6	55.4	34.8
Discussion	16.4	31.4	15.0

Source: Adapted from J. M. Ivancevich, "A Study of a Cognitive Training Program: Trainer Styles and Group Development," *Academy of Management Journal,* 17 : 435–437 (1974).

been immediately after training (16). Thus, the effects of human relations training may be retained, although this has not always proved to be the case.

Laboratory, Sensitivity, or T-Group Training

Three terms—laboratory training, sensitivity training, and T-Group training—tend to be used interchangeably, although in a technical sense the T-Group is a special technique within the broader context of a laboratory, or sensitivity, program. The approach is closely allied to human relations training, but has increasingly taken on certain objectives and procedures that have come to distinguish it from other types of training.

Laboratory training originated with a workshop conducted at the New Britain (Connecticut) State Teachers College in 1946 by staff members from the Research Center for Group Dynamics, then located at the Massachusetts Institute of Technology (1). In this early period, the major focus was on group discussions of various job-related problems brought in by the participants. These discussions were supplemented with some lectures, demonstrations, and role playing.

Very soon, the emphasis shifted from back-home problems to the processes occurring in the here-and-now group situation. It is this technique of learning about oneself and others through observing and participating in an ongoing group situation that is properly designated as T-Group training. Programs of laboratory training containing this element have been conducted at Bethel, Maine, under the auspices of the National Education Association, since 1947. Similar training is now offered at a number of universities and in many other locations. Companies have also set up programs containing individuals from the firm's managerial ranks, often managers who are closely associated in their everyday work.

Although lectures, role playing, problem-centered discussions, special projects, and the like have remained a part of the total laboratory experience, the major aspect is the T-Group. These groups meet for two or three hours daily over a period of a week, or longer. Although there is a leader, he or she does not impose a structure on the group and its activities; there is no specified task to be performed. At first, the members tend to be frustrated and embarrassed. They cannot see why they are there and want someone to tell them what to do. Gradually, however, the conversation turns to the group itself and its members. The leader tends to encourage frankness in the expression of feelings and reactions to others. Such matters as the effects of authority, the motives of others, and the need to be understood are discussed. The participants gradually open up and show themselves for what they are. Frequently, the ties between them become quite strong, and the group eventually develops its own structure. At points during this process, certain participants may become quite anxious. Whether there is likely to be a real threat to psychological adjustment remains a matter of some controversy, although in some cases there clearly can be (25).

ORGANIZATION DEVELOPMENT

Although one of its outcomes may be a revised organization structure as considered in Chapter 6, the approach known as organization development is in fact concerned with change of many kinds. It has its origins in the T-Group, especially the so-called family-group procedure; in certain respects, it moves back to the concern with job-related problems that characterized the very early efforts at New Britain State Teachers College.

Organization development, although it takes varied forms in different applications, is in essence a combination of T-Group procedures and more pragmatic organizational problem solving (13). Information is obtained from interviews, questionnaires, and other sources for use in the problem-solving process. The outcome of the series of group sessions is a program of planned changes in company policies and structures and eventually the implementation of these plans to achieve a more effective organization. As with the laboratory approach generally, there is characteristically a strong emphasis on participative, democratic procedures and thus an increasing equalization of power. A comprehensive organization development effort that permeates an entire company may require a number of years.

THE RESULTS OF EVALUATION

A number of studies have now been conducted to identify the impact of laboratory approaches. These have indicated that change often does occur (36). The findings presented in Table 14–2 are typical.

In this particular instance, individuals who had attended the Bethel program were compared with co-workers who had not some 8 to 10 months after returning to their jobs (8). A special questionnaire was administered to people who were in a position to observe both the experimental and control subjects in their work. The questionnaires were designed to elicit information on observed changes in behavior and attitude. The approach is an after-only one with a delayed posttest. The variables noted in Table 14–2 are those that revealed a statistically significant difference between experimental and control groups in the proportion of individuals exhibiting change. An additional four variables did not yield reliable results. Overall, approximately two-thirds of the experimental subjects changed in some respect, whereas only one-third of those who did not attend the Bethel sessions changed.

The stated goals of the laboratory procedures are to make the manager more sensitive to emotional reaction and expression in others, to produce greater skill in perceiving the consequences of actions through attention to one's own feelings and those of other people, to develop in a manager values

Table 14–2. Proportions of Experimental and Control Subjects Reported as Changed Subsequent to Laboratory Training

Area of Change	Proportions Changed	
	Experimentals (N = 229)	Controls (N = 112)
Receiving Communication—more effort to understand, attentive listening, understands.	.34	.16
Relational Facility—cooperative, tactful, less irritating, easier to deal with, able to negotiate.	.36	.21
Increased Interdependence—encourages participation, involves others, greater leeway to subordinates, less dominating, lets others think.	.38	.27
Self-control—more self-discipline, less quick with judgment, checks temper.	.26	.15
Awareness of Human Behavior—more conscious of why people act, more analytic of others' actions, clear perceptions of people.	.34	.16
Sensitivity to Group Behavior—more conscious of group process, aware of subcurrents in groups.	.24	.09
Sensitivity to Others' Feelings—more capacity for understanding feelings, more sensitive to needs of others.	.34	.10
Acceptance of Other People—able to tolerate shortcomings, considerate of individual differences, patient.	.49	.29
Tolerance of New Information—willing to accept suggestions, considers new points of view, less dogmatic, less arbitrary.	.42	.23
Comfort—relaxed, at ease.	.36	.23
Insight into Self and Role—understands job demands, more aware of own behavior, better adjusted to job.	.36	.24

Source: D. R. Bunker, "The Effect of Laboratory Education upon Individual Behavior," in G. G. Somers (ed.), Proceedings of the Sixteenth Annual Meeting (Madison, Wis.: Industrial Relations Research Association, 1964), pp. 225, 231.

of a primarily democratic and scientific nature, to provide information about interpersonal and group situations, and to foster behavioral effectiveness in dealing with others (4). The approach deliberately attempts to make those exposed to training value science, democracy, and helping others more than they have in the past. These are exactly the kinds of changes noted in Table 14–2 and in other similar evaluation studies.

On the other hand, studies conducted to evaluate laboratory training and organization development have produced some conclusions that are not favorable. There is a very good chance that role conflict will appear at some point; it may be of sufficient magnitude and duration to be truly dysfunctional for both the organization and the individual (21). Another consequence that has appeared frequently is a tendency for managers to abdicate the leadership role, thus leaving groups and organizations essentially un-managed and organizational goals less effectively pursued. Thus, even though many people are changed by the training, the findings as regards organizational relevance suggest that many companies will not in fact benefit from the changes. Maintenance goals may very well be fostered, but productivity goals can suffer (37). As a consequence, sensitivity training is not a highly popular management development technique in the business world at the present time (20).

Performance Appraisal, Coaching, and Conference Leadership Training

The techniques of performance appraisal, coaching, and conference leadership training are widely used to enable managers more effectively to evaluate and utilize their subordinates. They are primarily directed at the productivity goal, although other considerations may be involved as well.

Performance appraisal training is intended to teach the various methods of rating and evaluating employees used by the company. It is the basic method for installing many of the procedures discussed in Chapters 8 and 9. As noted previously, such training can be effective in achieving a reduction in the various sources of error that may creep into the rating process.

Closely related are the various coaching training programs that attempt to make a manager more effective in feeding back and utilizing appraisal data for the purpose of developing subordinates. Coaching training often involves teaching a manager how to guide a subordinate in setting his own objectives, or targets, for future performance. The subordinate is then expected to evaluate himself against these previously established goals with the help of his superior. Coaching training has become a basic part of the *management by objectives* approach, with its emphasis on planning and target setting.

Another method a manager may use to develop and more effectively utilize his subordinates is to conduct problem-solving conferences with them. This is part of the *participative management* approach that argues in favor of group decision making and group involvement in the managerial process rather than unilateral command. The essence of this view is that in many instances, decisions are never implemented, because the subordinates who would have to actually do the work are for one reason or another resistant. To overcome this resistance, it is necessary only to have the subordinates become involved in making the decision, so that they will perceive it as their own. It is recognized that this may result in a somewhat lower-quality decision, but in many instances this is preferable to not having a decision implemented at all.

To use the participative approach effectively and conduct conferences that lead to meaningful results is very difficult for many managers, especially those who believe strongly that decisions should be made individually by the person in charge. A number of firms have instituted training programs for their managers to change attitudes and develop skills in conference and discussion leadership. Just as coaching training has come to have a close association with the management by objectives approach, conference leadership training is an integral part of participative management. The two training procedures and managerial approaches can of course be used together.

Problem Solving and Creativity Training

A variety of different training programs have been developed to help managers become more original and effective in thinking of solutions to business problems (11). The emphasis tends to be on upgrading decision-making skills so that the manager will be able to reach more rational conclusions and thus make a greater contribution to a firm's profitability. In some instances, the training is intended to provide an impetus in the area of research and invention as well.

One such course has been offered through a specialized consulting firm (22). The training contains three aspects. First, there is instruction of a more or less conventional type, using lecture and discussion methods, aimed at providing a general understanding of the concepts and sequential steps in the problem-solving process. Then the participants work together on a simulated problem drawn from the business world. The conferences and conversations that form a part of this practice exercise are recorded. The final aspect of training, and perhaps the most important, is the feedback process. Here, the recordings are played back, and the efforts at problem solution critiqued. Thus, the manager has an opportunity to see where he may be going wrong and to learn new approaches.

In another approach, the participants are taught to defer judgment both at the problem definition and the problem solution stages, until they have a clear picture of the many alternatives. The procedure emphasizes a listing of all possible ways in which a problem may be stated, and only then a selection of *the* problem. The latter is broken down into as many aspects as possible, and alternative solutions are developed for each aspect. Thus, the manager learns a technique that stresses selecting from among a large number of known possibilities. Evaluation studies indicate that training of this kind does increase an individual's ability to develop original problem solutions of high quality. Furthermore, these changes are retained (11).

Motivation Training

Another group of training programs seeks to develop motives that are likely to contribute to success in managerial positions. Although in certain respects very similar to human relations training, these programs tend to focus on motives having little to do with power equalization and the shifting of decision making to lower organizational levels; in fact, in some instances, they may have just the opposite effect.

ACHIEVEMENT-MOTIVATION TRAINING

The objective of achievement-motivation training is to stimulate a desire to achieve of the kind that has been found to contribute to entrepreneurial business activity (25). The training begins with a presentation of research evidence regarding the impact of motivation on business performance. Participants then analyze their own achievement motivation, relate this knowledge to their work, and develop achievement-related goals. Exercises and simulations are completed, and examples of entrepreneurial success are presented.

One of the earlier applications of this approach was in attempting to stimulate increased economic activity in countries such as Mexico and India. Although not universally successful, these efforts were found to bring about the desired results in some cases; both achievement-motivation levels and efforts to start or expand business increased after training (25). More recently, evidence has been obtained that similar results can be expected when the training is given to minority group members in the United States (12).

MANAGERIAL ROLE-MOTIVATION TRAINING

A second procedure, known as managerial role-motivation training, has been rather extensively evaluated with consistently favorable results (28, 31). Training is conducted by the lecture method, plus a certain amount of directed discussion. A text, readings, and casebook are used (30). Emphasis is placed on the various factors in the individual, his work group, his family, the organizational milieu, the society as a whole, and the physical work situation that may contribute to ineffective performance in a subordinate. In this way, the manager's responsibility for maintaining satisfactory productivity levels among subordinates is stressed. In addition, the manager's own motivation to meet certain of the role requirements for his own job is increased.

Evaluation data on this course are presented in Table 14–3. The research and development managers exhibited a highly reliable increase in motivation to manage after training. The control group actually decreased in this regard. Although it was not possible to carry out a third follow-up testing on these groups, a follow-up was conducted over the subsequent five years using personnel records as a source of information. Experimental and control managers were compared in terms of the number who achieved success in the company after the training was completed. Success was defined as having at least one promotion in the five-year period or, if the manager left the company in the interim, a favorable separation rating in his file.

Table 14–3. Pretest, Posttest, and Follow-up Scores on the Miner Sentence Completion Scale for Groups That Did (Experimental) and Did Not (Control) Take Role-motivation Training.

Group	Mean Score at Pretest	Mean Score at Posttest	Mean Score at Follow-up
Research and development managers			
Experimental ($N = 56$)	4.66	6.77	—
Control ($N = 30$)	5.60	4.47	—
Business school students			
Experimental ($N = 129$)	3.40	6.67	5.90
Control ($N = 54$)	3.67	3.24	—

Source: J. B. Miner, Studies in Management Education (New York: Springer, 1965), pp. 98, 115, 122, and 127.

Experimental and control groups were at the same average grade level at the time of training and were considered to have the same potential for advancement. Thus, the two groups started the race at essentially the same point. Yet those who underwent role-motivation training were much more likely to win out, as the following data on the per cent achieving success indicate:

experimentals   81%
controls   51%

These findings suggest that in this instance the training was congruent with existing managerial role requirements and that encapsulation did not occur. The results for business school students are similar. Although there was some dropoff in motivation within the follow-up period, which averaged about a year, a reliable 70 per cent of the initial pretest-posttest change was retained. Unfortunately, the control subjects could not be tested a third time. As indicated in the preceding chapter, the change measure employed is a valid predictor of managerial success. Thus, this particular mediator does appear to contribute to company goals insofar as managerial performance is concerned, just as achievement-motivation training does with regard to entrepreneurial activity. There is reason to believe role training of this kind can be particularly valuable in introducing women to managerial work (6).

Simulation Procedures

Case study, role playing, business games, and similar procedures have in common that the manager is required to think and/or act in terms of a set of role prescriptions differing in some degree from those applying to his own job in the here and now. Thus, he is forced out of his current mold and exposed to new ways of thinking and acting. The result can be a considerable amount of new learning and attitude change. Simulations of this kind can be very close to the present job, dealing with role behaviors that are to be added to the existing patterns; they can also be quite distant, dealing with the role prescriptions for a position for which the trainee may some day qualify.

There are also major differences in the degree of reality inherent in the simulation. In case study, information is presented in written terms, and the participant must imagine the situation. At no point does he or she do any more than think through the role. In certain more complex types of simulations, considerable effort is devoted to reproducing the salient aspects of the situation, and the individual actually acts out his solution to the problem presented.

CASE STUDY

The case approach is one in which a problem is given in written form to a group for solution. The usual procedure is for the group members, individually to assume the role of the manager who is faced with the problem situation. The written statement stops short of a solution, and the participants in the training must then think through to the role behavior they feel to be desirable. The leader does not impose a specific solution. The emphasis is on individual or team problem solving, group discussion, and group critique.

The method is clearly more appropriate for certain purposes than others. It is helpful in teaching managers to identify and analyze complex problems and to make their own decisions. It permits coverage of a great deal of ground very rapidly in terms of diverse approaches, interpretations, and personalities. Making snap judgments and applying pat solutions to problems are discouraged, at the same time that learning is fostered. When the participants are sufficiently sophisticated and knowledgeable in the subject areas involved, it can serve as a basis for the development of general principles that may then be used in solving actual on-the-job problems. If the trainees do not have the background knowledge to come up with meaningful case solutions, or they lack any real understanding of the role the case requires them to assume, none of these objectives is likely to be achieved, and the use of the method should probably be avoided. Given such knowledge, however, case analysis has been shown to produce sizable improvements in performance (27).

THE INCIDENT METHOD

The incident method is a modification of the basic case study procedure (18). The class initially is given a very brief written incident and a statement of the role to be assumed in viewing this incident. The incident is then developed further by means of a question-and-answer process, with the leader supplying information as the trainees ask for it, or through outside reading. After the problem to be solved has been established, each trainee writes his own particular solution down on a piece of paper. These solutions are then sorted by the leader, and their authors are assigned to discussion groups on the basis of similarity of opinion. These groups develop the strongest statement of their members' mutual opinion that they can. The statements may then be presented in the form of a debate, or the groups may role-play their solutions.

Often, the leader presents what actually was done in the particular instance and, where possible, the consequences. A general discussion follows, with the focus on such matters as the factors accounting for accomplishments and difficulties, the possibilities of accomplishing more, methods of surmounting difficulties, and what can be learned from the case for transfer to on-the-job situations.

ROLE PLAYING

Basically, the role-playing approach may be considered as a type of case study in which actual individuals play the various roles of the persons in the case. All participants do not assume the same role, the role of the responsible manager, as with the typical written case. The fact that participants *behave* in roles rather than merely think in them tends to create a more realistic learning situation.

Usually role playing is done in groups of 10 to 20, with members taking turns acting and serving as analysts. The leader assigns individuals to roles. An oral or written briefing is given to put the audience and actors into the situation. Sometimes rather detailed role instructions are given; sometimes the actors actually read a skit up to a certain point; sometimes there is practically no structuring of this kind, and the participants largely develop their own roles. In any event, the actors eventually take over on their own, behaving as they see fit in the situation. The leader terminates the session when the audience has been emotionally involved and either the problem is analyzed or an impasse has been reached. A lengthy discussion that attempts to point up the objectives of training normally follows.

There are a great many variants in technique used by different trainers, even to the point of employing professional actors to take certain parts in a skit. In addition, the approach has been used in a number of different contexts, although the training of managers in leadership behaviors is most common, usually in conjunction with a human relations program. Specific applications have been made in connection with the handling of discharges, layoffs, merit ratings, and grievances, as well as in sales training.

Role playing can be very helpful in practicing role behaviors, provided a sufficient illusion of reality can be produced. Learning by doing is known to be an effective method of developing new skills, although it does not necessarily guarantee against encapsulation. Research evidence is available, indicating that when there is adequate discussion and critique of each role-playing episode, rather sizable changes in areas related to organizational maintenance goals can be achieved (39). These changes are similar to those produced by laboratory training, and in fact, role playing is often used as part of the total laboratory experience. It seems apparent, however, that role playing need not be oriented toward organizational maintenance considerations only. Roles can be constructed to emphasize factors directly related to productivity.

BEHAVIOR MODIFICATION

An approach to management development that has appeared quite recently builds upon the role-playing technique; it stresses behavior change as opposed to attitude or motivational change and utilizes a number of constructs from learning theory, such as conditioning and reinforcement, which are considered in greater detail in the following chapter. This approach is variously referred to as organizational behavior modification (o.b. mod.), behavior modeling, applied learning, or simply behavior modification (24).

As applied in management development, behavior modification may involve a sequence of modeling, role playing, reinforcement and feedback, and transfer training (15). The modeling phase utilizes films or videotapes that depict various desired managerial behaviors. Then the participants role-play these situations, thus rehearsing and practicing the specific behaviors to be learned. As this behavior comes closer and closer to the model provided in the film, approval and praise are given both by the trainer and by other participants. Finally, attention focuses on transferring the behaviors that have been learned to the actual managerial job situations where they might appropriately be used.

There are no lectures, but there is instead a strong reliance on participant involvement. The objective is to broaden the repertoire of behaviors that a manager can call upon in carrying out his job. This is accomplished through guided practice in doing new and unfamiliar things that previous analysis of the job has indicated can improve the effectiveness of performance. It is still too early to determine whether training of this kind does achieve the long-term changes in managerial behavior desired. Most of the arguments for the approach have been extrapolated from other contexts; there is very little research focused on management development applications directly. Furthermore, a number of criticisms have been advanced against the approach, both on ethical grounds and in terms of the applicability of operant-conditioning principles to the real world of human work (35). It may very well turn out that a behavior-focused, as opposed to a motivation-focused, approach to management development has a relatively narrow range of application.

BUSINESS GAMES

Another method of obtaining high levels of participant involvement is the business game, which may be viewed as a case spread out over time, with the consequences of decisions made apparent. The usual procedure is to first inform the trainees regarding the business objectives to be sought, the decisions to be made, and the rules that apply. This may be done orally, but it is common practice to provide written instructions as well. Each competing team organizes itself, studies the available information on operations to date, and makes its initial set of decisions. Each decision period is set equal to a unit of time—a day, week, month, or even a quarter or longer. After the first decisions are turned in, the trainers calculate the operating results, either manually or with the aid of an electronic computer, and feed them back to the teams, often with further environmental and competitive data added. This cycle is repeated several times, and the results are then discussed and critiqued at length.

Some of the available games deal with top-level decisions affecting the total enterprise. Others have been constructed with reference to specific functions and problems—personnel assignment, materials management, stock transactions, sales management, production scheduling, collective bargaining, inventory control, and bank management (43). The list is constantly increasing. Although the tendency is to deal with generalized and hypothetical business situations, there are a number of games constructed with specific reference to a particular firm or industry. In some instances, the decisions made by one team are *interactive* with the results obtained by other teams, in that constant mathematical probabilities have been built into the game as concomitants of particular types of decisions. This is not always done, however.

The results of a rather typical study evaluating the learning effects of a business game are given in Table 14–4 (41). Changes were identified from before training to afterwards in both groups—those who devoted most of their time to playing a business game, and those who concentrated on analyzing and presenting cases. However, the important finding is that the

Table 14–4. A Comparison of Learning Effects from Case Study and Business Gaming

Knowledge Measure	Mean Pretest Score	Mean Posttest Score	Change
Overall test score			
Business game group	10.6	25.9	+15.3
Case study group	10.4	19.9	+9.5
Mastery of principles and concepts			
Business game group	8.8	22.0	+13.2
Case study group	9.4	16.6	+7.2
Mastery of specific facts			
Business game group	1.7	3.9	+2.2
Case study group	1.1	4.0	+2.9

Source: Adapted from J. Wolfe, "The Comparative Learning Effects of a Management Game vs. Casework in the Teaching of Business Policy," *Academy of Management Proceedings*, 294, 296 (1973).

Table 14–5. Pretest-Posttest Changes in Mean Test Scores for Groups Exposed to Problem-oriented and Sensitivity Training

Test Measure	Problem-oriented Training	Sensitivity Training
General business knowledge	+13.9	+9.5
Complexity of thought	+1.7	−.5
Achievement motivation	+.7	−1.8

Source: Adapted from G. Gardiner, "Cognitive and Motivational Development in Two Experimental Undergraduate Programs in Business," *Academy of Management Journal,* 17 : 379 (1974).

change was significantly greater in the business game group. Furthermore, the data indicate that the major effect of the game experience was to improve mastery of principles and general concepts, not specific facts.

Results obtained comparing a variant of the usual business game approach with a course oriented around sensitivity training are given in Table 14–5 (14). The problem-oriented training involved searching for solutions to business problems by asking questions of a computer data bank containing detailed information regarding the companies noted in the problems and by reading related materials. The approach contains elements of both the incident method and business gaming. As opposed to the sensitivity-training approach, the problem-oriented procedure shows a clear superiority both in developing cognitive knowledge and skills, and in producing positive motivational changes. These cognitive effects are similar to those characteristically obtained with the more traditional business games.

University and University-type Programs

Although much management development is carried out in classrooms located on company premises near the workplace, there is also widespread utilization of university facilities. In part, this involves enrollment in regular courses carrying degree credit. Many universities offer a large number of evening courses for the specific purpose of meeting the demand created by business firms and their employees. Some companies even give time off during the day so that individuals may attend classes. Increasingly, policies are being developed that permit a person to take a leave to pursue graduate study on a full-time basis. This is a particularly common practice within research and development departments.

In some instances, the initiative behind this return to school comes from the employee; in some, from the company. Many firms pay a large proportion or even all of the costs under tuition-aid programs. Such programs have been increasing in number, so that now over 90 per cent of the larger companies have them. In many cases, the fact or amount of payment is tied directly to the grade received (9). Policies with regard to tuition aid vary tremendously, depending in large part on the company's need for individuals with various kinds of university training.

In addition, most universities are engaged in some type of management development effort on a noncredit basis. These are programs specifically structured to meet the needs of the business community. They vary from one-day conferences to year-long programs of the kind originated at the Massachusetts Institute of Technology in the early 1930s and since emulated by a number of other schools (7). In most instances, a company will send only one manager, or at most several, to a given university course, with the result that the groups tend to be quite heterogeneous in company representation. Occasionally, however, a university will offer a program specifically for the managers of a single company.

The subjects taught vary a great deal. One survey noted the following as frequently included in live-in university programs (33). The listing is in order of company views regarding importance.

1. Business policy.
2. Human relations.
3. General management functions.
4. Communications.
5. Financial management.
6. Problem solving and decision making.
7. Managerial economics.
8. Quantitative approaches.
9. Marketing.
10. Accounting.
11. Social responsibilities of business.
12. Industrial relations.
13. Government regulation.
14. Production.

Very little information is available regarding the change-producing effects of these programs. Most are intended either to impart new knowledge, in an area related to career objectives and of a kind that the managers do not currently possess, or to update existing knowledge. There is reason to believe that such learning does occur, but it may not be achieved as efficiently as in the regular university classroom. The reason for this is that in most instances examinations are not given, and no report on the managers' level of accomplishment is sent back to the company. A manager who really wants to learn will no doubt do so, but without question some individuals attend these programs with very little gain to either themselves or the firms that send them.

There are a number of programs in existence that closely parallel those offered by the universities but that are made available under other auspices. The American Management Association conducts a great many such courses, as do a number of other professional and managerial societies and consulting firms. Most of these are very similar to university offerings, but they more frequently utilize business managers themselves as trainers. Often, instruction is given in hotel meeting rooms, at private clubs, or at special facilities maintained by the organization.

Another approach that is being utilized by a number of the larger firms is for the company to establish what amounts to a "college" of its own. These facilities are generally located on former private estates or on similar properties. The teaching may be done by the company's own managers, by a special training staff, or by university professors hired as consultants. A group of managers may spend 10 weeks or more on the premises, and a new group comes in shortly after the last has finished. Perhaps the extreme in terms of this kind of company investment in education is represented by the degree-granting institutions, such as General Motors Institute. The latter is run by the company for its own employees, who attend on a cooperative work-study basis.

There is evidence that university-type programs can induce changes. A study of an eight-month program conducted by the American Management Association produced the results given in Table 14–6. Although a control

Table 14–6. Changes Induced During a University-type Program (N = 124)

Test	Pretest Mean	Posttest Mean
Guilford-Zimmerman Temperament Survey		
General activity	18.2	20.6
Ascendancy	18.2	20.7
Sociability	20.0	22.0
Emotional stability	17.8	20.0
Objectivity	18.0	19.4
Thoughtfulness	18.6	19.4
Personal relations	17.5	19.8
Study of Values		
Aesthetics	34.9	36.2
Leadership Opinion Questionnaire		
Structure	51.4	48.6
Consideration	56.1	58.0
Strong Vocational Interest Blank		
Sales	57.6	60.2
Business management	63.6	62.2
Technical supervision	57.6	55.3
Nature	42.0	44.2
Adventure	60.1	63.8
Teaching	52.1	54.6
Music	51.3	53.0
Art	52.6	55.5
Writing	53.0	55.1

Source: V. E. Schein, "An Evaluation of a Long-term Management Training Program," Training and Development Journal, 25, No. 12 : 30–31 (1971).

group was not employed and thus one cannot be certain, it looks very much as if the program, like the university program just described, may have moved the participants away from business and managerial interests to an interest in the arts (34). Yet, in spite of their questionable organizational relevance, it remains true that once again training does appear to have produced sizable changes.

DEVELOPMENT OUTSIDE THE CLASSROOM

Management development is not entirely a matter of classroom training. There are a number of other techniques that are utilized by companies with a view to improving the effectiveness of their members. Among these input-output mediators are job rotation, understudy assignments, committee participation, special reading assignments, and correspondence courses.

Job Rotation and Understudy Assignments

In job rotation, placements are not so much with a view to selecting the individuals who will perform most effectively on the job as with the idea of exposing to new learning experiences individuals who are thought to have good prospects of moving to higher levels of responsibility. The extent to which these assignments carry full operating responsibilities varies considerably (42). In some cases, the individual is rotated from one department to another, perhaps at yearly intervals, and takes over each job with all its role requirements. It is not uncommon for this sort of activity to occur at relatively high levels in the managerial hierarchy. The usual practice is to exercise rather close supervision over individuals who are being rotated for purposes of development and to give them a good deal of coaching. At the other extreme is an approach, used mostly with new management trainees, whereby the individual is assigned for varying periods to different types of work primarily for the purpose of observing and perhaps of carrying out special projects of a largely training nature. Here the development emphasis is primary, and there is only a very limited direct contribution to organizational goal attainment in the work the individual does.

Understudy assignments are normally used not so much for general broadening as to prepare a person for a specific position. Here, the emphasis is not on obtaining a general understanding of the total company operation or of several important segments of it, as in rotation. Understudies may be in a direct line relationship, serving as assistant managers, or they may hold positions as administrative assistants or assistants to a particular manager. In many cases, these jobs are created specifically for the purpose of training a successor to an incumbent manager and are abolished after promotion occurs.

In evaluating the various developmental techniques involving the use of placement procedures, it is important to remember that training that seriously hampers present operations is not really of much value. The ideal is to be able to carry out the training process with a minimum of disruption on the job. This means that throwing a person into a job that he knows nothing about, purely to gain the advantage of rotation, is normally to be avoided. Even if he does eventually survive and begin to grow, the loss in present efficiency may well be too great.

Also, rotations and understudy assignments in and of themselves have little worth. It is because they can offer opportunities for new learning and change that these procedures are considered to be of value. If, however, because of the way an immediate superior handles individuals in such positions, or for some other reason, very little learning is possible, then techniques of this kind are likely to do more harm than good. Thus, such placements are probably best restricted to certain groups and departments where there is known to be a high probability that development will in fact occur. Furthermore, the kind of individuals selected for rotation should be those who can be counted on to benefit from the experience. It is clear from what we know about individual differences that placement procedures of this kind will contribute little if applied on a universal basis.

Committee Assignments

Another means of exposing managers to new experiences, and thus opportunities to learn, is through the judicious use of committee assignments. Work on salary and grievance committees and in groups set up to study special problems can be of considerable value if these committees are made up of representatives with varied backgrounds.

A related approach is *multiple management*, as originally developed at McCormick and Company (38). This involves establishing what amounts to a junior board of directors, made up of from 10 to 20 members of middle management. Such a board deals with problems from the viewpoint of the overall company and makes recommendations directly to the board of directors in a variety of areas. Membership is rotated to a degree by virtue of the fact that the three least effective managers, as determined by peer ratings, are dropped off the board at regular intervals and replaced by new members. Recommendations to the board of directors must be unanimous, and if they are not accepted, the reasons for rejection must be stated in writing by the senior board.

Many firms that have adopted this technique have added factory boards, sales boards, and the like to deal with problems in particular functional areas. Subcommittees to handle such matters as executive actions, new products, human relations, training, and suggestions are often appointed. All this is done primarily for the purpose of development, although other objectives may be fostered as well.

Reading and Correspondence Courses

A number of training departments, although having primary responsibility in the area of classroom training, also assume the role of guide, or counselor, to management with regard to learning generally. This may well be done on a formal basis. The management-appraisal statement, as indicated in Table 8–1, normally ends with a series of development recommendations that may have reference to special reading assignments, as well as to certain correspondence courses sponsored by a university extension division, a private organization, or by the training department itself. Libraries are on occasion maintained on the premises to facilitate these activities. Sometimes companies will buy large quantities of a particular book or journal article and distribute them to management as required reading.

In addition to these more formal programs, training departments normally serve as a source of information regarding self-development. In some instances, various department members are assigned responsibility for keeping abreast of knowledge changes in the various subject matter areas relevant to the company's operations. These individuals recommend reading materials to appropriate members of management and in some cases provide synopses of new publications. The latter role, as knowledge broker, represents one of the important recent developments in the training field. It requires, however, that the personnel manager who specializes in the training area be a highly educated and well-informed person.

QUESTIONS

1. Why are control groups needed in evaluation of change studies? Can you think of any reason why it might be useful to have both a before-after control group and an after-only control group?
2. What do we know about the change-producing potential of the following training methods?
   a. Achievement-motivation training.
   b. Behavior modification.
   c. Business games.
   d. Performance-appraisal training.
3. Select five of the management development techniques discussed in this chapter and for each indicate what you believe the organizational relevance relationship would be in a highly productivity-oriented and profit-conscious company. Substantiate your conclusions.
4. Describe and discuss each of the following:
   a. Tuition aid.
   b. Multiple management.
   c. T-Group.
   d. Encapsulated training.
   e. Pretest sensitization.

5. There has been considerable controversy over the years regarding the relative value of the traditional lecture approach. Some of the techniques discussed in this chapter utilize a lecture approach; some do not. Review the research reported from this viewpoint. What is your conclusion regarding the lecture method?

REFERENCES

1. Back, K. W. *Beyond Words: The Story of Sensitivity Training and the Encounter Movement.* Baltimore: Penguin Books, Inc., 1973.
2. Baum, B. H., P. F. Sorensen, and W. S. Place. "The Effect of Managerial Training on Organizational Control: An Experimental Study." *Organizational Behavior and Human Performance,* 5 (1970), 170–182.
3. Belasco, J. A., and H. M. Trice. *The Assessment of Change in Training and Therapy.* New York: McGraw-Hill Book Company, 1969.
4. Benne, K. D., L. P. Bradford, and R. Lippitt. "The Laboratory Method," in L. P. Bradford, J. R. Gibb, and K. D. Benne (eds.), *T-Group Theory and Laboratory Method.* New York: John Wiley & Sons, Inc., 1964, pp. 15–44.
5. Blumenfeld, W. S., and D. P. Crane. "Opinions of Training Effectiveness: How Good?" *Training and Development Journal,* 27 (1973), No. 12, 42–51.
6. Brenner, M. H. "Management Development for Women." *Personnel Journal,* 51 (1972), 165–169.
7. Bricker, G. W. *Bricker's Directory of University-sponsored Executive Development Programs.* South Chatham, Mass.: Bricker Publications, 1975.
8. Bunker, D. R. "The Effect of Laboratory Education upon Individual Behavior," in G. G. Somers (ed.), *Proceedings of the Sixteenth Annual Meeting.* Madison, Wis.: Industrial Relations Research Association, 1964, pp. 220–232.
9. Bureau of National Affairs, Inc. *The Employer and Higher Education.* Personnel Policies Forum No. 99. Washington, D.C.: BNA, Inc., November 1972.
10. Carrol, S. J., F. T. Paine, and J. M. Ivancevich. "The Relative Effectiveness of Training Methods—Expert Opinion and Research." *Personnel Psychology,* 25 (1972), 495–509.
11. Davis, G. A. *Psychology of Problem Solving: Theory and Practice.* New York: Basic Books, 1973.
12. Durand, D. E. "Effects of Achievement Motivation and Skill Training on the Entrepreneurial Behavior of Black Businessmen." *Organizational Behavior and Human Performance,* 14 (1975), 76–90.
13. Friedlander, F., and L. D. Brown. "Organization Development." *Annual Review of Psychology,* 25 (1974), 313–341.

14. Gardiner, G. S. "Cognitive and Motivational Development in Two Experimental Undergraduate Programs in Business." *Academy of Management Journal,* 17 (1974), 375–381.
15. Goldstein, A. P., and M. Sorcher. *Changing Supervisor Behavior.* New York: Pergamon Press, Inc., 1974.
16. Hand, H. H., M. D. Richards, and J. W. Slocum. "Organizational Climate and the Effectiveness of a Human Relations Training Program." *Academy of Management Journal,* 16 (1973), 185–195.
17. Ivancevich, J. M. "A Study of a Cognitive Training Program: Trainer Styles and Group Development." *Academy of Management Journal,* 17 (1974), 428–439.
18. James, J. H. "The Critical Incident Method in Manager Education and Development." *Academy of Management Proceedings,* August 1975, 22–24.
19. Kearney, W. J. "Management Development Programs Can Pay Off." *Business Horizons,* 18 (1975), No. 2, 81–88.
20. Kearney, W. J., and D. D. Martin. "Sensitivity Training: An Established Management Development Tool?" *Academy of Management Journal,* 17 (1974), 755–760.
21. Kegan, D. L. "Organizational Development: Descriptions, Issues, and Some Research Results." *Academy of Management Journal,* 14 (1971), 453–464.
22. Kepner, C. H., and B. B. Tregoe. *The Rational Manager.* New York: McGraw-Hill Book Company, 1965.
23. Lana, R. E. *Assumptions of Social Psychology.* New York: Appleton-Century-Crofts, 1969.
24. Luthans, F., and R. Kreitner. *Organizational Behavior Modification.* Glenview, Ill.: Scott, Foresman and Co., 1975.
25. McClelland, D. C., and D. G. Winter. *Motivating Economic Achievement.* New York: The Free Press, 1969.
26. Maliver, B. L. *The Encounter Group.* New York: Stein and Day Publishers, 1973.
27. Mikesell, J. L., J. A. Wilson, and W. Lawther, "Training Program and Evaluation Model." *Public Personnel Management,* 4 (1975), 405–411.
28. Miner, J. B. *Studies in Management Education.* New York: Springer Publishing Co., Inc., 1965.
29. Miner, J. B. "The OD-Management Development Conflict." *Business Horizons,* 16 (1973), No. 6, 31–36.
30. Miner, J. B. *The Challenge of Managing.* Philadelphia: W. B. Saunders Company, 1975.
31. Miner, J. B. *Motivation to Manage.* Atlanta, Ga.: Organizational Measurement Systems Press, 1977.
32. Mosvick, R. K. "Human Relations Training for Scientists, Technicians,

and Engineers: A Review of Relevant Experimental Evaluations of Human Relations Training." *Personnel Psychology,* 24 (1971), 275–292.

33. Powell, R. M., and C. S. Davis. "Do University Executive Development Programs Pay Off?" *Business Horizons,* 16 (1973), No. 4, 81–87.

34. Schein, V. E. "An Evaluation of a Long-term Management Training Program." *Training and Development Journal,* 25 (1971), No. 12, 28–34.

35. Schneier, C. E. "Behavior Modification in Management: A Review and Critique." *Academy of Management Journal,* 17 (1974), 528–548.

36. Smith, P. B. "Controlled Studies of the Outcome of Sensitivity Training." *Psychological Bulletin,* 82 (1975), 597–622.

37. Stogdill, R. M. *Handbook of Leadership: A Survey of Theory and Research.* New York: The Free Press, 1974.

38. Watson, K. B. "The Maturing of Multiple Management." *Management Review,* 63 (1974), No. 7, 4–14.

39. Wexley, K. N., and W. F. Nemeroff. "Effectiveness of Positive Reinforcement and Goal Setting as Methods of Management Development." *Journal of Applied Psychology,* 60 (1975), 446–450.

40. Wikstrom, W. S. *Supervisory Training.* New York: Conference Board, Inc., 1973.

41. Wolfe, J. "The Comparative Learning Effects of a Management Game vs. Casework in the Teaching of Business Policy." *Academy of Management Proceedings,* August 1973, 291–298.

42. Zeira, Y. "Job Rotation for Management Development." *Personnel,* 51 (1974), No. 4, 25–35.

43. Zuckerman, D. W., and R. E. Horn. *The Guide to Simulations/Games for Education and Training.* Lexington, Mass.: Information Resources, Inc., 1973.

15   Skill Training and Retraining

At this point, it is desirable to differentiate between *training* and *education*. This is not an easy task. Both certainly are concerned with human change and learning, but they differ considerably in purpose. Training is basically role specific. It attempts to help those who are or will be performing a certain job achieve successful role behavior. On the other hand, education is tied to the goals of the individual more than to those of the organization, although some overlapping between the two sets of goals can be anticipated. Thus, education tends to take the individual, his growth, and the multiple roles that he may play in society as its starting point. Training starts with the requirements of a particular employing organization and, within that, of a given job.

Where the student is expected to pay tuition to obtain a learning experience he himself desires, as in the universities, we tend to speak of an educational process. Training normally is paid for by the employing organization, although both the individual and the company may benefit.

These distinctions leave the various management-development procedures discussed in the preceding chapter in a realm of considerable uncertainty. Clearly, they are intended to be training, or at least they should be. But managerial jobs tend to have rather broad role prescriptions, especially at the very top levels, where the demand for the generalist is greatest. Furthermore, there are companies that do not place very clear delimitations on the scope of various managerial positions. The result is that management development can easily become transformed into education, even when paid for by the company. That is, it becomes oriented more toward the individual than the company.

Such problems of definition do not characteristically arise at lower levels in the organization. In this chapter, the focus will be directly on training as a role-specific process. We shall be concerned with learning that in the ideal situation is (a) specifically applicable to the job, (b) complete in its coverage of job requirements, and (c) efficient in terms of the time, money, and resources utilized. The latter requirement implies that the training should not be continued beyond the point where perfectly adequate on-the-job performance is possible.

Because training of this kind must be commensurate with what is known about the processes of human learning, a brief treatment of the implications from learning theory must preface the discussion. A second section will take up methods of identifying training needs. Finally, a number of the techniques, procedures, and applications of industrial training will be covered.

LEARNING THEORY AND INDUSTRIAL TRAINING

This section contains a synopsis of what have been called the *principles of learning*. These principles presumably are as applicable to the management-development programs discussed in Chapter 14 as to the training procedures to be considered later in this chapter (7). Unfortunately, however, knowledge regarding specific applications of these principles is far from complete.

Most of these principles were developed originally within the psychological laboratory, often as a result of work with animals. Although subsequent studies have almost without exception extended into the human sphere, research has not always been conducted in an industrial setting. Thus, what follows must be considered a best estimate of how the principles apply in business organizations as of this point in time. As a best estimate, it is important for those who, because of operating necessity, must make decisions regarding the content and format of various training programs. However, there is good reason to believe these principles may not have universal application (17).

Motivation

Although there is some question whether all learning requires some motive that can be directly satisfied through the learning experience, it does appear certain that greater efficiency is achieved under these circumstances. Thus, if a training program represents a means to achieve some strong personal goal of the trainee, maximal learning is more likely to occur.

This means that training should be directly tied to the various motives known to characterize those who will be exposed to it. Among the motives that seem most frequently to foster learning in the business world are a desire for security, for acceptable working conditions, for social interaction with others, for personal recognition, for intrinsically interesting work, for a sense of accomplishment, for freedom in the workplace, and for achievement. To the extent a learning experience can be related to one or more of these motives, as when retraining on a new piece of equipment is presented as a means to increased job security, the overall goals of training will be fostered. Motivation is more likely to operate in the desired fashion if the material to be learned is meaningful to the trainee, and if it has some relationship to things he has experienced previously—also, if it is sufficiently varied to maintain motivation rather than produce satiation and boredom.

Reinforcement

Closely related to the matter of motivation is what has been called the *law of effect*. According to this law, behavior that is viewed as leading to reward, or that satisfies a motive, tends to be learned and repeated; behavior that seems not to produce a reward, or that yields punishment, tends not to be repeated. Any event that operates in this way, so as to change the probability of a particular behavior, is said to be *reinforcing*.

In general, rewards (positive reinforcers) appear to be more effective in producing learning than punishments (negative reinforcers). In fact, it may be more desirable merely to fail to reward a behavior that is incorrect in a particular situation than to punish it. This is because punishment, at least in its more extreme forms, can lead to a mere suppression of the undesired behavior, with the result that the behavior appears again when the punishment is removed. Punishment can also produce so much anxiety and anger that it disrupts all learning. Yet somewhat less intense punishment can have a favorable effect, especially if it follows closely on the behavior that is to be eliminated.

In this connection, it is important to remember that the law of effect applies within the context of a particular person's motivational system and what he considers rewarding or punishing. Thus, although praise is generally a positive reinforcer, it may not always act as such (16). If a trainer is frequently an object of contempt, praise from him for a particular type of behavior may produce only ostracism and ridicule from the group in training. The result can be that desired behavior is suppressed rather than positively reinforced by the praise, with the consequence that learning follows a course differing considerably from that originally anticipated.

Knowledge of Results

Learning is not only more efficient when appropriate motivation is present and when adequate reinforcement is given, but also when the trainee has a clear picture of how well he is doing. This process of feeding back information on the effectiveness of responses is what is called *knowledge of results*. It appears to help in part because the trainee can use the knowledge to sort out behavior that he should learn from behavior that he should not. Without knowledge of results, a person may well spend long periods of time learning to do things that appear at first to be appropriate but that subsequently turn out not to be.

It is also true that knowledge of results affects motivation. When an individual knows whether a given response was right or wrong, whether he is improving or not, he can set goals for himself, thus making a game out of the learning process and maintaining motivation at a high level. There is reason to believe that explicit goal setting in conjunction with knowledge of results can be particularly helpful where the material to be learned is rather difficult, and the goals are set at a high level (14).

A demonstration of how knowledge of results can facilitate learning is contained in Table 15–1. In this classic study, textile workers were given

Table 15–1. Waste Ratios for Textile Workers over a 145-week Period, Which Included Training with Knowledge of Results

Period	Mean Waste Ratio for Period
Pretraining (10 weeks)	2.50
Training (3 weeks)	1.50
Reinforcement (12 weeks)	.87
Posttraining I (14 weeks)	.94
Posttraining II (20 weeks)	1.05
Posttraining III (20 weeks)	1.03
Posttraining IV (20 weeks)	1.01
Posttraining V (20 weeks)	.71
Retraining (26 weeks)	.52

Source: W. McGehee and D. H. Livingstone, "Persistence of the Effects of Training Employees to Reduce Waste," *Personnel Psychology*, 7 : 36 (1954).

considerable training, aimed at reducing material wastage, over a 3-week period (15). The knowledge of results aspect of this training was extended for 12 more weeks through on-the-job reinforcement of the original learning: The employees were told what their waste rates were. There was a sizable reduction in the amount of waste from pretraining to training and a further reduction with reinforcement. These training effects were maintained over a long period of time. Yet subsequently, when a second training program similar to the first was introduced, the amount of waste was even further reduced.

Active Practice

It is almost axiomatic that learning requires repetition and practice. To the extent possible, this practice should be active and overt. The employee should do and say what he is expected to learn, rather than merely listen to repetitions of instructions. Active practice of this kind maintains attention and concentration. Thus, job skills are most effectively developed by repeatedly performing the task to be learned, and knowledge is best acquired by writing down the material or reciting it orally.

At least in the early stages of learning, it is desirable to guide or shape this practice, rather than let a trainee find out by trial and error which are appropriate behaviors and which are not. A great deal of time can be saved if the trainer directs the practice in this manner, so that desired responses are produced almost immediately. Because eventually the individual will have to perform the new tasks alone on the job, it is important not to carry close guidance too far into the learning process. Training should include considerable independent practice of the newly acquired role behaviors at some point before it is terminated.

Massed Versus Distributed Practice

In general, the available evidence indicates that spacing out training sessions is desirable, especially as an aid to retention. This assumes, of course, that there is a good deal to be learned. Short lists of instructions and the like are probably best learned in a single intensive session.

This principle of distributed practice is one of the most widely violated in industrial training. The reason for this is that when a decision is made to place a person on a particular job, every effort is normally made to move him to effective performance in as short a total time span as possible. This means that all his time is devoted to training in the new role behaviors. Where the job is quite simple, the result is repeated practice of essentially the same activities and relatively inefficient learning.

In many such instances, it is possible to obtain the advantages of distributed practice if an effort is made to do so. There are a number of approaches that can be used. Job training can be alternated with some useful activity that requires minimal skill, such as filing, cleaning, or loading.

When people are being retrained to operate new equipment, the retraining can sometimes be alternated with continued work performance on the old equipment. Another approach involves grouping the various aspects of the total training into separate packages and alternating among them. This is particularly appropriate if the job is complex and contains a variety of tasks to be performed at different times. Finally, some firms employ high school and college students on a part-time basis and use the work periods for training in activities that will be carried out subsequently, when full-time employment occurs.

Whole Versus Part Learning

Another principle, which is unfortunately somewhat "shaky" in terms of the evidence supporting it, states that whole learning is preferable to part learning. This refers to the size of the units of content employed. According to this principle, it is desirable to have the trainees deal with large and meaningful wholes, rather than small bits and pieces, which may not be very meaningful in and of themselves and which still must be combined eventually before effective job performance is possible.

Unfortunately, for those making decisions regarding training content, there is evidence that under certain conditions part learning is preferable. Thus, the guidelines for action are not entirely clear in this area (7). Yet some statements can be made. More intelligent trainees tend to handle large, self-contained units of content well, whereas the less intelligent may require a more segmented approach. After an individual has become accustomed to the whole method and has become practiced in its use, its advantages become more marked. Whole learning combined with distributed practice represents a particularly advantageous combination. The whole method is desirable only if the material to be learned does in fact form a meaningful, unified grouping. A job made up of a series of disparate activities without logical connection might best be learned in parts. Finally, because of the nature of most job-related learning, there will almost inevitably be aspects of the material that must be handled on a part basis, even if the initial approach is in terms of the whole. When a particular aspect of the total learning is very difficult, training must focus on this aspect even if some segmentation does result.

Transfer of Training

In Chapter 13, evidence was presented that indicated that certain psychological tests having considerable validity for the initial training situation often did not predict as effectively when an on-the-job criterion measure was employed. The reverse was also true. Such findings suggest that transfer from the training to the actual work situation may not be perfect in many instances—that what is learned during training, although it may be considered important there, may have very little relevance for job performance.

This is the *transfer of training* problem. Also, under what conditions will information that has been learned in order to do the old job be most relevant for a new job, should the position be redesigned and retraining carried out?

The principle that seems to work most effectively as an answer to these questions is that of identical elements. If the behavior required and the characteristics of a training situation (or of an existing job) have many elements identical to those on the job (or on the redesigned job), a person who performs effectively in the one instance should do so in the other. Thus, to maximize *positive transfer* of the kind that is normally desired, there should be a close resemblance in the behaviors produced and the meaning content of the relevant stimuli in the two situations. This does not necessitate perfect physical identity, as is evident from what has been said about simulation techniques, but it does require psychological identity in terms of the thoughts and emotions aroused in the two situations.

It is also possible, however, for *negative transfer* to occur. What has been learned on one job can be detrimental for another. What has been learned in training can actually hamper job performance if the training is not effectively designed, or if it is designed with reference to goals that differ sharply from those characterizing the job situation. Thus, what one learns during a college education *could* lead to less effective performance in a particular subsequent business position. Negative transfer of this kind tends to be most pronounced when the new job requires behavior that is just the opposite of what a person has learned to apply in comparable situations. The old behaviors seem to keep forcing their way back and thus disturbing performance. This means that in redesigning jobs and equipment, one should make every effort to avoid situations in which workers must make opposite or nearly opposite responses to familiar situations (18).

Intelligence and Learning

A final guide for the industrial trainer derives from what is known about individual differences and the nature of mental abilities. There is good reason to believe that those with higher ability levels will learn more rapidly than those with less ability, when the ability involved is closely related to the material to be learned.

This means that training will be most efficient to the extent that the teaching process can be adapted to the mental ability level of the individual. A very intelligent person can absorb new things very rapidly, and thus the materials to be learned should be presented at an accelerated pace. The less intelligent are likely to require much longer exposure to the same materials before achieving a comparable degree of learning. Ideally, therefore, training experiences should be individualized for maximum efficiency. If individualized instruction is not possible, and large job-related individual differences are known to be present in a trainee group, it is generally desirable to group the trainees into "fast" and "slow" classes. In this way, it is possible to avoid the wasteful overlearning that may occur among high-ability individuals who are forced to continue practice while waiting for those of lower ability to catch up. In addition, motivation is more easily maintained where *ability grouping* of this kind is carried out.

ESTABLISHING TRAINING NEEDS

To operate efficiently as an input-output mediator, training must be focused on individuals and situations where the need is greatest. This means that large gaps between role prescriptions and existing role behaviors must be identified. Then a decision must be made as to whether a significant reduction in the size of the gap might be achieved through training. Establishing training needs thus requires an answer to two questions: Is there a problem in terms of the level or type of performance? Can training be of any value in correcting such a situation?

In terms of sheer numbers, the training-needs problem is usually most pronounced among individuals just starting out on a new job. Thus, new employees, employees who have been shifted into a new position, and employees being retrained because the role prescriptions for a position have been changed, all can normally be assumed to have rather acute training requirements. Fortunately, requirements of this kind tend to be rather easy to identify, and the level of motivation to learn tends to be quite high.

A much more difficult problem arises in the case of existing employees who have been working on the current job for some time. Here, persistent deviations from role prescriptions must be identified on an individual basis. There is no single categorization, such as that of "new man on the job," to make employees with marked training needs highly visible. Furthermore, motivation for new learning may well be minimal. To be singled out for special training and to accept the need for this training represents a tacit admission that one has not been performing with maximum effectiveness in the past. Thus, the "experienced" employee may go to great lengths to cover up any training needs and may resist such training as he or she does receive to prove that he or she has been performing the job correctly all along. This is not a universal occurrence, but it is well for a personnel manager to be sensitive to the possibility.

Whether the training needs analysis is directed toward individuals who are just starting on a job or those who have been there for some time, it remains a very important factor in a firm's total effort to utilize human resources effectively, and it may well become even more important in the future. Union pressure has produced many job assignment systems based in large part on seniority. Furthermore, a number of companies are firmly committed to the concept of promotion from within. These plus other factors mean that job security is much greater today than it has been in the past, and training is often the only available procedure for correcting deficiencies in selection and placement. If this training is to be applied in an efficient manner, it must be directed into areas where clearly identified training needs exist.

Specific Techniques in Training-needs Analysis

Because the process of identifying training needs depends at least in part on establishing disparities between role prescriptions and role behavior, any of the various appraisal and evaluation techniques discussed in Part III can be of value. In addition, achievement tests and job samples can provide information regarding the extent to which knowledge and skill are below expected levels. Yet, historically, training needs have been identified largely as a result of requests for training from line management, or through more protracted discussions with those responsible for the performance of the individuals considered for training, or through direct observation of actual job performance. Probably, the latter techniques remain the most common ones today, although group production records, turnover statistics, and the like are also widely used to pinpoint areas of difficulty (7).

The important thing, irrespective of the approach employed, is to develop some conception not only as to whether performance deficiencies are present, but regarding the extent to which training can remedy such deficiencies and also the type of training that might be most appropriate for this purpose. Thus, a training-needs analysis should come before any attempt at establishing the method or content of training.

In attempting to develop a preliminary estimate of training needs in a particular group, it is very helpful to utilize some type of checklist along the lines of the one presented in Table 15–2. Answers to the questions posed

Table 15–2. Checklist for Identifying Possible Training Needs in a Particular Unit

Items to Be Considered by Training Coordinator	Training Need?
Is turnover excessive?	——
Are accidents excessive?	——
Is absenteeism too high?	——
Are grievances filed frequently?	——
Are disciplinary actions excessive?	——
Is production often behind schedule?	——
Are there frequent production bottlenecks?	——
Are quality-control standards maintained without excessive costs?	——
Are poor management practices in evidence?	——
Are there problems in communication?	——
Are there frequent interpersonal conflicts?	——
Is supervision effective?	——
Are objectives known and understood?	——
Is paperwork done on time?	——
Do supervisors use staff specialists effectively?	——

can be obtained using data and information from the various sources already noted. After possible training needs are established, the training specialist can then gradually narrow his analysis until he is able to deal with the specific needs of specific individuals in specific jobs.

Training Needs and Job Analysis

The content of training frequently is developed from detailed job-analysis data. These data may have been prepared for other purposes as well, or the job analysis may be a special one to get at training needs only. In either event, the idea is to identify task components and then build these components into the training in the optimal sequence for positive transfer to on-the-job performance.

Various approaches have been used to analyze jobs into the component tasks that are to be taught. In one instance, critical incidents were obtained from customers, and then a training program for retail sales clerks was developed based on these incidents (5). Another approach utilizes the data-people-things categories for job activities noted in Chapter 7 and illustrated in Figure 7–1. In this instance, the model serves to specify what kinds of skills must be taught if people are to be trained for higher-level positions and thus prepared for movement up a career ladder.

A related procedure deals with organization analysis, operations analysis, and individual analysis (16, 22). Organization analysis determines where in the organization the training emphasis should be placed. Operations analysis deals with what the content of training should be insofar as preparing an employee to perform specific tasks is concerned; this is the actual job-analysis aspect. Individual analysis seeks to identify the skills, knowledge, aptitudes, and the like a person needs to perform the tasks that constitute a specific job in the organization. Again, the emphasis is on pinpointing what needs to be taught.

The techniques of management by objectives also may be applied in establishing training needs (25). In this instance, the particular goals or objectives set for individual performance provide a basis for establishing what tasks need to be carried out and thus what needs to be learned.

METHODS AND APPROACHES IN TRAINING

With the discussions of learning principles and training needs as a background, it is now feasible to consider some of the methods and approaches used in industrial training and to attempt an evaluation of relative merit. Thus, this section will be concerned with such matters as on-the-job training, vestibule schools, apprenticeships, system or team training, teaching machines, programmed instruction, and job retraining.

On- and Off-the-job Training

The most common procedure is for training to be carried out on the job, particularly for new employees. The individual becomes accustomed to the machinery and materials that he will use in his subsequent work, and he learns in the same physical and social environment in which he will carry out his job duties later on. Usually, the training is done by an experienced employee or by a supervisor. On occasion, however, trained instructors are assigned for the specific purpose of teaching job skills.

Much on-the-job training still utilizes procedures similar to those developed for use in connection with the Job Instruction Training sessions conducted by the Training Within Industry Division of the War Manpower Commission during World War II (see Chapter 2). The JIT guidelines are given below.

1. Pretraining steps:
    (a) Have a timetable developed in terms of which skills are to be attained. Indicate the speed at which the various levels of attainment may be expected.
    (b) Break down the job into its basic components.
    (c) Have all materials and supplies necessary for the training process available and ready.
    (d) Have the workplace arranged in the same way that the worker will be expected to keep it.
2. Training steps:
    (a) Prepare the worker by putting him at ease; find out what he already knows and show him the relationship of his job to other jobs.
    (b) Tell, show, and illustrate the job to be performed.
    (c) Have the worker try to perform the job and have him tell and explain why he performs each specific operation of the job. This tends to clarify the key aspects.
    (d) Follow up on the trainee after he has been put on his own by checking him often and encouraging further questions.

On-the-job training of this kind is very attractive in a number of respects. It requires relatively little special attention, no extra equipment is needed, and the employee can do some productive work while he learns. Furthermore, it is consistent with several principles of learning. There is active practice, motivation should be maximal due to the more meaningful nature of the learning materials, and the problem of transfer of training from the learning to the job situation is almost nonexistent.

Yet there are major difficulties (23). There is a risk that expensive equipment will be damaged by inexperienced employees, and the accident rate among on-the-job trainees tends to be high. In the absence of specially assigned trainers, the instruction is often haphazard or neglected entirely. The pressures of the workplace may in fact leave little time for effective training. Some activities may actually be more difficult to learn on the job because of their complexity or as a result of the regulated speed at which the machinery operates.

For these reasons, it seems desirable, in many cases, to carry out a large portion of the training process away from the job. This is a widespread practice in the management development area, but it is considerably less common insofar as skill training is concerned. Only in the case of relatively simple production, clerical, and sales jobs does the use of on-the-job training alone seem appropriate. If it is necessary to restrict the learning process to the actual work situation, it is usually desirable to have specific individuals designated as training specialists and to relieve them of other job duties, at least on a temporary basis.

VESTIBULE TRAINING

An approach that is in a sense intermediate between on- and off-the-job training utilizes the vestibule school. Here, the trainee uses equipment and procedures similar to those he would use in on-the-job training, but the equipment is set up in an area separate from the regular work place. The intent of this special installation is to facilitate learning, not to obtain productive output. A skilled trainer is in charge, and new workers receive detailed instruction while practicing their new skills at a rate appropriate to each individual.

From the learning viewpoint, this appears to represent an ideal approach. There is evidence that it does reduce training time and yield more skilled work performance (16). But it is also expensive, especially if the number of people to be trained on a particular type of equipment is small. Then, too, it is not suitable for many jobs. Unfortunately, some companies have placed obsolete or even broken machinery in vestibule schools in an effort to avoid the expense of purchasing duplicate equipment. This tends to limit severely the value of the training. It may even yield negative transfer effects.

ORIENTATION TRAINING

Orientation programs are established to provide new employees with information on such matters as company organization, the history of the firm, policies and procedures, pay and benefit plans, conditions of employment, safety practices, names of top executives, locations of various departments and facilities, manufacturing processes, and work rules. On occasion, brief orientation programs are offered for experienced employees to bring them up to date on current procedures (11).

In many companies, this kind of orientation training is conducted by the personnel department during the first few days of employment. Handbooks, films, and other materials may play an important part in this initial effort to provide the employee with knowledge regarding the salient features of a new environment. In those cases where immediate supervision has primary responsibility for these matters, the training tends to become more individualized, more variable, and on occasion more superficial.

Standardized programs, including classroom sessions and group tours of facilities, would appear to offer major advantages. Yet there is little solid research on the subject, and the informal procedures may often be as effective as the formal.

Apprenticeship

Apprentice training offers an integration of on- and off-the-job learning that under ideal conditions appears to be extremely effective. It is used to prepare employees for a variety of skilled occupations of the kind noted in Table 15–3 (27). The apprentice agrees to work for a company, at a rate well below that paid to fully qualified workers, in return for a specified number of hours of training. In many instances, the conditions of training have been negotiated with the relevant union and are specified in the union contract. Most of the programs are registered with the federal Department of Labor, which has responsibility for promoting apprenticeship training throughout the United States, and with appropriate state agencies.

The actual content of the training is usually established by a local apprenticeship committee that specifies the number of hours of experience for

Table 15–3. Selected Apprenticeable Occupations Classified by Length of Apprenticeship

Two years
  Barber
  Cosmetician
	Four years
	  Boilermaker
	  Carpenter
	  Machinist
	  Printing pressman
	  Tailor

Two to three years
  Brewer
  Butcher
  Roofer	

	Four to five years
	  Electrical worker
	  Lithographer
	  Mailer

Two to four years Bindery worker	

Three years
  Baker
  Bricklayer
  Photographer
	Four to eight years
	  Die sinker

	Five years
	  Lead burner
	  Pattern maker

Three to four years
  Airplane mechanic
  Leatherworker
  Operating engineer
  Sheet-metal worker
	Five to six years
	  Electrotyper
	  Photoengraver
	  Stereotyper

Three to five years Draftsman-designer	

Source: U.S. Department of Labor. *The National Apprenticeship Program.* (Washington, D.C.: Government Printing Office, 1972), pp. 9–27.

each machine or kind of work. The classroom part of the apprenticeship is conducted at a vocational school, with an experienced journeyman in the trade acting as instructor. These courses emphasize applied mathematics, the physical sciences, and the techniques of the occupation. The classroom instruction may be offered during the work day or after hours. It may also be by correspondence. The on-the-job training is also given by a skilled journeyman, and insofar as possible, it is integrated with the classroom material. Thus, the apprentice is given an immediate opportunity to practice what he has been taught.

EVALUATION

Apprenticeships can be extremely effective where complex skills must be learned. Yet there is some reason to believe that many apprenticeship programs are unnecessarily long, with the result that a good deal of inefficient overlearning occurs. A number of the trades represented are not as complex and difficult to learn as their members would like to believe. Yet largely as a result of union pressure, extended training periods of the kind noted in Table 15–3 have become accepted. Evidence for the view that overlearning is widespread in apprentice programs comes from the fact that many individuals attain the same skilled positions through vocational high school and on-the-job experience. Also, a number of dropouts from apprentice programs nevertheless go on to enter the same trade, in spite of the abbreviated learning period (1).

It is also true that apprentice training is on occasion subverted by a desire among certain management representatives to obtain as much productive labor as possible at the reduced apprentice rate. On-the-job learning is deemphasized, and there is little concern as to whether the employee attends classes or not. The major stress is on the amount of work produced, with the result that the training objective is lost.

Perhaps the most difficult problem is that apprenticeships tend to take on a rigidity that is unsuited to the advent of shifting technology. Occupations are changing constantly, as skills must be combined and recombined to meet the demands of new working environments. There is some question under these circumstances as to whether the traditional skilled trade categories are any longer appropriate. This questioning has extended to the apprenticeships that prepare individuals for these trades. Many personnel managers would prefer to avoid formal apprentice training programs entirely and utilize a more flexible approach that could yield individuals with the specific combinations of skills needed to do a given job in the most efficient manner. Yet changes are gradually being introduced into the formal apprenticeship programs. And there is still widespread agreement that carefully integrated classroom and on-the-job training can be very effective, given a satisfactory method of keying learning materials to existing job requirements.

Individualized Instruction

The distinguishing characteristic of the various individualized instruction techniques is that the individual learns at his own rate, using materials specifically prepared to facilitate the instructional process. These materials include teaching machines, books, computer data banks, and workbooks. The earliest of the three approaches currently in use is programmed instruction; in contrast, computer-assisted instruction and the personalized system of instruction, or Keller plan, are relatively recent additions. All three approaches derive directly from the learning principles described earlier in this chapter.

PROGRAMMED INSTRUCTION

This is an individualized procedure that utilizes training materials organized into a series of frames, usually of increasing difficulty, with each successive frame building on those that precede. Information, questions, and problems are presented to the learner with the requirement that he either write in his answer or select the answer from multiple-choice alternatives. Then feedback is provided on the correctness of the answer. The material is developed in such a way that a high proportion of the questions will elicit the desired response and thus result in positive reinforcement. The frames are frequently presented in a teaching machine that utilizes film or sound tapes. There are also a variety of programmed books and other printed materials in which the trainee uncovers the successive frames manually.

Inherent in all programmed instruction, irrespective of the way in which materials are presented, are such features as active practice, a gradual increase in difficulty levels over a series of small steps, immediate feedback, learning at the individual's own rate, and minimization of error. Thus, a variety of learning principles are explicitly built into the technique. There is reinforcement, knowledge of results, active practice, and guidance. There can be distributed practice, and the material may be learned in a time period suited to the ability level of the trainee. If the material is selected from the job in an appropriate manner, there should be positive transfer. The only factor that seems to be missing is whole learning, and that may not be essential. Also, the routine nature of the training may on occasion serve to dampen motivation.

Given this degree of synchronization with learning theory, one would expect that programmed instruction would provide an extremely efficient method of training. Such evidence as is available does yield a generally favorable result, but there are important reservations (24). Consistently, programmed instruction has proved to be a more rapid method of learning than conventional methods. On occasion, it has produced more learning as well. However, superior performance at the end of training is not the typical result, and retention of what is learned appears to be about the same as with other approaches.

In general, the use of programmed instruction can be expected to prove most advantageous with individuals of rather high mental ability and also with those toward the low end of the intellectual range. The person in the middle range benefits less from this particular type of training (24). Furthermore, the advantages of programmed instruction are generally considered to relate to knowledge acquisition only, rather than attitude change, skill learning, and other common objectives of training (2). Finally, the approach is extremely costly if a new program must be written. A single frame takes up to an hour to write, and a total program can contain hundreds or even thousands of frames, depending on the complexity of the material and the desired size of the learning steps. This means that the approach is feasible only when a large number of employees must be trained for a given job.

COMPUTER-ASSISTED INSTRUCTION

Programmed instruction and computer-assisted instruction have much in common. However, the newer approach utilizes a computer to select and present material and evaluate responses. Interaction with the computer occurs through a teaching terminal. The computer adjusts instruction to known aspects of the individual; thus, the rate and nature of learning can be adapted to individual differences in abilities, prior knowledge, and the like. This flexibility and the great amount of information that can be brought to bear for learning, if needed, are major advantages. The computer can analyze mistakes and make the next presentation so as to facilitate understanding of the reasons for error. Thus, with its capacity to select alternatives derived from multiple branching, computer-assisted instruction offers the possibility of a highly individualized and effective approach to learning.

Yet at the present time, it must be said that this potential is rarely fully recognized in existing systems (7). To some extent, the approach has been oversold. Studies to date indicate that computer-assisted instruction yields outcomes very similar to programmed instruction, with much the same advantages and limitations. It has the appeal for industrial organizations that instructional quality can be maintained at many locations through a dispersed system of terminals. However, the expense to achieve this is sizable, and the complexity of the needed programming is such that progress to date has been slower than many had hoped (15).

PERSONALIZED SYSTEM OF INSTRUCTION

The most extensive applications of the personalized system of instruction to date have been within the educational context rather than in the business world. However, the approach does have potential for training in industry. The distinguishing feature as opposed to traditional classroom learning is that the individual goes through the material at his own pace. Learning occurs in modules, and one moves on to the next unit only after demonstrating mastery of the preceding one. Material to be learned is presented in written form. There is repeated testing at the end of modules and immediate feedback of test results. Tests are taken when the individual requests them, testing may be repeated several times until mastery occurs, and the tests are proctored.

Table 15–4. Final and Retention Examination Scores for Students with Personalized System of Instruction and Traditional Lecture Instruction

	Mean Final Examination Score	Mean Retention Examination Score (80 days after final)
Personalized system of instruction	41.8	34.0
Traditional lecture method	39.2	30.3

Source: Adapted from C. G. Chentnik and P. A. Weatherford, "Teaching Management by Management Exception," *Academy of Management Journal,* 17 : 98 (1974).

The data of Table 15–4 provide a picture of the results obtained when the personalized system of instruction and more traditional lecture teaching were compared in an introductory management course (3). The personalized system produced significantly greater learning, as indicated by examination scores, and a reexamination 80 days later indicated better retention as well. Not all studies have yielded as positive a result; however, this particular study is not unique in its findings either. The key ingredient for success appears to be adequate planning and administration (17). Constructing course materials and tests, and being sure that they are used correctly, requires considerable effort. When planning and effort expenditures are at the required level, the individualized nature of the approach appears to offer major benefits. On the other hand, the strong emphasis on testing may make the procedure less palatable for the industrial training of adults than it has been in the educational setting.

System and Team Training

The training of groups of individuals whose work tasks interact has developed primarily within the armed services. However, various types of work unit training are finding their way into industry, especially in the field of air transportation.

In general, when the systems concept is applied as a basis for organizing work, the term system or subsystem training is applied. In other instances, one hears of team or crew training. In either case, complex person-machine interactions may be involved.

Training of this kind is normally introduced relatively late in the overall learning sequence, when individual workers are reasonably knowledgeable and proficient on their own individual jobs. A task is developed that requires role behavior from a number of employees in interaction. Usually, the task is selected to focus on special problem areas within the total work effort. The training may be conducted in the real-life work situation or in a simulated environment with the salient features built in. At the end of the exercise, knowledge of results on total team performance is provided insofar as this is possible, and the team members discuss their own performance. To the extent possible, this feedback should be of both an individual and a group nature (7).

The intent in all this is to develop a cooperative effort and thus overall levels of effectiveness beyond those that can be obtained from individual learning alone. As training progresses through successive trials on various tasks, the individual becomes increasingly aware of how his role behaviors may help and hinder his co-workers. He also begins to view his own work in terms of its place in the total team effort. Thus, team training can permit a group to develop solutions to various problems, such as the overloading of a single member, with the consequent formation of a bottleneck in production. Solutions of this kind are rarely learned when the training program relies entirely on individual instruction.

Especially when simulations are used, and simulations can be of considerable value in focusing on specific work problems, training of this type tends to have much in common with the business games discussed in the preceding chapter. This parallelism even extends to the situation in which employees are trained in a simulated situation to subsequently take over the operation of a person-machine system, the machine components of which are still under construction. Business games also are often used prior to any assumption of actual job duties.

There are several major differences as well. For one thing, business games characteristically operate in fast time: Events occur much more rapidly than in the actual business situation. System training on simulators occurs in real time. Second, business games are normally played with peers. Either all those engaged are students or, if management groups are involved, the tendency is to select individuals from approximately equal levels. Under system concepts, all those engaged in the operation of the system as it relates to the specific problem simulated must participate in the training, irrespective of the level in the organization.

EVALUATION

Several arguments may be advanced against the use of this type of team training in the industrial situation. For one thing, it is extremely wasteful of time and money. Team training exercises almost invariably require role behavior from only a few members at a given point in time. The others act as observers or await their turn for participation. It is difficult to maintain alertness and motivation among these nonactive members. Thus, their time is often wasted, and labor costs increase with little return on the investment. In addition, there are the costs associated either with the use of machinery for nonproductive purposes or with the construction of adequate simulations.

Second, there are problems related to the identification of individual errors and the overall evaluation of results. It is often almost impossible to determine exactly what went wrong when difficulties arise. Thus, immediate feedback and knowledge of results may be hard to achieve, and the specific source of an error may not be identified. Also, suitable criteria of team performance must be established, so that an effective effort can be clearly differentiated from an ineffective one. This can be done, but an adequate backlog of information does not yet exist in this area, with the result that team standard-setting can become a major problem. Thus, the knowledge-of-results requirement tends to run into difficulties both at the level of the individual team member and at the level of the total team (7).

On the positive side is the fact that where cooperative effort represents a major aspect of the work, clear gains in efficiency above those obtainable with individual training do appear to result from the team approach. There are factors in any actual work situation, with its flow of work activities and its patterning of social interactions, that cannot be adequately handled through individual training. When considerations of this kind are marked, some group training seems to be a desirable adjunct to other procedures.

Retraining

One consequence of the accelerated rate of technological change that has characterized the past few decades is that skill training obtained before a worker enters the labor force, or shortly thereafter on the job, no longer provides a guarantee of continued lifetime employment. There is a very real risk that one's entire occupation will become outmoded, and it is almost certain that the skills required in an occupation will change considerably before a person reaches retirement age.

It is a rare company today, among those with sizable manufacturing components, that has not had some experience with the retraining of large numbers of employees to operate new equipment. Such efforts have been particularly extensive in the automobile industry. All the procedures discussed in preceding sections of this chapter appear to have been utilized, but there is almost invariably a considerable amount of classroom training. This means that acceptable levels of literacy must be assumed as well as some competence in mathematics.

Although one might expect that these factors would not create problems in the America of today, this has not turned out to be the case. Many companies have run into major difficulties with current employees, whose schooling has proved insufficient or inadequate—especially when it becomes necessary to carry out very rapid retraining to get new machinery operative as quickly as possible. In many instances, companies have not been in a position to provide the basic schooling required, with the result that the less literate employees are the ones most likely to be displaced by new equipment. On the other hand, companies that have attempted such a basic skills training program have had considerable success (21).

Although the content of retraining tends to vary with the shifting currents of technological change, certain subject matter areas and skills have taken on increasing importance. Hydraulics, lubrication, electricity, electronics, control circuits, and similar subjects appear frequently in company retraining programs, along with classes dealing with the specifics of automated equipment operation and maintenance.

In addition to activity aimed at preparing workers for new jobs within the company, there has been some pressure from unions to have companies take on the expense of retraining workers who are slated for layoff, to prepare them for new jobs in the community. This pressure has been successful in a few instances. However, it now seems unlikely that many companies will be forced to assume this burden in the future.

TRAINING FOR THE CULTURALLY DISADVANTAGED

The major impetus to increased federal involvement in the training field was the fear that automation and changing technology would lead to extensive unemployment among older workers whose skills were no longer appropriate to the tasks to be performed. This fear has generally proved to be unjustified. Technological unemployment has been much less extensive than originally anticipated. Yet federal support of various training efforts has continued, although the focus has shifted to training that would increase the employability of minority group members and the culturally disadvantaged in general. More recently, high unemployment levels have provided an additional spur (19).

Governmental Training and Retraining

Governmental support of vocational education was initiated with the Smith-Hughes Act of 1917. Until the 1960s, this support generally was concentrated at the high school and vocational school level, especially in the fields of agriculture and home economics. With the Area Redevelopment Act of 1961 and the Manpower Development and Training Act of 1962, government began to assume direct responsibilities for the training and retraining of individuals who were already in the labor force, although often as unemployed job seekers rather than as employed workers.

These acts provided not only training opportunities, but also subsistence payments, transportation allowances, and vocational counseling. The Area

Redevelopment Act programs were geared to prepare underemployed and unemployed workers in depressed areas for immediate employment. They were usually oriented toward entry jobs within the labor force and were an integral part of a total area redevelopment effort. The Manpower Development and Training Act (MDTA) programs are generally longer in duration and take a greater variety of forms. Selection for training is carried out by the state employment agencies.

An idea of the growth and scope of federally assisted programs is provided in Table 15–5. A number of these programs derive from the Economic Opportunity Act of 1964. This is true of the Neighborhood Youth Corps, which provides job training and remedial education for high-school-age youth; Operation Mainstream, which provides training and jobs in community betterment and beautification, primarily for older workers; the Concentrated Employment Program, which focuses on the hard-core unemployed in selected geographical areas; and of the Job Corps, which operates centers for the training of disadvantaged youths aged sixteen to twenty-one. The Work Incentive Program is intended for welfare clients and was an outgrowth of a 1967 amendment to the Social Security Act. The Public Employment Program resulted from the Emergency Employment Act of 1971 and focused on the hiring and training of previously unemployed individuals by state, county, and local governments. It is being replaced by Comprehensive Manpower Assistance as a result of the

Table 15–5. First-time Enrollments in Federally Assisted
Work and Training Programs (in thousands)

Program	Fiscal Year		
	1964	1969	1974
Comprehensive Manpower Assistance	—	—	43
Institutional training under the MDTA	69	135	110
JOBS (federally financed) and other on-the-job training	9	136	163
Neighborhood Youth Corps			
In school and summer	—	430	741
Out of school	—	74	72
Operation Mainstream	—	11	42
Public Service Careers	—	4	10
Concentrated Employment Program	—	127	70
Job Corps	—	53	46
Work Incentive Program	—	81	353
Public Employment Program	—	—	269
Veterans programs	—	59	111
Vocational rehabilitation	179	368	540
Other programs (primarily social service training for public assistance recipients)	21	267	789
Totals	278	1,745	3,359

Source: Manpower Report of the President (Washington, D.C.: Government Printing Office, 1971), p. 37 and (1975), pp. 114, 317.

passage of the Comprehensive Employment and Training Act in late 1973. This latter act also provides for the continuation of a number of the previously created programs, but decentralizes their administration to lower levels of government.

From the point of view of the personnel manager in a business organization, probably the most significant of the programs is JOBS (Job Opportunities in the Business Sector). Public Service Careers is a comparable effort in the governmental sector. The JOBS program is run by the Department of Labor in conjunction with the National Alliance of Businessmen and provides training and employment for the culturally disadvantaged. It is business's answer to the societal outcry for increased social responsibility. In some cases, JOBS training is supported by government contracts; in other cases, it is handled entirely at company expense. In addition, other on-the-job training is conducted outside the JOBS framework. JOBS contracts involving the government have emphasized training for upgrading into more skilled positions above the entry level (23).

The formation of the National Alliance of Businessmen in 1968 was a consequence of the quite considerable resistance that the government encountered in, its efforts to establish on-the-job training programs under the MDTA. Although the approach of involving business leaders directly in the program has been very successful, there are companies that do not choose to participate. The major problems appear to be associated with the need to give time off from work for training during working hours; with the major government involvement, which is interpreted as meaning bureaucratic "red tape'" and interference in the business; and with the perceived lower productivity of the culturally disadvantaged (6).

The Nature of Training

In spite of the various factors that make training of the culturally disadvantaged unattractive, a great deal has been accomplished as a result of social responsibility concerns. The more successful efforts have been surprisingly similar in content (7, 28). Included are basic education and skills training; counseling and other types of individual assistance, including help with personal affairs; preassignment training, dealing with work orientation and role requirements; and actual on-the-job training. Topics such as grooming and hygiene, money management, use of public transportation facilities, getting along with others, where to find help, career development, arithmetic, remedial reading, manners, grammar, spelling, and composition often are included. By definition, the culturally disadvantaged lack much of the early culture training that society tends to take for granted. It is becoming increasingly apparent that turning the hard-core unemployed into stable, effective workers requires a considerable effort to compensate for this lack of culture training.

There is evidence that if training for the disadvantaged is to succeed, it must be carried out in a consistently supportive climate (8). This may mean some downward revision of standards, extension of the period of trainee status, and acceptance of unconventional behavior. A social environment that conveys a desire to help and a belief in ultimate success appears to be very important.

Sources of Problems

Experience has revealed a number of specific types of problems that may arise in training the disadvantaged (9, 13). Trainees often have been found to want to personalize the training to a point where there is a breakdown in teaching effectiveness. Instructors, being from a different background, have some tendency to allow the trainees to use their disadvantaged background as a crutch, to the detriment of learning. Often, details are sacrificed to get the overall picture across. When trainees cannot see the relevance of what they are asked to learn, and when rewards for participating in the training are insufficient, learning suffers. Generally, abstract principles have little meaning unless illustrated repeatedly with practical examples.

Difficulties may well arise because the training is not supported by higher-level management and because of a need for double standards vis-à-vis regular workers (4). The fact that the culturally handicapped are permitted to continue employment without discipline in spite of high absenteeism rates and substandard performance can create considerable resentment among other workers, and among foremen, too. In fact, most of the problems associated with training the culturally disadvantaged appear to derive from conflicting expectations and requirements generated by both humanitarian and productivity values as held by other workers, foremen, higher management, and government representatives. When the trainee is placed in a role conflict situation of this kind and gets widely varying communications as to what is expected of him and how he is perceived, it is little wonder that he is very likely to leave. Yet it remains true that these on-the-job programs, with all their problems, have proved to be a successful approach to aiding the employment of the culturally disadvantaged (18).

CAREER PLANNING

A number of considerations have operated in recent years to involve personnel departments not only in individual training and development programs but in the sequential planning of such efforts over a span of years. In times past, such career planning was considered entirely an individual responsibility. Government pressures, shortages in certain kinds of human resources, and rapid changes in technology have made it a company concern as well (29).

Governmental pressures to hire, retain, and upgrade women and minorities have already been noted in several contexts. If upgrading is to occur so that affirmative action goals are met, companies must plan for the movement of people through a hierarchy of positions and for the sequencing of appropriate training efforts (10). A variety of activities, many closely related to the concept of career ladders, are carried out to this end. Individuals are helped through counseling and coaching to develop plans for their careers, including needed education and training, both within and outside the company.

A second consideration fostering company involvement in career planning is the current reality, or prospect of, imminent shortages in key personnel, such as effective managers (20). To the extent companies anticipate such shortages and do not believe that qualified people can be obtained in the external labor market, it becomes expedient to help current employees plan for their own development, so that they will possess needed skills and knowledge at the time when these are required.

Finally, there has been increasing concern with problems of obsolescence resulting from rapidly changing technologies and the development of new knowledge (12). Fields such as engineering are changing so fast that what is learned during a university education may well have little relevance a few years later. This is a problem for the individual, but it is a problem for the employing organization as well. There is evidence that certain kinds of people, such as those with high achievement motivation, are likely to take steps to combat obsolescence on their own (26). But others are not. With these people, company involvement in career planning to maintain capabilities through periodic retraining can be useful for all concerned.

As a result of these factors, a number of the larger companies have already involved their personnel departments in career-planning activities of various kinds. It seems likely that such efforts will increase in the future.

QUESTIONS

1. Rank the various principles of learning in terms of the degree of certainty with which they can be stated. Annotate your ranking with reference to research.
2. What is the role of training-needs analysis? Do you believe all training programs are based on such an analysis? Explain.
3. In what ways do programmed instruction, computer-assisted instruction, and the personalized system of instruction differ? What are the pros and cons of these approaches for training industrial production workers?
4. It has been said that apprenticeship is the key to the American production system. In what sense is this true? In what sense not true?
5. The government is generally assumed to have cut back its training efforts in the mid-1970s through a recognition of past failures. Discuss with reference to specific data.

REFERENCES

1. Barocci, T. A. "The Determinants of Completion in Apprenticeship," in G. G. Somers (ed.), *Proceedings of the Twenty-sixth Annual Winter*

Meeting. Madison, Wis.: Industrial Relations Research Association, 1973, pp. 159–169.

2. Carroll, S. J., F. T. Paine, and J. M. Ivancevich. "The Relative Effectiveness of Training Methods—Expert Opinion and Research." *Personnel Psychology*, 25 (1972), 495–509.

3. Chentnik, C. G., and P. A. Weatherford. "Teaching Management by Management Exception." *Academy of Management Journal*, 17 (1974), 90–100.

4. Cohn, E., and M. V. Lewis. "Employer's Experience in Retaining Hard-core Hires." *Industrial Relations*, 14 (1975), 55–62.

5. Folley, J. D. "Determining Training Needs of Department Store Sales Personnel." *Training and Development Journal*, 23 (1969), No. 7, 24–27.

6. Fottler, M. D., J. E. Drotning, and D. B. Lipsky. "Reasons for Employer Nonparticipation in Manpower Training Programs for the Disadvantaged." *Labor Law Journal*, 22 (1971), 708–712.

7. Goldstein, I. L. *Training: Program Development and Evaluation*. Monterey, Calif.: Brooks/Cole Publishing Co., 1974.

8. Goodman, P. S., P. Salipante, and H. Paransky. "Hiring, Training, and Retraining the Hard-core Unemployed: A Selected Review." *Journal of Applied Psychology*, 58 (1973), 23–33.

9. Gray, I., and T. B. Borecki. "Training Program for the Hard-core: What the Trainer Has to Learn." *Personnel*, 47 (1970), No. 2, 23–30.

10. Gruenfeld, E. F. *Promotion: Practices, Policies, and Affirmative Action*. Ithaca, N.Y.: New York State School of Industrial and Labor Relations, Cornell University, 1975.

11. Holland, J. E., and T. P. Curtis. "Orientation of New Employees," in J. J. Famularo (ed.), *Handbook of Modern Personnel Administration*. New York: McGraw-Hill Book Company, 1972, pp. 23-1 to 23-33.

12. Kaufman, H. G. *Career Management: A Guide to Combating Obsolescence*. New York: Institute of Electrical and Electronics Engineers Press, 1975.

13. Koch, J. L. "Employing the Disadvantaged: Lessons from the Past Decade." *California Management Review*, 17 (1974), 68–77.

14. Locke, E. A. "Personnel Attitudes and Motivation." *Annual Review of Psychology*, 26 (1975), 457–480.

15. McGehee, W., and D. H. Livingston. "Persistence of the Effects of Training Employees to Reduce Waste." *Personnel Psychology*, 7 (1954), 33–39.

16. McGehee, W., and P. W. Thayer. *Training in Business and Industry*. New York: John Wiley & Sons, Inc., 1961.

17. McKeachie, W. J. "Instructional Psychology." *Annual Review of Psychology*, 25 (1974), 161–193.

18. Mangum, G. L., and J. A. Walsh. *A Decade of Manpower Develop-*

ment and Training. Salt Lake City, Utah: Olympus Publishing Co., 1973.

19. *Manpower Report of the President.* Washington, D.C.: Government Printing Office, 1971, 1975.

20. Miner, J. B. *The Human Constraint: The Coming Shortage of Managerial Talent.* Washington, D.C.: BNA Books, Inc., 1974.

21. Molenkopf, W. G. "Some Results of Three Basic Skills Training Programs in an Industrial Setting." *Journal of Applied Psychology,* 53 (1969), 343–347.

22. Morano, R. "Determining Organizational Training Needs." *Personnel Psychology,* 26 (1973), 479–487.

23. Myers, C. A. *The Role of the Private Sector in Manpower Development.* Baltimore, Md.: The Johns Hopkins University Press, 1971.

24. Nash, A. N., J. P. Muczyk, and F. L. Vettori. "The Relative Practical Effectiveness of Programmed Instruction." *Personnel Psychology,* 24 (1971), 397–418.

25. Odiorne, G. S. *Training by Objectives.* New York: Macmillan Publishing Co., Inc., 1970.

26. Shearer, R. L., and J. A. Steger. "Manpower Obsolescence: A New Definition and Empirical Investigation of Personal Variables." *Academy of Management Journal,* 18 (1975), 263–275.

27. U.S. Department of Labor. *The National Apprenticeship Program.* Washington, D.C.: Government Printing Office, 1972.

28. U.S. Department of Labor. *Productive Employment of the Disadvantaged: Guidelines for Action.* Washington, D.C.: Government Printing Office, 1973.

29. Walker, J. W. "Individual Career Planning: Managerial Help for Subordinates." *Business Horizons,* 16 (1973), No. 1, 65–72.

16 *Monetary Compensation*

The primary intent of the different types of monetary payment programs for employees is to provide an input-output mediator that will serve to maximize motivation to contribute to company goals. Whereas training is directed toward *changing* people to make them more effective, payment programs should be designed to provide inducements so that individuals will try to make the best use of their *existing* capabilities. Pay practices also have an important function in recruiting; the beginning pay levels need to be such that people with the necessary or desired characteristics will be induced to join a firm and contribute to its goal attainment.

COMPENSATION AND MOTIVATION

It is clear that money has reward value in a purely economic sense, and that individuals expect to be paid for the work they perform in furthering the organization's goals. It seems safe to assume, then, that when monetary rewards are made available in appropriate relationship to job behavior, they can influence the level of motivation and thus induce a maximal contribution to the company effort.

There is considerable research evidence that people can achieve higher levels of task performance when there is the prospect of achieving a greater monetary reward commensurate with their efforts. But whether a particular type of monetary compensation program actually does operate as an effective input-output mediator is much less certain (17, 39). It appears that many people are paid in ways that do little to arouse motivation, and that as a result the potential value of the payment process as a mediator often is lost. An additional complicating factor is that money itself has different meanings for different people (47); the most carefully designed pay system cannot motivate a person for whom money has little value. In most business organizations, however, this type of person is likely to be rare. At least initially, most people accept jobs to earn money.

In recent years, a number of behavioral scientists have been studying the question of pay, its importance as a motivator, and its effect on performance (25). One group of studies involves *expectancy theories,* based on the premise that individuals have certain expectancies regarding the consequences of their own behavior, and that they will behave in such a way as to achieve a desired outcome. These studies have indicated that pay is considered a means to satisfying some motives and not others. It is most closely related to such motives as security, physiological gratification, status, esteem, and recognition. The implication is that pay policies will have the most impact on the performance of lower-level employees with the greatest need for money per se, and of those higher-level employees who value the status and esteem that money represents. Employees concerned primarily with satisfying social or self-actualization needs, however, are not as likely to be motivated by pay.

Even for individuals motivated by physiological and psychological needs responsive to pay, however, there are other factors necessary for pay to achieve its potential as an input-output mediator. For job performance to be affected by pay policies, employees must expect that good performance

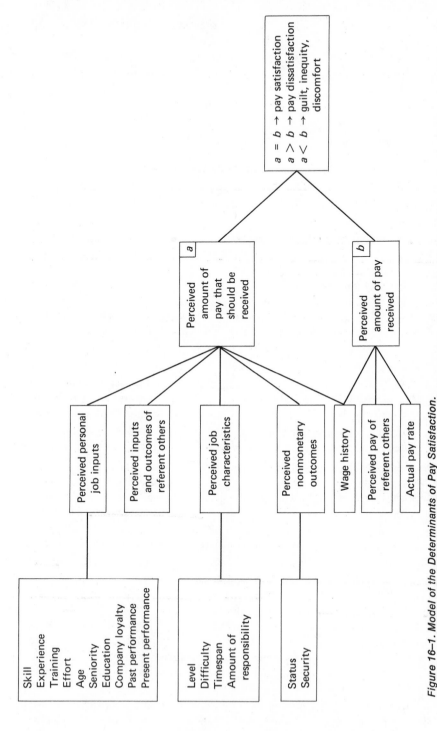

Figure 16–1. Model of the Determinants of Pay Satisfaction.
Source: From *Pay and Organizational Effectiveness: A Psychological View* by E. E. Lawler (New York: McGraw-Hill Book Company, 1971), **p. 215.** Copyright 1971 by McGraw-Hill Book Company. Used with permission of McGraw-Hill Book Company.

actually will yield high pay. Furthermore, employees must expect that it is possible to achieve such performance through their own efforts (21).

Another type of motivation theory that has generated a good deal of research is *equity theory* (14, 32, 36). According to this theory, employees are concerned not only with maximizing the amount of pay, but with the fairness of the pay *as they perceive it*. This perception is based on a comparison an individual makes between his own input into the job and what he is paid with the inputs and outcomes of another person or persons doing the same or comparable work. In both equity and expectancy theories, it is the employee's perception of his pay that relates to his satisfaction or dissatisfaction and ultimately to his motivation. Figure 16–1 illustrates the various elements that affect this perception.

While motivation theories such as those discussed, and others, deal primarily with the effects of pay procedures on individual performance, other theories of an economic nature relate to the overall compensation system as it exists in a given firm, labor market, or industry. These wage theories attempt to answer questions about differences in pay rates between companies for the same job, within the same company for different jobs, and even from one country to another. Before discussing the approaches involving individual compensation, it is necessary to outline the types of programs based on wage theory that companies undertake to determine their general pay policies.

WAGE LEVELS AND WAGE SURVEYS

Various procedures are used to establish (a) the general level of a company's payments to its employees relative to the payments made by *other* companies and (b) the relative grading or positioning of the jobs *within* a company in terms of pay. In the first instance, the concern is with the *wage level* of the firm, which is usually expressed either as an average figure for all jobs or through a gross comparison of job rates for various key jobs with rates for comparable jobs in other companies. In the second instance, the concern is with the internal *wage structure*, which is characteristically established in terms of various job grades or levels. Information used in determining a company's wage level is often obtained from *wage surveys* conducted within the industry or in the geographical locality. Information used in setting up a wage structure is usually derived from some kind of *job evaluation* procedure.

Considerations Related to the Company Wage Level

One might expect that traditional economic theory, or wage theory, with its emphasis on competition in the marketplace and conscious profit maximization would provide a sure guide for establishing the company wage level. This does not appear to be the case, however. Economic wage theory is helpful in understanding long-term shifts in wages within a particular country or wage differences between countries or regions. It has very little usefulness as a basis for short-term decisions where a single company is concerned. Furthermore, economic forces and labor market conditions do not necessarily result in what may be viewed as an "equitable" compensation system or "just" wages (30).

Among the specific factors that do appear to have some relationship to existing wage levels are union pressures, what other employers in the area or industry are paying, the average skill level of positions in the firm, minimum-wage legislation, the ease with which potential employees may be recruited, the number of positions that must be filled, the level of employee satisfaction, the degree to which product market competition exists, prospects for future profits, and company size. Which of these will exert the most influence depends on the particular circumstance, although it seems clear that the wage level is rarely a product of a single factor. Various studies at different times based on different samples of firms have related differences in wage structures to a multitude of factors, including changes in productivity, rate of profit, original wage level, extent of unionization, per cent of skilled labor in the work force, company size, and the degree to which output in the industry is concentrated in a few large companies (1, 40). While all these factors may have some influence on a particular firm's wage structure, those that seem to be most relevant are the ones that are a function of company size and location (24).

Changes in wage levels, at either the individual company level or the level of the entire work force of the country, are generally a reflection of the overall state of the economy. The inflationary pressures of the past decade have been both a cause and an effect of higher and higher wage levels and have resulted in severe problems in the administration of compensation policies—problems that were not resolved by the government's wage-control program (5, 28). In unionized firms, which traditionally have higher wage levels than nonunion companies, these pressures are even more acute, with the result that wage rates go up faster. A study of changes in total compensation, including benefit payments, between 1966 and 1972, for example, shows an increase in union establishments of 61 per cent— from $3.61 per hour in 1966 to $5.83 in 1972—compared to a 52 per cent change in nonunion establishments—from $2.32 in 1966 to $3.53 in 1972 (41).

The types of factors that are considered most important by company personnel executives in determining the general wage level are shown in Table 16–1. What the competition is paying for personnel is the most crucial factor, on an area basis for lower-level jobs and on an industry basis for managerial positions. The company's financial condition is more likely to be the most important factor in smaller companies and with reference to management jobs, and labor market conditions, such as the

Table 16–1. *Most Important Factors in Determining General Wage Levels*

| | Personnel Executives with | | | | | |
| | Small Companies (less than 1000 employees, N = 64) | | Large Companies (1000 employees or more, N = 120) | | All Companies (N = 184) | |
Factors	Per Cent Ranking Factor No. 1[a]	Weighted Rank	Per Cent Ranking Factor No. 1[a]	Weighted Rank	Per Cent Ranking Factor No. 1[a]	Weighted Rank
For nonmanagement jobs						
Competitive wages in the area	54	1.7	55	1.6	54	1.6
Competitive industry wages	21	2.6	27	2.0	25	2.2
Company financial condition	18	2.8	12	3.1	14	2.9
Labor market conditions	6	2.8	3	2.9	4	2.9
For management jobs						
Competitive industry wages	25	2.2	47	1.7	39	1.8
Competitive wages in the area	35	2.1	20	2.4	26	2.3
Company financial condition	21	2.7	18	2.8	19	2.7
Labor market conditions	12	2.6	5	2.9	8	2.7

Source: Bureau of National Affairs, Inc., *Wage and Salary Administration,* Personnel Policies Forum Survey No. 97, July 1972, p. 2.
[a] Percentages may not add to 100 because of nonresponses.

unemployment rate, are least likely to be the most important consideration when changes in wage levels are being considered (7).

WAGE CRITERIA

For purposes of establishing a company wage level, it is important to have some kind of yardstick that will indicate just how much of an increase (or decrease) in existing wage rates is appropriate. This is what the various *wage criteria* attempt to provide. Among the commonly noted criteria are

1. The results of wage surveys conducted either in the geographical area or in the industry. As indicated by Table 16–1, industry data are more commonly used by the larger corporations, and for management positions.
2. The Consumer Price Index published by the federal government. Many companies use this measure to adjust wage levels to cost-of-living changes on a periodic basis, a practice that has become increasingly popular in recent years (26).
3. Various ideal family budgets that specify the living-wage level required to maintain a standard of living judged to be adequate. The Urban Workers' Family Budgets prepared by the federal government are an example.
4. Company profit figures for the immediately preceding period, which are considered indicative of ability to pay.
5. Indexes of physical productivity for certain industries and for the economy as a whole developed by the U.S. Bureau of Labor Statistics. These specify a percentage improvement factor attributable to the combined effects of labor, management, tools, and materials.
6. Company turnover statistics, position vacancy data, and unemployment rates in the area that in combination provide information relative to recruiting difficulties and labor shortages.

Among these criteria, the results of wage surveys appear to be the most widely used. There is ample evidence that satisfaction with pay is dependent on relative rather than absolute wage levels. Although comparisons with other individuals in the same firm have a strong impact on perceptions of equity as regards pay, outside comparisons are also made—either with individual and average rates in the local area or with information regarding the industry or profession. In view of this strong tendency on the part of individual employees to use outside comparisons as a basis for determining whether pay is equitable, it is not surprising that such considerations have a strong impact at the level of management decision making as well as in union-management negotiations. Wage surveys are the means to obtain objective data in this area.

Wage Surveys

Wage survey data both from the local labor market and for the industry can be derived from a number of sources. Such surveys are conducted by individual companies, groups of companies formed specifically for this reason, employer associations created primarily for collective bargaining purposes, unions, consulting firms, professional survey companies, the federal government, and various professional societies.

When groups of companies are involved, it is important that the companies included be typical of the local area or industry, that enough companies be included to provide stable results, and that the group be relatively permanent, so the procedures and results become standardized over time. Although a company may conduct a spot survey by telephone if only one or two jobs are involved, mailed questionnaires are by far the most common data-gathering device. This is the procedure now used by the U.S. Department of Labor in conducting its Area Wage Surveys in more than 80 local labor markets throughout the country. In earlier years, the government got its wage survey data from personal interviews made by special field workers on company premises; at present, such interviews are used mainly to follow up on nonrespondents to the questionnaires.

DATA COLLECTION

For purposes of data collection, surveying all jobs in all companies would represent an almost impossible task, and the usual practice is to select a number of key jobs. These should cover the full range of positions, contain sizable numbers of employees, and be clearly defined in terms of content. The survey form should contain in each instance not only the job title, or job titles if more than one designation is in common use, but also at least a brief job description. This will help to ensure against the possibility that jobs that actually differ to a considerable degree might be grouped together because of similarities in their titles.

The information obtained on each job tends to vary considerably, depending on the needs of the companies involved. Perhaps most important is the *base rate* of pay for the job. This is defined for hourly workers as the wage per hour stripped of all overtime, shift differentials, and fringe benefits, but before deductions for taxes, social security, and the like. Salaries may also be changed into such an hourly base rate to permit comparability of all jobs under study. Incentive payments based on the actual amount of work produced may similarly be converted to a per-hour equivalent.

Other important figures are *hiring rates*—the amount paid to beginners who are just starting out in a given job; *earnings*—the total amount paid a worker per standard period of time, including overtime, incentives, shift differentials, and the like; *rate ranges*—the minimum and maximum amounts paid to workers on the particular job; and *wage changes*—recent shifts in either the amount or kind of payments made to various employee groups. Beyond these facts, information may be obtained on any other policies and practices of concern to the participating companies.

REPORTING RESULTS

The findings from a wage survey may be reported in any of a variety of forms. In general, a company will prefer to compare its own internal wage structure with that of various other firms. Figure 16–2 provides an abbreviated example of a format used for this purpose. An actual survey ordinarily would involve many more companies and many more jobs.

In this instance, anyone who knows the code designation for his own company can compare it individually with other companies included in the survey. One of the major disadvantages of the wage surveys conducted by

Job	Company A				Company B				Company C				Company D				Company E				Averages for All Companies (weighted by no. of employees)			
	Average	Minimum	Maximum	Employees	Average	Minimum	Maximum	Employees	Average	Minimum	Maximum	Employees	Average	Minimum	Maximum	Employees	Average	Minimum	Maximum	Employees	Average	Minimum	Maximum	Employees
Office Jobs																								
File clerk																								
Sorter operator																								
Typist																								
Factory Jobs																								
Loader																								
Welder																								
Drillpress operator																								
Sales Jobs																								
Sales trainee																								
Industrial salesman																								
Sales clerk																								

Figure 16–2. Example of Wage Survey Summary Report Form.

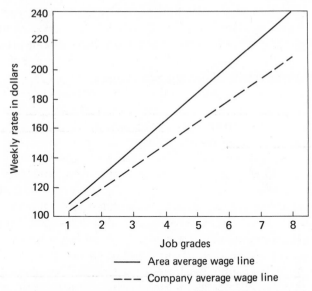

Figure 16–3. Comparison of Company and Area Average Rates.

the Department of Labor has been that they deal with averages and distributions of rates for each job but are not broken down by individual companies. This, plus the need for industry as well as geographical data, has tended to foster the use of private surveys.

When averages are used, it is often helpful to present the findings graphically, as in Figure 16–3. In this instance, the various jobs surveyed have been grouped into grade levels in accord with the specific company's job evaluation system. Then weighted averages were computed for each of the job grades, so that those jobs containing the largest number of employees received proportionately greater emphasis. It is apparent that although this particular company is relatively close to the industry average insofar as its lower-level jobs are concerned, it lags rather markedly in the higher job grades.

JOB EVALUATION AND WAGE STRUCTURES

It is possible to establish the internal wage structure of a firm entirely on the basis of wage surveys or even some less precise index of wage levels in the area labor market. There are a number of companies that do just this. The major difficulty is that the pay for any given job tends to vary considerably from company to company, depending in large part on the significance of the job for the operations of that particular organization. Thus, the market often provides an imperfect guideline at the level of the individual job. Furthermore, wage surveys usually focus on a limited number of key jobs. As a result, the majority of positions in a company will have to be priced without adequate knowledge of market conditions.

The consequence of these considerations is that companies that attempt to use the market as the only criterion for an internal wage structure are likely to find themselves without any real criterion at all. It is one thing to use market conditions as a guide to the overall wage level of the firm; it is quite another to use the market in determining the pay for each specific job. When this is attempted, there will almost inevitably be continuing dissension over pay scales—frequently with the union as a major participant. Thus, the inherent ambiguity of market considerations combines with insufficient knowledge to create internal stress, and organizational maintenance suffers.

Given the fact that pay can clearly be an important source of employee satisfaction and dissatisfaction, it seems desirable to structure the relationships among the amounts paid for various jobs within a firm, so that conflict is minimized. If the maintenance goal is to be adequately served, a system for relating jobs must be introduced that will be perceived as generally equitable by all parties and that will provide reasonably stable criteria for placing jobs in the structure. Thus, just as wage surveys make it possible to reduce feelings of inequity when a worker compares his earnings with those of others outside the firm, job evaluation can serve to reduce such feelings when internal comparisons are made.

Methods of Job Evaluation

As indicated in Chapter 7, job analysis provides the essential information on which job evaluation is based. Job evaluation takes the data set forth in the job description, and sometimes in the job specifications as well, and appraises these role prescriptions in terms of their degree of relationship to company goals. Thus, a rating of the job relative to productivity and maintenance goals is obtained that is in many ways similar to the rating an individual might receive relative to the role requirements of his specific position. As will become evident, the methods of job evaluation have much in common with the employee-rating systems discussed in Chapter 9.

In part because of space limitations and in part because advanced courses often cover this area, no effort will be made to present a detailed treatment of the different job-evaluation methods in current use. Only enough information to permit a general understanding of the four basic approaches will be provided, along with some appraisal of these methods. Of the four methods in general use, two—job ranking and job classification—are considered to be nonquantitative, and the other two—factor comparison and the point system—quantitative. Those who may wish a more extended discussion of a specific method can find the appropriate information in advanced texts in the area (3, 38).

JOB RANKING

In job ranking, the various jobs are arranged in order of merit, according to their worth as a whole. No attempt is made to separate out different factors within the jobs, although certain aspects, such as difficulty level, may be specified as criteria for the ranking. Usually, separate ranks are developed, using the job descriptions for each department and raters who know the work done in that department.

Either of two approaches may be used in developing ranks. The job descriptions may be sorted directly, so that a continuous-ordering results, or the paired comparison technique may be applied, and a ranking developed out of the various individual comparisons between pairs of jobs (see Chapter 9). In either case, the ratings made by two or more individuals must be combined by averaging to produce the final ranking for the department. Then, the data from all departments are dovetailed, either on the basis of the knowledge of a single individual who is well-informed regarding role prescriptions for the company as a whole or through committee action. The result is an ordering of all jobs in the organization.

JOB CLASSIFICATION

Grouping of jobs into various grades or levels may of course follow the use of the ranking approach. It is, in fact, common practice to do this. A similar assignment of jobs to categories of worth is also frequently used with the other methods to be discussed shortly. But in the job classification method proper, grades are established first, and then jobs are fitted into the appropriate classes, using preestablished grade descriptions or grading rules. Thus, the various groupings are not developed after some type of ordering process has already been carried out, but at the very outset.

Separate classification systems may be established for office, factory, sales, and managerial positions. Within each of these, descriptions are written that establish the bounds for the various grades. The number of grades so established will vary with the total range of job difficulty or complexity represented in the company, as well as with the fineness of differentiation desired. In general, between 7 and 15 classes will be required. The number of sales grades may, however, differ from those in the factory area, for instance. The crucial task of writing the grade descriptions or grading rules, against which individual job descriptions are subsequently compared, may be assigned to an individual or to a committee.

FACTOR COMPARISON

Factor comparison is in reality a complex variant of the ranking approach, because jobs are compared with each other rather than against category descriptions. The rankings are not done on a global basis, taking the whole job into account, but individually, in terms of various compo-

Table 16-2. Difficulty Rank Versus Money Rank for 16 Tentative Key Jobs

Jobs	Mental Effort Difficulty	Mental Effort Money	Physical Effort Difficulty	Physical Effort Money	Skill Difficulty	Skill Money	Responsibility Difficulty	Responsibility Money	Working Conditions Difficulty	Working Conditions Money
Gager	2	2	13	13	2	2	3	3	15	4
Pattern maker	1	1	12	12	1	1	1	1	16	16
Common laborer	16	16	1	1	16	16	16	16	1	1
Power shear operator	11	11	11	11	9	9	5	5	4	6
Plater	10	10	6	6	6	7	12	12	9	10
Riveter	12	12	3	3	12	12	14	14	8	9
Blacksmith	13	13	2	2	8	5	13	13	7	2
Punch press operator	14	14	4	4	13	13	15	15	5	7
Screw machine operator	4	4	8	8	3	3	2	2	13	14
Casting inspector	3	3	7	7	4	6	4	4	10	11
Millwright	9	9	10	10	5	4	6	6	11	12
Tool crib attendant	7	7	16	16	14	14	10	10	14	15
Arc welder	8	8	9	9	7	8	9	9	3	5
Electrical truck operator	6	6	15	15	11	11	8	8	12	13
Crane operator	5	5	14	14	10	10	7	7	6	8
Watchman	15	15	5	5	15	15	11	11	2	3

Source: D. W. Belcher, Compensation Administration, © 1974, p. 163. By permission of Prentice-Hall, Inc., Englewood Cliffs, N.J.

nent factors—usually skill, mental effort, physical effort, responsibility, and working conditions.

The initial step is to select some 15 to 25 key jobs that seem to be generally in the correct relationship to each other insofar as wage rates are concerned. Usually, these will be jobs that are widely distributed in level and that have not been a subject of controversy regarding payment rates. These key jobs are then rank ordered on each of the 5 factors. Thus, in the case of the 16 jobs noted in Table 16–2, the jobs rated highest on the particular factor noted are

1. Mental effort—pattern maker.
2. Physical effort—common laborer.
3. Skill—pattern maker.
4. Responsibility—pattern maker.
5. Working conditions—common laborer.

The jobs rated lowest are

1. Mental effort—common laborer.
2. Physical effort—tool crib attendant.
3. Skill—common laborer.
4. Responsibility—common laborer.
5. Working conditions—pattern maker.

Next, the present wage being paid on each of the key jobs is divided among the five factors, with the greatest proportion being given to the most important factor. This is as much a judgmental process as is the ranking. In both instances, averages of a number of independent ratings by different individuals should be obtained. With reference to the backup data for Table 16–2, given a present wage for gager of $6.16, this might be distributed among the factors as follows:

mental effort	$1.44
physical effort	.76
skill	2.04
responsibility	1.02
working conditions	.90
	$6.16

For pattern maker, the average of the judgments might be

mental effort	$1.80
physical effort	.78
skill	2.26
responsibility	1.20
working conditions	.46
	$6.50

The money amounts thus established may then be used to set up a second ranking on each of the five factors. The two rankings, on difficulty and money, are then compared as in Table 16–2. Where sizable disparities exist, as with gager (working conditions) and blacksmith (skill and working conditions), these jobs are eliminated from the list of key jobs.

The remaining jobs are then put into a job comparison scale. This scale indicates the money amounts associated with each job for each of the five factors. Thus, the key jobs become benchmarks against which other jobs may be compared. The appropriate pay for each nonkey job is determined by establishing which jobs it falls between on each of the five factors. The five money amounts thus identified are added to obtain the wage rate for the job. Each job in the company is related to the job comparison scale one factor at a time in this way, using the job descriptions for key and nonkey jobs. The result is not only an evaluation, but an actual pricing of the firm's job structure.

POINT SYSTEM

The point system is an extension of the job-classification approach that utilizes a variety of factors as a basis for classification rather than a single dimension. In one variant or another, it appears to be the most widely used of the job-evaluation methods (6). As with job classification, point systems are usually developed separately for different categories of jobs—factory, clerical, sales, and the like. The reason is that the relevant factors may differ considerably from one category of job to another. Thus, a single system for the whole organization could be extremely cumbersome and at the same time yield some rather incongruous results. The number and type of factors on which ratings are made tend to vary considerably between companies and even within companies between job categories. Among the factors that often occur are education, job knowledge, mental demand, effect of error, personal contact skill, initiative and ingenuity, physical demand, responsibility (in various areas such as safety, work of others, equipment, and materials), working conditions, hazards, and level to which the job reports. It is not uncommon to use as many as ten or even more factors in a single system.

When the factors have been established and defined, degrees are determined for each factor, so that those who subsequently rate jobs using the point manual may identify the amount, or level, of a factor in the particular job under consideration. Different numbers of degree differentiations may be used on the various factors, but in any case the definitions for each degree should be stated in considerable detail and should include if possible the titles of several key jobs falling at that particular level.

Table 16–3 provides an example of how points might be assigned after the appropriate factor and degree descriptions have been written. Judgments must be made as to how the total number of points should be allocated among factors. A common procedure is to start with 500 points

Table 16–3. Hypothetical Point Values for Job Factors

Factors	Lowest Degree	Next Degree	Next Degree	Next Degree	Highest Degree
Mental demand	15	30	45	60	75
Experience	20	40	60	80	100
Physical demand	15	35	55	—	75
Hazards	10	20	30	40	50
Education	10	20	30	40	50
Personal contact	10	30	—	—	50
Equipment responsibility	10	20	30	40	50
Initiative	10	23	37	—	50

and split this up in accordance with the importance of the various factors, to set the point values for the highest degrees. Then the lowest degrees are set, equal to one-fifth of the number of points used at the highest levels. Intermediate degree points are allocated in terms of arithmetically equal intervals. This interval varies in size, depending on the number of separate degrees identified on the factor.

Once a manual is developed describing factors and degrees and indicating points for each degree on each factor, jobs may be evaluated by comparing their descriptions against those in the manual. The points obtained on each factor are summed to yield a point total that indicates the value of the job. Usually, these point totals are then grouped to yield a series of job grades within each of which a single pay scale applies.

As previously indicated, a variety of point systems have been developed. Some use a few factors, some many. Some use more than 500 total points, some less. Some use statistical procedures for weighting the various factors. Some assign points to the degrees, using a geometric rather than an arithmetic progression. A point system that has been developed by a major consulting group in the area of wage and salary administration, called the Hay plan, is used extensively for high-level salaried and executive positions (6).

Although it seems desirable to develop a point manual that is adapted to a specific company situation, as the Hay plan is, there are many general systems that have achieved rather widespread use, particularly for lower-level jobs. Examples are the National Electrical Manufacturers Association and the National Metal Trades Association systems for factory jobs, the National Electrical Manufacturers Association system for salaried jobs, and the National Office Management Association system. In any case, it should be emphasized that no matter how great the statistical elaboration of the data, the point system, like other job evaluation procedures, remains primarily a judgmental process.

Selection of a Job-evaluation Method

The most crucial consideration in selecting among the various methods described is that the plan actually yield a stable job structure that is viewed as equitable and therefore minimizes controversy in the area of monetary payments (10). In all probability, the approach that will accomplish this in one company is not the one that will yield the same result in another. Employees in one firm may be conditioned to expect intensive study of each job along the lines of the factor comparison and point systems. In other instances, the major requirement may be that the procedures employed be simple and easy to understand, as with the job-ranking and job-comparison procedures. Where there is a strong need to recapitulate the current situation in any newly established job structure, the factor comparison method appears to offer some advantages, because it is directly tied to existing wage rates. In a small company with a limited number of positions, job ranking may be all that is needed to achieve a sense of equity.

Given these situational differences that may overrule all other considerations, the results of a number of studies bearing on the job-evaluation process can provide certain guidelines. For one thing, a single-factor, overall value accounts for the majority of the results obtained with the factor comparison and point methods. Thus, the single-factor approaches, such as job ranking and job classification, do not produce any great loss in precision. One problem with the more complex job-evaluation plans is that it is difficult to accommodate new jobs or changes in existing jobs. With the increasing rate of change in the ways in which both production and clerical jobs are performed, the traditional job-evaluation structures frequently are subject to criticism, particularly by union spokesmen (19). A number of new approaches have been developed, some of which are based on a single factor, such as problem solving or decision making, on which all jobs in a company can be evaluated (9, 20). This type of job evaluation also eliminates the need for separate classification systems for the different categories of employees; however, there is little evidence that single-factor approaches have been adopted to any degree to date (3).

If a multiple-factor approach is used, there seems little reason to go beyond three factors under any but the most unusual conditions (27). Experience, or time to learn the job, seems to be of the greatest importance in almost all situations. Hazards, education, initiative, safety responsibility, complexity of duties, and character of supervision may be added, depending on the company and the type of job covered. A major disadvantage of the use of multiple factors is the time and cost involved in rating jobs initially and in maintaining the system. Recent research compared the results of the four traditional job evaluation methods with a method using a number of job dimension scores from the Position Analysis Questionnaire (PAQ) used in job analysis (see Chapter 7). While all five methods provided comparable results, the method using PAQ data took less time and therefore was less costly than the point method used previously (37).

Studies dealing with the degree of agreement obtained with different judges or raters suggest that this is not a major problem. Independent ratings of the same jobs by different individuals tend to yield similar results. Thus, a large number of judgments need not be averaged. Three or four raters should be entirely adequate. Furthermore, the raters need not be experienced in the field of job evaluation. Studies indicate that inexperienced raters can achieve at least as high a level of agreement as the experienced (27). In fact, some companies have turned job evaluation over to the employees and have found that the resulting job hierarchy then is based on the factors that the employees themselves view as relevant and important. Where an employee group performs this task, this approach should result in increased equity of the system as perceived by the employees, and thus in increased effectiveness as an input-output mediator.

Establishing the Wage Structure

It is in the pricing process—the setting of a "price," or rate of pay, for each job—that wage structures and wage levels merge. The wage structure relates to the average pay assigned to each job. The wage level is the average pay for the firm, or the overall level of the wage structure. When the job structure, as determined by the evaluation process, is priced, this results not only in a wage structure but in the wage level as well. In the situation where a job-evaluation system is being installed for the first time, the initial wage structure that evolves may then be adjusted on the basis of appropriate wage criteria, such as results of area wage surveys, to determine the company's final wage level.

PAY GRADES

When job evaluation is carried out using any but the job classification method, it is possible to assign different money amounts to each individual job. This produces an extremely complex pay structure in any but the smallest firms, however, and for this reason is not a widely accepted approach. Normally, jobs are grouped as in job classification, and all jobs in the same group or grade level have the same rate of pay or rate range. While the content of the jobs in the same grade level may vary considerably from one department to another, presumably they will be at a similar level of difficulty as determined by a ranking, factor comparison, or point system of evaluation.

The number of pay grades in a given job structure will vary with the nature of the structure, and there appear to be no generally accepted standards to guide decisions in this area (11). In actual fact, one can find as few as 4 and as many as 60. Generally, however, something in the range of 10 to 16 seems to be adequate. Pay differentials between grades for hourly and clerical jobs tend to run at 5 to 7 per cent; for professional and administrative jobs, they are higher, in the 8 to 10 per cent range (3).

PRICING THE JOB STRUCTURE

Of the evaluation methods discussed, only the factor comparison approach yields a priced job structure directly. And even with this method, it is a frequent practice to convert the dollar amounts to some type of point equivalents to avoid the possible biasing effects of using existing wage rates in making the judgments. Whether the factor comparison or another job-evaluation method is used, the initial pricing of jobs may be done on the basis of the existing wage level. To do this, the average pay for all individuals working on jobs falling within a given pay-grade category is determined. This average is then established as the going rate for that pay grade under a single-rate system or as the midpoint of the range where rate ranges are used.

A common approach is to present the wage-rate data graphically by plotting the rates paid in terms of job class or evaluation points of the job and then establishing a wage line of the kind shown in Figure 16–4. When a job-evaluation system is first introduced in a company, it is likely that some of the existing pay rates will be out of line with the job structure as established by the evaluation process. These so-called red circle rates will be apparent when the job structure is presented graphically, and adjustments can then be made with a view to establishing a logically consistent

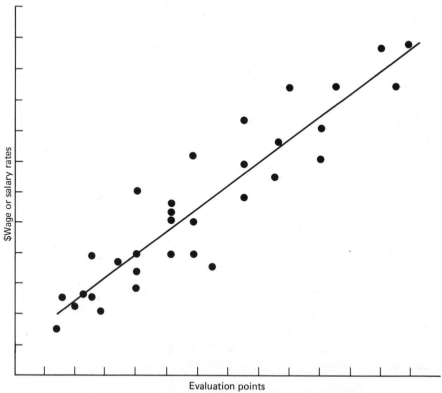

Figure 16–4. Comparing Present Wage or Salary Rates with Job Evaluation Values.

and equitable wage structure. In practice, red circle rates below the rate established for a particular job usually are raised to the minimum for the pay grade for the job. Thus, individuals being paid rates below the minimum are raised to that level, and new employees on the same job come in at the new rate. On the other hand, employees being paid rates that are above the established wage structure ordinarily do not receive a pay cut. These red circle rates are left in effect until such time as they correct themselves as a result of the retirement, separation, or promotion of the individuals receiving them. These rates also can be eliminated by withholding general wage increases from the workers involved until their pay rates are in line with the overall wage structure.

RATE RANGES

Nearly all wage structures involve rate ranges, with the notable exceptions of those in the heavily unionized basic steel and automobile industries, where single rates exist for all employees on a given job. Figure 16–5 illustrates a wage structure based on a point system of job evaluation with 12 pay grades. For each rate range, there is a 50 per cent overlap with

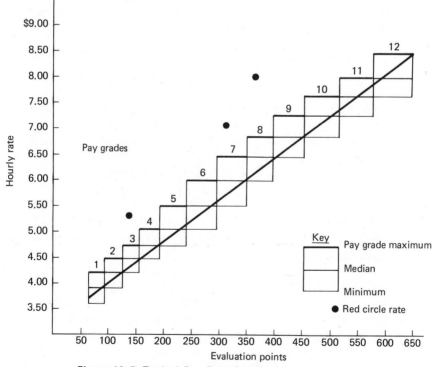

Figure 16–5. Typical Pay Rate Structure.

the next job class. Although many wage structures provide more of an overlap, 50 per cent or less is considered desirable, so that the same rate of pay is not possible in more than two pay grades (11). Otherwise, if an employee performing a grade 1 job can be paid the same rate as an employee on a grade 3 or 4 job, there is a serious question of job worth and the motivational value of the entire pay system.

Within each rate range, the usual practice is to specify a series of equal intervals or steps between the minimum and maximum rates. Each step indicates the amount by which an employee's pay will increase when he receives a raise on the same job. The number of steps usually is at least three and often as many as ten or more. The fewer the number of pay grades or job classes, the more steps are needed within the rate ranges, because the possibility of promotion to a higher job is less likely than when there are a large number of job classes.

In actual practice, at any given point in time, a high proportion of a company's employees are likely to be at the maximum of the rate range for the job, with the result that the incentive value of the rate range disappears. A solution proposed for this situation is to specify only a minimum rate for each pay grade and leave the maximum open-ended. Over the years, this would result in considerable overlap in the rates paid individuals in different job classes, but if the better performers on the job get the largest and most frequent raises, such a wage structure may be effective in motivating employees to higher productivity.

WAGES VERSUS SALARIES

In the discussion to this point, the term *wage* has been used in a general sense to include all monetary payment based on the time worked, but there is a more limited definition that ties wages to an hourly rate. Such hourly wages have been the tradition in factory employment, in contrast to the weekly or monthly salary that has been characteristic in the office situation. Where employment is intermittent and layoffs are frequent, there is probably good reason to maintain the hourly rate. But under more stable conditions, the use of a regular salary seems to offer a number of advantages.

Because of its association with certain high-status managerial and professional positions, the salary approach has considerable appeal to employees at all levels. As the proportion of white-collar, salaried employees has grown, a number of companies have questioned the traditional practice of compensating blue-collar workers with hourly pay and clerical and professional workers with a weekly or monthly salary. A report on the results in five companies that introduced salary plans for their production workers indicates an overall positive reaction on the part of the employees and management despite some increases in absenteeism and complaints on the part of first-level supervision about the additional burdens placed on them. A significant benefit of this approach is that it tends to minimize differences between employee groups and thus to reduce potential causes of conflict (18). From an organizational maintenance view, there is a strong case in favor of salaried payment, rather than hourly, in situations where a choice can be made.

SUPPLEMENTARY PAY PRACTICES

When employees are paid on a salary basis, an hourly wage rate usually is computed for each job or individual from the weekly or monthly payment. Such an hourly rate is necessary for employees subject to the wage-hour laws discussed in Chapter 5 in order to determine the pay for overtime work. In most companies, the overtime rate is one and one-half times the regular rate, although occasionally double time is paid, or even triple time in cases where the work extends beyond 10 hours.

Depending on the nature of the firm's business, there are a number of other supplementary pay practices that may be specified in the union contract or the employee handbook. While they are not an essential element of the basic wage structure, these payments do affect the individual employee's total earnings. In addition to overtime premiums, the most common of these payments are *premium pay for weekend or holiday work,* usually at the rates of time and one-half for Saturdays and double time for Sundays and holidays; *shift differentials,* providing extra pay on a cents-per-hour or percentage basis for work on the evening or night shift; *reporting pay* guarantees, which require a minimum payment (usually for four hours' work) when employees report in as scheduled and find work is not available; and *call-back* or *call-in* guarantees, which usually specify a minimum of four hours' pay for employees called in to work at some time other than a regularly scheduled shift.

From the employee's point of view, the regular or average total earnings, taking into account the various supplementary payments, probably are more crucial than the basic hourly rate of pay. Thus, companies that have changed to a four-day work schedule with employees putting in 10 hours a day instead of 8 hours a day for five days often have lowered the actual hourly pay rate. Because they are required to pay overtime for 2 of the 10 hours, a lower base rate ends up providing workers the same amount of pay on a weekly basis.

INDIVIDUAL WAGE PROGRESSION

No matter how carefully a company's wage structure is determined in terms of proper evaluation of the job hierarchy within the firm and in relation to what is being paid for similar work elsewhere, the compensation system will not work automatically as an input-output mediator fostering productivity. It is necessary for procedures used in administering the wage and salary program to be implemented in such a way that employees are motivated to achieve high levels of performance. In terms of the motivation theories discussed in the beginning of this chapter, the individual employee should perceive that his work behavior is related to his pay and that his pay is equitable in terms of other employees' work behavior and pay.

One of the determinants of pay satisfaction shown in Figure 16–1 is that of wage history, or what the employee has experienced in the past with respect to increases in his pay. Throughout a large segment of American industry, workers have come to expect sizable yearly pay raises as a result of union bargaining. This is true in nonunion firms also, as management decides to raise the general wage level and provide an across-the-board general increase to all employees. These increases often are pegged to changes in the cost of living since the last previous general increase, or they may be based on current area or industry wage-survey data. In companies with single job rates rather than rate ranges, this type of general increase is the only way an employee's rate of pay can be raised unless he gets promoted to a higher-level job. Because this type of increase is granted to all employees irrespective of their work behavior, it obviously has little motivational value from a productivity viewpoint. However, in times of rapidly rising prices and wages paid elsewhere, not to raise the general wage level would have serious consequences for organizational maintenance. And to the extent the better employees could be expected to be the first to leave for better-paying jobs in other firms, productivity would suffer also.

Merit Pay Systems

The type of pay increase that can be expected to have a positive effect on performance is one an individual employee receives in recognition of past performance; this is the rationale behind the establishment of rate ranges, and steps within the range, for each job class. Unfortunately, the potential incentive value of this approach often is lost, because there has been a marked tendency to move employees through ranges on the basis of seniority and experience rather than on the basis of merit as determined by performance appraisal techniques of the kind discussed in Chapters 8 and 9. One survey of the country's largest industrial firms indicates that although most companies say that job performance is the primary determinant of rate-range progression, more than half have no specific formal system for evaluating performance (12). Without such a system, the granting of "merit" increases tends to be almost automatic, and they come to be viewed as a reward for staying with the organization another year. An approach sometimes used is to give employees whose performance record has been satisfactory a one-step raise in recognition of service and to give a two-step increase to employees whose performance is judged superior. Another approach, used frequently for salaried employees, is to relate the size of, and the time intervals between, raises to different levels of performance. Figure 16–6 illustrates one way this can be achieved (28).

A major factor contributing to difficulties in the administration of merit pay systems is the role of the supervisor or higher-level manager, who often may try to avoid giving any employees poor performance ratings or denying them a salary increase and finds it difficult to communicate with employees on these matters. Because of different values between supervisors, even where two employees working in different departments are judged to have superior levels of peformance and to merit an increase on some objective basis, the amount of increase may differ, depending on the values of the boss. Another factor that may well influence salary-increase recommendation is the manager's perception of how the company has treated him or her; recent research indicates that managers who experience feelings of inequity about their own pay raises tend to be "tight" in making recommendations concerning increases for their subordinates (15).

There is other evidence that the supervisor has a definite impact on how merit systems work and how employees perceive them (2). One writer has suggested that the supervisor's key role in merit systems results in employee feelings of a dependent relationship that is "demeaning." He also points out that if merit plans were to operate as planned, there would be serious problems related to employees' self-esteem when they do not get the rewards—pay raises—they feel their performance justifies (31).

Guidelines for Relating Merit Increases to Individual Performance		Current position in salary range		
Expected distribution of individuals	Performance assessment	Lower third	Middle third	Upper third
15%	Exceptional	6–9 / 11–12%	9–12 / 11–12%	12–15 / 11–12%
20	Above expectations	9–12 / 9–10%	12–15 / 9–10%	15–18 / 9–10%
40	Meets expectations	12 / 7–8%	12–18 / 7–8%	18–24 / 7–8%
20	At minimum expectations	12 / 5–6%	12–18 / 5–6%	0
5	Below expectations	0	0	0
Increase as a percent of salary →		Months between increases		

Figure 16–6. Performance Ratings and Merit Increases.
Source: J. F. McIntosh. "Inflation—Your Salary Program's Nemesis," *Personnel Journal*, 54 (1975), 550.

An abundance of research has been conducted relating to pay satisfaction and the motivational role of pay and pay increases (16, 34, 45). Many studies involve reports of group differences; for example, females have been found to be more satisfied than males with their pay; the higher a person's educational level, the less satisfaction there is with pay; and the higher the organization level, the greater the satisfaction. Even these conclusions, however, appear to differ among occupations and in different types of organizations (44). To date, the results of research on pay satisfaction "appear to have only limited practical significance," according to the authors of one research report (45); these authors suggest that a great deal more needs to be learned about the determination of pay satisfaction before management uses this type of information as a basis for making changes in its personnel policies and procedures.

The Secrecy Issue

To increase the motivational role of pay for the individual employee, one specific suggestion is that pay procedures, pay rates, and actions taken in wage and salary matters be made more public, at least within the organization (21). It is argued that with less secrecy, employees would be able to see the relationship between performance and pay level more readily. One survey involving employees in job categories ranging from unskilled to managerial and professional in a number of industries does support this view. The employees in companies that were highly secretive about wage and salary data tended to believe that they were underpaid, while employees who had a high degree of access to such data tended to say that they were paid what the job was worth (4).

There is no doubt that secrecy about pay practices is the basic philosophy in most organizations in the private sector of the economy and at all levels of the organization (7). It also appears that in many instances the reasons for secrecy are that the pay system as it currently is administered would not be viewed as equitable if it were open to scrutiny, and that the superior performers are not always the employees who are rewarded with higher pay (33). There even is some question about what effect openness would have on high-level performers. A study of professional employees found that the better performers who also were better-paid preferred to keep pay secret slightly more than poor performers (43). This suggests that some employees might prefer to work harder and earn more money and yet not have to worry about the disapproval of their less hard-working peers.

As is the situation with regard to other motivational aspects of pay policies, the evidence on secrecy is not conclusive, and there obviously are some instances where the communication of salary information would contribute to more effective employee performance and instances where it would not.

INCENTIVE PAY SYSTEMS

The essential characteristic of incentive pay systems is that earnings are directly related to output. A standard of performance is established for each job in the case of individual incentives, or for an interlocking group of jobs in the case of group incentives. The employee's earnings are then promptly and automatically varied in accordance with some established formula that relates either individual or group performance to the standard.

Because reward is achieved in a relatively short time span and is closely tied to work output, incentive payment may be presumed to possess greater potential as an input-output mediator than the wage and salary approaches just discussed. This is true even when rate ranges and merit increases are used effectively to foster productivity. It is clear from a number of studies that the offering of individual financial rewards can affect productivity, and that individuals working on a piece-rate system often produce substantially more than those on an hourly rate pay system (21, 29). Incentive pay plans can be expected to achieve their motivational potential to the extent employees trust management, understand how the plan works, and perceive a close relationship between their pay and their effort (8).

Individual Incentive Systems

Over the past 70 or 80 years, many different types of individual incentive plans have been developed. Most have been created by industrial engineers and are closely tied to time study procedures. The basic approach is a piece-rate incentive, which is based on a measurement of what is considered normal or standard production on a given job. In the simpler piece-rate plans, employees are paid a specified rate for each piece produced; some plans call for a differential rate, with a low rate per piece below standard and a relatively high rate per piece above; and other incentive systems are based on the standard time required to produce one unit of output, with the employee being paid for any savings that result from above-average performance. The methods for measuring work and establishing time standards and piece rates vary considerably from one type of work to another, and many individual companies have developed their own special systems. As with job evaluation, the reader interested in more detailed information on these techniques should consult the more specialized texts (3, 50).

The piece-work incentive approach was developed originally to apply to direct production workers, and such pay plans are found predominantly in manufacturing operations. Similar incentive systems have, however, been extended to maintenance jobs, inspection, janitorial work, clerical jobs, and many other types of positions. In the sales field, the approach has been to pay commissions based on either the number of units sold, the total dollar volume of sales, or the gains and losses over the previous year's record in the same location—or perhaps even on number of new accounts secured.

In some sales occupations, these commission payments are set on top of a guaranteed base salary. It is also common practice to establish a drawing account, so that when a salesman's commissions are down, he can draw out an amount sufficient to bring his earnings up to a guaranteed base level. This money must be repaid later, when commission earnings are up. Such an approach is most applicable when wide fluctuations in sales are common, because of economic or seasonal factors.

Except in the sales situation, where the results of an individual's efforts are readily discernible, the advent of modern technology has presented difficulties in designing individual incentive pay systems. The piece-work approach is most effective for routine, repetitive jobs, many of which have been eliminated as the production line becomes more and more automated. Because the rationale behind most individual wage incentive plans is to motivate the employee, who presumably controls the pace of production, the elimination of these jobs has made such pay plans obsolete. This has led to new approaches to standard-setting, taking into account the fact that the role of the worker in highly mechanized installations is to keep the machinery operating. In addition, group incentive plans are being substituted for those of an individual nature. Some of these operate on a company- or plant-wide basis.

Group Incentive Systems

Group procedures offer the advantage that payroll and industrial engineering costs tend to be lower than with the individual plans. In addition, the group approach appears to permit more flexibility, in that resistance to technological changes seems to be less. On the negative side is the fact that paying members of a group, either equally or in proportion to job level, out of a pool determined by comparing group output with a group standard serves to reduce the motivational impact on the individual. Too much of what an employee makes depends on the work of others rather than on his own efforts. In very small groups, some direct motivational impact may remain; in large groups, it most likely does not. It is also true, however, that under certain circumstances a group will establish higher productivity aspirations and push its laggard members more under group than under individual incentives. Thus, the motivating effects of group pressure may be substituted for individual reward.

A number of the individual incentive plans can be adapted for group use, particularly those based on standard time savings. For this approach to operate effectively as a motivational force, the work of the various group members must be interlocking, membership must be stable, with little turnover, and the group must possess a certain cohesiveness. Given these factors, a work group incentive can be effective with as many as 40 people (3), although the larger the group, the lower the productivity to be expected (21).

THE SCANLON PLAN

The Scanlon plan is much more than a group incentive system. It operates at the plant or company level as a means of gaining union-management cooperation toward the goal of increased productivity. The incentive feature, however, is a bonus that is calculated from savings in labor costs. A standard ratio of payroll costs to sales value of production is developed from past records. Each month, current data are compared against this ratio to determine savings. Of the resulting amount, usually 75 per cent goes into a direct bonus paid to all employees, and 25 per cent is held to cover deficit periods. The latter fund is closed at the end of the year, with part going to employees and part to the company.

A major feature of the plan is its emphasis on suggestions for increased efficiency. These are evaluated by a complex committee structure that gives the union and management equal representation. Thus, management shares much of its normal control over the production process with the employees and with the union. The result can be a widespread concern with improved efficiency and increased output. While the Scanlon plan initially was most successful in companies experiencing financial difficulties during the depression years, more recently it has been adopted and has proved effective in a number of firms that were already economically healthy (35).

THE LINCOLN PLAN

For many years, the Lincoln Electric Company of Cleveland has utilized a cooperative plan that has not only received considerable publicity, but has also apparently proved extremely effective (50). Actual compensation is in terms of an individual standard time plan, which has been extended to cover all jobs that can possibly be standardized. There are, nevertheless, so many cooperative features in the total plan that it must be considered as basically a group approach. Among these features are extensive employee stock ownership, a sizable profit-sharing bonus at year end, an employee advisory board that has considerable influence on company policies and procedures, and a suggestion plan that yields sizable monetary awards. The bonus is distributed from year-end profits on the basis of a merit rating system that emphasizes cooperation, job knowledge, quality of work, and quantity of work. Thus, those who are seen as contributing most effectively to company goals receive the greatest rewards.

Problems Associated with Incentive Payment

The weight of the available evidence suggests that taken as a whole incentive plans have resulted in increased output and reduced costs (35).

Thus, such plans can operate effectively as input-output mediators, above and beyond what the usual time payment procedures achieve. Apparently, however, they do so less frequently when the work is extremely repetitive or boring and definitely disliked. Furthermore, there is some indication that workers paid under individual or group incentives are less satisfied with their pay than those paid on a time basis (45).

There are certainly many instances in which the full motivational potential of the incentive is not obtained. This occurs largely as a result of a quite conscious restriction of output by the workers themselves. Many work groups establish a group production norm that serves to set a very effective lid on output (48). Any worker who produces above this norm is likely to become the object of considerable group pressure and as a result will in most cases hold back on his output. The desire to maintain the respect and acceptance of the group appears to be a stronger motive for most workers than the desire for increased earnings. One writer has suggested that one way to deal with group pressures for restricting output is to share rewards among all employees in the work group for productivity above an established level (13).

In fact, it seems to be inherent in the very nature of incentive payment that although the approach does contribute to the goal it is directed to, namely productivity, it does so at some cost to organizational maintenance. Disputes and grievances related to inequitable standards are common in nearly every case in which incentive systems have been installed. Perhaps if a system could be devised that would reward an appropriate balance between productivity and maintenance considerations, this problem could be overcome. To date, however, little has been done in this area.

Other Incentive Plans

In addition to the individual and group incentive pay systems discussed above, there are other types of incentive plans related to the company's productivity goals, although not in as direct a fashion. Under these programs, employees are given monetary rewards for some aspect of their work behavior other than direct production, but the net effect is higher productivity. Suggestion systems like those involved in the Scanlon plan are an example, as are programs for paying awards to company scientists for inventions leading to patents.

Monetary awards, or bonuses, also may be paid to individuals or work groups for outstanding records in the areas of safety, quality control, housekeeping, attendance, and the like. The effectiveness of these programs in contributing to productivity may be enhanced by letting employees participate in establishing or modifying them. In one instance, where some work groups developed their own pay incentive plans to reward good attendance and these plans were then imposed on other work groups, attendance increased significantly only in the groups that had participated in the development of the plans (22).

Profit-sharing plans, under which employees get an annual bonus if the company realizes a certain level of profits for the year, often are considered incentive-type pay plans. While these plans may have an incentive value for the managers in control, for most lower-level employees it is difficult to equate their daily job performance with the company's profits. An exception is the Scanlon-type plan, where employees do share in control of the production process, and where bonuses are paid monthly. As most profit-sharing plans are constituted, however, their contribution probably is related more to organizational maintenance than to productivity goals, and they should be considered in the context of the employee benefit programs discussed in Chapter 20.

PAYMENTS TO MANAGEMENT
Top Management

At the very uppermost levels of the management hierarchy, salaries appear to be influenced in part by company size, in part by the specific industry, and in part by the contribution of the incumbent to the process of making decisions. Surveys have repeatedly indicated that the larger the firm (as defined by sales volume), the greater the payment to the top-level group (46).

It is also true, however, that there are sizable industry differences. The major differentiating factor appears to be the competitive environment that is characteristic. Thus, those industries that are more highly constrained by governmental regulation (banks, life insurance, air transport, meat packing, railroads, public utilities) pay relatively low salaries, and those that are more free to engage in unfettered competition (chemicals, department stores, automobiles, steel, textiles, appliances) pay well. The high-pay industries generally demand more decisions of top management, and the alternative courses of action available tend to be greater in number. At the other extreme, decisions are often so limited by external constraints that little if any discretion is left.

Although job evaluation is not employed at the upper levels by many companies that use it at lower levels, it still remains relatively common. The factors used, however, are different, emphasizing such things as accountability, decision making, organizing, planning responsibility, and supervision. In general, the chief executive's salary serves to limit the pay of those below him. Thus, the second man may receive 50 to 60 per cent of what his superior receives. Characteristically, staff managers receive somewhat less, all things being equal, than line managers at the same level.

BONUSES

A large proportion of companies pay bonuses averaging from 30 to 50 per cent of base salary to their top executives. These bonuses operate most effectively in increasing motivation when the following circumstances exist:

1. The amount paid is closely related to the level of individual performance.
2. The amount paid after taxes represents a clearly noticeable rise above the base salary level.
3. The amount paid is closely related to the level of company performance.
4. The amount paid is tied into base salary in such a way that combined earnings are equitable both in relation to internal and to external standards.
5. The amount paid is reduced drastically whenever an individual experiences a real and continuing decrease in performance effectiveness.
6. The amount paid is based on an easily understandable system of allocation, and the individual is provided with complete information on the relationship between bonus and performance.

In practice, however, these circumstances rarely do prevail. Where bonuses are paid to managers, they often amount to 10 per cent of salary or less and almost everyone gets a bonus regardless of performance, with the result that the bonus plan adds little if anything to the basic salary structure to motivate executives to better performance (49). Furthermore, the usual procedure is to discount the normal salary structure to some extent if a bonus system is in effect. Thus, the bonuses are not entirely in addition to equitable salaries. Most plans pay in cash, although some include stock. In some instances, the payment is deferred until retirement, so that the individual will not have to pay taxes on this income during a high-earnings period. This approach, however, removes the current reward value of the bonus and thus dilutes its impact as an input-output mediator.

Payment may also be in the form of options to buy company stock at some later date. Such purchases may be made at a specified current rate. If the stock goes up in value, the option may be exercised. Under some circumstances, there are income tax advantages related to stock options, but the individual has to have access to large amounts of cash in order to exercise certain kinds of options. Because of the big differences in income needs and tax status among top-level executives, there is increasing emphasis on a "cafeteria" approach to executive compensation, permitting the individual to select a pay package tailored to his desires (23, 42).

Middle Management

Below the top-management level, the major influence on salaries appears to derive from the national labor market. Many of these managers have special skills that have applications not only within the specific company or industry but on a much more widespread basis. This is particularly true of those with a professional background—accountants, lawyers, engineers, and the like. Sales skills also are widely transferable.

Middle-management positions are usually subjected to job evaluation, using techniques that represent modifications of the basic procedures discussed previously. At this level and above, rate ranges are almost universal, and increases are granted at least in theory on the basis of merit. In actual practice, however, the manager's previous history, cost of living factors, raises at lower levels, and internal equity considerations exert a strong influence.

Incentive payments above and beyond base salary take two forms at the middle-management level. On occasion, the type of bonus system described for top executives is extended down to considerably lower managerial levels. In other instances, incentive payments are made in terms of definite standards dealing with such matters as sales volume, production capacity achieved, and budgetary attainment. Generally, this latter type of system operates quite independently of company profit considerations. It pays in relation to the preestablished standard, no matter how well or poorly the firm is doing.

First-line Supervision

At the very lowest supervisory level, especially among production foremen and similar individuals whose training is not of a professional nature, the local rather than the national labor market exerts the greatest influence. In addition, pay levels at the next lower, nonsupervisory level have considerable impact, with the supervisor usually being paid 10 to 25 per cent above his highest paid subordinate. Maintaining this differential is one of the most difficult aspects of pay policies for supervisors, particularly where highly paid skilled workers are involved, and considerable overtime is worked.

Formal job-evaluation systems for lower grades are sometimes merely extended upward to include the first level of supervision. Even if this is not done, managers at this level are more likely to be covered by some type of job-evaluation plan than middle management. To the extent that flat rates rather than ranges occur at all in the ranks of management, they do so at this point. In many cases, even where ranges are used, a commitment to the merit principle seems to be totally lacking. Thus, in general, first-line supervisors are paid in ways that more closely resemble the procedures used with their subordinates than those used with managers higher in the hierarchy.

Incentive payments for supervisors are sometimes based entirely on the incentive earnings of subordinates. Under these circumstances, the supervisor is relatively easily integrated into the existing plan established for his group. There is, however, the risk that in an effort to increase his own earnings, a supervisor may exert what influence he can to obtain low standards and thus a higher incentive payment to subordinates. To circumvent this problem, a number of companies have resorted to multifactor systems emphasizing labor costs, quality of production, safety, absenteeism, and similar considerations. This method of divorcing incentives for first-line supervisors from incentive payments to subordinates, although costly in time and money, appears to be quite effective.

QUESTIONS

1. Compensation is treated as a productivity-oriented, input-output mediator. In what senses is this designation inappropriate? What other designations might also apply to the wage and salary process?
2. Define and describe the following:
   a. Wage criteria.
   b. Job grades.
   c. Red circle rates.
   d. Shift differentials.
   e. The Scanlon plan.
3. What is the secrecy issue in compensation? What are the pros and cons? How does this issue relate to the whole matter of the incentive value of pay?
4. At the present time, a number of methods of job evaluation are in use. Describe each and indicate what the various plans have in common.
5. A number of considerations involved in compensating managers do not operate below the managerial level. Discuss these considerations and show how they serve to produce differences between managerial and nonmanagerial compensation plans.

REFERENCES

1. Bailey, W. R., and A. E. Schwenk. "Wage Differences Among Manufacturing Establishments." *Monthly Labor Review*, 94 (1971), No. 5, 16–19.
2. Beer, M., and G. J. Gery. "Individual and Organizational Correlates of Pay System Preferences," in H. L. Tosi, R. J. House, and M. D. Dunnette (eds.), *Managerial Motivation and Compensation*, East Lansing, Mich.: Graduate School of Business, Michigan State University, 1972, pp. 455–476.
3. Belcher, D. W. *Compensation Administration*. Englewood Cliffs, N.J.: Prentice-Hall, Inc., 1974.
4. Boynton, R. E. "How Employees Measure Their Pay." *Compensation Review*, 2 (1970), No. 3.
5. Bronstein, R. J. "The Cost of Living and Salary Administration." *Personnel*, 52 (1975), No. 2, 11–18.
6. Bureau of National Affairs, Inc. *Job Evaluation*. Personnel Policies Forum Survey No. 113, June 1976.
7. Bureau of National Affairs, Inc. *Wage & Salary Administration*, Personnel Policies Forum Survey No. 97, July 1972.

8. Cammann, C., and E. E. Lawler. "Employee Reactions to a Pay Incentive Plan." *Journal of Applied Psychology,* 58 (1973), 163–172.

9. Charles, A. W. "Installing Single-factor Job Evaluation." *Compensation Review,* 3 (1971), No. 1, 9–21.

10. Dick, A. H. "Job Evaluation's Role in Employee Relations." *Personnel Journal,* 53 (1974), 176–179.

11. Dunn, J. D., and F. M. Rachel. *Wage and Salary Administration: Total Compensation Systems.* New York: McGraw-Hill Book Company, 1971.

12. Evans, W. A. "Pay for Performance: Fact or Fable." *Personnel Journal,* 49 (1970), 726–731.

13. Fein, Mitchell. "Restoring the Incentive to Wage Incentive Plans." *Conference Board Record,* 9 (1972), No. 11, 17–21.

14. Finn, R. H., and S. M. Lee. "Salary Equity: Its Determination, Analysis, and Correlates." *Journal of Applied Psychology,* 56 (1972), 283–292.

15. Goodman, P. S. "Effect of Perceived Inequity on Salary Allocation Decisions." *Journal of Applied Psychology,* 60 (1975), 372–375.

16. Greene, C. N. "Causal Connections Among Managers' Merit Pay, Job Satisfaction, and Performance." *Journal of Applied Psychology,* 58 (1973), 95–100.

17. Heneman, H. G., III, and D. P. Schwab. "Work and Rewards Theory," in D. Yoder and H. G. Heneman, Jr. (eds.), *Motivation and Commitment.* Washington: Bureau of National Affairs, Inc., 1975.

18. Hulme, R. D., and Bevan, R. V. "The Blue-collar Worker Goes on Salary." *Harvard Business Review,* 75 (1975), No. 2, 104–112.

19. Janes, H. D. "Issues in Job Evaluation: The Union View." *Personnel Journal,* 51 (1972), 675–679.

20. Jaques, E. *Equitable Payment.* New York: John Wiley & Sons, Inc., 1961.

21. Lawler, E. E. *Pay and Organizational Effectiveness: A Psychological View.* New York: McGraw-Hill Book Company, 1971.

22. Lawler, E. E., and J. R. Hackman. "Impact of Employee Participation in the Development of Pay Incentive Plans: A Field Experiment." *Journal of Applied Psychology,* 53 (1969), 467–471.

23. Lewellen, W. G., and H. P. Lanser, "Executive Pay Preferences." *Harvard Business Review,* 51 (1973), No. 5, 115–122.

24. Livernash, E. R. "Wages and Benefits," in *A Review of Industrial Relations Research,* Vol. 1. Madison, Wis.: Industrial Relations Research Association, 1970, pp. 79–144.

25. Locke, E. A. "Personnel Attitudes and Motivation." *Annual Review of Psychology,* 26 (1975), 457–480.

26. Lowenstern, H. "Adjusting Wages to Living Costs: A Historical Note." *Monthly Labor Review,* 97 (1974), No. 7, 21–26.

27. McCormick, E. J., and J. Tiffin. *Industrial Psychology,* 6th ed. Englewood Cliffs, N.J.: Prentice-Hall, Inc., 1974.

28. McIntosh, J. F. "Inflation—Your Salary Program's Nemesis." *Personnel Journal,* 54 (1975), 542–544, 550.
29. McManis, D. L., and W. G. Dick. "Monetary Incentives in Today's Industrial Setting." *Personnel Journal,* 52 (1973), 387–392.
30. Mahoney, T. A. "Justice and Equity: A Recurring Theme in Compensation." *Personnel,* 52 (1975), No. 5, 60–66.
31. Meyer, H. H. "The Pay-for-performance Dilemma." *Organizational Dynamics,* 3 (1975), No. 3, 39–50.
32. Milkovich, G. T., and K. Campbell. "A Study of Jaques' Norms of Equitable Payment." *Industrial Relations,* 11 (1972), 267–271.
33. Miner, M. G. "Pay Policies: Secret or Open? And Why?" *Personnel Journal,* 53 (1974), 110–115.
34. Nash, A. N., and S. J. Carroll. *The Management of Compensation.* Monterey, Calif.: Brooks/Cole Publishing Co., 1975.
35. National Commission on Productivity and Work Quality. *A Plantwide Productivity Plan in Action: Three Years of Experience with the Scanlon Plan.* Washington, D.C.: the Commission, 1975.
36. Pritchard, R. D., M. D. Dunnette, and D. O. Jorgenson. "Effects of Perceptions of Equity and Inequity on Worker Performance and Satisfaction." *Journal of Applied Psychology Monograph,* 56 (1972), 75–94.
37. Robinson, D. D., O. W. Wahlstrom, and R. C. Mecham. "Comparison of Job Evaluation Methods: A 'Policy Capturing' Approach Using the Position Analysis Questionnaire." *Journal of Applied Psychology,* 59 (1974), 633–637.
38. Rock, M. I. *Handbook of Wage and Salary Administration.* New York: McGraw-Hill Book Company, 1972.
39. Ronan, W. W., and G. J. Organt. "Determinants of Pay and Pay Satisfaction." *Personnel Psychology,* 26 (1973), 503–520.
40. Sawhney, P. K., and I. L. Herrnstadt. "Interindustry Wage Structure Variation in Manufacturing." *Industrial and Labor Relations Review,* 24 (1971), 407–419.
41. Scheible, P. L. "Changes in Employee Compensation, 1966 to 1972." *Monthly Labor Review,* 98 (1975), No. 3, 10–16.
42. Schuster, J. R. "Executive Compensation," in D. Yoder and H. G. Heneman, Jr. (eds.), *Motivation and Commitment.* Washington, D.C.: Bureau of National Affairs, Inc., 1975.
43. Schuster, J. R., and J. A. Colletti. "Pay Secrecy: Who Is For and Against It?" *Academy of Management Journal,* 16 (1973), 35–40.
44. Schuster, J. R., J. A. Colletti, and L. Knowles, Jr. "The Relationship Between Perceptions Concerning Magnitudes of Pay and the Perceived Utility of Pay: Public and Private Organizations Compared." *Organizational Behavior and Human Performance,* 9 (1973), 110–119.
45. Schwab, D. P., and M. J. Wallace. "Correlates of Employee Satisfaction with Pay." *Industrial Relations,* 13 (1974), 78–89.

46. Wallace, M. J. "Executive Compensation: Two Determinants." *Compensation Review*, 5 (1973), No. 4, 18–23.
47. Wernimont, Paul F., and S. Fitzpatrick. "The Meaning of Money." *Journal of Applied Psychology*, 56 (1972), 218–226.
48. Whyte, W. F., et al. *Money and Motivation*. New York: Harper & Row, Publishers, 1955.
49. Winstanley, N. B. "Management 'Incentive' Bonus Plan Realities." *Conference Board Record*, 7 (1970), No. 1, 35–39.
50. Zollitsch, H. G. "Productivity, Time Study, and Incentive-pay Plans," in D. Yoder and H. G. Heneman, Jr. (eds.), *Motivation and Commitment*. Washington, D.C.: Bureau of National Affairs, Inc., 1975, pp. 6-51 to 6-73.

The preceding chapters have dealt with input-output mediators that contribute to the productivity or profit goal either by changing the human input in some way or by increasing motivation to work toward the company's objectives. In this chapter, the focus shifts away from such maximizing processes to the somewhat more prosaic goal of maintaining organization members in good status as active contributors.

To keep employees producing at least at the level indicated by their potential when hired, it is necessary to prevent anything from happening to them that might result in a temporary or permanent reduction in output. The major types of such "happenings" are injuries and illnesses. Thus, it becomes important for business firms to take any steps possible to reduce accident frequency and severity and to eliminate anything that might contribute to the onset or prolongation of an illness. This is a humanitarian responsibility of any management, but it is also a factor in company goal attainment. Injuries and illnesses disrupt output and carry with them sizable monetary costs.

The current chapter will focus first on the various techniques that have been developed to prevent accidents, either by changing the environment to make it safer or by influencing the individual to make him or her less likely to fall prey to potential danger in the work area. A second major topic will be the peculiar proclivity some individuals exhibit to have accidents and incur injury. A final section will then take up preventive approaches in the health area and the role of the medical profession in this regard. The various legal influences on safety policies inherent in the workers' compensation laws and the Occupational Safety and Health Act were discussed in Chapter 5.

SAFETY-MANAGEMENT PROCEDURES

Although it is common practice to administer an accident-prevention program out of a safety division, usually located within the personnel structure, committees have become an important adjunct in this area, as they have in wage and salary administration. The primary reason for this development appears to be that widespread acceptance and cooperation are essential to the success of any safety effort. To the extent a large number of individuals distributed throughout the company can be involved in the program and made to feel a part of it, actual implementation of decisions related to safety is likely to be facilitated (23). It is important that those at the higher levels of management feel this sense of involvement, as well as those at lower levels (7).

Under normal circumstances, the highest-level safety committee is established on an interdepartmental basis and is concerned primarily with policy matters. This committee has responsibility for establishing safety rules, for investigating particularly hazardous situations, for making expenditures related to accident prevention, and for resolving disputes.

In addition, there usually are a number of departmental committees to deal with inspection and the correction of unsafe conditions. Unlike the policy committee, the latter groups are not restricted to managerial personnel. In fact, they appear to function more smoothly and effectively if there is a heavy representation from below the managerial level.

The departmental committees may also handle safety training and publicity, although frequently a separate committee structure is devoted to the specific purposes of developing and implementing programs to promote interest in safety, to obtain compliance with safety rules, and to disseminate safety knowledge. In some companies, safety training committees and those concerned with inspection have taken on a joint union-management character. Less frequently, the higher-level policy group also has union representation. In some instances, this joint approach is necessary and even helpful, especially if the union leadership is strongly concerned about safety matters, but it does tend to introduce a number of extraneous considerations into a group decision-making process that is often rather slow-moving and cumbersome even without this additional obstacle. The result is that the joint union-management committees can become so bound up in conflict that they are incapable of action.

Accident Statistics and Reports

Accident statistics are a valuable aspect of a total safety effort for two reasons. When calculated for the company as a whole, they permit comparison against the national and industry figures provided by such organizations as the National Safety Council and the U.S. Bureau of Labor Statistics. Thus, a company can determine its position relative to other firms and set its accident prevention goals accordingly. Where the comparative statistics suggest that a major problem exists, a sizable total investment in safety procedures may be warranted. Second, when rates are determined separately for the various work units within a firm, it is possible to pinpoint trouble spots and concentrate preventive efforts with these in mind. In this way, the accident prevention process may be focused where it will do the most good.

Most company accident statistics have been based on two rate formulas:

$$\text{injury frequency rate} = \frac{\text{number of disabling injuries} \times 1{,}000{,}000}{\text{number of man-hours worked}}$$

$$\text{injury severity rate} = \frac{\text{number of days lost} \times 1{,}000{,}000}{\text{number of man-hours worked}}$$

The usual practice is to use disabling or *lost-time injuries* only in these calculations, although rates for *minor injuries* may be determined separately. Lost-time injuries include deaths, permanent disabilities whether partial or total, and injuries that render a person unable to do his job for at least an entire work shift subsequent to the accident. Minor injuries are those that do not meet the above criteria but that do require first aid or treatment in a dispensary or physician's office. Because they may be used for workers' compensation claims and reflected in absenteeism statistics, lost-time injury data tend generally to be valid. Minor injuries, however, may go unreported. In calculating severity rates, standard time charges are used in the case of deaths and disabilities, and actual days lost for temporary conditions.

For many years, the U.S. Bureau of Labor Statistics published data, based on the formulas shown above for injury frequency and severity, using figures provided by employers voluntarily participating in the data-collection effort. With the passage of the Occupational Safety and Health Act (OSHA) in 1970, all employers except those with less than eight employees are required to keep accident records and to file an annual summary report of all accidents or injuries (34). Figure 17–1 is a guide for employers indicating what accidents or illnesses need to be recorded, and Figure 17–2 shows the section of the annual report form where these records are summarized.

Because of the extent of data now available, BLS abandoned the disabling injury frequency rate as the basis for safety statistics and developed a new measure called the incidence rate. This is the rate of occurrence of recordable occupational injuries and illnesses per 100 man-years of work (16). The formula used for calculating the rate is

$$\frac{N}{EH} \times 200{,}000$$

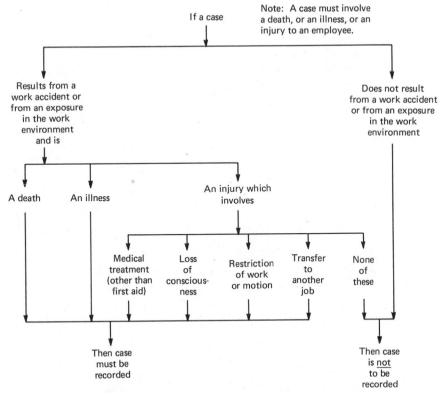

Figure 17–1. Guide to Recordability of Cases Under the Occupational Safety and Health Act.
Source: U.S. Department of Labor, Bureau of Labor Statistics, Occupational Safety and Health Statistics: Concepts and Methods, BLS Report 438 (Washington, D.C.; Bureau of Labor Statistics, 1975), p. 2.

where N = the number of injuries and illnesses, EH = the total hours worked by all the employees during the calendar year, and 200,000 = the base for 100 full-time equivalent workers (working 40 hours per week, 50 weeks per year).

Safety statistics for the years 1972 through 1974 based on the new formula are shown in Table 17–1. Although these figures are not comparable to those published in previous years, they indicate that construction, mining, and manufacturing are the most dangerous industries, as has been true over the years. An analysis of incidence rates by size of establishment, as illustrated in Figure 17–3, shows that the lowest rates are found in firms with fewer than 50 or with more than 1,000 employees, and the highest rates in companies with between 100 and 249 employees (33).

VIII. Injury and Illness Summary (covering calendar year 1974)

Instructions:
- This section may be completed by copying data from OSHA Form No. 102 "Summary, Occupational Injuries and Illnesses," which you are required to complete and post in your establishment.
- Leave Section VIII blank if there were no recordable injuries or illnesses during 1974.
- Code 30—Add all occupational illnesses (Code 21+22+23+24+25+26+29) and enter on this line for each column (3) through (8).
- Code 31—Add occupational injuries (Code 10) and the sum of all occupational illnesses (Code 30) and enter on this line for each column (3) through (8).

Code (1)	Category (2)	Fatalities (deaths) (3)	Lost workday cases Number of cases (4)	Lost workday cases Number of cases involving permanent transfer to another job or termination of employment (5)	Lost workday cases Number of lost workdays (6)	Nonfatal cases without lost workdays* Number of cases (7)	Nonfatal cases without lost workdays* Number of cases involving transfer to another job or termination of employment (8)
10	Occupational Injuries						
21	Occupational skin diseases or disorders						
22	Dust diseases of the lungs (pneumoconioses)						
23	Respiratory conditions due to toxic agents						
24	Poisoning (systemic effects of toxic materials)						
25	Disorders due to physical agents (other than toxic materials)						
26	Disorders due to repeated trauma						
29	All other occupational illnesses						
30	Sum of all occupational illnesses (Add Codes 21 through 29)						
31	Total of all occupational injuries and illnesses (Add Codes 10 + 30)						

(Codes 21–29 grouped under: Occupational illnesses)

*Nonfatal cases without lost workdays-Cases resulting in: Medical treatment beyond first-aid, diagnosis of occupational illness, loss of consciousness, restriction of work or motion, or transfer to another job (without lost workdays).

Comments: _____

IX. Report prepared by: _____   Date: _____
    Title: _____   Area code and phone: _____

Figure 17–2. Occupational Safety and Health Survey Form.
Source: U.S. Department of Labor, Bureau of Labor Statistics.

Motor vehicle accident rates are normally recorded on a separate basis for all company-owned cars or trucks. For purposes of motor safety, an accident is defined as any contact with the company vehicle causing either personal injury or property damage. The rate formula is

$$\text{motor vehicle accident frequency rate} = \frac{\text{number of accidents} \times 100{,}000}{\text{number of vehicle-miles operated}}$$

An attempt is usually made to compute separate rates for accidents that are chargeable against the company employee who was driving and those that do not appear to be his fault. There is some question, however,

Table 17–1. Occupational Injury and Illness Incidence Rates, U.S. Industry, Private Sector, 1972–1974

Industry	Incidence Rates Per 100 Full-time Workers [a]								
	Total Cases			Lost Workday Cases			Nonfatal Cases Without Lost Workdays		
	1974	1973	1972	1974	1973	1972	1974	1973	1972
Private Sector	10.4	11.0	10.9	3.5	3.4	3.3	6.9	7.5	7.6
Agriculture, forestry, and fisheries	9.9	11.6	n.a.	4.5	4.6	n.a.	5.3	7.0	n.a.
Mining	10.2	12.5	n.a.	5.1	5.8	n.a.	5.0	6.7	n.a.
Contract construction	18.3	19.8	19.0	5.9	6.1	6.0	12.4	13.6	12.9
Manufacturing	14.6	15.3	15.6	4.7	4.5	4.2	9.9	10.8	11.4
Transportation and public utilities	10.5	10.3	10.8	4.8	4.4	4.5	5.7	5.8	6.3
Wholesale and retail trade	8.4	8.6	8.4	2.8	2.7	2.8	5.6	5.9	5.6
Finance, insurance, and real estate	2.4	2.4	2.5	.8	.8	.8	1.6	1.6	1.7
Services	5.8	6.2	6.1	1.9	1.9	2.0	3.9	4.2	4.1

Source: U.S. Department of Labor, Bureau of Labor Statistics.
[a] The incidence rates represent the number of injuries and illnesses per 100 full-time workers and were calculated as $(N/EH) \times 200,000$ where

N = number of injuries and illnesses
EH = total hours worked by all employees during calendar year
200,000 = base for 100 full-time-equivalent workers (working 40 hours per week, 50 weeks per year)

n.a. = Not available.

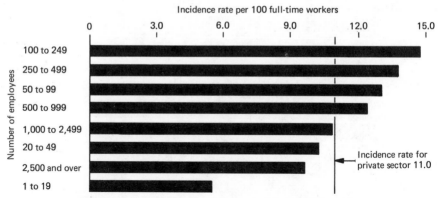

Figure 17–3. Injury and Illness Incidence Rates, by Employment-size Group, Private Sector, United States, 1973.
Source: U.S. Department of Labor, Occupational Injuries and Illnesses in the United States by Industry, 1973 (Washington, D.C.: Government Printing Office, 1975), p. 9.

whether such efforts at differentiation are ever entirely successful. Obtaining the required information is often difficult and almost always time-consuming.

ACCIDENT REPORTS

Statistics of the type discussed are developed from accident reports that are normally prepared by the immediate superior of the employee involved. The requirement that supervisors must fill out reports in this manner has the advantage that it makes the particular person who can do the most to promote safety aware of accidents occurring under his jurisdiction. Thus, it not only provides necessary information, but serves a useful educational purpose as well.

Many of the questions asked on an accident report form are noted in Figure 17–4. Several of these require explanation. For example, the accident is referred to as "alleged." This is done to protect the company against damage claims. Any report signed by a supervisor that refers in an unqualified manner to a specific accident can serve as evidence in court that the employer acknowledges responsibility in the case, whether or not the employer actually wishes to do so. And, of course, all such records can be subpoenaed. Thus, the use of *alleged* on a standard basis provides a defense against false claims.

The *agency* is the thing most closely associated with the injury. Examples are animals, boilers, chemicals, conveyors, dusts, electric apparatus, elevators, hand tools, flammable substances, hoisting apparatus, machines, radiations, and working surfaces. The *agency part* is that specific part or

Name of employee _____   Location _____

Address _____   Division _____

Sex _____ Age _____ Occupation _____

Married _____ Children _____ Wage rate _____

Date and time of alleged accident _____

Place of alleged accident _____

Description of alleged accident _____

_____

_____

_____

_____

_____

_____

Working on regular job? _____

Agency involved _____

Part of agency _____

Unsafe mechanical or physical condition of agency _____

_____

Accident type _____

Unsafe act _____

Unsafe personal factor _____

Safeguards provided _____

Safeguards in use _____

Nature and extent of injury _____

_____

_____

Days lost _____ Attending physician _____

Recommendations to prevent similar accidents _____

_____

_____

Prepared by _____ Date _____

Figure 17–4. Typical Accident Report Form.

aspect of the agency most closely associated with the injury. The *unsafe mechanical or physical condition of the agency* refers to the aspect of the agency that could have been guarded or corrected. The categories normally used are inadequate mechanical guarding, defective condition of the agency, unsafe design of the agency, hazardous processes or procedures, incorrect illumination, incorrect ventilation, and unsafe apparel.

The *accident type* refers to the type of contact of the injured person with the agency. Examples are caught in or between, struck by, struck against, fall of person, scratched, overexertion, and contact with either electricity, extreme temperatures, or noxious substances. The *unsafe act* is the type of behavior leading to the accident, such as working unsafely, performing unauthorized operations, removing safety devices, operating at unsafe speeds, use of improper equipment, using equipment unsafely, horseplay, and failure to use safe attire. The *unsafe personal factor* is the characteristic of the individual responsible for the unsafe act—unsafe attitudes, lack of knowledge, bodily defect, or disturbed emotional state.

Unfortunately, reports of this kind do not always yield completely valid information. The persons involved in an accident, including the supervisor in charge, may well be strongly motivated to cover up certain aspects of the case to protect themselves against anticipated criticism from higher management. Thus, it is often difficult to obtain objective data. Nevertheless, experience indicates that tabulations based on questions of the kind illustrated in Figure 17–4 can yield information that is at least sufficiently valid so that major sources of difficulty can be identified.

THE STUDY OF NEAR ACCIDENTS

The injury process may be described as a sequence running from a social environment or background, to a defect or fault of the person, to an unsafe act or conditions, to an accident, and finally to injury. In the great majority of cases, this sequence does not run its full course, and therefore no actual injury occurs. Yet the factors preceding are much the same as when the sequence is completed. Thus, the study of near accidents can provide useful insights that may be used to ward off future injuries.

Some companies go to considerable trouble to develop frequency and descriptive data on such near accidents. Either report forms or interviews with workers are used to collect the data. The approach has the advantage that because no actual loss occurs, attempts to cover up and protect against blame are less likely, and the true sources of danger can be established more easily. Furthermore, because near accidents are much more frequent, a study of them is particularly valuable in pinpointing those jobs, places, and individuals requiring the greatest attention.

Safety Training

There is evidence that, where the work situation is relatively hazardous, injuries are particularly likely to occur during the first few months of employment, when the worker has not yet learned how to protect himself against the dangers in his environment (12). Under such circumstances, it becomes apparent that any kind of training, whether directed toward orientation, skills, attitudes, or anything else connected with the job, can serve a preventive purpose insofar as accidents are concerned. To the extent such early training makes a new employee more capable of coping with his work environment, it will inevitably contribute to the safety goal.

In actual practice, training programs for new employees do characteristically contain considerable safety content. Items covered are special hazards in the work situation, examples of previous accidents, nature and use of safety equipment, availability of medical services, accident reporting, and safety rules. Where the work is particularly hazardous, first-aid procedures are often included.

Techniques used for safety training include most of those discussed in Chapter 15, such as lectures, demonstrations, and films. A recent study involving the operation of a small power tool indicates that the use of accident simulations may be more effective than training based on written instructions or demonstrations (30). In accident simulation, the tool operators performed an unsafe act and actually experienced an accident, using equipment modified to prevent injury. The training effect was successfully transferred to the use of unmodified equipment, and the trainees retained their superior safety record over a period of at least six months after the training. Simulation training could be expected to be particularly effective in high-hazard situations. One study of the types of human error involved in underground accidents in gold mines indicates that the dominant types of errors involve failures to perceive warnings of danger and underestimations of hazards (18). Accident simulation certainly should result in increased awareness of the dangers of the work place.

Some firms introduce more general discussions of safety off the job into the training process. This is done because most companies, as a result of their safety efforts, have produced a situation where injuries at work are less frequent than during the rest of the day. Factories are often safer than the home. Time lost because of off-the-job injuries may well be greater than for work-connected injuries. Under such circumstances, the tendency has been to include a rather broad treatment of accident prevention within the training context.

Another type of safety training is directed to specific situations where there has been a deterioration in accident rates. It is not uncommon for experienced employees to develop group norms that sanction the breaking of safety rules and a failure to use protective devices (20). When this happens, safety training becomes an important antidote. The usual procedure is to review safety rules in a series of discussions conducted by a safety specialist. Considerable opportunity is given for open criticism of existing rules and procedures, and on occasion, changes are introduced in response to group decisions. Every effort is made not only to impart safety information, but to get employees personally involved in the safety effort. Some companies carry out this type of retraining on a periodic basis with all workers, irrespective of the accident rate in the group.

Publicity and Contests

Safety publicity can take a variety of forms. Among those commonly used are posters, booklets, special memoranda, and articles in company publications. In many instances, these media are used to advertise contests that pit various work groups against each other in an effort to minimize the number of lost-time accidents.

A major source of posters for industry is the National Safety Council. Many companies also print their own posters and notices. Insofar as possible, these should concentrate on reminding employees of safe practices without arousing too much anxiety. Gruesome and disturbing material is simply avoided by many people; they do not look at it at all. The main function of a good poster is to attract attention and keep employees thinking about safety, not to scare them.

Company publications can be used to provide information on accidents that have occurred or on hazardous situations that have been corrected. Running accounts of the results of safety contests are often provided. All these serve to promote safety consciousness, and to the extent the average employee is kept aware of the possibility of injury, he is likely to exhibit safer behavior.

Safety rules and regulations often are printed in a separate booklet that is given wide distribution. Unfortunately, these booklets rarely achieve a readership even approximating their distribution. Furthermore, some of them actually create disrespect for safety procedures rather than promote them. The reason is that there is a strong temptation for management to absolve itself of responsibility in connection with accidents by proscribing all behaviors that might conceivably prove unsafe. As a result, many of the rules turn out to be entirely unrealistic, and employees break them without thinking, often with the tacit approval of their supervisors. When this happens, the whole system of safety regulation tends to become denigrated, with little differentiation being made between realistic and unrealistic rules. The only way to protect against this eventuality is to keep safety restrictions to a minimum and to recognize that a rule that no one will obey and that cannot be enforced is of little value to anyone. In fact, it can have a negative impact because of its influence on more appropriate regulations.

All manner of contests are conducted in the safety area, in most cases with considerable success. In general, the emphasis is on internal comparisons within a company, but there are some industry-wide contests, such as those conducted by the National Safety Council. Perhaps most common is a competition between departments with similar accident potentials as indicated by national rates. These contests may stress maintaining a low-frequency rate, or they may be concerned with the number of days without an injury. Sometimes, only lost time injuries are counted; sometimes, minor injuries as well. Departments may also compete against their own records for certain periods in the past. Awards are often given to individual employees working in high-accident occupations, such as truck drivers, for remaining accident-free over an extended time span.

Although contests do appear to have a generally salutary effect on injuries, there are certain negative aspects that should be recognized. One is the tendency to let down when a long accident-free period finally comes to an end. A rash of injuries can occur at such a time, if something is not done to divert interest to some new contest or record. Second, there is some tendency to cover up injuries when they occur in the context of a contest, especially if minor injuries are included. The result can be a failure to obtain needed first-aid and dispensary treatment. In addition, accident reports may not be filed when they should be, with a resulting distortion of statistics. Under certain circumstances, the harmful side effects of contests can outweigh the gains (14).

Control of the Work Environment

Design of the work place, and of equipment used in it, is probably the major approach to accident prevention and the most effective. Safety devices and the like have the advantage that they not only reduce accidents, but give employees a sense of confidence and security in the work place. Anxiety levels are reduced accordingly, and a potential source of performance disruption and failure is eliminated. This is a particularly important consideration in situations that would be extremely dangerous without accident prevention devices.

One of the major provisions of the Occupational Safety and Health Act calls for the government to set national standards for safety devices and other requirements related to a safe work environment. To date, however, many standards have yet to be issued because of disagreement among those responsible for developing them, and some of those that have been issued have been criticized as being too ambiguous to be enforced (1, 27). Much of the job of complying with the standards, once they are in effect, devolves on the safety engineers. An extended treatment of safety engineering techniques would take us well beyond the field of personnel management as it is usually defined; however, there are several basic points that can be made.

The most crucial consideration is that equipment be constructed so as to introduce barriers that make it very difficult, if not impossible, for the individual to expose himself to danger. Protective clothing, guards, covers, and the like can often isolate a person from a danger source, so that irrespective of what he does there is little chance of injury. In addition, controls should be designed and placed, so that opportunities for erroneous use are kept to a minimum. Devices that will yield information regarding any malfunctioning or breakdown of equipment should be installed wherever possible, and they should be readily visible. Self-correcting mechanisms and automatic shutoffs are, of course, the ideal, because then danger is eliminated without the need of human intervention. But if these cannot be installed, all controls, releases, gauges, and the like should be built so as to mesh to a maximal degree with the capabilities and characteristics of the human operator.

Equipment-design considerations probably constitute the major aspect of environmental control insofar as safety management is concerned, but there are other factors. Floors, stairs, ramps, elevators, and many other features must be constructed initially with safety in mind, and they must be inspected continually. Fire prevention and protection is also a normal safety division function, as is protection against catastrophes such as floods, windstorms, and nuclear attack. As previously noted, automobile accidents represent a safety management concern even when only property damage is involved. Safety considerations in the design of new products and such matters as air and water pollution may also contribute to the role prescriptions of a safety manager or engineer.

An example of the way in which environmental considerations may contribute to accidents is provided by a study undertaken to determine whether placing radiophones in company automobiles might be a source of danger (4). The answer appears to be in the affirmative. Telephoning and driving at the same time have little effect on routine driving skills that are well learned, but perception and decision making are impaired where automatic responses cannot operate. Installation of a device that makes it impossible to operate the telephone while the car is moving would appear to be an effective deterrent to accidents in this situation.

Inspection and Discipline

The Occupational Safety and Health Act calls for inspection of the work place for hazards by representatives of the Labor Department. Such inspection may be initiated by the government or as a result of a complaint by an employee (6). If hazards are found, action can be taken to enforce a change. In its enforcement of OSHA, the government holds employers responsible for making sure employees wear safety equipment such as hard hats, earplugs, and so forth. Employers, but not employees, are subject to legal citations and fines if hazards are found, even if there have been no accidents (10).

Many companies conduct their own regular inspections with a view to providing an early warning system against accidents and against OSHA citations. The inspections are carried out by supervisors, safety committee members, safety engineers, or often by representatives of insurance carriers handling the company's workers' compensation policies. These inspections are much more effective in identifying unsafe working conditions than unsafe practices; even in the former instance, the inspector must have considerable knowledge of the particular operations to be effective. Furthermore, inspection does little good if there is no follow-up to make sure that sources of danger have been corrected. Unfortunately, inspection reports requested from supervisors often are subordinated to more pressing production considerations.

When unsafe practices are identified, either as a result of inspection or in connection with an accident investigation, the usual first thought is some form of discipline ranging from a reprimand upward, although in cases of serious injury the conclusion usually is that the individual has suffered enough already. It must be recognized, however, that discipline may have little value in the accident context. In a study of problem automobile drivers, more severe punishments actually appear to have produced more subsequent traffic law violations—presumably because the punishment indicates that the person is a problem driver, and he drives accordingly (31).

ACCIDENT PRONENESS

No matter how much effort is spent in training, controlling the work environment, or other aspects of safety management, there appears to be no way to eliminate on-the-job accidents or unplanned events that do or could result in personal injury. In large measure, this is because people behave in ways that result in accidents. Although there is much disagreement about the concept of accident proneness (32), it is clear that some individuals have more accidents than can be reasonably attributed to chance (25). It also would appear that a person might be accident prone at one period of time during his or her life but not at another period of time. As indicated by Figure 17–5, accidents are most frequent in the age ranges from seventeen to thirty and decline steadily after that to reach a low point in the late sixties (11).

Other evidence indicates that individuals who have high injury rates in one year are the ones who are most likely to have high rates the following year (25). The data of Figure 17–6 are typical. In this instance, there is a steady increase in the number of accidents experienced during the second year as a function of the first-year frequencies. Those who had no accidents the first year had an average of only .69 the second year. Those who had nine accidents the first year averaged 5.14 the second year. The same trend appears in all the 11 separate departments represented in the combined data of Figure 17–6. Additional studies conducted to determine whether the hazards associated with specific jobs could account for these results produced negative results. When differences in job danger were controlled, the same pattern was still present in the data, as indicated by the dotted line in Figure 17–6.

Findings of this kind are consistent with the widely held opinion that injuries are not merely a direct function of the degree to which the working environment contains hazardous features. It is true that training deficiencies and the fact that younger workers are more likely to be new on

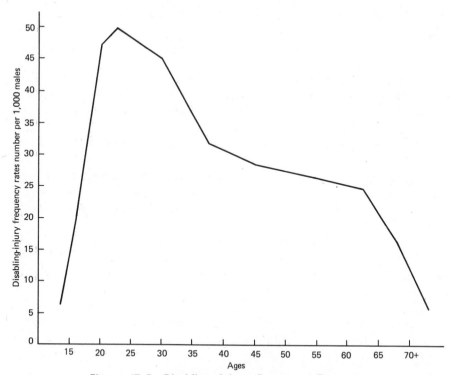

Figure 17–5. Disabling Injury Frequency Rates per 1000 Males in the Civilian Labor Force, California. Three-year Average (1960, 1965, 1968).
Source: Gordon, J. B., A. Akman, and M. L. Brooks, *Industrial Accident Statistics: A Re-examination* (New York: Praeger Publishers, Inc., 1971), p. 211.

the job could account for part of the injury-age relationship. But these cannot explain all the findings. For one thing, the increase during the early years is far too marked. For another, the injury rates do not reach their highest level until age twenty-one or twenty-two, even though skill deficiencies are most pronounced among those who are younger.

It seems, then, that contrary to the view that differences in accident frequencies could be accounted for in terms of chance fluctuations, there are certain individuals who are consistently more susceptible to injuries than others. As noted, however, this tendency may well be more pronounced during a specific period of a person's life. Research into the personality characteristics of individuals with high injury-frequency rates tends to support this conclusion. There do appear to be some consistent differences between these accident repeaters and those who do not have such a high injury potential.

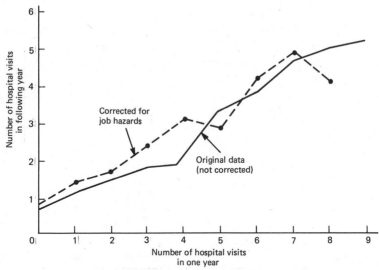

Figure 17–6. Relationship Between the Number of Hospital Visits for Two Successive Years Among About
9000 Steelworkers. The solid line represents the original data, while the dotted line represents the same
data "corrected" for differences in job hazards.
Source: Ernest J. McCormick and Joseph Tiffin, Industrial
Psychology, 6th ed. © 1974, p. 521. Reprinted by permission of Prentice-Hall, Inc., Englewood Cliffs, New Jersey.

Characteristics of the Accident Prone

An early study indicated that people with high injury-frequency and
-severity rates are likely to act with a high degree of muscular speed, even
though they lack the visual capacity to comprehend a situation with equal
rapidity (9). Thus, action often precedes perception and thought; such
people are often described as impulsive. This particular study was carried
out in the metal-working department of a large factory. More recent research attempted to relate this same tendency to react impulsively to the
frequency of accidents in which taxicab drivers are struck from behind (2).
A positive relationship was found.

Another factor in accident repetition appears to be the individual's
characteristic reaction to monotony. Among long-distance truck drivers,
those who tend to have difficulty concentrating and thus make more errors
on a monotonous task also are those who have more accidents on the road
(24). Again, the problem appears to be a difficulty in controlling thought
processes to use them for effective action. Those who tend to have accidents
also have more difficulty in perceptually differentiating a figure from its
background (3). People of this kind are known to think less analytically

and critically and become confused easily under stress. They do not think things through before acting.

Other research has focused directly on personality characteristics rather than on perceptual and behavioral relationships. In one such study, accident-prone individuals were found to be very negative in their attitudes (8). They dislike their superiors, their jobs, and work generally. Furthermore, they tend to be almost devoid of optimism and trust, and, in fact, have little positive feeling toward people at all.

Another investigation involved the testing of 54 individuals with extremely high injury-frequency rates (19). The lack of warm emotional relationships with others was again apparent. Most had a number of acquaintances, but they were not really close to these people. In addition, the negative attitudes toward those in positions of authority noted in the study just mentioned were once again present. These accident-prone individuals exhibited a marked, and often unreasonable, hatred of their superiors at work as well as of other authority figures.

There were certain other findings. The high-accident group was characterized by a great deal of concern about health matters, even though actual illness tended to be rare. There was a strong desire for increased social status coupled with very little accomplishment in this regard. Emotionally disturbing situations were often handled by misperceiving and distorting the world around them so as to make it less threatening. As a result, these people made bad mistakes in judgment rather frequently. Planning for the future was apparently minimal. They preferred to live from day to day and were, in fact, quite impulsive.

Taken together, these investigations and others of a similar nature yield a rather consistent picture of the accident-prone person, although it must be understood that a great many work injuries, perhaps the majority, involve people who do not have frequent accidents and who do not possess the characteristics found among these accident repeaters. The accident prone seem to be rather socially irresponsible and immature, although not really emotionally ill, in most cases. Because their high injury rates are not normally maintained throughout life, but only over periods of a few years, it seems most appropriate to view accident proneness as a transient personality maladjustment that is most likely to develop in the years before age thirty.

The major motivation behind the repeated accidents themselves would appear to be a desire to impress others by resorting to sudden and very risky decisions and behavior. Research has repeatedly demonstrated the very marked "adventuresomeness" of those with high accident frequencies (17). This impulsiveness is usually combined with a strong hatred of people at higher levels in the organization and a consequent defiance of the rules and policies established by these people. Thus, safety regulations are deliberately flouted, not only as a way of impressing others with one's skill or bravery, but as a means of attacking and resisting management. Under such circumstances, exposure to danger becomes unusually frequent for these employees. With an exposure level this high, it is not surprising that they are in fact injured on a number of occasions. By their own actions, they repeatedly place themselves in an extremely hazardous work environment, even though their jobs might not, under normal circumstances, be considered dangerous at all.

In some instances, this pattern may be supplemented as a result of certain additional personality processes. Hatred toward one's superiors can on occasion generate considerable guilt and a wish, whether conscious or unconscious, to escape this guilt by being punished. To the extent punishment is viewed as a means of atoning for one's sins, it may well be desired. For people such as this, an accident may be equated with punishment, and a real desire to suffer injury may develop at periodic intervals when guilt becomes too pronounced. Here, the accident is not merely a chance event in a personally created hazardous environment, but a specific outcome that is desired and directly caused. The need for self-preservation gives way before the need to expiate guilt, just as it often does in suicide cases.

Dealing with Accident Proneness

The question remains—What can be done to reduce the frequency of personally created accidents of this kind? To some extent, selection procedures may be used to screen the input on this basis, although this has not been widely done. Such an approach seems particularly desirable in high-accident-rate industries, such as mining and lumber. It seems less appropriate in safer industries, where it may not be economically feasible to invest heavily in selection—to screen out a limited number of accident-prone individuals who in all likelihood would not have an extremely high rate of injury in any event because of the lower danger level.

Given the fact, then, that because of a lack of, or the imperfections of, input screening, accident-prone people are likely to be employed by any company at least in limited numbers, what can be done to deal with the problem? As the age–accident frequency relationship suggests, accident proneness tends to correct itself eventually, but not until a number of injuries have occurred, large sums have been disbursed in disability payments, and in many instances sizable output and equipment losses have accrued.

Thus, some kind of direct action does seem to be called for. One approach is to reduce the danger in the work environment as much as possible. This will have only limited impact on those who really want to injure themselves to reduce guilt, but it will yield results among the high risk-takers, because there will be less chance for an accident to occur. In part, danger reduction can be achieved through equipment design and in part through transferring the accident-prone individual to low-hazard work.

Equipment design is of value, however, only to the extent it takes control of the safety factor out of the hands of the employee. Protective clothing and warning devices are of little help with the accident prone. Automatic shutoffs and fixed barriers, on the other hand, can be much more effective.

The second point relates to the hatred of people in positions of authority, which is known to characterize the accident prone. It is when they are forced into continuing close relationships with their superiors that these individuals are most likely to be injured. In view of this, managers should, insofar as possible, keep at a distance from those who have had high accident rates. Everything possible should be done to minimize conflict and resentment. To the extent the employee can work on his own with only limited restriction, control, and discipline, the chances of injury will inevitably be reduced. Appropriate supervisory techniques for use with the accident prone can be taught as part of various management development programs. If safety rules can be developed on a participative basis, rather than imposed from "on high," this too will help (26).

PREVENTIVE MEDICINE

Industrial medicine involves three major aspects. The first of these, the use of the physical examination in selection and placement, has been discussed in Chapter 13. A second, the elimination of health hazards and the prevention of illness, will concern us here. The third aspect, having to do with the diagnosis and cure of existing maladies, will be covered briefly in the next chapter.

Actually, treatment is not a major concern of most industrial physicians. Generally, firms do not offer continuing assistance of this kind to their employees. The normal procedure is to refer an individual who becomes ill to his own personal physician, after short-term, immediate treatment is provided as required. The exceptions to this occur primarily in those instances where the work is carried out in an isolated situation. Under such circumstances, when adequate medical services are not available in the community, they are often furnished by the company. In addition, there are a few firms that make it a policy to provide extensive treatment facilities for employees. Usually, though, preventive considerations remain paramount over those of a therapeutic nature.

Development of Industrial Medicine

In an earlier period, the primary duty of the industrial physician or nurse was to give prompt treatment in connection with accident cases (28). Gradually, however, the records of such treatments, which the medical staff maintained, became important as a source of information on specific situations that were particularly hazardous. At the same time, workers' compensation cases involving phosphorus and lead poisoning began to appear frequently, and the industrial physician assumed an important preventive role in this area. Subsequently, management came to recognize the potential value of the physical examination both for selection purposes and, when utilized on a periodic basis, in the early identification of disorders among current employees.

As indicated by the figures in Table 17–2, periodic physical exams are more common for managerial employees; in some companies, the practice is to offer regular exams to all managers and all employees over age forty or forty-five (5). A recent study of industrial medical programs indicates that an increasing number of companies offer such exams (22), and many companies are now using what are known as multiphasic health-screening procedures for their periodic physical examinations. These procedures involve the administration of a large number of regular diagnostic medical tests, such as X rays and blood tests, and the results are fed into a computer along with the employee's medical history and any other relevant data. If potential medical problems are indicated, the employee is referred to his or her personal physician for further examination and treatment (15). Another type of program that appears to be devolving on the company medical staff is that related to physical fitness. A number of firms have set up programs of exercise and other activities and offered them to employees, particularly

Table 17-2. Company Medical Services

Service	Per Cent of Companies (N = 204)
Physical examinations	
Preemployment	80
Periodic exams for—	
All employees	20
Managers only	39
Employees in certain jobs or over a certain age	22
Other medical services	
Medication (aspirin, etc.)	66
Shots for flu or other preventive measures	50
Blood bank or blood donor program	50
Dental exams	4
Company medical facilities and staff	
First-aid station	75
Sick room	55
Doctor—full-time	22
part-time	37
Nurse—full-time	53
part-time	6
visiting	4

Source: Compiled from Bureau of National Affairs, Inc., *Services for Employees,* Personnel Policies Forum Survey No. 105, March 1974, p. 2.

those whose physical exams indicate they are in high-risk groups for heart disease or other medical problems (36).

In recent years, the preventive role of the industrial medical department has spread to many other areas in addition to physical exams. The company doctor normally decides whether an employee can safely return to his job after an injury or illness. The work a handicapped person may perform is characteristically determined after a physical examination directed to this specific purpose. Recommendations regarding the shutdown or modification of hazardous situations often emanate from this source. So do company-wide programs of inoculations and similar preventive efforts.

Industrial physicians and hygienists also are concerned with calculations regarding gas, dust, fume, and smoke concentrations that may prove to be noxious. They make tests on chemical compounds and atmospheric conditions to determine toxicity. They deal with situations where noise levels may be such as to produce damage to the ear. They have become increasingly concerned with problems of radiation and with the detection of radiation hazards. These aspects of industrial medicine have expanded greatly with the advent of OSHA; national standards are being established for noise levels and the presence of gases and chemicals in the work place. While most major corporations already had extensive programs for monitoring such conditions, many smaller firms have had to install new programs in these areas (35).

Organization of Medical Services

There has been considerable discussion regarding the advantages of providing medical services through full-time professional employees who are on the company payroll, as against retaining outside specialists for this purpose. There are strong arguments pro and con. The inside physician is clearly at a disadvantage in dealing with representatives of higher management, because he is entirely dependent on them for his employment. The result can be some loss of effectiveness in this area. At lower levels, there may be problems in maintaining the traditional physician-patient confidential relationship because of the presence of a third party, the company,

On the other hand, it can be assumed that physicians who have accepted regular employment with a firm will not deliberately do things that are detrimental to that firm, even if on occasion, because of professional considerations, they do not contribute maximally to it. Private physicians, however, will normally feel a much greater commitment to the patient than to the company. Furthermore, they are not usually in a position to contribute a great deal to the prevention of illness and injury, and they may or may not be able to offer prompt treatment of injuries at the time they occur. For these reasons, most large corporations with sufficient demand for medical services at a single installation hire a professional staff and set up a dispensary. Smaller firms and installations of limited size within a much larger company are normally serviced by private physicians in the community, either on retainer or on a fee basis.

Even where a full-time physician is not employed, a dispensary may be operated. A local physician may be retained part-time, or a nurse may be put in charge. In larger dispensaries, a number of physicians and nurses as well as various medical technicians and clerical workers may be on the staff. In some cases, especially in foreign countries, companies operate full-scale hospitals for employees and on occasion for their dependents as well.

Recent federal legislation designed to encourage the growth of community medical facilities, particularly health maintenance organizations, or HMOs, may provide an answer to the problem of providing medical services in the smaller company. While there seems to be a definite trend toward companies' increasing the extent of medical services available to employees, there is some feeling that most business firms should not be in a medical role and might do better to spend their money supporting an HMO, which could provide better services (21). In some communities, a number of companies have gotten together and set up cooperative medical facilities to provide occupational health services. One such facility provides care in cases of occupational injuries, conducts environmental health surveys of the work place, and offers extensive preventive medical services to employees of the companies participating in the venture (29).

It is obvious that employers have a number of options in the type of medical program that can be provided for employees, and these options seem to be increasing. Such programs, particularly those emphasizing preventive measures, clearly can contribute to employee welfare and continued productivity much as preventive safety management does.

QUESTIONS

1. How does the new incidence-rate approach to safety statistics differ from the old injury-frequency- and injury-severity-rate approaches? Why do you suppose the change was made?
2. What are the most dangerous industries? What factors would account for the industry differences?
3. What is the relative effectiveness of safety training, contests, and control of the work environment in reducing accidents? Document your answer.
4. What evidence would argue for and against accident proneness as a psychological construct?
5. What are HMOs and what factors have contributed to their development? What are the advantages and the disadvantages of HMOs from a company viewpoint?

REFERENCES

1. Ashford, N. A. "Worker Health and Safety: An Area of Conflicts." *Monthly Labor Review*, 98 (1975), No. 9, 3–11.

2. Barbarik, P. "Automobile Accidents and Driver Reaction Pattern." *Journal of Applied Psychology,* 52 (1968), 49–54.
3. Barrett, G. V., and C. L. Thornton. "Relationship Between Perceptual Style and Driver Reaction to an Emergency Situation." *Journal of Applied Psychology,* 52 (1968), 169–176.
4. Brown, I. D., A. H. Tickner, and D. C. V. Simmonds. "Interference Between Concurrent Tasks of Driving and Telephoning." *Journal of Applied Psychology,* 53 (1969), 419–424.
5. Bureau of National Affairs, Inc. *Services for Employees.* Personnel Policies Forum Survey No. 105, March 1974.
6. Bureau of National Affairs, Inc. *The Job Safety and Health Act of 1970.* Washington, D.C.: BNA, Inc., 1971.
7. Carnahan, G. R. "Using Safety Committees Effectively." *Personnel Administrator,* 19 (1974), No. 2, 46–49.
8. Davids, A., and J. T. Mahoney. "Personality Dynamics and Accident-proneness in an Industrial Setting." *Journal of Applied Psychology,* 41 (1957), 303–306.
9. Drake, C. A. "Accident-proneness: A Hypothesis." *Character and Personality,* 8 (1940), 335–341.
10. Foulkes, F. K. "Learning to Live with OSHA." *Harvard Business Review,* 51 (1973), No. 6, 57–67.
11. Gordon, J. B., A. Akman, and M. L. Brooks. *Industrial Accident Statistics: A Re-examination.* New York: Praeger Publishers, Inc., 1971.
12. Greenberg, L. "Learning as a Factor in Accident Experience." *Personnel Psychology,* 24 (1971), 71–76.
13. Haddon, H., E. A. Suchman, and D. Kline. *Accident Research.* New York: Harper & Row, Publishers, 1964.
14. Hampton, D. R. "Contests Have Side Effects, Too." *California Management Review,* 12 (1970), No. 4, 86–94.
15. Holcomb, F. W. "IBM's Health Screening Program and Medical Data System." *Journal of Occupational Medicine,* 15 (1973), 863–868.
16. Inzana, J. T. "The New Survey of Occupational Injuries and Illnesses." *Monthly Labor Review,* 96 (1973), No. 8, 53–55.
17. Kunce, J. T. "Vocational Interests and Accident Proneness." *Journal of Applied Psychology,* 51 (1967), 223–225.
18. Lawrence, A. C. "Human Error as a Cause of Accidents in Gold Mining." *Journal of Safety Record,* 6 (1974), 78–88.
19. LeShan, L. L. "Dynamics of Accident-prone Behavior." *Psychiatry,* 15 (1952), 73–80.
20. Lippert, F. G. "Role Conflict and Ambiguity in Enforcing Safe Work Practice." *Journal of American Society of Safety Engineers* (1968), No. 5, 12–14.
21. Ludlow, H. T. "Becoming the Boss's Patient." *Conference Board Record,* 9 (1974), No. 7, 37–41.

22. Lusterman, S. *Industry Roles in Health Care.* New York: Conference Board, 1974.
23. Lyons, J. M. "Safety: The Company, the Committee and the Committed." *Personnel Journal,* 51 (1972), 95–98, 137.
24. McBain, W. N. "Arousal, Monotony, and Accidents in Line Driving." *Journal of Applied Psychology,* 54 (1970), 509–519.
25. McCormick, E. J., and J. Tiffin. *Industrial Psychology.* Englewood Cliffs, N.J.: Prentice-Hall, Inc., 1974.
26. Miner, J. B., and J. F. Brewer. "The Management of Ineffective Performance," in M. D. Dunnette (ed.), *Handbook of Industrial and Organizational Psychology.* Chicago: Rand McNally & Company, 1976.
27. Moran, R. D. "Are Job Safety Standards Understandable?" *The Personnel Administrator,* 19 (1974), No. 2, 22–25.
28. O'Brien, P. E. "Health, Safety, and the Corporate Balance Sheet." *Personnel Journal,* 52 (1973), 725–729.
29. Richmond, H. W. "Health Care Delivery in Cummins Engine Company." *Archives of Environmental Health,* 29 (1974), 328–335.
30. Rubinsky, S., and N. Smith. "Safety Training by Accident Simulation." *Journal of Applied Psychology,* 57 (1973), 68–73.
31. Schuster, D. H. "Two-year Follow-up of Official Action Taken Against Problem Drivers." *Proceedings, Seventy-ninth Annual Convention, American Psychological Association,* 1971, 505–506.
32. Shaw, L., and H. Sichel. *Accident Proneness.* Elmsford, N.Y.: Pergamon Press, Inc., 1971.
33. U.S. Department of Labor. *Occupational Injuries and Illnesses in the United States, by Industry, 1973.* Washington, D.C.: Government Printing Office, 1975.
34. U.S. Department of Labor. *Occupational Safety and Health Statistics: Concepts and Methods* (Report 438). Washington, D.C.: Bureau of Labor Statistics, 1975.
35. Wolkonsky, P., H. W. Spies, and P. D. Halley. "An Environmental Health Program." *Industrial Medicine and Surgery,* 42 (1973), No. 6, 5–10.
36. Yarvote, P. M., et al. "Organization and Evaluation of a Physical Fitness Program in Industry." *Journal of Occupational Medicine,* 16 (1974), 589–598.

18 *Performance Control*

THE CONTROL MODEL AND HUMAN PERFORMANCE
  Establishing Standards
  Performance Analysis
  Firing as an All-purpose Solution
A SCHEMA FOR PERFORMANCE ANALYSIS
  Intelligence and Job Knowledge
    INSUFFICIENT VERBAL ABILITY
    INSUFFICIENT SPECIAL ABILITY
    INSUFFICIENT JOB KNOWLEDGE
    DEFECT OF JUDGMENT OR MEMORY
  Emotions and Emotional Illness
    FREQUENT DISRUPTIVE EMOTION
    PSYCHOSIS
    NEUROSIS
    ALCOHOL AND DRUG PROBLEMS
  Individual Motivation to Work
    STRONG MOTIVES FRUSTRATED AT WORK
    UNINTEGRATED MEANS TO SATISFY MOTIVES
    EXCESSIVELY LOW PERSONAL WORK STANDARDS
    GENERALIZED LOW WORK MOTIVATION
  Physical Characteristics and Disorders
    PHYSICAL ILLNESS OR HANDICAP
    PHYSICAL DISORDERS OF EMOTIONAL ORIGIN
    INAPPROPRIATE PHYSICAL CHARACTERISTICS
    INSUFFICIENT MUSCULAR OR SENSORY ABILITY OR SKILL
  Family Ties
    FAMILY CRISES
    SEPARATION FROM THE FAMILY
    PREDOMINANCE OF FAMILY CONSIDERATIONS OVER WORK
    DEMANDS
  The Groups at Work
    NEGATIVE CONSEQUENCES ASSOCIATED WITH GROUP COHESION
    INEFFECTIVE MANAGEMENT
    INAPPROPRIATE MANAGERIAL STANDARDS AND CRITERIA
  The Company
    INSUFFICIENT ORGANIZATIONAL ACTION
    PLACEMENT ERROR
    ORGANIZATIONAL OVERPERMISSIVENESS
    EXCESSIVE SPAN OF CONTROL
    INAPPROPRIATE ORGANIZATIONAL STANDARDS AND CRITERIA

The preceding chapters of this part have dealt with a variety of functional input-output mediators, all of which are directed primarily toward the achievement of productivity and profit goals. These have been classified to differentiate between mediators that attempt to improve upon the quality of the original human input, mediators that are intended to maximize motivation relative to role requirements, and mediators that work toward an essentially hygienic function in that they serve to prevent output disruption from occurring. One further type of mediator remains to be discussed. An individual may in fact perform below the level of his initial promise, even to the point where a sizable disparity between role behavior and role prescriptions exists; he may fail to perform satisfactorily in one or more respects. At this point, concern tends to focus on the process of performance control and on mediators that may serve a corrective function.

The discussion that follows will first take up certain details of this control model in its application to human performance. A subsequent section will deal with the factors that may cause an individual to perform in an ineffective manner. Finally, the various mediators that may be used for corrective purposes will be considered. Special attention will be given to such approaches as moving the employee to another job, modifying existing personnel policy, discipline, counseling, and medical treatment.

THE CONTROL MODEL AND HUMAN PERFORMANCE

Procedures used to correct performance deficiencies are best understood when viewed in the context of the control model. This model serves to focus attention on those cases where some deviation from an established standard occurs. With regard to performance, this refers to the employee whose work behavior departs from role prescriptions so markedly that it falls below a minimum acceptable level. In specific instances of clear-cut ineffective performance, some type of corrective procedure is needed if the employee is to make any sizable contribution to company goal attainment. Thus, the process of performance control involves identifying individuals whose work is consistently below standard and taking action to restore performance to an acceptable level. In its major characteristics, it is essentially comparable to production control, quality control, inventory control, and cost control.

Establishing Standards

Minimum acceptable standards are established using a variety of performance indexes of the kind discussed in Chapters 8 and 9. Any type of appraisal or evaluation variable may be used, with the proviso that it should be related to organizational goal attainment.

The minimum acceptable level on each of the performance indexes, or criteria, may be established in either of two ways. The most common practice is for the immediate superior to set standards in his own mind on a judgmental basis. Under such circumstances, the minimum acceptable level of performance may vary somewhat from manager to manager and even at different points in time with the same manager. A second approach that avoids this difficulty involves a more objective standard-setting process carried out by some group, such as industrial engineering, on a company-wide basis. Unfortunately, however, suitable objective measures of the latter kind are not always available.

Performance standards, whether established judgmentally or in a more objective manner, relate to both the productivity and the organizational maintenance goals, although it is common practice for the former to be stressed. Thus, the greatest concern tends to be with the quantity and quality of output. Other important considerations are the extent of absenteeism, impact on the work of others, contribution to internal stress and conflict, and dishonest behavior.

Performance Analysis

In areas other than personnel management, the control concept has often been applied without giving detailed attention to determining the specific cause of the deviation from standard (17). The major concerns have tended to be with (a) establishing the standard, (b) measuring the deviation, and (c) setting up a feedback mechanism or some similar procedure to correct the deviation.

When the control model is applied in the personnel area, however, it becomes clear that corrective procedures cannot be effective unless information is available regarding the _causal_ factors that have operated to produce the performance failure. The situation is essentially comparable to that which exists in medicine. A physician must make a suitable diagnosis, which identifies the _cause_ of the failure to meet acceptable health standards, before he can select from among the numerous available treatments. He needs to know what specific disease entity he is dealing with. Otherwise, his treatment will be on a trial-and-error basis, and the chances for cure will be small.

Performance analysis is the name given to the process of identifying contributory causes, of diagnosing the factors that have combined to produce a given instance of performance failure (18). Basically what is involved is that a series of hypotheses are formulated regarding the possible strategic factors. Each hypothesis is then checked against what is known about the individual and either accepted or rejected. The result is a list of contributory causes that can serve to guide the selection of an appropriate corrective procedure.

Firing as an All-purpose Solution

As indicated in Chapter 10, selection procedures cannot achieve perfection. There inevitably will be some individuals hired who either immediately or at some subsequent date will fail to perform effectively. Thus, although a judicious use of selection techniques can reduce the incidence of performance failure, the problem will still remain. Performance control cannot be entirely circumvented by concentrating on achieving a high quality of input to the organization.

One other possibility does remain, however. Could not all those who become ineffective be immediately fired, thus eliminating any need for time-consuming and costly procedures such as performance analyses and corrective actions? The answer is that although firing is always a possibility, it has become hedged with so many constraints, both internal and external to the organization, that it is often not really feasible (9). In addition, it can well be as costly as taking corrective action. Thus, it must be considered a last resort in most cases.

Pressure against firing tends to be exerted because company payments toward unemployment compensation are based on an experience-rating procedure that penalizes a firm for high involuntary turnover rates. Furthermore, a number of companies have policies requiring severance payments to individuals who are separated against their will subsequent to an initial probationary period.

If there is a possibility that the dismissal represents an unfair labor practice, in that the firing occurred because of union activity, a firm may have to reinstate with back pay. This can be ordered by a Labor Relations Board or by the courts. Even if the company wins such a case, the investment in time and money is likely to be sizable. Similar considerations apply where there is a possibility of discrimination on the basis of race, religion, national origin, sex, or age. In any event, formal grievances are nearly always filed in discharge cases, and in many instances these require outside arbitration.

Strikes in response to a firing that is considered unfair are frequent in firms that do not have a clause incorporated in the union contract that bars such work stoppages. Even where a no-strike agreement does apply over the period of the agreement, slowdowns and other types of retaliatory action may occur. The only solution to these varied union pressures may be eventual reinstatement.

Internal pressures against firing need not, of course, be mediated through the union. Individuals or groups of employees may consider a discharge inequitable and take action to make things difficult for the responsible manager or retaliate against the company in some way. Even where a manager does not view such an eventuality as likely, he may hesitate to fire because of the enmity his action might create or because he himself would feel guilty were he to discharge the individual. Especially in the case of long-service employees, strong social pressures against firing are characteristic in the business world generally.

Externally, there is always the possibility that a company that frequently resorts to discharge may create an image for itself in the community that severely restricts the available labor market. The number and quality of applicants may be sharply curtailed, and recruiting costs may rise considerably. In some instances, too, antagonism toward the company resulting from a high discharge rate may influence the sale of products and other types of business dealings. Thus, both the product and the labor markets may suffer.

Finally, there are all the costs associated with personnel turnover of any kind:

1. The cost of recruiting and selecting a replacement.
2. The cost of training a replacement.
3. The costs associated with overpayment of the replacement during the period of learning, when he cannot produce at full capacity.
4. The cost of breakage and waste during the learning period and of any accidents that may occur.
5. The cost of any overtime work put in by others during the period be-

tween firing one employee and the achievement of full capacity by another.

6. The cost of production losses because of the lack of a worker to perform the job between firing and replacement, plus the similar costs attributable to the process of achieving an adjustment between the work group and its new member.

7. The costs resulting from a failure to fully utilize equipment during the replacement's training period.

Taken as a whole, this rather imposing array of factors exerts a strong pressure for performance control rather than discharge. Certainly, firing is not an impossibility, but it is often a last resort. As an all-purpose solution to ineffective performance, it is clearly inappropriate. As a solution when corrective action is known to be either impossible or inexpedient, it seems preferable to letting the employee stay on indefinitely while remaining entirely unsatisfactory.

A SCHEMA FOR PERFORMANCE ANALYSIS

Intensive study of cases where performance failures have occurred has resulted in the development of several schemata that cover at least the great majority of the factors that may prove strategic (19). The elements of such a schema may be treated as hypotheses that should be considered either implicitly or explicitly in the process of performance analysis or, to use the medical term, diagnosis. Each hypothesis is checked against all available information and either confirmed or rejected.

The number of confirmed hypotheses or strategic factors that will emerge from this process varies considerably from case to case. Job failure is rarely a result of a single cause. Usually, the number of contributory factors runs to something like four, but in an occasional instance it can be as high as seven or eight. People fail because, with their own particular pattern of abilities and personality characteristics, they become enmeshed in a specific constellation of circumstances. The problem is to spell out exactly which among these individual and environmental factors have in fact played a causal role.

Intelligence and Job Knowledge
INSUFFICIENT VERBAL ABILITY

The higher up in the job hierarchy a position is located, the greater its demand in terms of verbal ability or general intelligence. Given this circumstance, it is not surprising that on occasion people attain a level where the role requirements are intellectually beyond them. At such times, failure is likely to be reflected in a high incidence of errors and incorrect decisions.

The available evidence suggests that underplacement on the basis of verbal ability is not generally a problem. At least, it seems clear that a great many people work in jobs that demand much less intellectually than they could give (16). Yet under certain circumstances, especially where advancement opportunities are severely restricted, underplacement can be a source of difficulty, although usually in interaction with certain personality factors.

INSUFFICIENT SPECIAL ABILITY

Various jobs, irrespective of their level in the hierarchy, require widely differing types of intellectual abilities. Numerical, spatial, mechanical, clerical, and other abilities are relevant for some types of work and not for others. To the extent an individual lacks whatever such abilities may be required, he is likely to fail through an inability to think effectively and learn rapidly. Having abilities that are not utilized in a job constitutes less of a problem, unless the desire to use the ability is particularly strong.

INSUFFICIENT JOB KNOWLEDGE

Insufficient job knowledge cannot be attributed to lack of ability. The individual has the intellectual capacity to learn the job, but either because of inadequate training or for some other reason, he has not done so. In some instances, the difficulty stems from a lack of any real desire to take advantage of learning opportunities or from emotional blocks to learning.

DEFECT OF JUDGMENT OR MEMORY

In most cases, defects of judgment or memory reflect the interference of emotional factors with intellectual processes. On standard intelligence tests, the individual may score quite high, but when it comes to applying his intelligence on the job, the results are not as good. Defects of this kind are particularly frequent among those suffering from some type of emotional disorder, but they can also result from a disturbance in brain functioning, such as might occur as a result of a head injury.

Emotions and Emotional Illness
FREQUENT DISRUPTIVE EMOTION

As noted, emotions can serve to disrupt intellectual functioning to produce defects of judgment and memory. They can also, if intense enough and frequent enough, have a detrimental impact on many other aspects of job behavior. This is particularly true of negative emotional states, such as anxiety and fear, depression, shame, and guilt. But failure can also occur as a result of persistent anger, jealousy, and excitement. The individual need not be emotionally ill for a severe impact on the level of work performance to manifest itself. The result may be a number of errors, an inability to concentrate so that output is slowed, a tendency to be constantly immersed in controversy, or, and this is perhaps most frequent, a continuing avoidance of many required job behaviors.

PSYCHOSIS

Psychoses, like the neuroses to be discussed next, manifest themselves in a variety of symptoms that take on an inflexible character and serve to disrupt many of the ongoing processes of life. In a psychosis, the preoccupation with symptoms, emotions, and the warding off of unpleasant feelings becomes so intense that a real break with reality occurs, at least at certain times and under certain circumstances. Symptoms vary from incessant emotional states to disorders of physical functioning, to pathological behavior and speech, and even to extreme distortions of perception and belief. Although the various psychotic conditions represent relatively rare phenomena insofar as the work environment is concerned, their impact on performance is generally marked. Often, the individual cannot continue work at all while in the psychotic state.

NEUROSIS

The neuroses, although milder in their impact on the personality, may on occasion have just as detrimental an effect on work performance as psychoses. This appears to depend to a considerable extent on the job level, however.

True emotional health is found much more frequently at the higher occupational levels (18). In lower-level positions of a repetitive nature, symptoms of emotional disorder, primarily those associated with neuroses, are much more common, and in these particular jobs, the detrimental effects appear to be minimal. Thus, in such positions it cannot be presumed that if a neurosis is present, it will account for any ineffective performance that may appear. At higher levels, on the other hand, neuroses are typically quite disruptive. Whether the high incidence of poor mental health in low-level factory positions is primarily attributable to the impact of the routine work on the individual or to the fact that the emotionally ill gravitate to such jobs remains an open question. There is evidence for both views. In any event, it seems clear that people *can* be overplaced emotionally, as well as intellectually. In addition, it is apparent that given an appropriate job placement, even those who have suffered from quite severe emotional problems can recover sufficiently to perform satisfactorily (5).

ALCOHOL AND DRUG PROBLEMS

Alcoholism has been recognized as a major problem by many employers for a number of years. Because of drinking on the job, hangovers, and anxiety, alcoholics often turn out poor work. However, the major impact is in the area of absenteeism, where rates two to three times those of other employees are typical (18). In part, but only in part, these high absence rates are a function of accidents and physical disorders resulting from the alcoholic state. The overall effects on performance are most pronounced where there is a definite dependence on alcohol accompanied by the craving, loss of control, and withdrawal symptoms that indicate a true physical addiction. In cases of this kind, performance tends to deteriorate gradually to the point where employment is no longer possible.

In contrast to alcoholism, drug abuse is a relatively new concern for most companies, and adequate policies and programs in the area are a rarity. However, there is an increasing awareness of the problem, and a greater tendency to emphasize treatment upon identification, rather than immediate discharge, is emerging (26). Heavy use of any of the drugs currently in vogue, such as marijuana, amphetamines, the hallucinogens, and opiates, appears to have negative consequences insofar as employment is concerned. People under the influence of the drugs while at work can be expected to suffer performance decrements (15). In addition, certain physical disorders have been found to result from drug use, and where the drugs are very expensive and addictive, as with heroin, there is a sizable risk of theft.

Individual Motivation to Work
STRONG MOTIVES FRUSTRATED AT WORK

Probably the most common type of motivationally caused performance failure is the case where an individual wants something very much from his job and is unable to attain it. Among the things desired that seem to be important in this sense are success, the avoidance of all failure, domination of others, popularity, social interaction, attention, emotional support, and freedom from any anxiety that may have become associated with certain job aspects. When such motives are frustrated, the individual may leave his job, may stay on but make practically no effort, may become sullen and angry, or may attempt to achieve what he wants through behavior that is antithetical to effective job performance.

UNINTEGRATED MEANS TO SATISFY MOTIVES

Workers who resort to behavior that is not job-integrated may not actually experience any frustration of a strong motive at work. Many people almost immediately develop an approach to a new job that permits motive satisfaction, but at the expense of fulfilling role requirements. A secretary who desires social interaction may make friends rapidly and spend most of her time talking to others, to the detriment of their performance and her own. Similarly, theft and other forms of dishonesty may represent a rapid route to the goal of success.

EXCESSIVELY LOW PERSONAL WORK STANDARDS

Another possibility in the area of motivation involves the individual who sets very low work standards for himself, standards well below those considered minimally acceptable either by his superior or in the company as a whole. Individuals who have such low standards tend to be poor workers.

Apparently, they achieve a sense of personal success and accomplishment with a degree of effort far below that actually required.

GENERALIZED LOW WORK MOTIVATION

These are individuals whose motivational systems are so structured that their important desires tend to be satisfied outside the work situation, or at least through behavior that is not intended within the role prescriptions for any job. In such cases, there is practically no mesh between the individual and the world of work at all, and as a consequence the quantity, and perhaps quality also, of output will be low, quite irrespective of the position held.

Physical Characteristics and Disorders
PHYSICAL ILLNESS OR HANDICAP

The major avenue through which physical disorders contribute to ineffective performance is absence from the job, although quantity and quality of output may also be affected. And there may even be an increase in uncooperative, conflict-producing behavior, such as occurs with certain kinds of brain disorder. Handicapped employees have generally proved as competent as other workers if their handicaps do not bar working at all, but in some instances certain disabilities may contribute to failure in specific jobs. There are things that the deaf, the blind, those with heart conditions, epileptics, and other handicapped people just cannot do effectively. In general, performance failure is somewhat less likely among the physically handicapped than among the emotionally disturbed or the mentally retarded (28).

PHYSICAL DISORDERS OF EMOTIONAL ORIGIN

A number of physical symptoms, such as headaches, fainting, ulcers, high blood pressure, hay fever, backache, and skin disorders, may be caused by emotional factors. When this is the case, the symptoms and the work disruption are identical to those that would exist if no emotional element were present; only the causation is different. Yet, to select an appropriate corrective action, disorders of this kind must be differentiated from those due entirely to physical illness or handicap.

INAPPROPRIATE PHYSICAL CHARACTERISTICS

Inappropriate physical characteristics are the features of bodily proportion and aesthetics that although not widely significant may become strategic in certain jobs. A large person may have difficulty working in a cramped space, as may a small man in a truck cab with the seat far removed from the controls, or an unattractive woman in a modeling position. Many physical characteristics are less important today, what with the advent of human engineering and the consequent emphasis on designing equipment to fit the human operator, but these factors can become crucial at times.

INSUFFICIENT MUSCULAR OR SENSORY ABILITY OR SKILL

A variety of muscular dexterities and abilities, as well as the purely intellectual abilities, may influence job performance. Where there is a deficiency in some ability of this kind that is required by the job, ineffectiveness can result. Strength and physical dexterities do appear to have decreasing relevance as automation advances, but they still can be a factor in failure on some jobs. Defects and deficiencies of vision and hearing also remain a significant source of problems in many cases. Competence in driving a truck, for instance, is strongly influenced by such sensory abilities.

Family Ties
FAMILY CRISES

There are a number of significant events occurring in the home environment that can have an impact on the personality of certain individuals that is sufficient to disturb work performance. Among these are desertion, divorce, threatened divorce, illness of a family member, death, or criminal prosecution. Normally, these effects are transitory, but on occasion the performance decrement is maintained for a considerable period. Unfortunately, such crises do not always come to the attention of a personnel manager, and as a result, the frequency with which they are strategic may be markedly underestimated.

SEPARATION FROM THE FAMILY

The mere fact of extended separation from either the parental family or a spouse and children can produce a very intense homesickness in some individuals. Business trips, temporary assignments out of town, management-development programs at universities, and the like induce considerable anxiety in some people, especially those who have rarely been away from home before. The result can be a severe disruption of performance during the period of absence, with frequent errors, poor decisions, and difficult interpersonal relationships.

PREDOMINANCE OF FAMILY CONSIDERATIONS OVER WORK DEMANDS

In contrast to the family crises, there are factors that do not represent a threat to the family's unity or survival. Yet they can, and frequently do, have a considerable impact on performance. A demanding spouse can require so much of the other marital partner's time that little is left for work. Or a wife may become disturbed at leaving her home town, or going to a foreign country, and impose a severe burden on her husband as a result. Certain family situations are little short of chaos, and some carryover into the work situation is inevitable. Competition between father and son or wife and husband may well produce emotional reactions that permeate the job.

The Groups at Work
NEGATIVE CONSEQUENCES ASSOCIATED WITH GROUP COHESION

Restriction of output within a cohesive group can yield a low level of production that is, nevertheless, socially sanctioned. Although it is common to observe a generally centralizing tendency among group members when restriction occurs, it is also true that some individuals may be forced below the minimum acceptable level of output by the restricted standard. These are typically low producers who are incapable of gauging their work sufficiently well to remain above the unacceptable level when a low group standard is established.

Also, groups with a marked sense of cohesiveness or belongingness can reject members whom they believe to be deviant. Although such ostracism may have no effect on some people, it is extremely threatening to others. The result can be intense anxiety or anger that constantly disrupts work.

INEFFECTIVE MANAGEMENT

Varying managerial styles can influence performance in different ways (17). Managers who are extremely inconsiderate of subordinates, and those who fail to establish and enforce standards may well have low-producing groups. Laissez-faire managing, where very little if any supervising occurs, is particularly detrimental. It is also apparent that these styles can contribute to the ineffective performance of specific subordinates. It is not at all uncommon for supervisory action to conflict with subordinate personality patterns and as a result actually produce failure, even where just the opposite result is desired.

INAPPROPRIATE MANAGERIAL STANDARDS AND CRITERIA

As previously indicated, the criteria on which subordinates are judged are usually set by their superiors, as are the performance standards used to determine effectiveness. In certain cases, these may be established without any reference to organizational goals. Thus, failure may be embedded in the evaluative process rather than in the individual. Because of supervisory biases, standards may be set at an unrealistically high level. Or the criteria employed may be totally irrelevant to role prescriptions and the company's goals. In such instances, the failure may be by definition only. This is one of the few cases where only one factor may be strategic.

The Company
INSUFFICIENT ORGANIZATIONAL ACTION

Job failure may occur or be perpetuated because the company does not take the kind of corrective action required. Medical treatment, training, and the like simply may not be provided, either intentionally or through some oversight. In either case, the lack of action on the part of the company or its representatives in the personnel area can become strategic.

The decision not to invest in corrective action may be based on various considerations. The cost may be too high. The time required to restore effective performance may be too long, as with certain kinds of education and training. The chances of success, if the best available type of corrective action is applied, may be far from good. This is true, for instance, of psychotherapy with certain kinds of emotional disorders. Finally, potentially effective replacements may be readily available, so that any sizable investment in correction that may be required seems to be unwise.

PLACEMENT ERROR

Placement error probably appears in more cases than any other. It is particularly prevalent where random assignment policies, seniority, or union pressures govern the placement process, and where there is accordingly little effort to put individuals with known characteristics in appropriate jobs. If intellectual, emotional, motivational, or physical factors are strategic, there is nearly always a placement error.

ORGANIZATIONAL OVERPERMISSIVENESS

On occasion, a company will operate under such lax and permissive personnel policies and procedures that employees are actually encouraged not to work. When circumstances of this kind exist, individuals with certain types of motivational patterns may become ineffective as a result.

A company may, for instance, encourage insubordination through a lack of discipline. Excessive training, far beyond that required for complete learning, can foster a feeling that actual on-the-job production is unimportant. Liberal sick-leave policies can result in excessive absenteeism (10). In all these cases, there is a deficiency in organizational action of a kind that interacts with individual motives to produce job failure in specific employees.

EXCESSIVE SPAN OF CONTROL

In some cases, a manager may fail to deal effectively with a particular subordinate and thus contribute to a performance failure, not because of any inadequacy in himself as a manager, but because there simply is not sufficient time. The number of individuals supervised, the span of control, may be so great that the manager cannot deal with his subordinates as individuals, carrying out performance analyses and the like. Here the deficiency is not in the manager, and thus a group factor is not strategic. Rather, the organizational structure has been established in such a way as to preclude effective action by a superior aimed at preventing performance failure.

INAPPROPRIATE ORGANIZATIONAL STANDARDS AND CRITERIA

Inappropriate organizational standards and criteria are the counterparts of the inappropriate managerial standards and criteria category discussed under the work group heading. In this instance, however, the focus is on standards set as a result of organizational policy or high-level decisions, rather than on those established by individual superiors.

Society and Its Values
APPLICATION OF LEGAL SANCTIONS

"Application of legal sanctions" is introduced to cover those cases in which an individual is unable to perform his job duties because he has committed a crime and been sent to jail. Under such circumstances, societal values are strategic, in the sense that they form the base on which the legal structure is erected.

ENFORCEMENT OF SOCIETAL VALUES BY MEANS OTHER THAN THE LAW

Although society obtains compliance with its values in large part through the agency of the legal process and police action, it is also true that pressure may be exerted outside the law. Thus, a salesman may fail because no one will buy from' him after he has committed some act that his potential customers consider unethical or immoral. In cases of this kind, it is the enforcement of the societal value structure that produces the ineffective performance, but the source of enforcement is not connected with the legal process.

CONFLICT BETWEEN JOB DEMANDS AND CULTURAL VALUES

The most frequent type of strategic factor involving societal values is the situation in which an individual holds strong convictions that are in conflict with the role prescriptions for his job. Intense commitments to equity and fair play, to individual freedom, and to morality can contribute to job failure, even though all are highly valued in the society as a whole. It is not uncommon for industrial scientists, for instance, with a strong belief in freedom of inquiry to become incensed at the restrictions of a bureaucratic organization. Similarly salesmen with a particularly strong sense of honesty may fail because they view the behavior required of them on the job as basically dishonest.

The Work Context and the Work Itself
NEGATIVE CONSEQUENCES OF ECONOMIC FORCES

Negative consequences of economic forces usually occur in conjunction with an emotional or motivational factor. Competing firms, or economic conditions generally, operate to produce a situation in which an employee cannot achieve at a level consistent with his standards. As a result, he becomes emotionally distressed, and eventually his performance does not even come up to what could realistically be expected under the existing circumstances. Problems of this kind are particularly common among salesmen who are assigned to economically depressed territories or who face sharp price cutting by competitors.

NEGATIVE CONSEQUENCES OF GEOGRAPHIC LOCATION

A similar type of reaction may occur as a result of being forced to work in an inappropriate geographic location. Being sent to a foreign country is very disturbing to some individuals because of the strangeness of the world and people around them. This reaction may be totally unrelated to the fact of separation from loved ones at home. Some people experience debilitating physical symptoms in certain climates, and a sailor who is prone to seasickness may well never achieve a satisfactory performance level when he is at sea. In all such cases, something associated with the geographic location of the work makes effective performance impossible.

DETRIMENTAL CONDITIONS IN THE WORK SETTING

Many of the environmental forces impinging on an individual on the job derive from the various groups of which he is a member—his family, the work group, the company, society. Others derive from aspects of the work context (24). Already noted are other economic organizations and the geographic location. Equally effective as situational forces are the physical characteristics of the actual working environment—the noise level, the amount and type of illumination, the temperature, and various aspects of the design of the work place or the equipment in it. To the extent this working environment contains features that do not mesh with the physical capacities and characteristics of the individual, or on occasion with his intellectual, emotional, or motivational makeup, it can contribute markedly to employee performance failure.

EXCESSIVE DANGER

One aspect of the physical work context that appears to be sufficiently important to warrant separate attention is the danger level. The preceding chapter dealt with this topic at some length. A work environment with a high built-in accident potential can contribute to excessive absenteeism. It can elicit anxiety, too, and thus interfere with output.

It is also true that an individual may read much more danger into a situation than actually exists. Fears associated with heights, airplanes, closed places, and the like are common. Almost any aspect of the work context can serve to produce such reactions in certain people. And when this happens, the individual experiences emotions comparable to those aroused under really dangerous conditions. Subjective danger situations of this kind stimulate sufficient anxiety in some instances to make any work effort impossible.

In other cases, the emotion serves only to distract, producing errors and reduced output.

PROBLEMS IN THE WORK ITSELF

People may fail because of the basic nature of the work itself. In these cases, individual characteristics are involved and so too may be the way jobs are designed and people assigned to them. But above and beyond this is a residual factor represented by the nature of the overall work to be done. This work may be divided in many ways, but there is still a set "something" that has to be accomplished that is inherent in the task goal and that varies from the health care of a hospital to the sales processes of a retail store. This factor is a function of the nature of the organization, but at the level of the individual, it is the nature of the work itself, and this work can be inherently antithetical to effective performance for certain people.

Role of the Industrial Clinical Psychologist in Performance Analysis

It should be apparent that precise answers to the questions posed by the preceding schema for performance analysis can be obtained only when there is considerable information available regarding the individual. The more that is known about an employee, the better the performance analysis. In large part, the required information can be obtained by observing behavior on the job and by talking to the employee and others who know him or her. This any competent manager can do, although training can make for greater effectiveness in this regard (2).

There is, however, another source of data that normally requires extensive psychological training to utilize effectively. A battery of psychological tests combined with an intensive clinical interview can provide much information. However, to use these tools well requires a background in personality theory and considerable knowledge of various psychological tests. Projective measures are particularly helpful, but using them effectively in connection with a performance analysis is a complex task. Normally, work at the graduate level in personnel management, industrial psychology, and clinical psychology is required. Such an industrial clinical psychologist can make a major contribution in carrying out difficult performance analyses, where the strategic factors are numerous and complexly interrelated. Even in somewhat simpler cases, a psychological evaluation can expedite the finding of a solution.

CORRECTIVE PROCEDURES

A number of the input-output mediators discussed in preceding chapters may be used as corrective procedures to restore effective performance in a person who has failed. Because applications of these mediators in the area of performance control were not noted previously, it seems appropriate to do so now. Subsequent sections will then take up corrective techniques that have a more specific connection with the performance control process.

One obvious approach is to redesign the job so that it more closely approximates the individual's capabilities. Thus, through the processes of organization planning and job analysis, new role prescriptions may be established to fit the intellectual, physical, or personality characteristics of a specific person. Behaviors that the individual finds difficult or impossible are no longer required; new behaviors that are within his repertoire are introduced. This is feasible, of course, only within certain limits. Beyond these, transfer to a new position is usually more appropriate.

In addition to this application of structural mediators, a number of the functional mediators, discussed previously may be used as corrective procedures. Thus, management development and training may serve to overcome knowledge lacks, to change an individual's motivation relative to job requirements, and to introduce new skills of a physical nature. Furthermore, management development as applied to the ineffective individual's immediate superior may so change the superior that he becomes capable of restoring effective performance in his subordinate. In this way, management development is used to improve the leadership environment.

When motivation is strategic, alterations in the payment process may prove useful. Shifting an employee from salary to a partial or total incentive may arouse appropriate motivation. In other instances, the security of a guaranteed salary may be what is needed. In general, where motivational problems are present, and pay is known to be a relevant factor, providing an opportunity to earn more money in return for effective job-integrated behavior appears to be an appropriate solution. For instance, various systems for rewarding attendance financially have proved valuable in reducing excessive absenteeism (21).

Transfer, Promotion, and Demotion

The changing of an employee from one position to another may occur for a number of reasons (8). It may be that, owing to shifts in technology, new product lines, or a reorganization, certain jobs must be eliminated. Expanded or contracted operations almost always involve numerous job changes. The process of *bumping*, whereby individuals with greater seniority move down to lower-level positions when layoffs are required, is commonly provided for in union contracts. Reassignments for training and development purposes are also widespread. Thus, moving a person into a new position is not merely a way of correcting performance deficiencies, although this is a common consideration.

When such a change of job is carried out, it may be done to overcome the impact of almost any type of strategic factor. The important thing is that the new position have role prescriptions that the individual can meet. Thus, in the intellectual area, a demotion is usually required if the employee has been overplaced on verbal ability, but a lateral transfer will normally be sufficient to overcome deficiencies in other abilities. Jobs with emotional, motivational, and physical requirements that are more appropriate to the individual can often be located. When separation from the family is a problem, this can be corrected by transferring the employee to a job in which separation is not necessary. A more suitable work group or type of supervision can be achieved through reassignment. So, too, can a value climate better fitted to the individual, or a more appropriate working context.

The only strategic factors that cannot under any circumstances be overcome by placement changes are some in the company, or organizational, category. In these cases, the causal process continues to operate irrespective of the particular job, because it reflects company-wide policies or philosophies as applied to all positions.

In actual practice, however, placement change is not the all-purpose corrective action it appears to be. Most firms, especially the smaller ones, do not have enough kinds of positions available to permit the transfer of all their ineffective workers to more appropriate jobs. Thus, the potential value of reassignment as a corrective procedure is limited by the kinds of openings that can be found in any given company.

TRANSFER

Strictly speaking, a transfer involves shifting an individual to another job at the same grade level, as determined by job evaluation. In some companies, such shifts are relatively easy to accomplish, if they appear to provide an adequate means of improving performance. In other cases, they are so restricted by seniority provisions, supervisory prerogatives, and craft demarcations that there is little a personnel manager can do, even when he is sure he has a potential solution to a particular failure situation. In any event, it is important that supervisors not be permitted to foist their unsatisfactory workers on unsuspecting colleagues without reference to performance considerations. A transfer will achieve a corrective purpose only if there is good reason to believe the person will succeed in the new position. In general, transfer is most easily accomplished and appears to work best in a remedial sense when the person is in an entry-level, early career position, and when there is a clear alternative in which his or her capabilities can be used (19).

PROMOTION

It may seem strange to consider promotion as a solution to problems of performance failure, yet in clear-cut cases of underplacement, where an employee is strongly motivated to do the things a higher position requires and perhaps also to achieve the status that goes with such a job, promotion can work. On the other hand, where the employee seems hesitant about moving up in the job hierarchy, promotion is normally not a good solution.

In handling any promotion, there is always the problem of the unsuccessful candidates. This difficulty is accentuated in cases in which an employee who is failing in his current job is to be the one selected. Organizational maintenance considerations may, in fact, weigh so heavily that promotion cannot be applied as a solution even though it is clearly appropriate on all other grounds. If the employee can be promoted into a different work unit, this may help to minimize conflict. Certainly the crucial consideration is that he actually make good. Promoting a poor performer who then merely continues to fail will inevitably create long-term dissension and feelings of inequity.

DEMOTION

Moving an employee to a lower-level position is a more common solution to performance deficiency than promotion. It is most appropriate when there has been overplacement either on intellectual or emotional grounds. At such times, resistance to the change is likely to be minimal if the employee has actually experienced failure in his current position over a continuing period. In fact, in the writer's experience, actual requests for demotion under such circumstances are not at all uncommon. Even when the employee does resist, this reaction is normally short-lived if he is able to perform satisfactorily on the new job and achieves a sense of freedom from the anxieties associated with failure. Should this not be the case, however, continued and often vociferous resistance can be expected. The demotion solution must achieve its goal in order to be effective.

Personnel Policy Modification

Policies are formulated to apply to all employees of a company or, on occasion, to certain clearly defined groups. They limit the discretion of individual managers by serving as commands when certain indicated circumstances arise. They provide decision-making criteria, so that consistency of action can be maintained across the company, and thus they obviate the need for frequent repetition of an extended decision-making process. In this sense, they foster economy of time and effort. In some cases, they represent abstractions or generalizations that are in fact retrospective recognitions of existing decision guides. But in other cases, policies are a means to establishing new role prescriptions and thus a source of organizational change.

Yet a policy can contribute to ineffective performance, either because it is poorly thought out and formulated or because in a given instance it happens to have a negative impact on a specific individual (4). In the former case, policy modification means changing the policy or perhaps eliminating it. When this is done, it may be possible to carry out actions with regard to an employee in areas such as placement, discipline, payment, training, and the like, that were not previously possible. In company-caused instances of failure where transfer, promotion, or demotion are inappropriate as solutions because all jobs are affected equally by a policy, modification of this kind may be the only answer.

Changing or eliminating a policy is not an easy task, and at times it is clearly not desirable. An appropriate alternative may be to modify the policy only in the sense of permitting an exception. Such an exception can allow for the solution of a relatively unique instance of ineffective performance while leaving the overall policy structure intact. In general, exceptions to policy should be kept to a minimum and sanctioned only at the highest levels. They should be recorded in writing, so that if a number of exceptions are required in the same area, this fact can be ascertained, and a basis for policy revision provided (25).

The sources from which personnel policies emerge, and thus the points at which modifications can be made, vary considerably. Many firms have high-level personnel policy committees; others subsume this function under a general management committee. In some cases, policy emerges from the decisions of individual executives, usually those with specific responsibilities in a particular policy area. The result of this approach can be a lack of integration among the policies applied to different personnel problems. Some chief executives attempt to overcome this failure of coordination by making the personnel policies themselves, or at least by exerting a strong influence on the policy-making process. In some instances an ad hoc approach predominates. Companies that operate in this manner attempt to distill policy out of the decisions of the past, using various records, minutes of meetings, and memoranda. Whatever the approach, it is important that procedures for obtaining feedback on the effects of a policy at lower levels be introduced and that provision be made for modification either through permanent revision or special exception.

Threat, Punishment, and Disciplinary Action

One type of corrective action that may be applied in instances where motivational factors are strategic is the use of managerial power either to threaten or actually invoke sanctions against an individual. In this way, motivation appropriate to job role prescriptions may be aroused and effective behavior restored. This approach is particularly useful when standards of conduct or productivity are low, and new standards must be introduced. Unfortunately, however, threat and discipline are often applied in cases where the failure is not due to motivational causes that can be corrected in this manner. At such times, where the performance analysis has been faulty or nonexistent, the use of punishment may do more harm than good.

A resort to negative sanctions in an effort to restore effective performance may take one of two courses, although in any given case both may be invoked eventually. One approach is for a supervisor or personnel representative to demand improved performance and couple this demand with a threat of future managerial action if improvement does not occur. The threat may be implicit or explicit, but the entire process is relatively informal and does not usually involve any written statement or record.

FORMAL DISCIPLINARY ACTION

The alternative to this is a formal disciplinary action carried out in the manner specified by company rules or in the union contract. In many instances, this results in an appeal through the grievance machinery. Actions of this kind are normally recorded in writing and become a part of the individual's personnel file. The entire approach is strongly legalistic, especially when a union is involved (3).

Disciplinary actions take varying forms, depending on the nature and frequency of the behavior defined as ineffective. Tables 18–1 and 18–2 contain data on the severity of the punishments applied to various offenses, and

Table 18–1. Types of Offenses Causing Disciplinary Action in Order of Perceived Severity

Actions most frequently causing discharge on *first* offense
  Theft
  Falsifying employment application
  Possession of narcotics
  Willful damage to company property
  Possession of firearms or other weapons
  Falsifying work records
  Fighting
  Outside criminal activities
  Failure to report injuries
  Unauthorized strike activity
  Subversive activity
  Punching another employee's time card
  Intoxication at work
Actions most frequently causing discharge only after *second* offense
  Sleeping on the job
  Abusive or threatening language to supervision
  Insubordination
  Gambling
Actions most frequently causing discharge only after *third* offense
  Horseplay
  Unauthorized soliciting
  Leaving without permission
  Failure to use safety devices
  Smoking in unauthorized places
  Slowdown of production
Actions most frequently causing discharge only after *fourth* offense
  Carelessness
  Chronic absenteeism
  Unexcused absence
  Unexcused/excessive lateness

Source: Adapted from Bureau of National Affairs, Inc., *Employee Conduct and Discipline*, Personnel Policies Forum Survey No. 102, August 1973, p. 6.

Table 18–2. Typical Progressions of Disciplinary Actions for Various Sample Offenses

Type of Offense	First Offense	Second Offense	Third Offense	Fourth Offense
Unexcused absence	Warning	Warning	Suspension	Discharge
Unauthorized soliciting	Warning	Suspension	Discharge	
Theft	Discharge			
Carelessness	Warning	Warning	Suspension	Discharge
Sleeping on the job	Warning	Discharge		
Insubordination	Warning	Discharge		
Leaving without permission	Warning	Suspension	Discharge	
Slowdown of production	Warning	Suspension	Discharge	
Willful damage to company property	Discharge			
Unexcused/ excessive lateness	Warning	Warning	Suspension	Discharge

Source: Adapted from Bureau of National Affairs, Inc., *Employee Conduct and Discipline*, Personnel Policies Forum Survey No. 102, August 1973, p. 6.

on the sequence of punishments for different offenses when they are repeated, derived from a survey of 160 companies (6). The general sequence of warning, suspension, and discharge for successive infractions appears to be widely accepted.

At one time, it was common practice to insert an expanded table similar to Table 18–2 directly into the union contract, specifying the required penalty for each type of violation. At present, the tendency is to vary the penalty somewhat, depending on circumstances, and to leave the basic contract open on these matters; supplementary agreements at the local level are common, and plant or shop rules normally go into the specifics of disciplinary action. Usually, there is at least a reference in the master contract to management's right to apply discipline for *just cause.* The implication is that there must be grounds for the action in the employee's behavior, and that the punishment should be appropriate to the violation. In actual practice, supervisors do not resort to disciplinary actions nearly as often as they could in view of the actual infractions that occur (27). This may be due to a recognition that discipline is not an appropriate corrective procedure in many cases, but it may also reflect a fear of employee retaliation or the anticipation that support for the action will not be forthcoming at higher managerial levels. Whatever the reason, it is very clear that first-level supervisors are relatively unlikely to resort to severe discipline as compared to other managers; top management actually favors discipline the most (23).

The mildest of the formal disciplinary actions is an official warning. This is prepared in writing and signed by the employee, usually in the presence of a union representative. If the employee does not sign, the case goes immediately into the grievance procedure.

Disciplinary layoff, or suspension without pay, for varying periods is a common practice. Most companies do not normally suspend in this manner for more than a week, but longer periods are utilized on occasion. This is the most extreme type of discipline available to management short of discharge. And discharge is not a corrective action, but an admission of failure.

Demotion may also be used in a disciplinary sense, although this is relatively rare. The question of whether the employee will do any better on the new lower-level job than he did on the old one must be considered, and the answer is often negative. Temporary demotions with an understanding that good performance would result in the employee's being restored to his old position could be used, but these are difficult to administer in the legalistic context that has come to surround the disciplinary process.

THE EFFECTIVENESS OF DISCIPLINE

It is clear that different circumstances surrounding the offense tend to elicit discipline in varying degrees (22). What is not so clear is how effective discipline usually is.

The most consistently positive evidence comes from the area of absence control. Spot checks at home by visiting nurses can prove useful in uncovering and correcting sick-leave abuses (12). Studies have also demonstrated the value of formal discipline in holding down absenteeism (1).

Another approach to the evaluation of discipline as a corrective procedure has been to follow the performance of individuals who were discharged for disciplinary reasons and then reinstated by an arbitrator on appeal. Do people who have had such an experience improve after it?

Although among employees suffering from emotional problems the impact has been minimal, studies dealing with individuals whose discharges resulted from a much greater variety of causes produced results more favorable to the disciplinary approach (14). Very few were discharged a second time, and most maintained at least minimally satisfactory performance levels. It is apparent from this research that discipline can work, although not with everyone. Among those with whom it often does not work are employees whose problems involve addiction and, as indicated in Chapter 17, those who frequently violate safety rules.

Personnel and Psychological Counseling

The history of counseling in industry began with a department established in the Ford Motor Company in 1914 to advise employees on personal affairs and to assist them with health, legal, and family problems. The approach was strongly directive and permeated with Henry Ford's own personal philosophies. The result was considerable employee resistance and an eventual abandoning of the program. Similar large-scale efforts have been initiated in a number of firms, most notably the Western Electric Company, where counseling was introduced as an aspect of the Hawthorne studies. In almost every instance, these comprehensive programs have failed to survive over an extended period.

In recent years, industrial counseling has tended to focus more on specific types of employee problems, has involved the industrial clinical psychologist to a much greater extent, and has been more widely viewed as a corrective procedure for ineffective performance than as a means of increasing employee satisfaction or dealing with nonjob problems. Under these conditions, limited-scale programs have prospered and appear to have made sizable contributions to the productivity goal. It is now recognized that the needs of an individual and the goals of an organization may well be in conflict, and that for this reason certain kinds of counseling activities should usually be performed outside the employment context (11).

COUNSELING TECHNIQUE

Although in dealing with some types of problems a counselor must of necessity be somewhat directive, in that questions must be answered and information conveyed, the general approach in industry where emotional or motivational factors are strategic has been to stress *nondirective counseling*. Under the nondirective approach, the employee is encouraged to express his feelings, to gain an understanding of himself, and eventually to solve his own problems. The counselor listens and occasionally reformulates what the employee has said to permit greater understanding of the true emotional meaning of certain words. The counselor may also repeat certain phrases or sentences to stimulate the employee to continue and to lead him to concentrate on certain topics.

In the business context, counseling of this kind tends to focus on matters of performance and on social relationships at work, although family and other considerations may be treated if they subsequently prove relevant. Recently, an emphasis on career planning and guidance designed to correct inappropriate occupational choices has been added (13). Often, the counselor serves as an upward communication channel between the employee and the organization, correcting distorted communications and misunderstandings. The emphasis is on working out relatively mild problems that may be blocking performance effectiveness (20). More severe emotional disorders are normally referred to a psychotherapist working outside the company. If the problem appears to require more than perhaps 10 or 15 one-hour sessions, the employee is almost invariably advised to seek help on a private basis. Some firms, in fact, reject all internal adjustment counseling of this type, on the grounds that such matters are the sole responsibility of the individual. A recent survey indicated that only about 45 per cent of the companies made provision for counseling on job-related problems (7).

EXECUTIVE COUNSELING

At the higher managerial levels, counseling is usually carried out by an outside psychological consultant rather than a professional on the regular company staff. Although in some instances this counseling represents an attempt to cope with a performance failure, it is also true that many top-level managers are emotionally alone and thus in real need of someone with whom they can discuss problems. Under these circumstances, an industrial clinical psychologist may continue to counsel an executive at intervals over an extended period of time. The approach, in contrast to that of a regular management consultant, tends to be nondirective, with the executive increasingly learning to understand himself and the motives behind his actions.

RETIREMENT COUNSELING

In general, retirement counseling is intended to prepare employees for retirement, although on occasion it may be directed toward the rehabilitation of older workers whose performance has fallen off sharply with the approach of retirement. The counseling tends to be rather directive, emphasizing information on pension plans and other benefits. The counselors usually do not have psychological training. Counseling of this kind may be initiated as much as five years before the anticipated date of separation, and it appears that such early initiation is a desirable procedure (8).

Medical and Psychiatric Treatment

As indicated in the preceding chapter, medical treatment is not likely to be a major aspect of the industrial physician's job. Companies are much more prone to invest in selection through the physical examination and in preventive measures. Thus, although medical treatment is the major corrective procedure in cases where physical illness disrupts performance, this treatment does not represent a specific personnel management function. It is performed outside the company.

Similarly, psychiatric treatment for psychoses and neuroses is usually not provided by the company, although some firms do have psychiatrists on the regular staff. In certain instances, however, a company will take an active role in arranging for the treatment of a high-level executive and will pay all bills incurred. Also, there are companies that maintain special facilities for the treatment of alcoholics or contribute to the support of such facilities. It is not at all uncommon for a firm to maintain a close liaison with a local

Alcoholics Anonymous chapter and to arrange for a representative of that organization to be constantly available to assist employees.

PRODUCTIVITY MEDIATORS AND PERSONNEL STRATEGY

Of the three major types of productivity-oriented mediators, those of an input-improving nature can be expected to be the most expensive to utilize. A strategy that emphasizes job analysis and organization planning, coupled with extensive training and development and a compensation system having real incentive value, is a very costly matter. It requires a full-range output emphasis as well, since pay must be closely linked to organizational contribution. Normally, such a strategy would not be combined with an input emphasis, since it would then become redundant in many respects. The choice of an input-improving strategy insofar as productivity goals are concerned is often an alternative to the input-oriented approach, which is adopted because recruiting and selection do not appear to be working effectively to produce a truly competent labor force. Rather than increase the input investment further, a decision is made to shift to an emphasis on input-improving mediators.

Input-sustaining mediators are less expensive to utilize, because they do not attempt to do as much. Training is limited to necessary retraining and updating; much of it is on the job. Compensation levels are set with a close eye to the market, the main consideration being to ward off extensive turnover. Preventive programs in the health and safety areas are an important component of the strategy, since the major objective is to keep people on the job and working. Such an approach cannot hope to yield high levels of productivity—unless, and this is an important qualification, the individuals involved are already highly qualified and have strong internal motivation. This, of course, is what a really effective input emphasis should provide.

Input-controlling mediators are less costly than those of an input-improving nature for reasons differing considerably from those that operate in the case of input-sustaining mediators. In the latter instance, the effort is merely tuned down, so that less is attempted. With an input-controlling emphasis, the effort may well be just as strong as with improving mediators, but the saving is achieved by applying it to a much smaller segment of the applicable group—the individuals who are failing.

It is, of course, possible to use all three types of mediators to foster productivity goal attainment. Moreover, to the extent an input-improving strategy is implemented effectively, it should reduce the need for input-sustaining and -controlling approaches in many areas. Just as selection cannot obviate performance failure, neither can an input-improving emphasis, but it can reduce ineffective performance. Thus, staffing to provide many types of corrective actions should be less necessary. To the extent corrective procedures are needed, they often can be secured on an outside basis.

QUESTIONS

1. Describe an instance of job or scholastic failure that you have observed. Using the schema for performance analysis as a checklist, see if you can identify the various key factors contributing to this particular failure.
2. Should a first-line supervisor be able to fire a worker as he or she desires? Discuss with reference to legal, company, and societal ramifications.
3. Companies have established priorities with regard to discipline, just as nations have in their legal systems. What considerations appear to underlie these priorities? How do you feel about the punishments applied to different company offenses?
4. There are sharp differences between companies with regard to how they feel about the matter of employee counseling. Why should these disparities exist? What do the disparities imply about company goal orientations and attitudes toward the individual?
5. It is contended that an industrial clinical psychologist can make a significant contribution in performance analysis. Looking at the schema presented, in what areas would you expect this contribution to be the greatest?

REFERENCES

1. Baum, J. F., and S. A. Youngblood. "Impact of an Organizational Control Policy on Absenteeism, Performance, and Satisfaction." *Journal of Applied Psychology*, 60 (1975), 688–694.
2. Belasco, J. A., and H. M. Trice. *The Assessment of Change in Training and Therapy*. New York: McGraw-Hill Book Company, 1969.
3. Black, J. M. *Positive Discipline*. New York: American Management Association, Inc., 1970.
4. Brown, D. R. "Do Personnel Policies Alienate Employees?" *Personnel Administration*, 33 (1970), No. 1, 29–37.
5. Burden, C. A., and R. Faulk. "The Employment Process for Rehabilitants: Two Studies of the Hiring of Emotional Rehabilitants." *Personnel Journal*, 54 (1975), 529–531, 548.
6. Bureau of National Affairs, Inc. *Employee Conduct and Discipline*. Personnel Policies Forum Survey No. 102, August 1973.
7. Bureau of National Affairs, Inc. *Employee Performance: Evaluation and Control*. Personnel Policies Forum Survey No. 108, February 1975.
8. Conner, R. D., and R. L. Fjerstad. "Internal Personnel Maintenance," in D. Yoder and H. G. Heneman, *Staffing Policies and Strategies*. Washington, D.C.: Bureau of National Affairs, Inc., 1974, pp. 4:203–243.
9. Fisher, R. W. "When Workers Are Discharged—An Overview." *Monthly Labor Review*, 96 (1973), No. 6, 4–17.
10. Heneghan, M., and S. G. Ginsburg. "Use of Sick Leave." *Personnel Administration*, 33 (1970), No. 4, 46–50.

11. Hunt, R. G. *Interpersonal Strategies for System Management: Applications of Counseling and Participative Principles.* Monterey, Calif.: Brooks/Cole Publishing Co., 1974.

12. Johnson, E. H. "Control of Sick Leave." *Personnel Administration,* 32 (1969), No. 1, 35–39.

13. Korman, A., and R. Tanofsky. "Organizational Counseling: A Research-based Approach." *Personnel Journal,* 54 (1975), 25–26, 49, 68.

14. McDermott, T. J., and T. H. Newhams. "Discharge-Reinstatement: What Happens Thereafter." *Industrial and Labor Relations Review,* 24 (1971), 526–540.

15. McGlothin, W. H. "Drug Use and Abuse." *Annual Review of Psychology,* 26 (1975), 45–64.

16. Miner, J. B. *Intelligence in the United States.* Westport, Conn.: Greenwood Press, Inc., 1973.

17. Miner, J. B. *The Management Process: Theory, Research, and Practice.* New York: Macmillan Publishing Co., Inc., 1973.

18. Miner, J. B. *The Challenge of Managing.* Philadelphia: W. B. Saunders Company, 1975.

19. Miner, J. B., and J. F. Brewer. "The Management of Ineffective Performance," in M. D. Dunnette (ed.), *Handbook of Industrial and Organizational Psychology.* Chicago: Rand McNally & Company, 1976.

20. Noland, R. L. *Industrial Mental Health and Employee Counselling.* New York: Behavioral Publications, 1973.

21. Nord, W. "Improving Attendance Through Rewards." *Personnel Administration,* 33 (1970), No. 6, 37–41.

22. Rosen, B., and T. H. Jerdee. "Factors Influencing Disciplinary Judgments." *Journal of Applied Psychology,* 59 (1974), 327–331.

23. Shaak, P. C., and M. M. Schwartz. "Uniformity of Policy Interpretation Among Managers in the Utility Industry." *Academy of Management Journal,* 16 (1973), 77–83.

24. Steele, F. I. *Physical Settings and Organization Development.* Reading, Mass.: Addison-Wesley Publishing Co., Inc., 1973.

25. Steiner, G. A., and J. B. Miner. *Organizational Policy and Strategy.* New York: Macmillan Publishing Co., Inc., 1976.

26. Ward, H. *Employment and Addiction: Overview of Issues.* Washington, D.C.: Drug Abuse Council, Inc., 1973.

27. Wohlking, W. "Effective Discipline in Employee Relations." *Personnel Journal,* 54 (1975), 489–493, 500.

28. Wright, G. N., and A. B. Trotter. *Rehabilitation Research.* Madison, Wis.: University of Wisconsin, 1968.

VI INPUT-OUTPUT MEDIATORS: TECHNIQUES FOSTERING ORGANIZATIONAL MAINTENANCE

19 *Approaches in Labor Relations*

The area with the greatest potential for stress and conflict within business organizations is that of labor relations. Since the 1930s when, with the assistance of favorable legislation, unions first achieved a stable foothold in American industry, personnel management has had a continuing concern with the development of policies and approaches calculated to reduce labor-management conflict. In some instances, these efforts have been devoted to creating a relatively conflict-free relationship with unions already representing groups of employees, and in other cases, to thwarting the organizing attempts of unions desiring to achieve such representation.

The use of the various approaches that attempt to foster organizational maintenance is conditioned by several considerations that should be specified at the outset. For one thing, the goal in this area has normally been not so much to maximize maintenance aspects as to achieve a suitable level, while pursuing productivity and profit to the maximum degree possible. This means that companies do not normally devote their energies to conflict reduction at all costs. It is important, for instance, that management not sign a contract with a union that would impose internal constraints making it impossible to remain competitive in the industry, even if, by doing so, continuing labor peace and high levels of employee satisfaction could be guaranteed. The primary objective, then, in using the approaches to be discussed in Part VI, is to attain the least internal conflict and stress possible while at the same time maintaining maximum control over all aspects of human resources utilization and productivity. Firms that have devoted themselves to internal conflict reduction almost exclusively, without adequate concern for the external realities of the marketplace and a competitive economy, have often committed themselves to give away so much as to make continued survival impossible.

In this chapter, the major focus will be on approaches that have been developed to deal with unions. In subsequent chapters, fringe benefits, such as retirement and health insurance plans, will be discussed, as well as the various employee communications procedures that companies have introduced. All these have as their goal the reduction of employee dissatisfaction and the minimization of conflict within the organization. Only rarely are they directly concerned with increasing productivity and profit.

As it has developed over the past 40 years, the field of labor relations is far too extensive to cover in detail in a text such as this. Almost all universities offer more specialized courses in the area, which concentrate on various aspects of labor relations exclusively. For this reason, the coverage here will be restricted to major problems and concepts, with particular emphasis on some of the more recent developments.

Two important aspects of labor relations have been treated in earlier chapters. The history of the union movement in relation to the evolution of personnel management has been discussed in Chapter 2. Legal constraints on labor relations decisions and the current status of labor legislation were covered in Chapter 5.

THE EXTENT OF UNIONIZATION

As noted in Chapter 1, a personnel manager should be thoroughly familiar with the field of labor relations whether the firm's employees are unionized or not. Although less than a quarter of the nation's total labor force is represented by a union at the present time, a high percentage of the production workers in nearly all the larger and more consequential manufacturing operations are organized. Furthermore, wage rates, working conditions, and fringe benefits gained by the unions at the bargaining table tend to have considerable influence on personnel practices throughout an industry or area of influence—in union and nonunion firms alike.

Then, too, there is the continuing prospect that a union may attempt to organize a segment of a firm or even the total work force. Since the end of World War II, during which the labor movement experienced its most pronounced expansion, many personnel managers have increasingly concentrated on approaches that might improve employee satisfaction and consequently keep the unions at a distance. The effectiveness of these efforts may well account in large part for the slowdown in union growth since the mid-1950s.

As shown in Figure 19–1, union membership increased steadily from the mid-1930s to the mid-1950s, the only major exception being the 1948–1950 recession period. In 1956, union membership in the United States reached 17.5 million, or 24.2 per cent of the total labor force of 69.4 million. From then through the early 1960s, union membership declined to 16.5 million in 1963, when it again began to climb, reaching 19.4 million in 1972. In terms of per cent of the total labor force, however, union membership was higher in 1956; the 1972 union membership represented 21.8 per cent of the 72.8 million labor force (45).

Aside from more effective personnel management, there undoubtedly are a number of other reasons for the relative ineffectiveness of union organizing efforts and the general slowdown in the growth rate. There has, for instance, been a shift away from production employment to white-collar workers, and a larger proportion of the work force are women. Both these groups have traditionally resisted union membership. Second, a number of firms have moved from heavily unionized areas to locations that have characteristically been more opposed to union membership. However, a number of writers have suggested that it is primarily during periods of crisis, such as war or severe economic problems, that union membership experiences rapid growth (17). The upswing in union membership in the late 1960s came during a time of rapidly rising prices, and the wage controls

(a) Membership of national unions.

Excludes Canadian membership but includes members in other areas outside the United States. Members of AFL-CIO directly affiliated local unions are also included. For the years 1948– 1952, midpoints of membership estimates, which were expressed as ranges, were used.

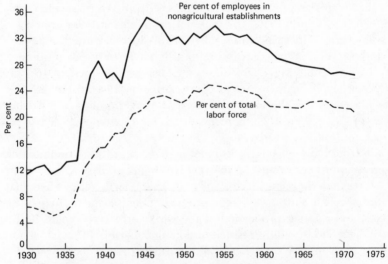

(b) Union membership as a per cent of total labor force and employees in nonagricultural establishments. (Excludes Canadian membership.)

Figure 19–1. Trends In Union Membership, 1930–1972.
Source: Bureau of Labor Statistics, U.S. Department of Labor, *Directory of National and International Labor Unions in the United States, 1972* (Washington, D.C.: Bureau of Labor Statistics, 1974), pp. 71, 72.

program of the early 1970s triggered another spurt in union organizing success, especially among white-collar groups (35).

FACTORS RELATED TO A UNION'S CONFLICT POTENTIAL

There seems little question that the preferred approach to organizational maintenance insofar as labor relations are concerned has beeen to keep the unions out, if at all possible. And personnel managers have devoted, and still are devoting, considerable effort toward just this end. The reason is that any situation involving a union represents a potential source of internal conflict. The mere presence of the union restricts management's freedom of action in many areas.

Although American labor unions have traditionally shown little interest in assuming a managerial role in the firms with which they deal, their goals are clearly antithetical in many ways to those of the companies. Not only do the unions seek to win higher wages and fringe benefits, thus cutting into profits, but they also attempt to ensure that all employees are treated on the same basis in such matters as work scheduling, promotions, discipline, and the like. In the absence of a union, these matters can be handled in terms of the individual and his particular capabilities. The unions argue, however, that the individual has relatively little power, if he has any at all, in dealing with the business firm when management acts in an arbitrary or inequitable manner. Thus, an employee will fare much better with the collective power of the union membership behind him.

It is, in fact, this collective power of the membership that provides the unions with their real strength in dealing with the management of a single firm; it is also the basis for the political strength of the labor movement as a whole. But there are other factors contributing to the strength, and thus to the conflict potential, inherent in a specific union in a particular situation. These factors are related to the nature of the union itself.

The Nature of the Union and Its Power

In what follows, an attempt will be made to identify some of the ways in which unions may be categorized, especially as these relate to matters of union power. Thus, the discussion will take up the various types of unions, the matter of affiliation, and certain other aspects of union membership, as well as differences in style of union leadership.

TYPES OF UNIONS

Most unions may be classified as *craft* or *industrial*, depending largely on the kind of workers making up the membership. The earliest labor organizations were of the craft type, with the members almost entirely restricted to workmen within a single job skill, such as carpentry or bricklaying. The original American Federation of Labor (AFL) was an affiliation of these craft groups.

Industrial unions, such as the United Auto Workers and the United Steelworkers, tend to include in their memberships only workers of a given industry and do so whether the employees are skilled, semiskilled, or unskilled. These are the unions that disaffiliated from the AFL in the mid-1930s and formed the Congress of Industrial Organizations (CIO). Actually, however, some of the traditional craft unions have organized plants on an industrial basis also; the Machinists Union, for instance, represents all workers in a number of factories, particularly in the aircraft industry.

It is primarily in the building trades that the craft unions still operate in their original form. Because they often work for many employers for relatively short periods of time, the members of these crafts tend to look to their unions for assurances that they will be hired for the specific skill required, that skills will be acquired through appropriate apprentice training, and that high wage rates plus fringe benefits will be maintained. Industrial unions, on the other hand, are more likely to be as concerned about matters related to job security, such as seniority and grievance procedures, as they are about wages and fringe benefits. This is not surprising in view of the more stable nature of their members' employment relationships and their lower average skill levels, which make unemployment a realistic threat.

A third type of union that has emerged in recent years is the *professional union*, which encompasses groups such as scientists, engineers, and teachers. These groups tend to be particularly concerned with preserving professional status as related to such matters as salary and the special privileges of the profession.

AFFILIATION

The majority of all local unions are associated with a national or international union, which is in turn affiliated with AFL-CIO. The latter organization was formed when the two major components of the labor movement merged in 1955. Of the more than 19 million union members in the United States in 1972, about 15 million belonged to AFL-CIO affiliates. Another 4.2 million belonged to national unions not affiliated with the AFL-CIO. These latter include several that were expelled from the AFL-CIO for various reasons—notably the Teamsters, whose membership of nearly 2 million is the largest of any single union in the United States. Other unions with sizable memberships include the United Auto Workers and the Steelworkers, each with almost $1\frac{1}{2}$ million, the International Brotherhood of Electrical Workers, with 957,000, the Carpenters, with 820,000, and the Machinists, with 750,000 (45).

A very small proportion of union members belong to unaffiliated local unions, usually an independent group limited to the employees of a single company. In a number of cases, these unions began as company-sponsored employee associations. This pattern is particularly prevalent in the petroleum industry. The Bureau of Labor Statistics does not include these unions in its standard estimates of union membership, and for this reason these groups are not represented in the statistics cited previously.

The affiliation of an employee group can have a sizable effect on its strength. Nearly all the national unions have large funds available for strike benefits, and they can provide a variety of full-time staff members to aid in organizing efforts, in negotiating contracts, and in handling grievance or arbitration procedures. At the same time, a national organization can exert considerable control through the threat of withholding these benefits and services, if the local membership acts in a manner inconsistent with its desires.

ADDITIONAL FACTORS

Although the type and affiliation of the union are perhaps the most significant factors contributing to conflict potential and influencing the issues over which conflict is likely to be joined, there are other factors more closely tied to the local plant situation. A newly organized union often has considerable power in dealing with management, especially if the workers have given the union overwhelming support in the representation election. Where the union has been in the plant for some time and has gained much of its membership through a union shop agreement, which forces new employees to join, the potentiality for concerted action may be less. Workers who become union members and pay dues voluntarily may give their leaders greater support than those who are required to join as a condition of employment.

A second factor is whether the union represents all or only a segment of the firm's nonmanagement employees. If all the production, maintenance, and perhaps white-collar workers are represented, this gives a union considerable power, because the threat of a strike implies a total shutdown. For the same reason, representing the employees in several plants of a multiplant company also tends to buttress union power. The total potential impact on the firm is greater.

On the other hand, there are situations in which a relatively small union group within a plant can achieve a degree of strength entirely out of proportion to its size. This happens if the location of the group in relation to the production process is particularly strategic, as with a small maintenance unit represented by a craft union, or if the group is able to utilize the allegiances of other workers in support of its demands.

DIFFERENCES IN UNION LEADERSHIP

The conflict potential, and the power, inherent in a given union is also influenced by the nature and the position of its leadership. In some cases, a labor leader will have the rank and file solidly behind him—in which case he may have considerable power, but little need to exhibit it. In other cases, the leadership may be less secure in its position. At such times, a militant membership can force a union leader into actions that are clearly inappropriate, but that he must take to maintain his position in the union. Or a leader may take a belligerent attitude toward management merely to demonstrate to the rank and file that he is standing up for their rights. At such times, he may be well aware that his position is untenable on economic or other grounds. Under such circumstances, it is often difficult for management to assess the true strength of the leadership in relation to the internal "political" situation in the union itself. Such an assessment becomes crucial when management must make decisions in the face of a strike threat.

Environmental Factors and Industrial Conflict

The potential for conflict varies considerably from firm to firm, from area to area, and from one point in time to another. Although the relative strengths of company and union do represent important determining factors, there are other considerations. Some of these are set forth in Table 19–1, which is based on an extensive study of collective bargaining relationships involving parties of relatively equal strength (28). There are indications that some of these factors may have changed since this study was published; recent research, for example, has found that strikes were more frequent in medium-sized plants than in plants with less than five hundred or more than one thousand employees (10). However, it can be assumed that many of the factors still are relevant, particularly those involving the community and political environment of the parties. Clearly, many of the circumstances noted are beyond the control of personnel management.

Figures on union membership provide some indication of where "union towns," as noted in Table 19–1, would be likely to predominate. More than one-half of all the union members in the United States reside in six states— New York, California, Pennsylvania, Illinois, Ohio, and Michigan. Unionized work forces are most characteristic in the Northeast, the Great Lakes region, and the Far West. In the Southeast and the Great Plains areas, a relatively small proportion of the labor force is represented by a labor organization.

In addition to these geographical differentials, there are others associated with the particular industry. In 1972, about 60 per cent of manufacturing employment was unionized, one-fourth of nonmanufacturing, and one-fifth of government (45).

THE UNIONIZATION PROCESS

Historically, labor-management conflict has been most acute during union organizing efforts. Management typically has used every available weapon to avoid the necessity of bargaining over wages, conditions of employment, and the like. With the passage of the Wagner Act in 1935, however, many

Table 19–1. *Environmental Factors* and Industrial Peace†*

Factors	Frequently Favorable Circumstances	Frequently Unfavorable Circumstances
Industrial environment		
1. Size of plant and company	Medium-sized company	Industrial giant
2. Production pattern	Steady	Seasonal; intermittent; production crises
3. Technological advance	Moderate	Severe
4. Nature of the jobs	Skilled; responsible	Assembly line type
5. Cost factors	Inframarginal plant	Marginal plant
6. Market factors	Expanding; cyclically insensitive; inelastic demand	Contracting; sensitive to cycle; elastic demand
7. Locational factors	Relatively immobile plant	Relatively mobile plant
Community environment		
1. The work force	Steady; tractable	Inconstant; combative
2. The plant and the labor	Metropolitan area	One-industry town
3. Local wage levels	Low-wage community and high-wage industry	Low-wage industry and high-wage community
4. Industrial climate	"Union town"	"Open shop town"
"Political" environment of the parties		
1. The union	Secure union; secure leaders; homogeneous membership; local autonomy; pattern following	Insecure union; insecure leaders; heterogeneous membership; external domination; pattern setting
2. The employer	Pattern following; in employers' association; local autonomy in noncontractual matters	Pattern setting; lone bargainer; strong central domination of local plant
Time as an environmental factor	Origins in peaceful period; old relationship	Origins in warlike period; new relationship

Source: C. Kerr, "The Collective Bargaining Environment," in C. S. Golden and V. D. Parker, eds., *Causes of Industrial Peace Under Collective Bargaining* (New York: Harper, 1955), p. 22.
* The full range of environmental conditions is not set forth in this table, which presents only conditions that appear to relate to the prospects for industrial peace.
† Reference is made here to "industrial peace" developed by parties of relatively equal strength, not arrived at because of domination by one side or government.

antiunion tactics were barred, and as a result it became increasingly difficult to deal with this threat to organizational maintenance through exclusion.

Yet there are many companies that have been able to avoid unionization entirely, or at least in some of their facilities. Most of these firms have faced repeated organizing attempts, and in spite of the slowdown in such union efforts during the 1960s, they can no doubt anticipate many more. A number of the unions representing production workers are seeking to extend their influence to white-collar groups, and there have been some concerted drives aimed at certain traditionally nonunion areas and industries. A related type of conflict involves the situation in which an established local union is either weak or considered to be weak, and another union attempts to establish its jurisdiction over the same employee unit. There are also cases where two or more unions may attempt to organize the same group. In these latter instances, where interunion conflict is added to that between labor and management, the internal stress on an organization may become considerable.

Motives in Union Membership

A large proportion of new members presently join unions automatically because it is required under a union shop contract as a condition of employment. Undoubtedly, many of these workers give relatively little thought to this action, especially if they were raised in a prounion environment. In the past, however, such automatic membership was uncommon, and it is not always the case today, especially where employees select a new union as their bargaining agent. Under such voluntary conditions, it seems apparent that union membership can provide for the satisfaction of important motives.

Over the years, scholars have advanced numerous theories of union membership. The earlier theories were predicated primarily on economic grounds. The assumption was that, as individuals, workers are at the mercy of their employers, particularly in times of job scarcity. Only by joining forces and forming a union can workers achieve the power to force an employer to provide fair wages and adequate working conditions. Furthermore, under prosperous economic conditions, when profits are high, the union's power in collective bargaining can give the workers a means of obtaining what they consider to be a fair share.

More recently, however, investigators have found that the desire for economic gain may not be the primary factor in union membership. A variety of social and psychological needs are satisfied as well. The union can provide a worker with a sense of security, perhaps some status, a feeling of independence in relation to his employer, and the satisfactions of group membership. Even in a well-managed firm that pays good wages and offers ideal working conditions, union membership may have considerable appeal solely because it frees the employees from a sense of being dependent on their employer. This is particularly likely to be the case when the union is well established and has achieved some status in the community.

It is generally conceded that the employees most likely to be susceptible to union organizing appeals are those who are dissatisfied. This dissatisfaction may relate to wage rates, to the lack of available channels for complaints regarding unfair treatment, and to many other things. Thus, dissatisfaction may be primarily economic in nature, but it may also be associated with a variety of social or psychological considerations. In many instances, employees are not really aware of the true sources of their dissatisfaction.

In any event, if through appropriate personnel policies and procedures a company can keep its employees satisfied with their jobs and with management's actions, a union will find it much more difficult to become established. On the other hand, union leaders will almost certainly attempt to capitalize on any signs of dissatisfaction within an employee group they are attempting to organize. It is for this reason that many companies conduct attitude surveys to ascertain the extent and sources of employee discontent, whenever they believe a threat of unionization exists. With such knowledge, it is often possible to blunt the appeals of the union.

Smaller firms generally have been considered to have an advantage over larger companies when it comes to heading off a union organizing effort, on the assumption that employees in small companies are closer to management. However, data on the outcome of union representation elections indicate that this potential advantage often is not realized; the smaller the employee unit involved, the more likely the union is to win the election (38). In units of less than 10 employees, the union won 66 per cent of the elections, whereas in units of 100 employees or more, the union was the victor in 52 per cent. In this particular study, there were relatively small differences in elections won in different regions of the country, but the highest percentage was in the South, which traditionally has been viewed as having a more negative attitude toward unions than other parts of the country.

White-collar Unionization

Many factors involved in the unionization process may be illustrated with reference to the current situation within the white-collar group, which is understood to include office employees, retail store clerks, engineers, teachers, and government employees. (3). Until the mid-1950s, the white-collar workers were consistently a minority of the nation's labor force; since that time, they have outnumbered blue-collar workers. In fact, the gap has been continually widening as automation has reduced the demand for factory employees.

Recognizing this shift in labor force composition as a basic threat to the strength of the labor movement, a number of unions have initiated extensive organizing campaigns within the white-collar sector. Some of these unions are composed entirely of white-collar employees—the Office and Professional Employees, the Retail Clerks, and the Government Employees, for example. In other instances, office workers are represented by an industrial union, such as the United Auto Workers, that also represents the production workers of the same company. Finally, certain unions whose membership was originally restricted to a quite different group have turned their efforts in this direction. Among these, the Teamsters, initially a union of truck drivers, has been especially active.

Initially, these white-collar organizing drives were not spectacularly successful. From 1956 to 1960 there was, in fact, a decline in the number of white-collar union members from 2.5 to 2.2 million, but by 1972 the total had increased to 3.4 million (45). Most of the growth in union membership in the 1960s was in the white-collar unions in retail trade, communications, and public service. The unions have been extremely successful in organizing government white-collar workers over the past 10 years.

There seem to be several factors related to the success or failure of organizing efforts in the white-collar units. One factor would appear to be the structure of the labor movement, with its stress on craft differentials. Even in the industrial unions, some internal structural changes were made to appeal to the white-collar employees. These workers may be organized most effectively by professional associations, such as the National Education Association and the American Nurses Association.

At a more basic level, however, the problem for the unions has related to the attitudes that have traditionally prevailed in the white-collar group. In part, this situation is attributable to the large percentages of women engaged in this type of employment. In the past, the majority of women viewed their work as a short-term matter; they were not career-oriented and thus expected little benefit from the dues they had to pay a union. Furthermore, they viewed unions as essentially male organizations. This conception often was fostered by the unions themselves; little was done to recruit female members except in industries with predominantly women workers. As more women come to think in terms of lifetime careers, it may be expected they will find more reason to become union members. Thus far, however, there is little evidence of such occurrence. While the number of female union members increased during the 1960s, the ratio of women union members to the total number of women in the labor force remained about the same (45).

An additional cause of antiunion attitudes among white-collar workers was the higher status these employees usually enjoyed. Many felt much closer to management than to production workers. Working conditions generally were good, and opportunities for advancement and recognition on an individual basis were frequent. Why should a person join a union when he or she could achieve as much or more without resort to collective action?

As white-collar units in the business world increase in size, however, much of this has changed. Groups of office workers as large as those on production lines, and whose work may be just as routine, have emerged, and in many cases these groups are as far removed from management as their blue-collar counterparts (48). Much of the differential in wages and benefits has been eliminated by union gains, so that many firms now treat their unionized blue-collar and nonunionized white-collar employees alike. In one case, where a union was successful in organizing a group of office workers, the two major reasons for dissatisfaction were the fact that white-collar employees were not given the same pay raises as unionized production workers and the lack of a satisfactory method for handling complaints, such as the grievance procedure provided for union members (21). Where the higher status of the office worker cannot be protected, opportunities for promotion maintained, and provision made for upward communication, the appeal of the union for white-collar employees has increased sharply. Sociological factors, such as the increasing respectability of membership in unions, particularly when they are known as professional employee associations, also point to a continued upsurge in white-collar unionization. Thus, the matter of faculty unionization has become a major issue facing universities (14).

The Union Organizing Drive

The impetus for a union organizing campaign may derive from a group of employees within the company, especially if there has been considerable discontent. Far more frequently, however, the campaign is initiated by a national union as part of an overall effort in the particular industry, or by a union that already represents one segment of the company's work force and desires to extend its jurisdiction into other areas. Usually, a union will attempt to contact individual employees first, emphasizing any known sources of dissatisfaction, such as wage rates or working conditions. After sufficient interest is aroused, the union will hold a mass meeting to discuss the advantages of membership and to solicit signatures in support of union representation.

In most cases, management becomes aware of the organizing effort at an early point, either through the rumor transmission process or because of the appearance of union literature. The actions of management at this point are subject to a number of constraints of a legal nature. The company cannot discriminate on the basis of union activity and cannot interfere with the formation of a labor organization among employees. Under the *free speech* provisions of the Taft-Hartley Act, however, management can communicate with employees regarding an organizing drive as long as threats are not used and rewards are not offered for rejecting the union. A further deterrent to management action was introduced by the Landrum-Griffin Act of 1959, which requires employers to report to the Secretary of Labor all expenditures for outside labor relations consultants who aid management at the time of an organizing drive.

After a union has obtained signed authorization cards from 30 per cent or more of the employees in the company unit it seeks to represent, it can petition the National Labor Relations Board for a representation election. If such an election is held and the union wins a majority of the votes, it is certified as the bargaining agent. It is entirely permissible for the company to recognize a union without such an election if it chooses, but as a practical matter most employers prefer the election, to be certain that the union does have a majority and because after one NLRB election has been held another cannot be scheduled in the same bargaining unit for at least a year. The costs to the employer of an NLRB election can be sizable, however (25). Besides supervising the election, the NLRB also determines the appropriateness of the bargaining unit, should there be a dispute on the matter. This can be a very important consideration. If a particular group of employees is known to be strongly prounion, it is to management's advantage to have them excluded. Similarly, the inclusion of an antiunion segment of the work force may swing the election, so that the organizing effort fails. Thus, attempts to have the bargaining unit defined in favorable terms often represent an important aspect of management strategy in dealing with a union threat to organizational maintenance.

Because similar efforts normally characterize the union approach also, the early stages of an organizing drive may involve numerous petitions and counterpetitions to the NLRB, aimed at obtaining a favorable ruling in this regard. Yet the judgments rendered by the NLRB in such matters are far from arbitrary. Decisions are reached in accordance with certain very definite guidelines related to common employment interests and any previous bargaining history.

Thus, governmental constraints in connection with an organizing effort do not operate entirely on management. Unions are also restricted. This is particularly true with regard to picketing. If a union initiates picketing as part of an organizing campaign, it must petition for an NLRB election within 30 days or cease picketing. After an election has been held, *organizational picketing* is illegal for a year, whether the union has won or lost. When one union has been certified as bargaining representative, other unions may not engage in organizational picketing.

JURISDICTIONAL DISPUTES

Rivalry between two or more unions attempting to represent a group of employees can produce one of the most difficult labor relations problems for management. When jurisdictional disputes of this kind develop, a serious threat to organizational maintenance is posed without management's being in any sense a party to the controversy. Even when an employer clearly prefers to have the employees represented by a particular union, it is illegal to overtly proclaim this preference or to provide support to a particular union.

Jurisdictional problems have plagued the labor movement for decades. When the AFL and CIO merged in 1955, there was some hope that this particular type of difficulty would diminish. Yet it was not until 1962 that a workable plan for handling internal disputes evolved. Since that time, most controversies between unions affiliated with the AFL-CIO have been resolved, although not always before the company involved has experienced considerable internal stress. Disputes with independent unions, particularly the Teamsters, however, became increasingly frequent.

Managerial Attitudes During an Organizing Drive

In terms of organizational maintenance, a union organizing drive can be a devastating experience for a firm. Few companies welcome the presence of a union. After a union wins the right to represent a group of employees, management's authority is challenged, and its freedom to act is restricted in many areas.

Thus, when faced with a union representation election, most managements will do everything possible to keep the union out. In this connection, it is important to refrain from any actions that might be interpreted as interference with a union's rights under the law. If the union loses the election and can claim management interference, the company may be faced with an NLRB unfair labor practices charge, and another election may be ordered. The period of internal strife will be prolonged accordingly, and management may lose employee goodwill to the point where the second election goes against it.

In attempting to avoid legal difficulties and minimize internal stress in the firm, management normally relies upon its own labor relations experts or, in the case of smaller companies, outside consultants. It is important for these individuals to keep all levels of management, from first-line supervision up, fully informed as to what can and cannot be done or said during the organizing drive. There have been many instances when, at such times, uninformed and overzealous managers have done their companies irreparable damage. On the other hand, companies have succeeded in winning NLRB elections through concerted communications efforts at all organizational levels (12).

It is almost always difficult to remain unemotional in the organizing situation. Managers often feel that employees are being ungrateful or disloyal if they even consider a union, especially if the firm is already providing good wages and fringe benefits. Many firms have succeeded in avoiding unionization through effective personnel management, but successes have been most notable in those industries and geographical areas that were the least heavily unionized initially. Thus, there are instances in which the union will almost inevitably achieve its goal. At such times, a personnel manager may find himself shifting from mere personal involvement, which is quite natural under the circumstances, to highly defensive behavior, as the campaign progresses. A union victory may become in his mind clear-cut evidence of his own personal failure to perform effectively.

Yet by doing all it can to minimize tension and avoid feelings of bitterness, management will be in a far better position subsequent to an election. If the union should win and be certified as a bargaining agent, the company is legally bound to negotiate on the terms of employment. This process of collective bargaining is considerably easier if hostile relations and personal animosities built up in the past do not provide a backdrop for the negotiations.

COLLECTIVE BARGAINING

Assuming that excluding the union has either failed as a strategy or has not been attempted in the first place, the next approach to labor-management conflict reduction must be collective bargaining. Although the form such bargaining actually takes is highly variable from situation to situation, its use in some form is required by law, given the fact that a union has been certified as a bargaining agent. Because of this legal constraint, collective bargaining is now the major approach to organizational maintenance in the labor relations area, at least in the United States. Thus, management is required as a matter of public policy to bargain with the union and to do so in "good faith" (9).

This does not mean that management must relinquish its right to direct the company, or that it must accede to union demands. The extent to which a union can persuade a firm to grant its demands depends in large part on the relative power balance between the two parties. After this has been established and an agreement is reached, a contract outlining terms of employment for a specified period of time is prepared and signed.

Approaches to Bargaining

The particular individual or individuals who deal with the union, either in collective bargaining or in day-to-day administration of the contract, vary considerably, depending on the size and complexity of the firm and the extent to which it is unionized. Labor relations may be handled by the personnel manager, the plant manager, or even the company president, in the case of a small company dealing with a single union. On the other hand, a large multiplant corporation bargaining with many unions in several locations may have an entire department staffed with experts in wage and salary administration, insurance and pension planning, contract negotiation, labor law, and the like. A number of these individuals will be located at corporate headquarters, but others may be distributed throughout the firm. In some areas, employer associations staffed in a similar manner handle relations with unions for groups of firms.

THE NEGOTIATING COMMITTEE

A company bargaining committee normally contains anywhere from two to six people, including at least one personnel representative and at least one representative from the line organization. The company president usually retains final authority to accept or reject the agreement reached by his negotiating committee but does not sit in on the bargaining itself. It is common practice for the president to indicate to the committee exactly how far it can go in making concessions. Within the limits thus established, the committee, in effect, has full authority to negotiate a final agreement. Although it is by no means a universal practice, some firms include first-line supervisors and other managers in negotiations on a rotating basis to provide these individuals with a better understanding of union and management viewpoints.

The union bargaining committee tends to be larger and includes some or all of the officers of the local union, one or more shop stewards or specially elected committeemen, and a representative of the national union. Local craft unions employ a full-time *business agent* who acts as the chief negotiator in all bargaining conducted by the local.

Unlike the company bargaining committee, the union negotiators do not have authority to accept a final agreement. When bargaining is initiated, the union committee presents a set of demands originally prepared by the executive board or some similar group in the local. These demands must have the approval of the membership. Similarly, any final agreement must also be ratified by a vote of the membership. In most cases, the union bargaining committee is well aware of what the membership will accept. Thus, the ratification requirement does not constitute a major barrier to settlement. There have been a number of instances, however, in which the membership has rejected a proposed agreement, particularly in situations involving multiplant or industry-wide bargaining, where the negotiators have been top officials of national unions. Apparently, these individuals had difficulty keeping attuned to the sentiments of the rank and file.

The current trend appears to be for larger and larger units to be subsumed under the same bargaining process, either on an area-, industry-, or corporation-wide basis. In the past, the usual union tactic was to concentrate on obtaining a settlement with an industry leader and then to attempt to obtain essentially the same agreement from other firms in the industry. In most cases, these other firms accepted the original pattern rather than suffer a strike and a loss of market position to the leader, who already had a contract. Although such *pattern bargaining* is still common, there are a number of industries in which the leading firms have banded together and now bargain as a single unit, as well as instances where several unions representing different bargaining units of a multiplant corporation coordinate their bargaining on major issues. In addition to such *coordinated bargaining* efforts, which result in separate contracts with common provisions, there also have been situations involving *coalition bargaining*, where two or more unions bargain with an employer for a common master agreement (40).

In most instances of coordinated bargaining, some provision is made for negotiation on local issues. Nevertheless, bargaining of this kind does concentrate power in the hands of the top union officials and serves to reduce the power of the individual employer and of local plant management. It also tends to increase the probability of some kind of governmental intervention in the bargaining process, because a major segment of the economy often is involved.

With the growth in the number and the economic strength of multinational corporations, there has been considerable discussion of the prospects for multinational unions to engage in collective bargaining with these firms (20). One comprehensive case study of the results of a company transferring production from plants in this country to plants overseas indicates that unions are at a severe disadvantage in bargaining with the typical conglomerate multinational firm (5). Because of the barriers involved in such factors as different legal requirements and differences in wage levels in different parts of the world, however, the growth of international unionism has not been material in extent (44).

PREPARATIONS FOR BARGAINING

For many years, the typical approach was for the union to present a series of demands, which the company would subsequently either accept, attempt to modify, or reject outright. Often, a company would await these demands and then formulate a response. In recent years, it has become common practice for a company to spend considerable time and effort preparing for negotiations and even to take the initiative by presenting proposals for contract changes that would be beneficial to management. An extreme version of this approach, in which management presents its proposals on a "take-it-or-leave-it" basis and refuses to change the terms of the initial offer in subsequent bargaining, is called "Boulwarism," after General Electric's former vice-president for employee and public relations, Lemuel Boulware (37). However, this approach as used by GE was found to be a violation of the Taft-Hartley Act.

In determining what, if any, changes might be warranted with regard to wages and fringe benefits, companies tend to utilize survey data on competitive practices in the industry and area. This information may be readily available within the company (see Chapter 16), or special surveys may be conducted for bargaining purposes. To pinpoint sections of the existing contract that may represent sources of difficulty, grievances and arbitration awards are studied; supervisors are polled for suggested changes. Company negotiators are usually provided with information on the company's financial position, on the cost to the company of various changes in wages and fringe benefits, and on the power position of the union.

The union, too, will study wage and other information before entering upon negotiations. All the major unions maintain staffs at national and regional headquarters for the sole purpose of collecting information on recent wage settlements and on changes in the cost of living. In the case of the larger unions that bargain with major segments of an industry, the union demands may be announced publicly well in advance of actual negotiations to gain public support, if possible, or at least to determine the trend of public sentiment.

The Bargaining Relationship

A number of studies have been conducted dealing with various bargaining relationships (8, 30). In general, the emphasis has been on the identification of those types of relationships that are and are not conducive to industrial peace. The definitions of bargaining relationships range from open conflict to containment, accommodation, and cooperation. The most common of these appears to be containment, in which every effort is made to contain the union's power and preserve the rights of management to the extent permissible within the law.

One further relationship that has existed in the past and that no doubt still exists in some localities is one in which management makes certain special arrangements with the union leaders, usually without membership knowledge or approval. The leaders may agree to forego a wage increase in return for a union shop. Where racketeering elements are present, a small employer may agree to sign a contract under threat of being forced out of business. In many of these situations, the union leaders have an inordinate amount of power. It was to correct such abuses that the Landrum-Griffin Act was passed in 1959.

The type of bargaining relationship does not always remain stable. Often, feelings of resentment created during an organizing drive are difficult to erase, and an open conflict relationship may persist for years. Then, with a change in union leadership or management personnel, a more effective approach may evolve. In other cases, a firm may prefer a policy of containment but on occasion work with the union on an accommodation basis for a particular purpose. Joint safety committees established to deal with a sharply rising accident rate represent a case in point. Factors influencing the union may also produce a change in the character of the bargaining relationship. In bad times, when jobs are scarce or when the company is in a precarious competitive position, a union may utilize accommodating or cooperative procedures. In good times, when profits are high and there is full employment, the same union may engage in open conflict.

Irrespective of the overall relationship between a company and a union, it is almost inevitable that conflict will arise during the collective bargaining process itself, simply because the parties have different desires and expectations as regards the final solution. This concept is illustrated in Figure 19-2. In most negotiations each party begins by listing its demands for contract changes. These constitute the desired solution. The demands are normally accompanied by supporting facts and figures. The primary task then becomes one of determining the tolerance limits of the respective parties, thus establishing the bargaining zone (41).

There are a number of problems that characteristically arise and con-

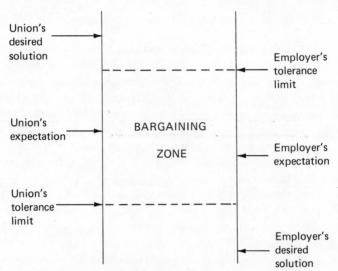

Figure 19–2. Desires, Expectations, and Tolerance Limits That Determine the Bargaining Zone.
Source: From *Psychology of Union-Management Relations* by Ross Stagner and Hjalmar Rosen, p. 96. © 1965 by Wadsworth Publishing Co., Inc., Belmont, Calif. Used by permission.

tribute to conflict. Primarily, these are communications problems resulting from faulty perceptions and differences in the personalities, backgrounds, and motives of the management and union negotiators. Other sources of difficulty are the ritualistic formality of the bargaining situation (which tends to thwart new approaches), the need of both sets of negotiators to convey a favorable impression to their constituencies, and the lack of appropriate support (which may arise on either the management or the union side) (49). One study indicates that a negotiator's personal inclination to settle for a new contract is related to a number of noneconomic factors, such as the nature of interpersonal relationships within the negotiating team (43).

A number of approaches have been suggested and used to minimize bargaining conflicts (2). Sometimes, training programs designed to produce awareness of communications problems can have a positive effect. For example, if company negotiators can recognize when the union leaders are pressing a demand merely to placate the national officers, the vehemence of their counterresponse may well be reduced considerably. Outside consultants sometimes work with both parties along these lines with a view to reducing the incidence of conflict.

The Settlement Process

On occasion, the bargaining relationship is influenced by the intervention of a third, outside, party, either at the request of the other two parties or as a result of direct governmental action. This usually occurs when the negotiations have seemingly failed, and a strike deadline is near. It is common practice for union members to vote a strike authorization to become effective should there be no settlement by a certain date, usually the expiration of the current contract. As the deadline approaches, the union may extend this date should a settlement appear imminent. If this is not the case, the contesting parties may ask for outside help before moving into a strike situation. In actuality, the majority of settlements are achieved without resort to either strike action or outside intervention, but cases of bargaining failure are most likely to achieve mention in the press.

The usual process through which an impartial outside party helps to break a deadlock in negotiations is *mediation* or *conciliation* by a governmental representative. Such a mediator has no power to force a settlement, but he can work with the parties separately to determine their respective positions, explain a position more fully to the opposition, point out bases for agreement that may not have been apparent previously, help in the search for solutions, and generally facilitate the reaching of an agreement. In effect, the mediator acts as a communications catalyst, and his effectiveness depends on his impartiality and on his capacity to win the trust of both parties.

While a number of states have mediation services, the majority of mediators are provided by the Federal Mediation and Conciliation Service, which was established as an independent agency by the Taft-Hartley Act in 1947. Either or both parties can seek the assistance of the FMCS, or the Service can offer help should it feel the situation warrants it. Federal law requires that 60 days prior to the expiration of a contract, any party wishing to change the contract must give notice of this intention to the other party. If no agreement has been reached 30 days prior to the expiration date, the FMCS must be notified. Thus, the FMCS is informed in cases in which strike action seems imminent and is likely to take action on its own if not asked to do so. This is particularly common when large numbers of employees are involved or when the public interest is clearly at stake.

Another related process is *arbitration*, under which unresolved bargaining issues are submitted to an impartial arbitrator or board of arbitrators whose decision is binding on both parties. In practice, arbitration is used primarily in settling grievances that arise under an existing contract, rather than to determine the terms of the contract itself. Very few labor contracts provide for arbitration of contract issues, although in an increasing number of states, arbitration of such issues is compulsory in areas of public interest, government employment, hospitals, and so on (23).

With the growth of union membership and greater emphasis on labor relations in the public sector, a technique called final offer arbitration has been developed for resolving bargaining disputes without resort to a strike. The arbitrator must choose, as the final bargaining settlement, the final position of one of the two parties without modification. The result usually is that each party tries to make its final offer as reasonable as possible (14). Additional experience with this type of arbitration could result in its being adopted more widely in the private sector. Research designed to study the effects of mediation versus arbitration as an intervention in the negotiating situation indicates that the prospect of arbitration in the event of an impasse may lead to greater concessions and more agreement, particularly on the part of the union negotiators (26).

NATIONAL EMERGENCY DISPUTES

Further government intervention in the bargaining process with a view to facilitating a settlement may be initiated by the President in cases in which a threatened strike would "imperil the national health or safety." When this occurs, the Taft-Hartley Act provides for an 80-day postponement of any strike action, during which time a fact-finding board must investigate the dispute and report to the President. The NLRB is to poll the employees as to their willingness to accept the company's last offer. If a majority reject this offer, the President may approach Congress for further authority to deal with the situation.

In the first 20 years of the Taft-Hartley Act, emergency dispute provisions were invoked 28 times, most commonly in the longshoring and defense industries. None of the parties involved appears to have been satisfied with the procedure, and there is almost inevitably a controversy as to whether a particular strike would actually "imperil the national health and safety." To date, however, no acceptable alternative approaches have been advanced (6).

THE LABOR-MANAGEMENT AGREEMENT

The settlement reached in collective bargaining is incorporated in a legal document, a contract. In an earlier period, these contracts were relatively short and dealt almost entirely with hours of work and rates of pay. Over the years, the size of the bargaining arena has expanded. More issues have been included, and more complex settlements reached. Contracts now sometimes run to 50 pages or more, and many companies issue supplementary guides to explain the various provisions.

Another noticeable trend is for contracts to apply over a longer period of time. The standard used to be one year, but by 1960 two-year agreements were most common, and by 1970 nearly two-thirds of the agreements were for three years. Nearly all of these extended contracts provide for a second wage increase at some date during the term of the agreement, usually a year after the initial effective date, or for a reopening of negotiations on wage issues only at a specified time (4).

The longer-term contracts have both pros and cons from the management viewpoint. On the one hand, management can avoid the internal stress of repeated strike threats and can save the time and money associated with yearly negotiating sessions. On the other hand, the buildup of change proposals over several years can be considerable. Thus, the renegotiation process may be much more difficult, and the chances of a strike increased disproportionately. Various approaches have been developed to alleviate this situation and still maintain the longer contract duration. In the basic steel industry, a joint union-management study committee has been established to make recommendations, prior to the start of negotiations on a new contract, regarding provisions that are known to be potentially troublesome.

Management Rights

The question of whether to include a provision in the contract aimed at protecting the basic rights of management has long been a subject for debate. Some companies take the position that because certain rights and responsibilities are inherent in the very process of management, there is no need to spell these out in the agreement. To attempt to do so might actually be restrictive, in that anything not mentioned could be interpreted as outside the exclusive domain of management.

More than two-thirds of union agreements contain a statement on management rights (4). Some of these are very general in nature, on the theory that a more detailed treatment might be restrictive; others list specific areas (sometimes as many as 15 or 20) in which management retains its freedom to act; some even contain such a listing plus a proviso that the items noted are not all-inclusive. The more frequently noted rights in contracts with a detailed statement are those concerning the closing or relocating of facilities, the framing of company rules, the instituting of technological changes, and the determining of employee duties.

On the other hand, most contracts also include a statement to the effect that management has no rights that are in conflict with the terms of the agreement. Thus, there may be explicit restrictions limiting management's freedom to act in such areas as subcontracting, carrying out technological changes, and (in a small percentage of contracts) shutting down or relocating plants. Although most of these provisions do not actually prohibit management from taking action in these areas, they do require prior discussion with the union, the retraining of affected employees, and job guarantees.

In practice, what the contract specifies in the way of management rights may be a moot point. Whether the contract requires it or not, companies frequently do notify the union of job changes, make special arrangements for affected workers when operations are moved or equipment is changed, and otherwise act in accordance with many union expectations. They do so on the theory that these actions will minimize disruptive effects and contribute to organizational maintenance.

Actually, the trend in arbitration awards and court decisions has been toward reinforcing the view that any management decision affecting the employment relationship should be discussed with the union unless such discussion has previously been waived by both parties. The assumption is that in exercising its rights management must take into account the rights that workers have built up over the years as employees. It is in situations in which management has ignored these considerations, usually in connection with subcontracting, plant relocation, or technological change, that union protests have been supported.

Union Security

Just as provisions relating to management rights may be critical from the employer viewpoint, those relating to union security are of paramount importance to the union. After a union has been successful in organizing a group of employees and gaining recognition, union security stipulations in the contract, requiring union membership of all employees in the bargaining unit, provide the best assurance of continued strength. Management generally is opposed to such provisions because they force employees to join or pay dues to the union whether they wish to or not. However, for many years union security was the major noneconomic issue advocated by the unions. Under the threat of strikes and other stresses, many firms agreed to some type of union security. More than 9 out of 10 contracts provide some form of union security (4).

One approach management has used to avoid compulsory union membership is to influence state legislatures to enact "right-to-work" laws, which forbid union shop agreements. Such laws are explicitly condoned in the Taft-Hartley Act. They exist in 20 states at the present time, although most of these are not heavily industrialized. The South and Great Plains are the major areas of the country represented.

Types of Union Security Provisions

The most common form of union security is the *union shop*, under which all employees in the bargaining unit are required to join the union and to maintain membership as a condition of employment. Some agreements permit certain exceptions. Thus, employees who were not members as of the contract's effective date may be allowed to stay out, but all persons hired after the agreement goes into effect are required to join. Provisions of the latter kind are referred to as a *modified union shop*.

Another approach is known as *maintenance-of-membership*. Employees who choose to join the union are required to maintain membership as a condition of employment, but joining the union is not essential. Furthermore, there is usually some provision for an escape period at the time of contract negotiations. At this time, anyone who wishes to resign can do so without losing his job.

The *agency shop* requires employees who do not join the union to pay the union a fee equal to union dues. This type of arrangement came about as a result of union objections to "free riders," who benefited from negotiations without paying dues to support the union. A number of states that forbid compulsory union membership do permit agency shop arrangements.

Other hiring arrangements, including the *closed shop, requiring that only union members be employed*, and the *preferential shop, requiring that union members be given preference in filling job openings, were outlawed by the Taft-Hartley Act* and thus no longer appear in collective bargaining agreements. Nevertheless, some contracts still contain references to union hiring halls and to certain requirements involving apprenticeships, which in effect do give preference to union members.

Most union security provisions are accompanied by the *checkoff*, an arrangement whereby the company agrees to deduct union dues, and sometimes initiation fees and assessments, from the member's paycheck and submit this money to the union. For such provisions to become operative, members must sign an authorization form, which is usually irrevocable for the term of the contract.

REGULATION OF UNION ACTIVITY

Although not classified specifically as union security, many provisions of a related nature may be scattered throughout the contract. These are aimed at regulating various activities of the union on company premises, or at providing special status for union representatives in carrying out the terms of the agreement. Among the former are provisions guaranteeing access to the plant by union representatives who are not company employees (sometimes with the stipulation that there be no interference with production), restrictions on the use of union bulletin boards, bans on membership solicitation or dues collection on company time, and limitations on the number of union representatives who may function within a company facility.

Provisions relating to union representatives may include such things as superseniority in matters of layoff, overtime, transfer, and holiday assignments; leaves of absence for union business; pay for time spent in processing grievances; and in some cases the use of company telephones or office space to conduct union affairs. Increasingly, such provisions are being included in labor contracts. Presumably, companies consider them to be worthwhile in terms of improved union relations and conflict minimization, although implementation of these provisions is often a source of conflict in itself (31, 50).

Job Security

Another matter of importance for the unions is job security. Provisions relating to discipline and discharge are of great significance to the union insofar as job security is concerned. Almost all contracts list grounds for action in this sphere. There are also provisions for such procedures as warnings, notice to the employee and the union, hearings, and appeals.

From the union viewpoint, seniority appears to be the most important aspect of job security. Under most agreements, employees in the bargaining unit are ranked on the basis of seniority for purposes of preferences in promotion, transfer, choice of shift, layoff, and recall from layoff. In some instances, the seniority unit may be limited to a single department, particularly where special skills are involved, but there are plant-wide units as well. As noted in Chapter 9, seniority and merit may carry varying weights in various types of employment decisions.

In years past, when there was the prospect of loss of jobs through technological displacement, unions pushed for a considerable broadening of seniority rights. Thus, in some cases, where a company decided to shut down one of its operations, the union insisted that employees have an option to transfer to another plant on the basis of overall company seniority. If a company decided to transfer an operation to a new location, the union position has often been that the new jobs should be offered to those previously employed at the old plant in terms of seniority. As noted in Chapter 5, in more recent years a matter of concern with regard to seniority is that of the adverse effect on minorities and women in times of large-scale layoffs of the type experienced in the 1974–1975 recession. In many instances, the traditional union view that layoffs should be based strictly on seniority was in direct conflict with the requirements of employers' affirmative action plans.

Wages and Hours

Although wage increases have traditionally been the major economic goal of unions in collective bargaining, most agreements do not include detailed rates and ranges. Generally, any increase negotiated by a union is added to the existing rates on the basis of either a cents-per-hour, across-the-board raise for all, or a percentage raise, with a larger total amount going to the higher-rated job classifications. For many years, the former approach was followed almost exclusively, with the result that pay differentials for skilled work diminished markedly in percentage terms. This became a major source of conflict within the union movement, especially within the industrial unions. Under pressure from the more skilled groups, there has been a gradual shift, so that percentage increases are now more common.

Most contracts that run for more than a year provide for certain automatic wage adjustments. These are sometimes called *improvement factors,* or *productivity increases,* and usually become effective at yearly intervals. *Escalator clauses,* requiring automatic wage adjustments at quarterly intervals on the basis of changes in the cost of living, are found in a small percentage of agreements. Both of these types of automatic wage increase provisions became more popular during the inflationary period of the late 1960s and early 1970s.

The union agreement also usually contains provisions relating to the supplementary wage practices described in Chapter 16 that relate to work performed by those in the bargaining unit and that regulate the hours of work.

Employee Benefits and Services

Any so-called *fringe benefit* that can be considered of economic worth to employees or that influences working conditions is bargainable in a legal sense. Consequently, contracts normally deal at great length with paid vacations, holidays, insurance plans, pensions, and the like. These and other employee benefits will be considered in detail in Chapter 20.

Strikes and Lockouts

More than half of all union contracts contain unconditional no-strike clauses, banning work stoppages during the term of the agreement. Another one-third provide that the union will not strike except under specified conditions, such as exhaustion of the grievance procedure, violation of the contract terms, or failure to enforce an arbitration award. No-strike provisions often include statements to the effect that the union must take positive action against any unauthorized strikes if it is to avoid liability. Also, there are likely to be penalties for individual employees who participate in such unauthorized strikes. Nearly all no-strike clauses are accompanied by a comparable ban against lockouts by the company (4).

Grievances and Arbitration

Nearly every agreement establishes procedures for handling employee complaints and disputes over the interpretation of contract terms. In most cases, these procedures include arbitration of unresolved differences by an impartial third party. Grievance handling is a continuing process and represents the primary source of union-management contacts at times other than when negotiations are in progress. As such, it may easily become embroiled in conflict. Efforts to minimize this eventuality will be considered in the section that follows.

ADMINISTERING THE CONTRACT

The contract provides a backdrop and a guide for day-to-day relations between union and management. But it does not inevitably eliminate conflict in these relations or provide a blueprint for subsequent events in all cases. It is not at all uncommon for a company to give the union a great deal more than it is actually entitled to under the contract. This is an effort to minimize conflict and maintain friendly relations. Situations of this kind are most frequent when the union is new on the scene and the leaders are militant. As the bargaining relationship matures, the trend is for management to reassert its rights under the contract and to insist on stricter enforcement.

In many plants there is considerable informal cooperation between local management and union representatives on a continuing basis. At times, there are even private agreements to ignore major provisions of the contract in the interest of harmonious relations. Although practices of this kind are often helpful at the moment, the long-term result may well be continuing union pressure for informal concessions to the point where productivity goals are seriously imperiled. Thus, the advances in organizational maintenance are achieved at a heavy price. Eventually, as personnel changes occur, administration of the contract may verge on the chaotic.

Under a more formal approach, local plant managers are encouraged to notify top management of any contract provisions that are creating problems so that they may be modified through collective bargaining, rather than subverted on an informal basis. Another aspect of such an approach is for management to act on a unilateral basis, except as consultation with the union is specifically required in the contract. The union may then protest under the grievance process, if it desires. Thus, the grievance machinery, which was originally established to insure equity in handling the complaints of individual employees and to provide a channel for upward communication, is used in addition as a method of interpreting the contract (13). The preponderance of grievances, however, involve disputes relating to employee discipline rather than to contract interpretation (32).

Grievance Procedures

The grievance process is set in motion through the discussion of a complaint by the employee, either alone or in conjunction with the steward, and his immediate supervisor. From there, the complaint is processed through successively higher levels of management and union officials to a point where an outside arbitrator may be called upon to resolve the issue. Settlement may of course occur at any point in this upward movement. The details of the procedure between the first and final steps vary from company to company. As indicated in Figures 19–3 and 19–4, the number of steps tends to be a function of company size.

Besides the number of steps, other differences from company to company concern such matters as time limits at each level, requirements for presenting complaints in writing (usually this is first required at the second step), pay to union representatives for time spent in grievance handling, and personnel responsible for different phases of the total activity. Some procedures call for a joint labor-management grievance committee to meet on a regular weekly or monthly basis.

In nonunion facilities, or for groups of employees not represented by a union, some firms have established procedures that are in many ways com-

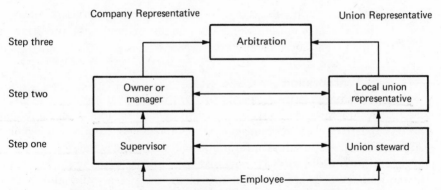

Figure 19–3. Grievance Procedure for a Small Company.

parable to union-negotiated grievance procedures. Some of these utilize higher-level line and staff executives (the latter primarily in the personnel area), some provide for a grievance committee elected by employees, and some specify a board of review consisting of company executives. Arbitration by an outsider is not normally included as a final step. These formalized grievance processes in nonunion situations are found primarily in large corporations. In addition, certain firms have informal appeal systems per-

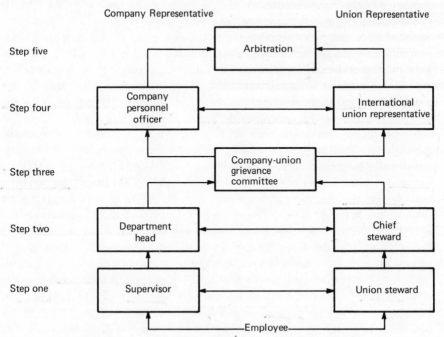

Figure 19–4. Grievance Procedure for a Large Company.

mitting some complaints to go beyond the immediate supervisor. Nevertheless, the majority of nonunion companies do not make specific provision for the handling of employee complaints.

Arbitration

Nearly all union contracts specify that grievances that are not resolved by the parties themselves must be decided by arbitration—a quasi-judicial process that has both advantages and disadvantages from a management viewpoint (11). Although arbitration provides an orderly method of settling disputes and is ordinarily accompanied by a union no-strike pledge, which is unquestionably beneficial to management, the process, may also serve to limit severely a company's freedom of action. For this reason, a number of firms have insisted on contract provisions that clearly establish the scope of arbitration. These usually specify a limitation to matters involving the interpretation of the contract or exclude such concerns as general wage issues, production standards, and management rights.

In general, the arbitrator is chosen on an ad hoc basis; that is, a different individual may be selected for each case. Some contracts call for an arbitration board, consisting of union and management representatives, with an impartial chairman. In some large companies or where an association-wide agreement exists, a permanent umpire or arbitration panel may be appointed to handle all disputes during the term of the contract. This has the advantage that the arbitrator can become familiar with contract provisions and problems and thus will not have to spend the same time acquiring background information that an ad hoc appointee would. The arbitrator must be a mutual choice of both parties. Usually, if agreement on an individual cannot be achieved, the contract will require that the arbitrator be appointed by an impartial agency, such as the Federal Mediation and Conciliation Service or the American Arbitration Association.

The expenses associated with arbitration can be considerable; normally the costs are shared equally by union and company, although some contracts require the loser to assume the whole burden. In addition to the mounting expense, arbitration procedures have been criticized for being too legalistic and too lengthy. According to one report, by the time a grievance has gone through arbitration, the worker involved may be dissatisfied and frustrated even if the decision is in his favor (47). Frequently, it is six months or more before there is a decision. An approach to reducing the cost and time of processing grievances has been undertaken by a number of large companies, including the major steel producers. This "expedited arbitration" requires that hearings in routine cases be held within 10 days and that an award be handed down within 2 days of the hearing (16). Another system of expedited arbitration has been established between the U.S. Postal Service and four unions for handling disciplinary grievances (22). Experience to date with these new procedures is highly favorable, and the savings in time and money have been substantial.

Effectiveness of Grievance Machinery

The grievance procedure is usually the most important aspect of labor relations insofar as conflict minimization is concerned. When the process operates fairly and efficiently, employees will have little need to resort to slowdowns, strikes, and similar disruptive actions to draw attention to their problems. The grievance machinery provides a readily available channel for upward communication.

By studying the use of the grievance procedure, a personnel manager can often become aware of potential focuses of conflict before they become disruptive. Any time there is a decided increase in grievance activity at a particular location or in an employee group, it can be assumed problems exist that may subsequently become critical. There may be an overeager union steward trying to make a name for himself through the expansion of minor incidents into full-scale grievances; there may be a concerted attempt to "get" an unpopular foreman; there may be considerable and widespread discontent over a change in production standards. In any event, increased grievance activity is likely to portend trouble. One study of grievance rates in the various departments of a large manufacturing company over a five-year period showed that the departments with high grievances were more likely to experience work stoppages (1).

Yet a complete lack of grievances can also raise questions. There have been numerous instances in which foremen have permitted employees to violate the contract repeatedly to keep grievances down and avoid an image of dissension at higher levels. Thus, extremely low grievance rates may reflect supervisory overpermissiveness and may be obtained at considerable cost in other areas.

Because grievances almost invariably begin with a complaint to first-line supervision, and because the attitudes and behavior of supervisors have a direct relationship to the grievance rate, it is extremely important to keep the lower levels of management well informed in this area. This is particularly crucial in large organizations, in which foremen often feel that they have little voice in contract negotiations. It is not "their" contract, and they may tend to reject it merely because they do not understand the reasons for certain provisions. Management-development programs dealing with contract changes, grievance settlements, and arbitration awards are widely used to serve this need for continuing information.

In spite of these efforts, many firms are not able to make the grievance machinery operate effectively as a method of draining off anger and reducing controversy. Foremen often become disillusioned when their decisions are reversed at a later stage of the grievance process. The next time, they may decide not to take disciplinary action, enforce production standards, or risk antagonizing their subordinates in some other way. The prospect of being reversed once again is more than they wish to face. Such difficulties can be overcome through effective communication among those responsible for management's answers at various steps in the grievance process. Unfortunately, however, this is not always achieved, and as a result the grievance machinery may serve to foster ineffective supervision much more than it serves to reduce conflict.

Another contributory factor in instances in which the grievance approach fails to achieve its full potential can be the nature of the relationship between union leaders and union members. In a sample of four hundred arbitration cases, it was found that almost one out of every four derived from a union political-strategic person (34). A union steward or higher official may push an employee complaint to arbitration even though it is apparent to him that there is little likelihood of success. This is done to prove to the employee involved, and to others, that the leadership of the union does in fact have the interests of the membership in mind. Ironically, this sort of action tends to occur most frequently when union-management relations are tranquil, and the leadership may feel it is under some pressure to demonstrate a degree of militancy. Furthermore, there are times when it is difficult to convince an employee that his grievance has no merit. Under such circumstances, it is often easier to let an arbitrator tell him than to withdraw the grievance against his opposition. A high proportion of grievances going to arbitration is often indicative of a leadership that feels powerless relative to the rank and file. This assumes, of course, that the union has a sizable treasury and can afford to use the arbitration process to placate the membership.

A number of different approaches have been developed to improve the effectiveness of the grievance machinery. Many of these involve some type of management-development effort stressing aspects of the communications process. One company required the union to submit all grievances in writing and then made it mandatory for the foreman involved to consult with the personnel department before taking any action. In this way, the company was able to assure that the foreman acted with full knowledge of relevant contract provisions and company policy. In another instance, the approach was reversed. The formal writing of grievances was suspended; union and management representatives were encouraged to settle employee complaints orally and on the spot. The result was that the number of grievances submitted for arbitration was reduced substantially (33).

A fact-finding step has been introduced in some grievance procedures at the point where the grievance is put in writing. The purpose of this step is to collect and discuss all the relevant facts at the beginning of the procedure rather than at the point the grievance reaches arbitration; the result has been a sharp reduction in the number of grievances actually submitted to arbitration (27). Another aspect of the fact-finding technique at one company is that at the first step of the procedure there are no grievances, merely "mutual problems," unless the union wishes to go beyond fact-finding.

Other companies have resorted to what amount to group therapy sessions in which supervisors discuss their grievance-handling methods and the reasons behind them. At Lockheed Aircraft Corporation, the company provides special training in grievance administration for union stewards as well as for supervisors (36). Clearly, unique aspects of each situation contribute to the effectiveness of these approaches. What works to make the grievance process function more efficiently as a means to organizational maintenance in one firm may not achieve the same result in another.

UNION-MANAGEMENT CONFLICT

Situations leading to major disputes between management and a union may result from an organizing drive, from an impasse during collective bargaining, from unresolved grievances, or from widespread employee dissatisfaction. When such disputes are not resolved to the satisfaction of the unionized employees, open conflict can result. The ultimate weapon available to the union at such time is a strike or some other type of work stoppage. A sizable breakdown of organizational maintenance can occur, and contributions to productivity goals are decreased or eliminated.

During the 1930s, the major factor in instances of open conflict was some kind of organizing effort. As indicated in Table 19–2, this situation has now changed. In recent years, work stoppages have resulted primarily from disputes over general wage changes and other bargaining issues (46). This is true at least in part because most contracts include some type of no-strike pledge from the union. Because these pledges hold for the duration of a contract, it is only when an agreement has terminated, without a new one's

Table 19–2. Work Stoppages by Major Issue, 1972

Issue	Stoppages (%)
General wage changes	40.3
Supplementary benefits	1.8
Wage adjustments	5.0
Hours of work	.1
Other contractual matters	1.9
Union organization and security	10.2
Job security	4.6
Plant administration	23.4
Other working conditions	4.3
Interunion or intraunion matters	7.9
Not reported	.6

Source: Bureau of Labor Statistics, U.S. Department of Labor, *Analysis of Work Stoppages, 1972* (Washington, D.C., 1975), p. 21.

Table 19–3. Time Cycle of Strike Causes

Time Sequence of Union Demands*	Primary Strike Issues
Formative stage	Recognition Jurisdiction
Early years	Wages Hours
Maturing union	Seniority Job security Working conditions Fringe benefits
Mature union	Any of the prior issues Organizational goals other than historical ones

Source: From *Management Under Strike Conditions* by John G. Hutchinson, p. 114. Copyright © 1966 by Holt, Rinehart and Winston, Inc. Reprinted by permission of Holt, Rinehart and Winston, Inc.
* Once a demand is secured, it will be retained as succeeding demands are presented.

being signed, that the union can strike, unless it is willing to take the risk of being held liable for damages.

Table 19–3 shows how the issues involved in work stoppages change over time as the bargaining relationship matures (24).

Union Tactics in Conflict

Strike actions may be categorized on a number of bases. The major consideration is the nature of the demand made on the company. An *economic strike* is one in which the demands relate to wages, fringe benefits, or some other factor having economic value. Usually, it is an outgrowth of bargaining. An *unfair labor practices strike* represents a protest against an alleged illegal labor practice involving management, such as discrimination on the basis of union membership. *Jurisdictional strikes* may result when there is a dispute over representation—one of the unions involved uses this tactic to enforce a demand for recognition as the sole bargaining agent. *Sympathy strikes* occur when a union has no direct dispute with the company but merely wishes to register support for the demands of other strikers.

In any of these cases, the strike may be *authorized,* in that it has been approved by a vote of the membership and by the national executive board, or *unauthorized,* in that such support has not been obtained. Unauthorized strikes are frequently referred to as *wildcat strikes.* Employees participating in them take considerable risk because they may be disciplined by the union as well as the company.

The *slowdown* is another tactic that may be used by any group of employees, whether unionized or not, to indicate protest and to provide pressure in support of demands. Usually, the employees stay on the job but slow production in various ways; sometimes they report sick in disproportionately large numbers. Approaches such as these are used during the term of a contract when a no-strike clause bars more direct action, and when the situation does not appear to warrant the risks of a wildcat strike.

Unions may engage in *picketing* either in conjunction with a strike or separately. This tactic provides a means of informing outsiders regarding the nature of a labor-management dispute, with a view to discouraging buying, cutting off suppliers, or gaining support of sympathy strikers. Picketing against a company with which the union has no dispute, merely to force the company not to handle products of another firm with which it does have a dispute, is considered a *secondary boycott* and is illegal under federal labor law.

Ordinarily, a company that is struck can retaliate with a *lockout,* excluding all workers, whether on strike or not. This is frequently done in association bargaining; the union will strike one plant or company, and the association responds with a lockout extending throughout its ranks. The union is thus faced with a considerably increased burden in terms of strike benefits.

Generally, management has a fairly good idea as to whether a union is in a position to strike in an effort to achieve its demands. Yet there are times when, even though the union clearly has the backing of its members and the resources to conduct a strike, the issues at stake are of such fundamental, long-term significance to the organization that there is, in fact, little choice. Management can lose more by giving in to a union than it could possibly lose by accepting a strike.

Both sides have much to consider before forcing such an open conflict. The union is much more likely to risk a strike in times of high employment and profits, when internal problems facing the leadership are minimal, when membership support for such action is strong, where the national union has given its approval and made strike funds available, and in an environment in which community and general public support can be anticipated. (See Table 19–1.) One of the most common and most serious miscalculations on the part of management relates to the support of the membership. In a number of cases in which there has appeared to be dissension within the union ranks, a firm stand by the company has served to polarize opinion and unite the membership against management.

Alternatives to Conflict

There is reason to believe that certain unions, at least, are finding strikes less attractive, especially in industries such as chemicals, petroleum, and the utilities, where operations are increasingly automated, and production can continue at near normal levels despite a walkout (42). Furthermore, many current issues appear to be far too complex to be solved under the pressure of a strike. Accordingly, companies and unions in a number of industries have experimented with new approaches involving formal plans for cooperation, either written into the contract, or supplementing it, or in a few instances entirely outside it.

In the 1950s and early 1960s a major impetus for trying different approaches to bargaining and contract administration was the threat of automation; management wanted to be competitive in a technological sense, while the unions wanted to protect workers' job rights. A widely discussed agreement with regard to automation was one covering longshoring operations on the West Coast. In return for the right to change work methods and introduce labor-saving devices on a large scale, the employers guaranteed a certain amount of work or pay and set up funds to encourage early retirement. An important aspect of the agreement was the provision for port arbitrators charged with handling disputes on the docks, with the result that for a period of about 10 years, day-to-day conflicts diminished and actual work stoppages were rare. The peace came to an end in 1971, however, with a lengthy strike over issues related to the handling of containerized cargo.

Nearly all attempts for long-term union-management cooperation have involved some provision for continuing contact between the parties, usually with a third party representing the public. There is no doubt that they result in greater understanding and a good deal of problem solving. It also seems clear, however, that much of the success of these efforts in the 1960s can be attributed to economic conditions. With a low unemployment rate and an expanding economy, workers whose jobs were eliminated by automation had little trouble finding employment. On the West Coast docks, even with the introduction of new methods, there was little if any decline in employment until the economic downturn in early 1970.

One of the key issues in labor-management relations in the 1970s is directly related to the nation's economic problems. This is the issue of worker productivity, particularly as it relates to inflationary pressures. Much has been written about the possibility of productivity bargaining, under which management attempts to elicit union cooperation in new and more efficient work methods in exchange for higher pay or other gains (18, 39). There also have been reports of unions agreeing to forego scheduled wage increases or to permit changes in pay practices or fringe benefits in situations where jobs were threatened because of the company's financial situation (19).

At the same time, there has been continued concern about the effects of large-scale strikes. In a number of bargaining situations, new procedures often involving arbitration are being experimented with in efforts to avoid crisis bargaining. The U.S. Postal Service and the four major postal workers unions have such an arrangement, and so does the steel industry. The steel agreement provides for a two-tiered bargaining procedure; at the national level, unresolved bargaining issues are submitted to arbitration, but at the plant level, strikes or lockouts are permitted over unresolved local issues. The result is that any strikes that occur will not affect the whole industry (7).

Despite such efforts, there is continuing discussion about alternatives to the strike, particularly in the public sector, and there are frequent suggestions for legislation requiring compulsory arbitration of bargaining issues. Such legislation does apply to unions representing government workers in many areas, but the prospects appear to be slim for such legislation in the private sector of the economy. The traditional union view is that there is no alternative to the strike. According to one union spokesman, "a free enterprise system without the right to strike is a contradiction in terms" (29, p. 57). As long as American unions have the political strength they have had over the past 30 or 40 years, strikes will remain potential threats to organizational maintenance.

QUESTIONS

1. What trends in union membership have been evidenced over the past 10 years? What factors might account for these trends?
2. Distinguish among the different kinds of union security provisions and among the different kinds of strikes. Why are these distinctions important?
3. Describe the various purposes for which arbitration may be used in the labor relations area. How is arbitration related to the grievance machinery and to mediation?
4. In what ways does the state of the economy appear to influence labor-management conflict? What issues are likely to come to the fore during prosperity? During recession?
5. Describe and discuss the following:
   a. Industrial union.
   b. Union town.
   c. Business agent.
   d. Boulwarism.
   e. Secondary boycott.

REFERENCES

1. Ash, P. "The Parties to the Grievance." *Personnel Psychology,* 23 (1970), 13–37.
2. Balke, W. M., K. R. Hammond, and G. D. Meyer. "An Alternate Approach to Labor-Management Relations." *Administrative Science Quarterly,* 18 (1973), 311–327.
3. Blum, A. A., M. Estey, J. W. Kuhn, W. A. Wilman, and L. Troy. *White-collar Workers.* New York: Random House, Inc., 1971.
4. Bureau of National Affairs, Inc. *Basic Patterns in Union Contracts,* 8th ed. Washington, D.C.: Bureau of National Affairs, Inc., 1975.

5. Craypo, C. "Collective Bargaining in the Conglomerate, Multinational Firm: Litton's Shutdown of Royal Typewriter." *Industrial and Labor Relations Review,* 29 (1975), 3–25.

6. Cullen, D. E. *National Emergency Strikes.* Ithaca, N.Y.: New York State School of Industrial and Labor Relations, Cornell University, 1968.

7. Cushman, B. "Current Experiments in Collective Bargaining," in G. G. Somers (ed.), *Proceedings of the Twenty-sixth Annual Winter Meeting.* Madison, Wis.: Industrial Relations Research Association, 1974.

8. Dubin, R. "Industrial Conflict: The Power of Prediction." *Industrial and Labor Relations Review,* 18 (1965), 352–363.

9. Dunlop, J. T. "Structure of Collective Bargaining," in G. G. Somers (ed.), *The Next Twenty-five Years of Industrial Relations.* Madison, Wis.: Industrial Relations Research Association, 1973.

10. Eisele, C. F. "Organization Size, Technology, and Frequency of Strikes." *Industrial and Labor Relations Review,* 27 (1974), 560–571.

11. Elkouri, F., and E. Elkouri. *How Arbitration Works.* Washington, D.C.: Bureau of National Affairs, Inc., 1973.

12. Ellis, D. S., L. Jacobs, and C. Mills. "A Union Authorization Election: The Key to Winning." *Personnel Journal,* 51 (1972), 246–254.

13. Ferris, F. D. "Contract Interpretation—A Bread-and-butter Talent." *Public Personnel Management,* 4 (1975), 223–230.

14. Feuille, P. *Final Offer Arbitration.* Chicago: International Personnel Management Association, 1975.

15. Feuille, P., and J. Blandin. "Faculty Job Satisfaction and Bargaining Sentiments: A Case Study." *Academy of Management Journal,* 17 (1974), 678–692.

16. Fischer, B. "Arbitration: The Steel Industry Experiment." *Monthly Labor Review,* 95 (1972), No. 11, 7–10.

17. Ginsburg, W. L. "Union Growth, Government and Structure," in W. L. Ginsburg, et al. (eds.), *A Review of Industrial Relations Research,* Vol. I. Madison, Wis.: Industrial Relations Research Association, 1970, pp. 207–260.

18. Goldberg, J., et al. *Collective Bargaining and Productivity.* Madison, Wis.: Industrial Relations Research Association, 1975.

19. Henle, P. "Reverse Collective Bargaining? A Look at Some Union Concession Situations." *Industrial and Labor Relations Review,* 26 (1973), 956–968.

20. Hershfield, D. C. *The Multinational Union Challenges the Multinational Company.* New York: Conference Board, 1975.

21. Hilgert, R. L. "When an Office Is Unionized—Its Meaning for Management Policy." *Personnel Administration,* 28 (1965), No. 2, 33–38.

22. Hoellering, M. F. "Expedited Grievance Arbitration: The First Steps," in J. L. Stern and B. D. Dennis (eds.), *Proceedings of the Twenty-seventh Annual Winter Meeting.* Madison, Wis.: Industrial Relations Research Association, 1975, pp. 324–331.

23. Horton, R. D. "Arbitration, Arbitrators, and the Public Interest." *Industrial and Labor Relations Review,* 28 (1975), 497–507.

24. Hutchinson, J. G. *Management Under Strike Conditions.* New York: Holt, Rinehart and Winston, 1966.

25. Iberman, W. "How Expensive Is an NLRB Election?" *MSU Business Topics,* 23 (1975), No. 3, 13–18.

26. Johnson, D. F., and D. G. Pruitt. "Preintervention Effects of Mediation Versus Arbitration." *Journal of Applied Psychology,* 56 (1972), 1–10.

27. Kagel, S., and J. Kagel. "Using Two New Arbitration Techniques." *Monthly Labor Review,* 95 (1972), No. 11, 11–14.

28. Kerr, C. "The Collective Bargaining Environment," in C. S. Golden and V. D. Parker (eds.), *Causes of Industrial Peace Under Collective Bargaining.* New York: Harper & Row, Publishers, 1955, pp. 10–22.

29. Kheel, T. W., et al. "Exploring Alternatives to the Strike." *Monthly Labor Review,* 96 (1973), 33–68.

30. Kornhauser, A., R. Dubin, and A. M. Ross. *Industrial Conflict.* New York: McGraw-Hill Book Company, 1954.

31. Leahy, W. H. "Landmark Cases Involving Union Representatives." *Personnel Journal,* 51 (1972), 241–245.

32. McGuckin, J. H. "Grist for the Arbitrators' Mill: What GM and the UAW Argue About." *Labor Law Journal,* 22 (1971), 647–664.

33. McKersie, R. B. "Avoiding Written Grievances by Problem-solving: An Outside View." *Personnel Psychology,* 17 (1964), 367–379.

34. Peterson, D. J. "Why Unions Go to Arbitration: Politics and Strategy vs. 'Merit'." *Personnel,* 48 (1971), No. 4, 44–49.

35. Peterson, D. J. "Labor Trends: White-collar Unionization and the Pay Board." *Personnel,* 49 (1972), No. 4, 34–39.

36. Pettefer, J. C. "Effective Grievance Administration." *California Management Review,* 13 (1970), No. 2, 12–18.

37. Roberts, H. S. *Roberts' Dictionary of Industrial Relations.* Washington, D.C.: Bureau of National Affairs, Inc., 1971.

38. Rose, J. B. "What Factors Influence Union Representation Elections?" *Monthly Labor Review,* 95 (1972), No. 10, 49–51.

39. Rosow, J. M. "Now Is the Time for Productivity Bargaining." *Harvard Business Review,* 50 (1972), No. 1, 78–89.

40. Schwartz, P. J. *Coalition Bargaining.* Ithaca, N.Y.: New York State School of Industrial and Labor Relations, Cornell University, 1970.

41. Stagner, R., and H. Rosen. *Psychology of Union Management Relations.* Belmont, Calif.: Wadsworth Publishing Co., Inc., 1965.

42. Tagliaferri, L. E. "Plant Operations During a Strike." *Personnel Administration,* 35 (1972), No. 2, 47–51, 61.

43. Tracy, L. "The Influence of Noneconomic Factors on Negotiators." *Industrial and Labor Relations Review,* 27 (1974), 204–215.

44. Ulman, Lloyd. "Multinational Unionism: Incentives, Barriers, and Alternatives." *Industrial Relations,* 14 (1975), 1–31.

45. U.S. Department of Labor, Bureau of Labor Statistics. *Directory of National and International Labor Unions in the United States, 1973.* Washington, D.C.: the Bureau, 1974.

46. U.S. Department of Labor, Bureau of Labor Statistics. *Analysis of Work Stoppages, 1972,* Bulletin No. 1687. Washington, D.C.: the Bureau, 1975.

47. Usery, W. J. "Some Attempts to Reduce Arbitration Costs and Delays." *Monthly Labor Review,* 95 (1972), No. 11, 3–6.

48. Vogel, A. "Your Clerical Workers Are Ripe for Unionism." *Harvard Business Review,* 49 (1971), No. 2, 48–54.

49. Walton, R. W., and R. B. McKersie. *A Behavioral Theory of Labor Negotiations.* New York: McGraw-Hill Book Company, 1965.

50. Yaffe, B. "The Protected Rights of the Union Steward." *Industrial and Labor Relations Review,* 23 (1970), No. 4, 483–499.

20   *Employee Benefits and Services*

The number and variety of benefits and services provided by companies for their employees have grown rapidly over the years to the point where items of this kind represent a major factor in total compensation. These so-called fringe benefits range from costly insurance and retirement programs to the use of company facilities in connection with the activities of various employee groups. They may be provided by the company on an entirely unilateral basis, or they may emerge out of extended bargaining with a union. They may have as their immediate goal the improvement of working conditions (music in the plant), the provision of more leisure time (vacations and holidays), or the guaranteeing of security in times of personal adversity (group hospitalization insurance and supplemental unemployment pay).

Although part of the total compensation package, these items are not intended to encourage task motivation. Little effort has been made to use fringe benefits as inducements or rewards, with a view to maximizing the effectiveness of role behavior. Thus, differentials related to merit or productivity are not a characteristic aspect of their application. The ultimate goal of employee benefits and services is to further organizational maintenance by contributing to high morale, a sense of security, and the general job satisfaction of employees. In this way, stress within the organization is minimized, but there is no reason to believe that productivity will necessarily be fostered as a result. In addition, benefits may be used as an inducement to continued organizational membership. A further objective, which is often noted, is that such benefits are a valuable asset in recruiting potentially effective employees.

The latter factor may not be as important as many have believed. Young people just entering the labor force, in particular, are unlikely to be influenced by liberal retirement provisions and life insurance plans. Even more mature job seekers are often not as concerned with such matters as with basic wage rates and advancement opportunities. Furthermore, the firms with the most liberal benefit plans also tend to be the ones with the highest wage scales and the most desirable working conditions (29). In other words, a good place to work is a good place to work, and employee benefits are unlikely to be the deciding factor when an individual agrees to accept employment. On the other hand, a program in this area that is markedly deficient, relative to those of other companies, may make this a salient concern for a prospective employee, who may accept work elsewhere.

This same consideration—that benefit programs can hurt a company if they are below expectation levels but contribute very little to goal attainment in a positive sense if they are more liberal than expected—applies to existing employees as well. Yet some benefits clearly do contribute to a more stable work force. Thus, such things as the length of paid vacations and the amount of monthly retirement payments are normally dependent upon length of service and therefore do make a contribution to organizational stability.

Irrespective of the significance benefit programs may have for maintenance and recruiting, they nevertheless do represent a major aspect of the personnel function in most firms. Much time and effort is spent on surveys and studies of alternative benefit practices, in negotiating with unions on such matters, and in administering existing programs. Furthermore, a high percentage of all payroll costs are paid out in this form.

THE PATTERN OF GROWTH

Various programs providing benefits and services to employees have been in existence since the beginnings of industrialization. Thus, it is not so much the existence of these practices that differentiates the present from the past as the frequency with which they are found and the costs involved.

Types of Benefits

The earliest employee benefits, such as company housing and company stores, were provided largely out of necessity where adequate facilities were not otherwise available to employees. By the first years of the present century, there were occasional instances of companies' giving paid vacations and holidays, and even retirement and insurance benefits. These spread still further during the 1920s with the advent of so-called paternalism. The benefits were usually granted unilaterally by the company, although it can be assumed that in some cases the primary intent was to prevent unionization. Actually, however, the most pronounced increase occurred among white-collar and, salaried groups. In any event, many benefit plans inaugurated during the 1920s were short-lived. The depression produced major cutbacks in this area, so that by the mid-1930s few firms provided benefits of any real significance. For production workers, they were almost nonexistent (32).

Yet at the present time, practically all employees in the United States, at all levels, enjoy several paid holidays and a paid vacation each year, more than half are enrolled in some type of private pension plan, and about three-fourths are covered by a health and welfare program. This very marked change over the past 30 years can be attributed in large part to policies adopted by the federal government and to the constraints on company personnel decisions that have resulted.

GOVERNMENTAL EFFECTS

As noted in Chapter 5, various laws of the New Deal era had considerable impact. The Social Security Act influenced pension planning; the wage-hour law increased premium pay; the Wagner Act served to support unionization, and thus ultimately gave unions the strength to bargain for fringe benefits. During World War II, and again during the Korean War, the fiscal policies of the federal government were important. Under the wage controls in effect at these times, companies were discouraged from raising wages, but they were often permitted to provide longer vacations, additional paid holidays, and other fringe items. Excess profit tax provisions served to encourage companies to set up retirement or health and welfare funds, because this could be done at very little immediate cost.

UNION EFFECTS

Although these governmental actions encouraged the growth of employee benefits, even forcing them upon companies in some instances, the effects were often mediated by the unions. Until the end of World War II, the major union emphasis was on raising wages; on benefits related to wages, hours, and work schedules, such as shift differentials, rest periods, and cleanup time; and on benefits requiring paid time away from work, such as holidays, vacations, and certain kinds of leaves. After the war, perhaps influenced by the number of plans established unilaterally by companies under the favorable wartime tax laws, the major unions began to demand bargaining with regard to retirement plans and health and welfare programs.

Initially, there was considerable doubt as to whether these union demands were legally justified. However, in 1948, the National Labor Relations Board ruled in favor of the unions, indicating that companies must bargain on such matters.[1] Consequently, the decade that followed produced a dramatic growth, both in the number of companies providing retirement and health benefits and in the level of the benefits themselves. The wage controls and tax provisions invoked during the Korean War of the early 1950s gave additional impetus to this upswing.

By the mid-1950s, pension and welfare plans were well-established throughout most of manufacturing. Union attention then shifted to methods of providing worker security against seasonal layoffs, as well as against technological displacement. In the automobile industry, demands for a guaranteed annual wage produced extensive supplemental unemployment benefits at company expense. In other industries, where automation threatened job security, union demands centered on benefits such as retraining allowances and severance pay, again with some success. However, the majority of these items are tailored to the specific problems of a particular industry. Thus, none has achieved widespread acceptance. In recent years, the primary source of growth in the employee benefits area has been the increase in the level of existing provisions—longer vacations, additional insurance, higher retirement payments, more paid holidays, and the like.

With the growth in benefit plans, both in terms of groups of employees covered and in level of benefits, management is facing a new dilemma. Increasingly, these benefits are viewed as social obligations, in that an employer in hiring an individual is expected not only to pay an adequate wage for his services but also to provide him assistance in the event of illness or layoff and to help prepare for old age (1). As industry succeeded in doing this by covering large numbers of workers with adequate benefits, the pressure for governmental action along these lines has been minimal. Recently, however, there has been concern that the nation's population is becoming divided into the haves and have-nots with respect to various welfare and retirement provisions. People with steady positions in large corporations can look forward to having their security needs taken care of

---

[1] *Inland Steel Company* v. *NLRB*, NLRB77, 1 (1948).

for the rest of their lives, whereas the hard-core unemployed or those with erratic work histories have to rely on public welfare. The high levels of benefits being provided by private employers have made the disparity between the two groups more pronounced; with every increase in private benefits, management faces the prospect of more public pressure for governmental legislation to provide for the social needs of those not regularly employed.

Costs of Benefits

One method of measuring growth in employee benefits is in terms of their cost to employers. Because of differences of opinion regarding the specific items to be included and varying methods of computing costs, it is often difficult to make meaningful benefit comparisons between companies (11). However, the Chamber of Commerce of the United States has conducted reasonably standardized surveys of fringe benefit costs every two years since 1947, and these findings are useful as a general indicator of trends over time.

The results of the 1975 survey indicated that payments for employee benefits and services ranged from less than 18 to over 60 per cent of payroll. The average for all companies included in the survey was 35.4 per cent of payroll, 193.2 cents per payroll hour, or $3,984 per year per employee (9). By contrast, the best available estimate of average benefit costs for the year 1929 is 3 per cent of payroll.

The figures in Table 20–1 and Figure 20–1 are based on benefit costs reported by the 152 companies that have been included in all Chamber of Commerce surveys since 1955. In absolute terms, these results presumably are not typical of industry as a whole, but the trend of the data does provide a good index of growth. Because of rapidly rising wages over the period, the increase as a percentage of payroll amounted to 78 per cent; the actual increase in company costs, in terms of cents per payroll hour, as shown in Table 20–1, was 394 per cent.

As illustrated in Figure 20–1, most of the increases took the form of pension and welfare benefits and payments for time not worked, the two areas in which the unions have been most active. One forecast of the future of employee benefits anticipates increased government, as well as union,

Table 20–1. Comparison of 1955–1975 Employee Benefits: Cents per Payroll Hour

Industry Group	1955	1965	1975
All industries (152 companies)	46.7	86.6	230.9
Manufacturing (65 companies)	44.3	86.0	238.4
Nonmanufacturing (87 companies)	48.2	87.0	226.4

Source; U.S. Chamber of Commerce, *Employee Benefits 1975* (Washington, D.C., 1976), p. 27.

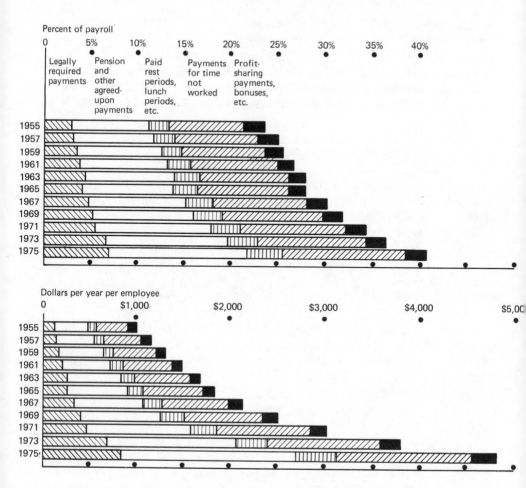

Figure 20–1. Comparison of 1955–1975 Employee
Benefits for 152 Companies.
Source: Chamber of Commerce of the United States, Employee Benefits 1975 (Washington, D.C., 1976), p. 28.

pressure to raise benefit levels, with the result that the costs of benefits will amount to 50 per cent of payroll by 1986 (17).

Legally Required Payments

Included in the Chamber of Commerce figures are payments required of employers by state or federal law. Such payments serve to provide Social Security benefits at retirement, medical care for the elderly, compensation for injury on the job, and support for the unemployed. These legally required plans are of interest primarily as they influence the specific private benefit programs developed by various companies, and as a payroll cost over which management has no direct control.

Table 20–2. Federal Social Security (Old Age, Survivors, Disability, and Health Insurance) Provisions. Past and Future Financing Provisions

Period	Maximum Taxable Earnings ($)	Combined Employer-Employee Tax Rate (%)			Self-employed Tax Rate		
		OASDI	HI	Total	OASDI	HI	Total
1937–1949	3,000	2	—	2	—	—	—
1950	3,000	3	—	3	—	—	—
1951–1953	3,600	3	—	3	2.25	—	2.25
1954	3,600	4	—	4	3	—	3
1955–1956	4,200	4	—	4	3	—	3
1957–1958	4,200	4.5	—	4.5	3.375	—	3.375
1959	4,800	5	—	5	3.75	—	3.75
1960–1961	4,800	6	—	6	4.5	—	4.5
1962	4,800	6.25	—	6.25	4.7	—	4.7
1963–1965	4,800	7.25	—	7.25	5.4	—	5.4
1966	6,600	7.7	.7	8.4	5.8	.35	6.15
1967	6,600	7.8	1.0	8.8	5.9	.5	6.4
1968	7,800	7.6	1.2	8.8	5.8	.6	6.4
1969–1970	7,800	8.4	1.2	9.6	6.3	.6	6.9
1971	7,800	9.2	1.2	10.4	6.9	.6	7.5
1972	9,000	9.2	1.2	10.4	6.9	.6	7.5
1973	10,800	9.7	1.0	10.7	7.0	1.0	8.0
1974	13,200	9.9	1.8	11.7	7.0	.9	7.9
1975	14,100	9.9	1.8	11.7	7.0	.9	7.9
1976	15,300	9.9	1.8	11.7	7.0	.9	7.9
1977	16,500	9.9	1.8	11.7	7.0	.9	7.9
1978–1980	*	9.9	2.2	12.1	7.0	1.1	8.1
1981–1985	*	9.9	2.7	12.6	7.0	1.5	8.35
1986–2010	*	9.9	3.0	12.9	7.0	1.5	8.5

Source: Social Security Administration.
* From 1975 on, the taxable wage base is adjusted annually for cost-of-living changes.

In contrast to unemployment and workers' compensation payments, which are paid for solely by employer contributions, benefits under the Social Security system are financed by a tax, half of which is paid by the employee and half by the employer. The amount of this tax has increased steadily over the years, as shown in Table 20–2. As indicated, an additional tax was added in 1966 to pay for health insurance, or Medicare, benefits for retired workers.

DIRECT MONETARY BENEFITS

A major category commonly included within the definition of employee benefits involves various direct payments to employees. These may occur (a) as part of regular earnings, (b) in lieu of regular earnings in cases associated with layoffs, and (c) in addition to regular earnings, as with certain types of bonuses. In unionized situations, such payments are a matter for negotiation and are specified in the contract. Generally, nonunion firms attempt to maintain these direct monetary benefits at levels that are typical for the specific labor market and/or industry.

Payments Related to Time Worked

As noted in Chapter 16, almost all companies make some payments to their hourly workers that are in addition to the straight time rate for hours spent on the job. Included are payments for daily or weekly overtime at rates above those for straight time; differentials for work on a second or third shift; premium pay for work on weekends, holidays, or under hazardous or undesirable conditions; call-in, reporting, and call-back pay; pay for wash-up or travel time; and paid coffee breaks, rest periods, or lunch hours.

Some of these are required by law. Other payments related to time worked are specified in the union contract. Still others are provided by the company at its own discretion as a contribution to organizational maintenance. In large part, the extent of such payments depends on the nature of the firm's operations. A manufacturing plant on a 24-hour day and a 7-day week will have much higher costs in this area than a nonmanufacturing organization on a regular work week.

Paid Time Off

Another group of benefits includes items designed to provide employees, whether hourly or salaried, a certain amount of time off without loss of pay. Holidays, vacations, and leaves are all of this kind.

HOLIDAYS

Nearly all firms give their employees at least 6 paid holidays; about two-thirds give 9; two-fifths give 10 or more a year. Employees (other than managers and professionals) required to work on these days are normally compensated with an extra day's pay or more. Usually, eligibility for holiday pay is contingent on the employee's working his regularly scheduled day before and after the holiday.

The most common holidays are Christmas, Thanksgiving, July Fourth, Labor Day, New Year's Day, and Memorial Day. Beyond these there is a great deal of diversity. Days off range from Election Day to various state holidays to the employee's birthday (7). Figure 20–2 shows how the number of paid holidays has increased under union contracts. In the past, employees in offices and in nonmanufacturing operations usually enjoyed more paid holidays than those in manufacturing plants, but over the years union demands have resulted in the virtual elimination of this differential.

Rather than extending the number of isolated holidays, the trend in recent years has been to group holidays in clusters and around weekends. Frequent examples are the day after Thanksgiving, the day before Christ-

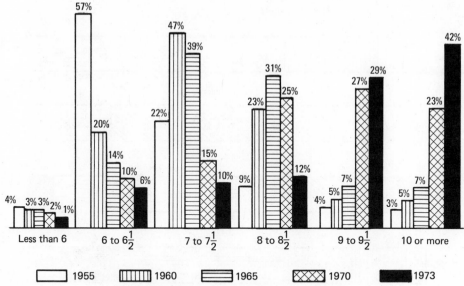

Figure 20-2. Holiday Trends, 1955-1973: Per Cent of
Collective Bargaining Agreements with Specified Num-
ber of Holidays.
Source: Adapted from Basic Patterns in Union Contracts
(Washington, D.C.: Bureau of National Affairs, Inc., 1975),
p. 57.

mas, and a "travel day" taken on the last working day before or the first
working day after an employee's vacation. A growing number of companies
provide what is called a "floating" holiday, where one or more of the paid
holidays are observed on different days each year. In a year in which
Christmas falls on a Thursday, for example, the day after could be designated as the floating holiday. Much of the impetus for longer weekend
and floating holidays came from legislation calling for certain holidays,
such as Washington's Birthday and Memorial Day, to be observed on
Mondays for all government employees. Such practices can contribute to
both maintenance and productivity goals. If, for reasons of organizational
maintenance, an employer decides to provide another paid holiday, productivity will suffer least by granting a day like the day after Thanksgiving, when absenteeism ordinarily runs high.

VACATIONS

Provisions for paid vacations, varying in length from one to six weeks,
are now a standard practice throughout industry. In nearly all cases, the
length of the vacation depends on the duration of employment with the
company—for example, 1 week after 1 year of service, 2 weeks after 3 years,
3 weeks after 10 years, and 4 weeks after 20 years. As indicated in Figure

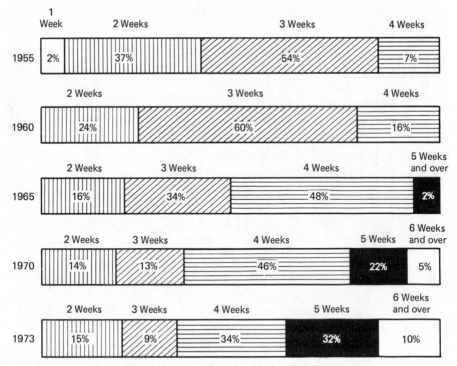

Figure 20–3. Vacation Trends, 1955–1973: Percentage of Collective Bargaining Agreements with Specified Maximum Vacation Allowances.
Source: Adapted from *Basic Patterns in Union Contracts* (Washington, D.C.: Bureau of National Affairs, Inc., 1975), p. 107.

20–3, the maximum vacation allowance has increased considerably since 1955. As with holidays, employees must usually meet certain work requirements to be eligible for a paid vacation. Some companies close down operations for vacation periods. Where this is not the practice, employees are likely to be given some choice in the scheduling process. First choice normally goes to those with the most seniority.

In industries characterized by casual employment, such as construction, employer associations or unions may establish a vacation fund from which workers receive benefits based on the number of hours worked during the year. In the business world generally, it is not uncommon to make payments in lieu of a vacation, especially if an individual terminates employment prior to exhausting his allotted number of days. Thus, vacations are increasingly taking on the status of an earned right.

A concept involving periodic extended vacations, or so-called sabbaticals, was introduced in the steel and related industries in the mid-1960s. Aimed at providing more jobs for younger employees, cutting down on layoffs, and encouraging earlier retirements, the plan calls for 10 weeks' vacation, in addition to the regular 3 or 4 weeks, once every 5 years. There is little indication that such plans have expanded to any marked degree beyond the confines of this one industry (7).

LEAVE

Unscheduled time off with pay, due to personal illness or to death or illness in the family, is provided by a number of companies. This type of benefit is most likely to apply to salaried employees, but many hourly production workers are now covered by insurance plans that accomplish much the same results. Time off to vote, required by law in a number of states, and time for jury duty are additional forms of paid leave often provided.

In addition, there are a variety of unpaid leaves that, although they involve only negligible costs to the company, have important implications for job security. Thus, most firms permit employees to take unpaid leaves of absence for such reasons as maternity, military service, union business, civic duty, education, or merely "personal reasons" without any loss in seniority (8). In recent years, a number of companies have adopted formal plans permitting employees to take leave time to participate in political or social action programs (12).

Payments in Lieu of Earnings

Several types of benefits are designed to maintain some income for employees during periods when work is not available. Some companies guarantee all regular employees a certain number of hours or a certain amount of pay per week. Or they guarantee so many weeks of work during the year. Provisions of this kind have been in existence for as long as 30 or 40 years. More recently, certain unions have negotiated plans calling for the payment of supplemental unemployment benefits (SUB). Generally, these plans are financed by company contributions to a trust fund and, as the name implies, the benefits are paid as a supplement to state unemployment compensation. Thus, during the period of layoff, such as the annual retooling period in the automobile industry, employees are able to maintain an income level close to their regular earnings.

In the first 10 to 15 years the SUB plans were in operation, they were quite effective in cushioning the effects of layoffs in the auto and other industries characterized by cyclical unemployment. The cost to management was relatively small and limited to a predetermined level of contributions to the SUB trust fund. With the large-scale, indefinite layoffs in the auto industry during the 1974–75 recession, the trust funds dropped to the point where payment of benefits was suspended and many auto workers were without unemployment benefits of any kind. Consequently, the union asked for higher company contributions to the funds.

Other benefits, such as severance or separation pay, retraining allowances, and technological adjustment pay, serve to maintain income to employees who are separated. The idea is to help them in the process of finding new employment, although some such payments extend well beyond the period normally required for this purpose. The minimum amount would appear to be about two weeks' pay; the maximum, approximately a year's pay. Length of prior service is the determining factor in establishing the total payment.

Payments in Addition to Regular Earnings

Other types of cash payments, although not as widespread as those previously noted, are found in some companies. These usually take the form of a Christmas or year-end bonus. The amount of such a bonus may or may not be related to profits, but it is common practice to do so. Other factors that may influence the amount received are the total time worked during the year, length of service, and job level. A number of profit-related plans carry a provision that all, or a large share, of the bonus go into a trust fund, so that actual payment does not occur until retirement or termination of employment. Thus, profit sharing becomes a means to enforced savings.

There are, in addition, a number of savings or *thrift plans* that do not necessarily have this enforced character. The usual practice under these plans is for the company to match a certain proportion of the employee's pay, which he chooses to contribute into the fund. Thus, an employee may put in perhaps 5 per cent of his earnings, and the company will contribute an equal amount. There is a set maximum that the employee can allocate for this purpose, and it is not uncommon to provide the company share in the form of stock, usually nonvoting. In most cases, payment of the company contribution is contingent upon some length of service requirement. Thus, this benefit is used to foster continued employment; organizational maintenance is directly involved.

Finally, mention should be made of various cash bonuses paid for long-term service to the company, for good attendance, as prizes for the winners of employee contests, and as awards under suggestion systems. In some cases, such payments have an incentive quality that is closely tied to productivity. Many, however, represent an attempt to foster continued employment and employee satisfaction in a general sense. As such, they contribute to the maintenance goal.

GROUP INSURANCE

The greatest activity over the last 30 years, insofar as employee benefits are concerned, has occurred in the area of retirement planning and group insurance. In the latter instance, the growth rate, whether computed in terms of the number of firms involved, the number of employees covered, the types of plans in force, or the amount of insurance provided, has been little short of phenomenal. Even when the company does not pay a share of the cost, group insurance of this kind represents a sizable benefit to the employee. He or she obtains the saving associated with group rates, and certain kinds of protection that are not practicable on an individual basis now become available.

Types of Group Insurance

Most group insurance available today through company programs falls into three categories—life, medical, and disability.

LIFE INSURANCE

Life insurance policies provide either a lump-sum payment, or a guaranteed income, or some combination of the two to an employee's family in case of his death or, frequently, for dismemberment also. Special provisions may relate to accidental death, or separate insurance may be available for this purpose. In some instances, there is an opportunity to insure the lives of other family members in addition to that of the employee.

MEDICAL INSURANCE

Medical insurance policies are extremely diverse. They cover costs associated with hospitalization, medical and surgical treatment, visits to a physician's office, and so on. Although many policies have relatively limited coverage in terms of costs, there are also *major medical* plans that provide protection against the costs associated with medical catastrophe and extended treatment. A typical plan might, for instance, pay 80 per cent of all costs not covered by other forms of medical insurance, up to a maximum of $50,000 a year. Frequently, the basic protection and major medical benefits are combined in what is known as a comprehensive medical insurance policy. Special kinds of medical coverage are offered by a few companies; these include dental care, prescription drug, and eye care insurance plans (5).

Another approach to providing medical benefits for employees is to pay part or all of their membership in a group practice plan or a Health Maintenance Organization (HMO) that provides a full spectrum of medical services. Federal legislation passed in 1973 is designed to encourage the establishment and growth of HMOs and stipulates that in communities with HMOs meeting certain standards, employers providing medical benefits must offer employees a choice between HMO and insurance coverage. To the extent the HMO membership costs more than the employer has been paying for medical insurance, the employee may be required to pay the difference (27).

DISABILITY INSURANCE

Insurance benefits designed to tide employees over during periods of disability caused by sickness and accident are of two basic types—short term and long term. Policies of the first type pay weekly benefits based on a percentage of regular earnings to employees who are temporarily disabled. The benefits usually are paid for a maximum of 26 weeks; employers are required to provide this type of benefit under compulsory disability benefit laws in a few states.

Long-term disability, or LTD, plans have become increasingly popular (3). Under these plans, benefits also are based on a percentage of regular pay, but they usually do not begin until the employee has been disabled for a period of time, often three to six months, during which time he or she may be covered by a paid-sick-leave policy or by short-term benefits. Benefits may be payable for life or until age 65, when retirement benefits become available; such plans also are known as income-protection plans.

Financing Employee Insurance Benefits

The decision making associated with establishing and administering an employee insurance program can become an extremely complex process. There are hundreds of plans available through different private insurance companies in each of the three major categories, all with variable benefit amounts at variable costs. For this reason, many companies, particularly smaller firms, provide insurance benefits through a trust fund established on an industry or area basis. These funds may be administered by representatives of the member companies, by a corporation or partnership made up of insurance specialists, or by a joint union-management committee— or, on occasion, they may be controlled by the union alone. The company pays into the fund on the basis of a cents-per-hour-worked formula, or as a percentage of total payroll. The trustees of the fund establish the types and levels of benefits to be paid within the limitations imposed by the union-management contract. Usually, insurance is purchased commercially to guarantee these payments; sometimes, the fund operates on a pay-as-you-go basis through what amounts to self-insurance.

In some areas and industries, union-controlled funds have expanded to a point where they now cover all types of medical expenses, including prescriptions, dental care, and psychiatric treatment. There are a number of union-operated clinics. Under such circumstances, the company not only loses control insofar as specifying the benefits to be provided for its employees, but the union rather than the company tends to be credited with making the benefits possible. Furthermore, in most cases only employees represented by unions are eligible to receive benefits from the fund, with the result that nonunion employees including management must be covered in some other way. In instances of this kind, certain immediate advantages in terms of ease of administration and greater predictability of benefit costs are achieved at considerable expense in other respects. A major opportunity to obtain a maximum return on investment, in terms of employee satisfaction and company loyalty, is lost.

EMPLOYEE CONTRIBUTIONS

Although there is a strong feeling that employees are more aware of benefits and more appreciative of them when they contribute part of the cost, there is a clear trend for companies to assume more and more of this burden (25). One reason is that for group insurance plans to operate at any savings over individual plans, a certain percentage of the total employee group must be covered. In the case of life insurance, for example, if the employee group includes a large proportion of women without dependents, who would not choose to be covered if they had to pay part of the cost, the only way to obtain coverage for employees who desire it, at any saving, is for the company to pay the premium. One approach to this problem is for the company to pay the full cost of basic levels of insurance and then make certain additional benefits available on a contributory basis.

Dependent coverage is usually provided on such a contributory basis for most types of medical insurance, the company paying only the employee portion. Yet in some cases companies assume all premium costs for the individual and his or her family. Retired employees continue to be covered by company insurance programs in many cases, although usually life insurance benefit amounts are reduced. The matter of continuing to cover the retired for health benefits is of less concern now that Medicare has been established under Social Security.

PENSIONS AND RETIREMENT

Retirement plans, like group insurance, have experienced a sizable growth since the late 1940s, when they became clearly established as a union bargaining goal. Even those company plans that existed prior to that time have undergone drastic changes as a result of union pressures. As indicated by the figures in Table 20-3, employees in unionized companies still are much more likely to be covered by a private pension plan than are nonunionized employees (2).

Financing Retirement Plans

Most retirement plans that have been negotiated with a union are established so as to provide certain specified monthly benefits payable to the employee on retirement. The matter of how to guarantee these payments normally is left to the company. In the case of contributory plans, where the employee pays part of the cost, the contribution is a set amount or percentage of salary, and the company's share is the remaining amount

Table 20–3. Employees in Establishment Groups with Private Retirement Plans

Industry or Other Characteristic of Establishment	Establishments with Retirement Plan Expenditures as a Per Cent of Total Employment, 1972
All industries	63
Manufacturing	79
All nonmanufacturing	55
Mining	89
Construction	60
Transportation and public utilities	73
Finance, insurance, and real estate	76
Trade and services	48
Employee Groups	
Union	91
Nonunion	52
Office	72
Nonoffice	58
Number of Employees in Establishments	
Less than 100	38
100 to 499	76
500 and over	93

Source: D. R. Bell, "Prevalence of Private Retirement Plans," *Monthly Labor Review*, 98 (1975), No. 10, p. 17.

necessary to provide the specified benefits. Such contributory plans are more commonly applied to nonunion, salaried workers and to management than to a unionized work force. If the pension is paid through a deferred profit-sharing arrangement, of the kind discussed previously under direct monetary payments, the monthly benefit payable at retirement depends on the equity built up over the years of employment by the individual employee.

Depending on such factors as the level of the benefits specified, the company financial position, and the average age of the work force, pensions may be financed on a pay-as-you-go basis, by establishing a trust fund, and/or through the purchase of annuities. One type of funding, which is being encouraged by favorable tax treatment, involves Employee Stock Ownership Trusts (ESOT). Basically, an ESOT invests company contributions to employees' retirement in company stock ownership (20). The financial aspects of pension planning are complex and subject to many tax and legal constraints. Thus, decisions in this area normally involve financial executives and/or consultants knowledgeable in areas other than personnel management. Although tax considerations do have implications for a company's retirement program, personnel managers in general have been much more concerned with the various ways in which retirement provisions may be related to internal stresses and organizational maintenance.

Normal Retirement

The original Social Security legislation established age sixty-five as the earliest point at which monthly retirement benefits could be paid. This subsequently became the standard retirement age under most private plans. Some firms made retirement at sixty-five compulsory; others consider this as normal, but do not require retirement until age sixty-eight; still others attempt to maintain a flexible policy, with the compulsory provision invoked only when it is clearly required in a particular case.

Compulsory retirement at a fixed age, such as sixty-five, does have certain advantages in that all employees are treated alike, and thus complaints of unfair treatment are kept to a minimum. From a social viewpoint, it serves to increase turnover during periods of high unemployment and thus provides opportunities for younger workers with families to support. If new technology results in a reduced manpower need, the required attrition can be handled in many cases through normal retirement, and less-senior workers do not have to be released.

A flexible approach is much more difficult to administer, and it can become a source of dissension if certain employees feel that the policy as applied to them is unjust. Yet it does permit the retention of older individuals who remain effective. Senior employees need not be forced out, if they are clearly capable of making a contribution, and many, without doubt, are extremely capable. This is a particularly important consideration in times of labor shortage when older employees are likely to possess skills that are difficult to locate in the available labor market. Thus, it would seem that the flexible policy places greater emphasis on productivity considerations, whereas a fixed retirement age tends to foster organizational maintenance through a reduction in internal dissension.

There are various formulas for computing pension payments, most based on either flat amounts or a percentage of average annual earnings times years of service (4). In either case, longer service with the company makes for a higher level of retirement pay. Yet even with relatively long service, the normal pension often amounts to only between one-half and two-thirds of previous earnings. This situation was improved somewhat during the 1960s, when pension benefits rose sharply as a result of changes in the formulas for determining the monthly payments in many of the largest companies; however, much of this improvement was negated with the steep inflation of the early 1970s. An approach designed to increase benefit levels is to use an average earnings figure based on the years just prior to retirement rather than an average based on the employee's total service. Under most plans, however, benefit levels are increased by increasing the specified dollar amounts (22).

Another consideration is that most plans pay the same monthly benefits for the remainder of the individual's life, irrespective of changes in living costs. Some of the earliest plans negotiated with unions provided a flat monthly amount that included Social Security payments. Thus, raises in the federal benefits as a result of revisions in the law did not serve to increase the amount received. Most such plans have now been altered, and certain changes have also been introduced in some cases to adjust for the rising cost of living.

Disability and Early Retirement

Another aspect of most retirement plans is a provision for payments of benefits before normal retirement age under certain circumstances. Most commonly, there is some kind of protection against permanent and total disability. To be eligible for such a disability pension, the employee must generally have a specified amount of service; frequently, the employee must also have reached a certain age, such as fifty.

Early retirement for reasons other than disability is also permitted under most plans. Employees are allowed to retire voluntarily at age sixty, fifty-five, or even younger provided they have the required length of service. Increasingly, employees are electing to take early retirement even at high levels, where retirement involves a substantial reduction in income (31).

Where the company has no great interest in encouraging early retirements, the monthly benefits tend to be lower than those provided with normal retirement. However, a number of companies have considered early retirement attractive as a method of reducing the work force, when technological changes produce decreased manpower requirements. It is minimally disruptive and creates few problems with the unions. Under such conditions, companies have tended to escalate the rewards for accepting an early retirement. There have been instances, however, where companies have been found in violation of age discrimination laws when they have forced employees to take early retirement, even with full benefits.

Vesting Provisions

Over the years, there has been considerable discussion regarding the effects of pension provisions on labor mobility. Partly out of economic considerations and partly out of a desire to foster a stable labor force, companies tended to withhold the *vesting* of pension rights as long as possible. Thus, they attempted to delay the point at which an employee attained a full right to the company's contribution to the retirement fund and therefore the time when he could be sure of achieving a full pension.

The issue of vesting provisions was one of several aspects of private pension plans that led to the passage of the Employee Retirement Income Security Act (ERISA), mentioned in Chapter 5. The vesting issue became more acute as it became evident that many employees do not spend their entire working career with one company even if they want to; the cutbacks in the aerospace industry in the early 1970s resulted in large numbers of scientists and engineers being terminated and losing rights to various benefits that had built up over many years.

The Employee Retirement Income Security Act gives employees options for vesting of pension rights; depending on the option chosen, with 10 to 15 years of coverage by a retirement plan, employees must be fully vested. The law also attempts to solve another problem inherent in private pensions, the problem of companies' closing down or going out of business. In such situations, retired employees who looked forward to pension payments for life and employees who had built up benefit credits over long periods of time are threatened with losing the benefits. A special plan termination insurance fund is provided under ERISA to take care of such situations. In addition to setting standards related to financing and requiring certain communications to employees covered by pension plans, the law provides that individuals can finance their own retirement benefits through individual accounts to which they can contribute up to $1,500 per year (6).

EMPLOYEE SERVICES

In contrast to direct monetary benefits, group insurance, and pensions, the various employee services are much more likely to be given at management's discretion, are not in any sense a reflection of public policy, are usually of limited concern to unions in collective bargaining, and are provided at relatively low cost to the company. A number of the services now available were initiated before the depression of the 1930s as part of the paternalistic emphasis that characterized that period. Recreation programs are typical. Some services are a function of plant location—for example, transportation and eating facilities. Type of industry is clearly a factor in granting employee discounts on company products because only consumer goods manufacturers have anything to offer in this regard. Certain services, such as free medical examinations, are closely related to other aspects of the personnel function. In some instances, there is a good possibility that the company may benefit as much as the employee. This is particularly true of tuition refund programs and other types of educational sponsorship. It is probably impossible to mention all such employee services, but the following listing is reasonably comprehensive. Any one company, of course, will provide only a limited number of these:

1. *Services related to type of work performed,* including subsidies for the purchase and upkeep of work clothes and uniforms, as well as for various types of tools used in connection with the work.
2. *Eating facilities,* including company restaurants, cafeterias, lunchrooms, and vending machines. Under certain circumstances meals may be pro-

vided free of charge. More frequently the charge is at cost or somewhat below.

3. *Transportation and child care facilities,* including parking lots, bus service, company cars, assistance with arrangements for car pools, and day-care centers for employees' preschool children.

4. *Housing services,* including company-owned or company-constructed housing projects, rental lists, assistance with home financing, guarantees on the purchase of homes owned by employees transferred to new locations, and payment of moving expenses.

5. *Financial and legal services,* including sponsorship of credit unions, help in preparing income tax forms, and many types of legal assistance available through the company legal department. In addition, a number of companies operate loan services for employees, although these are usually restricted to hardship cases. Group automobile insurance sometimes is offered on a payroll deduction basis, and group legal insurance plans recently have been developed.

6. *Purchasing services,* including company-owned or -operated stores and discounts on company products and services.

7. *Recreational, social, and cultural programs,* including sponsorship of company athletic teams, social clubs, summer camps, country clubs, recreational areas, orchestras, libraries, discounts on tickets to cultural or sporting events, and travel clubs, which permit employees to get the advantages of charter rates on air fares and accommodations.

8. *Medical and community services,* including plant infirmaries, clinics, and hospitals, with the more extensive facilities being found largely in isolated areas or foreign countries. In addition, companies provide physical examinations, visiting nurses, counseling services, and referrals to various community social service agencies.

9. *Educational services,* including sponsorship of off-hours courses, educational leaves, tuition refund plans, and scholarships or educational loans for employees and their children. Under certain conditions, companies operate complete educational systems for the children of their employees.

10. *Out-placement services,* including making contacts with other employers in the area, help with writing up résumés, and secretarial assistance. Such services usually are provided only where large numbers of technical or professional employees are being terminated.

BENEFIT PROGRAMS FOR MANAGEMENT

In the matter of employee benefits, as in many other aspects of the personnel function, special considerations and policies typically apply in the case of management, particularly at the higher levels. It is not at all uncommon for a firm to have an entirely different benefit structure for individuals in the ranks of management. This is due in part to the fact that many legal constraints, such as overtime payment requirements, do not operate at this level. In addition, collective bargaining agreements do not apply to management in most cases, although they may cover foremen in certain industries, such as construction and printing. Finally, different traditions and requirements exist with regard to management employees; for example, holidays and paid vacations were well established for them long before they were applied to hourly workers. On the other hand, many of the services noted in the previous section have little meaning for managers.

Although there is considerable variability from one company to another, benefit levels tend to be somewhat higher for nonproduction and managerial employees; the differential, however, does not reach that in the salary area. In the matter of temporary disability, salaried employees are usually guaranteed paid sick leave, under which the company continues their full salary for a specified period. Hourly workers are more likely to be covered by a sickness and accident insurance policy that pays benefits below the level of weekly wages.

On the other hand, salaried employees generally, and managers in particular, are, more likely to contribute part of the cost of insurance and retirement benefits. Whether this will remain the case in the future is an open question. One argument in favor of noncontributory benefit plans is based on tax considerations. Employee contributions are part of taxable income for the individual, whereas company payments into pension and welfare funds are treated as an operating expense and thus are not subject to taxation, provided they meet certain Internal Revenue Service criteria.

Tax considerations become increasingly important generally as one moves up the management hierarchy. Thus, many complex executive benefits, like certain types of productivity-oriented compensation (see Chapter 16), have evolved as ways of deferring income and otherwise providing a tax shelter.

THE BENEFIT PROGRAM AS A WHOLE

Aside from the ever-increasing cost aspects of employee benefits and services, the major problem for personnel management in this area relates to matters of planning and control (24). Union pressures combined with a natural desire to maintain a competitive position vis-à-vis benefits offered by other firms have created a situation in some companies that borders on the chaotic. Pronounced imbalances exist between the various benefits, and the relationship of the total benefit package to organizational goal attainment is often unclear (19).

More than any other consideration in collective bargaining, fringe benefits have been used to achieve face-saving settlements by union and management alike. When demands for wage increases could not be justified, union leaders have often turned to employee benefits instead, even though the specific item had little appeal to the rank and file. Under such circumstances, the leadership could at least point to some gain to compensate for an unchanging paycheck, although the gain might not actually be realized until after retirement.

On the other hand, a number of companies have succumbed to a "follow-the-leader" approach in bargaining on fringes. Rather than risk a strike, they have granted benefits negotiated elsewhere without concern for cost considerations that are unique to a particular situation. On occasion, this approach has resulted in an agreement to provide benefits that make no sense at all when applied to a specific employee group. Or there may be a sizable overlap with programs already in effect.

The result of these processes has been that a number of firms have found themselves saddled with a hodgepodge of benefit programs, the costs of which are clearly unreasonable in relation to what is gained in employee satisfaction and organizational maintenance. In one instance, when a bank analyzed its benefits program, it found that it was paying part or all of the costs of 47 different benefits. Furthermore, nearly half of all expenses for benefits was spent for postemployment payments that only those no longer employed would receive (30). There is little doubt that a more positive approach is needed. The cost of each fringe item should be determined, the objective in granting it to employees should be established, and a total package should be formed that provides the greatest return to the company in terms of its goals.

Administration of the Benefit Program

The technicalities of most employee benefits and the amount of clerical work involved in their administration can present a sizable problem. For small employers, the costs of administration can come to more than the amount paid for the benefits themselves. This is one reason why multi-employer arrangements that establish benefit funds are so attractive to smaller firms. The processing of forms and the handling of employee complaints regarding payments for all member firms are the responsibility of the fund's administrators. The economies of scale, insofar as administrative costs are concerned, are considerable.

Benefits specified in a union contract can represent a major source of grievance activity. Rights to vacation or holiday pay, for instance, may be questioned where the eligibility requirements as stated in the agreement are ambiguous and subject to multiple interpretations. Loose contract language can also result in overlapping benefits. A worker may be eligible to collect weekly benefits as paid sick leave and as workers' compensation for the same period of time, unless the contract is very clear on this point. Thus, he could receive a higher income while absent than while present on the job, and the whole amount, ultimately, could be charged completely to the company. Such difficulties can be minimized with care in contract wording, particularly in dealing with eligibility requirements for various benefits.

In larger firms, administrative difficulties are particularly frequent when benefit practices vary from plant to plant or department to department. This problem becomes especially acute when the firm has grown by acquisition and thus taken on a great diversity of benefit packages. Even where one policy is in effect, this policy may be interpreted differently at various company locations. On occasion, several departments or divisions within the firm may be involved in administering benefit programs, with the result that conflicting statements are issued to employees. All this argues strongly for the centralization of responsibility for benefit planning and control in a single profit center, which can provide for effective policy communications and coordination.

Employee Attitudes

Company benefit programs are often criticized for including items that fulfill no real employee need and that accomplish little in terms of goal attainment. A number of benefits that were initiated as legitimate motive satisfiers have now become standard in most firms. Against the background of current practice, it would appear that liberalizing them further has very little appeal for employees. After benefits reach a certain level, wage increases are preferred to more benefits (13). On occasion, union leaders have had to sell the membership on the value of a particular fringe item, particularly where there is some feeling that a wage increase has been traded for a benefit that might well not be realized personally, as with higher retirement pay. Benefit plans that require employee contributions may, in fact, have a negative impact on employee attitudes. It is not particularly pleasant to find money deducted from one's paycheck for benefits that are not desired, even if, under a certain amount of social pressure, one has signed an authorization form.

Nevertheless, it can be assumed that many benefits are considered important by the majority of employees. This is illustrated in Table 20–4. In a few instances, such as major medical, there apparently was a strong motive that was not being met on a widespread basis (it can be assumed that the situation is different today because major medical coverage has become much more common as an employee benefit in the years since this study was conducted). On the other hand, group life insurance was ranked at the very bottom of the various insurance benefits, even though 70 percent of the firms provided it.

Among the noninsurance benefits there are some discrepancies also. One of the most notable is in the case of profit sharing, which was ranked fourth by the employees but was provided by only 15 per cent of the firms included in the study (18).

The significance of various work-force characteristics has been investigated in a number of studies of employee preferences for certain types of benefits or employee choices among benefits or pay increases. In one research study, employees were asked to indicate their choices between a pay increase and seven benefit options, all of which were of approximately equal

Table 20–4. Employee Preferences for Selected Employee Benefits

Benefits	Employee Rank	Employees in 111 Firms Indicating That the Benefit Was of Great Importance (per cent)	Total Firms Providing the Benefit (per cent)
Insurance benefits			
Hospitalization	1	79.6	93.2
Doctor bill	2	73.9	94.4
Major medical	3	64.8	45.7
Retirement plan (other than Social Security)	4	63.5	70.4
Disability income	5	61.3	53.7
Accidental death and dismemberment	6	58.8	53.1
Group life	7	55.9	70.4
Noninsurance benefits			
Paid vacation	1	87.0	81.5
Paid holidays	2	81.0	98.1
Paid sick leave	3	54.1	25.9
Profit-sharing plan	4	42.2	15.4
Credit unions	5	38.7	24.1
Paid rest periods, lunch	6	38.2	71.0
Other paid leaves	7	38.0	46.9
Free medical exams	8	31.0	30.2
Layoff allowances, SUB	9	28.0	11.1
Stock options	10	20.6	8.6
Merchandise discounts	11	18.0	55.6
Free or low-cost meals on premises	12	14.5	n.a.

Source: M. R. Greene, *The Role of Employee Benefit Structures in Manufacturing Industry* (Eugene, Ore.: School of Business Administration, University of Oregon, 1964), pp. 24–25.

economic value (10). Overall, the preference was for longer paid vacations, with the pay increase the second choice, and an increase in the monthly pension benefit third. Results based on a number of demographic variables are shown in Table 20–5. As would be expected, older employees are more likely to prefer the pension benefit increase and provisions for early retirement, and married employees, particularly those with four or more dependents, have a higher preference for the dental insurance plan. There is some evidence, however, that preferences found in this type of study may not be stable; they may change considerably in relatively short periods of time (26).

Because of differences in employees' needs and preferences with regard to fringe benefits, there has been widespread discussion of ways to give the individual worker a choice among benefits or even between benefits and pay increases. This is frequently referred to as a "cafeteria" or "smorgasbord"

Table 20–5. Employee Preference for Compensation Options (ranking based on results of paired comparisons)

Employee Variables

	Age			Marital Status		Sex		Dependents			Years of Service			Job Title	
Compensation Option	18–35 (N = 52)	36–49 (N = 58)	50–56 (N = 39)	Single (N = 52)	Married (N = 97)	Male (N = 114)	Female (N = 35)	0 (N = 33)	1–3 (N = 60)	4 or more (N = 56)	1–10 (N = 48)	11–20 (N = 63)	21 or more (N = 38)	Clerical (N = 48)	Operating (N = 101)
Extra vacation	1	2	2	1	1	1	1	2	1	1	1	1	2	1	1
Pay increase	2	1	3	2	2	2	3	1	3	3	2	2	3	2	2
Pension increase	6	3	1	3	3	3	2	3	2	4	4	3	1	3	3
Dental plan	3	4	7	7	4	4	7	8	5	2	3	4	6	6	4
Early retirement	7	5	4	4	5	5	5	4	4	6	5	5	4	5	5
10 Fridays	5	6	5	5	6	6	4	5	6	7	6	7	5	4	7
Four-day week	4	7	6	6	7	7	6	6	7	5	7	6	8	7	6
Shorter workday	8	8	8	8	8	8	8	7	8	8	8	8	7	8	8

Source: Adapted from J. B. Chapman and R. Otteman, Employee Preference for Various Compensation and Fringe Benefit Options, ASPA Foundation, Berea, Ohio, 1975.

approach to compensation. A young, single worker might take a pay raise, for example, a married employee with dependents would prefer more insurance benefits, and the older worker would contribute the money available to his pension fund. So far, most employers who have offered any choices have limited them to options relating to one specific benefit, such as the purchase of additional life insurance or different types of health insurance, or to a choice of extra pay in lieu of a particular benefit, such as another paid holiday or more vacation. In part, the problems, such as different tax treatment, and additional costs of administering any program based on wide choices have made them unattractive to management, but this could change with increasing computer capabilities. One writer suggests that employers are going to have to move to individualized benefits, or psychological fringes, now that the basic security needs have been taken care of by most health and welfare plans (15).

Another problem with a cafeteria-type program of benefits is that of educating the employee so that he can make an informed choice (16). Even among the higher-level members of the work force, there are those who do not have the interest, do not want to take the time, or do not feel capable of making decisions between a number of options. Often, also, there are specified time limits for exercising options, age limits after which certain benefits are no longer available or are more costly, or length-of-service requirements governing employee eligibility. The experience of TRW, which instituted a Flexible Benefits Program in 1974, indicates that employees can make intelligent choices, however, and that the vast majority do desire changes in their benefit coverage when given the opportunity to make them (14).

Irrespective of what benefits and services a firm provides, and whether or not employees have any choice in the matter, the communications aspect of the benefit program is crucial (23). The benefits have little value as a means to encouraging pride in the organization, loyalty, and satisfaction unless employees know about and understand them. Many workers are entirely unaware that the company pays for unemployment compensation and contributes sizably to Social Security. A large number appear to have little knowledge of the private benefits available to them through the company, or the actual dollar value of the benefits provided (21). Frequently, a union receives the credit for employee benefits and services, particularly those administered under union sponsorship, even though the funds derive entirely from company sources.

Thus, it becomes important to inform employees regarding the nature of the benefits provided and the company's role in their financing. This does not mean that a firm should claim full credit for benefits that are in fact provided at least in part as a result of legal constraints or union pressure, but it is desirable to make employees aware of what they are getting and of the costs incurred as a result of benefit payments. Where items are provided on a unilateral basis by the company, employees should know of this.

To get maximum return from an investment in fringe benefits, a company must have an effective communications program to inform employees regarding what is available, when they are eligible, and what procedures are involved in obtaining benefits. It is especially important that communications to employees on these matters be clear and correct; employers often have been taken to court by disgruntled employees who thought they were entitled to certain benefits on the basis of statements in company handbooks. At times, these statements have proved to be incomplete or at variance with the provisions of the official text of the benefit plan (28). As a result, one of the major requirements of the Pension Reform Law (ERISA) is that employees be provided with descriptions of benefit plans and regular reports on their operation. Furthermore, the law specifies that these communications be prepared so that employees can clearly understand them (13).

Managers in particular should be able to speak with knowledge about the benefits program because employees normally turn to their immediate superior in search of information about all aspects of their relationship with their employer. The various approaches that are used for this purpose and the techniques of internal communications are discussed in the next chapter.

QUESTIONS

1. What do the various types of benefits and services contribute to a company? Do they contribute in the same way as monetary compensation? Explain.
2. Describe and discuss the following:
   a. Monday holiday law.
   b. Sabbaticals in industry.
   c. SUB.
   d. Thrift plans.
   e. Comprehensive medical insurance.
3. What is vesting, and how does it work? How has ERISA influenced vesting? What social concerns appear to have motivated this type of legislation?
4. What are the various ways in which benefit programs for managers and production workers tend to differ? What might account for these differences?
5. What are some of the pitfalls that companies often succumb to in setting up and administering their total benefit programs? How might these pitfalls be avoided?

REFERENCES
1. Allen, D. *Fringe Benefits: Wages or Social Obligation?* Ithaca, N.Y.: New York State School of Industrial and Labor Relations, Cornell University, 1969.

2. Bell, D. R. "Prevalence of Private Retirement Plans." *Monthly Labor Review*, 98 (1975), No. 10, 17–20.
3. Brennan, J. H. "What Makes LTD a Special Benefits Problem." *Compensation Review*, 5 (1973), No. 1, 26–34.
4. Bureau of National Affairs, Inc. *Pensions & Other Retirement Benefits.* Personnel Policies Forum Survey No. 103, October 1973.
5. Bureau of National Affairs, Inc. *Employee Health & Welfare Benefits.* Personnel Policies Forum Survey No. 107, October 1974.
6. Bureau of National Affairs, Inc. *Highlights of the New Pension Reform Law.* Washington, D.C.: BNA, Inc., 1974.
7. Bureau of National Affairs, Inc. *Basic Patterns in Union Contracts.* 8th ed., Washington, D.C.: BNA, Inc., 1975.
8. Bureau of National Affairs, Inc. *Paid Leave and Leave of Absence Policies,* Personnel Policies Forum Survey No. 111, November 1975.
9. Chamber of Commerce of the United States. *Employee Benefits 1973.* Washington, D.C.: Chamber of Commerce, 1974.
10. Chapman, J. B., and R. Ottemann. *Employee Preference for Various Compensation and Fringe Benefit Options.* Berea, Ohio: ASPA Foundation, 1975.
11. Ellig, B. R. "Determining Competiveness of Employee Benefit Systems." *Compensation Review*, 6 (1974), No. 1, 8–34.
12. Finley, G. J. *Policies on Leave for Political and Social Action.* New York: Conference Board, 1972.
13. Fleming, S. "ERISA and the Employee's Right to Know." *Personnel Journal*, 54 (1975), 346–349.
14. "Flexible Benefits: How One Company Does It." *Personnel Administrator*, 10 (1974), No. 8, p. 51.
15. Foegen, J. H. "Fringe on the Fringe." *Personnel Administration*, 35 (1972), No. 1, 18–22.
16. Goode, R. V. "Complications at the Cafeteria Checkout Line." *Personnel*, 51 (1974), No. 6, 45–49.
17. Gordon, T. J., and R. E. LeBleu. "Employee Benefits, 1970–1985." *Harvard Business Review*, 48 (1970), No. 1, 93–107.
18. Greene, M. R. *The Role of Employee Benefit Structures in Manufacturing Industry.* Eugene, Ore.: School of Business Administration, University of Oregon, 1964.
19. Harris, R. L. "Let's Take the 'Fringe' Out of Fringe Benefits." *Personnel Journal*, 54 (1975), 86–89.
20. Hearst, P. S. "Employee Stock Ownership Trusts and Their Uses." *Personnel Journal*, 54 (1975), 104–106.
21. Hettenhouse, G. W., W. G. Lewellen, H. P. Lanser, and H. L. James. "Communicating the Compensation Package." *Personnel*, 52 (1975), No. 6, 19–30.

22. Hodgens, E. L. "Key Changes in Major Pension Plans." *Monthly Labor Review*, 98 (1975), No. 7, 22–27.
23. Ives, C. S. "Benefits and Services—Private," in D. Yoder and H. G. Heneman, Jr., *Motivation and Commitment*. Washington, D.C.: Bureau of National Affairs, Inc., 1975.
24. McCaffery, R. M. *Managing the Employee Benefits Program*. New York: American Management Association, Inc., 1972.
25. Meyer, M., and H. Fox. *Profile of Employee Benefits*. New York: Conference Board, 1974.
26. Milkovich, G. T., and M. J. Delaney. "A Note on Cafeteria Pay Plans." *Industrial Relations*, 14 (1975), No. 1, 112–116.
27. Snider, Paul. "Health Maintenance Organizations—A Can of Worms?" *Personnel*, 51 (1974), No. 6, 36–44.
28. Srb, J. H. *Communicating with Employees About Pension and Welfare Benefits*. Ithaca, N.Y.: New York State School of Industrial and Labor Relations, Cornell University, 1971.
29. Tilove, R. "Pensions, Health, and Welfare Plans," in L. Ulman (ed.), *Challenges to Collective Bargaining*. Englewood Cliffs, N.J.: Prentice-Hall, Inc., 1967, pp. 37–64.
30. Yount, H. H. "Total Compensation—Cost, Comparison and Control." *Compensation Review*, 3 (1971), No. 4, 9–18.
31. Walker, J. W. "The New Appeal of Early Retirement." *Business Horizons*, 18 (1975), No. 3, 43–48.
32. Wistert, F. M. *Fringe Benefits*. New York: Van Nostrand Reinhold Company, 1959.

Internal Communications

This chapter will consider those communications procedures that personnel management can utilize directly to foster goal attainment—a limited perspective in comparison with a discussion of organizational communication processes as a whole. Yet personnel management cannot be all things to all people. If it attempts to be so, it loses its identity as a separate area of study. Just as with such topics as leadership, employee motivation, and work group dynamics, extended treatment of organizational communication generally seems more appropriately left to courses in management and organizational behavior. The present focus, then, will be on those internal communications techniques that a personnel manager can bring directly to bear in utilizing a company's work force effectively. With only a few exceptions, communications procedures of this kind have been directed toward the goal of organizational maintenance.

Although the present chapter will devote little space to the matter of superior-subordinate communications as they occur on a day-to-day basis in the work place, it should not be assumed that interactions of this kind are totally unrelated to personnel management. As a part of the general management process, they are of concern to managers in all aspects of the business, including managers in the personnel area. In addition, such topics as semantics in communications, communications skills, barriers to communications, and two-way communications are widely included in management-development programs. It is thus indirectly, through its responsibility for effective communications training for managers, that personnel management achieves much of its impact on the primarily productivity-oriented superior-subordinate communications process (22).

The tremendous growth in recent years in the amount of research and general literature on communication processes in organizations has not yet been reflected in many changes in business organizations themselves. As a start toward developing a general communication system, it has been suggested that companies make an audit of all internal and external, formal and informal, verbal and nonverbal communications activities as they relate to the goals they are expected to achieve (15). As illustrated in Table 21–1, there are four basic types of objectives of communications activities that combine to form communications networks. The *regulative* network has the goal of securing conformity to plans and assuring achievement of productivity through such communications as policy statements, procedures, and rules. The *innovative* network is concerned with problem solving and change through such techniques as suggestion systems and meetings. The *integrative* network is directly related to employee morale and organizational maintenance considerations and uses methods ranging from the informal grapevine to formal presentations by the company president. The *informative* network relates to employee effectiveness and productivity through direct dissemination of information and training programs.

In Table 21–1, the internal verbal communication activities—the activities most likely to be associated with the personnel department's responsibilities—are classified by network and by whether they are interpersonal between two individuals, relate to small groups within the company, or are organization-wide. The major responsibility of personnel in the area of employee communications in most companies would involve the activities shown in the organization-wide group, particularly those under the informative network, but to a lesser degree those in the innovative and integrative networks also. Generally, the formal aspects of communication programs are classified as downward or upward in nature.

COMMUNICATIONS DOWNWARD

Various techniques are used to transmit information from the higher levels of an organization directly to individual members, with the objective of creating a sense of belonging. The overall cohesiveness of the company as a social unit is fostered, and presumably employees will be more satisfied

Table 21–1. *Internal Verbal Communication Activities Classified by Number of Participants and Communication Network Objectives*

Number of Participants	Regulative Network	Innovative Network	Integrative Network	Informative Network
Interpersonal (2 persons)	Supervisor directions and requests Supervisor-subordinate meetings Job descriptions and standards Annual appraisal Special problem sessions Reports on operations Memoranda	Ad hoc problem resolution Supervisor-subordinate idea development meetings Annual goals determination in work planning program Informal get-togethers, as in-house lunch meetings Reports on visits to other organizations, conventions, seminars	President's welcome letter to new employee Grievance discussion Progress review in work planning program Annual appraisal Informal meeting of two organization members Superior-subordinate informal conversation on personal matters	Hiring interview New employee orientation Memoranda Oral and written reports Cross-functioning
Small Group (3–10 persons)	Meetings: directors, executive committee, departmental; crisis-type meetings, as in fire, flood, strike	Meetings: directors, executive committee, departmental, interdepartmental, problem-solving, sales development, crisis-type, budget, group lunch	Meetings: participative work group, interdepartmental, coffee break, group lunch	Meetings Training in small groups

Organization-wide				
	Organization plans	Suggestion program	In-house publications	In-house publications
	Policy statements	Problem-finding program	Holiday social function	Bulletin board notices
	Standard procedures	Operations audit reports as to general and specific areas of the organization	The grapevine	Staff meetings
	Regulations		Literature available to personnel concerning plans, etc.	Employee information booklets
	Union contract		President's talk to all employees	Benefits brochure
	Chart of organization		Supervisory staff meeting	Statements of standard procedures
	Staff memos			Union contract
	Organization chart			Organization policy statements
				The grapevine

Source: H. H. Greenbaum, "The Audit of Organizational Communication," *Academy of Management Journal,* 17 (1974), p. 748.

with their work situation. Downward communications should pull the entire organization together and unite it behind particular task objectives. Occasionally, this may require a concerted effort to subvert the goals of a union, which represents or is attempting to represent the company's employees, because unions can produce a major divisive force within the firm.

The media used by different companies to achieve these goals vary considerably. Among them are company magazines and newspapers; mass meetings, for all or groups of employees; employee letters, sent directly to the home or inserted in paychecks; information racks containing circulars and pamphlets; employee handbooks and manuals; bulletin boards and posters; bulletins and memoranda to management; and tours of company facilities. Annual reports, news items in the popular media, and even commercial advertising are used on occasion to communicate with employees. (In such cases, external media are used for internal purposes.) Other downward communications techniques involve the use of speeches, telephone, teletype, films, public-address systems, slides, radio, and television.

It is important that the internal communication system operate rapidly and with maximal validity. To the extent the system produces information that later proves to be incorrect, or lags and so yields its data subsequent to public or other media, it will be viewed as lacking in value by employees and will lose much of its audience. Without an audience, it can have little impact as an input-output mediator.

The Selection of Media

Any medium of communication must meet certain requirements to be effective. It must reach all employees for whom it is intended. It must be official in the sense that the information is perceived as originating with individuals consistently, so that employees will look to this source when they desire to know about a particular matter.

Given these conditions, is there any evidence that some media are inherently more effective than others in getting information to employees? The data of Table 21–2 bear on this point. In this instance, three separate studies were conducted—one with a large group of college students enrolled in a public speaking course at Purdue University; one with the production employees of a building materials manufacturing plant; and one with the employees at a single facility of Spiegel's, a mail order-chain store organization (9). The same information was transmitted in various ways, including oral presentations by professors or supervisors, written handouts or letters, and posting on a bulletin board. Information retention was measured with a 10-item questionnaire administered approximately two days after the original communication. In all cases, a control group was included that could learn only through the grapevine. The bulletin board method was not used in the manufacturing plant.

Table 21–2. Mean Accuracy of Recall Scores for Information Transmitted Using Various Media

Method of Presenting Information	College Student Sample		Manufacturing Employee Sample		Retail Store Sample	
	Mean Recall Score	Number	Mean Recall Score	Number	Mean Recall Score	Number
Oral and written	6.54	281	7.30	30	7.70	102
Oral only	5.31	161	6.38	13	6.17	94
Written only	4.58	279	4.46	28	4.91	109
Bulletin board	3.52	152	—	—	3.72	115
Grapevine only	2.88	157	3.00	13	3.56	108

Source: T. L. Dahle, "An Objective and Comparative Study of Five Methods of Transmitting Information to Business and Industrial Employees," Speech Monographs, 21 : 24, 26, 27 (1954).

The results are surprisingly consistent. A combination of written and oral media is clearly preferable. As between the two, however, oral presentations at a meeting are more effective. Posting an item on a bulletin board appears to accomplish relatively little, being indistinguishable from the grapevine, when standard tests of statistical significance are applied.

The superiority of oral face-to-face communication does not appear to be limited to information transmission. There is good evidence that employees prefer it (13). In one study, comparisons were made between two almost identical plants, one of which relied upon regular monthly meetings conducted by foremen to transmit information, whereas the other did not. As might be expected, the employees in the plant with the meetings were much more likely to feel well-informed, and they were also more likely to feel that they really belonged in the company (62 vs. 29 per cent) and to be highly satisfied with it as a place to work (45 vs. 20 per cent) (16). Thus, the meetings not only served to provide information; in doing so, they made a sizable contribution to organizational maintenance.

It should be emphasized that in this specific instance, the meetings involved a two-way communications process. Employees were encouraged to ask questions, either with a view to clarifying points made by the foremen or for the purpose of eliciting new information. In general, such an approach seems to be highly advantageous in fostering employee satisfaction. A one-way system can create considerable frustration if the material is at all ambiguous or important aspects are omitted, whereas providing an opportunity for questioning can increase understanding. It can also produce a greater feeling of trust, openness, and belonging as regards the company. One major difficulty with written media is that it is very difficult to integrate them with communication upward in a meaningful way. Thus, they appear to be most useful for transmitting information of a routine nature (10).

In using oral communications, with or without a two-way approach, a great many companies go to considerable trouble to stage and program their presentations. Materials are often prepared in advance, and the manager who is to do the speaking may receive coaching from various training specialists. Presentations involving the company's financial position, in conjunction with the annual report, are particularly likely to involve considerable preparation. In other cases, information may be transmitted to management via various memorandums or bulletins. The latter then serve as a basis for oral communications to appropriate employee groups. During union negotiations, a strike, or an organizing attempt, these management bulletins appear quite frequently.

A firm that refuses to provide any information, or does so on a very minimal basis, will almost certainly suffer negative consequences. But given that communication is attempted at some meaningful level, the crucial considerations are how and what rather than how much. The advantages of a two-way approach have already been noted, and certainly the tone inherent in any communication can influence attitudes. But even more important is the content. Certain kinds of information may well make employees less satisfied, as, for instance, the knowledge that the firm has been put up for sale or merger. If no effort is made to utilize the communication system to convince employees that they are part of a worthwhile organization, then favorable attitudes are unlikely to result. Neutral communications may increase information tremendously but have little impact on how employees feel about the company.

The choice of communications media can influence how employees are likely to react to the information being transmitted, and some methods of communication obviously are more suited to certain types of information than others. Table 21–3 provides data in this regard (6). The figures in the table indicate the percentages of more than 200 companies using various techniques for six different categories of information communicated downward to employees. For many of the types of information included in the table, it is apparent that most companies use more than one method to reinforce getting the message across.

Combining oral and written media to convey a piece of information with maximum effectiveness will contribute to goal achievement only if the information is of a kind that creates favorable attitudes. This is not to say that unpleasant information should be withheld or distorted. It is important that employees trust management and its information channels. A communication system that does not yield important information that is expected of it will soon lose its audience. But communication procedures can appropriately be used to encourage pride in the organization; to point up real advantages of employment, such as benefits and services; to state company, as opposed to union, viewpoints; and to demonstrate the advantages of the economic system that makes the company's existence possible (7).

Table 21–3. Methods Used to Communicate Different Types of Information to Employees

Method of Communication	Percentage of Companies (N = 219) Using Method to Communicate—					
	Change in Wage or Salary Levels	Change in Employee Benefits	Individual Employee Benefits Status	Changes in Operations That Might Result in Layoffs, etc.	Changes in Top-level Personnel	Status of Union Negotiations
Individual verbal communication	45	13	52	31	5	19
Group meetings	29	39	8	44	13	41
Memos or letters to employees	31	65	30	21	44	48
Articles in employee publications	14	41	3	13	43	15
Posted on bulletin boards	12	19	1	12	36	16
Through union	13	7	3	8	0	13
Special individual benefits statement	n.a.	n.a.	23	n.a.	n.a.	n.a.
Other (local press, teletype network, public-address system, recordings)	5	0	0	0	8	9

Source: Adapted from Bureau of National Affairs, Inc., Employee Communications, Personnel Policies Forum Survey No. 110, July 1975, pp. 16–17. n.a. = not applicable.

Company Magazines and Newspapers

Almost all large corporations and a great many smaller ones publish a company magazine or newspaper, usually on a monthly basis, that goes to all employees (6). Many firms have additional publications for separate departments, geographical regions, or plants. When these internal media are combined with those of an external nature directed to stockholders and the public, the total journalistic effort is very comprehensive indeed.

Yet, for many years, these publications said practically nothing about the company as an organization and did little to develop favorable employee attitudes. During and after World War II, there was some shift away from chitchat and personal news of individual employees, but much still remained. Even when information about the company, including such matters as its economic position, organization, products, equipment, methods, benefits, and services, was included, it was usually presented in an entirely factual manner. There was little attempt to provide employees with a company viewpoint and thus to encourage cohesiveness and loyalty.

Comparisons of union and company publications consistently point up the differential emphasis on economic matters, bargaining issues, and political action. Company magazines practically never deal with these matters, whereas union publications invariably devote considerable space to them. Yet during a strike, companies are much more likely to move into the center of the communications arena. The company magazine may now take up the issues, letters are sent to employees at their homes, and the public media may be used to present the company viewpoint. Thus, the typical pattern is complete silence on labor relations matters prior to open conflict and then considerable utilization of company publications for persuasive purposes.

The reason often given for avoiding persuasive material, and even information regarding the company as an organization, is that too much stress on such matters will result in a loss of readership. Many company editors have maintained that if an employee does not find frequent mention of himself or people he knows in the pages of the magazine or newspaper, he will cease to read it. In particular, they have argued that "propaganda" should be avoided. The feeling has been that the audience must be held at all costs, and this cannot be done if one moves directly into the realm of organizational maintenance. This viewpoint involves certain quite testable assumptions about the nature of employee readership preferences and patterns. And, in fact, evidence does exist regarding reading differentials for material that is totally unrelated to company goals, company-oriented material, and material that is persuasive to a company viewpoint.

READERSHIP SURVEYS

One relevant study dealt with readership patterns among employees of The Atlantic Refining Company (28). Fifteen articles, which proved to be relatively evenly spaced along a scale of company orientation, were selected from various prior issues of *The Atlantic Magazine* and reprinted in a questionnaire. Scale position was determined by judges. None of the items dealt with economic, political, or union considerations, so that persuasion to a company viewpoint on such matters was not a factor in this particular study. Headlines for typical items judged to be highly company-oriented, in the middle range, and not company-oriented follow.

1. Company-oriented:
   (a) Retirement System Ends 25th Year.
   (b) New-Products, Applications, Customers.
   (c) Questions and Answers on Company's Recent $55 Million Issue of Debentures!
2. Middle range:
   (a) Safe Drivers Are Honored.
   (b) Atlantic Congratulates Its Faithful Employees Who Celebrate Service Anniversaries.
3. Not company-oriented:
   (a) Two at Pittsburgh Avid Stamp Collectors.
   (b) Egg Magic (four recipes).

In each instance the employee was asked to indicate whether he or she usually or only rarely read this particular type of item in the magazine. Questionnaires were sent to a representative sample of 600 employees; 251 were returned. Subsequent follow-up studies of the nonrespondents indicated that had all 600 employees returned questionnaires, the readership results obtained would not have differed from those derived with the 251. The response rate obtained in this study is typical for readership surveys, although rates as high as 67 per cent and as low as 10 per cent have been reported (20).

The findings presented in Table 21–4 indicate that the employees not only did not object to company-oriented material, they actually preferred it. The major conclusion derived from the study was that the company magazine was viewed as the primary source of information regarding the firm's level of success. Thus, through such company-related material as appeared, employees could determine whether they were associated with an effective organization that could provide them with both security and opportunity. With the exception of the female employees, most of whom were young and would not stay long, there was a consistent tendency toward more widespread readership of the company-oriented articles. There was no evidence that chitchat was necessary to maintain readership—quite the opposite.

It seems apparent that the widespread assumptions regarding loss of readership when company publications are oriented specifically to the goal of organizational maintenance do not meet the test of the research evidence. Articles of the kind described as company-oriented in *The Atlantic Magazine* can be used. In fact, this is what many employees appear to want from

Table 21–4. Rank-order Correlations Between Scale Values on Degree of Company Orientation for 15 Company Magazine Articles and Extent of Readership of the Articles

Group	N	Correlation
Total sample	251	.72
Sex		
Male	218	.70
Female	33	.40
Job level		
Supervisory	58	.72
Nonsupervisory	193	.74
Company service		
0–10 years	92	.79
11–20 years	65	.68
21+ years	94	.77
Education		
0–11 years	67	.63
12 Years	79	.72
13+ Years	96	.79
Unknown	9	—

Source: J. B. Miner and E. E. Heaton, "Company Orientation as a Factor in the Readership of Employee Publications," *Personnel Psychology,* 12 : 615 (1959).

company publications. The recent trend toward greater concern with such matters as community problems, race relations, and pollution in company publications is consistent with this mandate (39).

Yet there is one important consideration if employee attitudes are to be influenced. The company magazine must not be viewed as an organ of extremism. It must be considered a trusted source of information; it must be accepted as a legitimate medium for transmitting the particular kind of material it contains; it must have a reputation for moderation and not be viewed as "always preaching" (33). Given these conditions, there is every reason to believe that an appropriate selection of content along the lines suggested can make company publications a meaningful factor in organizational goal attainment.

The Problem of Readability

During the late 1940s and early 1950s, there was a rather widespread concern in the business world regarding the reading level of material published for employees. A number of studies indicated that much of what was produced as part of the downward communication process was far above the comprehension level of the intended audience. Although the emphasis on this topic did yield considerable change in readability levels, the matter remains an important one. An employee who is continually exposed to material that he finds difficult or impossible to understand is unlikely to view the source of this material favorably. Such communication is most likely to

Table 21–5. Comparison of Flesch Reading Ease Grades for Employee Handbooks in 29 Organizations, 1949 and 1964

	Number of Handbooks	
Reading Ease Grade	1949	1964
Very easy	—	—
Easy	—	—
Fairly easy	—	1
Standard	1	4
Fairly difficult	10	6
Difficult	16	17
Very difficult	2	1

Source: K. Davis, "Readability Changes in Employee Handbooks of Identical Companies During a Fifteen-year Period," Personnel Psychology, 21 : 416 (1968).

yield feelings of inferiority and defensive criticism of the publication, perhaps also of the company as well.

The readability problem appears to arise because employee publications are written by individuals with at least a college education, to be cleared by managers both within and outside the personnel area, who are equally well-educated. Thus, handbooks, magazines, and practically anything else written for employees can easily represent difficult reading for those whose education is more limited. Industrial editors have become increasingly conscious of this problem, and at the same time the educational level of the population has been rising. Thus, the gap is narrowing. However, as Table 21–5 indicates, increases in readability since the problem was first recognized have not been very pronounced (11). The major contribution to narrowing the gap has come from the increased educational level of the population.

The matter of readability is particularly acute with regard to employee handbooks because they are viewed as the basic source of information about the company, and they are designed to be a more permanent type of communication than newspapers, magazines, or memos to employees (8). Frequently, the handbook lists company rules and disciplinary procedures and describes working conditions, pay practices, and benefits; as noted in Chapter 20, it is important not only from an employee relations point of view but frequently also from a legal point of view that these matters be clearly understood by employees. Companies sometimes publish more than one employee handbook because of different policies that apply to different employee groups or because of varying educational levels of certain employee groups (21).

COMMUNICATIONS UPWARD

Communications from the bottom to the top of the organizational hierarchy are of significance for two reasons. First, it is primarily through some type of feedback process that management is able to obtain the information needed to evaluate and perhaps correct its downward communications. Feedback of this kind is needed to determine whether employees have received and understood the messages directed to them through the company media and supervisory channels. Second, without some mechanisms through which employees can ask questions, express dissatisfactions, register complaints, or make suggestions regarding company policies and procedures, management may remain completely unaware of major problem areas and threats to organizational maintenance for extended periods of time. The consequence can be a continual festering of problems leading to open conflict, mass resignations, or even disintegration of the organization.

In contrast to downward communications, techniques of communicating upward are rather limited in number, and it is often difficult to control them, so as to keep the focus on goal-related information. As noted in the last section, the content of items initiated from the top can easily shift to areas, such as bowling leagues and cooking, that have little to do with company goals; this problem is accentuated many times when transmission is initiated at lower levels.

In part the difficulties of upward communication are inherent in the nature of business organizations, with their stress on hierarchy and their underlying premise that those at the upper levels should tell individuals below them what to do and how to do it, not the reverse. Furthermore, because a manager or supervisor has the power to control the work situation in many of its aspects, employees are not likely to communicate upward anything that might reflect negatively on them. Should an individual complain to his superior, or make a suggestion, he can have no feeling of certainty that the matter will go to higher levels (35). The supervisor may consider it unimportant or be too busy to take any action, or he may deliberately fail to report it to his superior because it implies that his own performance has been less than perfect. Even within the ranks of management, upward communications may be severely stifled or distorted.

Techniques in Upward Communication

From what has been said, it is apparent that the barriers and distortions that plague downward communications are magnified many times in the upward situation (2, 3, 31). Because of the uncertainties associated with the use of the superior-subordinate channel, various techniques have been devised that permit employees to bypass their immediate superiors in registering complaints or making suggestions. A type of program that has become popular in recent years is often called a private or "hot" line system; it provides a way for employees to discuss or question anonymously any company matter of concern (17). Through the use of a special telephone line or special company mail forms, questions are directed to the company official with the responsibility or expertise required to provide accurate information. The employee making the inquiry receives a prompt and direct reply; ques-

Table 21–6. Upward Communications Techniques

	Per Cent of Companies ($N = 219$)	
Technique	Using Technique	Considered Most Effective
Informal inquiries or discussions with employees	86	31
Exit interviews	81	6
Discussions with first-level supervisors	78	22
Grievance or complaint procedures	66	7
The "grapevine"	59	*
Union representatives [a]	56	6
Counseling	49	6
Formal meetings	40	5
Suggestion systems	37	*
Formal attitude surveys	30	9
Question and answer column in employee publications	16	*
Gripe boxes	8	*
"Hot" line or recording systems	6	*

Source: Adapted from Bureau of National Affairs, Inc., Employee Communications, Personnel Policies Forum Survey No. 110, July 1975.
* Less than 3, per cent.
[a] Figures are percentages of companies with some union-represented employees.

tions of general interest often are discussed later in employee publications. Thus, both upward and downward communications become involved.

While special upward communications devices are being used in many companies, it is clear from the data in Table 21–6 that the informal, face-to-face channels are still considered the most effective, despite their inadequacies. None of the formal techniques was viewed as most effective for upward communications by as many as ten per cent of the more than 200 personnel executives responding to the survey (6). Although about one-half the companies with unionized employees rely on union representatives for information, this source is not considered the most effective except in a small percentage of these companies.

Among the techniques that are used extensively but not rated as being effective is the "grapevine." Over the years, there have been numerous studies of this informal communication network because of its obvious existence and the need for management to try to control it and to use it (24). One report indicates that while employees perceive the grapevine as very influential, they also tend to have negative feelings about it (29). This could account for the assessment by personnel executives that it is not effective as an upward communications channel.

Formal attitude surveys, including exit interviews, as an upward communication technique will be considered separately in the next section. This is an area where considerable research has been done and the amount of knowledge that has accumulated is sizable. The use of such surveys in evaluating managers was considered in Chapter 8. Several of the other techniques noted in Table 21–6 have also been discussed previously.

Employee counseling was considered in Chapter 18 as one of the corrective procedures used in connection with performance control. Although counselors will rarely transmit specific problems of specific employees to higher management, because in doing so they might create mistrust and thus prevent other employees from coming to them in the future, they may provide general impressions of employee attitudes. If a company does utilize counseling on a wide scale, this can be a valuable upward communications technique. Yet counseling is rarely, if ever, introduced for its upward communications value alone. The communications aspect tends to emerge subsequently, as a by-product.

Grievance handling was considered at some length in Chapter 19 as an approach in labor relations. Procedures of this kind may also be viewed as devices to facilitate upward communications, even though when used with any frequency, they tend to reflect a breakdown or blockage within the superior-subordinate channel. The major difficulty from a communications viewpoint is that the grievance machinery may be used largely to further union goals. Thus, it may not provide valid information on real sources of employee dissatisfaction.

Suggestion Systems

A rather widely used technique for upward communications is the suggestion system. In many respects this approach is unique. It is not characteristically designed to provide feedback with regard to downward communications; those at lower levels must initiate largely in terms of their own ideas. It is not intended as a means to the expression of complaints so much as to permit employees to communicate upward in a positive and constructive fashion. The ideas communicated may relate to their productivity or maintenance goals; they may deal with more efficient production methods or with procedures for improving job satisfaction. Yet the existence of an effective suggestion system per se contributes primarily to organizational maintenance. The use of this technique can well yield a considerable feeling of involvement in the organization, a belief that one's contributions count and will be rewarded. Thus, loyalty, cohesiveness, and commitment are likely to be fostered. On the other hand, suggestion systems may also function to provide financial rewards for creative effort. Under these circumstances, they are more than a technique of upward communication.

Suggestion systems may take a variety of forms. In some cases, they are tied to specific objectives, as with work-simplification and cost-reduction programs, or they may be built into an incentive payment procedure, as in the Scanlon plans, discussed in Chapter 17. The system may be company-wide, or it may apply only to a segment of the work force. Thus, some companies maintain entirely independent suggestion systems for production, office, and managerial employees. Usually, operation is continuous, but on occasion a definite time limit is established. In such cases, the scope may also be restricted, to ideas related to safety, for instance.

OPERATING PROCEDURES

Suggestion systems need to be carefully administered if they are to make a positive contribution to organizational maintenance. There is always a risk that feelings of inequity and injustice will be aroused, with the result that conflict may be the only observable consequence. For this reason, most effective suggestion systems have standard forms for employees to use in submitting ideas. They set specific time limits for acknowledging the receipt of suggestions, investigation by the department concerned, and acceptance or rejection by the suggestion committee. They establish procedures to ensure the anonymity of those making suggestions during the review process. The suggestion committee itself is usually constituted primarily from among rank-and-file employees; often the only management representative is someone from the personnel department. However, to the extent top management can be involved, support for the suggestion system is likely to be increased. The union may well have formal representation, although this is by no means a universal practice.

Applicable rules and regulations normally attempt to ensure that the employee who first submits a suggestion receives credit for it, and that suggestions are not rejected without a full explanation. The usual practice is to exclude ideas that fall within the normal scope of the individual's job. Thus, if the role requirements are such as to indicate that ideas of a certain kind *should* be produced by a particular individual, such ideas are ineligible for a suggestion award.

AWARDS

Probably the most difficult aspect of suggestion systems is determining the award for an acceptable suggestion. Most plans provide for awards in cash, although some firms award an equivalent amount in savings bonds or company stock certificates. There are also plans which make no formal provision for payment. The employee receives only a certificate of merit or a letter of commendation. But a copy of this goes in his personnel file. Thus, pay raises, promotions, and other personnel actions may well be influenced, even though direct payment is lacking.

Where cash awards are made, the minimum payment can vary from $15, or in some cases even less, to $25; the maximum can go as high as $10,000, or there may be no specified upper limit. Employees whose suggestions yield measurable savings to the company ordinarily receive an award amounting to a percentage, usually 10 or 20 per cent, of the anticipated savings during the year subsequent to adoption. Such awards may well run into thousands of dollars. Some companies conduct a special review at the end of the first

```
                                                    Suggestion No. _____

Nature of Benefit                                              Points

  1. Has definite therapeutic value.                          16 to 20
  2. Results in a definite improvement in safety.             16 to 20
  3. Produces a marked improvement in operations.            16 to 20
  4. Improves employee relations.                              6 to 15
  5. Improves working conditions.                              6 to 15
  6. Has only limited importance—minor improvement.           1 to  5

Distribution of Value of Benefit
  1. Company-wide application.                                21 to 25
  2. More than one department or installation.               16 to 20
  3. Single department or installation.                       6 to 15
  4. Single operation or section.                             1 to  5

Ingenuity
  1. Very resourceful.                                        11 to 25
  2. Average.                                                  6 to 10
  3. Uninventive.                                             1 to  5

Cost of Adoption
  1. Less than $25.                                              0
  2. $25 to $100.                                               -5
  3. Over $100.                                                -10

Effort Involved
  1. Considerable personal research.                         11 to 15
  2. Average substantiation.                                  1 to 10
  3. No research at all.                                         0

Completeness of Proposal
  1. Facts clearly presented, so that little further effort is required
     to put idea into effect.                                 11 to 15
  2. Basic facts are sound, but needs some refining to put into effect.  6 to 10
  3. Facts not completely or clearly presented, thus requiring consider-
     able clarification.                                      1 to  5

                                                Total points
```

Award Scale

Less than 25 points	$ 5	61 to 64 points	$ 55
25 to 28 points	$10	65 to 68 points	$ 60
29 to 32 points	$15	69 to 72 points	$ 65
33 to 36 points	$20	73 to 76 points	$ 70
37 to 40 points	$25	77 to 80 points	$ 75
41 to 44 points	$30	81 to 84 points	$ 80
45 to 48 points	$35	85 to 88 points	$ 85
49 to 52 points	$40	89 to 92 points	$ 90
53 to 56 points	$45	93 to 96 points	$ 95
57 to 60 points	$50	97 to 100 points	$100

                                                Total $

Figure 21–1. Typical Form for Evaluating Suggestions with Intangible Value.

year to determine actual savings. Should these be greater than originally anticipated, a supplemental award is made; should they be less, the employee is permitted to keep all money paid on the estimated savings.

An idea of the extent of these monetary awards can be obtained from data on the General Motors suggestion plan (5). During one year a total of 724,551 suggestions were submitted and 194,937 were adopted. The amount paid out in awards was $13.4 million, and 60 employees received the maximum of $10,000. Since its initiation in 1942, this plan has paid out over $155 million.

Determining awards for suggestions where the value cannot be stated in monetary terms, even though there is some intangible value to the firm, is more complex. Unfortunately, in many employment situations, suggestions of this kind are much more frequent than those involving identifiable savings. The usual procedure is to award points to the suggestion in terms of the particular factors considered to be relevant. The approach has much in common with certain types of job evaluation. The points awarded on each of the factors are totaled, and this point score is then converted to a dollar amount using a standardized award scale. An example of a typical form used in evaluating intangible suggestions is provided in Figure 21–1.

FACTORS IN EFFECTIVENESS

It is widely recognized that, in spite of their tremendous potential contribution, many suggestion plans exist in a semidormant state. Few suggestions are submitted, and the contribution to goal attainment is probably not sufficient to justify the cost of maintaining the machinery. This is particularly likely to be the case where monetary awards are minimal or nonexistent, but it can occur under other circumstances as well.

A major factor in effectiveness appears to be the attitude of first-line supervision. Does the supervisor create the impression that good suggestions are desired and important? Or does his attitude imply that submitting suggestions is merely a troublesome method of attempting to curry favor? Even in departments where supervision actively promotes the suggestion system, it may not operate very effectively. One study was designed to show the relationship of the work environment, including supervisory supportiveness, to innovation as demonstrated by suggestions submitted and adopted. The results indicate that employees with certain characteristics, such as high levels of creativity, are likely to participate regardless of the supervisory environment (30).

Aside from the attitudes of supervision and characteristics of the employees, there are other factors associated with effectiveness. Most of these represent aspects of downward communication. The suggestion system should be actively promoted in the downward media. Information regarding awards should be publicized. Special attention should be given to particularly meritorious ideas. In this way, high-quality participation can be stimulated. Also, management must take steps to ensure that employees feel entirely free to submit suggestions. An idea that would almost certainly leave a man without a job, or result in layoffs for others, or reduce incentive payments, is not likely to be submitted. There must be guarantees against negative consequences such as these.

ATTITUDE SURVEYS

Although attitude surveys are used for various purposes, historically they have been employed most extensively to provide a gauge of the extent and sources of dissatisfaction within an organization and as a means of communicating this information upward to management. Frequently, the reason for seeking such data has been a desire to determine what steps should be taken, if any, to thwart a possible union organizing attempt or to minimize union militancy (38). In one company, where an attitude survey had been conducted just prior to a strike affecting three of the five plants surveyed, it was possible to compare attitude scores between plants that had a strike and those that did not. It was found that the survey results could provide predictions of labor unrest and also could indicate changes management needed to make to head off employee relations problems (36).

A question arises as to why information on employee attitudes should be obtained from the individuals themselves, rather than from superiors. Why cannot managers rate their subordinates in the attitude area just as they do in the productivity area? A partial answer is that in many instances they do. Many rating systems contain questions dealing with attitude, cooperativeness, and the degree to which job dissatisfaction may be manifest in behavior.

On the other hand, these management estimates may not prove very reliable. Supervisors may not wish to inform higher management regarding any widespread dissatisfaction within their groups for fear this condition will reflect on their own competence, or they may not be aware of the degree of discontent. For whatever reason, management estimates and employee reports on their own attitudes have often proved to be surprisingly disparate. Typically, supervisors underestimate the degree of dissatisfaction in their groups (27). This tendency appears consistently among supervisors who on other grounds are viewed as poor in the area of employee relations. Thus, in just those situations where valid attitude data are needed most, the tendency to misperceive or distort appears to be greatest. It is for this reason that many firms have moved beyond management estimates and ratings to more direct attitude measurement procedures.

Interviews

One obvious approach is to ask employees how they feel. The difficulty is that many will hesitate to express negative attitudes because of fear of retaliation. Various techniques have been devised to deal with this problem, but it still remains the major barrier to effective attitude measurement.

Many companies have found it desirable to have interviews conducted either by a consulting firm or representatives of a university. In this way, they hope to reassure the employees that responses will not serve as a basis for retaliation against individuals. In addition, efforts are made to ensure anonymity insofar as management is concerned. Thus, only the outside organization receives information on the names of those interviewed. The company's management is given a report in terms of group frequencies, rather than individuals' attitudes.

Interviews may be *guided* or *unguided*. In the latter instance, the interviewer encourages the employee to express himself in various areas but does not follow a definite format. Questions may be worded quite differently when asked of different employees. Attitudes are assessed by the interviewer based on what happens in the interview as a whole.

The problems here are maintaining comparability across interviews and minimizing the effects of interviewer bias. A talkative worker provides information differing in many ways from that derived from a reticent individual. Questions inevitably will be worded differently, and the interviewer may well react much more favorably toward an employee who is willing to talk, thus making the interview easier to conduct.

Because unguided interviews are difficult to quantify, the tendency has been to resort primarily to the guided approach. This approach tends to approximate the questionnaire procedure, to be discussed in the next section, but the questions are asked orally. Administering such a standard questionnaire in an interview situation is costly, but it has the advantage of ensuring a high response rate within a group. Employees are much more likely to give answers to an interviewer than to return a mailed questionnaire. Thus, the bias that results when a nonrepresentative set of responses is obtained from a particular work unit tends to be reduced.

EXIT INTERVIEWS

Some firms make it a regular practice to conduct exit interviews with employees who are leaving the company voluntarily in order to assess attitudes in the groups where they worked. The assumption is that these people will talk freely because they have nothing to lose and that, therefore, the information obtained from them is more valid.

Research, however, does not support this assumption. One study compared exit interview data with data obtained from questionnaires six months after separation (26). It was evident that many individuals have a strong tendency to "clam up" in the exit interview. There were widespread discrepancies between initial and follow-up reasons for termination, and many who could give no specific reasons for leaving at the time did give reasons later. Production pressures were rarely mentioned in the exit interview, but frequently mentioned later. Similar results were obtained in another study, in which information from exit interviews of professional employees who had voluntarily resigned was compared with subsequent questionnaire data and with information obtained through interviews conducted by an outside consultant. Not only did the reasons for leaving frequently differ from the initial exit interview to the questionnaire and the reinterview, but the consultant's interviews elicited more negative attitudes toward management per se. These attitudes were not in evidence when company managers conducted the exit interviews (19).

The problem appears to be that most of those who are terminating are so defensive at the time that they do not in fact reveal their true attitudes. Many, no doubt, are still unsure as to their employment future. They do not want to eliminate all possibility of reemployment by the company. They may also need references later and to ensure a good report will avoid any criticism of the former employer.

In addition, there are those who feel guilty about leaving their jobs and to justify doing so will exaggerate negative factors in the work situation. Thus, the blame for the separation is shifted from the individual to the company. Again, the exit interview emerges as a poor source of valid information on attitudes.

Questionnaires

In the past, it has been a common practice to enclose attitude questionnaires with paychecks, to mail them to the employee's home, or even to hand them out at quitting time. These procedures rarely elicit a response from more than 50 per cent of a group, usually considerably less, and it is difficult to know what the results mean. Because anonymity is usually protected in order to foster valid answers, it is not possible to follow up on those who do not return completed forms. A more desirable procedure, now widely adopted, is to assemble the employees in groups and have them complete the forms on company time. In this way, response rates comparable to those obtained with personal interviews can be obtained. Some companies follow up on the results obtained through questionnaires by conducting personal interviews with a small sample drawn from different components of the firm (14).

The topics covered in an attitude questionnaire vary with the particular needs of a company at a given time. Thus, firms may carry out surveys because they are concerned about labor relations problems, attitudes toward fringe benefits, and so on. In these cases, the questionnaires should be constructed to fit the specific problem.

Where more general coverage is desired, some of the standardized forms that are available commercially may be preferable. These have the advantage that information on response frequencies in other companies is available for comparison purposes, although it has been pointed out that it is difficult to explain some of the results to employees using national normative data (40).

Topics that are often considered in a comprehensive survey include:

1. Working conditions.
2. Job demands.
3. Pay.
4. Employee benefits.
5. Supervision.
6. Communications.
7. Promotions.
8. Status and recognition.
9. Security.
10. Relations with co-workers.
11. Hours of work.
12. Opportunity for growth and development.
13. Personnel policies.

Table 21–7 contains data on the sources of greatest dissatisfaction reported by a group of over 1,500 individuals selected to represent the U.S. labor force as a whole (18). Items of the kind noted with higher frequencies are particularly important and should be included in any survey aimed at uncovering sources of discontent.

Attitude questionnaire items are of two basic types: fixed-alternative and

Table 21–7. Workers' Reports of "Single Biggest Problem Faced on the Job"

Type of Problem	Per Cent Reporting
Technical problems in getting the work done	18
Too much work; work is too hard or too fast	14
Interpersonal problems (excluding supervisory relationships)	10
Worker is given inadequate resources to do his job	9
Problems with being supervised	8
Problems with pay or fringe benefits	7
Problems with supervising others	7
Problems with physical working conditions	5
Problems with psychological rewards provided by the work (work is boring, routine, etc.)	5
Problems with hours or work schedule	3
Problems with job security	2
Problems with promotions or status	2
Problems with transportation to, from, or during work	1
Problems with maintaining good health	1
Other problems	8

Source: N. Q. Herrick and R. P. Quinn, "The Working Conditions Survey as a Source of Social Indicators," Monthly Labor Review, 94, No. 4 : 17 (1971).

open-ended. In the former category are questions with simple Yes or No alternatives as well as those of a multiple-choice nature. Open-ended questions either ask for a free-written answer or require that blanks be filled in. In either case, the responses must be categorized after the answers have been obtained.

Open-ended questions can be expensive to use because of the need to construct categories (similar to multiple-choice alternatives) afterward and to code responses into these categories. On the other hand, if one is not sure what alternatives should be included in a fixed-alternative measure, the open-ended approach may be preferable. Often it takes as much time and money to conduct preliminary studies aimed at setting up appropriate multiple-choice alternatives as it does to categorize free responses.

Attitude Scales

Attitude scales are frequently utilized in instances where a more precise and reliable measure is desired than can be obtained from a few questionnaire items. Measures of this kind have been developed for a great variety of purposes. There are several procedures, but all have in common the fact that various scores or weights are attached to different alternatives to indicate the degree of feeling that characterizes a person who responds in a particular manner.

Perhaps the most frequently used approach is that developed by Thurstone (37), or some variant of it. The first step is to write out a great many statements bearing on the attitude to be measured, let us say satisfaction with one's present job. A number of people are then asked to serve as judges and to classify these statements in terms of their favorableness. Traditionally, 11 categories are used ranging from 1, indicating the least favorable viewpoint, to 11, the most favorable.

The *scale value* of each statement is the average of the category numbers assigned by the various judges. Not all the statements are normally used in the final attitude scale, however. It is important to select items indicating all variants of opinion. Thus, those finally used should be spread evenly throughout the range, from a scale value close to 1 to a scale value close to 11. Also, statements on which the judges cannot agree must be discarded. If several indicate that a statement should be in category 2, and the others have it in various categories up to 9, then agreement is clearly minimal, and the item should not be used. The scale of Figure 21–2 represents what remains from an original 246 statements (4).

If the Brayfield-Rothe scale were administered without the five multiple-choice alternatives for each item, and employees were asked merely to check those of the 18 items that applied to them, then we would have a typical Thurstone scale. The score for an individual would be the sum of the scale values for the statements checked. Items like 5 and 12 carry high-scale values, whereas items like 4 and 18 carry low values.

Some jobs are more interesting and satisfying than others. We want to know how people feel about different jobs. You are to cross out the phrase below each statement that best describes how you feel about your present job. There are no right or wrong answers. We should like your honest opinion on each one of the statements. Work out the sample item numbered (0).

0. There are some conditions concerning my job that could be improved.
   Strongly agree   Agree   Undecided   Disagree   Strongly disagree
1. My job is like a hobby to me.
   Strongly agree   Agree   Undecided   Disagree   Strongly disagree
2. My job is usually interesting enough to keep me from getting bored.
   Strongly agree   Agree   Undecided   Disagree   Strongly disagree
3. It seems that my friends are more interested in their jobs.
   Strongly agree   Agree   Undecided   Disagree   Strongly disagree
4. I consider my job rather unpleasant.
   Strongly agree   Agree   Undecided   Disagree   Strongly disagree
5. I enjoy my work more than my leisure time.
   Strongly agree   Agree   Undecided   Disagree   Strongly disagree
6. I am often bored with my job.
   Strongly agree   Agree   Undecided   Disagree   Strongly disagree
7. I feel fairly well satisfied with my present job.
   Strongly agree   Agree   Undecided   Disagree   Strongly disagree
8. Most of the time I have to force myself to go to work.
   Strongly agree   Agree   Undecided   Disagree   Strongly disagree
9. I am satisfied with my job for the time being.
   Strongly agree   Agree   Undecided   Disagree   Strongly disagree
10. I feel that my job is no more interesting than any other I could get.
   Strongly agree   Agree   Undecided   Disagree   Strongly disagree
11. I definitely dislike my work.
   Strongly agree   Agree   Undecided   Disagree   Strongly disagree
12. I feel that I am happier in my work than most other people.
   Strongly agree   Agree   Undecided   Disagree   Strongly disagree
13. Most days I am enthusiastic about my work.
   Strongly agree   Agree   Undecided   Disagree   Strongly disagree
14. Each day of work seems like it will never end.
   Strongly agree   Agree   Undecided   Disagree   Strongly disagree
15. I like my job better than the average worker does.
   Strongly agree   Agree   Undecided   Disagree   Strongly disagree
16. My job is pretty uninteresting.
   Strongly agree   Agree   Undecided   Disagree   Strongly disagree
17. I find real enjoyment in my work.
   Strongly agree   Agree   Undecided   Disagree   Strongly disagree
18. I am disappointed that I ever took this job.
   Strongly agree   Agree   Undecided   Disagree   Strongly disagree

Figure 21–2. Brayfield-Rothe Job Satisfaction Questionnaire.
Source: A. H. Brayfield and H. F. Rothe, "An Index of Job Satisfaction," *Journal of Applied Psychology*, 35 : 309 (1951). Copyright 1951 by the American Psychological Association, reproduced by permission.

In this particular instance, a modification of the standard Thurstone procedure has been introduced that allows employees to express the degree of agreement. Statements with scale values above 6 (positive statements) were scored 5 for a "strongly agree" response, 4 for "agree," and so on down to 1 for "strongly disagree." Statements with scale values below 6 (negative) are scored in the reverse direction, with a 5 given for "strongly disagree." Thus, total scores range from 18 to 90.

In addition to the Brayfield-Rothe scale, there are several other measures of job attitudes available that have been developed and tested in numerous settings (32).

Indirect Measures

Most of the approaches to attitude measurement discussed to this point attempt to deal with the tendency of employees to suppress unfavorable feelings by protecting the anonymity of respondents. Thus, groups rather than individuals must be compared against existing role prescriptions.

The indirect measures attempt to solve the problem of suppressed attitudes in a different manner: one which does permit individual evaluation. The approach is comparable in certain respects to that employed in forced-choice rating. The employee does not know what he is revealing about his attitudes. As a consequence, he cannot withhold that which he might not wish to say.

PROJECTIVE METHODS

Here, the essential element is that the employee "projects" himself into a situation portrayed by a picture or by a written statement and in responding to this situation reveals his attitudes. He may be required to describe a picture or to tell a story or complete a statement of some kind. In any event, he tends to ascribe to the situation and the people in it characteristics that belong to himself.

In general, these techniques are administered in an interview situation, but measures can be devised to fit the questionnaire format. The major problem is to be absolutely certain that the attitude measured is what one wants to measure. Devising a good projective attitude index requires considerable training and experience, and unfortunately little in the way of standardized measures related to job problems is available commercially.

STRUCTURED DISGUISED MEASURES

A second approach requires the employee to respond to a series of questions that appear to constitute a test of general information or intelligence. However, the questions are so constructed that there either are no correct answers or the employee could not possibly be aware of the answers. Thus, any choice between alternatives must be based on attitudes. Employees are encouraged to guess.

The major difficulty with the use of these techniques in industrial situations is that, unlike the other approaches discussed, they are often deliberately misleading. Considerable resentment may result should employees become aware of the fact that management is not being entirely honest. Especially in unionized firms, the losses can be greater than the gains. For this reason, a personnel manager should give considerable thought to the pros and cons before undertaking an attitude survey with a structured disguised measure. Procedures of this kind have not seen extensive use in recent years.

Sociometry

Although sociometric procedures have not been widely utilized in the business world, they appear to have considerable potential, especially as an aid in establishing the degree of attachment to a work group or organization—what has been called the cohesiveness of the group. They should provide particularly valuable information regarding a tendency to resort to escape behavior as a solution to discontent.

The sociometric questionnaire, in its most common form, merely asks each member of a group to indicate which among the other members he would like to have as a companion in some activity, such as teaming up on a job or eating lunch. Usually, negative choices are also requested. Thus, each employee also indicates those he would not want as a companion. These choices provide valuable information regarding an individual's ties to his group, whether he is accepted by others, and whether he feels close to certain group members. An index of the pull of the group vis-à-vis external social forces may be obtained if the questionnaire is designed so as to permit choices both within and outside the specific work unit.

Feedback of Attitude Survey Data

A question that arises frequently in connection with the utilization of attitude survey data is whether results should be fed back to those who provided the information in the first place. Somehow, it is always easier to ask people to complete questionnaires if feedback of results is guaranteed, but it is also very hard to follow through on such a commitment when the results are not very complimentary to the organization and its management.

Such research as has been done is clearly favorable to the feedback approach (23). Employee reactions and perceptions regarding management's taking positive actions based on the survey are more positive when feedback occurs. The response to meetings is better than for written feedback, and it appears that these meetings should be conducted by immediate supervisors rather than personnel managers. The focus should be on data for the immediate department, more than one meeting should be conducted, and open discussion should be permitted (1). These studies clearly indicate that a lack of feedback of attitude survey results can serve to frustrate employees and confirm their belief that management never intended to act on the findings in the first place.

Resistance to Attitude Surveys

Perhaps, in part at least, because of inadequate feedback, or none at all, a number of companies have found it difficult to maintain a system of periodic attitude measurement. Many firms have at one time or another instituted continuing procedures aimed at obtaining data relative to the organizational maintenance goal. For various reasons, a number of these have discontinued the procedures after a relatively brief trial.

Part of the difficulty seems to be that, historically, organizational maintenance has never attained quite the same stature as productivity. Thus, a number of managers have considered attitude survey results relatively unimportant. Although appreciation of the significance of this goal is now on the upswing, attitude measurement in the past has not had the support that other evaluation techniques have enjoyed.

Perhaps related to this consideration is the fact that if attitude surveys are to be of real value, they must be tied to action (12, 34). When a number of employees in a unit are discontented, and a survey identifies the source of the difficulty, an effort should be made to improve the situation and thus to improve attitudes. Unfortunately, this has not always been done. Accordingly, periodic surveys have often yielded almost identical results, time after time, to the point where measurement was finally discontinued because no new information was obtained.

Finally, and perhaps this is the underlying difficulty, what management may really want from attitude measurement is individual employee evaluation of the kind produced by rating procedures. Yet the commonly used procedures yield group results only. Although these group data do have considerable value in appraising managers and in pinpointing labor problems, the return on the investment may be insufficient to convince some managers that continuing measurement is warranted. There is reason to believe, however, that information on job attitudes of individual employees can be a good predictor of subsequent turnover (25). Research results such as these may lead to increased use of individual measures in the future.

When these managerial considerations are combined with the long-standing and not too surprising union resistance to the use of attitude surveys, rather than union leaders, as a major upward communication channel, the fact that the use of attitude surveys has seen little expansion cannot be considered unexpected. What expansion has occurred is almost entirely at the managerial level.

MAINTENANCE MEDIATORS AND PERSONNEL STRATEGY

For most organizations, the preferred strategy is to invest in maintenance mediators only to the extent required by internal and external stresses.

Thus, the various approaches in labor relations, benefit programs, and personnel communications techniques are utilized as input-sustaining and input-controlling mediators, but no attempt is made to maximize in terms of maintenance considerations. The maintenance mediators are introduced first to head off or prevent debilitating conflict and then to correct the conflict condition should it occur. The idea is to keep conflict from seriously interfering with the pursuit of productivity goals.

An attempt to move maintenance mediators upward into the input-improving sphere, and thus to make employees highly satisfied without reference to their contribution to productivity goal attainment, can yield either a reduced return on the investment or a negative impact on productivity, depending on the circumstances. For instance, an extremely attractive benefit program may do no more to attract and retain good employees than a somewhat less attractive one. Once a certain level is reached insofar as benefits are concerned, the incremental return on the additional investment begins to fall off sharply. Once a company has used benefits to attract and retain competent employees, more and more benefits can add very little.

Under other circumstances, the investment in making maintenance mediators input-improving may actually interfere with productivity and profit attainment. There is always the cost of the investment per se, but in addition one can give so much in the course of collective bargaining or to ward off a union organizing attempt that the conduct of work is severely hampered. This sort of thing was relatively common during World War II, when many companies were operating on cost-plus government contracts with a guaranteed profit margin, and the only crucial requirement was to avoid strikes. Faced with a return to a peacetime competitive market, a number of firms found that they had given so much for maintenance purposes to their employees and the unions that they could not control production processes and output sufficiently to achieve a profit.

As with productivity mediators, those of a maintenance nature may on occasion be subordinated to either an input or an output emphasis. The input-oriented approach involves a stress on recruiting and selecting those individuals who are least likely to contribute to internal conflict. Thus, some firms have deliberately moved facilities or located new plants in rural areas, where a less conflict-prone labor force is more likely to be found. As a result, they have been able to operate without unions or with less militant locals. Such a strategy can be extremely costly and is becoming subject to an increasing number of constraints of a legal nature. Furthermore, a corporate environment that facilitates an input-oriented strategy in the maintenance area at one point in time may well change later on; there may be a shift in the community from antiunion to prounion attitudes, for instance. In general, therefore, a primary input emphasis as regards maintenance seems desirable only when the input emphasis can be extended to the productivity sphere as well.

Legal constraints may also serve to hamper the use of an output-oriented strategy in the maintenance area. Many of these constraints on firing were considered in Chapter 18. Firing for union activity has long been proscribed, and disciplinary actions that result in termination are often reversed by arbitrators. Thus, both input and output strategies for minimizing conflict and stress within an organization are becoming increasingly difficult to apply effectively. The result is that most companies of any size have little choice but to adopt a strategy emphasizing the maintenance mediators. It is mainly the very small firms, especially those that are not unionized, that can afford to realistically consider the input- or output-oriented alternatives at the present time. This is in part because their total need for employees is less and in part because of their limited visibility.

QUESTIONS

1. What are the various types of communications networks in a company? How do the communications activities of the personnel department relate to these networks?
2. Describe and discuss the following:
   a. Readership surveys.
   b. Readability levels.
   c. The hot line system.
   d. Grapevine.
   e. Exit interviews.
3. What are the most frequently used communication techniques, both upward and downward? Can you account for the popularity of these techniques?
4. What considerations are important in designing and maintaining an effective suggestion system?
5. Discuss the various approaches to attitude measurement. What are the pros and cons of the various procedures and techniques? Of what value is it to a company to obtain good measures of employee attitudes on a periodic basis?

REFERENCES

1. Alpin, J. C., and D. E. Thompson. "Feedback: Key to Survey-based Change." *Public Personnel Management,* 3 (1974), 524–530.
2. Athanassiades, J. C. "The Distortion of Upward Communication in Hierarchical Organizations." *Academy of Management Journal,* 16 (1973), 207–226.
3. Athanassiades, J. C. "The Sounds and Silences of Employee Communication." *Journal of Business Communication,* 10 (1973), No. 4, 43–50.
4. Brayfield, A. H., and H. F. Rothe. "An Index of Job Satisfaction." *Journal of Applied Psychology,* 35 (1951), 307–311.
5. Bureau of National Affairs, Inc. *Bulletin to Management* No. 1153, March 16, 1972, p. 2.

6. Bureau of National Affairs, Inc. *Employee Communications.* Personnel Policies Forum Survey No. 110, July 1975.
7. Coffin, R. M., and M. S. Shaw. *Effective Communication of Employee Benefits.* New York: American. Management Association, Inc., 1971.
8. Cowan, P. "Establishing a Communication Chain: The Development and Distribution of an Employee Handbook." *Personnel Journal,* 54 (1975), 342–344, 349.
9. Dahle, T. L. "An Objective and Comparative Study of Five Methods of Transmitting Information to Business and Industrial Employees." *Speech Monographs,* 21 (1954), 21–28.
10. Davis, K. "Success of Chain-of-command Oral Communication in a Manufacturing Management Group." *Academy of Management Journal,* 11 (1968), 379–387.
11. Davis, K. "Readability Changes in Employee Handbooks of Identical Companies During a Fifteen-year Period." *Personnel Psychology,* 21 (1968), 413–420.
12. Dawis, R. V., and W. Weitzel. "Worker Attitudes and Expectations," in D. Yoder and H. G. Heneman, Jr., *Motivation and Commitment.* Washington, D.C.: Bureau of National Affairs, Inc., 1975, 6-23 to 6-49.
13. Gelfand, L. I. "Communicate Through Your Supervisor." *Harvard Business Review,* 48 (1970), No. 6, 101–104.
14. Goode, R. V. "How to Get Better Results from Attitude Surveys." *Personnel Journal,* 52 (1973), 187–192.
15. Greenbaum, H. H. "The Audit of Organizational Communication." *Academy of Management Journal,* 17 (1974), 739–754.
16. Habbe, S. "Does Communication Make a Difference?" *Management Record,* 14 (1952), 414–416, 442–444.
17. Harriman, B. "Up and Down the Communications Ladder." *Harvard Business Review,* 52 (1974), No. 5, 143–151.
18. Herrick, N. Q., and R. P. Quinn. "The Working Conditions Survey as a Source of Social Indicators." *Monthly Labor Review,* 94 (1971), No. 4, 15–24.
19. Hinrichs, J. R. "Measurement of Reasons for Resignation of Professionals: Questionnaire Versus Company and Consultant Exit Interviews." *Journal of Applied Psychology,* 60 (1975), 530–532.
20. International Association of Business Communicators. *Readership Surveys.* Akron, Ohio: the Association, 1970.
21. Jones, D. E. "The Employee Handbook." *Personnel Journal,* 52 (1973), 136–141.
22. Kirkpatrick, D. L. "Personnel Department's Role in Communication." *Personnel Journal,* 51 (1972), 279–282.
23. Klein, S. M., A. I. Kraut, and A. Wolfson. "Employee Reactions to Attitude Survey Feedback: A Study of the Impact of Structure and Process." *Administrative Science Quarterly,* 16 (1971), 497–514.

24. Knippen, J. T. "Grapevine Communication: Management and Employees." *Journal of Business Research,* 2 (1974), No. 1, 47–58.
25. Kraut, A. I. "Predicting Turnover of Employees from Measured Job Attitudes." *Organizational Behavior and Human Performance,* 13 (1975), 223–243.
26. Lefkowitz, J., and M. Katz. "Validity of Exit Interviews." *Personnel Psychology,* 22 (1969), 445–455.
27. Losey, M. R. "What Do Your Employees Really Think?" *Personnel Administration,* 34 (1971), No. 2, 4–7, 60–61.
28. Miner, J. B., and E. E. Heaton. "Company Orientation as a Factor in the Readership of Employee Publications." *Personnel Psychology,* 12 (1959), 607–618.
29. Newstrom, J. W., R. E. Monczka, and W. E. Reif. "Perceptions of the Grapevine: Its Value and Influence." *Journal of Business Communication,* 11 (1974), No. 3, 12–20.
30. Pizam, A. "Some Correlates of Innovation Within Industrial Suggestion Systems." *Personnel Psychology,* 27 (1974), 63–76.
31. Roberts, K. H., and C. A. O'Reilly. "Failures in Upward Communication in Organizations: Three Possible Culprits." *Academy of Management Journal,* 17 (1974), 205–215.
32. Roberts, K. H., and F. Savage. "Twenty Questions: Utilizing Job Satisfaction Measures." *California Management Review,* 15 (1973), No. 3, 82–90.
33. Schupp, W. "Any Company Can." *Personnel Journal,* 52 (1973), 629–632.
34. Sirota, D. "Opinion Surveys: The Results Are In—What Do We Do with Them?" *Personnel,* 51 (1974), No. 5, 24–31.
35. Sussman, L. "Perceived Message Distortion or You Can Fool Some of the Supervisors Some of the Time . . ." *Personnel Journal,* 53 (1974), 679–682.
36. Thompson, D. E., and R. P. Borglum. "A Case Study of Employee Attitudes and Labor Unrest." *Industrial and Labor Relations Review,* 27 (1973), 74–83.
37. Thurstone, L. L., and E. J. Chave. *The Measurement of Attitude.* Chicago: University of Chicago Press, 1929.
38. Vogel, A. "Your Clerical Workers Are Ripe for Unionism." *Harvard Business Review,* 49 (1971), No. 2, 48–54.
39. Walker, A. "Recent Findings Reveal Rising Involvement of Communicators." *Industrial Press Research Report,* Special Report, Fall 1970.
40. Wheatley, B. C., and W. B. Cash. "The Employee Survey: Correcting Its Basic Weakness." *Personnel Journal,* 52 (1973), 456–459.

PERSONNEL MANAGEMENT IN PERSPECTIVE

22 Future Needs for More Effective Personnel and Industrial Relations

---

BEHAVIORAL SCIENCE AND PERSONNEL RESEARCH
  Company Research
  Behavioral Science Research and the Future
THE EVALUATION OF PERSONNEL ACTIVITIES
  Current Approaches to Evaluation
  Cost Effectiveness
DEVELOPMENT OF MEASURES FOR COMPARISON PURPOSES
  Unavailability of Comparison Data
  Approaches to a Solution: Absenteeism Statistics
CONTROL OVER HUMAN RESOURCE ACTIVITIES
  The Role of Motivation to Manage
  Professionalization
EXPANDED PERSONNEL ROLES IN SMALL BUSINESS
  Strategies for Small Business
  The Need for Personnel Managers
THE PERSONNEL AND INDUSTRIAL RELATIONS MANAGER OF THE FUTURE

The objective in this final chapter is to develop some guidelines with regard to the future of the personnel and industrial relations field. The discussion here is not necessarily a projection of where the field *will* go in the years ahead. Others have already attempted to grapple with that task (27). Rather, the intent is to indicate what appears to be needed if the field is to continue to grow and prosper, and thus to provide some indications as to where personnel and industrial relations *should* go. This is done with full realization that some individuals, even among those highly knowledgeable regarding the field, may well differ with certain of the recommendations. At the very best, however, the topics considered are deserving of extended discussion and debate. In several cases, this discussion and debate already has begun.

BEHAVIORAL SCIENCE AND PERSONNEL RESEARCH
It seems likely that what personnel management ultimately becomes will depend in large part upon the achievements of behavioral science and personnel research. Opportunity, however defined, will be available only to the

extent that research generates useful theories, knowledge, techniques, and approaches for the practitioner. To achieve increasing status and growth, personnel management has to expand what it has to offer to users of its services.

Research related to personnel and industrial relations problems derives from a number of sources—companies and firms of all kinds, government, nonprofit research organizations, and universities. Company personnel research units are a major source. So, too, are university faculties in such areas as personnel management, industrial relations, labor economics, industrial sociology, and industrial psychology. These two types of organizational groupings, company personnel research units and university departments, form the major foci of careers in behavioral science and personnel research. Typically, a researcher spends an entire working life in one context or the other, although there is some movement back and forth, and an occasional individual will conduct studies while employed both in a university position and in the business world.

Company Research

Company personnel research sometimes is contracted out to organizations specializing in this activity or to individual consultants, but much is done on an in-house basis by company staff members. Usually, there is a separate unit within the personnel department, although there are instances of combining personnel research with physical science research or with market research.

By no means do all companies conduct personnel research. Clearly, the size of the company is a major determinant (25). Historically, personnel research has been almost entirely the domain of the large corporation. However, governmental pressures for validation of selection techniques and the increasing sophistication of personnel practitioners have combined to extend personnel research activities increasingly to the medium-sized and even smaller firms.

In addition to size, other determinants appear to be the extent of decentralization, the personnel orientation, and the research orientation of the firm (6). Although one occasionally finds personnel research units in decentralized divisions, they are much more frequent where there is a large corporate personnel staff. Personnel research also is more common where human resource considerations are particularly important, as in firms with large sales forces and where there is a strong commitment to research in general. Thus, such units appear most frequently in such industries as automobile, insurance, oil, and aerospace (2).

Generally, the personnel research staff is not large. The average number of researchers is three or four, and very few companies employ over ten (2, 6). When one considers that much of the time of even these individuals is devoted to nonresearch activities, as indicated in the job description of

Table 22-1, it is apparent that the amount of research done is not large in comparison with the average company's output of economic, marketing, and physical science research.

At the present time, personnel research is dominated by industrial psychologists, most of whom have doctorates. One survey indicated that 90 per cent of those conducting company personnel research are psychologists (6). The remainder, most of whom are sociologists, economists, or business administration graduates, often have doctorates as well. The type of research done tends to be applied rather than basic and closely tied to short-term payoffs. It is concerned primarily with selection and placement on the one hand and opinion and attitude measurement on the other. These are the major traditional areas of industrial psychological practice. However, some companies are doing research related to training, management development, organization planning, management appraisal, motivation, and leadership.

Behavioral Science Research and the Future

In view of the strong, and entirely appropriate, orientation of company research to immediate practical applications, and the fact that growth in both the number and size of personnel research staffs has been slow (2), it seems unlikely that the kind of breakthrough research that the field of personnel management appears to need for continued growth and development can be generated primarily by company research staffs.

There have been urgent pleas for more research for a number of years (10, 25). The type of research envisaged in these pleas will almost inevitably have to come from the university faculties of the future. Thus, for those with interests in more basic research into personnel and industrial relations problems, the greatest opportunities are likely to be on the faculties of the major universities. Appointments to such faculties invariably require a doctorate either in some relevant area of business administration or in one of the social sciences, such as psychology, sociology, economics, or anthropology.

In any event, there can be little doubt that the personnel specialist of the future, whether employed in a company, a consulting firm, a government unit, a university, a hospital, or elsewhere, will be faced with the problem of keeping abreast of a continually growing wave of research findings. A perusal of recent issues of the various periodicals noted in Chapter 2 makes it clear that such research is, in fact, currently forthcoming. The major need for the future is that the research contribute more than it has in the past to the solution of important personnel and industrial relations problems.

THE EVALUATION OF PERSONNEL ACTIVITIES

The link between personnel research and procedures for evaluating the effectiveness of the personnel function is a close one. Validation studies,

Directs the division's program of personnel and organizational research, using techniques and methodology from the behavioral sciences to assure that the abilities, capabilities, education, and experience of all employees are utilized as fully as is practicable. Job duties may be categorized under five general headings:

I. Research
   A. Designs or reviews the design of all research projects.
   B. Conducts research projects.
   C. Analyzes and evaluates data: prepares reports summarizing the results of research.
   D. Reviews all data analyses and interpretations as well as all final reports coming from the department, to assure that they meet current professional standards.
   E. Discusses the implications of research with management, and participates in planning future activities suggested by research results.
   F. Coordinates outside behavioral science research activities with universities, other corporation units and governmental agencies.
   G. Suggests areas where research might profitably be conducted.
II. Professional Activities
   A. Keeps up to date on developments in the behavioral sciences.
      1. Attends appropriate conventions, meetings, special seminars.
      2. Reviews professional journals and literature.
      3. Maintains personal professional contacts.
      4. Discusses specific research techniques and methodology with outside consultants when necessary.
   B. Provides professional consultation and/or assistance upon request to areas throughout the division.
   C. Represents the division in outside professional contacts.
III. Testing
   A. Establishes testing policies and procedures for the division.
   B. Directs the continual review of tests used, testing procedures, testing facilities, etc., to assure that they meet or exceed accepted professional standards at all times.
   C. Administers the Controlled Testing Center for the Psychological Corporation.
   D. Maintains all test records of personnel employees.
IV. Departmental Effectiveness
   A. Conducts development of discussion sessions with staff members as necessary, to assure that departmental efforts meet or exceed professional standards at all times.
   B. Conducts periodic assessment of the goal attainment of the department and plans future activities and research.
V. General
   A. Participates in discussions of and makes recommendations regarding personnel policies, procedures, or programs.
   B. Maintains close contact with those areas in personnel whose activities relate to departmental efforts.
   C. Circulates selected articles dealing with personnel and organization to top management.
   D. Publicizes the activities and capabilities of the department to areas both inside and outside of the division.

Source: Reprinted by permission of the publisher from AMA Research Study No. 91, The Uses of Personnel Research, by W. C. Byham, © 1968 by the American Management Association, Inc.

evaluation of training efforts, attitude surveys, and the like all may be carried out with the objective of determining whether current programs and procedures are in fact contributing to the attainment of the organization's task and maintenance goals. But beyond the question of whether existing activities are making any positive contribution is a much more difficult problem: Is the return on the investment, the benefit received, the greatest that could reasonably be expected? Evaluation of a program is not merely a matter of determining if an approach is working; it is a matter of contrasting it with possible alternatives, to see if it is the best program that can be used.

Current Approaches to Evaluation

Table 22-2 presents the results of two surveys of company practices in evaluating personnel activities (3, 22). Although the surveys are not entirely comparable, they do bring out several points collectively. For one thing, the proportion of companies using any one approach is small in both surveys. In fact, many firms do no evaluation at all. Furthermore, the preponderance of the approaches focus on organizational maintenance goals. This tendency reflects a long-standing emphasis in the audit and evaluation of personnel programs (17).

In view of the fact that strong arguments have been advanced in favor of a management-by-objectives approach in this area (23), it is surprising that so few firms use it. In this instance, accomplishments of the personnel department are evaluated against previously established goals. The reference point or standard of evaluation is entirely internal to the company.

Table 22–2. Results of Two Surveys of Methods Used in Evaluating Personnel and Industrial Relations Activities (10 most frequently mentioned methods)

Survey of 100 Companies Nationwide		Survey of 279 Indiana Companies	
Method Used	Per Cent of Companies	Method Used	Per Cent of Companies
Periodic review	25	Turnover	22
Evaluating against goals	24	Grievances	21
Surveys, discussions, interviews	20	Performance standards	17
		Absenteeism	11
Turnover	16	Accident rate	11
Grievances	8	Employee opinion survey	7
Management by objectives	7	Departmental reports	6
Cost analysis	6	Interviews	6
Training effectiveness	5	External comparison	5
Accident rate	5	Management by objectives	4
Feedback from managers	5		

Source: Adapted from Bureau of National Affairs, Inc., The Personnel Department, Personnel Policies Forum Survey No. 92, November 1970, p. 11; M. S. Novit and E. G. Williams, Personnel Administration in Indiana. (Indianapolis; Indiana State Chamber of Commerce, 1973), p. 21.

Cost Effectiveness

There is little question that personnel and industrial relations activities need to be evaluated if only to permit relative comparisons with the contributions made by other areas of the business (21). However, recognition of the need has not produced the reality. In many cases, personnel departments have been the first to be cut back when the profit picture became bleak, simply because they could not show a clear, direct relationship of their activities to profits (12).

Yet there is ample evidence that doing one thing and not another in dealing with human resource problems can produce sizable savings (26). Furthermore, the fact that personnel staff costs are approximately one to two per cent of payroll, and human resources overall account for between 40 and 70 per cent of total costs in most companies implies that considerable leverage is possible through the use of effective personnel and industrial relations procedures (7). The problem is to demonstrate this leverage relative to approaches that stress monetary or material resources. Because the value of these other approaches typically is established in cost-effectiveness terms, personnel managers will have to do the same if their function is to progress and make the contribution to company goals that it can.

As indicated in Table 22–2, costing various personnel programs is not a widespread practice. However, some breakthroughs are occurring. An approach developed by Xerox provides an example of what can be done (7). The procedure involves the following steps:

1. Define and describe all personnel programs either currently in existence or proposed for future implementation. For each specify—
   a. Objectives of the program.
   b. Employee group involved.
   c. Schedule for implementing.
2. Separate out and assign top priority to all of the programs that are legally required. These would include programs involving payroll, safety, reporting to the government, affirmative action, etc.
3. Evaluate the remaining programs for feasibility, as follows:
   a. Determine the state of the art with regard to the program including the availability of needed skills.
   b. Determine how difficult it would be to implement the program in terms of acceptance by the management of the affected group.
   c. Determine the expected net economic benefits using the best available data on (1) potential revenue impacts, (2) the probability of these impacts' occurring, (3) tangible costs of the program, and (4) the probability of these costs' occurring. In addition, intangible benefits and costs are noted where dollar values cannot be specified.
   d. Determine the economic risks of not implementing the program.

4. Combine the four types of data from the feasibility analysis into an overall evaluation, and rank order all programs.

When this procedure is carried out with care, it yields a priority schedule that includes information on timing, net annual dollar benefits, and cost/benefit ratios. The procedure is by no means perfect, but it does offer a basis for selecting and deleting personnel programs and making comparisons with existing and proposed programs in other parts of the company. As data develop from pilot projects, actual implementation, and other sources, dollar values can be attached to benefits and costs with considerable precision.

Some effort of this kind seems absolutely essential if personnel and industrial relations departments are to monitor their own activities effectively and demonstrate their true value to overall company operations.

DEVELOPMENT OF MEASURES FOR COMPARISON PURPOSES

An essential ingredient for the evaluation of personnel activities is that output measures be available that are closely related to productivity and maintenance goals and to which dollar values can subsequently be attached. In order to determine whether a company is improving or failing, doing well or poorly on a given measure, however, comparison data are needed. There should be an opportunity both to contrast current performance with past performances within the company, and to contrast company performance with that of other firms, especially close competitors. In many cases, it would be extremely useful to make such comparisons on individual difference variables known to be closely related to output, as well as on the output variables themselves. This would facilitate establishing the causes of variances. Unfortunately, this kind of comparison data is not widely available; it is badly needed.

Unavailability of Comparison Data

The major source of comparison data in the United States is the Bureau of Labor Statistics in the Department of Labor, which provides information on unemployment, the cost of living, and the like. However, these statistics are developed primarily for purposes of governmental policymaking (8). The measures used are not of the kind that companies can use to appraise their personnel activities effectively.

For example, data on turnover are published that are very useful in determining labor force mobility. They say nothing, however, regarding whether companies are losing people they want to keep or people they want to get rid of. A company using a delayed selection strategy will inevitably have high turnover; what indicates ineffective human resource management is disproportionately high turnover among the better employees. Table 22–3

Table 22–3. Turnover Rates of Employees Leaving During Year as a Per Cent of Total Number of Employees at Year-end, Broken Down by Desirability of Retention for a Six-year Period

Bases for Calculating Turnover Rates	Year					
	First	Second	Third	Fourth	Fifth	Sixth
Company overall	17	11	13	14	11	16
Individuals judged "sorry to have leave" by immediate superior	6	4	8	6	5	7
Individuals judged "not sorry to have leave" by immediate superior	11	7	5	8	6	9

provides data from one such company for a six-year period. In only one of these years was the turnover rate higher for the people the company wanted to keep than for those it did not. But how good is good? There simply are no data from other companies to answer that question.

The same situation is in evidence with regard to most of the other types of output measures discussed in Chapters 8 and 9. There is a need for appropriate comparison data, so that when a company determines it has certain numbers of people at various levels of effectiveness, this distribution can be checked against distributions for other companies. Only on the basis of this type of data can a statement be made as to whether the company is doing a good or a poor job in the human resources area.

Furthermore, comparable statistics are needed over time to determine whether the personnel effort is increasing or decreasing in effectiveness. The company noted in Table 22–3 seems to have maintained a relatively stable level of effectiveness (or ineffectiveness) over the six-year period studied. However, such an interpretation would have to be questioned if average turnover rates in the same industry had shifted from 9 per cent to 2 per cent over the same period in the "sorry to have leave" category.

Even at the national level, the lack of relevant statistics over time represents a problem. Much has been made of the "blue-collar blues" and the "white-collar woes," and how these factors have contributed to decreasing levels of work performance (24). Yet a recent analysis can find no evidence to support this hypothesis (11). The fact of the matter is that the comparative data needed to answer the question at the level of individual worker effectiveness simply are not available.

The need is equally great for individual-difference data to permit a company to determine its position in relation to comparable firms and to evaluate this position. Relative deficiencies of the work force on output measures may then be traced to such factors as insufficient knowledge, intellectual abilities, motivation, and physical capability. The measurement of these factors also requires comparative data so that a company can determine where it stands. To some extent, this can be accomplished through the use of normative tables provided by psychological test publishers, in the same way that a school district may be evaluated by comparing pupil achievement test scores with national norms. Unfortunately, the available norms are limited, and in some areas even the needed individual difference measures have not yet been developed.

Approaches to a Solution: Absenteeism Statistics

An example of the kind of approach to the problem of obtaining comparison data that is needed is provided by some recent efforts in the area of absenteeism statistics. The U.S. Department of Labor has been obtaining data through Census Bureau interviewers, using certain questions asked at the employee's home (14). This type of information has very limited usefulness for individual companies, and in any event has not been made available on a regular basis.

Recently, the Bureau of National Affairs, Inc., introduced a quarterly survey of companies requesting absenteeism data using a standardized computation formula and criterion of absence. The data are reported quarterly (4). The sample of responding companies has now been expanded with the cooperation of the American Society for Personnel Administration, making breakdowns into additional categories possible.

Using this approach as a model, it should be possible to obtain comparative measures of a standardized nature in a number of areas. The essential requirement is that some central source, such as a reporting service or professional association, monitor the collection of data, analyze it, and publish the results.

CONTROL OVER HUMAN RESOURCE ACTIVITIES

As indicated in Chapter 1, the authority that the personnel department exercises often is rather limited. The result is that it may be extremely difficult to utilize effectively the expertise residing in the personnel staff, and companies often make decisions in the human resource area that should not be made. This is detrimental to the personnel function and to the company as a whole; the situation obviously needs to be changed. The personnel function should exercise as much control over human resources as the controllership function does over monetary resources. Such is not currently the case in most companies (15). Some indication of the rather limited authority role of personnel managers is provided by the fact that on the average, the personnel budget amounts to only one per cent of the total company budget, a cost of slightly more than $200 per employee (5).

The Role of Motivation to Manage

Although there are some signs of increasing personnel influence, especially in the areas of recruiting and selection, compensation, and training and development, there is a need for much more influence (9). A major barrier appears to be the relatively low motivation to manage of many personnel and industrial relations managers.

Data relative to this point are given in Table 22–4. Within personnel management, as in other areas of management, individuals with the strongest motivation to manage are most likely to succeed; they tend to be in higher-level positions and to make more money (20). However, when contrasted with groups of managers drawn from a diverse array of other functions, a cross-section of personnel managers proved to have less motivation to manage than the other managers (19). They also were more negative toward authority, less competitive, less assertive, and less responsible in carrying out routine administrative functions. The most pronounced difference was in assertiveness, where the personnel managers were particularly lacking.

Obviously, it is impossible to say which came first—whether the limited authority of the personnel function attracted people with less managerial motivation, or the relatively low levels of motivation to manage of those entering the field caused them to assume less authority. In any event, it is clear that the kind of person now employed in a personnel position is on balance not likely to push for greater influence over human resource decisions, although in certain individual cases, especially at the top levels, this may not be true.

The current situation creates both a problem and an opportunity. It is a problem in that greater influence and authority is badly needed; it is an opportunity in that individuals with high motivation to manage can expect to do very well in the personnel and industrial relations field. Such people do get rewards, the field needs them, and the competition is currently less intense than in other functional areas.

Professionalization

In recent years, a great deal has been written about the professionalization of the personnel and industrial relations field. Many arguments have been presented to support such a development. Certainly, as one looks at the data on the backgrounds of personnel managers, as presented in Chapter 1, some approximations to a profession are in evidence. A college education is typical, although not necessarily in a particular field of specialization. A set of core courses can be identified that are viewed as important and frequently taken, irrespective of the actual major. Furthermore, a degree in business administration is becoming increasingly frequent.

Many personnel managers have not spent their entire career in the field, but an increasing number are doing so, and many of those who have worked

Table 22–4. Ranking on Motivation to Manage and Related Characteristics for Personnel Managers and Samples of Managers Outside the Personnel Area (Note: 1 = highest score and 7 = lowest score)

Sample	N	Expected Ranking of the Samples	Actual Ranking of the Samples				
			Motivation to Manage	Favorable Attitude to Authority	Desire to Compete	Assertiveness	Sense of Responsibility
Top Personnel Managers	50	1	4	4	3	6	5
Middle Managers [1]	30	3.5	1	2	1	2	1
Middle Managers [2]	30	3.5	2	3	4	4	3
Middle Managers [3]	37	3.5	3	1	2	1	2
Middle Personnel Managers	51	3.5	7	7	5	7	7
Lower Managers [1]	50	6.5	5	5	6	3	6
Lower Managers [2]	117	6.5	6	6	7	5	4

Source: Adapted from J. B. Miner, "Levels of Motivation to Manage Among Personnel and Industrial Relations Managers," Journal of Applied Psychology, 61 (1976), p. 424.

in other functional areas did so rather briefly. If given an opportunity to transfer to some other area, most personnel managers would prefer not to take it. In one survey of personnel administrators, 85 per cent indicated a desire to remain in personnel and industrial relations permanently (13). Thus, there is some sense of career permanency. Furthermore, the strong concern with integrity that has been found is consistent with a professional identification.

Although these considerations do not provide a picture of a fully developed profession such as law or medicine, some movement in the professional direction is in evidence. On the other hand, there are certain strong antithetical pressures. Chief executives and other company officers typically want personnel managers to have line experience and to understand general management problems. Furthermore, many companies rotate managers through personnel assignments for purposes of broadening, and they want to continue this practice as part of their total management-development effort. Thus, there are strong organizational pressures to open personnel positions to nonprofessionals and to put personnel people in nonprofessional positions. Added to this is the fact that many people working in the field already identify with other professions—law, psychology, accounting, medicine, engineering, education. Many of these individuals have little interest in having a second profession in personnel management.

Overall, the trend appears to be toward increased, but not full, professionalization. In particular, there is an emphasis on a common body of knowledge (21). This is reflected in the accreditation program recently introduced by the American Society for Personnel Administration (1).

Such a professionalization process, emphasizing as it does increased knowledge rather than job control, can in fact contribute to a greater expert power in the hands of the personnel manager, and thus greater influence and authority. To the extent it attracts to the field those who are essentially professionals rather than managers, there is a risk, however, that this potential for influence may not be realized in the hierarchic, competitive organizations where personnel managers must of necessity operate. In this sense, professionalization may prove to be a mixed blessing.

EXPANDED PERSONNEL ROLES IN SMALL BUSINESS

Because many of the human resource strategies used by larger firms are not applicable to the very small enterprise, there has been some tendency to accept the no-strategy option in small business (18). Necessary personnel and industrial relations functions are distributed among managers in other functional areas who know little about them, and the remainder are not performed at all. Yet effective strategies can be developed under such circumstances, and the techniques are available to carry them out (6).

Strategies for Small Business

An especially common problem for the smaller firm involves the selection process. The traditional validation procedures require a large enough number of individuals who are hired for and who work at a given job to carry out a meaningful study. In small business, the number of people working at any one job tends to be small, and the hiring of new employees does not occur often enough to spread the cost of a validation study over sufficient cases to justify it.

The standard solutions in such instances are to do a synthetic validity study using a number of similar jobs within the firm or to study the same job in several firms, usually working through a trade association. In addition to these strategies, another approach is to utilize delayed selection with a strong output emphasis. The initial hiring is carried out with a very minimal investment in selection. The real selection occurs later on the job, during a probationary or training period. To use this approach well, a detailed job analysis must be carried out to establish what must be done, and then performance evaluated with considerable precision. Those who do not meet job requirements at an acceptable level within a given period of time are separated and replaced with another person. Ultimately, a competent stable work force is developed. Such a strategy is particularly appropriate for small companies.

A very similar problem, also related to the small number employed in a single occupational category, occurs in the training area. The large firm that requires many people with certain capabilities can initiate a training program to develop them. The cost per person is likely to be prohibitive in a small company. On-the-job training may solve the problem at lower levels, but at higher levels, there may be no one who can or has the time to train in this manner.

In this situation, the small company does best to seek fully trained expertise elsewhere, often in the ranks of a larger firm. This substitution of a recruiting strategy for training and development may well require a rather high compensation level to attract the desired people, but this cost is spread over time, while training costs are concentrated. If updating or development of current employees is needed subsequent to hiring, courses at universities or similar institutions should be used so that the cost is shared.

In large corporations, the preferred approach to dealing with anticipated talent shortages is human resource planning. However, these approaches are not cost-effective for many small companies because the expense of planning cannot be spread over a sufficient number of personnel actions. Thus, the small employer does best to concentrate on filling needs as they occur. The best approach is to maintain an inventory of people working elsewhere, who might be hired if vacancies develop. The small company may not be able to afford procedures that predict when shortages can be expected, but it can establish contingency plans, so as to respond rapidly to a situation once it occurs.

In dealing with job dissatisfaction and any resultant union organizing attempts, union militancy, or excessive voluntary turnover, small companies have certain strategic advantages. For one thing, they can make much better use of face-to-face discussions and meetings simply because of their size. They do not need to resort to the less effective formal communication procedures, such as magazines and newspapers, as the larger companies do.

Furthermore, legal and union pressures make it very difficult for large companies to handle "troublemakers" by screening them out or firing. Company visibility, the existence of grievance and arbitration procedures, social pressures, and various other constraints often combine to make it difficult to deal with internal dissension by keeping those who might cause it from employment. Small business, with fewer employees and much less visibility, is in a much better position to utilize individualized strategies, rather than broad overall policies. This flexibility makes it possible to protect against dissension through a strategy of judicious selection and retention.

The Need for Personnel Managers

These examples of small business strategies are by no means exhaustive, but they do illustrate the need for qualified personnel and industrial relations expertise. It may be that the type of knowledge most in demand may differ from large to small firms, but the need for someone who can develop and carry out appropriate human resource strategies is just as great as the need for someone who can handle financial resources. Until this fact is more widely recognized, the small business failure rate is certain to remain high, and the field of personnel management will not make the contribution to the business system as a whole that it is now capable of.

It is apparent that the small company should hire somewhat more of a generalist as a personnel manager simply because it cannot afford a full-time staff of specialists in the various areas. This means that where highly specialized expertise is required, it should be obtained from outside consultants on a pay-for-time-worked basis.

Here again, however, the appropriate strategies for small and large firms differ. Often, large companies are best served by the general management consulting firms that send in teams to carry out intensive analyses in a limited time span. The small company on the other hand typically needs an independent specialist who continues to work on problems in his area of expertise on an intermittent basis for a considerable period of time. In this way, the consultant gets to know the company and its problems and contributes the needed specialized knowledge without the company's having to pay for a great deal of professional time that it does not require.

THE PERSONNEL AND INDUSTRIAL RELATIONS
MANAGER OF THE FUTURE

If the needs and recommendations considered do in fact become a reality, the personnel and industrial relations practitioner of the future may be rather different than he is today. He will know more about research and will have access to a greater body of knowledge to help him in the conduct of his job. Evaluation of personnel activities in terms of their cost-effectiveness will be widespread, and accordingly the contribution of these activities to overall company profitability will be much more widely recognized and appreciated. Because a variety of standardized comparison data are available, it will be much easier to determine how well a given personnel effort is doing. The personnel manager will exercise considerably greater authority and influence within the company over human resource matters. He will be much more likely to be located in a small company or working in a consultant capacity.

The personnel and industrial relations manager role thus defined would be closely integrated with overall company objectives and values. As a result, it seems safe to predict, the levels of both financial compensation and intangible rewards of personnel executives would be much greater than they are today.

QUESTIONS

1. In what ways do company personnel research and university research on personnel topics tend to differ? Can you cite examples of each to document your position?
2. Why is it important for personnel departments to be able to demonstrate the cost-effectiveness of their programs? What are the consequences of not doing so?
3. List as many measures that would be useful for comparison purposes as you can. What problems would you foresee in developing data banks over time and across a number of companies for these measures?
4. What advantages would accrue to personnel management were it to become highly professionalized? What disadvantages?
5. Describe several personnel strategies that are particularly suited to the needs of small businesses. To what extent do these strategies require an experienced personnel specialist for their development and implementation?

REFERENCES

1. ASPA Accreditation Institute. *ASPA Accreditation Program*. Berea, Ohio: the Institute, 1975.
2. Berry, D. F. *The Politics of Personnel Research*. Ann Arbor, Mich.: Bureau of Industrial Relations, University of Michigan, 1967.

3. Bureau of National Affairs, Inc. *The Personnel Department*. Personnel Policies Forum Survey No. 92, November 1970.
4. Bureau of National Affairs, Inc. *Bulletin to Management*, March 14, 1974, and quarterly thereafter.
5. Bureau of National Affairs, Inc. "ASPA-BNA Survey No. 23: Planning and Budgeting the Personnel Program." *Bulletin to Management*, June 6, 1974.
6. Byham, W. C. *The Uses of Personnel Research*. AMA Research Study 91. New York: American Management Association, Inc., 1968.
7. Cheek, L. M. "Cost Effectiveness Comes to the Personnel Function." *Harvard Business Review*, 51 (1973), No. 3, 96–105.
8. Claque, E. "Developments in Labor Statistics," in G. G. Somers (ed.), *The Next Twenty-five Years of Industrial Relations*. Madison, Wis.: Industrial Relations Research Association, 1973, pp. 37–46.
9. Coleman, C. J. "Personnel: The Changing Function." *Public Personnel Management*, Vol. 2, (1973), No. 3, 186–193.
10. Dunnette, M. D., and B. M. Bass. "Behavioral Scientists and Personnel Management." *Industrial Relations*, 2 (1963), 115–130.
11. Flanagan, R. J., G. Strauss, and L. Ulman. "Worker Discontent and Work Place Behavior." *Industrial Relations*, 13 (1974), 101–123.
12. Foulkes, F. K. "The Expanding Role of the Personnel Function." *Harvard Business Review*, Vol. 53 (1975), No. 2, 71–84.
13. Harris, O. J. "Personnel Administrators—The Truth About Their Backgrounds." *MSU Business Topics*, 17 (1969), No. 3, 22–29.
14. Hedges, J. N. "Unscheduled Absence from Work—An Update." *Monthly Labor Review*, 98 (1975), No. 8, 36–39.
15. Henning, D. A., and R. L. Moseley. "Authority Role of a Functional Manager: The Controller." *Administrative Science Quarterly*, 15 (1970), 482–489.
16. Loen, E. L. *Personnel Management Guides for Small Business*. Washington, D.C.: Small Business Administration, 1974.
17. Luck, T. J. *Personnel Audit and Appraisal*. New York: McGraw-Hill Book Company, 1955.
18. Miner, J. B. "Personnel Strategies in the Small Business Organization." *Journal of Small Business Management*, 11 (1973), No. 3, 13–16.
19. Miner, J. B. "Levels of Motivation to Manage Among Personnel and Industrial Relations Managers." *Journal of Applied Psychology*, 61 (1976), 419–427.
20. Miner, J. B., and M. G. Miner. "Motivational Patterns of Personnel Managers." *Industrial Relations*, 15 (1976), 225–234.
21. Miner, M. G., and J. B. Miner. *A Guide to Personnel Management*. Washington, D.C.: BNA Books, 1973.
22. Novit, M. S., and E. G. Williams. *Personnel Administration in Indiana*. Indianapolis: Indiana State Chamber of Commerce, 1973.

23. Odiorne, G. S. "Evaluating the Personnel Program," in J. J. Famularo (ed.), *Handbook of Modern Personnel Administration*. New York: McGraw-Hill Book Company, 1972, pp. 8-1 to 8-7.

24. O'Toole, J., et al. *Work in America: Report of a Special Task Force to the Secretary of Health, Education and Welfare*. Cambridge, Mass.: The MIT Press, 1973.

25. Paul, R. J. "Constructing Personnel Research Programs," in J. J. Famularo (ed.), *Handbook of Modern Personnel Administration*. New York: McGraw-Hill Book Company, 1972, pp. 81-1 to 81-20.

26. Wittreich, W. J., and J. B. Miner. "People: The Most Mismanaged Asset." *Business Horizons*, 14 (1971), 69–77.

27. Yoder, D. "Personnel Administration," in G. G. Somers (ed.), *The Next Twenty-five Years of Industrial Relations*. Madison, Wis.: Industrial Relations Research Association, 1973, pp. 141–156.

Author Index

A

Aaron, B. J., 120
Abbott, R. D., 325
Abrahams, N. M., 324
Ace, M. E., 121
Akman, A., 434f, 442
Albright, L. E., 86, 253t, 259, 296f, 302
Alexander, R. A., 258
Allen, D., 541
Allenspach, H., 177
Alper, S. W., 279
Alpin, J. C., 572
Alutto, J. A., 22
American Society for Personnel Administration, 18t, 22
Anastasi, A., 84
Anderson, H. E., 324
Anderson, H. J., 121
Andrews, I. R., 303
Appel, V., 302
Armenakis, A. A., 41
Arthur, R. J., 325
Ash, P., 121, 257, 324, 325, 511
Ash, R. A., 177
Asher, J. J., 302, 325
Ashford, N. A., 441
ASPA Accreditation Institute, 591
Athanassiades, J. C., 572
Athos, A. G., 282

B

Back, K. W., 355
Baggaley, A. R., 232
Bagley, E. R., 147
Bailey, W. R., 416
Balke, W. M., 511
Barbarik, P., 442
Barnako, F. R., 121
Barocci, T. A., 381
Barrett, G. V., 442
Bartlett, C. J., 233
Bartol, K. M., 84
Bass, A. R., 232
Bass, B. M., 57, 86, 592
Bassett, G. A., 206
Bassford, G. L., 257
Battalia, Lotz, and Associates, 22
Baum, B. H., 355
Baum, J. F., 470
Baum, S. J., 177
Baxter, B., 257
Baylie, T. N., 232
Beatty, R. W., 57
Beaumont, R. A., 138f, 148
Bedeian, A. G., 41
Beer, M., 416
Belasco, J. A., 22, 355, 470
Belcher, D. W., 396t, 416
Bell, D. R., 530t, 542
Bellows, R., 41
Belt, J. A., 22
Bemis, S. E., 280
Bemis, S. S., 325
Benne, K. D., 355
Bergman, B. A., 326
Bergmann, B. R., 121
Berkshire, J. R., 232
Bernstein, I., 41, 121

National Labor Relations Board, 117t, 122
Naylor, J. C., 241f, 258
Nemeroff, W. F., 357
Neumann, I., 324
Newhams, T. H., 471
Newstrom, J. W., 574
Noland, R. L., 122, 258, 471
Nord, W., 471
Nordlund, W. J., 281
Northrup, H. R., 122
Novit, M. S., 581t, 592
Nuttall, R. L., 85

O

Oberg, W., 230t, 233
O'Brien, P. E., 443
O'Connor, E. J., 258
Odiorne, G. S., 383, 593
Oldham, G. R., 178
Oliver, R. L., 303
O'Meara, J. R., 122, 123
O'Reilly, C. A., 574
Organt, G. J., 418
Orife, J. N., 178
Orpen, C., 326
Osburn, H. G., 71t, 86
O'Toole, J., 593
Ottemann, R., 542
Ouchi, W. G., 149
Owens, W. A., 296f, 302

P

Paine, F. T., 355, 382
Papier, W., 123
Paransky, H., 382
Parker, V. D., 483t, 513
Parrish, J. B., 149
Patton, A., 23
Patz, A. L., 207
Paul, R. J., 593
Peres, S. H., 303
Peters, L. H., 303
Peterson, D. A., 302
Peterson, D. J., 259, 513
Pettefer, J. C., 513
Petty, M. M., 148
Pizam, A., 574
Place, W. S., 355
Porter, L. W., 85, 86
Powell, R. M., 357

Prather, R. L., 233
Prentice-Hall, Inc., 259
Prien, E. P., 178
Pritchard, R. D., 418
Pruitt, D. G., 513
Pursell, E. D., 233
Pyron, H. C., 303

Q

Quinn, R. P., 565t, 573

R

Rachel, F. M., 417
Rahe, R. H., 325
Raia, A. P., 178
Rajaratnam, N., 258
Ramser, C., 23
Reeser, C., 207
Reid, G. L., 281
Reif, W. E., 574
Reis, A. J., 121
Rezler, J., 23
Rice, G. H., 149
Richards, M. D., 85, 356
Richards, S. A., 233
Richardson, J. A., 22
Richmond, H. W., 443
Ritzer, G., 24
Roach, D. E., 303
Roberts, H. S., 513
Roberts, K. H., 574
Robey, D., 178
Robinson, D. D., 418
Rock, M. I., 418
Roethlisberger, F. J., 42
Ronan, W. W., 178, 418
Root, F. R., 86
Rose, J. B., 513
Rosen, B., 281, 471
Rosen, H., 494f, 513
Rosenbaum, B. L., 259
Rosenblum, M., 149
Rosenfeld, C., 276t, 281
Rosenzweig, J. E., 58
Rosow, J. M., 513
Ross, A. M., 84t, 85, 513
Rothe, H. F., 567f, 572
Rouleau, E. J., 178
Roush, S. L., 324
Roy, S. K., 80t, 85, 86, 87
Rubinsky, S., 443
Ruch, F. L., 259, 303

Subject Index

A

Abilities
  individual differences in, 61–75
  job performance and, 449–450
  tests of, 311–317
Ability grouping, 365
Absenteeism, 201, 451
Absenteeism statistics, 585
Accident proneness, 433–438
Accident statistics, 201–202, 421–428
Accidents, 420–438; see also Safety
Accounting measures in management
  appraisal, 198–199
Achievement-motivation training, 343
Achievement tests, 323–324
Active practice, in learning theory, 362
Advertising, recruitment, 265–266
Affirmative action programs, 261, 275–
  279; see also Equal Employment
  Opportunity
AFL-CIO, 36, 480, 488
Age, ability and, 71–73
Age discrimination, 97–98, 100t
Age Discrimination Act of 1967, 91t,
  97–98
Alcoholics Anonymous, 469
Alcoholism, 451–452, 468–469
Alphabetical Index of Industries and
  Occupations, 167
American Arbitration Association, 504
American Compensation Association, 39
American Federation of Labor (AFL),
  28, 33, 480
American Management Association, 39,
  350–351
American Nurse Association, 486
American Psychological Association, Di-
  vision of Industrial and Organiza-
  tional Psychology (Division 14), 39
American Society for Personnel Admin-
  istration (ASPA), 18, 20, 38, 585,
  588
American Society of Training Directors,
  39
American Telephone and Telegraph
  Company (AT&T), 105, 171, 194,
  225
Angell, James, 29
Application blanks, 291–298
Appraisal, 180–206
Apprentice training, 370–372
Arbitration, 495–496, 501–505
Area Redevelopment Act of 1961, 377–
  378
Army Alpha, 30
Army Beta, 30
ASPA, 18, 39
Assessment centers, 194–196
Atlantic Magazine, The, 553
Atlantic Refining Company, 552
Attitude surveys, 203–204, 562–570
Attitudes toward benefits, employee,
  537–541
Automation, 510

B

Bargaining unit, determination of, 488
Behavior checklists, 221–225
Behavior modification, 347